Edited by

JOHN B. WILLIAMSON
Boston College

LINDA EVANS
Central Connecticut State College

MICHAEL RUSTAD
Northeastern University

SOCIAL PROBLEMS

THE CONTEMPORARY DEBATES

FOURTH EDITION

LITTLE, BROWN AND COMPANY

Boston   Toronto

Library of Congress Cataloging in Publication Data
Main entry under title:

Social problems.

    Bibliography: p.
    1. United States—Social conditions—1980–   —Ad-
dresses, essays, lectures.   2. Social problems—Addresses,
essays, lectures.   I. Williamson, John B.   II. Evans,
Linda.   III. Rustad, Michael.
HN65.S5753   1985   973.92   84-26109
ISBN 0-316-94376-2

Library of Congress Catalog Card Number 84-26109

ISBN 0-316-94376-2

9 8 7 6 5 4 3 2 1

ALP

Published simultaneously in Canada
by Little, Brown & Company (Canada) Limited

Printed in the United States of America

Acknowledgments

Thomas Sowell, "Government and Minorities," from *Markets and Minorities* by Thomas Sowell. Copyright © 1981 by The International Center for Economic Policy Studies. Reprinted by permission of Basic Books, Inc., Publishers.

Joe R. Feagin, "Social Problems," from *Social Problems: A Critical Power-Conflict Perspective.* Copyright © 1982 by Joe R. Feagin. Reprinted by permission of Prentice-Hall, Inc., Englewood Cliffs, New Jersey.

Robert B. Reich, "The Next American Frontier," from *The Next American Frontier.* Copyright © 1983 by Robert Reich. Reprinted by permission of Times Books/The New York Times Book Co., Inc.

George Gilder, "The Bullheaded Brewer," from *Wealth and Poverty.* Copyright © 1981 by George Gilder. Reprinted by permission of Basic Books, Inc., Publishers.

Barry Bluestone and Bennett Harrison, from *The Deindustrialization of America.* Copyright © 1982 by Barry Bluestone and Bennett Harrison. Reprinted by permission of Basic Books, Inc., Publishers and John Brockman Associates, Inc.

Jeremy Main, "The Hazards of Helping Toxic Waste Victims," from *Fortune*, October 31, 1983. Copyright © 1983 Time, Inc. All rights reserved. Reprinted by permission of Time, Inc.

Ken Geiser, "Toxic Times and Class Politics," from *Radical America*, Vol. 17, Nos. 2 and 3. Reprinted by permission of Radical America, Somerville, Massachusetts.

Ernest van den Haag, "The Death Penalty: Arguments For," from *Punishing Criminals*. Copyright © 1975 by Basic Books, Inc., Publishers. Reprinted by permission of the publisher.

David Hoekema, "Capital Punishment: The Question of Justification," from *The Christian Century*, March 28, 1979. Copyright 1979 by Christian Century Foundation. Reprinted by permission of the Christian Century Foundation.

B. Bruce-Briggs, "A Catechism of Strategic Defense," from *National Review*, October 5, 1984. Copyright © 1984 by National Review, Inc., New York, New York. Reprinted by permission.

Andrew Winnick, "Rapid Deployment and Nuclear War: Reagan's New Military Strategies," from *Socialist Review*, Number 73 (Vol. 14, No. 1) January-February 1984. Copyright © 1984 by Socialist Review, Inc., Berkeley, California. Reprinted by permission.

W. Norton Grubb and Marvin Lazerson, excerpts from *Broken Promises: How Americans Fail Their Children*. Copyright © 1982 by Basic Books, Inc., Publishers. Reprinted by permission of the publisher.

Brigitte Berger and Peter L. Berger, "The Family and Democracy," from *The War over the Family*. Copyright © 1983 by Brigitte Berger and Peter L. Berger. Reprinted by permission of Doubleday & Company, Inc.

Peter Steinfels, "The Search for an Alternative," from *Commonweal*, November 21, 1981. Reprinted by permission of the publisher.

Charles Hartshorne, "Concerning Abortion: An Attempt at a Rational View," from The Christian Century, January 21, 1981. Copyright 1981 by Christian Century Foundation. Reprinted by permission of the Christian Century Foundation.

Catharine MacKinnon, "The Male Ideology of Privacy: A Feminist Perspective on the Right to Abortion," from *Radical America*, Vol. 17, No. 4, July–August, 1983. Reprinted by permission of Radical America and the author.

James Q. Wilson, "Heroin," from *Thinking about Crime*. Copyright © 1975, 1983 by Basic Books, Inc., Publishers. Reprinted by permission of the publisher.

Andrew Weil, "Marijuana Reconsidered," from *The Marriage of the Sun and Moon*. Copyright © 1980 by Andrew Weil. Reprinted by permission of Houghton Mifflin Company.

Bruce K. MacMurray, Thomas M. Shapiro, and Maureen E. Kelleher, "Decriminalization: The Law, Society, and the User," by permission of Bruce K. MacMurray, Thomas M. Shapiro, and Maureen E. Kelleher, Department of Sociology-Anthropology, Northeastern University, Boston, Massachusetts.

O. Ruth Russell, "The Case for the Legalization of Euthanasia," from *Freedom to Die*, Chapter 9. Copyright © 1975 by Human Sciences Press, Inc. Reprinted by permission of Human Sciences Press, Inc., New York, New York.

John B. Williamson, Linda Evans, and Anne Munley, "Why the Legalization of Euthanasia Is Feared," from *Aging and Society: An Introduction to Social Gerontology*. Copyright © 1980 by Holt, Rinehart and Winston. Reprinted by permission of Holt, Rinehart and Winston, CBS College Publishing.

Herbert A. Simon, "The Consequences of Computers for Centralization and Decentralization," from *The Computer Age* edited by Michael Dertouzos and Joel Moses. Reprinted by permission of The MIT Press.

Judith A. Perrolle, "Computers and Capitalism," by permission of Judith A. Perrolle, Department of Sociology-Anthropology, Northeastern University, Boston, Massachusetts.

A. P. Simonds, "On Being Informed," originally appeared in *Theory and Society 11* (1982) (Elsevier Scientific Publishing Co., Amsterdam). Copyright © 1982 by The American Political Science Association. Reprinted by permission of The American Political Science Association.

Ithiel de Sola Pool, "Technologies of Freedom," reprinted by permission of the publishers from *Technologies of Freedom* by Ithiel de Soal Pool, Cambridge, Massachusetts: The Belknap Press of Harvard University Press, Copyright © 1983 by the President and Fellows of Harvard College.

Pope John Paul II, "On Human Work: Laborem Exercens," reprinted by permission of Libreria Editrice Vaticana.

Peter Rachleff, ''Working the Fast Lane: Jobs, Technology and Scientific Management in the U.S. Postal Service,'' from *Radical America*, Vol. 16, Nos. 1 and 2, January-February, and March-April, 1982. Reprinted by permission of Radical America, Somerville, Massachusetts.

PREFACE

This reader, like our previous editions, is designed for those who wish to examine social problems from a variety of perspectives. We have been delighted to learn that included in the group of interested parties are instructors and students from debate and rhetoric, political science, American studies, and general "core curriculum" courses, as well as from traditional sociology courses. Rather than selecting articles in which the authors provide what we consider a "balanced" analysis of the issue, presenting and weighing the alternative perspectives, we choose to let the proponents of divergent perspectives speak for themselves. The authors, or "debaters," have been given a good deal of space in which to develop their arguments fully. The fourth edition, then, is characterized by lengthier, more substantive debates than previous editions. Special care has also been taken to update; the emphasis of this edition is on *contemporary* debates.

Our aim in employing the debate format remains that of stimulating classroom discussion. We feel that students enjoy participating in the evaluation of the different perspectives. We seek to demonstrate in our text that strong arguments can be made about the same topic from competing perspectives. Nevertheless, discovering which argument is the most persuasive tends to provoke comments. Please keep in mind that while each chapter stands independently, what one garners in the course of one chapter (for instance, information about the conservative position) can be used to understand the substance of another chapter. For example, Brigitte and Peter Berger argue against government interference in family life in one chapter. In another debate, Jeremy Main argues against government interference to solve the problem of toxic wastes. One may gather, then, that the conservatives find the role of the government problematic in solving issues.

In the fourth edition, we have added debates on a number of new issues, like computer-generated social problems; the possibility of nuclear war and how to avert one; and the problem of staying informed by way of the mass media and new technologies. We also spend a good part of the text covering the traditional social problems like racism, sexism, poverty, crime, and housing, but in a new fashion. Our look, or we should say our authors' method of looking, at traditional social problems tends to be through larger issues or problems. For example, Thomas Sowell, a black economist, investigates the relationship between the government and minorities. In discussing this general issue, however, he focuses in on a variety of specific social problems, like poverty, racism, and housing availability. In another debate, radical economists Barry Bluestone and Bennett Harrison discuss the deindustrialization of America, and explain why crime rates soar in healthy, "boom" economies as well as in "bust" economies. Yet another example can be seen in "On Being Informed," the piece by A. P. Simonds, who is a professor of political science at the University of

Massachusetts/Boston. Particular concerns about our reading and television viewing habits emerge in the context of the larger discussion of the relationship between democracy and information.

We have been assisted by a number of people in the preparation of this edition. We first want to thank the professors from across the country who responded to the Little, Brown survey concerning revisions for this edition. We hope we have satisfactorily incorporated their suggestions. For technical assistance, we wish to thank Chryss Knowles; John Demeter of *Radical America*; the Daughters of St. Paul (Boston); and Brad Gray and Anne Bingham of the College Division at Little, Brown and Company. We appreciated the helpful suggestions that came from Andrew Herman and Charles Derber of Boston College; Rusty Simonds and Linda Gordon of the University of Massachusetts/Boston/Harbor Campus; Judy Perrolle, Tom Koenig, Wini Breines, and Maureen Kelleher of Northeastern University; and Catharine MacKinnon of the University of Minnesota School of Law.

One last point that we are obliged to make is that for some pieces, particularly book excerpts, the footnotes have been deleted in the interests of space and editorial consistency. One should refer to the original source listed in our acknowledgments.

CONTENTS

Chapter 8 / Decriminalization: Healthy, Wealthy, and Wise 251

Chapter 9 / Should Euthanasia Be Legalized?   284

PART III / SCIENCE, TECHNOLOGY AND WORK   303

Chapter 10 / Computers: What Is Their Social Impact?   305

INTRODUCTION

| SOCIAL PROBLEMS: |
| A MATTER FOR DEBATE |

WHAT IS A SOCIAL PROBLEM?

To some readers the answer may seem obvious. They see this question as unnecessary and irrelevant, of the sort with which sociologists too frequently concern themselves. In the words of one newspaper columnist:

Sociology, as we all know, is a scholarly discipline which elevates the obvious to the esoteric. A sociologist will devote several years to a study which eventually will disclose that most men and women like sex, in one form or another. A sociologist will pontificate on the inequitable distribution of wealth in language neither the rich nor the poor will understand. These savants who relentlessly pursue things-everyone-knew-in-the-first-place often exceed their own seemingly infinite capacity for revealing revealed truths.[1]

Our method is to begin with what appear to be obvious answers. These answers may satisfy some people, but they will not satisfy most sociologists. We will point out the flaws in the obvious answers and go on to discuss conservative, liberal, and radical alternatives. Our argument should convince the reader that there are no objective and neutral guidelines for defining social problems. Social problems cannot be defined outside of strongly held political perspectives.

This text presents several different theoretical and ideological perspectives for each social problem because we see social problems as political statements. These contradictory positions are not just differences of opinion. They are the dominant political and social debates of our time. They are the perspectives that have profound implications; they determine what conditions are ultimately defined as problems as well as how people can deal with them. Before describing the features of conservatism, liberalism, and radicalism, it is necessary to compare our approach with traditional treatments of social problems.

POSITIVISM: SOCIAL PROBLEMS AS SCIENCE

Today many sociologists have an image of themselves as working in the province of science rather than politics. The view that sociologists should not get caught up in politics comes from the classic tradition of positivism. August Comte (1798–1957) coined the term *positivism* to define a new intellectual epoch in which scientists would replace armchair philosophers as the gatherers of knowledge.[2] Comte assumed that sociologists would assemble all objective sources of knowledge from all of the sciences to solve social problems. The positivism of Comte was tied to the belief that science was a more rational basis for public policy than the musings of philosophy. Comte saw sociologists as practical activists in contrast to the useless project of speculative philosophy.[3]

Emile Durkheim (1857–1917) was the most influential follower of Comte's positivism. Durkheim abandoned Comte's idea that sociologists should be the high priests of a new religion of humanity. Rather, the role of sociologists was to gather social facts. By monitoring such social stresses as suicide, the breakdown of community, and the upheaval of traditional institutions, sociologists could lend reliable knowledge to the solution of social problems.[4]

Durkheim's quest for rational intervention in the solution of social problems was illustrated in his study entitled *Suicide* (1897). Durkheim eschewed the musings of philosophers who associated the problem of suicide with climate, geography, national character, or psychic predisposition. Durkeim patiently tested and rejected all of the traditional beliefs about suicide. Through a careful analysis of governmental data from such European regions as Bavaria, Burgundy, and Prussia, Durkheim associated suicide rates with the social fact of integration. His general finding was that suicide was positively related to social integration. Social contacts such as religious membership, occupational group, and family ties insulated the individual from the psychic pain that leads to suicide.

Durkheim found that various types of suicide were associated with the magnitude of social integration. Durkheim was most interested in the form of suicide which he called *anomic suicide*. Anomic suicide occurred when social stresses such as migration and dislocation wrenched individuals from their social bonds. The obvious solution to the social problem of anomic suicide was to construct new social bonds for the dislocated. If social contact could be reestablished for victims of disaster, war, and other forms of depression, the suicide rate would drop. Of course, this is the theory that underpins crisis intervention and suicide hot lines. The purpose of crisis intervention is to help lonely persons find social bonds which will insulate them from the chasm that leads to suicide.

Whether the problem was suicide, the division of labor, criminal behavior, or educational concerns, Durkheim found social solidarity to be a significant social fact. Whenever the social fabric was ruptured, social problems were likely to occur. Like Comte, Durkheim thought it was the job of sociologists to reconstruct the moral foundation of society.[5]

A third figure important to the positivist tradition was Max Weber. Weber thought that sociology should be value-free. He believed that researchers had value preferences which influenced the choice of research topics. But once the topic had been selected, the social scientist should be dispassionate. Social research can and should be conducted according to the norms of scientific research—objectivity, verifiability, and value-neutrality. Researchers must follow their data and present the results even when those results do not satisfy their ideological preferences. If objective value-free research has been achieved, another researcher with a very different value orientation should be able to replicate the results. Weber believed that sociologists should test their hypotheses and leave politics to others.

Weber's belief in an objective social science assumed that facts could be separated from values. In other words, "ought" statements cannot be drawn from "is" statements.

American sociologists of the first decades of this century were hardly value-free. *Social Darwinists*, as they were called, used the theory of natural selection as justification for the huge disparities of wealth associated with maturing capitalism:

In Britain, the plutocracy embraced the ruminations of Spencer as evidence that, by an iron law of nature, they had "survived" best because they were morally and intellectually "fittest."[6]

Herbert Spencer adapted Darwin's theories to British society. He saw the elites of British society as the pinnacle of evolution. As Ronald Chester correctly notes, Social Darwinism was filled with value judgments and rife with contradictions:

Nowhere in Spencer's publications do we find a direct explanation of how the fittest could be determined in a society where inherited concentrations of wealth made starting points so unequal. At the end of the century, Britain, like America, was hardly in a "state of nature," where each individual could fight the social struggle on relatively equal terms.[7]

It is difficult to overestimate the significance of Herbert Spencer on American social thought in the first decades of this century. The judicial philosophy of the Supreme Court was influenced by Spencer and his American counterpart, William Graham Sumner. Spencer argued for noninterference by the state. He thought that noninterference would guarantee that those human groups best adapted to produce offspring would survive. Inferior social groups would decline. He thought that the best guarantee of liberty was freedom of contract. From the beginning of the century throughout the 1930s, the Court followed the Social Darwinists when it struck down many state laws which sought to protect the health of employees and consumers. For instance, in *Lochner v. New York* (1905), the Court invalidated a New York labor law which sought to limit the workweek of bakery employees to sixty hours a week. Justice Peckham argued in the majority opinion that the state should never restrain the liberty of employees to freely contract with employers. Liberty of contract presumed that employers and employees bargained on equal terms. Justice Oliver Wendell Holmes castigated his colleagues as enacting Mr. Herbert Spencer's *Social Statics*, rather than considering the case on constitutional grounds.[8]

The American sociologists who followed Spencer used biological analogies to develop highly partisan notions of public policy. Darwin's "survival of the fittest" concept was used to justify the exclusion of Eastern and Southern European immigrants. Some sociologists thought that eugenics was the only alternative to root out these unfortunate people. In short, Social Darwinism was anything but value-free.

Today Social Darwinism has long since been discredited by modern positivists. In fact, many positivists regard the freewheeling libertarian politics of the Social Darwinists as an example of the very great danger of partisanship. Max Weber's position still has a strong influence on American sociology; it is often repeated in introductory textbooks. Here is one example:

Sociology is a categorical, not a normative, discipline; that is, it confines itself to statements about what is, not what should or ought to be. As a science sociology is necessarily silent about questions of value; it cannot decide the directions in which society ought to go, and it makes no recommendations on matters of social policy.[9]

Today there are at least three uses of the term positivism. Anthony Giddens distinguishes the positivism of Comte from the positivists of the Vienna Circle. The Vienna Circle is a school of philosophy which sees itself as carrying on the spirit of Hume and Comte, but equipped with more modern logical tools. Such figures as Karl Popper, Rudolph Carnap, and Otto Neurath argue that social science's power came from its loyalty to the logic of science.[10] Karl Popper's famous argument is that social science is separated from metaphysics insofar as its findings are capable of being exposed to empirical tests; he calls this the "principle of falsification." Knowledge comes from discarding hypotheses that pass for truth rather than from grand theory.[11]

Giddens's third use of the term positivism interests students of social problems. This is what Giddens dubbed "positivistic sociology."[12] Positivistic sociology borrows much from Comte and much from the Vienna Circle, yet it has a character of its own. We see positivistic sociology in today's social problem textbooks. Many texts provide the student with a definition that assumes that all sociologists accumulate knowledge in the vision of Comte, Durkheim, and Weber. They see "ideology" as inapplicable to the building of sociology in the tradition of the Vienna Circle. Positivists shun any ideology whether it be conservative, liberal, or radical because they see themselves as value-free in the tradition of Max Weber. Jerome Manis offers the following definition representative of scientific sociology: "Social problems are those social conditions identified by scientific inquiry and values as detrimental to human beings."[13] On its face, the definition seems simple enough. It says that the definition of social problems is unproblematic. It is a simple matter to define social problems according to this view. A sociologist need only poll people about what they regard to be harmful. Another recent text argues that scientific research provides a guide for distinguishing social problems. "A social problem is a social condition that has been found to be harmful to individual and/or societal well-being. It is a condition that originates in social behavior and that proves to have harmful consequences."[14]

These definitions share a tacit assumption that sociologists agree on what a social problem is and how it shall be resolved. Many definitions seem to involve a "public opinion" conception of social problems: social problems are defined as those conditions that deviate from society's major norms and values.[15] The definition by Joseph Julian that follows is representative of this conception. "In order for a social condition to become a social problem, a significant number of people—or a number of significant people—must agree both that this condition violates an accepted value or standard *and* that is should be eliminated, resolved, or remedied through collective action."[16] Jerome Manis would consider this a public opinion conception in that it implies some sort of head count to decide on society's major social problems.[17] It is admitted that some people's opinions count more than others, but the general thrust is that one can get a reasonably accurate assessment of contemporary social problems by administering a public opinion survey in which people are asked to indicate what they consider to be society's major social problems. If such a survey were carried out following scientific procedures of sampling, questionnaire construction, and the like, the result would be a reasonably accurate conception of the major social problems facing society at that time.

Definitions of the sort just given, while common in contemporary social problems textbooks, are by no means unproblematic. To demonstrate this we will take a close look at each component of the above definition.

Julian's definition specifies that a "significant number" of people must agree that the condition is problematic. We might ask, How many is a significant number? It turns out that there is no precise answer. But we can say something about the factors that affect the extent to which the criterion is met.

One is the size of the community being considered. If we are dealing with a local community, such as a town of 5000 residents, and it turns out that 3000 consider the pollution caused by a local refinery undesirable, then this pollution is a social problem for the community. On the other hand, if we are considering the national community (the nation as a whole) and find that only 3000 people consider a specified condition undesirable, then it would typically not be considered a social problem.

Julian qualifies his definition with a reference to the alternative of "a number of significant people." This qualification is added because it is assumed that the condition is more likely to be considered a social problem if the people affected are influential. When a condition begins to affect the middle and upper classes, the chances of its being considered a social problem increase substantially. Addiction to hard drugs had been an urban, lower-class black phenomenon for quite some time before it reached the suburban, white middle class. When this began to occur, addiction's salience as a social problem dramatically increased.

A rapid increase in the number of people affected is as important as the absolute number of people affected. We become accustomed to the prevailing levels of crime, pollution, and urban congestion, but a sharp increase in the intensity of the problem and in the number of people affected often leads to the condition's being defined as a social problem.

The reference to "a significant number of people" in the definition is useful so as to exclude what are considered individual or personal problems. The loss of a job is a personal problem for Mr. Butler and his family, but it is not a social problem. In contrast, if half the wage earners in the community are out of work, the community has a social problem. Thus Mr. Butler's personal problem may be a symptom of a community social problem.

A second criterion mentioned by Julian is that the condition "violates an accepted value or standard." Note that a reasonably strong societal consensus on values and standards is being assumed. This assumption legitimates the values of those with a vested interest in the status quo. The view that a social problem exists when there is a gap between the values of the dominant majority and the existing reality tends to reduce the opportunity for minority groups (e.g., blacks or homosexuals) and those taking atypical ideological perspectives (e.g., Marxists or ultraconservatives) to define conditions they consider problematic as social problems.

The radical left faces this difficulty in its attempt to have imperialism defined as a social problem in the national community. Despite the conservative drift of recent years, liberalism remains the dominant political ideology in America today. From the liberal perspective American commercial involvement in the developing nations is not imperialism. Rather the investments of American corporations in these countries are viewed as mutually beneficial. The capital that American corporations can supply to a poor nation is needed to develop local industry and provides the means of extracting available natural resources. The resulting profits can be divided so that both parties benefit from the "cooperation."

But from the perspective of the radical left, the country in which these investments are made is often a victim of exploitation. One argument is that American companies frequently make deals with a small local elite. These elites become rich, but there are few benefits for the common people. Another argument from this perspective is that the American corporations develop an interest in maintaining the status quo and in protecting their investments; thus they often support repressive local elites (or right-wing dictators) and oppose popular peasant movements.

The same logic can be applied to issues of concern to other minority groups. Consider the gay community. If we use the criterion that the condition "violates an accepted value or standard," it is clear that the social problem in this case would be defined as sexual deviation. But from the perspective of the gay community the problem is discrimination against gays. In short, the general definition of a social problem that we are considering does not provide for the opinions of population subgroups that hold values and standards that differ from those of the majority. For those who believe that the rights and values of minority group members need to be protected, this is a very serious flaw.

According to Julian another criterion for a social problem is that a significant number of people feel it requires collective social action. This does not mean that people help deal with the situation personally. Generally they will support the establishment of an institution, such as the police, the welfare department, or the department of public health, to deal with the problem.

This criterion rules out individual action taken to deal with personal problems or with the infrequent acts of highly deviant individuals. When airline hijacking first occurred most people felt that is was too unlikely an event to justify elaborate search procedures to control it. But as hijacking became more frequent, it was defined as a social problem and collective social action was taken to deal with it.

Also according to this criterion a social problem is not one that the community fatalistically accepts. Floods, droughts, and epidemics, for example, are accepted by everyone in a primitive tribe as acts of nature over which they have no control. Sociologists have frequently used this example to argue that adverse conditions that are fatalistically accepted do not constitute social problems for the society in question.

What if members of the tribe say prayers designed to ward off such natural disasters? Would we consider this a form of collective action? Some would say it is. People in primitive societies tend to be more fatalistic than those in advanced societies. It is very difficult to find examples of adverse conditions affecting large numbers of people in the United States which are not being dealt with through some form of collective social action.

Even when many people feel collective social action is called for, however, such action will not necessarily take place. Some people in the community will always feel that their interests are best served by the status quo. Others may in principle support efforts to deal with the social problem, but may be unwilling to pay the higher taxes needed to finance such efforts. Still others may fail to back a proposed measure because they feel the approach being proposed will not have any real effect on the problem.

Positivists believe that values can be kept from influencing the investigation of social problems. They assume a false empirical-analytical world in which sociologists can agree about what is wrong with society and what should be changed.

Howard Becker is one of the best-known liberal critics of the positivist goal of value-free social science. He argues that is impossible to conduct social research "that is uncontaminated by personal and political sympathies," and that "we cannot avoid taking sides for reasons firmly based in social structure."[18] He views society as characterized by hierarchical relationships: "In the case of deviance, the hierarchical relationship is a moral one. The superordinate parties in the relationship are those who represent the forces of approved and official morality; the subordinate parties are those who, it is alleged, have violated that morality."

We generally conduct research from the perspective of one layer of the hierarchy, never including the perspectives of all layers. As a result the conclusions do not present a full picture, but a partisan viewpoint. Becker argues that by presenting the analysis from the perspective of one group (e.g., drug addicts) the researcher is often tacitly sympathizing with this group.

Alvin Gouldner, who in the past has attacked the "dominant professional ideology of positivism: that favoring the value-free doctrine of social science,"[19] shifted his perspective, partly in response to Becker's article and the strength of the support it received. Gouldner stated, "I fear that the myth of a value-free social science is about to be supplanted by still another myth, and that the once glib acceptance of the value-free doctrine is about to be superseded by a new but no less glib rejection of it."[20]

Gresham Riley has also attacked Becker's position.[21] His major point is that Becker has considerably overstated the case in asserting that all social science research must be partisan. He does not deny that much social research is partisan; rather he argues that much social research is *not* partisan. There are many sociological propositions that cannot in any clear way be linked to the perspective of one of the partisan groups Becker refers to.

Becker refers to a *hierarchy of credibility*. By this he means that the superordinates in a hierarchy are assumed to be more credible because they have a more complete picture of the organization (or society). Sociologists are likely to be considered biased if their conclusions differ from those of people higher up. This judgment holds true for any segment of the population that decides to disagree with their superiors. When the antiwar protesters criticized the handling of the war in Vietnam by Presidents Johnson and Nixon, their views were considered biased not only by the government decision makers, but also by a wide segment of the general population who accepted the president as a more credible source. Nixon and Johnson did not hesitate to capitalize on this hierarchy of credibility in their efforts to deal with criticism from antiwar factions. President Reagan uses this advantage in his Central America policy.

Is moral indifference a necessary consequence of efforts to achieve objectivity in social research? Does a goal of value-free research free sociologists from moral responsibility for their work? Consider first the case of physics. Among physicists there has long been strong normative support for value-free scientific research. The individual physicist was not to be held responsible for the use to which his or her discovery might be put. The development and use of the atom bomb led many physicists to become highly critical of the moral indifference that had previously been highly valued. Some chose not to work on projects that clearly involved the development of destructive weapons. Others continued their work feeling that it might be put to constructive uses (e.g., nuclear power) and as private citizens became activists for a different policy on the use of such knowledge.

The policy implications of the findings of sociological research have never been so dramatic as the development of the ability to split the atom. But the same issue does exist on a more modest scale. An example are the researchers who sympathize with a segment of society they study and come up with some research findings that they consider potentially harmful to the group. The finding may not be detrimental if taken with all the necessary qualifications, but the researcher may know that the popular press will emphasize some aspects of the results and ignore these qualifications.

For some time now sociologists have placed a high value on objective social science. What have been some of the consequences of this effort? Gouldner points out that "the value-free principle did enhance the autonomy of sociology; it was one way in which our discipline pried itself loose—in some modest measure—from the clutch of its society, in Europe freer from political party influence, in the United States freer of ministerial influence."[22] Although sociology has not been kept value-free, sociologists are sensitive to the way in which values can cause bias in social research. Another consequence has been an increased emphasis on sophisticated statistical methods. Some sociologists assumed that bias could be avoided if the appropriate statistical procedures were employed. In reality the problems of value bias remain. Ideological values influence social research at all phases, from conception to publication.

IDEOLOGY AND INTEREST GROUPS

Ideology plays an important role in determining which social conditions are singled out as social problems. To the radical Marxist, America's social problems stem from its capitalistic economic system. Ideology determines how a social problem is defined.

Each political perspective determines just what a social problem is and what creates it. For instance, activists on the left blame the capitalist system for social problems such as environmental hazards, youth unemployment, and the monotony of work. Marxists are a sub-type of radicals who argue for a fundamental transformation to greater worker control of production as the solution to social problems. The term *radical* is often applied to Marxists, Social Democrats, and Critical Legal Theorists, who blame the system rather than individuals for social problems. Despite the radicals' inability to agree on the specifics of a strategy for transforming capitalism, they do share certain ideological assumptions. Radicals believe that corporate power, militarism, and imperialism are among America's most pressing social problems. By contrast, conservatives want "America to stand tall" and be the dominant military power. They support United States economic involvement in other nations, increases in the defense budget, and military solutions to many international problems, but they deny that the United States engages in imperialism or militarism and for this reason do not consider them social problems.

Ideology influences beliefs as to which issues are worthy of serious debate. Commonly, those taking an opposing ideological perspective on an issue or debate will deny that the issue is important or relevant. Consider the following questions:

Is capitalism basically a rational or basically an irrational form of economic organization?
Are the goals of social responsibility and profit maximization compatible for American corporations?
Does American investment in Third World nations tend to contribute to their long-run economic growth or does it constitute a new form of imperialism?

Radicals feel these questions need serious consideration. Liberals consider such issues worthy of debate, but give them a lower priority. Most conservatives would not consider them worthy of much attention, and certainly not in an introductory college course on social problems.

Ideology determines how a social problem is defined. Conservatives, liberals, and radicals can agree that America has a poverty problem, but they cannot agree on a specific definition of the problem. Conservatives will discuss the problem in terms of the low intelligence, lack of motivation, lack of ability to delay gratification, and other personal characteristics attributed to the poor. Liberals emphasize the lack of opportunity faced by the poor. Radicals say that poverty is a direct and logical consequence of a capitalistic economy.

Ideology also affects any discussion of solutions to a social problem. Consider again the poverty problem. The conservative is likely to argue that many of the poor are responsible for their poverty and deserve only charity or perhaps very temporary assistance until they find employment. Liberals argue that the poor need assistance, whether special education programs, job training, job creation, or some form of income maintenance. The objective of such programs is to give the poor who can support themselves the skills they will need to enter the mainstream of American society. Radicals call for a shift to or toward a socialist economy. The objective is to deal directly with the characteristics of the economy that generate and perpetuate poverty. Thus agreement that poverty is a social problem in no way assures agreement on possible solutions.

In view of the importance of ideology to the analysis of social problems, we will present a brief outline of conservativism, liberalism, and radicalism, the three perspectives that come up most frequently in the debates considered in this book. When appropriate, other ideological perspectives, such as feminist or Roman Catholic, are introduced. Some social problems are more appropriately analyzed in terms of opposing interest group perspectives, so we will also discuss interest groups and their relevance to the study of social problems.

Conservatism

Conservatism is often treated as a unified ideology. This is possible if some inconsistency among tenets is accepted. This inconsistency can be reduced by arguing that there are two basic conservative ideologies in America today: (1) individualist-conservatism, with the major emphasis on individual freedom, particularly freedom from government coercion; and (2) organic conservatism, emphasizing a reverence for and reification of society as the product of the traditions, institutions, and cumulative wisdom of the past.[23]

Several ideas are shared by almost all conservatives. One of the most fundamental is a pessimistic view of human nature.[24] People are seen as irrational, competitive, and motivated by self-interest. "History," wrote Edmund Burke, "consists for the greater part of the miseries brought upon the world by pride, ambition, avarice, revenge, lust, sedition, [and] hypocrisy." People are not considered perfectible. Conservatives distrust any utopian scheme that assumes people are basically good and does not take the baser side of human nature into account.

Individualist-conservatism draws heavily upon nineteenth-century capitalism and nineteenth-century liberalism. Basic to this ideology is the belief in the free market as a source of economic and political freedom.[25] In a free market economy there is marked decentralization of political power. The market allows freedom of choice and self-improvement. The result of these millions of individual choices is more harmony and greater satisfaction, but the total amount of satisfaction is greater in a free market than in any collectivistic alternative.

The individualist-conservative ideology is also opposed to coercion of the individual. The principal source of coercion in this context is the federal government. The individualist-conservative will therefore oppose government regulation of the economy and federal social welfare programs. Even when such programs are introduced for the highest of motives they invariably require extensive coercion.

Individualist-conservatives value cultural diversity. Inequality is viewed as necessary for diversity. Diversity in turn is essential to the evolution of culture; for example, the cultural achievements of ancient Greece would not have been possible without inequality supporting a leisured aristocracy. The individualist-conservative is intensively critical of socialist collectivization and economic leveling in general. Such efforts are considered coercive and a threat to individualism, motivation, and creativity.

Organic conservativism values past wisdom in dealing with today's problems. Society has a life and needs of its own; it is separate from the people that compose it. It is often viewed as an intricate and delicate mechanism that may be tampered with only with the greatest trepidation. Although it may not work perfectly, some imperfection is better than the risk of major upset of the existing social order. A case in point for the organic conservative is the marked discrepancy between the utopian ideals of nineteenth-century communists and the totalitarianism of the Eastern European countries in which an effort to realize these ideals was made.

Authority, social order, and freedom are all central concepts in the organic conservative ideology. Authority is essential to social order. Social order involves what is generally called law and order and a general acceptance of the existing relationships within institutions and among various segments of society (this is mainly an acceptance of the existing system of social stratification). Freedom is possible only when there is social order.

The term *freedom* is used by the organic conservative in a rather unusual way. People are free when they are not dominated by their baser tendencies and those of their fellow citizens. When these base tendencies (such as violence, irrationality, selfishness, and laziness) are controlled, people are free to live more creatively and meaningfully, contributing to the society. A similar argument is that people are free when they choose to act in the way they know they should.

The organic conservative believes that there are moral laws or principles by which people ought to guide their lives. One can never know exactly what these principles are, but the traditional wisdom of the past as reflected in custom, laws, and religion is usually a reliable guide.

The organic conservative favors social change when existing institutions must be adapted to changing conditions. Such change should take into consideration the wisdom of the past. The conservative frequently opposes proposed changes as rash or unnecessary. Social change may not be social reform; change can be bad as easily as good.

For the individualist-conservative, the basically selfish nature of humanity is not a liability. Some even say that selfishness is a positive virtue.[26] It is viewed as necessary for the operation of a free market. In contrast, the organic conservative believes the self-seeking nature of humanity must be controlled in the interests of a civilized existence. To the former selfishness is essential to freedom; to the latter it must be controlled if there is to be freedom.

The individualist-conservative wishes to maximize the freedom of individuals in society. He or she will therefore criticize proposals for government intervention in people's private affairs except for the preservation of law and order. The organic conservative wishes to preserve the social order rather than the freedom of individuals in society to do what they want. A strong central government able to control threats by the baser aspects of human nature to the social order would be consistent with the organic conservative ideology. The individualist-conservative ideology tends to be democratic; the organic conservative ideology tends to be elitist in arguing that very few people in society know what decisions are most appropriate for its preservation.

Both individualist and organic conservatives oppose communism and communist expansion; both emphasize military strength. The individualist-conservative is motivated by a desire to protect the citizens of the country against communist domination by an "evil empire" that would eliminate the free market and introduce collectivization and intolerance of individualism.[27] For the organic conservative the motivation is much the same—to protect society from radical change.

Private property and the protection of property rights is a concern of both conservative ideologies. To the individualist-conservative, property is the just reward for individual effort. To the organic conservative, the preservation of property relations is basic to the maintenance of social order.

Liberalism

Liberalism can be traced back to John Locke's *Second Treatise of Government* (1690), in which he defends the rights of the emerging mercantilist middle class to own property and conduct business with a minimum of government interference. During the nineteenth century, liberalism became strongly identified with capitalist ideology. But liberalism was more general, endorsing capitalism in the economic sphere and representative democracy in the political sphere.[28]

Today our economy involves more government regulation and is further from the ideal of the free market than it was in the nineteenth century. Political decision making has also undergone considerable change. But liberal ideology has kept pace with these changes and fully supports today's economic and political institutions.

Liberalism views human beings as motivated primarily by economic self-interest and defends their right to seek the maximization of private goals. This includes belief in the efficacy of the free market and in the right to private property. The liberal value on individualism is reflected in the political as well as the economic sphere. Civil liberties, due process, and other such rights are viewed as means for protecting the individual against the power of the state.

Liberalism sees the political system "as a free market for the exchange of demands, support, and public policies. Each individual has his specific wants and equivalent purchasing power—one vote. He 'buys' the policies and candidates of his choice in the competitive market on election day."[29] Politicians' desires to win elections encourage them to work out compromises among the interests of diverse constituents. These compromises co-opt many by giving them some of what they are seeking, but generally not complete satisfaction.

The liberal's image of political power in America is sometimes referred to as *pluralism*.[30] Power seems to be dispersed among a wide range of interest groups rather than concentrated in the hands of a "power elite" or a ruling class.[31] These interest groups are sometimes voluntary associations, but they can also be unorganized racial, ethnic, or occupational groups. From the pluralist perspective the decision-making process involves much coalition building and bargaining among interest groups.

The result is considerable compromise. Decisions and policies are likely to reflect the middle of the range of alternatives. The liberal position depends as much on the range of alternatives being proposed as it does on any general liberal tenet. Liberalism reflects a faith in the orderly give and take of decision making. The mechanisms of compromise contribute to political stability. This stability and the avoidance of violent conflict are basic liberal objectives.

Civil liberties and due process are also central to liberal ideology. Among the most basic civil liberties are freedom of speech, freedom of the press, and freedom of assembly. The right to due process ensures that a person's liberty and property cannot be taken without following clearly specified legal procedures; for example, guilt must be established on the basis of evidence that an existing law has been violated. The objective is to protect the individual from the exercise of arbitrary power by government.

Equality has always been a basic liberal value, but its meaning has shifted over the years. Our founding fathers referred to political and legal equality among adult white males. Men were equal if they had equal right to participate in the political process and were subject to the same laws. In time equality in this sense was extended at least formally to blacks and then to women. During the 1960s concern grew over the discrepancy between the formal rights to political participation and equal treatment before the law on the one hand and actual situation on the other. It became evident that in some areas highly effective informal mechanisms had been developed to restrict the political participation of blacks. Therefore the federal government took steps to remove the barriers to participation by blacks.

The 1960s also saw more emphasis on equality of economic opportunity. It became evident that those who were born poor had substantially less opportunity to achieve economic success. This lack of opportunity came to be viewed as a violation of the liberal ideological commitment to equality. Thus equality had come to include, if not complete equality of opportunity, at least equal opportunity to enter the American mainstream.

In recent years anticommunism has been a major tenet of liberal ideology. Communism is viewed as a threat to our capitalist economic system and our democratic political system, to say nothing of its consequences for individual freedom. Communism's willingness to use unscrupulous means to obtain control of a country and its ideological commitment to eventual world domination are major justifications of anti-communism. In light of the communist threat there is liberal support for a strong defense posture. The belief that all communist nations are controlled by Moscow was another tenet for many years, but it has broken down in recent years owing in large measure to the split between Communist China and the Soviet Union.

Liberals seek a world in which there are few international conflicts to disrupt American investments abroad. They seek a world where there is a stability of business transactions led by America's megacorporations. Liberals support right-wing dictators only because they make it easy for corporations to build export markets and cheap armies of workers. For instance, liberals fear the Sandinistas in Nicaragua because that government is perceived to threaten American business interests in Latin America. While liberals may abhor right-wing death squads in El Salvador, they favor military aid to the anticommunist government. There are limits to the liberals' support of interventionism on behalf of American business interests. When the cost in lives and money of the Vietnam War became too protracted, many liberals demonstrated against the war. Liberals may be opposed to a given intervention as too costly, but they broadly support American interventionism against left-wing movements if this objective can be achieved at a modest cost and without many American combat troops. American liberals view American domination of foreign governments as consistent with a national security that protects American markets.

Liberalism as we have presented it up to this point does not adequately describe the ideology of those who actively support efforts to deal with poverty, racism, sexism, and other forms of social inequality in America. Concern over the extent of social inequality and support for efforts to do something about it are characteristic of those who are referred to as *reform liberals, liberal reformers*, or (as we shall refer to them) *left-liberals*, On most basic ideological values left-liberals and other liberals are in agreement. In particular both accept capitalism and democracy as they exist in America today. Left-liberals call for reforms in the political and economic systems, but do not question the overall framework. They are quite willing to press for change using established procedures within the system.

The left-liberal supports efforts to make political decision making more responsive to the will of those supposedly being served. One form this view took during the 1960s was support for the Community Action Program, an effort to make local government more responsive to the needs of the poor, particularly the black poor.[32] Another form it has taken is support for legislation to regulate election campaign financing. Of particular concern has been evidence that large donations are often made with an implicit or explicit understanding of later special favors.

Left-liberals have been very interested in more equitable distribution of income and wealth. In recent years the most frequently proposed mechanism has been the guaranteed income (or the negative income tax, which always includes as a central component a guaranteed income). Although the idea was first proposed by Milton Friedman, a conservative economist, most subsequent proposals and support for the idea have come from left-liberals.[33]

The power of large corporations is more problematic to left-liberals than to other liberals. They are particularly disturbed by evidence of (1) collusion between corporations to limit competition and increase price and profits, (2) large contributions to the election campaigns of candidates for federal and state office to buy support for the industry's interests, and (3) strong lobbying against health and safety measures in industry and demands for curtailment of environmental pollution.

The left-liberal is more likely than other liberals to question United States involvement in the internal conflicts of developing nations. The left-liberal often sees such conflicts as nationalistic efforts to overthrow a foreign-dominated autocratic elite in favor of a regime that is responsive to the needs of the people. Knowledge that the insurgents have communist support does not seem sufficient grounds for United States intervention. Communism seems less threatening to left-liberals than to other liberals partly because they believe that there is increasing autonomy among communist nations.

Radicalism

There are almost as many radical ideologies as there are radical theorists. In particular, many ideologies are referred to as Marxism or neo-Marxism. To outsiders the distinctions between these ideologies often seem relatively unimportant; to insiders these distinctions are grounds for heated debate. For this discussion we will greatly simplify these distinctions by reducing radical ideology to *Marxism* and the *new left*. The ideology we refer to as Marxism might more appropriately be called *American neo-Marxism*. We will not discuss orthodox Marxism separately. The ideology of the new left is a synthesis of recent American radical ideologies generally not classified as Marxist.[34]

The term *Marxist* refers to those who believe that the economic structure of society basically determines social reality. One authority says it refers to those who:

1. see the character of economic organization as the basic factor in shaping a society's value system, social class structure, and political institutions and practices;
2. see a capitalist economy as creating profit-oriented, materialistic values and a class structure in which wealthy owners constitute a ruling class that uses the power of the state, both at home and abroad, in exploitative and selfish ways; and
3. believe that such a social system is unjust, unnecessary, inconsistent with man's nature, and should be eliminated—peacefully or, if necessary, by force.[35]

The Marxist conception of human nature is very different from that of the conservative or liberal. Conservatives have a basic distrust of human nature. People are viewed as naturally selfish, irrational, and untrustworthy. Liberals do not have as jaundiced a view of human nature, but do share with conservatives the belief that people are basically competitive and primarily motivated by self-interest. This trait is sometimes portrayed in a negative light, but more frequently it is portrayed as essential to an effective capitalist economic system. By contrast, Marxists have a very positive view of human nature: people naturally cooperate and search for fulfilling nonabrasive relationships with others.

Many Marxist criticisms of capitalism pertain to the consequences of the need for a constantly increasing supply of goods. Among the most frequently mentioned consequences are consumerism, militarism, and imperialism.

Economic power in America is much more concentrated than it was during the nineteenth century. The term *monopoly capitalism* refers to this more advanced stage of capitalism. In the earlier stage most market relations were competitive. But today the typical productive unit is not the small family firm or family farm producing an insignificant share of the market; it is the large corporation producing a sufficient share of the market to give it considerable control over prices.[36]

Greater economic concentration has led to a greater economic surplus (the difference between what a society produces and the cost of production). The absorption of the surplus is a major problem for monopoly capitalism. It can be consumed (as cars, schools, or military aircraft) or it can be invested. The logic of capitalism requires investment for greater future profits. As long as new markets and new sources of investment can be found, the surplus increases; but the Marxists argue that eventually such opportunities will be exhausted and the whole process will come to a grinding halt. For the Marxist this is the basic contradiction of the capitalist system.

The economic surplus can be absorbed through increased consumption. Advertising can create a demand for goods that people do not really need. But satisfication does not necessarily increase with consumption stimulated by advertising. The Marxist criticism goes deeper, calling the capitalist economy irrational for wasting so much production (surplus) on created needs while neglecting so many basic needs.

The Marxist believes the federal government is mainly subservient to corporate interests. In response to corporate needs the government has taken on a major responsibility for stimulating aggregate demand. In a more rational society, the Marxist say, the government would emphasize spending on social welfare needs. But in our society such needs have a lower priority because they do not contribute to the economic surplus. However, defense spending does contribute and in so doing it creates profits for corporate interests.

The Marxist believes defense spending is directly linked to imperialism.[37] A strong defense posture enables us to protect our overseas markets and sources of raw materials. The Marxists argue that the United States depends heavily on the ability to control the economies of other nations, particularly the less developed nations. They also argue that the affluence of the United States and Western Europe is mainly due to imperialism, whether past or present.

The liberal often defends American intervention in the less developed countries on the grounds that we should protect their political freedom. The Marxist argues that such intervention is basically economic. This is sometimes obvious, as when American war materials or even troops are used to prevent a takeover by those who are hostile to our business interests. In other instances our involvement is based on long-term economic interests. One of the justifications given for American involvement in Vietnam was the need to demonstrate to the major communist powers that we would not tolerate efforts to undercut governments favorable to our interests.

Marxists disagree on many issues. One of the most important disagreements is on the means of effecting the radical transformation of society for by Marxist ideology. Some say that in the United States the use of electoral politics is the only promising approach. Others argue that there is no hope at all for the United States in the foreseeable future. Still others argue that the revolutionary vanguard will be the peoples of the less developed nations of the world, not the poor or the working class in America. Some believe that radical transformation is possible without violence, but others believe that violent conflict is inevitable.

We are using the term *new left* to refer to recent American radicals who cannot appropriately be grouped with the Marxists.[38] We do not mean that they have not been influenced by Marxist ideology. Rather their critique goes substantially beyond the economic institutions and structures of American society. The ideology of the new left is not unified, but several tenets are repeatedly mentioned by its spokespeople.

The new left shares the Marxist objection to the "dehumanizing" consequences of our capitalist economy. It sees such goals as efficiency and profit maximization as being vigorously pursued with too little attention to the human costs involved. The new left shares the Marxist view that people are by nature cooperative and good; it also shares the view that extralegal means may be necessary for radically transforming society.

Herbert Marcuse speaks for many in the new left in saying that the technology and bureaucracy of modern society, both socialist and capitalist, have had disastrous consequences for human nature (the human spirit). Modern technology could have an immense liberating effect on humanity according to Marcuse, but as industrial society has evolved, people have been shaped to the needs of technology. They have been manipulated by the mass media to seek fulfillment in the material goods that must be consumed to keep the economy running smoothly. Materialism so pervades society that people usually define themselves in terms of their consumer goods.[39]

The new left sees American society and its institutional structures becoming increasingly centralized and bureaucratized. C. Wright Mills says that our society has become dominated by a power elite in each of three highly centralized and interconnected spheres of power: the military, business, and politics. A few leaders at the top of these bureaucracies make the important decisions in our society.[40] This view differs from the Marxist opinion that such decisions are made by the corporate elite alone and from the liberal idea that such decisions are compromises among a wide range of interest groups each pushing for its own objectives.

The highly bureaucratic nature of modern society causes alienation. People are alienated because they are so far from the centers of power and because the bureaucratic structure they encounter every day are so unresponsive to their needs. As antidotes to the alienation of bureaucratic society the new left proposes an emphasis on participatory democracy and community.[41] Radicals favor a more democratic structuring of work and more participation in all other social institutions. The goal of participatory democracy is to decentralize power and the decision-making process, that is, to return power to the people. Participatory democracy is an objective not only in the political sphere, but in all areas of life that are presently dominated by highly centralized bureaucratic structures.

A second response by the new left to the alienation of contemporary society is to seek a sense of community. This alternative has been taken up by many who have rejected materialism and competition in favor of such values as cooperation and brotherhood. For people to have a sense of community society must be organized around cooperation and mutual trust rather than around competition. In this framework, progress does not equal more sophisticated technology and material goods, but greater human liberation, freedom from alienation, and freedom from the abrasiveness of human interaction that so characterizes modern society.

References

1. See Ritchie P. Lowry, *Social Problems: A Critical Analysis of Theories and Public Policy* (Lexington, Mass.: D. C. Heath, 1974), p. 3.

2. The description of August Comte's project is drawn from Anthony Giddens's paper entitled, "Positivism and Its Critics," which appears as Chapter Seven in Tom Bottomore and Robert Nisbet, *A History of Sociological Analysis* (New York: Basic Books, 1978), pp. 237–86.

3. Ibid., pp. 240–41.

4. The materials on Durkheim's positivism are derived form Edward A. Tiryakian's paper entitled "Emile Durkheim," which appears as Chapter Six in Bottomore and Nisbet, *History of Sociological Analysis*, pp. 187–286.

5. Giddens, op. cit., pp. 243–45.

6. Ronald Chester, *Inheritance, Wealth, and Society* (Bloomington, Ind.: Indiana University Press, 1982), p. 31.

7. Ibid.

8. *Lochner* v. *New York*, 198 U.S. 45 (1905).

9. Robert Bierstedt, *The Social Order* (New York: McGraw-Hill 1970), p. 11.

10. Giddens, op. cit., pp. 237–38.

11. See Dorothy Emmet and Alasdair MacIntyre. *Sociological Theory and Philosophical Analysis* (London: The MacMillan Press, 1970). See especially Chapter Five, "Methodological Individualism Reconsidered," by Steven Lukes, pp. 76–88.

12. Giddens, op. cit., pp. 237–38.

13. Jerome G. Manis, *Analyzing Social Problems* (New York: Praeger, 1976), pp. 6–7.

14. Michael Bassis, Richard J. Gelles, and Ann Levine, *Social Problems* (New York: Harcourt Brace Jovanovich, 1982), p. 15.

15. The reader who is familiar with the sociological perspective of *functionalism* will recognize that what we are referring to as the "public opinion" perspective turns out to be a functionalist perspective. Functionalism is a consensus theory that tends to assume general societal agreement with respect to basic values.

16. Joseph Julian, *Social Problems*, 2nd edition (Englewood Cliffs, N.J.: Prentice-Hall, 1977), p. 3.

17. Manis, *Analyzing Social Problems*, pp. 18–19.

18. Howard S. Becker, "Whose Side Are We On?" *Social Problems* vol. 14 (1967), pp. 239–47.

19. Alvin W. Gouldner, "Anti-Minotaur: The Myth of a Value-Free Sociology," *Social Problems*, vol. 9 (1962), pp. 199–213.

20. Alvin W. Gouldner, "The Sociologist as Partisan: Sociology and the Welfare State," *American Sociologist*, vol. 3 (1968), pp. 103–16.

21. Gresham Riley, "Partisanship and Objectivity in the Social Sciences," *American Sociologist*, vol. 6 (1971), pp. 6–12.

22. Gouldner, "Anti-Minotaur," pp. 199–213.

23. Kenneth M. Dolbeare and Patricia Dolbeare, *American Ideologies* (Chicago: Markham, 1971), pp. 207–27. Our discussion draws upon their analysis of the distinction between organic and individualist conservatism.

24. Andrew Hacker, "On Original Sin and Conservatives," *New York Times Magazine*, February 25, 1973.

25. Milton Friedman, *Capitalism and Freedom* (Chicago: University of Chicago Press, 1962), pp. 7–21.

26. Ayn Rand, *The Virtue of Selfishness* (New York: New American Library, 1966).

27. Barry Goldwater, *The Conscience of a Conservative* (Shepherdsville, Ky.: Victor Publishing Company, 1960).

28. Dolbeare and Dolbeare, *American Ideologies*, pp. 5–106.

29. Ibid., pp. 5–53.

30. Robert A. Dahl, *Pluralist Democracy in the United States: Conflict and Consensus* (Chicago: Rand McNally, 1967).

31. C. Wright Mills, *The Power Elite* (New York: Oxford University Press, 1956).

32. Peter Marris and Martin Rein, *Dilemmas of Social Reform* (New York: Atherton, 1969).

33. Robert Theobald, ed., *The Guaranteed Income* (Garden City, N.Y.: Doubleday, 1966); Christopher Green, *Negative Taxes and the Poverty Problem* (Washington, D.C.: Brookings Institution, 1967).

34. Dolbeare and Dolbeare, *American Ideologies*, pp. 145–206. For a more thorough treatment see their discussion of the new left and American Marxism.

35. Ibid., p. 185.

36. Paul A. Baran and Paul M. Sweezy, *Monopoly Capital* (New York: Modern Reader Paperbacks, 1966), p. 6.

37. Harry Magdoff, "Militarism and Imperialism," *Monthly Review*, vol. 21 (February 1970), pp. 1–14.

38. The designation *new left* is not entirely satisfactory as it is typically used in reference to the radical student movement of the late 1960s. The term is being used here because the perspective being described

was in fact strongly influenced by the new left of the 1960s. Today there is no generally agreed-to term for this group. Cumbersome but more accurate designation might be the *non-Marxist radical left*. Even this designation, however, would be problematic, as it would tend to deny the very real link with the Marxist perspective.

39. Herbert Marcuse, *One Dimensional Man* (Boston: Beacon Press, 1969).
40. Mills, *The Power Elite*, Chap. 12.
41. Dolbeare and Dolbeare, *American Ideologies*, pp. 159–62.

PART I

SOCIAL PROBLEMS AND PUBLIC POLICY

CHAPTER 1

CAN THE GOVERNMENT SOLVE
SOCIAL PROBLEMS?

The quarrel between the liberals, conservatives, and radicals about the role of government in solving social problems is a guiding theme for all that follows in this book. The articles selected for this chapter present the strongest argument for each of the conflicting perspectives.

Senator Edward M. Kennedy's report on hunger is a restatement of the modern liberal position on the role of government regulation as the key to a humane society. Modern liberals emphasize the positive aspects of liberty. They believe that group goals such as the abolition of poverty and racism can be accomplished through innovative public policies. While liberals accept the central tenets of the capitalist system, they are quick to concede that the free market can also be a destructive and cruel predator to those unemployed by an unstable economy. Senator Kennedy views many of our social problems as emanating from a relentless recession combined with heartless cuts in government programs by the Reagan administration. He sees hunger on the rise because the state has abdicated its positive role in providing a safety net for those displaced and dispossessed by a "high-tech" economy. Kennedy, like other liberals, believes it is the role of the state to squarely confront social problems created by the economic sphere.

Thomas Sowell's examination of the government in its relations with minorities reveals government itself as the problem because it threatens to paralyze the free market. Sowell argues that poverty, criminality, unemployment, racism, housing shortages, and problems of work are only a few of the social problems created or worsened by the intervention of big government. Sowell, a black economist, cites slavery as an example of the evils of official government policy. He opposes the liberal idea of accomplishing group goals through government action and is confident that social problems can be solved eventually through the freedom of choice afforded by the private sphere. Sowell believes that democratic egalitarianism never works. He is suspicious of government programs because of the history of interventionism, which, in his view, has only made things worse. Sowell believes that government regulation can only lead to paternalism and the loss of liberty.

The debate between the liberals and conservatives on the role of government is seen as beside the point by radicals. Joe R. Feagin's section links today's social problems such as poverty to the capitalistic mode of production. To Feagin, social problems will never be solved until the fundamental inequality of capitalism is finally transformed. The government spending advocated by reform-minded liberals to alleviate social problems interferes with the accumulation of profit and is inevitably cut back. Yet when the government fails to intervene, as conservatives recommend, the effectiveness of the major legitimating prop of capitalism is diminished. The roller coaster ride never ends: social problems are never solved.

We can place the three perspectives in a nutshell by remembering that the liberal reformer favors government action aimed at curbing the excesses created by the private sphere; the conservative is confident that a free market is the ultimate solution to social problems; and the radical feels social problems are inherent to the capitalist system.

1. GOING HUNGRY IN AMERICA

**Report by Senator Edward M. Kennedy
to the Committee on Labor and Human Resources
United States Senate, December 22, 1983**

> About the twenty-third or the twenty-fourth of the month, the refrigerator is empty, and I often will not eat at all myself.
>
> Ms. Geraldine Smith, Pittsburgh, Pennsylvania
> November 21, 1983; Kennedy Forum on Hunger

INTRODUCTION

Over the past three years, the United States has endured a severe recession and unprecedented unemployment. At the same time, record budget cuts were being made in federal assistance programs for the needy. The National Bureau of Economic Research reported that the recession officially ended in November 1982. But Congress continued to receive reports of a different and more ominous sort from across the country—that more and more families were going hungry in America. The Reagan administration urged us to stay the course of its economic policy; they offered soothing reassurances that the reports of hunger were anecdotal, and that the truly needy were truly protected.

The reports of need persisted, and finally, a year into the recovery, I decided to see for myself. In a six-day period just before Thanksgiving 1983, I visited five different cities and communities in urban and rural America to investigate the facts.

The evidence I found of hunger is not anecdotal, but overwhelming; it leads to three fundamental conclusions:

1. For the first time since the 1960s, and perhaps since the Great Depression, hunger is on the rise again in America. After years of slow but steady progress in the war against hunger in this country, the momentum has shifted against us and the enemy is advancing.

2. The principal causes of the problem are the recession of 1981–82, which was the longest and deepest since World War II, and the simultaneous cutbacks in funds for basic federal nutrition programs and other measures to help the poor. At a time when record numbers of Americans were enduring severe deprivation because of the recession, deep cuts in the federal budget were stretching the safety net until it was too thin to protect the needy. The effect of the budget cuts was to rub salt in the wounds of the recession, and the heroic efforts of local agencies and private charitable organizations have not been able to undo

the damage. For millions of families facing Ronald Reagan's choice of sacrificing food, shelter, clothing, health or heat, food is the first necessity to go.
3. Hunger is not a new phenomenon in America, but it is one problem we know how to solve. The landmark federal initiatives of the 1960s launched nearly two decades of steady progress against hunger, and the sixteen recommendations in this report have been carefully developed to restore the path of progress. The goal is modest, and it is attainable at reasonable cost—approximately $2.5 billion a year—to hard-pressed federal, state, and local taxpayers.

More important that the cost is the renewed national commitment that goes with it. America has grown complacent about hunger; the hungry have again become invisible in our midst. As Thomas Jefferson wrote in the Declaration of Independence, "Let facts be submitted to a candid world." In that spirit, I offer the results of this investigation on hunger, confident that when America knows the facts, America will act.

FINDINGS

In November 1983, I held forums on the extent and consequences of hunger in five different areas—San Francisco, Minneapolis, Detroit, Pittsburgh, and eastern Kentucky. *There is clear, undeniable, authoritative evidence of widespread and increasing hunger in America.*

The Increase in Hunger

At every location more and more people are seeking food assistance on a regular basis. Social services agencies began to experience rapid growth in requests for food late in 1981 and those requests have in most cases at least doubled over the last year. In many areas the increases were even greater.

- According to the Kentucky Task Force on Hunger, 350 emergency food programs reported increases ranging from 75 to 400 percent.
- Since 1982, emergency food providers in the Twin Cities area are reporting a 150 to 400 percent increase in demand for emergency food assistance since 1981.
- In the San Francisco Bay Area, soup kitchens and dining halls for the needy report 200 to 400 percent increases. For example, the St. Vincent de Paul dining room, which served 4000 meals per month in 1980, is now serving over 25,000 meals per month, a sixfold increase.
- Soup kitchens in Pittsburgh and Detroit report a 300 to 400 percent increase in the number of people using their services from 1979 to 1983. In no case has utilization declined and in several instances the increases exceed 500 percent. In Pittsburgh, emergency pantries report a 200 percent increase in demand for services in each six-month period.

The New Poor

At the same time, the nature of those relying on public food distribution has changed, and many of them now come from intact families—the new poor. There was absolutely no evidence in our forums, or anywhere in any authoritative study or report, of people relying on soup kitchens even though they had sufficient funds to pay for their own food. Indeed, there has been a need to establish separate emergency food programs in order to serve the new poor. This shift in emphasis was reported by emergency food providers in each city. . . .

FINDINGS

The Reagan administration came to office after two decades of progress in the battle against hunger in America. Since then, we have lost ground in the battle, as a so-called supply-side economics has failed to supply even the most minimum level of nutrition for many who are among the most truly needy.

Witness after witness told the forums I chaired how they did not eat at all for a few days a week, or for a week or two at the end of every month. Soup kitchens and food assistance centers reported not only steady increases in the total number of individuals in need, but dramatic increases in the needy during the last two weeks of each month. In March 1983 the Pilot City Food Shelf in Minneapolis received 730 requests for food in the first two weeks of the month—and 1762 requests in the last two weeks of the month. In September, Holy Rosary Soup Kitchen served 147 guests in the first two weeks of the month and 412 guests during the last two weeks. In Detroit, one soup kitchen is serving 600 meals a day during the first two weeks of the month—and 1000 meals a day during the last two weeks. At every stop, the forums confirmed the findings of a May 1983 study commissioned by the United States Department of Agriculture—a study which revealed that emergency food agencies experience increased requests for help toward the end of every month, "often tripling the number of clients served the previous two weeks."

Moreover, the dedicated individuals involved in providing food for the needy are themselves nearing the end of their resources. Limitations on the availability of food and inadequate distribution facilities now make it impossible to serve a significant number of local agencies that request food to feed the hungry. Emergency food pantries report that demand and limited supplies mean harsh restrictions on recipients. In most instances, needy individuals and families are eligible to receive emergency food no more than *once* every six months. The food distribution effort is primarily a voluntary undertaking to meet a need that suddenly emerged; it is not a permanent system and there is reason to believe that it is strained near the breaking point. Volunteers are overworked; the hungry are underfed; and providers are fearful that they cannot sustain even present efforts if demand does not decline.

Much of the problem and much of the solution can be found in the same place— federal food programs. They have been cut back at fearful human cost. They are, in a sense, old programs; they are, in the best sense, liberal programs—and most of all, they are programs that were working. They showed that we could solve the problem of hunger—not by throwing money at it, but by spending money on it. There is no such thing as fighting hunger on the cheap.

The steps I recommend in this report will cost approximately $2.5 billion a year—or only one-twentieth of the $50 billion increase the Defense Department is seeking for military spending in the next year alone. Presumably that increase is supposed to advance the national defense. But surely the defense of this nation includes the health of our families as much as the size of our bombs; it means freedom from hunger for our own citizens at least as much as military assistance for Central America.

Forty years ago, an American President spoke of Four Freedoms as fundamental purposes of our national life. One of them was Freedom from Want. Today want stalks the communities of this land as it has not in many years.

During these forums, I saw families standing in the cold rain for hours in Minneapolis, waiting for a few pounds of cheese and butter. That cheese line, and others like it, are a rebuke to the American promise. Those families, and so many others like them, deserve Freedom from Want—and from the fear of going hungry in America. . . .

MINNEAPOLIS, MINNESOTA

I. Background

The economic crisis over the past few years in the United States has seen Minnesota lose more jobs by percentage than any other state in the country, resulting in 386,000 Minnesotans living at or below the poverty level. Unemployment is particularly severe in northern Minnesota, where the Iron Range is located. The state government has instituted an innovative jobs program involving both the public and private sector and has appropriated $70 million to this Emergency Employment Program. This program began in July of this year and it is anticipated that it will be several months before the program's impact is seen in lasting jobs.

The primary providers and organizers of emergency food programs in Minnesota are the church organizations. The corporate and philanthropic sectors have been extraordinarily active in supporting emergency food efforts. These emergency food services, food shelves, and meal programs experienced dramatic growth in 1983 due to the economic crisis.

In the metropolitan Twin Cities area, there is a reported increase of 150 to 400 percent demand for emergency food services since 1982. More than a half-million people have been fed through these services in the first eight months of this year. Metro food banks and food shelves report an increased use of their services by whole families, heavy use at the end of the month, and many repeat users, rather than one-time "emergency" cases. One food shelf director commented on the increase in the number of men—husbands and fathers—coming to the food shelf as compared with mostly single mothers and single men who had typically used the shelf. According to data gathered by the food services from the recipients, many people are using the food shelves to supplement diets monthly because of the inadequacy of federal food assistance programs or because they cannot participate in food assistance programs.

The metro area hot meals programs are run mainly by the Loaves and Fishes organization, which began in January of 1982. Over 130 churches participate in providing meals to 176,000 men, women, and children so far this year. Each church is responsible for preparing a meal for one of the five sites on a rotating schedule. Members of the congregations volunteer their time and efforts to provide food to the needy.

In northern Minnesota, the Iron Range is experiencing a critical emergency and what appears to be an insurmountable problem. Of the 15,000 steel workers, 1,500 presently have jobs. The unemployed are going into their second and third winters without employment.

In 1950 the natural iron supply was depleted and the Range went into a time of unemployment. Then taconite mining began and towns and cities on the range grew again.

Now that taconite is depleted, there appears to be no hope of future jobs on the Range, and with heavy industry being phased out across the country, their skills are not readily transferable. The unions have job retraining programs that are touching only one-tenth of the people. Attempts are being made to relocate people to the Twin Cities.

People living in northern Minnesota are struggling to meet mortgage payments on their houses and frequently sacrifice basic necessities such as food and clothing to hold on to their homes.

Iron Range Emergency Food Service statistics are staggering considering its small population—about 8.5 percent of the total state population. In 1981 with the first layoffs, there were big efforts to help their own people. But now, only the most severe cases are taken care of with money contributions. The food shelves report that they have all drawn down on their cash reserves and no new money is coming in. This constitutes a major crisis as they go into this winter. 15,705 families have been served to date this year (October). Duluth food shelves served 3785 families in 1982 and almost doubled the number of families served in 1983. Duluth hot meals programs have increased their monthly service by 100 percent in 1983.

Two Food Shelves in Duluth
        April through December 1981   —   803 families served
        January through September 1982   —   2241 families served
        January through September 1983   —   6937 families served

Cases of malnutrition have been referred by doctors to the food shelves on the range. Several doctors offer free medical care to the unemployed after office hours. One doctor expressed his fear and concern for the emotional and psychological well-being of the people in his town. In just one week in October he had "seen the regular yearly quota of people (4) experiencing critical psychological problems.'' He had treated and referred a young child who was threatening suicide, and young adolescents with depression and drug dependency. This was not typical for his practice. The doctor felt that these problems were directly related to the unemployment situation and that he was ''just beginning to see the tip of the iceberg.''

Other assistance to the Range has come from farmers who, while experiencing their own crisis, have donated food by the semitrailer load. Farmers who work the South for the winter have sent up citrus products—trailers of grapefruits.

Small metropolitan cities have ''adopted'' Range cities and towns in order to provide them with assistance.

In rural Minnesota, the north central and southern parts of the state, communities are trying to meet the growing needs of their citizens. Forty-four percent of all Minnesotans live outside the seven-county metro area and 65 percent of these people are living below the poverty level. Emergency food programs are just beginning to reach these areas. Rural hunger poverty is hidden and services aren't as accessible. Many rural counties have limited or no federal food assistance programs. Nine counties have no WIC programs and some country commissioners have refused the school lunch program.

Increase in the number of people using rural and suburban emergency food programs does not show up in thousands. One small food shelf in Elk River served an average twenty families per month in 1982 and presently in 1983 it serves a hundred families per month, mostly young couples living in mobile homes in the area. The food shelf director reported a change in recipients over the last year from mostly single mothers with children to whole families.

Status of Public Assistance Programs in Minnesota.   In Minnesota, 578,000 people receive 1.9 pounds of food each month through the Commodities Distribution Program. Minnesotans are forced to stand in long lines for sometimes over four hours in all kinds of weather—rain, snow, and temperatures of fourteen degrees below freezing.

Although the commodities program does provide Minnesotans with some cheese, butter, honey, and sometimes cornmeal, the program does not take into account adequate nutritional needs. Decisions on what will be distributed is based on surplus, not what is needed nutritionally.

In Minneapolis there are areas where people are waiting in long food lines around the corner from huge warehouses where surplus commodities are stored. Storage, refrigeration, transportation, and handling costs for the commodities are enormous problems. Some emergency food programs do not take the free commodities available to them because it takes all their time to get it, store it, actually use it (due to packaging), and complete the intricate paperwork. They just don't have the manpower to do this.

According to an Emergency Needs Project report recently published by a Minneapolis community group, the state estimates that 102,201 women and children are eligible for WIC, a conservative estimate. Through the federal Emergency Jobs

Bill this summer, funds were made available for program expansion in the state. The state made money available to currently operating programs and funded new programs in fourteen unserved counties. These new projects were only beginning service in September 1983. Nine of Minnesota's eighty-seven counties still do not have WIC programs.

USDA has developed a new funding formula and proposes to fund Minnesota at the September participation rate. This new funding formula will leave Minnesota short of funds to serve 26,000 women, infants, and children at the current participation rate.

Along with inadequate WIC funding, federal maternal and child health program funds, and critical preventative health services have been cut back up to 18 percent in Hennepin County alone, due to recent budget cuts. In one county in the Twin Cities area, many children have dropped out of the school lunch program due to federal cutbacks. Many of these children were previously eligible for free meals and are not participating because the reduced meals' price charges doubled. The Minneapolis School Department estimates that raising the cost of their school lunches eliminated 40 percent of the children who formerly participated in the reduced price lunch program. Average daily breakfast participation in Hennepin County fell by 25 percent from the 1981/1982 school year to the 1982/1983 school year.

Although the Minneapolis School Department reports little difference in total participation, other changes have been reported. Less schools offer breakfast programs than in the past for a variety of reasons, and school nutritionists are observing increased chronic underfeeding. There appear to be greater numbers of children whose only meals per day are the school meals, particularly toward the end of the month.

The Minnesota Child Care Food Program (CCFP) experienced its biggest cuts in 1981. Day care centers and homes limit children to two meals and one snack, even in full-day programs. Reduced reimbursement levels are forcing some programs to turn to food banks and are making it more difficult for them to serve nutritionally balanced meals.

Minnesota congregate and home-delivered meals program have been able to expand to serve all senior citizens who wanted to participate due to carry-over funds in the state. These carry-over funds will be used up by next year. Many programs will be cut back or eliminated if there is no increase in federal funding for next year. Food stamp participation has increased by 27 percent since 1980 in the Minneapolis area. It is difficult to estimate the number of people who have lost their food stamp benefits due to tightened eligibility. According to the Minnesota State Food Stamp Office, at the same time that people were cut off from benefits, an increased number of other people were applying. However, as of July 1983 only a little more than half of the potentially eligible persons in Hennepin County were participating in the food stamp program. This does not take into account the many needy people who cannot get food stamp assistance because of the severely restricted eligibility levels. Along with tightened eligibility, many food stamp recipients are experiencing a long waiting period before these benefits start. It has been reported that people whose applications may not be processed and benefits provided within the mandated times, are being referred to food shelves for help during this time.

II. Forum and Other Activities

Commodities Distribution Site Visit.   At 9:00 on Saturday morning, I visited a commodities distribution site at the Hamilton School in Minneapolis. At the Hamilton School, I saw hundreds of area residents lined up in the driving rain waiting to receive five pounds of cheese and two pounds of butter on a first-come first-serve basis. Honey was also scheduled to be distributed but due to red tape it was not released from the warehouse ten miles away from the distribution site. People had started to arrive at 7:30 A.M. and by 12:00 noon up to 1564 people had been served. I spoke to many senior citizens, families, and handicapped individuals as they waited outside to get less than one day's supply of food.

The Forum.   Following the commodities distribution site visit, I arrived at the Plymouth Congregational Church in Minneapolis, where I conducted a forum on hunger in Minnesota. Fourteen people came together from across the state to tell about Minnesotans who are hungry and of their efforts to help these people.

Cyndie Tidwell, coordinator of Minnesota Food Share, presented an overview of the statewide efforts of emergency food systems to meet the needs of the more than 100,000 people now depending on these services for their basic needs.

Cyndie reported that the majority of emergency food programs, food shelves, and hot meals programs started in 1982 and 1983 in response to economic crisis and severe unemployment in the state. She said than "many long-standing emergency providers in the metro area report an increase of 150 to 400 percent in demand for services since 1982."

Cyndie described other efforts of the communities to provide emergency food, specifically the Metro Food Share drive, which took place this past February. Cyndie told of how the religious community, corporate food producers, food shelf providers, and many other groups worked together to reach a goal of collecting 200,000 pounds of food for metro area emergency food services. During that month of February, "the community responded overwhelmingly with the final grand total of 1.8 million pounds of food collected." This was supposed to be a one-time effort but Cyndie said she is now coordinating a statewide food share drive for this coming February.

Cyndie also commented on the Commodities Distribution Program:

. . . it's obviously bitterly cold here December to April. On a first-come, first-served basis to receive less than a one-day supply of food is a publicly humiliating act and causes additional hardship.

Cyndie told me that the community is now asking, "What is an emergency?" She said that the emergency food programs have now become critical lifesaving services instead of emergency services. She said the community is asking, "What is the appropriate role of the community?" Cyndie said that the community is greatly concerned with the fate of the hundreds of thousands of their fellow citizens who are depending on them to eat. "What if the all-out community effort wanes?"

I then heard from eight Minnesotans regarding the problems they were experiencing and how they came to use the emergency food programs.

— Lois and Melvin Perkins told me of the emotional and physical strains they have experienced since Mr. Perkins was laid off in December 1982. Melvin had been working at a furniture company for fifteen years and was earning $24,000 annually before being laid off.

They are behind in their rent again. Because Melvin has been called back to work once in a while for one or two days, they do not qualify for many assistance programs.

Lois said she uses the food shelf in Elk River, a rural suburb where they live with one of their two daughters. Mrs. Perkins said that they ate pancakes for a week because they didn't have any other food.

Lois said that their eldest daughter, who attends community college, has been having grand mal seizures daily and that she thinks it is the result of the emotional strain on the family. Melvin experienced a mental collapse on New Year's Day because he was so distraught over his unemployment.

Lois has cancer. She did not go to a scheduled checkup two months ago. She said that she has been having some physical problems and discomfort recently. They do not have any medical insurance.

— Ruth Rice is sixty-seven years old and lives in an efficiency in Minneapolis. She said she goes to the local church soup kitchen four nights a week.

Ruth told me that she ate only one meal a day all last year. She said she was hospitalized in February and the doctor told her that her poor diet contributed to her health problems. Ruth receives $365 a month from Social Security and pays $225 in rent per month. Ruth works two hours a week at the church day care center for $8.00. She periodically sits with a senior citizen for $10.00 a day. "Not in my whole life did I think I would be like this." Ruth said she would probably go back to eating one meal a day if she couldn't go to the soup kitchen.

—Mary Smith is twenty years old and lives in a shelter in downtown Minneapolis. Mary was laid off from a secretarial job in August of last year. In the ensuing months, Mary lost her apartment and sold her furniture. She continued to look for a job.

Mary told me that she ate yogurt and water for a month. She said she lived on just water for three days before she went to the shelter. One night Mary sat in a hospital waiting room and then found an empty bed to sleep in. The hospital staff referred her to the shelter.

Mary said that she always had plenty of everything when she was growing up: "Let's put it this way, my mother gave me a new color TV set each Christmas. As I got bigger, so did the set."

Mary divorced her husband last year but while married, Mary said that their combined income was $35,000 annually. Mary said it is "very scary to be like this."

—Carol Burdick is thirty-six years old and lives in St. Paul with her two school age children. Mrs. Burdick is recently unemployed. She receives $100 per month in unemployment benefits and $80 per month in food stamps.

Carol told me that she worries about her children's nutrition. She said she eats popcorn in the afternoon before they come home from school and tells them that she is not hungry so they will have enough to eat for dinner. "I will beg to make sure my children have enough to eat."

Carol goes to a food shelf in St. Paul. "A friend and I walked seven miles home from the food shelf carrying the groceries." She said that people make cruel comments in the store when she pays for food with food stamps. "I told one woman that I hoped she never had to use food stamps."

Carol said that she is a survivor and a fighter and that she wasn't going to give up.

—Robert Voht is thirty-nine years old and a Vietnam veteran. He was laid off six months ago and receives $182 per month in unemployment benefits. He pays a $412 mortgage payment every month, plus utilities. His wife Vicky works fifteen hours a week as a maid and earns $4.65 per hour.

Robert, Vicky, and their two children eat at the local church soup kitchen four nights a week. Vicky said that she "wouldn't know what to do if it wasn't there." The Vohts do not qualify for food stamps. Mrs. Voht told me, "We both cry a lot and can't sleep at night."

The Vohts are trying to hold on to their house. They lived in a trailer for four years in order to save enough money to purchase their home. Mr. Voht said "it would be just too much if we lost our house."

—Rod Scarborough is fifty-three years old and lives in a rooming house in downtown Minneapolis. He has had chronic back problems due to an injury when he was young. In 1973, he lost his job, his house was repossessed, and he became a hobo. In September he arrived in Minneapolis on a freight train and a policeman sent him to the General Assistance Office and to a shelter.

Rod told me that he has lived under bridges, along railroad tracks, and in missions. He said he's eaten out of garbage cans and lived on soda crackers for weeks at a time. He said he's sold blood to eat and, "At one time I stole food and sold it . . . may God forgive me."

Rod said he never thought he would be like this until it happened. He said that things are just as bad as the Depression.

I then heard testimony from two people who are providing emergency food services to hungry Minnesotans on a day-to-day basis.

—Sadie Bronson is an LPN and nutritionist who is the director of the food shelf in Itaska County, a rural area in northern Minnesota with high unemployment. She has been working in conjunction with the University of Minnesota on documentation of nutritional needs using diet recall surveys.

Sadie talked about the people who come to the food shelf. She said many are unemployed and have come from the Iron Range· and have moved back in with relatives. "I have seen sixteen people living in one small house." Sadie said that a woman and her daughter who live in a tent use the food shelf and "a man who lives in his car also comes to our shelf." Sadie said that a young couple who lost their home came into the food shelf asking for "only food they could cook over a campfire." Sadie talked about the many people that come to the shelf who are acutely unemployed and are on a waiting period of six to eight weeks for benefits.

Sadie also described many of the food shelf users as "senior citizens on fixed incomes who can't make it." She said she had recently serviced an elderly couple who had been eating cat food.

Sadie said that she had seen an increase in people's diet recall and feels that it is a result of those people using the food shelf. She told me that she believes that outreach is very important and that the only way that people find out about the services now is through friends. She also stated that nutrition education and use of food, particularly the Federal Commodities, is essential.

—Mary Jo Knox is a neighborhood worker at the Branches, a drop-in center run by Catholic Charities. Mary Jos is in charge of the on-site eating programs for all three "Branch" locations. They see 150 to 200 people per day for meals at each center.

Mary Jo told me about the problems people are having "in the cities." She said she services the chronically unemployed, the sporadically chronically unemployed, and those with bad job records.

Mary Jo said she is seeing more young people, eighteen to twenty-five, and more women with two to three children coming to the Branches. She has a pregnant mother with six children coming in who can't stretch her food stamps and who is living in one small room. "It's as if they won't give them enough assistance and watch them suffer. The system makes them cheat."

A year ago a man named John came into the Branches. He was a laid-off computer worker who came in to eat. He set up an appointment to talk with me. He said he didn't want to lose his self-respect and dignity like he saw other people at the center had. He was asking for help. Well, it's a year later and he has lost his dignity, has gone downhill just as he feared. He's having a difficult time.

Mary Jo said, "These people have a lot of pride and there is a stigma to being at the center. Some people know that jobs may never be there."

Mary Jo talked about the malnourished children she has seen at the Branches:

Malnourished means when I see kids with blotchy skin, pasty-looking, gray complexions. Their hair is thin with no luster and they have bald patches. Some children are very skinny and sometimes they look obese and bloated.

A lot of women with children are not coming in. Transportation is a problem and they have to cart all their children with them.

Mary Jo stated that one of the problems in the city is that "there are only small convenience stores located in most of the neighborhoods. These stores don't carry a wide variety of fresh fruits and vegetables. They carry lots of junk food and at twice the price as larger stores and those stores in the suburbs. Five dollars in food stamps doesn't go nearly as far as it would in the suburbs."

Mary Jo cited another problem in the city as the "high crime rate area" that a lot of people live in. Because of the low amount of general assistance and AFDC, these people live in the worst part of town. Mary Jo said it prevents a lot of people from using congregate dining and prevents mothers from taking their children to soup kitchens for evening meals.

Mary Jo described the emergency food system as "only a Band-Aid on the crisis."

Four medical professionals and nutritionists testified regarding the problems they were seeing in their patients and clients in the area of nutrition and health.

—Dr. Johanna Miller, a pediatrician at the Pilot Cities Health Clinic in Minneapolis, told me that the WIC program is vital to the health and well-being of most of the women, infants, and children she sees. "This program is a carrot to primary health care for these people."

Dr. Miller refers mothers and children to the food shelf three and four times a week. She said there is an increase in referrals to the shelf near the end of the month when benefits, WIC, and food stamps have been exhausted.

Dr. Miller said she prescribes tea, Kool-Aid, and juices from the food shelf for children who come in with temperatures and infections because the mothers do not have any fluids at home for the children. Dr. Miller also gives out cans of formula to mothers from the free formula supply the clinic receives from companies. She said food shelves don't have cans of formula.

Dr. Miller talked about the noticeable increase in the number of young children coming to the clinic exhibiting nonorganic "failure to thrive." She said that this may be a result of the tension surrounding food or lack thereof at home and eating may take on a negative meaning for the child.

—Dr. Edward Ehlinger, director of Personal Health Services for the Minneapolis Health Department, talked about "a disturbing reality in Minnesota—the reality that not all groups are sharing equally in the benefits of our health and social service system. The reality of inequity is particularly evident in minority and low-income populations." He said that this inequity can be seen in Minneapolis infant mortality rates for blacks and Native Americans which were two and a half times that for whites in the three-year period between 1979–1981. "In low-income neighborhoods in Minneapolis, the infant mortality rate is twice that of more affluent neighborhoods."

Dr. Ehlinger cited recent economic and social policy changes as having added many people to the ranks of the disadvantaged: "Increased employment, loss of insurance coverage, tightened eligibility for welfare, decreased reimbursement for medical assistance, and elimination of some health and social service programs have had a tremendous impact on the poor and near-poor and the health and social service agencies that remain to work with them.''

The doctor told of the consequences of cutbacks in services on his clients. He said the number of potentially preventable infant deaths in Minneapolis more than doubled over 1981 to 1982. He said he has recently seen women opt for no prenatal care or for a home delivery solely for financial reasons. Many mothers have postponed immunizations for their children and have not taken them for regular checkups. Dr. Ehlinger told of his concern for his clients if further cuts are made: ''. . . Even without further cuts we can't keep up with the increasing demand for our services from people who have lost health benefits because they are unemployed. . . .''

Dr. Ehlinger concluded that an increasingly large number of people in Minneapolis, particularly mothers and children, are at increasingly high risk for adverse health outcomes and that the most vulnerable of these people are the poor and minorities:

. . . It will be a sad commentary on our health and social service system because we have demonstrated in the past through programs like the Maternity and Infant Care and Children and Youth Projects, Neighborhood Health Centers, and WIC that we can improve the health of all Americans. It will reflect the fact that we are ignoring all that we have learned over the last twenty years. It will reflect the fact that we as a society are ignoring the plight of the disadvantaged.''

—Patricia Milhous, a registered dietician and head of the Nutrition Unit of Minneapolis Health Department, is responsible for managing the WIC program. She told me that the Hennepin County WIC program is the largest WIC program in Minnesota.

Pat presented statistics gathered from a large outreach campaign and special WIC enrollment clinics made possible this summer by the Emergency Jobs Bill money. She said that up to 70 percent of the women enrolled in the WIC program this summer had income levels below the federal poverty level. Pat cited statistics on the percentage of women, infants, and children enrolled through the summer special clinics who had anemia.

	Women	Children	Infants
Special summer WIC clinic	33%	21%	13%
Typical WIC clinic	28%	11%	5%

Pat also told of the growth problems that these children and infants were having. She said that the infants under one year of age demonstrated a great need in this area and that babies of that age are very nutritionally vulnerable. She reported that 14 percent of infants had low weight for their age.

Pat concluded by telling me that despite this demonstrated high need in Hennepin County, a freeze was placed on the WIC program on October 1st. She said that in a three-day period of the past week, more than eighty-five women, infants, and children with inadequate diets were placed on a waiting list.

WIC services continue to be needed. . . . However, WIC dollars have not increased at the same rate. Individuals recovering from nutritional problems and women, infants, and children with poor quality diets are no longer served. WIC then becomes a therapeutic, or treatment program, and the original intent of the program—that of nutritional prevention—is lost.

—Katherine Cairns, a public health nutritionist and director of the St. Paul/ Ramsey County Nutrition Program, reported on the status of over 13,000 preschool and school-age children from all income levels throughout Ramsey County seen at preschool screening from January 1980 through September 30, 1983.

Kathy said the surprising finding was "the poor nutritional health of the non-WIC population." She described these children as supposedly well nourished, assumed to be in good health with few nutritional problems, of higher income status, and more likely to live in higher income suburbs of St. Paul. "We found that their nutritional status was actually worse than that of some of our new, unserved, low-income WIC clients."

Kathy stated that the declining health and nutrition status of these higher income clients could be traced back to 1980 and that significant changes were occurring in short stature, underweight, and overweight.

Kathy said that although short-stature problems declined in 1981–1982, they are beginning to see an increase again in 1983. According to Ms. Cairns, this statistic suggests evidence of more long-term nutrition problems. She further reported that underweight problems are increasing "with a dramatic increase developing in 1983." Along with these statistics, Ms. Cairns reported data which detailed the dramatic increase in low protein levels, low vitamin A and C levels, and low calcium levels in these children.

Kathy summarized her findings by saying:

. . . as a Public Health Nutritionist, I have serious concerns about those children in our community that are not considered to be low income. They may be the corridor poor, middle, or high income. Regardless, we have documented increasing levels of nutrition problems in these children. Further investigations of these trends is warranted."

Conclusion

From the testimony and statistics of increased emergency food program use presented at the forum, it is clear that many people in Minnesota are not able to obtain enough food. Along with people who have consistently lived below the poverty line, individuals who were typically able to provide for themselves and their families have joined the growing number of hungry people in the soup kitchen and food shelf lines. These people are unemployed and underemployed. Most have solid work histories. They have a desire to work, to support their families, to hold on to their homes or apartments. They talk about the shame they feel going to the soup kitchens, standing in food lines, using food stamps for the first time. "But you learn to survive, to do what you have to do" was a statement heard again and again.

People on the Iron Range are selling their homes for $10,000 and moving back in with relatives. People in rural Minnesota are living in tents or in their cars asking the food shelves for "only food we can cook over a fire."

Evidence was given on the impact of the cutbacks in federal assistance programs. Food stamps are running out before the end of the month for many people as documented by increased use of food shelves and hot meal programs in the second half of the month. The WIC program is servicing only 15 percent of the eligible woman, infants, and children in Hennepin County alone. Due to cuts in funding, their case load has been frozen and people are being taken off the program and put on waiting lists. Nine counties in Minnesota still do not have a WIC program.

Perhaps the most disturbing evidence of the hunger problem in Minnesota and the danger it is posing to people's health was given by the medical community. Doctors and nutritionists testified to the declining health and nutritional status not only of individuals using federal assistance programs but also of individuals, particularly children, from all income levels.

Dr. Ehlinger of the Minneapolis Health Department called his department's recent findings on the anemia rate of women, infants, and children enrolled in the WIC program this summer "shocking," and described the findings as further evidence that "there is hunger in this country." The Department reportedly "hasn't seen this kind of anemia level since back in the early 1970s when the anemia rate was about 12 percent instead of this year's 20 percent."

Katherine Cairns, director of the St. Paul/Ramsel County Nutrition Program, reported that the nutritional status of preschool and school-age children from all income levels was actually worse than that of new, unserved low-income WIC clients. Ms. Cairns summarized her findings by saying:

. . . Malnutrition is increasing in what many people define as middle-income Americans. I urge you to . . . realize that hunger in America, which was documented in low-income children in the 1960s, has reappeared in the 1980s to impinge on the health of the low- and middle-income children."

Both the government and the community in Minnesota are very aware of the existence of hunger in their state. In response to the increase in need for emergency services over the past two years, the government and community have been actively seeking ways to meet these needs.

—In 1982 Governor Perpich convened an Emergency Task Force to study the alarming increase in demand for emergency food services.

—In February of 1983, the Greater Minneapolis Council of Churches in conjunction with other religious organizations, private foundations, and the corporate sector conducted the Metro Food Share and raised 1.8 million pounds of food.

—The Minnesota Public Health Department is presently completing a study of Minnesota's use of emergency food services, the nutritional status of these users and the impact of federal food programs in Minnesota.

In July 1983, representatives from the religious, philanthropic, and corporate sector, emergency service providers, volunteers, and advocacy groups formed the Emergency Needs Project in order to gather data and address the growing need for emergency food in Hennepin County.

Minnesota has sophisticated emergency food networks in place and tremendous community support for helping the hungry and the needy. Those volunteers, congregations, and agency staff are asking why these emergency food programs have become critical services, not just one time a year but every month. They are reporting that an emergency has become "chronically inadequate income for many families." Cyndie Tidwell, coordinator of the Minnesota FoodShare summarized the feelings of the community.

It is a confusing and ironic image of America—a nation that had to put nearly one third of selected croplands in "idle" to try to reduce surpluses of basic commodities, and still ends up "holding the bag" so to speak, with warehouses bulging with excess food—while we here in Minnesota, part of the breadbasket of the world, have hundreds of thousands of our brothers and sisters unable to put adequate food on the table, or to meet other basic needs on a secure basis. We ask if it is possible to say that every person as a member of the community has inherent rights and claims on the resources of the community in a just society. That seems to be an emergency consensus of the community here—and might it not be reasonable to assume that it would also be the consensus of this nation?

CONSERVATIVE: NO

2. GOVERNMENT AND MINORITIES

Thomas Sowell

Government has three roles in the economy that bear on the economic fate of ethnic groups: (1) government provides a legal framework within which transactors can make their own economic (and other) decisions; (2) government can reduce the options available to the transactors; and (3) government can redistribute the fruits of economic transactions.

Government is inextricably bound up with politics, even in non-democratic nations. Therefore, the role of government is greatly influenced by the incentives and constraints facing those individuals who pursue politics as a career. This simple fact is often overlooked in policy discussions in which the government is treated as if it were an external agency correcting the deficiencies of other institutions — more or less "the public interest" personified. While public spirit and self-sacrifice have characterized some statesmen, to expect this to be the sole or dominant incentive among political decision-makers as a whole is to ignore thousands of years of human history.

GOVERNMENT AS FRAMEWORK

The diffusion of knowledge and the concentration of power can be reconciled by having economic decisions made by individual transactors, and the terms agreed upon enforced by the government. In addition to these explicitly contractual agreements, there are virtually universally shared desires — such as security of person and belongings — which can be treated as implicit contracts to be enforced by the government. Depending upon the specific nature of the government, the population (or segments thereof) may have more or less "rights" — meaning, empirically, options for which government force is available to the individual.

The stable framework of behavioral expectations provided by government enables individuals to interact with less fear of physical or economic harm from one another, fewer and less costly precautions, and more willingness to undertake joint actions whose benefits accrue in the future. Much of this beneficial effect comes from the stability of the framework rather than the intrinsic merits of its specific provisions. For example, driving on the right-hand side of the road may be no more advantageous than driving on the left-hand side of the road, but either system may be far preferable to *ad hoc* decisions by each driver.

In the case of low-income ethnic groups attempting to rise, the degree of stability of the governmental framework is especially important. Typically, low-income ethnic groups are relative newcomers — either to the country or (in the case of blacks or American Indians) to the urban economy and society. It is difficult enough to adjust to a new situation, but adjusting to a situation that is itself continually changing is obviously even more of a problem. To what extent has the government maintained stable "rules of the game," within which ethnic minorities could adjust? A brief historical sketch of blacks may suggest some of the problems.

Initially, Africans brought to the United States in the early seventeenth century became indentured servants, like most white immigrants, and were freed at the end of a few years. Somewhere around the middle of the seventeenth century, this was changed to perpetual slavery. Free blacks in the early seventeenth century had essentially the same rights as their white contemporaries, but these rights came to be taken away, one by one, with the development of slavery and its attendant efforts to control and humble the entire black population. The post-Revolutionary War era led to abolition of slavery in the North, and a relaxation of restrictions on "free persons of color." But within a generation, new government restrictions began to be imposed on the occupation, mobility, legal status, etc., of free Negroes. Moreover, the enforcement of these state laws was highly varied with respect to both time and place. Free blacks were voting, even in some southern states, in the 1820s but, by the mid-nineteenth century, all southern and even many northern states were barring blacks from voting — but in less than a generation these laws were repealed. In the South, Reconstruction saw blacks holding political office on a large scale, from local officials to the Congress of the United States. Just one generation later, Jim Crow laws and extralegal terrorism against black voters almost totally eliminated black officials from southern political life. In the national government, the slow progress of black employees over the decades was suddenly reversed by the Woodrow Wilson administration, which introduced segregation among federal employees and began a drastic cutback of blacks in nonmenial jobs. In the war of 1812 Commodore Perry's crew had been one-fourth black, but by the 1920s there was literally not one black in the navy. In the 1930s, the New Deal began a slow reversal again, toward better treatment of blacks — a pattern now a little more than a generation old.

In broad historical terms, government has changed the rules of the game for blacks in virtually every generation. These have been fundamental changes stretching across the spectrum from education to housing to jobs to voting. Nor have blacks been unique. The changing interpretations and violations of Indian treaties are an historical scandal. With respect to European immigrants, the largest and most open migration in human history was suddenly brought to a screeching halt in the 1920s. Japanese Americans, who were initially welcomed as workers in California in the nineteenth century, were later segregated in the schools, barred from numerous occupations, forbidden to own land, locked up *en masse* during World War II — and then, in less than a decade, all these trends reversed. Residential segregation of Orientals collapsed, high rates of intermarriage with whites followed, along with national political office holding — and then even preferential treatment as "disadvantaged" minorities, while earning above-average incomes.

The point here is not so much the individual merits or demerits of these various policies considered in isolation. The point is the sheer *volatility* of government policy toward ethnic groups. Nor is the United States unique in this. Similar patterns have occurred in other multi-ethnic societies. Political authorities in many countries have often turned against ethnic minorities once allowed to prosper in peace. The brutal mass expulsions of East Indians under the Amin regime in Uganda, the slaughter of the Ibos in Nigeria, and the severe current official discrimination against the Chinese in Indonesia are recent examples of a pattern of volatile government policy changes toward minorities that goes back for centuries. Historically, Germany was one of the most open, tolerant, and favorable countries in the world for Jews — until the generation of Hitler and the Holocaust. American Jews were so favorably disposed toward Germany as of World War I that the U.S. government cracked down on Jewish newspapers in the United States on grounds of undermining the war effort. From World War I to World War II was less than a quarter of a century.

In view of the historic unpredictability of government policy toward ethnic minorities, it is perhaps unsurprising that some of the most dramatic rises from poverty to affluence in United States have been among groups who did *not* attempt to use the political route to economic advancement — notably the Chinese, the Japanese, and the Jews. Chinese American leaders long ago made a deliberate decision to keep out of the political arena, while concentrating on economic progress. Conversely, the group with the longest and most intimate involvement with the U.S. government — American Indians, especially on reservations — have long been at the bottom of the economic ladder by such indices as family income or unemployment rates, not to mention restrictions on the use of their own property and other paternalistic policies of the Bureau of Indian Affairs. The most politically successful American ethnic group — the Irish — was also the slowest rising of the nineteenth-century European immigrant groups.

Nevertheless, it is taken as axiomatic in many quarters that political action is the key to economic advance. Even writers who use the recent economic advancement of blacks through government policy as proof of the power of group political action nevertheless note — as an isolated curiosity — that northern blacks have had *declining* voter registration and voter turnout since 1940. Southern blacks of course vote much more often than before — but this is a consequence rather than a cause of federal government policy.

At particular historic junctures, government policy may be beneficial to particular ethnic groups. It is the long-run reliance on political action that is questionable in view of the unpredictability of political trends in general. It has been said that in politics "overnight is a lifetime." Even in governmental institutions less subject to electoral shifts — the Supreme Court, for example — profound changes can take place in a span that is relatively short in historical perspective. Throughout much of the nineteenth century, advocates of the cause of blacks looked upon the Supreme Court as a bitter enemy rather than a protector of rights — and decisions from *Dred Scott* in 1857 to *Plessy* v. *Ferguson* in 1896 gave ample support to this view. However, in the twentieth century, the Supreme Court has become the primary hope of civil rights advocates. In an even shorter time frame, restrictive covenants were upheld by the Supreme Court in 1926 and declared unconstitutional just twenty-two years later. The same attorney who attacked restrictive covenants before the Supreme Court in 1926 defended school segregation before that Court in 1954. In short, the supposedly stable legal and constitutional framework is also subject to drastic changes, which are still more common in electoral politics.

All this has a bearing on a subsidiary theme of some, that there is an establishment relentlessly pursuing its aims behind the political scene. There are special interest groups of whom this is true, and politicians who engage in corruption and cover-up. What has been lacking — certainly as regards ethnic groups — is any stable, long-run policy, whether benign or sinister.

GOVERNMENT REDUCTION OF OPTIONS

Economic analysis would lead us to expect that people would more fully satisfy their own respective preferences with a larger set of options, where the larger set includes all the items in a smaller set. Yet there are many government laws, regulations, and policies whose effect is simply to reduce existing options without adding any new ones. Minimum wage laws, rent control, and interest rate ceilings, for example, simply outlaw certain ranges of transactions terms. Housing codes, occupational licensing laws, or Jim Crow laws have made certain kinds of transactions illegal, regardless of their terms. None of these laws and policies add any options. They simply remove some existing options.

Housing Quality

In housing, such government programs as "slum clearance" or urban renewal have been justified by studies showing former slum dwellers living in "better" housing. But this is no new option. Slum dwellers always had the option of moving into better housing, at the sacrifice of some non-housing goods they were purchasing. All that "slum clearance" has done is force them to make a trade-off they did not want to make — i.e., to become worse off by their own preference standards.

In special circumstances, the negative effects of some transactions on non-transacting parties may justify option-reduction applied to transactors — precisely in order that the excluded preferences of non-transactors be taken into account. Air and water pollution are classic examples of these external effects. In such cases, there is no net reduction of options of all the affected parties, even though the options of the immediate transactors may be reduced. Housing has sometimes been alleged to be another case of external effects, as in the proposition that "slums breed crime."

That criminality and slums have gone together down through history is demonstrable, but the direction of causation is by no means clear. The same attitudes that create crime may also create slums. It is not a question of which theory sounds more plausible *a priori* but (1) what different consequences follow from the two different theories, and (2) which set of consequences is found in factual data. To make such an empirical test possible, "slums" must be defined independently of the amount of crime taking place in neighborhoods with structures of given physical characteristics. It is possible to make crime-breeding slums a circular conclusion by simply defining physically run-down buildings or neighborhoods without high crime rates as not "really" slums. The great problem with circular statements is that what they are explicitly saying — which is nothing — is irrefutable, while what they are insinuating may be fraught with meaning and completely wrong.

As the proportion of physically substandard housing units declined in the 1960s, the crime rates soared. New York's Chinatown was once one of the lowest crime rate sections of the city, despite older and more run-down buildings than in Harlem. The later crime increase in New York's Chinatown — and Chinatowns in other cities — was not associated with housing deterioration but with the arrival of new Chinese immigrants from a different culture in Hong Kong.

The central role of people and their values — rather than physical surroundings — raises the question of whether much of the physical deterioration is not itself a result of the same set of values, or lack of values. Brand-new government housing projects around the country have become instant slums as former slum dwellers moved in. All the characteristics of old-fashioned slums — filth, noise, violence, and physical destruction of property — have reappeared in government housing projects. Even such a zealous nineteenth-century reformer as Jacob Riis, who called slums "nurseries of crime," also noted that some people "carry their slums with them" wherever they go."

Labor

In labor markets as well as in housing markets, government reduces options in general — and the options of low-income ethnic groups in particular. In nineteenth-century American cities the lowest jobs, as well as the worst slum housing, belonged almost exclusively to the various immigrant groups from Europe. On the West Coast, such jobs and such housing was also the fate of immigrants from China, and in the South it was the fate of newly freed blacks.

Government regulation of labor markets has included occupational licensing laws, minimum wage laws, regulation of working conditions, and child labor laws. We have also seen . . . how minimum wage laws reduce the price of discrimination, thereby increasing the quantity. Such laws also harm low-income ethnic groups in their role as less skilled or less productive workers for whatever reason (inexperience, cultural patterns at variance with industrial requirements of punctuality, discipline, cooperation, etc.). Restrictive occupational licensing laws also reduce the employer's cost of discrimination by creating a surplus of job applicants. In addition, occupational licensing standards may themselves be discriminatory. For example, during the 1930s, when many skilled Jewish refugees were entering the United States, "a U.S. citizenship requirement was added to most occupational licensure laws." In the South, around the turn of the century, licensing examinations for black plumbers were conducted by white examiners, who almost invariably "failed" them, even though the same individual blacks "have easily met the requirements elsewhere." With the rise of government-supported labor unions having complete dominance over particular occupations — notably in the railroads and the construction trades — union membership was tantamount to occupational licensing, and was used to keep out (or drive out) blacks.

In both the craft union situation and in explicit occupational licensing, it was the turning over of governmental powers to private interests that was the key to the effectiveness of the exclusion. Occupational licensing boards are almost invariably in the hands of existing practitioners. With the Wagner Act in 1935, the government made employer recognition of existing employees' unions mandatory, and therefore put into the hands of incumbent workers the power to exclude other workers.

Government control of working conditions would seem to be racially or ethnically neutral, but historically its impact has been quite different for different groups, regardless of whether or not this was the intent. In the nineteenth century, the prime target of government regulation of working conditions was the "sweatshop" where long hours in run-down buildings was the rule. These sweatshop workers were almost entirely immigrants, and the classic examples were the sweatshops among the Jewish workers on the lower east side of New York. Again, the government did nothing directly to create better conditions — that would have cost vast sums of money — but instead simply outlawed some existing conditions, or reduced the options open to the transactors. One of the other options was to have the work performed in the home, where it was more difficult for government inspectors to monitor hours or working conditions.

A contemporary account of a typical nineteenth-century east side tenement mentioned, along with "smells of cabbage, onions, or frying fish" on every floor, also "whirring sewing machines behind closed doors, betraying what goes on within. . . ." The men, women, and children — mostly Jewish in this era — worked long hours in their homes. But, although reformers and historians have spoken of this as "exploitation," they also acknowledged that (1) the sweatshop owners themselves made little money, despite long hours of work, and (2) among the Jewish workers on New York's lower east side, the long hours were hardly necessary to keep body and soul together, despite their low pay, "more than half of which goes into the bank." In short, despite the sinister innuendos and indignant language which have become standard in describing this situation, the actual evidence suggests nothing more than employers and employees making the most of such limited options as they had, given the technology, skill, and wealth at their disposal. Government added to none of these three requisites, but only reduced their ability to optimize according to their own knowledge and preferences. In view of the later economic progress of Jews, it is by no means clear that their understanding of their situation was not at least as good as that of the reformers, who tried vainly to stop them from doing what they felt they had to do.

Nor is it obvious that the greater success of twentieth century reformers in forcing contemporary low-income minority youths out of the labor force has been a blessing, especially given the evidence of a correlation between youth unemployment and crime. These reform efforts have included not only control of working conditions, but also compulsory school attendance laws, which make full-time work illegal for those of school age. Here, at least, the claim can be made that the government adds to the available options by providing schooling free of charge to the users. However, the forced retention of teenagers who do not want to be in school is hardly costless to the other students, or to the process of education. A study of changes in the compulsory attendance law in Britain showed that the oldest group retained in school had the highest delinquency rate, both before and after that age was raised — thirteen-year-olds before, and fourteen-year-olds after. It was apparently not the fact of being age thirteen or fourteen that was crucial — it was the length of time being forcibly retained past the point where the process had become counterproductive for both the student and the school.

It is often taken as axiomatic that more years in school is "a good thing" virtually without limit, in defiance of the economic logic of diminishing returns and of inherent trade-offs between one good and another. But, once the idea of trade-off is accepted, it is easy to understand that the terms of trade-off may differ from individual to individual and from group to group, implying that different amounts of schooling may be optimal in different circumstances. Moreover, those closest to the situation — the parents and children — may have more knowledge of their options than distant social theorists. But when the decision as to length of schooling is made by third-party observers and enforced by government, it is more likely to reflect some crude compromise between what the poor prefer and what the middle class prefer — very much like "decent housing."

Insofar as such reform efforts are spearheaded by the educated, and by educators — and seconded by labor unions, with a vested interest in restricting the labor supply — the tendency of compulsory attendance laws is to keep youths in school well past the point where they and their parents would have preferred that they be working. Evidence for this hypothesis includes both high rates of truancy and in-school delinquency in low-income ethinc neighborhoods — much more than in past periods, when the school-leaving age was lower.

Transactions Terms

More direct government intervention, with the explicit intention of affecting ethnic minorities, has been evident in such laws and policies as Jim Crow laws in the South, and "equal opportunity" laws and "affirmative action" policies more recently at the federal level.

Deliberately discriminatory laws have been part of the history of the United States, and many other countries. If such laws were always effective, Jews and Chinese would be poverty-stricken around the world, instead of generally prosperous. Even in the antebellum South, where severely restrictive laws kept the "free persons of color" out of many occupations, the economic advancement of this group continued on up to the Civil War, and their descendants continued to prosper and provide a disproportionate amount of twentieth-century black leadership. The problems facing a government seeking to enforce discrimination as a social policy are very similar to those facing governments seeking the social betterment of some groups: (1) insufficiency of knowledge, (2) monitoring costs, and (3) individual transactors' incentives to behave at variance with the government policy.

Discrimination, like any other government policy, requires a certain amount of knowledge of current conditions and of future trends to be effective. When Jews were kept out of many occupations central to the landed economy of feudalism, they were forced into commercial and industrial occupations peripheral to feudalism but central to later emerging capitalism, giving the Jews an historic advantage — obviously contrary to the purposes of the policy. Even where government has a generally accurate assessment of conditions and trends, it faces the problem of monitoring numerous transactors who have incentives to behave differently from the way government wants them to behave. The difficulties of enforcing conditions deemed appropriate to urban slaves in the antebellum South indicate something of the magnitude of the monitoring problem, even when those being monitored are easily distinguished from the general population by skin color.

The historic poverty of postbellum southern blacks may seem to suggest the effectiveness of the discriminatory policies of southern states. However, given the enormous racial difference in initial wealth and — perhaps even more important — in human capital immediately after the Civil War, even with an ideally non-discriminating government, it would have taken unprecedented achievements for blacks to have closed the gap in a few generations — especially since white income was growing all the while. As it was, with governments that were very far from ideal, black income grew at a higher rate than white income after the Civil War. In short, black-white income gaps are hardly an accurate measure of the effectiveness of discriminatory government policy. Conversely, the highly controversial "affirmative action" government policies in recent years have produced little overall pay or employment changes for blacks relative to whites, as measured empirically by a number of economists. The point here is not to claim that all government discrimination has been totally ineffective. Economic questions are generally incremental rather than categorical.

Why have government policies — whether discriminatory or preferential — had less impact than anticipated? The uniform transactions terms (including no transactions in some high-level positions) preferred by a discriminatory government are almost certain to differ from the variety of transactions terms preferred by individuals in differing circumstances and having preferences differing from one another as well as from the government. Moreover, economic competition especially rewards those who find cheaper ways to produce, or ways to make more sales — including producing with proscribed workers and selling to proscribed customers (racial "block-busting" in real estate, for example). Those potential transactors facing the greatest barriers tend to offer the most favorable terms, by agreeing to work for lower wages or to pay higher rents.

Monitoring millions of individual transactors who have incentives to circumvent government policy is a formidable task in any context, including Prohibition. Even in South Africa, policies to exclude black workers from various higher positions have been eroded despite restrictive laws against Africans and government quotas for Europeans. To effectively maintain apartheid in the economy, the government has had to resort to laws which appear on the surface to be non-racial — minimum wage laws and equal pay laws — but which serve the key purpose of reducing monitoring costs, by eliminating the incentive to evade the discrimination policies. It is relatively easy to monitor observance of wage minima and equal pay for equal work and, insofar as this is done, it is far less necessary to monitor hiring practices, for the incentive to hire native Africans is eliminated, once their pay has been raised to parity with Europeans.

"Equal opportunity" laws and policies — hiring "without regard" to race, color, or nationality — represent less interference with ordinary economic incentives than either discriminatory or preferential policies. It is therefore, perhaps not surprising that they seem more effective. Black income as a percentage of white income rose significantly after passage of the Civil Rights Act of 1964 — whether because of that Act or because the changed public opinion which made the Act possible also made possible a reduction in hiring discrimination. There were many independent contemporary indications of changed public opinion on race and ethnicity.

Housing Distribution

In consumer markets, the effect of political versus market decision making can be seen in the very different history of housing for Jews in Europe and blacks in the United States. Historically, the term "ghetto" originated in medieval Europe, where Jews lived in sections of town designated by political authorities, and surrounded by walls and gates that were locked at night. Black neighborhoods today are called ghettos only metaphorically, by extension. As the Jewish population grew, the ghetto simply became more crowded, except for political decisions permitting expansion at infrequent and unpredictable intervals. By contrast, every northern urban ghetto in the United States has developed out of neighborhoods that were white at the turn of the century. Harlem, the oldest and most famous of the northern black urban communities, was still predominantly white as late as 1910. Black ghettos expanded much more steadily and rapidly through market transactions in the United States than did Jewish ghettos through political processes in Europe.

These empirical results are at variance with frequently reiterated assertions that government action in general, and court action in particular, are essential if blacks are to obtain desegregated housing. To have housing decisions made through the market, rather than through the political process, means "abandoning the Negro to the slum-ghetto that 'private enterprise' has made ready for him," according to this viewpoint. This conclusion was treated as axiomatic, so there was no need to examine evidence comparing the consequences of political versus economic modes of decision making. Once it was decided that the economic results were displeasing, the next step was the familiar *non sequitur* that political results would be better.

In practice, however, . . . the era of the greatest residential integration in American cities was the last quarter of the nineteenth century — at a time when racially restrictive covenants were legal, when courts took little interest in the rights of blacks, and when black political power was negligible (especially in the northern cities that were residentially integrated). Conversely, although the Supreme Court's striking down of racially restrictive covenants in 1948 was hailed as a landmark in the struggle for integrated housing, in cold fact it made very little difference in the amount of residential segregation.

Historically, government has itself been a major promoter of residential segregation. A number of municipal governments made residential segregation official policy early in the twentieth century, and the Federal Housing Administration *required* racial segregation as a precondition for federally insured loans on into the late 1940s. The current swing of the political pendulum is in the direction of residentially mixing not only races but social classes. However, insofar as this takes the form of simply reducing options, it may be relatively ineffective. For example, a judge ordered that 75 percent of the public housing built in Chicago be so located as to place black tenants in white neighborhoods — but the only net result was to halt public housing construction in Chicago. Nor is the issue necessarily racial. Black middle-class residents have bitterly fought the building of low-income housing projects near them, and there is a great difference in the general public's reactions to housing for the elderly from their reactions to housing for low-income families of any race or ethnicity:

Subsidized housing, which does not carry the threat of crime, vandalism, or deterioration of local schools, can be built almost anywhere without much protest, but any sizable project for poor families has always been extremely hard to plant in a neighborhood where people are paying their own way.

In short, the *behavior pattern* of a group is the crucial variable in both racial and non-racial contexts. It was the crucial variable in the residential racial integration of northern cities in the late nineteenth century, in the severe segregation that succeeded it after the massive migration of southern blacks, and in the *internal* segregation of different classes of blacks, Jews, Mexicans, etc., from other members of their own respective groups. Individuals whose behavior patterns differ most from that of their own racial or ethnic group suffer most from group sorting and labeling, and it is precisely such individuals who have spearheaded the drive for housing "integration" — meaning, in fact, class segregation. Racial segregation inhibited class segregation by lumping all blacks together. Once government policy begins to mean random redistribution of people, black middle-class "integrationists" oppose it.

There has never been random distribution of people, whether in housing, jobs, or other activities. Jewish immigrants from different countries or at different stages of acculturation and socioeconomic mobility likewise separated residentially. There was a "separateness and discontinuity" of these local Jewish areas from one another, and sometimes a repeated migration of individuals from one to the other in response to their own acculturation or to the inflow of less acculturated newcomers: "he becomes irritated by the presence of his fellow-Jews, more Jewish than himself" — all this to the accompaniment of mutual recriminations.

Among Italian immigrants, residential clustering occurred according to the province, city, or even village of origin in Italy. This reflected the highly localized loyalties of southern Italy, from which most Italian Americans originated. They only begin to think of themselves as Italian after reaching America.

Among the present-day descendants of southern European immigrants, half would have to relocated if a random distribution of people were to be achieved. This much residential "segregation" from the larger society persists half a century after mass immigration from that part of the world ended. The very phrase "segregation" is ambiguous — lumping together both *ex ante* restrictions and *ex post* results. One reason why even a successful "open housing" campaign changes residential clustering patterns very little is that many people prefer being clustered, even when they are not segregated by the large society.

Neither the market nor the government has "solved" the "problem" of residential clustering. The very conception of a problem with a solution may be fallacious here, as in many other areas of decision making. There are highly disparate values within and between groups, and one way of coping with these differences is separation — spatial or psychic. It has long been noted that there is usually less spatial separation between blacks and whites in the South because there are such well-developed psychic mechanisms of separation there. Studies have shown that even those blacks or Jews who express belief in integration prefer living where half the people are members of their own group. But such a result is incompatible with the preferences of other groups. There is no reason to expect that there exists anything that can be called a "solution" in such circumstances. There may be something that meets the standard of Pareto optimality — a situation in which each individual is as well off as he can be, by his own standards, without making others worse off by their standards. There is no reason to expect a government-imposed reduction of options to move the situation in that direction.

In addition to housing segregation, government policies affect low-income ethnic groups in other ways. Both historically and at present, low-income ethnic groups have arrived in the cities after others have had first choice of locations, and have typically occupied the most desirable ones. In addition to occupying larger individual quantities of the most desirable urban land, the more affluent classes typically also make recreational use of vast amounts of land in the countryside, in such activities as camping, hunting, boating, and skiing. While the residential land is typically allocated through economic processes, recreational land is more likely to be allocated through political processes — as state and national parks and forests, or land "protected" by laws on coastal preservation or zoning. The land owned and kept out of the market by state or national government is far from negligible. In California, for example, more than half the land in the state is government-owned, and in Alaska more than 90 percent of the land is owned by the federal government.

While the affluent, by definition, have individually larger amounts of money than the non-affluent, the sheer numbers of the latter put far more total financial resources at their disposal. Economic transactors who are seeking to maximize their total profit would much rather make ten million dollars from 10,000 people who are not rich than to make one million dollars from one millionaire. The net result is that ethnic groups newly arriving in the city bid great quantities of land and housing away from the affluent, either directly or through realtors, banks, landlords, or other intermediaries. The arrival of Irish and German immigrants in New York in the 1840s brought a transfer of property in the central city from the affluent natives to the impoverished newcomers, and an expansion of the city as a whole, with the affluent leading the exodus. The same scenario was to be followed again and again, in innumerable urban centers, for more than a century, with blacks, Hispanics, Orientals, and others taking on the role of urban newcomers in later times.

No such pattern has been evident in the vast recreational land area under political control, despite the widespread assumption that the poor are at an advantage in the political process and at a disadvantage in the economic process. But in the economic process it is the *total* financial resources that count, while in the political process it is often the *average* level of understanding of the issues that is critical. If an issue is very clearly understood by all, the numerous poor have a political advantage over the few rich. But many political issues are quite complex — or lend themselves to being made complicated by rhetoric and obfuscation — and in these cases the poor, the less educated, the newly arrived, can be at a decisive disadvantage in the political process.

In the case of recreational land use, the issue is not even posed in terms of alternative sets of people competing for given land. Instead, the affluent who make up such groups as the Sierra Club pose the issue as one of disembodied principles about "the environment," "ecology," "congestion," or preventing the "misuse" or "spoiling" of "nature." That these goals have some positive value is neither unusual nor decisive; it is typical of economic competition that different sets of values are weighed against each other. Clearly, if half the land in a state is kept off the market by the government, the price of the other half is going to be far higher than otherwise, and this means far higher prices for buying houses or renting apartments throughout the state. Where the land along the coast is either government-owned or kept from being used for small homes or apartments by coastal commissions or zoning boards, this means that other people stay bottled up in the inner city away from fresh air. Insofar as the affluent succeed politically in blocking the construction of power plants, this raises electricity rates. Insofar as they block construction of highways or motels near the wilderness areas, they keep access to such areas limited to those with the time, money, and leisure to hike in or to maintain clubs or other private facilities in the area. In short, the policies of affluent recreational interests ("environmentalists") do involve a trade-off between the well-being of different sets of people, even though phrased in highly abstract principles about "nature," "ecology," etc. Although this has been going on for generations, it is only quite recently that any question has been raised about such things from the standpoint of low-income ethnic groups. Differences in the average level of understanding and promotion of self-interest (suitable packaged as the general well-being) often put low-income ethnic groups at more of a disadvantage in the political arena than in the economic arena.

In economic transactions, it usually matters little how much the individual transactor understands about the underlying process involved. He needs only know his own preferences and alternatives. The extreme example would be the immediate postbellum blacks in the South, who were illiterate, unable to count, and largely unprotected by the law — and who still were able to get improved housing and higher pay through ordinary market transactions. The underlying processes behind transaction terms need not be understood by both sides, so long as those transactors who do understand have to compete with each other. But the low-income labor market and the low-income housing market are too vast for transactors to be anything other than competitors.

GOVERNMENT REDISTRIBUTION

The redistribution of income by government is one area in which political activity seems most promising for low-income minorities. However, even here the picture is not nearly as clear-cut as it might appear for a number of reasons:

1. The great variety of progressive and regressive government transfers makes their net effects uncertain.

2. All that is taken from the taxpayers for the benefit of the poor does not in fact go to the poor.
3. Transfers are not simply added to the earnings the recipient would have otherwise; remaining below some officially defined level of income is a precondition for receiving many forms of government transfer payments, and transfers are reduced as earnings increase.
4. When losses of earnings due to various other government programs are balanced against income transfers, it is uncertain whether there are any net gains.

Historically, governments have subsidized many activities, including activities from which ethnic minorities were excluded or did not use for various reasons. The antebellum "free persons of color," for example, were taxed to support public schools from which their own children were excluded. Various Catholic ethnic groups have also been taxed for public schools which their children did not attend. While their lack of use of the public schools was voluntary, in some nineteenth-century schools the religious emphasis was so heavily Protestant that many Catholic parents felt that they had to educate their children elsewhere.

A wide variety of goods and services rarely used by low-income ethnic groups are subsidized by government out of taxes to which the latter contribute — recreational land use (state and national parks and forests), airport facilities, maritime subsidies, state universities, federal grants to higher education, tax shelters of many sorts, etc. On the other hand, a disproportionate share of welfare and public housing goes to low-income minorities. What is the net? *We do not know*. Different methods of computing it give different results. A revealing study of government money flowing in and out of a low-income black ghetto in Washington D.C., showed that — despite huge welfare payments and expenditures on the public schools, as part of nearly $46 million of government spending there — there was an *outflow* of $50 million in taxes, so that this ghetto *lost* more than $4 million on net balance. A cessation of all government transfers would have somewhat alleviated rather than aggravated their poverty.

The amount necessary to lift every man, woman, and child in America above the poverty line has been calculated, and it is *one-third* of what is in fact spent on poverty programs. Clearly, much of the transfer ends up in the pockets of highly paid administrators, consultants, and staff as well as higher income recipients of benefits from programs advertised as anti-poverty efforts.

In order to qualify for many government programs, one must be unemployed, earning below the official poverty level, or otherwise disadvantaged. This provides incentives to forego present earning — and with it, forego human capital formation for the future. The government money currently received is not all net gain.

Finally, because minorities are, by definition, only part of a larger society, and many other groups with claims on government receive concessions whose economic impacts on minorities may offset all transfers put together. To make a very rough estimate of just one government activity, take the restrictive licensing of taxicabs. The number of taxis in Los Angeles is only one-fifteenth the number of taxis in Washington, D.C., even through Los Angeles is more than seven times the size of the nation's capital. If there were only five times as many taxis in Los Angeles as there are under restrictive licensing, that would mean thousands more jobs for which low-income minority members would be eligible instantly. When one considers that there are approximately 3000 licensed occupations, the impact of this one government restriction looms very large.

There is no compelling reason to believe that government activity has benefitted ethnic minorities on net balance, even when that has been its purpose. The volatility of government policy suggests that determining its purpose over some meaningful span of time is also no easy task.

IMPLICATIONS

When the government chooses between policy A and policy B, it is making a choice in which the personal interests of the decision maker are involved. Rewards for both elected and appointed officials — whether in money or in kind — come from increasing the demand for their services. If policy A will achieve a certain result largely through the individual efforts of the citizens themselves, and policy B requires the presence, activity, and visibility of politicians, clearly it is to the politicians' advantage to advocate policy B. It is also to the advantage of political organizations, individual "leaders," or various "movements" to favor the kinds of policies which promote their visibility and apparent importance.

Whatever the merits of demerits of particular government policies, nothing seems surer from history that that those policies will change. Within a period of twenty years, various state governments have permitted, prohibited, and then required racial and ethnic designations on employment records. Within the same span, the federal government has permitted, required, and then prohibited racially restrictive covenants in housing. The representation of minorities in the military and the civil service has undergone similarly extreme changes in a few decades. Questions about the role of government are not simply questions about whatever particular policies are being followed at a given time, but involve longer-run considerations about the effects of generating uncertainty about the ground rules within which individual plans and transactions can be made.

RADICAL: NO

3. SOCIAL PROBLEMS

Joe R. Feagin

BACKGROUND: THE THOUGHT OF KARL MARX

A growing number of American social scientists are today becoming aware of the importance of Karl Marx and Marxist intellectual traditions for building an adequate understanding of U.S. society, including its serious social problems. More so than in most European countries, Marxist and new-Marxist ideas, books, organizations, and college teachers have been repressed in the United States since the late 1930s. In the 1940s and 1950s, which have been termed the era of McCarthyism, many thousands of people were fired from their jobs or prevented from taking jobs (such as college teachers) if there was the slightest indication that they held a radical power-conflict point of view. There were official witchhunts for "disloyal" (which meant "critical") Americans in many institutions, including government agencies and universities. This political repression had a chilling effect on the social sciences. so much so that it has only been since the late 1960s that some American scholars and researchers have felt they had the freedom to discuss and write about the ideas and impact of the Marxist and other radical power-conflict traditions. Even today, in many parts of the country, there is not complete freedom to discuss these ideas.

Karl Marx (1818 – 1883) was perhaps the first major social science thinker to put power and class conflict issues at the center of his thoroughgoing interpretation of the social structure of capitalist societies. Capitalistic societies, at their most fundamental level, are characterized by ongoing class conflict between two major antagonistic social classes called the capitalist class (owners and controllers of the means of production) and the proletariat (workers). Marx recognized numerous classes, such as mom-and-pop grocery store owners (petty bourgeoisie), but he gave emphasis to this fundamental split between owners (controllers) of factories and offices and those who work for these owners (controllers) in those same factories and offices. The capitalistic structure of production and distribution has resulted in the direct control and exploitation of great masses of struggling workers by a small group of (wealthy) capitalist owners (or controllers) whose profits in effect are stolen from (the result of) the hard work of workers, who must sell their labor so that they and their families can survive. For Marx, this unequal class structure greatly influenced the development of politics, law, and education in capitalistic societies such as Great Britain and the United States.

Marx emphasized that human beings are born into social classes and ideological frameworks not of their own making; individuals and their basic needs for material goods, as well as their needs for self-mastery and creativity, are the core reality, but human beings are hemmed in by the actions of others. Thus, exploited workers often find themselves fighting for their interests, for better wages or working conditions, in an ongoing struggle with capitalists. Because of its ownership and control over the means of production (such as factories), the capitalist class has much greater resources and power than do the workers. The capitalists' ideology, their view of the world, becomes the ruling ideology in the society. This great power and resource imbalance, Marx argued, will periodically generate worker protest, including large-scale movements, even occasionally revolutions, on the part of the workers who become conscious of unnecessary workplace exploitation. Ongoing and recurring economic and political conflict are fostered by the presence of clear class enemies and of good communications within one's own class, be it capitalists or workers. Neither individual pathologies and maladjustments nor large-scale disasters are necessary for social problems to occur. The class conflict shaping problems is a basic underlying feature of a capitalist society. To understand major problems in societies, Marx argues, look for social relations of exploitation between groups and thus for the inevitable and regular conflicts in basic class interests.[1]

A critical feature of Marx's analysis, and of those in his tradition ever since, is the view that government under capitalism is not an independent force somehow separated from the capitalist class. Rather, the state under capitalism is not neutral. It is substantially dominated by the capitalist class both directly through actual participation and indirectly through the requirements and needs of a capitalist economy to which government officials (whatever their class) must respond. Unlike most academic corporate liberals . . . those in Marx's tradition see the state as greatly and inevitably biased by its links to capitalism. Basic societal problems, thus, cannot be solved at their most fundamental level by appeals to government. A bit more government regulation here, a few more social welfare programs there, can make life more bearable for ordinary people, but worker-forced government programs are always in danger of being compromised or rolled back. Capitalist nations have governments which reflect in their programs the struggles between capitalist and ordinary working people, but they remain capitalist states.

Most Americans know this is a troubled society with major problems. Most know that many of their own basic needs are not being met. And many are aware that their personal and family problems are linked to the larger social context. But this larger social context is often seen through a haze of vague explanations. The declining work ethic, lazy individuals, big government, foreign competition, inflation — often hazy explanations such as these are offered to explain our societal troubles. A basic reason why most people do not understand how and why many social problems are grounded in the larger societal realities of capitalism, racism, and sexism is that they have been misled by teachers, politicians, business leaders, and the mass media.

Traditional sociological approaches to major societal problems have often emphasized order and stability in the society. The dominant viewpoint lying behind much social science in the United States reflects a basic commitment to the existing social order of capitalism. This viewpoint has evolved from a *laissez-faire* perspective in the nineteenth century to a *corporate liberalism* today. Basic to traditional sociological approaches is some type of strain theory of social problems. The breakdown of traditional authority and norms is one source seen as likely to create social problems. These social scientists often see government as the neutral judge of competing groups, as the instrument to restore order and stability within the framework of the existing capitalistic, racist, sexist system. Conventional approaches to social problems reject the idea that the problems are rooted so deeply in the society that *massive* society-wide changes in class, race, and sex structures will be required to eradicate the problems.

Since these social scientists accept the basic contours of this capitalistic society, they often argue for a value-free, "social engineering" approach to the study of social problems. For this mainline approach, the task of social problems analysis is to build up a body of empirical facts which can be used by existing policymakers to devise remedies to "fix" existing social problems. Since the 1960s the social engineering approach to social problems has been strong in the United States. Social scientists are seen as the experts who can, apolitically and scientifically, collect data on social problems and provide data on which current government policymakers can act wisely.

Those who adopt the mainline approach are generally unwilling to explore the far-reaching implictions of a thoroughgoing power-conflict approach for understanding major societal problems. . . . A radical (from the Latin, *radix*, "root") power-conflict perspective looks critically at the often-hidden roots of social problems in exploitative, discriminatory, and alienating social arrangements.

Today power-conflict social scientists are a diverse group, including not only Marxists and neo-Marxists (who tend to emphasize class), but also radical feminists (who emphasize sex exploitation) and radical nationalists (who focus on race exploitation).

THE CAPITALIST STATE

The power and resources of corporate America, particularly of top officials in larger corporations, have shaped the structure and character of government. The U.S. government is a capitalistic state, which also reflects the race and sex stratification patterns we have discussed elsewhere. Thus the legal system protects the property held by the propertied classes. And the federal government is substantially controlled at the top by those with close ties to corporate America. Members of presidential cabinets, top congressional committee chairpersons, many members of Congress, and even many presidents have been top executives or senior managers in corporations, professionals (e.g., lawyers) servicing corporate America, or politicians groomed for political service by corporate interests. Moreover, most other top government officials hold values that usually parallel those of the leaders of corporate America, even where there are no direct personal or corporate ties. Some may be more liberal on certain issues than others, but the coordination of business and government is a major goal of top capitalists and their political allies. Indeed, over the last decade we have seen a regular presentation of the view that government should be redirected so that it operates even more effectively than now to promote business interests. For example, one goal is even less regulation and taxation for businesses than they now endure. . . . Most local government officials, from state legislatures to city councils, also have close ties to, or hold values supportive of capitalistic interests. Even local school boards frequently have ties to business values and interests, a fact that has long shaped the character of American education.

That federal, state, and local governments in the United States reflect the interests of the propertied class can be seen in many of the governmental programs which are currently in operation. The growth of government has been very important to the expansion and growth of capitalism, particularly corporate and monopoly capitalism. The state, according to James O'Connor, has had to take over more and more of the social and other costs of modern capitalism, even though the social surplus (e.g., profits) of business still are privately controlled. Monopoly capitalism, in particular, increasingly requires that government pay many of the costs of continuing economic growth.

Government under modern capitalism must try to meet certain different obligations: (1) enhancing capital accumulation (rate of profit), and (2) maintaining the legitimacy of the system in the eyes of the general public. Capital accumulation is fostered by government projects and services that increase productivity of labor and the rate of profit, such as government subsidized industrial development parks, urban renewal projects, airports, and many highway and utility projects built to facilitate business needs. Firms using these facilities, as well as those constructing the facilities, profit greatly from these governmental expenditures. Moreover, much scientific research and development and the education of skilled laborpower, both needs of business, are paid for by government. And many types of government regulation (e.g., regulation of stock market trading) have been implemented under capitalists' pressures for government to stabilize, to make more orderly, the once intensely competitive capitalism. Thus state funds provide many goods and services for which capitalists and corporations do not have to pay. The general public shares much of the costs of these programs. Capital accumulation (rate of profit) may also be increased by government programs of social insurance (for accidents or old age) in which the workers and taxpayers in general pay some or all of the costs business would otherwise be pressured to pay. Social insurance also reflects worker pressures, and it provides a sense of security among employed workers, thus protecting the legitimacy of the capitalistic system.[2]

Other critical government expenditures also help legitimize the capitalistic system. One important category of state expenditures, such as those for unemployment assistance and welfare programs, helps protect the capitalistic system from distressed workers who might otherwise protest or riot. And some police expenditures are also necessary to protect the capitalistic system from its unorganized and organized enemies in the working class.

The growth of governmental intervention in the economy and the society since the early 1900s reflects both working-class pressure for reform and the fundamental needs of monopoly capitalism in this century. The social welfare reforms associated with corporate liberalism have been implemented and shaped by those government officials whose views were close to those of leading capitalists, as a way of defusing socialistic and other workers' movements. The regulatory reforms have also reflected the desire of these same leaders to see capitalism become more orderly and less wildly competitive, to make the marketplace become more stable by ridding it of the most unscrupulous capitalists. Corporate-liberal capitalists have gradually come to support government benefit programs and expanded police forces ("carrot and the stick") in order to reduce strikes and labor unrest. Some have also accepted moderate unions as a way of reducing labor unrest. The older *laissez-faire* (government hands-off) perspective has gradually been replaced by support for government intervention by virtually all capitalist and managerial officials. Corporate liberals, some of whom are now called "corporatists," accept government intervention on behalf of business and some (or substantial) action on behalf of ordinary working people. Those capitalist leaders who today call themselves "conservatives," for the most part, also accept government intervention on behalf of corporations and other businesses, although they are less (or a lot less) supportive of government action in the form of social welfare programs. All accept government intervention in the marketplace; the disagreements are over how much, and what type of, intervention.

The growth of large corporations has been accompanied by a drive to expand and control markets overseas. This drive for expansion has been coupled with huge and growing U.S. government military forces (army, navy, air force) designed in large part to protect the overseas markets required by corporations. Moreover, the monopoly sector of capitalism periodically creates surplus capacity and thus lays off surplus workers, generating serious problems of unemployment and poverty. Pressure from those workers has required an expansion of government social service programs such as welfare.

In many ways government is a battleground for class conflict. Corporations and capitalists want the general public to pay for the industrial development and urban renewal projects. Small businesses want the general public to pay for small business loans. Many working-class Americans want better social services in the areas of unemployment and health care. All classes want to pay less in the way of taxes. Not suprisingly, then, there have been increasing government fiscal crises. Governments simply cannot meet the needs of corporate America for capital accumlation and worker demands for better services (and tax relief) at the same time. . . .

THE IDEOLOGY OF INDIVIDUALISM AND THE POOR

Poor Americans not only have suffered the indignities of underemployment, low incomes, inadequate food, and rundown housing, but they have also suffered from considerable stereotyping and hostility directed at them by better-off Americans. The gospel of individualism is central to the dominant value system. Widely accepted beliefs include the following:

1. that each person should work hard and strive to succeed in material terms,
2. that those who work hard will in fact succeed, and
3. that those who do not succeed (e.g., the poor) have only themselves to blame: their laziness, immorality, or other character defects.

Closely related to these individualistic beliefs are others relating to private property and "free" enterprise. While there are alternative beliefs, these values are strongly held and widely influential. With the emphasis on the ideology of individualism, a development that has paralleled the growth of capitalism, has come not only the positive view of the successful as virtuous but also the negative view of poverty as punishment for those who were not virtuous. A distinctive folk myth has developed: the self-made rags-to-riches Horatio Alger type. Yet deeply worked into the texture of the American belief system has also been a folk villain: the self-made lazy and immoral poor person. Attacks on the poor in the last two decades have focused commonly on the welfare poor, who are often seen as the most serious violators of the work ethic. While significant numbers of Americans are now questioning these hyper-individualistic beliefs, many still accept them, perhaps with minor qualifications. . . .

Consequences of These Rationalizations for Poverty

Given the strength and pervasiveness of these views, a question arises as to the functions or consequences of both the traditional view of the poor and the traditional antiwelfare sentiment view imbedded in the individualistic ethic. What do these beliefs accomplish? What have been their consequences for this society in the past and in the present? Antiwelfarism and antipoor attitudes among large numbers of Americans, particularly in the working class, may be a partial sign of a lack of awareness of their own basic interests.

As we have seen in previous sections, most poverty is linked to structural conditions, particularly to underemployment, unemployment, and race and sex discrimination. So antipoor and related individualistic views offer a distorted picture of the social and economic world, views that have long buttressed the structure of capitalism in the United States.

Culturally ingrained exhortations to work hard — seen as leading toward material success — have been important in stimulating the work effort of workers under Western capitalistic development. One indication of a poorly developed awareness of class exploitation among many workers can be seen in their strong acceptance of the individualistic focus on personal success. Their attention has been focused on signs of individual success — which often take the form of private consumption (e.g., clothing and car) — rather than on control and exploitation of workers by the capitalist and managerial classes. Moreover, the view of poverty as reflecting laziness and immorality has been a strong motivating force behind the work of the average worker in capitalist countries. The fear of falling into material poverty was twice buttressed, once by the specter of economic deprivation itself and again by the shame and stigma that such economic deprivation would bring.[3]

A second and related consequence of antipoor perspectives among middle-income workers has been to focus hostility on poor workers, so much so that accusations of immorality and denials of proper work attitudes direct attention away from one's own economic problems and one's own exploitation. Schorr, grappling with the level of hostility expressed by many against welfare recipients, argues that the relatively harsh public attacks on, and treatment of, these recipients can be explained in terms of scapegoat theory. Under tension, particularly recurrent economic tension, ordinary Americans have selected this disadvantaged group to receive their concentrated hostility. This scapegoating process also takes the heat off the staus quo — off the structure of class inequality detrimental to the lives of all workers, but beneficial to the capitalist class. By this means, antipoor sentiments help legitimize the existing class structure. Welfare and other government expenditures for the "immoral" poor and the high taxes they allegedly require are thus seen as a conspicuous and much discussed public burden, whereas the much higher proportion of taxes going for such things as military expenditures, business subsidies, and middle-income workers (e.g., education) receives less intense attention. Antipoor views help depoliticize the society and forestall conflict by concentrating the attention of middle-income workers on the poor workers at the bottom, diverting the animosity of the bulk of workers downward rather than upward.[4]

The emphasis on individual success and antipoor views also works to separate workers from one another by reinforcing the divisive status lines between workers. Such views retard joint action by poor and middle-income workers toward goals of major social change. The development of a vigorous antipoor, antiwelfare ideology has diverted the attention of the middle-income workers from their own inequality and to the status differences between themselves and the poor, reducing the likelihood of their joining together with the poor in large-scale protest efforts. The general work ethic has the same effect, because there an emphasis on competition among individuals contributes to the inability to work collectively for major economic change.[5]

What seems to characterize the views of many rank-and-file workers, thus, is a significant degree of false consciousness, a heavy focus on diversionary issues coupled with a relatively weak consciousness of their own class interests and the dynamics of their own economic oppression. These diversionary beliefs include the complex set of misconceptions held about poverty and welfare, those myths and exaggerated generalizations that indicate a distorted view of the capitalistic world. Yet false consciousness is not an "all-or-nothing" phenomenon. Many workers reflect some mixed feelings about the poor; most also have some awareness of the role that capitalists and managers play in their own economic problems — an awareness that has fluctuated significantly with economic upheavals such as those manifest in the Great Depression of the 1930s.

Ideological Socialization

Have average Americans come to these antipoor views in a vacuum? What reinforces the false consciousness of many ordinary Americans? Why do many workers hold to rather conservative views on matters such as poverty and welfare? Who benefits the most from this acceptance of individualism? It seems that the individualistic ethic has been taught with care to most Americans over the course of their lives. This ideology and its associated beliefs — such beliefs as those about welfare, private property, and free enterprise — have been propagated vigorously by Western capitalists and their political allies directly and through the mass media and public schools for a long time. With the acceleration of Western capitalism in the nineteenth century, the dominant classes intentionally reinforced the ideology of individualism and propagated it aggressively throughout the U.S. population. Beliefs justifying this capitalistic system became ruling ideas, and they have come to appear more and more as part of the natural order of things. While those in the most advantaged classes have vigorously supported the ideology of individualism, majorities in other classes have long been persuaded by much of it as well. Once the beliefs became dominant, they had an inertia of their own.[6]

Advertising agencies and the mass media have routinely reinforced prevailing ideologies. Advertising campaigns on productivity and the need for greater work effort, as well as routine accents on individualism and competitiveness by corporate and other business sources in the mass media, illustrate the importance of this influence on American values. A major function of business advertising is to maintain, directly or indirectly, allegiance to the American system and its core values. Television and radio advertising, as well as programs, reinforce competitive and individualistic values from an early age.[7]

Government officials have been very important in propagating and reinforcing the individualistic ethic. News releases and speeches by elected officials at the various levels of government have circulated much propaganda not only about individualism and competition but also about welfare programs and the poor. From time to time some more progressive officials and professionals, particularly those in welfare agencies, have tried to counteract poverty sterotypes by issuing research reports or by public comments, but their counterattacks have so far only partially offset the antipoverty views. The public educational system, as well, has played an important role in indoctrinating basic antipoverty values in successive generations of the young.

Many powerful organizations do not have ideological repression as a central function: it is usually a side effect of their operations. Once the gospel of individualism became part of this society, its propagation became part of the normal operation of major institutions. As with objects, basic beliefs seem to have their own law of inertia. Once set into motion, they tend to persist. Reinforcement of individualistic and related values has not always been completely consistent on the part of corporate and other business leaders, but the indoctrination process has contributed to the hardy persistence of ideological individualism.[8]

GOVERNMENT INTERVENTION: THE BROAD SUBSIDY SYSTEM

Some analysts of U.S. society have accented what they see as the "dramatic progress" the United States has made since the 1930s in "redistributional" reform, particularly in social security, social insurance, and related programs for workers and in the establishment of public assistance and health programs for the poor. Other analysts express concern over the slow pace of this development. Thus Wilensky and Lebeaux have described the United States as the "most reluctant welfare state."[9] And still other observers remain unconvinced that the much touted U.S. welfare state is any more than a meager substitute for significant changes in the distribution of major economic and political privileges and benefits. From this viewpoint the rhetoric of government redistribution has not been matched by the wealth, resource, or organizational shifts that could lead to a significant decrease in economic and other inequalities.

The Context of Aid for the Poor

The contemporary public assistance ("welfare") system for the poor was inaugurated by the 1935 Social Security Act, a major part of the New Deal. Even this modest step was taken against great opposition; more conservative business and government officials expressed the fear that such legislation would destroy individual initiative. Southern legislators were concerned with protecting the low-wage structure of the South against generous assistance levels and also with ensuring that federal officials, who might be more sympathetic to needy blacks, would have less to say about how programs were operated than would local officials. Administration of new aid-for-the-poor programs was to remain firmly in the hands of local officials.

Federal grants-in-aid were provided for the states and localities to help finance a sizable portion of costs under major welfare assistance programs. An approach that limited cash assistance only to certain categories of the poor was used. This approach was based on the assumption that relief had to be restricted and that the major reasons for poverty that should concern government were blindness, old age, and dependent children. Consequently, the original legislation provided aid programs only for three groups: Aid to the Blind, Old Age Assistance, and Aid to Dependent Children (ADC).

Since 1950 major changes have included the establishment of a program called Aid to the Permanently and Totally Disabled, a program for adults caring for dependent children (AFDC), and a program for needy children with unemployed parents (AFDC-U). There has been substantial state legislative reluctance to take on some new programs; this reluctance has reflected the objectives of maintaining a supply of low-wage workers and of keeping state public aid expenditures low. As of 1980, about half the states had no program of aid to families with unemployed fathers.

From recent political campaigns and from the mass media, one sometimes gets the impression that the poor are the major recipients of government dollars. This is not the case. There is a vast array of subsidies provided by federal, state, and local governments for groups above the poverty line. This aid has aptly been termed "welfare for the affluent" and "welfare for the rich." The irony of this type of aid can be seen in one news story. In the late 1960s a news report revealed that James Eastland, a conservative senator from Mississippi and a critic of welfare, had received more than $150,000 in federal subsidy payments for keeping his land idle. In that same year an average Mississippi mother who could not find employment could not receive more than $500 in federally subsidized welfare aid for herself and her family. Similar figures could be calculated for the 1980s.[10]

Billions in aid, moreover, go each year to businesspersons in the form of agricultural subsidies to farmers; investment tax credits for corporations; large subsidies or loan guarantees to auto corporations, shipbuilders, aircraft companies, and railroads; indirect subsidies to resource industries (e.g., tax relief for the oil industry); and substantial (capital gains) tax relief for corporate investors. Much aid does not take the form of direct government spending but, rather, is made possible by the existence of special tax loopholes, resulting in large savings for some well-off Americans and increased taxes for ordinary workers. One observer has wryly noted that "there are no more persistent and successful applicants for public assistance than the proud giants of the private enterprise system."[11]

Then there is the extensive government aid for a broad array of educational and health care programs, with most of the money targeted for nonpoor Americans. In the 1960s and 1970s, federal expenditures increased dramatically for human resources and income transfer programs, for all programs including grants to local governments for education and training, health, cash assistance, food stamps, and the like. Surprisingly, however, most of these governmental expenditures have not been targeted at the poor. In 1961 nearly $34 billion was spent by the federal government for all these programs, but $29 billion of that was for programs that were aimed substantially at the nonpoor (e.g., social security). By 1976 the federal government was spending $232 billion for human resources programs,with only $34.5 billion, or about 15 percent of the total, for programs aimed exclusively at the poor. Most human resources expenditures by the federal government, today as in the past, substantially benefit middle-income and upper-income persons.[12]

The United States now has a broad subsidy-for-many system. One part of the system, government aid for rich and middle-income Americans, is seldom thought of as a subsidy or welfare program and is usually seen as very worthwhile. Another major part of the system, public assistance for the poor, is considered to be a government welfare program and is often viewed as wholly or partially *illegitimate*. The less egalitarian subsidy programs, aid for business and industry, and even social security, have historically been the most favored; the most truly egalitarian programs, such as direct cash assistance to poor families, have been relatively starved.[13] . . .

Making "Slums"

Profit-oriented real estate operations have contributed significantly to the creation of contemporary "slums"* in central city areas. Ghettos and "slums" with slowly or rapidly deteriorating housing are sometimes seen by social scientists as the result (1) of disorganized poor people without the means to keep up the property or (2) of the inevitable, natural invasion and succession process whereby one group of people becomes more affluent and moves out and another group moves in behind them. From this traditional perspective "slum" problems are creations either of the poor themselves or of natural city processes.

Yet there is another view of this societal problem of slum making. This degradation of central cities is in part the result of intentional profit making on the part of those who invest in central city real estate. While most sum landlords operate on a small scale, making small (or no) profits, a significant minority engages in buying and selling property for very lucrative depreciation and speculation purposes. This activity often creates dilapidated, later even abandoned, residential areas. There are big profits to be made in this activity. For example, one Washington, D.C., savings and loan association grew from $30,000 in assets in 1952 to $57 million in 1967, in part by loaning money to speculators reselling Washington, D.C., poverty areas. Such profit making can involve outside speculators by means of real estate syndicates; some wealthy doctors, corporate lawyers, and business executives

---

*The word "slum" . . . [here] refers to geographical areas in which poor people are concentrated.

buy into a "slum" investment scheme because the very large depreciation allowed by the Internal Revenue Service on such building can sharply reduce their taxes on other income. "Slums" can be created by this profit-centered activity, as upkeep on the purchased buildings is kept low to keep profits and other benefits high for the investors in the real estate syndicate. The quality of the housing can be irrelevant to this type of real estate speculation. Run-down poverty area tenements can bring in as much profit, because of depreciation and mortgage advantages, as better quality housing elsewhere.[14]

Shaping Suburbia

Today the lot-and-block patterns of development can be seen clearly in the suburban patchwork quilt that sprawls out from the edges of central cities. So far the great suburban migration has involved more than 50 million people. In the 1970s the rise in land prices each year, for land moved from rural to suburban use, was estimated at $14 – 20 billion. By the year 2000, an estimated 40 – 60 million acres of U.S. land will be withdrawn from other uses for urban development, mostly for suburban growth around cities. This suburbanization is seriously depleting farmland. Indeed, a recent study released by the U.S. Department of Agriculture calls for the federal government to stop financing suburban development on farmlands. This study estimated that 3 million acres of farmland each year is lost to urban development such as highways, shopping centers, subdivisions, and airports; one-third is very productive farmland. Over the last decade New England lost half its farmland. The report makes it clear that the United States no longer can afford this destruction of agricultural land, for population growth means that the more than 400 million acres now being farmed will have to be expanded to meet the food needs of an increasingly urban population.[15]

Suburbs are often seen in conventional social science as a result of a freewheeling market system in which middle-income workers play the major role as they bid for better housing. From this viewpoint the demand for single-family housing, together with the government subsidization of home mortgages and utilities, has created suburbanization. "In this view, businesses have no independent decision-making role, but merely do the bidding of consumers in the most efficient manner."[16] Yet an influential developer often buys the land, lays out a suburban development, then markets it, before consumers can have a role in the decision-making process about the location and arrangement of the subdivisions. A capitalistic market economy can provide certain types of basic goods and services, but only in the form this market find profitable. Among the commodities available is a certain type of single-family housing, much of it in suburbanized developments. Generally speaking, business interests are interested in meeting only certain material needs of urban consumers, and not other needs such as the need for mass transit, a vibrant community, or for an unpolluted living environment.[17]

Moreover, suburban growth has involved considerably more planning and purpose than the traditional view suggests. The acts of profit making by powerful developers, builders, and land speculators have radically shaped both central city and suburban development. Suburban real estate operators function as a critical group of capitalists filling the ownership gap between agricultural land and urban land. Pressures at the urban fringe around cities eventually force agricultural owner-users (e.g., farmers) to sell out, usually to speculators and developers willing to hold the land for later suburban development. A number or research studies have illustrated the high profits made by many speculators buying up such farmland. In areas like California land developers have bought out farmers by offering $200 – $6000 more an acre than they paid for it. Such sales push up the property taxes on surrounding farmlands not yet sold to speculators. Tax pressures, coupled with the water runoff and pollution problems of suburban development, force even the most committed farmer to eventually sell out. As a result, the rise in residential land prices, particularly in many suburban areas, has been 200 – 400 percent faster than the price of housing in the same areas. In some areas, such as Los Angeles, the price of residential land went up at the rate of 40 percent a year in the 1970s, in part the result of profit-oriented speculative activity.[18]

According to Downie, real estate people in Los Angeles admit that *sprawl* development there was heavily shaped by the quest for capital accumulation, that the sprawl pattern was "merely the easist, fastest, most lucrative way to cash in on the motor-age California land rush: Buy a tract of vacant land, wait a short time for the population and roads to move toward it, subdivide it into lots for cheaply built single-family homes, and sell them to builders at prices that total several times the land's original cost — then take your profit and buy another, larger tract of land farther out to begin the process all over again."[19] The drive toward profit created the sprawling freeway system, with its severe congestion and pollution problems.

Suburbanization has also involved industrial and commercial enterprises. Shopping malls signal an increasingly common type of construction being put on large tracts of suburban land, some of which was bought up previously by speculators. Often huge, air-conditioned malls are advertised as the new "central business districts" of American cities. For example, Phoenix, Arizona, has one hundred decentralized mall areas and a declining central business district.

Some power-conflict analysts see suburbanization, at least in part, as an attempt by powerful actors to absorb or co-opt the managers and the more affluent fraction of workers into the system and make them committed to the unequal ownership of private property. After all, only managers and the more affluent workers can afford to buy in most of the sprawling suburbs. The rising cost of single-family housing rations housing according to income. This has long been the case, but recent increases in the price of residential housing have further segregated Americans by income. Income segregation, unlike racial segregation, is quite legal. Well-heeled suburbs can sometimes frustrate central city attempts to incorporate them. Thus managers and the upper strata of workers can often secure better school and other governmental services than can those remaining in the city.

Workers do demand better housing. Pressure from ordinary workers for better housing has been important in generating housing development in central cities and suburbs. Since the nineteenth century, worker pressures have forced politicians to develop mass transit systems, public housing, and government assistance in buying private housing. An example of this government assistance can be seen in the Federal Housing Administration and Veterans Administration loans that have enabled many working people to get better housing over the last four decades. Better housing for the working class has resulted from this pressure. However, our capitalistic system has often shaped this demand for housing into a form of private consumption as seen by the detached homes in sprawling suburb. This "privatized" consumption has been profitable for the powerful land-interested actors, but it has retarded the development of important housing alternatives — such as more centrally located, moderately priced row housing — that could better meet the needs of all Americans, including less affluent and lower-income workers. Indeed, some Americans now recognize that sprawling suburbs have been costly to the society in the destruction of valuable farmland and in their link to high energy consumption in the form of big commuter automobiles and home heating and cooling.[20] . . .

Urban Renewal and Revitalization

Working with powerful business leaders, governmental officials have created major problems for working-class people, black and white, in the process of urban renewal. Spending billions of dollars, the federal Urban Renewal Agency has managed to reduce sharply the amount of housing available to working people, particularly low-income and low-middle-income workers, in cities. In the 1960s and 1970s hundreds of thousands of homes were destroyed in the urban renewal process; the majority of those displaced were nonwhites. Relatively little low-income and moderate-income housing was built in renewal areas. Rather, government frequently provided a way to get poor people off the land needed for business to develop. Hotels, high-rise apartments, convention centers, and office buildings (privately and government owned) sprang up where the working poor had once lived.

Urban renewal reflects a class struggle: it uproots certain urbanites to benefit others. Areas are intentionally labeled "blighted" or "slums"; such labels are frequently the first step toward large-scale bulldozing. Urban renewal usually signals that a powerless group is being shoved aside by a powerful group of capitalists and allied actors. Large-scale urban renewal, generated largely by business officials, landowners, speculators, and allied government officials, has remade large areas of many American central cities. For example, in the 1950s a major urban renewal project bulldozed more than 500 acres of outmoded apartment houses in the southwestern region of Washington, D.C., forcing black families out. Housing for no less than 10,000 working-class families was torn down and replaced with expensive apartments and federal office buildings. "Negro removal" has become a common term for this renewal process since that time.[21]

Two detailed examples of the character and effects of government-facilitated urban revitalization can be given: one in Boston in the late 1950s and early 1960s and the other in San Francisco in the 1970s and 1980s. In his research study *The*

Urban Villagers Herbert Gans documented the impact of urban renewal on a working-class Italian-American community in downtown Boston called the West End. Looking at this low-rent area, Gans found that it had been defined negatively and unfairly by business leaders and government officials as a "slum." This process raises a serious question about who controls the urban definition process, for once an area has been defined publicly as a "slum," it has frequently been an easy next step for powerful agents to bulldoze the area and rebuild it according to their undemocratic development schemes. This Boston urban renewal plan had been approved by government officials in the mid-1950s; soon only debris existed where thousands had once lived; by 1962 new residents had begun to move into the luxury housing that replaced the homes of the Italian Americans. The despair, the grieving for a lost home, that another researcher, Marc Fried, found among those forced to move from the West End is not surprising in light of the vital social ties that existed there prior to urban renewal. Interviewing five hundred people forced to move, Fried found that nearly half the women and 38 percent of the men expressed severe grief reactions about losing their homes. comments were like the following: "I felt as though I had lost everything." "I felt like my heart was taken out of me." "I felt like taking the gaspipe," "Something of me went with the West End." The sense of loss felt encompassed not only lost friends and community networks, but also the loss of a familiar physical space and a sense of continuity with the past. Urban renewal was dangerous to the health of these uprooted urban residents, perhaps even contributing to premature deaths among a few older residents. Such data indicate the importance of urban space and social structure, including peer group networks, in providing workers and their families with a sense of belonging within the urban context. By removing these networks, urban renewal has frequently created other major social problems.[22]

Perhaps the best documented recent study of government urban renewal is that by Hartman and his associates in regard to the Yerba Buena Center renewal project in San Francisco. In the early 1970s public relations releases extolled the virtues of a large-scale renewal project in central San Francisco: a "center city redevelopment to include a sports arena, 800-room hotel, office buildings, and parking for 4000 cars . . . going up only a few blocks from the San Francisco Hilton."[23] What is missing from the glowing advertising are answers to a string of critical questions about who loses and who profits from such large-scale developments.

This renewal project was approved by the San Francisco Board of Supervisors and went through a number of stages: the issuing of a plan for the area in 1954, federal approval of a planning grant in 1962, securing a federal loan and grant contract for development in 1966, the beginning of resident displacement and building demolition in 1967, the formation of a Tenants an Owners in Opposition to Redevelopment (TOOR) in 1969, a series of legal battles between TOOR and city and federal agencies over inadequate relocation plans and replacement housing for the displaced, and a 1973 agreement between TOOR and the San Francisco Redevelopment Agency in which the agency reluctantly agreed to develop 400 low-rent housing units as part of Yerba Center and 1500 – 1800 low-rent units in other parts of the city.[24]

The area at issue is a central city area, called the "South of Market," adjacent to the downtown corporate center of San Francisco. Beginning in the World War II period, San Francisco became a multinational corporate center. San Francisco has headquarters for Southern Pacific, Standard Oil of California, Transamerica Corporation, Crown Zellerbach, Del Monte, Foremost-McKesson, Levi Strauss, Potlach Forests, the Bechtel Corporation, and the Bank of America, to name just a few. A major administrative and finance center of modern capitalism, San Francisco has a growing corporate "need" for support facilities such as office buildings, convention centers, and hotels. Corporations "need" room, in the form of skyscrapers, not only for top executives but also for a large number of support workers, including public relations people, accountants, and secretaries. The common justification for pushing aside existing working-class residents, including the elderly, is that the land can be put to a "higher and better use." As Justin Herman, director of the Redevelopment Agency put it, "This land is too valuable to permit poor people to park on it."[25] Private profit is the guiding principle, even for the many government officials operating in support roles for business redevelopment. In addition, official justifications for large-scale land clearance often take the form of arguing that new buildings will improve the city's tax base, will make the city look better, and will bring new jobs.

In 1950 the San Francisco Planning and Urban Renewal Association was created as a private group, including major corporate executives, designed to generate business interest in urban renewal plans. In the association's "Prologue for Action," it was made clear what the effects of the changes desired by the corporate business elite would be: "If San Francisco decides to compete effectively with other cities for new 'clean' industries and new corporate power, its population will move closer to 'standard white Anglo-Saxon Protestant' characteristics. As automation increases the need of unskilled labor will decrease. Economically and socially, the population will tend to range from lower middle-class through lower upper-class.[26] . . . Working through the governmental redevelopment agency, these business executives intended to accomplish that class-biased goal.

The San Francisco Redevelopment Authority (SFRA), like other local government renewal agencies, has broad powers to coordinate private and public action. Creating and carrying out its renewal plans, it can move urban residents around, bulldoze areas, and advertise its projects with little democratic input or control. The agency has kept close ties with San Francisco's business elite. In the 1960s several large renewal projects were carried out, resulting in the displacement of 4000 families, mostly working-class blacks and Japanese.

The Yerba Buena Center development was designed to expand the city's financial district to the south; it garnered the interest of a number of important corporations and other investors. Selling it to the general public was more difficult. Speculative real estate operators and adjacent landowners stood to gain much from this land clearance, but getting public support for governmental expenditures required the help of local newspapers. Local San Francisco newspapers strongly supported the Yerba Buena development editorially and, in their news coverage, generally supported the point of view of the business leaders. For example, the *San Francisco*

Examiner attacked the residents of the South of Market area as follows in an October 15, 1971 editorial:[28]

Nor do we believe that such people should have the right — in the absence of some compelling reason deeply rooted in the public good — to delay and quite possibly kill a major public project of profound importance to the economic well-being of a city that is not really their home community, that they have built no stake in, that they make no attempt to adorn, and to which they are on the whole an unsought burden.

But who are the thousands displaced to provide great profits to a few dozen individuals and multinational corporations? The South of the Market area had been an area of retired working men's lodging. Most of the 5000 residents of this area were single, primarily older men living on small pensions. Forty-eight residential hotels provided these retired or disabled men with low-rent housing, which was generally decent and in sound condition. Many of the hotels were in need of some rehabilitation, but the proposed massive clearance was not required to significantly improve the housing for existing residents. The area was close to the transportation and other service facilities that these older men needed. The area was home, a place where single men could find friendship and support services.[29]

Yet, as in Boston's West End, in the renewal process this area was often inaccurately described as a "skid row" or "transient area." Stereotypes were intentionally aimed at these poor retired workers in an attempt to persuade other (particularly white-collar) workers in San Francisco of the justice in this case of urban renewal. Retired workers were conspicuously absent from the planning process for the Yerba Buena Center project. Nonetheless, the people in the area did organize against the massive problems about to be visited on them. Two years after the beginning of resident displacement and building demolition, Tenants and Owners in Opposition to Redevelopment (TOOR) was formed and fought legal battles with city and federal agencies over inadequate relocation plans and replacement housing for the displaced. They won a limited victory in the form of an agreement with the Redevelopment Agency in which the Agency agreed to develop 400 low-rent housing units as part of Yerba Buena Center and 1500 – 1800 low-rent units in other parts of the city mentioned earlier. By 1979, however, only 150 units of replacement housing had been built. The city leaders got their project, but for virtually the first time in urban renewal history they had to make some concessions to a people's movement against renewal.

Using Government Programs

Land clearing is not the only federal government program that lends itself to corporate control and profit making. A variety of government housing and development programs have been used to make a private profit. Writing in the *Harvard Business Review*, corporate executive Eli Goldston has described how a gas company made a good profit by participating in renewal and housing programs in Boston's black ghetto. The article explains in cost accounting terms how corporate developers make money from federal programs. A company takes some risk in going into ghetto areas, but the federal government's underwriting of projects with tax dollars makes this type of land and housing speculation less risky. Goldston emphasizes the valuable tax shelter advantages that flow from investments in housing developments in central city areas. In the Boston case, several thousand apartments were rehabilitated, with the gas company providing substantial financing for the project. In return the gas company got many new customers and a major "spillover" tax shelter benefit; both together provided the company with a "respectable profit." At the same time black construction workers got employment, and a significant number of black families got renovated housing.[30]

But the financial advantages to corporations are the primary consideration. As Goldston puts it, the "principal factor in most speculative real estate development is the spillover tax shelter, by which tax losses on cash-producing real estate can be used to reduce taxes on income from other sources." What he has in mind is the fact that federal tax laws permit corporate investors to take a rapid depreciation on rehabilitation projects, thus creating huge losses (usually on paper only) in the first few years of ownership that can be used to reduce or eliminate taxes that would otherwise have to be paid on income from other sources. When the tax advantages run out, the corporate investor can get out of the project. In addition, federal programs for poverty areas make it easy to get relatively low-interest government-insured loans from banks so that very little cash investment is required from corporations and others getting into these housing investments. Indeed, Goldston shows how a rehabilitated eighty-unit building worth $1 million can be bought and rehabilitated for only $38,000 in investment money. Given normal occupancy rates and reasonable rents, this eighty-unit builing will pay back, in tax savings and rentals, the entire $38,000 investment in less than two years and will pay back a total of nearly $100,000 in ten years. Here is a cold cost accounting defense of the profits to be made in central city housing rehabilitation projects.

In his recommendations to other companies seeking to make "respectable profits" in central city areas, Goldston recommends that they not only look at building codes and population trends but also at the relations the local community officals have with federal government housing and renewal agencies, those agencies with money for such rehabilitation developments. He even suggests ways in which to manipulate tenant organizations for rehabilitated apartment buildings so that they become "a forum for educating tenants in landlords' problems" and so that they "may even come to provide the self-regulation and control lacking in typical low-income rental situations."[31] He warns too that black militancy may make it difficult for landowners to get all their "traditional legal rights, obligations and enforcement procedures" upheld in the local courts. These are some of the risks to corporations seeking profits in government programs in central city areas.

It is clear from these recommendations by Goldston that government social programs are not just programs designed to benefit ordinary Americans, such as poor workers and their families. Both urban renewal and housing programs, as well as many others, have been used by corporate executives to make reasonable, sometimes handsome, profits. The proud giants of free enterprise also feed at the trough of government "handouts." The benefits to working people of this intervention are to some extent offset by the corporate concern with "control" and "self-regulation" and by the short-term commitment to ghetto problems. After the depreciation tax shelter is gone, in about ten years, corporations may well pull out of these investments. Such housing may then deteriorate as it is passed along from one investor to another until it is no longer useful as a tax shelter. . . .

THE BENEFICIAL IMPACT ON SOCIAL PROBLEMS

A democratic-socialist society with a nonracist, nonsexist structure could go a long way toward changing the underlying conditions that have generated or shaped most social problems . . ., from problems of income inequality and chronic unemployment, to problems of racial and sexual inequality, to problems in education, health care, and urban renewal. . . . Many American grass-roots movements have already pointed the way to democratic socialism. Large-scale democratic-socialist restructuring of this society would doubtless have far-reaching effects.

Eliminating a capitalistic system would mean an end to the existence of a small elite at the top of the society that controls enormous amounts of wealth in the form of such things as factories, offices, land, stocks, money savings, and housing. This in turn could mean that more income and wealth would be available to low- and middle-income Americans. Poverty could be eliminated. More important than the wealth itself is the power over the entire society that ownership and control of wealth-creating facilities confers. If such things as plants, offices, stores and natural resources (e.g., oil and minerals) were owned publicly *and* controlled democratically, then the people of the United States would no longer be at the mercy of decisions made by a small class of capitalists and its immediate subordinates with their interests in mind. People themselves could decide how their plants and organizations would be run, how their natural resources would be developed and used, and how social surpluses would be used.

While any society is going to have planning and distribution problems, a democratic-socialist society would not have severe recessions or depressions in which the bottom two-thirds of the society would suffer while capitalist and managers work out their investment and private profit difficulties. There would be no capitalist class to hold off on investment now to make better profits later on. If hard times came, the suffering could be broadly shared by all citizens. Jobs could be guaranteed. Most unemployment and underemployment could be eliminated.

A democratic-socialist society would not have a class-structured system of education. An alienating society is one with troubled schools. A democratic-socialist society could have decentralized community schools oriented toward a cooperative ethic rather than an individualistic ethic. Children could learn in a cooperative environment where class, race, and sex stratification would no longer track students into segregated educational environments and job channels. Moreover, education could be much more of an omnipresent, lifelong process. There would be no educational or workplace hierarchies to break down communication between individuals and groups. Knowledge would not be hoarded as much for private profit by corporations and other businesses. There would be far more decentralized schools scattered throughout neighborhoods, workplaces, and communities around the nation; there would be no need for large centralized educational institutions.

A reasonably equal distribution of wealth and income, and thus of dignity, would reduce crime by removing the causes of much property and personal crime. There would be less economic pressure for the poor or unemployed to steal, and the economic reasons for such crimes as assault and murder would be reduced substantially. In addition, much of the economic and political pressure for oppressed minorities and the poor to revolt and riot would be removed from the society. This could reduce much civil disobedience now labeled ''crime.'' Corporate crime would be eliminated from the society, since there would be no secretive corporate class that could charge artificially high prices or dump dangerous products on unsuspecting consumers. Many other kinds of crimes could also be eliminated from the society.

References

1. See Karl Marx, *Capital*, Vol. I, trans. Ernest Mandel (New York: Vintage Books, 1978); Lewis A. Coser, *Masters of Sociological Thought*, 2nd ed. (New York: Harcourt Brace Jovanovich, Inc., 1977), pp. 42–52; Charles Tilly, *From Mobilization to Revolution* (Reading, Mass.: Addison-Wesley Co., Inc., 1978), pp. 13–14.

2. This section draws on James O'Connor, *The Fiscal Crisis of the State* (New York: St. Martin's Press, 1973), pp.5–9 and passim.

3. Charles H. Anderson, *Toward a New Sociology*, rev. ed. (Homewood, Ill.: Dorsey Press, 1974), p. 125.

4. Alvin L. Schorr, ''Problems in the ADC Program,'' unpublished paper in author's possession, n.d.; Richard C. Edwards, ''Who Fares Well in the Welfare State?'' in *The Capitalist System*, eds. Richard C. Edwards et al. (Englewood Cliffs, N.J.: Prentice-Hall, Inc., 1972), p. 250.

5. Alan Wolfe, *The Seamy Side of Democracy* (New York: David McKay Co., Inc., 1973), pp.136–137.

6. Charles H. Anderson, *The Political Economy of Social Class* (Englewood Cliffs, N.J.: Prentice-Hall, Inc., 1974), p. 60.

7. Wolfe, *The Seamy Side of Democracy*, p. 133.

8. Anderson, *The Political Economy of Social Class*, p. 60.

9. This section draws heavily on Joe R. Feagin, *Subordinating the Poor* (Englewood Cliffs, N.J.: Prentice-Hall, Inc., 1975), pp. 50–72; Harold L. Willensky and Charles N. Lebeaux, *Industrial Society and Social Welfare* (New York: The Free Press, 1965), pp. xvi–xvii; Richard E. Edgar, *Urban Power and Social Welfare* (Beverly Hills, Calif.: Sage Publications, 1970), p. 10; Edwards, ''Who Fares Well in the Welfare State?'' p. 244.

10. Robert M. O'Neill, *The Price of Dependency* (New York: E. P. Dutton & Co., Inc., 1970), p. 292.

11. Ralph Miliband, *The State in Capitalist Society* (London: Weidenfield and Nicholson, 1969), p. 78; see also Milwaukee County Welfare Rights Organization, *Welfare Mothers Speak Out* (New York: W. W. Norton & Company, Inc., 1972), pp. 17–21; Philip M. Stern, *The Rape of the Taxpayer* (New York: Random House, Inc., 1973), pp.60–306.

12. Henry J. Aaron, *Politics and the Professors: The Great Society in Perspective* (Washington, D.C.: Brookings Institution, 1978), pp. 11–13.

13. A. Dale Tussing, ''The Dual Welfare System,'' *Society*, 11 (January–February 1974), 53.

14. Leonard Downie, *Mortgage on America* (New York: Praeger Publishers, Inc., 1974), pp. 32–40.
15. Seth S. King, "Action Is Sought to Help Protect U.S. Farmlands," *The New York Times*, January 18, 1981, Section 7, p. 9; Marion Clawson, *Suburban Land Conversion in the United States* (Baltimore, Md.: Johns Hopkins University Press, 1971); Joseph Ackerman et al., eds., *Land Economics Research* (Baltimore, Md.: Johns Hopkins University Press, 1962).
16. Larry Sawers, "Urban Form and the Mode of Production,"*Review of Radical Political Economics*, 7 (Spring 1975), 57.
17. Stuart Ewen, *Captains of Consciousness* (New York: McGraw-Hill Book Company, 1976), pp. 188–190.
18. Downie, *Mortgage on America*, p. 88.
19. Ibid., p. 10.
20. Sawers, "Urban Form and the Mode of Production," p. 59; Matthew Edel, "Rent Theory and Labor Strategy: Marx, George and the Urban Crisis," *Review of Radical Political Economics*, 9 (Winter 1977), n.p.
21. Downie, *Mortgage on America*, p. 65.
22. Herbert Gans, *The Urban Villagers* (Glencoe, Ill.: Free Press, 1962); Marc Fried, "Grieving for a Lost Home," in *The Urban Scene*, 2nd ed., ed. Joe R. Feagin (New York: Random House, Inc., 1979), pp. 167–182.
23. Chester Hartman, *Yerba Buena* (San Francisco: Glide Publications, 1974), p. 13. The next few paragraphs draw on this book.
24. Ibid., pp. 23–27.
25. Quoted in ibid., p. 19.
26. Quoted in ibid., p. 43.
27. Ibid., pp.48–50.
28. Quoted in ibid., p. 93.
29. Ibid., p. 97.
30. Eli Goldston, "BURP and Make Money," *Harvard Business Review*, 47 (September–October 1969), 99.
31. Ibid., p. 93.

CHAPTER 2

DO WE NEED A
NEW INDUSTRIAL POLICY?

Liberal theory, in its unadorned Hobbesian version, begins with the assumption that each of us desires as much as he or she can obtain. We are inclined to grasp everything within reach, without consideration of the desires or interests of others. Nevertheless, we find that our desire for more will generally be thwarted in the war of all against all. We solve this dilemma, according to liberal theory, by surrendering some of our autonomy to the state in return for security in our possessions. This exchange is called a social contract, and it is intended to engender peace between the parties involved.[1]

Pax Americana is the term employed by economists Bluestone and Harrison to refer to our dominance in global affairs after World War II. It was, they claim, a period that afforded American capital maximum opportunity to expand overseas. However, labor union discontentment manifested in strikes threatened to interfere with managerial strategy. Thereupon, a "social contract" between business and organized labor emerged. This "cease-fire" constituted a give-and-take process for both parties: capital gained more control over decision making in the workplace but at the cost of recognizing the legitimacy of labor unions.[2] Peace was short-lived because by 1970 American corporate hegemony was over. Competition from abroad put capital in a new mood, unfavorable to making labor concessions. Bluestone and Harrison argue that the current spate of plant closings and community abandonment indicates that capital has quit giving even lip service to the great postwar social contract, and is openly fleeing high-priced labor and social responsibility.

Robert B. Reich agrees that America is not coping well with foreign competition. He argues that Americans have suffered consequences the not adapting to the need for change. His discussion of the inability of the educational system to prepare students for highly skilled work is most interesting.

George Gilder, in contradistinction to the other authors considered, does not advocate a new industrial policy, nor does he defend an old one. Gilder argues against the plausibility of "risk-free" solutions; he relies instead on individual "heroism" to cope with national problems.

References

1. MacPherson, C. B., *The Political Theory of Possessive Individualism* (London: Oxford University Press, 1962), pp. 9–106. Also see Coleman, Frank M., *Hobbes and America: Exploring the Constitutional Foundations* (Toronto and Buffalo: University of Toronto Press, 1977).
2. Nissen, Bruce, "U.S. Workers and the U.S. Labor Movement," *Monthly Review* 33, No. 1 (May 1981), p. 25.

4. THE NEXT AMERICAN FRONTIER

Robert B. Reich

Americans tend to divide the dimensions of our national life into two broad realms. The first is the realm of government and politics. The second is the realm of business and economics. Our concerns about social justice are restricted to the first realm; our concerns about prosperity, to the second. Issues of participation, equality of opportunity and civil rights, public education and mass transit, social security and welfare, housing, pollution, and crime are seen as aspects of government and politics—the substance of our civic culture. Issues of productivity and economic growth, inflation and unemployment, savings, investment, and trade are seen as aspects of business and economics—the substance of our business culture. Democrats and liberals traditionally lay claim to the first realm; Republicans and conservatives, to the second.

Americans whose principal frame of reference is the civic culture charge business with undermining civic values by compromising politicans with campaign contributions, polluting air and water, and endangering workers and consumers. Americans whose principal frame of reference is the business culture feel that government and politics intrude mischievously on the free market, at best distracting businessmen from the vigorous pursuit of national prosperity, at worst subverting the system of individual enterprise.

Our civic culture embodies a vision of community, premised upon citizenship. Its concern with democratic participation and the sharing of wealth stems from a conviction that such commitments enrich life and affirm the interdependency of individual lives. The profit motive is anathema to this vision because it apparently gives selfishness precedence over the common good. The pursuit of profit cannot be the sole guide to behavior, so this vision holds, because there would then be no firm distinction between productive enterprise and robbery, between voluntary trade and coercion. Unleashed fear and greed would destroy the fabric of community.

The business culture embodies a moral vision of its own — one of individual responsibility and freedom. According to this vision, the market offers a superior organizing principle for society because it promotes the common good while preserving individual autonomy. The market rewards endeavors to the extent that they contribute to others' well-being. Because their efforts enrich them, people willingly apply their talents and energies to the common good — a Frank Sinatra to entertain us or a Thomas Edison to invent for us. Incompetence, carelessness, and laziness are not rewarded. Collectivism is anathema to this vision because it seems to discourage such unforced efforts and to rely instead on more intrusive, less efficient incentives, such as coercion, compassion, or patriotism. Such a society, according to the business culture's moral vision, would offer both less prosperity and less freedom.

In countless ways Americans are called upon to choose between these two sets of central values — social justice or prosperity; government or free market; community or freedom. A debate over environmental pollution becomes a contest between the vision of a restored community flourishing within a scenic and healthly environment and the opposite vision of unfettered entrepreneurs whose ambition and daring would create new products and processes to benefit all. A debate over taxes and government spending becomes a divisive dispute over the relative value of business investment versus such intangibles as education, public health, and income security. . . .

[Our] central theme . . . is that in the emerging era of productivity, social justice is not incompatible with economic growth, but essential to it. A social organization premised on equity, security, and participation will generate greater productivity than one premised on greed and fear. Collaboration and collective adaptation are coming to be more important to an industrialized nation's well-being than are personal daring and ambition. And at an even more fundamental level, the goals of prosperity and social justice cannot validly be separated. America's well-being is a function of the quality of life enjoyed by all our citizens; it is only indirectly a function of abstract rates of investment and economic growth. Social concerns are the ends that economics seeks to serve. It is perverse to relegate them even implicitly to a separate and subordinate status.

America has a choice: It can adapt itself to the new economic realities by altering its organizations, or it can fail to adapt and thereby continue its present decline. Adaptation will be difficult. America's current patterns of organization were once so successful that they have endured long after they have outlived their usefulness. To change the way we conduct our businesses and our government implies a more general change of customs, attitudes, and values which are parts of our cultural heritage. This more fundamental change is emotionally difficult. It becomes even more difficult as economic decline sets in because then change threatens the economic security of people who are desperately trying to hold on to what they have. A new consensus is difficult to achieve when each person seeks to preserve his standard of living but finds that he can only do so at the expense of someone else. But failure to adapt will rend the social fabric irreparably. Adaptation is America's challenge. It is America's next frontier. . . .

Over the course of the past century American industry perfected a wholly new organization of production, geared to manufacturing very large quantities of relatively simple, standardized products. The key was long production runs with each step along the way made simple and routine. Sometimes the long runs were on an assembly line carrying materials continuously from one stage to the next; sometimes the process involved very large batches of chemical compounds; sometimes it was based on continuous-process machines that automatically turned out parts or whole products. But however the principles were embodied, this new organization of production moved materials through the manufacturing process at an unprecedented velocity. As the scale of production increased, the cost of producing each unit plummeted. . . . Between 1900 and 1920 the rate of increase in output per worker (and per person) in the American economy declined by approximately 50 percent from the rate prevailing over the previous decade. This deceleration marked the end of the first era of American productivity. The enormous spurt in productivity of the late 1880s and 1890s had been due to an extraordinarily efficient mobilization of resources into high-volume production: machinery which incorporated new technology; disciplined workers from the farm and from overseas; and advances in transportation and communication that enabled goods and materials to flow continuously through the manufacturing process and into distribution. But the processes underlying the surge of mobilization could not sustain the dynamic they had set in motion.

In sum, the problems that stalled the next stage of industrialization stemmed from failures of organization. When America's new engine of production began to overrun its capacity to distribute, market, and consume, business sought to remedy the problem through mergers and consolidations. But this reorganization did not suffice. Some of the mergers let manufacturers reduce capacity and limit competition without any real gains in the efficiency of production, distribution, or marketing. Even the combinations that did yield new efficiencies were suspect in the eyes of many Americans, who doubted their accountability either to the market or to the political process. And many of the risks of overcapacity remained.

The shop floor itself suffered from organizational inadequacy. Foremen's authority over their subordinates was arbitrary and unchecked, resulting in worsening labor unrest and mounting difficulties in coordinating production within the firm.

A third organizational failure plagued public administration. American government lacked the capacity to respond efficiently and equitably to many of the social ills of industrialization. The result was the beginning of a sharp ideological cleavage between the ideals of social welfare and industrial growth.

The evolving American economy required systems of organization that could give it stability and legitimacy. Large, newly consolidated enterprises needed an institutional structure that could confirm their new role and help shield them against the ravages of the business cycle. Within their own enterprises, businessmen required a system of rules and policies to check the arbitrary actions of foremen, legitimize their authority in the eyes of workers, and aid them in coordinating production within the firm. And within society at large, popular acceptance of industrialization depended on a system of public administration to soften its social impact.

In the absence of these organizational systems, the continued growth of high-volume production in America was stymied. Labor unrest, social disruption, and political turmoil in the first decades of the new century constrained productivity and raised fundamental questions about the role of the large corporation in American life. America searched for an answer to what appeared to be an impasse in its politics and economy. The answer came in the form of a new political and economic vision: that of management. . . .

World War II plunged the federal government far more deeply into industrial management than it had ever been before. At the height of the war 40 percent of everything manufactured or grown in the nation went to the war effort. Planning on the scale the war required had never been attempted. But all the institutional precedents were there — the superstructures of industrial management, in the form of trade associations, industry commissions, boards, regulatory agencies, and labor unions. They needed only modification and enlargement to meet the industrial challenge of war mobilization.

Unlike the First World War, however, the Second failed to end with the last shots. Instead, it became a permanent mobilization, punctuated by Korea and Vietnam. Many of the superstructures of industrial management were incorporated into a permanent defense production system. Others migrated to the departments of Commerce and Interior. Anticipating the war's end the Commerce Department's Business Advisory Council, for example, estimated postwar production levels industry by industry, devised programs to cushion companies and workers against the decline in the defense market, and encouraged large firms to integrate their plans with suppliers and customers.

Soon after the Korean War the Commerce Department established a Business and Defense Services Administration. Its role, in the words of Sinclair Weeks, Secretary of Commerce under Dwight D. Eisenhower, was "to see to it that, while private business, of course, cannot dictate government policy and plans, it be placed in a position where it can effectively approve or disapprove of the implementation of such policy and plans from the standpoint of their practical workability in everyday industrial operation." In practice, the agency allocated materials required in military and atomic energy programs and advised the president on accelerated tax depreciation schemes, loan assistance, stockpiling, and other forms of federal support for industry.

By organizing the Business and Defense Services Administration along industrial lines, the Commerce Department sought to give each industry "its own special division for receiving government information service." Each division was, naturally enough, dominated by the industry's major firms. The staff of the Aluminum and Magnesium Division, for example, came from the three largest integrated producers — Alcoa, Kaiser, and Reynolds. The Forest Products Division was staffed by the vice-president of the Weyerhaeuser Company.

Other government departments had their own business committees. The Department of the Interior, for example, inherited the Petroleum Industry War Council, which had served as part of the War Production Board. During peacetime its membership — including every major American oil company — supervised voluntary industry agreements on the allocation of oil transportation facilities and equipment. Every other raw materials industry had a similar committee within the Interior Department. A 1956 survey found more than 5000 business advisory committees spread throughout the federal government, many of them carrying out delegated responsibilities for managing their industries.

The Pentagon's role in industrial mangement was perhaps the most important of all. Unlike the other superstructures of management — which delegated to industries the authority to coordinate production — the Pentagon spawned superstructures that contracted directly with the government. It was American industry's largest single purchaser. In 1952, 11.6 percent of the nation's gross national product was purchased for defense. In the next two decades the percentage never fell below 6 percent.

The government provided a substantial market for several industries. In 1977, for example, government purchases accounted for 56 percent of all U.S. aircraft shipments, 56 percent of the sales of radio and communications equipment, 12 percent of engineering and scientific instruments, and 12 percent of transmitting electron tubes. By the end of the era the Pentagon was funding approximately 30 percent of all U.S. research and development and more than 80 percent of all government-financed research. For basic research with few immediate commercial applications, federal funding exceeded two-thirds of the total. In some industries, government research support reached particularly high levels. In 1977, for example, the government funded 70 percent of research and development in the aircraft industry and 48 percent in the communications equipment industry.

Significantly, government purchases not only underpinned old industries but also shaped the development of new ones. Large-scale defense and aerospace contracts provided emerging industries in the United States with a ready market that let them quickly expand production and thus gain scale economies and valuable experience. The Pentagon's willingness to pay a high premium for quality and reliability, moreover, helped emerging industries bear the cost of refining and "debugging" their products. Largely as a result of government contracts, for example, the U.S. semiconductor industry was able to reduce its unit costs quickly during the 1960s and emerge as a commercial leader in the world market. Because the arms race and the moon race both demanded smaller, faster, and more reliable memory units, the Defense Department and the National Aeronautics and Space Administration became the largest purchasers of semiconductors, together accounting for almost one-third of the market by 1967. While in 1962 an integrated circuit cost $50, by 1968 its cost had dropped to $2.33, making it commercially attractive for use in many consumer products. Over the same period the semiconductor market grew from $4 million to $31 million.

Many other emerging industries followed the same pattern. In 1950 government purchases accounted for 92 percent of aerospace sales. Advanced aircraft originally developed for the military were adapted to civilian uses, the Boeing B-47 and B-52 bombers evolving into the Boeing 707; the Douglas A-3D, A-4D, and B-66 military aircraft becoming the DC-8. The nascent computer industry also relied on federal support. In 1954 the government was the only major purchaser of computers; by 1962 the government market still represented almost one-half of total computer sales. Defense purchases and research support spurred other industries as well: hard plastics, synthetic rubber, lasers, fiber optics, nuclear power, radio and television communications equipment, and optical and scientific instruments.

In many industries, military contracts reinforced the dominance of the largest producers. Although defense contracts often required that firms cooperate on research projects or subcontract the work to smaller manufacturers, the Pentagon tended to rely on the largest firms by awarding them contracts without competitive bidding. Even when firms had to submit bids, they were often rendered meaningless by routine cost overruns. And major defense contractors developed the specifications on which future contracts were to be based, thus guaranteeing their continued favored status.

In his farewell address President Eisenhower warned the nation of growing military-industrial complex which was gaining enormous power. Yet the superstructures of industrial management spawned by the Pentagon's permanent war mobilization were in fact little more than larger versions of the superstructures that had already dominated the American economy for decades. There was nothing inherently mischievous about these superstructures. On the contrary, they were necessary for efficient high-volume production. The Pentagon's purchases and research subsidies enabled new industries, like electronics and jet aircraft, to gain high-volume scale quickly. Innovation may have been slowed in some instances, but so long as America's economic growth was based not on industrial change but on ever greater production of standardized goods, these superstructures were central to the nation's economic health. . . .

With the close of the management era America has abruptly faced a stark challenge of economic transformation, but the old organization of business, labor, and government has resisted change. High-volume, standardized production was the engine of prosperity for so long that fundamental change threatens the well-being of too many people. So the nation has pretended that the management era has not really ended. America has dismissed its economic troubles as the work of OPEC and the oil shocks of 1973 and 1979. It has blamed regulations, inflation, taxes, government deficits, and subsidized imports.

As the trusted formula of high-volume, standardized production has ceased to deliver prosperity, America has been ready to embrace any explanation but the most obvious: The same factor that previously brought prosperity — the way the nation organizes itself for production — now threatens decline. Everywhere America has looked, it has seen the symptoms of its economic impasse, but the nation has been unable to recognize the problem because its roots are deeply embedded in the organization of America's business enterprises, labor unions, and government institutions.

Government regulation served as a convenient rhetorical scapegoat in the 1980 presidential election but offers no real explanation. Environmental laws indeed require firms to invest in new equipment, but those requirements have imposed only modest costs. Safety regulations also add some costs to operations, but the reduction in accidents has meant savings in time and expense that go far to offset these extra costs. Capital expenditures on pollution control and safety combined have never exceeded 6 percent of industrial investment and may be blamed for at most around a tenth of the slowdown in productivity. Significantly, pollution control and mandatory safety laws have been more stringent in many other countries, including Japan, that have still surpassed American rates of productivity growth

As we shall see, during the 1970s Japanese steelmakers spent almost twice as much as their American counterparts on pollution control and worker safety. Finally, many critics of regulation underscore the obvious when they claim that safety and a clean environment cost something. The issue is whether they are worth it. Considering the relatively modest cost of the regulations and the importance Americans place on these aspects of their well-being, the claim that measures to maintain the environment and protect workers are responsible for a declining American standard of living is simply not plausible.

Nor do government deficits explain any major part of America's problem. There is no evidence that deficits have been nearly large enough to discourage private investment and economic growth substantially. What matters is not the total dollar debt but its relationship to the economy's size. In the period from 1956 to 1973, when the U.S. public sector mushroomed, the rest of the economy also grew in proportion. After 1973, as overall growth slowed dramatically, the government's share of the economy stabilized. Today's debt is less than 30 percent of the nation's gross national product, about the same proportion as it was in the late eighteenth century. By comparison with other industrial countries that have outpaced America, the U.S. government sector has stayed quite small as a proportion of the economy. Indeed, throughout the 1970s the governments in West Germany, Japan, and France maintained a larger public debt in proportion to their national economies than did the American government. And tax revenues as a percent of national product increased substantially more in every other major industrialized country than in the United States.

Inadequate capital formation has not been the problem either. Between 1965 and 1980, even in the face of inflation, America continued to invest about 10 percent of its gross national product in plant and equipment; since 1977 the rate has exceeded 11 percent, and in the first quarter of 1982 it reached 11.7 percent — its highest level since 1928. Indeed, investment in *manufacturing* as a percent of the total output of goods in manufacturing increased substantially — from 10.8 percent between 1960 and 1964 to 14.8 percent between 1973 and 1978. This level of manufacturing investment was not significantly below that of America's foreign competitors.

Nor can other proposed explanations really explain America's decline. Investment in research and development declined from 3 percent of the gross national product at the start of the 1970s to 2 percent at the start of the 1980s. But this decline stemmed mostly from the slowdown in publicly financed defense and space programs which affected American industry only indirectly. And U.S. expenditures for research and development were still higher than those of its competitors. In any event, the decline in America's productive growth actually began in the late 1960s, well before any cutback in research expenditures. Nor can responsibility be placed on escalating energy prices. The oil shock affected all nations, many of which were much more dependent on imported energy resources than was the United States. Even more to the point, America's economic decline predated the oil embargo.

Nor was it the inevitable drop in output from the nation's mines; or the slowdown in the movement of American labor out of agriculture; or the entrance of women and young people into the labor force; or unfair competition by foreign manufacturers. Even taken together these explain only a small part of America's gradual, steady economic decline relative to other leading industrial nations. They fail to take into account the worldwide reorganization of production and America's failure to adapt to it. . . .

Other industrialized nations of course confront the same competitive threat. Since the mid-1960s European industries have faced an ever grater challenge from low-wage production in developing countries. Since the late 1970s Japan has been challenged as well. Japan is no longer a low-wage nation — the real earnings of Japanese workers are approaching those of their European and American counterparts.

Japan, West Germany, France, and other industrialized countries have sought to meet this challenge by shifting their industrial bases toward products and processes that require skilled labor. Skilled labor has become a key barrier against low-wage competition for the simple reason that it is the only dimension of production in which these countries retain an advantage. Technological innovations may be bought or imitated by anyone. High-volume, standardized production facilities may be established anywhere. But production processes that depend on skilled labor must stay where that labor is. The competitive fate of British industry over the last twenty-five years illustrates this pattern. Great Britain has consistently led the world in major technological breakthroughs, like continuous casting for steel, monoclonal antibodies, and CAT-scanning devices. But because its businesses lacked the organization and its workers lacked the skills necessary to incorporate these inventions into production processes quickly enough, they have reaped no real competitive advantage from them.

Industrialized countries are therefore moving into products like precision castings, specialty steel, special chemicals, process control devices, sensor devices, and luxury automobiles as well as into the design and manufacture of fiber-optic cable, fine ceramics, lasers, integrated circuits, and aircraft engines.

Some of these products or processes require precision engineering, complex testing, and sophisticated maintenance. Others are custom-tailored to the special needs of particular customers. The remainder involve technologies that are changing rapidly. These three product groups are relatively secure against low-wage competition because they depend on high-level skills rather than on standardized production.

Precision Products.   Products that require precision engineering, testing, and maintenance cannot easily be made in most developing countries. In the precision casting industry, for example, highly skilled labor is required first for making the dies and tools and then for forming, finishing, and correcting the resulting products. Because these highly skilled jobs must be performed in the same place as the rest of the production process and because they involve a significant percentage of the total labor required to produce precision castings, the whole process is protected against low-wage competition. The assembly of process control devices similarly demands exacting mechanical adjustments, which can be undertaken only by skilled technicians.

Custom Products. Products custom-tailored to buyers' specific needs are also immune to rapid competitive decline. Turned out in relatively small batches and in close coordination with their customers, these products inevitably depend more on the skill and knowledge of their designers, fabricators, and marketers than on unskilled labor. Examples include numerically controlled machine tools and multipurpose robots; auto body sheet steel that is resistant to corrosion on the inside and smooth and paintable on the outside, made in a small-batch process that coats galvanized sheet on one side; steel rods and bars, which are produced from scrap metal in minimills; telecommunications switching equipment, each installation requiring a separate, customized software system; computer hardware and software systems designed to solve specific problems, like inventory control; made-to-order semiconductor chips designed to fit into particular machinery; special chemicals prepared for particular industrial uses; and custom-designed office equipment.

Computers can add to the efficiency of small-batch, customer-tailored production by controlling the pace and performance of various machines. This innovation permits skilled workers to make rapid changes in product design after short runs and avoids expensive retooling. The inherent analytical strength of computers complements uniquely human advantages in recognizing patterns, assessing complex problems, and making intuitive leaps to new situations. For example, computerized machinery has been installed in a new Canadian chemical plant that custom-blends a wide range of alcohol products for use in carpets, soaps, and containers. Rather than have all possible blends programmed into the machinery in advance, the computers provide teams of workers with technical and economic data for refining their own decisions about which blends are needed and how they should be produced. The production process is thus constantly changed and upgraded.

When computers are used in predetermined ways, however, the production process does not need skilled workers. Computer-aided manufacturing processes that do not rely on skilled workers are migrating to developing countries in which low-wage labor or cheap raw materials can reduce the cost of product still further.

Technology-Driven Products. The third group of products that are relatively protected against foreign competition is that that depends on rapidly changing technologies. When major innovations occur so frequently that new product generations appear every few years, high-volume, standardized production confers little competitive advantage. By the time high volume is reached the product has already been outdated. Mass production can still yield economies of scale (Japanese production of semiconductor chips is prime example), but real competitive advantage derives from technological advances. Under these circumstances, production facilities must be in close contact with research and development efforts, so that the latest innovations can be incorporated quickly and efficiently. Examples of products or processes that depend on rapidly changing technologies computers, integrated circuits, biotechnologies, fiber optics, lasers, and ceramics.

These three product categories — precision-manufactured, custom-tailored, and technology-driven — have a great delay in common. They all depend on the skills of their employees, which often are developed within teams. And they all require that traditionally separate business functions (research, design, engineering, purchasing, manufacturing, distribution, marketing, sales) be merged into a highly integrated system that can respond quickly to new opportunities. A useful shorthand term for this general type of production ''flexible system.''

Flexible-system production has an advantage over high-volume standardized production in any enterprise in which production costs can be reduced more sharply by solving new problems than by making routine the solution of old ones. The unit costs of producing simple, standardized products like cotton textiles, basic steel, or rubber tires generally decline more with long production runs than with improvements in the production process. Manufacturers of these products therefore do well to emphasize large capacity, cheap labor, and cheap raw materials rather than flexible systems.

This does not mean that industrialized countries must abandon their older industries, like steel, chemicals, textiles, and automobiles. These industries are the gateways through which new products and processes emerge. It is far easier to move into flexible-system production by upgrading manufacturing skills and know-how and by elaborating networks of suppliers, distributors, and customers already in existence than by leaping into a totally uncharted sea of products and processes unrelated to an industrial base of the past. Rather than abandoning these older industries, America's industrialized competitors are seeking to restructure them toward higher valued and technologically more sophisticated businesses — like specialty steel, special chemicals, synthetic fibers, and precision-engineered automobiles and auto components. . . .

America's industrial base must change radically. If American prosperity is to be truly restored, a substantial fraction of capital and labor must shift toward flexible-system production. But the organization of high-volume, standardized production permits change in only one dimension: toward greater scale and a larger volume of the same standardized products. As shall be discussed, because America's professional managers are ill equipped to undertake the necessary shift, they have resorted to various ploys designed to maintain or increase their firms' earnings without new productive investment. Paper entrepreneurialism of this kind merely rearranges industrial assets while wasting the time and abilities of some of America's most talented people.

Organized labor, meanwhile, also resists industrial change, ready to sacrifice growth and even to roll back wages as the price of preserving America's old industrial base. The superstructures of industry-wide management, dominated by the largest and most entrenched firms within each industry, have joined in coalition with organized labor to lobby — successfully — for protection against imports. . . .

And America's social welfare and employment policies continue to seek stability rather than social change, thereby relegating the poor to permanent poverty and making the prospect of economic change particularly threatening to everyone whose economic well-being depends on older industries. Failing to adapt to skill-intensive labor implies, by default, an adaptation to dead-end labor. . . .

The shift has been slow and painful because America is simply not organized for economic change. Its organizations are based on stability rather than on adaptability. The extraordinary success of high-volume, standardized production during the half century of the management era has left America a legacy of economic inflexibility. The institutional heritage of our past success now imperils our future. . . .

America's system of public education is similarly inadequate to the task of preparing citizens for skill-intensive production. Because public schools are financed largely by local property taxes, schools in the poorest neighborhoods and in regions particularly hard hit by economic decline are least able to provide their students with the basic skills necessary for job mobility. In America's largest cities the middle class has all but abandoned the public school system, sending its children to private schools instead; left behind, in underfunded, decaying facilities, are the working class and the poor. The decay of America public education resembles other facets of the current impasse. In response to America's economic decline, public schools have been starved of resources. And as its public education degenerates, the erosion of its economic base accelerates.

The result is hardly surprising. Nearly 13 percent of the young in New York City are now functionally illiterate. Between 1963 and 1982 the median score on the verbal Scholastic Aptitude Test declined from 478 (out of a possible 800) to 426; on the mathematics SAT, from 502 to 467. The National Assessment of Education Progress reports that today's high school students are less able than their counterparts of a decade ago to understand and analyze what they read.

In fields of knowledge directly related to America's competitive position in the world economy, the decline in educational quality has been particularly dramatic. Fewer than one-fifth of the nation's high school students now study a foreign language, and only 4 percent study one for more than two years. Only 8 percent of American colleges and universities require some minimal competence in a foreign language for admission (down from 34 percent just fifteen years ago). Only one out of six high school students has any math or science training beyond tenth grade. Fewer than 10 percent of U.S. high school students study physics. Only 3 percent study calculus. While in 1960, 59 percent of American high school students took at least one science course, by 1977 the proportion was only 48 percent.

Part of the problem is the scarcity of suitable teachers. There are only 10,000 high school physics teachers to cover 17,000 American school districts. Chicago has only one physics teacher for every two high schools. High school mathematics and science teachers are fleeing the schools for higher-paying jobs in industry.

Public schools have been denied the resources to come anywhere close to matching industrial salaries, and scarce talent is drawn into immediate production at the expense of the future. In 1981 alone 1000 physics teachers — 10 percent of the total — left the classroom for jobs in industry. Many of those who remain are unqualified to teach math or science: More than half the 2000 high school principals surveyed in 1981 by the National Science Teachers Association judged their math teachers to be unqualified. In the same survey officials from 600 teacher-training schools reported a 77 percent decline since 1971 in the number of high school mathematics teachers they graduated, and a 65 percent decline in the number of science teachers.

The same "brain drain" is occurring in U.S. universities. American engineering schools in particular are badly understaffed. Across America, 2500 of 20,000 faculty positions in engineering remain unfilled. Even prestigious MIT cannot fill faculty positions in microelectronics and computer engineering. At San Jose State University, in the heart of California's "Silicon Valley," one-third of the engineering faculty positions are unfilled, and the department must turn away half of the qualified applicants. Nearby electronics companies, meanwhile, suffer from shortages of engineers — shortages that current trends promise to worsen. (It is ironic that both California and Massachusetts, the two states that have most successfully parlayed first-rate public health and educational systems into regional centers of skill-intensive industries, have succumbed to tax revolts that starve the sources of the skilled workers these industries will need in the future.) And as a result of reductions in federal funding, university science and engineering laboratories are grossly outdated. In sum, American students are not obtaining the education they need for leadership in flexible-system production.

Neglecting public education has the most damaging results for the children of less affluent Americans. Local school districts in the poorest areas of the country now have even fewer resources. Proposed tax credits for parents who send their children to private schools would further erode middle-class support for public education. And many American universities face pressure to accept students on the basis of their ability to pay. America's future work force is being doomed to start out handicapped.

Underlying these disturbing trends is another factor, having more to do with the way American education is designed and administered than with its funding. Even if America were to devote more resources to education, simply more of the same would not prepare its youth for roles in flexible-system enterprises. At best, the current system of education prepares young people for preexisting jobs in high-volume, standardized production. Some students are sorted into professional ranks, and trained in the manipulation of abstract symbols. Others are prepared for lower-level routine tasks in production or sales. Few students are taught how to work collaboratively to solve novel real-world problems — the essence of flexible-system production.

U.S. education has been modeled on scientific management. Students are sorted, programmed, and controlled in a high-volume, standardized production process essentially like any other. Knowledge is divided and subdivided into discrete units, delivered according to preset instructions, and monitored at regular intervals through standardized examinations — precisely Frederick Taylor's prescription of specialization by simplification, preestablished rules, and feedback information. Students move through high schools and universities as if they were on a conveyor belt.

American education has followed the form of American business. As businesses have merged and consolidated, so, too, have schools and universities — into centralized "comprehensive" school districts and giant university campuses. Increasingly America's educational curriculum is planned and monitored by professional administrators and delivered by teachers whose low salaries and tedious, repetitive jobs are coming to resemble those of production workers in a traditional American factory.

These trends toward consolidating physical plant and separating the planners and providers of education have had predictable results: Professional education administrators now spend a large portion of their time dealing in abstract rules and numbers, distilled to the point of being disconnected from the real processes of learning. Countless efforts are made to measure and quantify educational achievement. Professional administrators start from these measures to devise standard rules and procedures for teachers and students. Success in American education is coming to be measured largely by the degree of order and management control in the classroom.

Collaborative and innovative problem-solving skills simply cannot easily be learned in a routine and tightly controlled environment. People cannot be trained to participate in flexible-system enterprises when their daily lives are dominated by high-volume, standardized institutions. Children cannot learn to take responsibility and to work creatively within an atmosphere that discourages personal responsibility and rewards rote responses. America's schools and universities have come to mirror American firms — rigid systems for achieving economies of scale, impressively efficient but incapable of imaginative responses.

The value of education transcends it economic dimension, of course. Knowledge does not need to be justified in instrumental terms. But in our present period of fiscal belt tightening, it is well to remind ourselves of the connection between education and our collective well-being. A decline in our citizens' capacity to analyze, innovate, create, and communicate will condemn us all to a meager existence as it impoverishes our cultural and civic life together. . . .

The conservative vision of a market economy in which people are propelled solely by greed and fear is crippling the U.S. economy. A society that simultaneously offers its members both the prospect of substantial wealth and the threat of severe poverty will no doubt inspire occasional feats of dazzling entrepreneurialism. But just as surely, it will reduce the capacity of its members to work together to a common end and to adapt themselves collectively to new conditions. The ideology of wealth and poverty, to which some Americans still cling, is suited to a simple frontier economy in which social progress depends on personal daring. It may well have been a fitting ideology for America's early era of mobilization. But a social ethos shaped in a virgin continent is the wrong vision to guide and motivate the members of an increasingly complex industrial economy.

It is becoming clear that America's economic future depends less on lonely geniuses and backyard inventors than on versatile organizations. Our abundance of Nobel laureates attests to American cleverness. Technical advances originate disproportionately in America — semiconductors, videocassette recorders, and automobile stamping technologies, to name only a few. Our problem is that we are not consolidating this technological leadership into enduring commerical leadership because our industrial organization is not adaptable enough.

The kinds of productive systems that will sustain America's future prosperity are technically intricate. They demand an exacting degree of teamwork. They are vulnerable to individual sabotage in the form of active resistance, the stagnant inefficiency of resentful time servers, or the cynical manipulation of legal and financial symbols. Likewise, our national economy is ever more exposed to sudden global changes. Responding to these challenges requires an engaged and adaptable citizenry. We all are at the mercy of recalcitrant minorities who fear change (when we ourselves are not members of such minorities).

Under these circumstances, the incentives of greed and fear are having perverse effects: Many Americans are resisting change, resorting instead, to strategies of historic preservation. Lacking mechanisms for negotiating and ensuring the fairness of collective response, we are eschewing collaboration and seeking security and gain in schemes of paper entrepreneurialism and ploys of "beggar thy neighbor." We struggle to avoid sacrifices and burdens we believe others are successfully evading, and we refuse to support social services the direct beneficiaries of which are different from ourselves. And we seek to gain personal benefits at the expense of society at large, benefits like those we suspect others are already obtaining. The social fabric is slowly unraveling.

The challenge of adapting to the era of human capital exemplifies the paradox of civic virtue. To the extent that people cooperate — willingly sharing their knowledge, skills, and resources with one another — each person is rendered better off than he would be without such cooperation. The collective power of everyone's talents and resources is greater than the mere sum of the individual talents and resources involved. But each person is aware that he can be even better off if everyone *but* himself acts with an eye to the common good, so that he can benefit from the result without bearing any part of the mutual burden. If each person follows this logic and rationally opts for personal gain at the expense of everyone else, there will be no cooperation. Everyone will be worse off. What is rational for the individual is tragically irrational for the society as a whole.

Any society that hopes to escape this grim logic — or the despairing solution of blunt coercion — must equip itself with ideals and institutions that inspire citizens to work together without fear of being victimized. The confidence that underpins cooperation depends on effective codes of fairness and on institutions that nurture a sense of economic citizenship — in short, on a potent concern with civic virtue.

The notion that an atmosphere of civic membership and obligation is a requisite for prosperity may seem quaintly old-fashioned in an age of robots and microcomputers. But the logic is timeless: Civic virtue is not a matter of charity or ethics; it is the adhesive of social and economic life.

CONSERVATIVE: NO

5. THE BULLHEADED BREWER

George Gilder

To the mind that doubts that decisive role of genius, courage, and chance in the past, the future usually seems impossible: the Western world appears doomed to decay and coercion as its growing populations press against a closing frontier and science and technology meet the law of diminishing returns. A sociology of despair is emerging, based on spurious science, incomprehension of the hardships of all human history, and blindness to the perennial sources of human triumph. While physicists begin to concede freedom for microscopic particles, social scientists still begrudge it to human beings. Atomic structure is allowed room for the random and incalculable; but social structure is supposedly under siege by mechanistic forces of entropy and exhaustion, playing out their logic in a "closing circle" of ecological decline.

These attitudes lead to systematic distortions of vision and policy. The mind-set that prompts a man to see the future blighted by coercion and scarcity also inclines him to believe that the present can be made as free of risk and uncertainty as the past, receding unchangeably in the lenses of hindsight. Because an intelligible logic is seen to have determined the past and is predicted to shape the future, the modern political thinker wants to impose a similar pat rationality on current events. He calls on government to create an orderly and predictable economy, with known energy reserves always equaling prospective needs; with jobs always assured in appropriate geographic and demographic patterns; with monetary demand always expanding to absorb expected output of current corporate goods; with disorderly foreign intruders banished from the marketplace or burdened by tariffs and quotas; with factories controlled by workers and prohibited from rapid movement of change; with invention and creativity summoned by bureaucrats for forced marches of research and development; with inflation insurance in every contract, unemployment insurance in every job, and bankruptcy insurance for every corporation; with all windfall wealth briskly taxed away and unseemly poverty removed by income guarantees. In this view, held in varying but essentially discernible forms by every "humanist" intellectual, risk and uncertainty are seen to be the problem and government the solution in a fail-safe quest for a managed economy and a quiet and predictable world.

These notions deeply affront the most essential conditions of economic growth and human progress. The quest for calculable rationality in human affairs defies the incalculable subjectivity of human beings and the danger and indeterminancy of all human life. In economics the problem surfaces most clearly in the failures of planning, which in turn are perhaps most vividly on display in the small and struggling economies of the Third World. Here contemporary ideas are applied with an abstract directness that is not feasible in the dense and multifarious societies of the industrialized northern hemisphere. With a passionate devotion to the ideals of welfare and central control, and an undeniable need for public works and investments, the developing countries provide continuing lessons in the perplexities of rational management.

Albert O. Hirschman, an economics professor at Harvard and Princeton who has long specialized in the study of retarded economies, launched, some fifteen years ago, an analysis of the development schemes and achievements in some fifty less-developed countries. He discovered, as might have been expected, a morass. He met "comprehensive programs" that parlay a medley of vain hopes, expert jargon, and jaded pieties into a "multipronged" agenda of "development"; he found spuriously "imitative" ventures, envisioning any random river valley as a site for "another TVA"; he saw grandiose steel mills and automobile plants looming over insulated little national markets. There was usually an elegant plan and a sophisticated rationale, followed by a dismal or unexpected result.

In other words, Hirschman found all the usual pretensions and fatuities of economic uplift in the Third World. It would have been perfectly possible for him to issue the usual report, applauding the ambitious schemes and aspirations, while criticizing the faulty execution, the lack of technical skill, the absence of adequate capital, the inhibitions of primitive culture, and the parsimony of the industrial world that prevent the carrying out of the Western prescriptions for growth. But instead he discovered in the trials and errors — and occasional successes — of these countries, a crucial principle of economic progress.

His key finding was that it is not only the failed projects that do not fulfill expectations. Most of the *successful* projects also drastically diverge from the plans and intentions that give them birth. A factory will be built in the midst of a bamboo forest to exploit this source of pulp. The bamboo will all go bad and the factory will thrive instead on scrap pulpwood shipped by water to the plant. A hydroelectric station is built to stimulate industrial development in a rural area. No industrial development occurs and the station seems a complete fiasco, until transmission lines are provided to deliver the power to a neighboring country. Demand grows so much that the station must be twice enlarged.

Recounting scores of examples, Hirschman proposed as a theory "the principle of the hiding hand." Economic plans and projects rarely come to their intended fruition. But leaders in Third World countries need them nonetheless. They can muster in themselves and their followers the confidence and willpower to commence a major undertaking only if its dangers and difficulties are obscured. This "hiding hand" takes the form of a plan, a show of expertise, often vastly overestimating the benefits and underestimating the difficulties. The authoritative scheme and agenda serve to persuade a timid leadership that all problems have been anticipated and the solutions are known.

Such a "hiding hand" seems to have been active in the industrial development of the United States during the first half of the nineteenth century. Economic historian John Sawyer has observed that "miscalculation or sheer ignorance" of costs and difficulties was the key to launching a number of great and successful enterprises, from canals and railroads to mining and manufacture.

Again folly seems to bear fruit. What is happening here? Do these experiences mean that economic advance is essentially accidental, the statistically predictable outcome of innumerable trials and errors, a random accretion of chances, building on one another like a Darwinian process of natural selection among probabilistic mutations? There are better explanations, and Hirschman gives us a key to them.

Success in any difficult undertaking is always a product of human creativity. But

creativity always comes as a surprise to us; therefore we can never count on it and we dare not believe in it until it has happened. . . . Since we necessarily underestimate our creativity, it is desirable that we underestimate to a roughly similar extent the difficulties.

[Then we will undertake tasks] which we can, but otherwise would not dare tackle. . . . The Hiding Hand is essentially a mechanisn *which makes a risk averter take risks* and turns him into less of a risk averter in the process.

Of course, the entrepreneurs themselves will not see it this way. They will not imagine that they may have stumbled into their greatest achievements. As Hirschman puts it, in a linguistic *aperçu*: "We fall into error, but do not usually speak of falling into truth."

Hirschman has fallen into some of the most vital truths of human society, but he does not quite dare to extend them beyond the less-developed world or seek to explain their deeper meaning. Things are different, he seems to assume, in modern economies.

He implies (though he surely knows better) that in modern societies planning is successful: costs are correctly estimated and benefits clearly foreseen. Yet it is apparent that if he had directed his attentions to the advanced industrial world, he would have discovered the same pattern that he found in nineteenth-century America and in the Third World: growth is an effect not of detailed plans and predictable processes but of individual leadership, initiative, and creativity. Planning is always necessary, often useful, but rarely adequate. The essential unpredictability that Hirschman took to be a malady of underdevelopment is, in fact, the incalculable condition of all economic progress. Progress and creativity cannot be forced or prescribed except for short periods and at costs far beyond the reach of any Third World country or any competitive firm anywhere. There is no way to escape for long the necessity of openness and risk.

This truth is anathema to those who seek a risk-free scheme of development and growth, whether they be unlettered leftist generals assuming control of small nations or smooth-talking corporate leaders in the United States. The rule of risk applies alike to national planning and private business, to advanced technical industries like lasers and microprocessors, and even to the movies.

John Gregory Dunne's extraordinary book *The Studio* tells of the foibles of planning during a year of high expectations under new leadership at Twentieth-Century Fox. In preparation — and preoccupying the executives — were several "sure things," including *Doctor Doolittle* with Rex Harrison, *Star!* with Julie Andrews (coming off her *Sound of Music* bonanza), and *Hello, Dolly!* with Barbra Streisand. The "sure-thing" superhits, however, would nearly have bankrupted the company, if it had not been for an afterthought cheapie (several times nearly cancelled in the interests of economy) named *Planet of the Apes*. *Star Wars* was later to perform a similar miracle for the studio. This experience is not untypical of business success. As clothing executive Richard Salomon told *The Wall Street Journal*, "Everybody praises carefully tested methods and long-range planning. Yet the most successful moves are often on-the-spot responses to completely unexpected situations, taking a company to places it never before imagined."

In this respect, microeconomics converges with macroeconomics, the economics of the firm with the economics of the nation. Unpredictability dictates openness as a prime prerequisite of growth, and it requires flexibility as a key to successful planning. Closed systems of enterprise can sometimes succeed in manipulating markets or governments, in making incremental advances of productivity, or in initiating the innovations of others. But these systems rarely generate new enterprises or substantial growth.

Aaron Wildavsky in a celebrated study of national plans could not find a sure success anywhere. From France to the Philippines, plans are propounded, given lip service, and flouted. Countries such as Taiwan and the Ivory Coast, which leave room for uncontrolled private ventures, grow faster than their centralized neighbors. In the late 1970s, while many centrally managed and financed European economies were stagnating, Italy, with its chaotic government and haphazard system of taxation, accommodated a huge and thriving black market making textiles, shoes and even automotive parts in abandoned basements and attics — raising the national product by as much as one-third. With this *lavoro nero* as a leading sector of growth, Italy's economy outperformed those of Britain and Sweden with their unionized work forces, "social contracts," and armies of dutiful bureaucrats.

The center of Italy's underground prosperity, ironically enough, was the Communist province Emiglia Romana. As *Forbes* magazine observed: "Beneath a public veneer of collectivism, there is a bubbling free-enterprise sector, probably as productive and healthy as its counterparts in right wing havens like Hong Kong or Singapore. And . . . even Communist politicians acknowledge it as an engine of national economic recovery."

It takes more, however, than a system of openness and low taxes to launch economic growth. Through most of human history, taxes have been low and governments incompetent without evoking enterprise. Enterprise, in fact, seems most improbable where it is most needed: in a depressed or undeveloped economy, with low "demand" and little evidence of opportunity. How ventures emerge under these conditions is a key question of economics. In an attempt to answer it, David McCord Wright has speculated on the reasons why "a brewer, say, might build a new brewery even though the volume of total beer sales, or the price of beer, or both, were falling. There are three causes: the better beer, the cheaper beer, and . . . the 'bullheaded brewer'" who "may simply feel he is smarter than the market. . . ." His supplies can create demand in accordance with Say's Law. "It is undeniable that his courage and the stimulus of the construction he is carrying through may start the economy once more expanding."

The bullheaded brewer is essentially responsible for *the entrepreneurial accelerator* that Hirschman and Sawyer found in nineteenth-century American economic development. During this crucial period "collective overestimations" of returns "operated to accelerate the processes of growth and often, in varying measure, produced the result" that in retrospect made their initial overestimates valid. This phenomenon goes to the heart of economic development.

David McClelland sums up the point with reference to the building of railroads across the American continent:

When they were built they could hardly be justified in economic terms, as the subsequent ruin of many stockholders demonstrated. Furthermore, they would never have been economically justified if the country had not been "swarming" with thousands of small entrepreneurs who repeatedly overestimated their chances of success, but who collectively managed to settle and develop the West while many of them individually were failing.

. . . it is hard to explain in rational economic terms why men settled in the Middle West in the 1860s and 1870s. Trollope (1862), in his travels down the Mississippi River could never stop marvelling at why people who knew better would voluntarily choose to live under such primitive conditions in caves or sod huts. He found them laboring from dawn to dark just to keep alive and with no immediate prospect of improvement in their lot. Yet they were cheerful about the future and did not want to return to "civilization," even though they were under no compelling reasons to leave it in the first place. Their behavior is the more impressive by contrast with peoples in South America and Java who have refused to leave crowded urban centers for fertile, unsettled lands not far away.

In the United States today, a similar defiance of the odds impels economic creativity. The Internal Revenue Service estimates that some 4700 small manufacturers are spawned in this country each week, while 4500 others fail. More than two-thirds of all ventures collapse within five years, and the median small businessman earns less than a New York City garbage collector. Of the thousands of plausible inventions, only scores are tested by business, and only a handful of these are an economic success. By some estimates, 90 percent of trade hardcover books lose money for the publisher, and a still higher proportion represent a net loss for the author; an even greater number, comprising untold months or years of labor, are never published at all. But such waste and irrationality is the secret of economic growth. Because no one knows which venture will succeed, which number will win the lottery, a society ruled by risk and freedom rather than planning it, can call forth an endless stream of invention, enterprise, and art.

In order to have growth, openness must be joined by a certain "bullheadedness," some Keynesian "animal spirits," and an essential optimism and willingness to risk. In order to take the hill, someone must dare first to charge the enemy bunker. Heroism, willingness to plunge into the unknown, in the hope that others will follow, is indispensable to all great human achievement. Indeed, such human qualities have been evident during most periods of progress, under most governmental and social systems. But they are supremely the human qualities of capitalism.

The attempt of the welfare state to deny, suppress, and plan away the dangers of uncertainties of our lives — to domesticate the inevitable unknown — violates not only the spirit of capitalism but also the nature of man. Even the most primitive societies invent forms of gambling (dice in many places preceded the wheel). The government devoted to suppressing uncertainty finds itself forever having to channel or repress the human will to risk. The effect is often to drive it from positive and creative avenues into negative or destructive ones.

In this country the impulse to gamble and risk is often diverted from the economy, from serious life, into fantasy and frivolity — games and wagers — or deflected from productive activity into courtroom assaults against the productive. One of the best remaining ways to strike it rich — the best remaining scene for gambling, with the odds against the productive stacked ever higher by government — is the civil suit: malpractice, product liability, discrimination, antitrust, libel, pollution — whatever. The government has created a vast new sweepstakes open to the man willing to play for high stakes and to the law firms that join in the new champerty.

Among the most mischievous of these opportunities for profit is the product-liability suit. Under the worker's compensation law an employee can sue the original manufacturer of machinery, regardless of how old, how much altered, or how often resold it is. Small companies are particularly damaged, with annual insurance rates rising a hundredfold or more to cover this threat and driving many firms out of business. In a good many cases the victims of such suits and insurance rates are men of ingenuity and courage who dare to risk their own money to bring a new product or service to the public. *Caveat productor* is the new rule.

For citizens without the means or litigious bent to sue for a living, the state is widely setting up simpler lotteries of it own, opening in every neighborhood a storefront for the gambling impulse, advertising on billboards the government games. And everywhere it tells the insidious lie that its lottery affords a better deal ("where no one has a better chance that you"), a fairer opportunity than the real and continuing lotteries of lower-class life; that it is more promising to place your wagers on "The New York Bets" than in the U.S. economy. This effect is to trivialize and stultify the will to risk and work that is the only real hope of the poor.

Similarly with the rich, the government makes the dubious claim that it can use wealth more productively than a free capitalist; so its tax policy raises the always adverse odds of enterprise to the point where they may no longer invite the investor. While the poor man swings between welfare and the state lottery, the rich man alternates between personal gambling and municipal bonds The stochastic margin of progress — the frontier of the economy — can be closed off by obtuse taxation and bureaucracy.

Most redistributive activity is based on serious misunderstandings of the nature and sources of wealth and innovation. Seeing the high levels of evident chance involved in each particular business success, many officials and intellectuals conclude that most large capital gains are in a sense both unearned and unanticipated, and are not a factor in either personal motivation or efficient allocation of resources. Two of the nation's leading thinkers on the left, Lester C. Thurow and Christopher Jencks, ended their ambitious studies of inequality with the conclusion that crucial in most fortunes, great and small, is luck. The beneficiary, like a raffle winner, was at the right place at the right time, and in a rational system he should not be permitted to convert his luck into real economic power, any more than the myriad losers should suffer more than limited liability for their losses.

These are several problems with this approach. The first is that these economists use luck as a kind of residual category, containing any factors that they do not understand. Since there is much that they do not comprehend in the economy, they naturally exaggerate the importance of chance.

A more serious error, however, is a misunderstanding of the nature of chance itself. Critics of capitalism often imagine that they have discovered some great scandal of the system when they reveal its crucial reliance on luck: its distribution of benefits and attainment of riches by unpredictable and irrational processes—its resemblance at some level to a lottery. Chance, to many economists, is something bad, arbitrary, haphazard — a descent to aimlessness or chaos and a domain for the remedies of government. At best, by a strained Darwinian analogy, the chance happenings so frequent in successful enterprise are assigned the role of "mutations," randomly produced, that are "selected" when particularly fit for their environment. This theory explains the complex and dynamic structures of capitalism no better than it comprehends the prodigally various plenitude of the natural world.

Chance, however, is not the realm of the anarchic and haphazard but the area of freedom and the condition of creativity. It taps the underlying and transcendent order of the universe. We call it chance because it is beyond the ken of ordered rational processes, part of "the mysterious" realm that Einstein called "the cradle of true art and true science." When Hirschman writes that "creativity always comes as a surprise to us," he is acknowledging this essential quality of invention. Any attempt to reduce the world to the dimensions of our own understanding will exclude novelty and progress. The domain of chance is our access to futurity and to providence.

Capitalism succeeds because it accommodates chance and thus accords with the reality of the human situation in a fundamentally incomprehensible, but nonetheless providential, universe. Economists who attempt to banish chance through methods of rational management also banish the only sources of human triumph. It is no coincidence that the most deeply pessimistic of economic and social analysts are the advocates of radical and comprehensive systems of planning.

John Kenneth Galbraith in 1979 as much as gave up on the economic development of much of the Third World. According to Galbraith, the prime obstacle to progress is what he calls the "accommodation" of the poor to their plight. He does not object to this attitude. He finds in it a reasonable "refusal to struggle against the impossible. . . . They accept [their poverty]. Nor is such acceptance a sign of weakness of character. Rather it is a profoundly rational response." Galbraith is exactly right. As long as men are "profoundly rational," economic development will seem "impossible" and it will not occur. Instead, as Galbraith shows, there will persist "an equilibrium of poverty" and the best way to escape it is to emigrate to the industrial world, which fortunately has not yet fully accepted the rationality of resignation.

Nonetheless, there is a movement of economists and sociologists who urge "accommodation" by the West as well. Essentially neo-Malthusian or Doomsday Adventist, they recite, in tones of portentous revelation, the long familiar asymptotes of rational despair. Economist Robert Heilbroner predicts despotism and war as the almost certain outcomes. Marvin Harris, making a bid for anthropology as the truly dismal science, proposes a prospect of cannibalism and infanticide (a vista brightened, though, by the possible end of sexism).

In two books Barry Commoner has popularized a biological doom theory, *the closing circle* of ecological limits to growth, that requires the adoption of socialist planning in the United States to prevent the familiar catastrophes. All in all, *The Limits to Growth* may have been revised and amended by its authors in the wealthy and prestigious precincts of the Club of Rome, but it remains the crucial book of our time. While its graphs and computations have been discredited, its emotional symbolism and trajectory were uncannily on target, and it has reverberated throughout our culture and politics ever since its publication.

These attitudes, for all their appeal to secular America, are nothing less than fatuous. Economic and technological breakthroughs always seems impossible in the calculus of closed rationality. Anyone having the slightest familiarity with the history of either science or capitalism knows that leading analysts, generation after generation after generation, have always predicted the exhaustion of capitalist dynamism and the end of technological progress.

In the fifteenth century the longbow — with its unlimited supplies of ammunition, its rapid-firing capacity (twelve shots per minute), and its long range of some two hundred yards — was regarded as the ultimate weapon. Leading seventeenth-century intellectuals imagined that all the available inventions were already behind us. In the eighteenth century even Adam Smith himself envisaged the eventual decline of capitalism into a stationary state. Sismondi thought economic development was all over in 1815 and John Stuart Mill supposed that we had reached the end of the line in 1830. In 1843 the U.S. Commissioner of Patents thought that the onrush of inventions might "presage [a time] when human improvement must end." Alvin Hansen and scores of other economists predicted socialist stagnation as the likely human prospect after World War II. Even Thomas Edison believed that the major inventions had all been accomplished during his own lifetime.

Decade after decade experts have predicted exhaustion, first of wood fuel, then of coal, and now of oil and gas. Today, when there is a wider variety of new energy sources available or in view than ever before in our history, and when most of the world has yet to be explored for fossil fuels to one-tenth the degree the United States has been explored, there is a prevailing idea that we are running out of energy and must revert to a preindustrial reliance on wind and sun. At a time when radically important new technologies are being spawned on every hand, leading experts imagine that we are entering a technological climacteric, a period of diminishing scientific returns. Such views are suitable for analysis not in the universities (where they often prevail) but on the couch.

The most obvious source of such beliefs is the individual life cycle. Because human beings become exhausted and decline as they grow older, they are inclined to believe that societies do as well. It is a kind of pathetic fallacy: the ascription of individual human characteristics to large group phenomena. Many intellectuals, moreover, like to support that human evolution reached some climactic pinnacle with their own publications and that nothing very important will follow them. As they grow older, they lose track of new developments and find it easier to dismiss them than attempt to master their implications.

The chief problem, however, is a profound incomprehension of the human situation. Human life itself, from any rational and scientific perspective, is wildly unlikely — in fact, impossible. Modern civilization is hopelessly contingent and problematical, subject to destruction any day by possible climatic reversals, astrophysical mishaps, genetic plagues, nuclear explosions, geological convulsions, and atmospheric transformation — all conceivable catastrophes originating beyond the ken of plausible remedy or control.

People like to speak of the "delicate balance" of nature, as if the present natural order represented some static consummation rather than an ongoing struggle of survival. Natural history is a saga not of balance but of convulsive changes, wiping out whole species left and right, transforming continents, evulsing mountains, and flooding vast plains and valleys. There is no such thing as equilibrium, in ecology any more than in economics. Any static stat is doomed to disaster. Our supposed current crises of energy and protein pale before the perpetual crisis of human existence itself.

At any time in human history, a rational calculus of our possibilities would lead to a prediction of doom. But over the millennia, the race has flourished. It has thrived, however, chiefly on one condition, one cluster of conditions, combining faith and freedom with risk and work. It is chiefly when we give up on chance and providence, when we attempt to calculate and control our own destinies through ever greater regulation by a demiurgic state, that disaster occurs.

Marvin Harris's grim catalog of the rise and fall of previous societies dramatizes this reality. He describes a recurrently vicious cycle of population growth and resource depletion. The climax always begins with an intensification of productive activity, followed by a still faster rise in population and by industrial, agricultural, or hunting pursuits taken beyond the point of diminishing returns. The usual result is a dearth of protein and other sustenance and the emergence of ever more brutal social arrangements, marked by war and infanticide, and leading at last to cannibalism and other bestiality.

The worst of all the societies he describes were the *hydraulic dictatorships*, which arose in narrow river valleys or other enclosed regions and created huge bureaucracies and mass mobilizations to build and manage great waterworks and irrigation projects. Although Harris does not emphasize this point, the result is the commitment of the entire social order to rigid bureaucratic and administrative systems, which respond to the worsening crunch by raising taxes and increasing controls. Every new measure of desperation by the prevailing powers raises still higher the obstacles to innovation and progress and makes the final disaster still more ineluctable.

Amazingly, though, Harris ends his book by calling for expanded regulation and controls to meet the new crises of scarcity in America. He sees little possibility of solving the problems as free men. What he fails to comprehend is that the visibly possible breakthroughs, the clearly available resources, have always been measured and discounted. At any time in the history of the race, the extended future has usually appeared to be hopelessly grim, uninhabitable by free humans. All plans based on the calculable present, on the existing statistics, necessarily presume a declining field of choice, a diminishing of returns — entropy and decay.

To combat these exigencies, the planner will always see a need for regulation of ever more intimate and intrusive kinds, invading the family and the home. in the end, as reserves expire, the planner becomes a tyrant and a killer — the Moloch of the closing circle.

Like the anthropophagus dictatorships of the Aztec kingdom and the other monstrous hydraulic despotisms described by Harris, a state that responds by confiscation and coercion to the inevitable crises of closure, the inexorable pressures of population against the land, ends by consuming its own people. The rates of taxation climb and the levels of capital decline, until the only remaining wealth beyond the reach of the regime is the very protein of human flesh, and that too is finally taxed, bound, and gagged, and brought to the colossal temple of the state — a final sacrifice of carnal revenue to feed the declining elite. This is the destination of all dictatorship, unless it is saved by the unanticipated boon, the serendipitous cavalry of providence that awaits only the bugle of freedom and faith.

Leszek Kolakowski, the expatriate Polish philosopher, in another context has well depicted the essential human predicament. We are in convoy, lightly but adequately equipped to cross a stretch of desert if all goes well. But it doesn't. We misread our maps and go astray. Sandstorms erupt. The camels balk. Water runs out. But we have hope, a belief in providence, a "myth." Our faith calls forth a kind of

Fata Morgana which makes beautiful lands rise before the eyes of the members of the caravan and thus increases their efforts to the point where, in spite of all their sufferings, they reach the next tiny water hole. Had such tempting mirages not appeared, the exhausted caravan would inevitably have perished in the sandstorm, bereft of hope.

It is a powerful image and richly suggestive, but I do not believe that the point is exactly right. We do not need "myths" so much as we need religious beliefs, which, for all their dubious "irrationality," bear in their symbolic depths the greatest of pragmatic and historical truths. They tell us that free humans with faith in the future and a commitment to it will prevail.

RADICAL: YES

6. THE DEINDUSTRIALIZATION OF AMERICA

Barry Bluestone and Bennett Harrison

Underlying the high rates of unemployment, the sluggish growth in the domestic economy, and the failure to successfully compete in the international market is the deindustrialization of America. By *deindustrialization* is meant a widespread, systematic disinvestment in the nation's basic productive capacity. Controversial as it may be, the essential problem with the U.S. economy can be traced to the way capital — in the forms of financial resources and of real plant and equipment — has been diverted from productive investment in our basic national industries into unproductive speculation, mergers and acquisitions, and foreign investment. Left behind are shuttered factories, displaced workers, and a newly emerging group of ghost towns.

The traces of widespread disinvestment show up in an aging capital stock at home and in the diversion of investment resources to American corporate subsidiaries operating abroad. In 1979 the average age of the capital stock from sprawling factories to intricate machine tools, was 7.1 years. Hence, much of our productive equipment was put in place when oil prices were much lower. As a consequence, much of the capital stock is energy-inefficient and, for this reason, outmoded. In the steel industry, the capital situation is particularly serious. According to industry experts, the steel companies are modernizing their equipment at less than half the rate needed to keep plants up to date on a twenty-five-year cycle. Across all sectors in the economy, the average rate of new investment has not even kept pace with the growth in the labor force.

This does *not* mean that corporate managers are refusing to invest, but only that they are refusing to invest in the basic industries of the country. U.S. Steel has billions to spend, but instead of rebuilding steel capacity, it paid $6 billion to acquire Marathon Oil of Ohio. General Electric is expanding its capital stock, but not in the United States. During the 1970s, GE expanded its worldwide payroll by 5000, but it did so by adding 30,000 foreign jobs and reducing its U.S. employment by 25,000. RCA Corporation followed the same strategy, cutting its U.S. employment by 14,000 and increasing its foreign work force by 19,000. It is the same in the depressed automobile industry. Ford Motor Company reports that more than 40 percent of its capital budget will be spent outside the United States, while General

Motors has given up its plans to build a new multibillion-dollar plant in Kansas City, Missouri, and instead has shifted its capital spending to one of its facilities in Spain.

The movement of capital can take many forms that progress from the virtually invisible to the drastic and dramatic. The most subtle policy consists of the redirection of profits generated from a particular plant's operations without management tampering with the establishment itself. For example, the managers of a multibranch corporation may decide to reallocate profits earned from a particular plant's operations to new facilities or for new product development. Such "milking" of a profitable plant turns out to be especially common among conglomerates, whose managers are trained to treat certain of their acquired subsidiaries as "cash cows" (a term they themselves use). The older plant is not run down or dismantled in the short run. However, the loss of control over retained earnings increases the subsidiary's chances of encountering trouble in the future. A step beyond the milking operation is the conscious decision to reallocate capital by running down a plant simply by failing to replace worn out or obsolete machinery. In this case, management not only uses the profits from an existing operation, but its depreciation reserves as well, for investment elsewhere. Of course, this type of capital reallocation produces a self-fulfilling prophesy. A plant that is not quite productive enough to meet the profit targets set by management will very soon be unable to make any profit at all.

Another method for shifting capital involves physically relocating some of the equipment from one facility to another, or selling off some of the old establishment's capital stock to specialized jobbers. The plant remains in operation for the time being, but often at a much lower level of production. Indeed, the equipment may not even be moved or sold, but simply turned off when the managers decide to subcontract (or "outsource") to another firm part of the work that used to be done in the plant. The physical capital is still there, but from the point of view of production this is also a case of disinvestment.

Finally, management can move capital by completely shutting down a plant. It can sell as many of the old facility's assets as possible. In a few cases it may even load some of the machinery onto flatcars or moving vans and set up essentially the same operation elsewhere. . . .

Deindustrialization does not just happen. Conscious decisions have to be made by corporate managers to move a factory from one location to another, to buy up a going concern or to dispose of one, or to shut down a facility altogether. These things never happen automatically nor are they simply a passive response to mysterious market forces. The planning behind such decisions is usually intricate, often costly, and extensive.

Deindustrialization is the outcome of a worldwide crisis in the economic system. The very successes of the long postwar expansion generated conditions that ultimately turned the normal, and often healthy, disinvestment process into a torrent of capital flight and wholesale deindustrialization. During the boom years, U.S. economic expansion abroad generated enormous short-run profits, but in the course of doing this it helped to establish excess (unused) productive capacity in one basic industry after another. Through their multinational subsidiaries and the profitable sale of patents and licenses to foreign enterprises, the leading American firms even helped to generate their own future competition. In the 1970s this competition came back to haunt them in virtually every major industry: steel, automobiles, shipbuilding, and electronics, to name a few.

With no rational way to divide up the international market, U.S. firms found themselves subject to intense world competition and as a consequence, shrinking profits. One possible reaction to this situation would have been to try to meet the new competition in the old-fashioned way — an active search for new markets, increased research and development, and investments in more efficient technology. Some American firms took this route, but many more decided instead to abandon the competition altogether (as in electronics), to reduce their investments (as in steel), or to focus all their energies on reducing labor costs and circumventing public sector taxes and regulations. In a desperate attempt to restore, or preserve, the rates of profit to which they had become accustomed in the halcyon days of the 1950s and 1960s, American corporate managers in the 1970s went to extraordinary lengths to shift capital as rapidly as possible, from one activity, one region, and one nation to another. In the process, the industrial base of the American economy began to come apart at the seams.

To be sure, capital flight has always been a tactic that management wished to have at its disposal in order to "discipline" labor and to assure itself of a favorable business climate wherever it set up operations. But only in the last two decades has systematic disinvestment become, from management's perspective, a *necessary* strategy, and from a technological perspective, a *feasible* one.

It is crucial to view this development in the light of post–World War II economic history. It was not only international competition that was threatening corporate profits. The postwar series of labor victories that successfully constrained the flexibility of management by regulating the workplace and forcing the corporate sector to underwrite part of the costs of the "social safety net" also contributed to the profit squeeze.

From the middle of the 1930s to the 1970s, organized labor in the United States won major concessions on a broad set of issues that ultimately limited capital's flexibility in its use of labor. One indicator of this loss of flexibility and of the subversion of unquestioned managerial discretion can be found in the sheer size of the contract documents negotiated between unions and employers. The initial agreement between the United Automobile Workers (UAW) and General Motors (GM), signed in 1937, covered less than one-and-a-half pages and contained only one provision: union recognition. By 1979 the UAW-GM contract, with its extensive array of provisions covering each of the company's 140 production units, contained literally thousands of pages printed in proverbial small type. In exacting detail the contract specifies hundreds of items from wage scales and a cornucopia of fringe benefits to limits on subcontracting and the pacing of each machine and assembly line; it even goes so far as to establish some rules governing the introduction of new technology.

Each of these rules and regulations was forced into place by labor for the explicit purpose of increasing job security and limiting the discretionary power of management. With the important — indeed absolutely critical — exception of limiting the right of management to reduce the aggregate size of its labor force, these incursions by organized labor were highly successful. As long as management *had* to deal with labor where workers were well organized, it was constrained to operate within the set of rules that unions had long struggled to secure.

Moreover, using the power of the State, labor won important concessions from industry through the regulatory process. Minimum wages, fair labor standards, occupational health and safety provisions, equal employment opportunity, extended unemployment benefits, and improvements in workers' compensation constitute only a partial list of the gains made by labor during this period. Taken together, these victories limited management's ability to extract the last ounce of productivity from labor and thus the last ounce of profit.

During the heyday of American economic power, from 1945 to about 1971, industrialists were able to reap healthy profits while affording these concessions to organized labor. The so-called social contract between labor and management even proved advantageous to the corporate sector, for it assured some semblance of labor peace needed for continued economic expansion. Corporations did not complain as bitterly in the early 1960s when they were earning an average annual real rate of return of 15.5 percent on their investments. Their attitudes changed dramatically, however, when profits began to slip near the end of the decade. By the late 1960s, the profit rate for non-financial corporations had declined to 12.7 percent. It fell further as the result of increased international competition. By the early 1970s, the average rate had declined to 10.1 percent, and after 1975, it never rose above 10 percent again.

Management found that it could no longer afford the social contract and maintain its accustomed level of profit. Instead of accepting the new realities of the world marketplace, one firm after another began to contemplate fresh ways to circumvent union rules and to hold the line on wages. Of course, labor was not initially ready to concede its hard-won victories; therefore to accomplish its goal of reasserting its authority, management had to find some mechanism for disarming organized labor of its standard weapons: the grievance process, various job actions, and work stoppages. The solution was capital mobility. If labor was unwilling to moderate its demands, the prescription became ''move'' — or at least threaten to do so. For one enterprise, this entailed disinvestment. When entire industries adopted this strategy, the result was deindustrialization.

The capital mobility option had always been available to some extent. The early American canal systems and the coming of the steam locomotive allowed the transfer of production to new communities along the new transportation routes. What is different today is the distance and speed over which that transfer can take place. Satellite-linked telex communication and wide-bodied cargo jets provide a technical environment that has allowed production to become far more spatially ''footloose'' than ever before. The linking of communications systems to computers permits central management to coordinate worldwide operations at lightning speed, while jet aircraft permit the movement of physical commodities at near the velocity of sound — a far cry from the 3.2 mile per hour of barge traffic on the Erie Canal in the 1840s.

The capital mobility option provided by the new technology has shifted the fulcrum of bargaining power in favor of capital to an unprecedented degree. It gives employers the ability to effectively insist upon smaller wage improvements or, as has been seen in an increasing number of core industries, actual wage rollbacks. In essence, the capital mobility option provides industry with the power to make "take it or leave it" propositions stick. There are some signs in the auto, steel, and rubber industries that the strategy is actually beginning to work. But the cost to workers and communities in the form of plant closings and labor displacement has been enormous.

The capital mobility strategy is not merely aimed at organized labor. The newly enhanced ability to move capital between regions within the same country provides corporate management with the necessary economic and political clout to insist upon reductions in local taxation, and therefore cuts in community services and the social safety net. The competition between local governments to retain existing capital or to attract new private investment is leading to an extraordinary retrenchment in social programs as we have known them. The most noteworthy victories of the corporate sector in this regard are found in Proposition 13 in California and Proposition 2½ in Massachusetts. These substantial tax cuts were actively supported by the banking and business communities of each state, which suggested that failure of passage would seriously undermine the "business climate" in their regions. The interregional rivalry to attract capital, in light of the high degree of threatened or real capital mobility, has led the business press to write that the nation is in the midst of a new civil war — a new "war between the states." Without the heightened ability to move capital, this could not have happened.

The election of Ronald Reagan elevated the "civil war" to a new level. To reindustrialize America, the federal government is insisting on creating a "good business climate" in the United States through extreme cuts in corporate taxes, drastic reductions in the government's guarantee of the social safety net, and the virtual deregulation of the private sector. Washington has joined the corporate sector in declaring a class war on workers and their communities. . . .

Just after the Second World War, in one fell swoop the Chance-Vought Division of United Aircraft moved an entire industrial complex from Bridgeport, Connecticut, to Dallas, Texas. This particular relocation, which had financial assistance from the federal government, has been described as one of the most spectacular migrations in industrial history — fifteen hundred people, two thousand machines, and fifty million pounds of equipment were involved.

The relocation of Chance-Vought was an especially dramatic example of the "runaway shop." Even today, when companies literally pick up and move, the wholesale disruption of people's lives garners newspaper and TV headlines. Especially when the move is from the "Frostbelt" — the states of the old industrial

Northeast and upper Midwest — to the "Sunbelt" or overseas, it reinforces the popular impression that "capital flight" is a matter of manufacturing firms literally relocating their plants and equipment into areas where wages are lower, unions are weaker, and local government provides the good business climate that corporate managers dream about. And there is no question that such dramatic relocations *do* occur; during the decade of the 1970s, we estimate that between 450,000 and 650,000 jobs in the private sector, in both manufacturing and non-manufacturing, were wiped out somewhere in the United States by the movement of both large and small runaway shops. But it turns out that such physical relocations are only the tip of a huge iceberg. When the employment lost as a direct result of plant, store, and office *shutdowns* during the 1970s is added to the job loss associated with runaway shops, it appears that more than 32 million jobs were destroyed. Together, runaways, shutdowns, and permanent physical cutbacks short of complete closure may have cost the country as many as 38 million jobs.

The process of capital disinvestment in older plants, industries, or regions, and reinvestment in other activities or places, can take many forms. For example, when General Electric builds a new steam iron factory in Singapore and subsequently sells an older one outside of Los Angeles, thus eliminating nearly a thousand jobs in the process, that is capital shift. Or when Pratt & Whitney Aircraft or the Ford Motor Company transfers subcontracts for machine-tooled parts from local suppliers to shops located in other countries, causing widespread layoffs in Connecticut and outright plant shutdowns in Michigan, that, too, is capital flight. Private disinvestment in a particular locale occurs when a conglomerate buys a business that was operating profitably in one place and moves it to another, as Norton Simon has done with the Max Factor cosmetics firm, shifting production from California to Tennessee. The loss in social productivity is even greater — going beyond the mere shifting of existing facilities around the map — when a conglomerate acquires a profitable company, milks it of its cash, runs it into the ground, and then closes it down altogether. By all accounts this is what happened to the Youngstown Sheet and Tube Company, a steel mill in Ohio's Mahoning Valley, after it was acquired by the Lykes Corporation (now itself part of the giant Ling-Temco-Vought (LTV) conglomerate).

Remarkable as it may seem, in a country whose national census bureau regularly pokes into the minutest details of people's private lives, measuring how many children they have or why their mothers did not to go work last week, the government makes only the most minimal demands on private companies to report their investment transactions. Data on the investment decisions by managers in the service sector are almost completely nonexistent, even though hospitals, supermarkets, and television stations obviously buy and sell buildings and machinery, too. Because companies are virtually allowed to select depreciation schedules from a menu offered by the Internal Revenue Service to fit their cash flow requirements, official published statistics on the extent to which an industry's capital stock is being run down by its managers have become artifacts of the political process, almost useless for measuring actual disinvestment.

Few people have the necessary time, access, or money to pierce the veil of secrecy that firms have thrown up around their investment transactions. With the federal government unwilling to require companies to disclose the details of their investment activities, direct measurement of all of the many different forms of capital movement is virtually impossible. What we *can* measure now — thanks not to any government program, but to the availability of information generated by the private sector itself, for its own internal use — are plant (as well as office, store, shop, and warehouse) relocations and shutdowns.

Over the decade of the 1970s, in twelve states, plant closings shut down more jobs than were added through new start-ups. Elsewhere, jobs created by the opening of new business establishments barely offset the losses connected with the closings of older ones (except in those states containing the mining and energy industries, where the net growth was considerable). But even where more new plants were opened than shut down, millions of workers, their families, and their communities experienced severe economic and emotional dislocation. Typically, the businesses that started up were located in different places and were in different industries (usually services rather than manufacturing); they required different skills, paid lower wages, provided less job security, or simply would not hire the people who had been laid off. . . .

While the impact of disinvestment on individual workers and their families is probably the correct place to begin any inquiry into the social costs of unregulated deindustrialization, it cannot be the end of such an inquiry. For when mills or department stores or supermarket chains shut down, many other things can happen to a community. These can be extraordinarily costly as they ripple through the economy.

The primary effects are, of course, visited on those closest to the production unit that ceases operations. The unit's own employees lose salaries and wages, pensions, and other fringe benefits; supplier firms lose contracts; and the various levels of government lose corporate income and commercial property tax revenue. These in turn result in a series of secondary shocks including decreased retail purchases in the community, a reduction in earnings at supplier plants, and increased unemployment in other sectors. Finally, these events produce tertiary effects in the form of increased demand for public assistance and social services, reduced personal tax receipts, and eventually layoffs in other industries, including the public sector. What begins as a behind-closed-doors company decision to shut down a particular production facility ends up affecting literally everyone in town, including the butcher, the baker, and the candlestick maker. By the time all of these "ripple effects" spread throughout the economy, workers and families far removed from the original plant closing can be affected, often with dramatic consequences.

Some of these ripple (or multiplier) effects are felt immediately, while others take time to work through the economy. Some will dissipate quickly (especially if the local economy is expanding), while others may become a permanent part of the local economic environment. The extent of the impact of any particular closing will depend also on whether the plant or store was a major employer in the area, or an important purchaser of goods and services produced by other area businesses. All of these indirect impacts will be multiplied if a number of closings or cutbacks occur in the area simultaneously.

Systematic research that statistically accounts for all of these crucial ecological factors is, like the data on plant closings themselves, almost totally nonexistent. Nevertheless, it is possible to assemble bits and pieces of evidence that provide at least some sense of what can be involved at the wider community level when a major employer shuts down or leaves town. Here the experiences of just a few places — Newark, New Jersey; Youngstown, Ohio; Detroit, Michigan; Johnstown, Pennsylvania; Cortland County, New York; and Anaconda, Montana — must suffice. This is not because there are only a few isolated instances of economic disaster associated with capital mobility, but because social scientists have not had the foresight or the resources to produce more than a handful of studies. In fact, literally hundreds of communities have gone through the trials faced by the towns and cities considered here.

J. Wiss & Son, a large cutlery manufacturer, had been in business in Newark, New Jersey, since 1848. When it was acquired by a Texas conglomerate and relocated to North Carolina in 1978, the state AFL-CIO decided to undertake a community-impact assessment, using methods and data suggested by the U.S. Chamber of Commerce. The direct loss of 760 manufacturing jobs, according to this study, cost the city an additional 468 jobs "in stores, banks, bus service, luncheonettes, taverns, gas stations, and other local businesses." More than $14 million in purchasing power was removed from the local economy, half of which had resided in local bank deposits used for loans to finance mortgages, home improvements, purchases of automobiles, televisions, refrigerators, and other major appliances.

Even charities suffered. No longer available were the annual contributions of $22,000 by the Wiss employees or the $11,000 corporate gift. Among the losers were the community's retarded children who were aided by these funds, the Associated Catholic Charities, the Jewish Community Federation, the Red Cross, the Salvation Army, the Presbyterian Boys Club and Hospital, and the Cerebral Palsy Foundation — all of which were associated with the Essex and West Hudson County United Way. . . .

Thus far, the quantifiable social impacts of business closings have been stressed. But other, and in some respects more profound, impacts are not so easily expressed in numbers — let alone in numbers of dollars.

In terms of a variety of standard indicators, the Brockway closing in upstate New York had a relatively minor impact on the Cortland County community. Nevertheless,

The situation in Cortland appears to have had very adverse effects on the social cohesiveness of the community. A repeated assertion by members of the community was that: "the psychological effects outweighed the real effects" of the shutdown. Soon after the Brockway termination, a bumper sticker began to circulate that reflected this anomie — "The last person to leave Cortland please shut out the lights." The shutdown was coincident with the departure of the Montgomery Ward store from downtown Cortland, compounding the "depression psychology" prevalent in the community. The gas shortage, retrenchment in the [State University] system affecting Cortland State in 1977, the short workweek of many municipal workers — all resulted in a poor job market for Cortland and impeded efforts to help the Brockway dischargees as a group with special needs.

The state of "anomie" described for Cortland County — evident in community disorientation, anxiety, and isolation — is found almost universally in case studies of plant closings. Those who observed Hopedale, Youngstown, Anaconda, Detroit, Johnstown, Hartford County, and other communities hit by deindustrialization all come to the conclusion that the social "psyche" is damaged by the sudden loss of economic security. The damage, in many cases, has far-ranging consequences beyond the apparent emotional response of anger, frustration, or victimization. Victims lose faith in the "system," leading to a kind of dependency that precludes redevelopment of their communities. Although some struggle heroically to salvage what is left after a major shutdown, there is often the widespread attitude embodied in the statement of one victim: "We put thirty years into building this mill and this community, and it has all come to naught. I can't see that I've the energy to start all over again."

There is a strange silver lining behind all of this — for management. Compelling evidence exists that the layoffs created by plant closings can actually improve the business climate. The swelling of the ranks of the unemployed creates a reserve of malleable workers and even potential strikebreakers. The memory of such drastic dislocation can have what labor relations experts call a "chilling effect" on future labor-management negotiations. Surviving firms in the area gain the advantage of being able to hire the most highly skilled of the dischargees without having to bid them away from their former jobs. This obviously creates the conditions for the previously cited finding that workers experiencing sudden unemployment almost always suffer a significant drop in earnings, at least on their next job.

The strength of the labor relations impact of the three New York state plant closings studied by Aronson and McKersie seems to have especially impressed these researchers. With respect to the GAF closing in Binghamton, they note that "local union leadership felt that the uncertainty regarding GAF's future, and a pool of 1100 potential strikebreakers in the displacees, severely constrained its ability to strike successfully." In the wake of the Cortland shutdown, the researchers reported that they repeatedly encountered an "anti-union animus" related to the widespread belief in the community that it was "the local union's 'exhorbitant' demands and 'intransigent' position in the negotiations" before the shutdown that caused the closing.

Further, it was rumored that the pall cast over other negotiations by this anti-union sentiment and the fear of job loss had induced other unions bargaining with local firms to settle negotiations quickly.

Finally, perhaps the most "socially disconcerting" finding of all was the

"blacklisting" of Brockway workers. . . . Employers were hesitant to hire persons accustomed to high wages and union benefits, while the community at large felt that the militant stance and strike by the union had caused the closing. In short "they got what they deserved."

Whether it is "what they deserve," when deindustrialization occurs, the overwhelming weight of the evidence suggests that workers receive a heavy blow, only a part of which can be systematically quantified. A large majority of those directly affected endure at least temporary income loss, while a significant minority suffer long-term damage to their standards of living and to their physical and emotional well-being. Through the employment and income multiplier effects, a slew of innocent bystanders are victimized as well. . . .

Few people, and certainly not those who have spent any time in cities like Youngstown and Detroit, or in towns like Anaconda, Montana, would deny that deindustrialization is an agonizing experience for the families and communities that must contend with it. Yet the belief lingers that disinvestment is somehow a necessary precondition for the constant renewal and reinvigoration of the economy. It is part of the grand scheme of creative destruction — a reminder that omelettes can be made only by cracking eggs.

The omelettes, in this case, are presumably cities like Houston, the southern metropolis that *U.S. News & World Report* claims is "bursting out all over." Indeed the economic juices of the nation seem to be flowing swiftly to areas like Houston, and millions of transient families are following the flow. Youngstown's loss seems to be Houston's gain, so that on average the nation prospers.

But does it? A closer look at America's new boomtowns suggests that not all is well there either. The movement of capital imposes enormous social costs on the "winners" just as it does on the "losers." Like the boomtowns of the nineteenth-century Wild West, much of the glitter is true gold, but not everyone in town is overjoyed with the social conditions that accompany its discovery.

No one can deny the fact that explosive economic growth in the Sunbelt has brought "the good life" to many of the region's residents and to those who have migrated to the area. Yet this is only one side of the Sunbelt story. To leave off here would be to totally ignore the other side of the "boomtown syndrome" — the often destructive consequences of unplanned rapid development.

With a deliberate policy of enacting no zoning laws and doing practically no planning, Houston and other boomtown cities have been virtually overrun by the influx of capital. Growth has occurred so rapidly and haphazardly that boomtown metropolises now paradoxically exhibit many of the same urban woes that plague northern central cities. To most city planners, "Houston's sprawling growth represents how not to do it. In Houston, developers can build what they want, when they want, where they want. While such laissez faire certainly engenders boom-town vitality, it also creates boom-town problems."

Among these are highway congestion, air pollution, water shortages, overcrowded schools, and a housing crisis marked by some real estate prices that have tripled in a matter of a few years. Twenty-five percent of the city's streets remained unlighted, 400 miles were unpaved, and 29 percent of the poor lived in substandard housing — even as recently as 1978. Every day nearly 200 newly registered cars join the armada that clog Houston's freeways. As a result, a commute that took thirty minutes five years ago takes an hour today. And there is no alternative way to get to work. What passes for the bus system, according to *Newsweek*, is "a joke"; the more charitable *Wall Street Journal* calls it merely "decrepit." Only eighty-two buses — four-fifths of them paid for by the federal government — serve Houston's 400,000 residents. This situation is typical of many Sunbelt cities built during the age of the internal-combustion engine. In neighboring Albuquerque, New Mexico, 95 percent of all trips in and around the metropolitan area are done by car.

Other city services suffer as well. Annexation of suburban communities, combined with successful attempts at limiting property-tax levies to lure yet more industry, leave many a boomtown with inadequate revenues for even the most basic social services. This is certainly true in Houston where there is only one policeman for every 600 people and the average police response time to an emergency call is twenty-six minutes. (This amounts to one-third of the police protection of Philadelphia and less than half of that found in other big cities.) The frighteningly slow emergency response time in Houston is almost surely due to the fact that a total of only seven police stations service the city's 556 square miles!

Yet perhaps the worst legacy of uncontrollable boomtown expansion is not in poor social services but in the violence done to a community's social fabric. As a consequence of the hyper-investment boom, the disparity between rich and poor is becoming increasingly evident throughout the Sunbelt, creating a dualism reminiscent of the pre–Civil War South. In 1978 the richest 5 percent of the Sunbelt population enjoyed a far larger share (16.4 percent) of income than the top 5 percent in any other region, and the bottom 20 percent have less (only 4.8 percent) than anywhere else. The wealthiest one-fifth of the southern population has nearly nine times the aggregate income of the poorest fifth. Outside the South, that differential is 7.4 to 1.

Reflecting on these data, Georgia State Senator Julian Bond fears "the creation of a permanent underclass in the new South." *Fortune* magazine, a champion of Sunbelt development, admits that the black population (16 percent of the Sunbelt) has "scarcely shared in the economic upsurge." Again the statistics tell a gloomy story. In spite of boom conditions all around them, over *one-third* (35.1 percent) of all blacks in the South — more than 4.8 million — were still below the official poverty line in 1980. More than a quarter (27.3 percent) of what the Census Bureau calls the "Spanish-origin" population shared the same fate. In Houston the poverty has been described in particularly graphic terms:

Left behind in Houston's headlong flight toward growth and economic success are an estimated 400,000 people who live in a 73-square-mile slum that, says a college professor, has an infant mortality rate "that would have embarrassed the Belgian Congo."

As a partial consequence of extreme income inequality, acutely visible in the juxtaposition of new industrial wealth and old rural squalor, the new boomtowns are experiencing a crime wave. In 1979, reports the FBI, Houston distinguished itself with one of the highest murder rates in the country: 40.4 killings per 100,000 residents, two-thirds higher than New York City's homicide record. It is at least partly for this reason that the Commission on the Future of the South — made up of bankers, a judge, college presidents, and regional politicians — concluded that the South is a "time bomb" ready to go off. The unmet need for services for new residents is so staggering that the whole urban system may be on the brink of an explosion. The Fantus Company, which helps businesses select new plant locations, has even gone so far as to lower its official assessment of Houston's business climate, precisely because of poor public services. The city's own residents agree. In a recent University of Houston survey, only 26 percent of those who live in the city now think the impact of rapid growth has been "good."

Houston's problems are not unique. In many ways, they can be found in all of the boomtowns that have become the victims of too much unplanned development too fast. Atlanta has even sorrier stories to tell. And so do many of the cities in Florida. Every six minutes, the equivalent of a family of four moves to the Sunshine State seeking jobs or a retirement home. The new residents require housing, roads, schools, sewers, and water. Given the extremely fragile ecology of Florida, fresh water is a real problem — as it is in the booming Southwest. The Florida aquifer, the water table underlying the state, is down to its lowest level in recorded history. Fresh-water wells are being destroyed by salt-water seepage and some lakes are down by as much as 12 feet. Air pollution is killing Dade County's palm trees, while the state's rivers are dying of chemicals, sewer waste, and algae. The water and sewage system is simply overloaded and many experts fear a real environmental calamity. A leading Florida newspaper editor summed up his assessment of the situation to a group of state planners saying, "[Florida] is going to die of thirst or choke to death on a glut of people, exhaust fumes, concrete, and sewage unless the public wakes up."

Silicon Valley, California, the bustling home of the computer "chip" in Santa Clara County, suffers from the same boomtown syndrome. At the end of World War II, Santa Clara County was known for its fruit orchards and Stanford University. Today, it is blanketed with 500 electronics firms that make components for everything from the cruise missile to Space Invader computer games. Between 1960 and 1975, employment in the valley grew by 156 percent — three times the national rate and twice that of California. High-tech workers flocked into the area the way that retirees headed for Florida. And with the influx came the same problems.

By 1980 there were over 670,000 jobs, but only 480,000 housing units in the county. As a result the *average* price for a house soared to well over $100,000. Cheaper houses were bid up in price so rapidly that low-income families were displaced in the process. With no viable mass transit, the freeways became jammed and the average commuting time reached three hours or more for workers living in the southern parts of the county. Federal air-quality standards are now violated at least 10 percent of the time. With land prices out of control and the air spoiled, the fruit orchards have entirely disappeared.

This drama of industrialization that has gone haywire seems quite ubiquitous across the Sunbelt. University of California regional economist Ann Markusen estimates that between 5 and 15 million Americans are now involved in rapid-growth boomtowns in the Southwest and Mountain states alone. In many of the thousands of smaller communities, particularly where new capital-intensive energy investment is leading to exaggerated boom-bust cycles, long-time residents are finding themselves evicted from their homes, and the competition for land is resulting in the direct displacement of agricultural and tourist related jobs. The newly introduced production techniques and skill requirements often mean that the higher-wage jobs created in the capital-intensive sector are not available to those who lose their jobs in more traditional lines of work. . . .

American corporate leaders realized almost immediately after World War II that their new national and international opportunities for profit could more easily be pursued if their domestic relations with labor could be stabilized. The trade union movement had been growing since the late 1930s. Labor militancy ebbed somewhat during the war but revived explosively immediately afterwards. In 1946 more Americans went out on strike than in any other year in the nation's history.. If labor peace could be secured — by either breaking the unions or coming to an accommodation with them on matters of wages and fringe benefits — it could give corporations the breathing space needed to undertake the major investments and work reorganizations necessary for launching their global reach. If they were successful, the wealth accumulated in the process could even be shared with the American working class, at least to the extent necessary to nullify the further organizing capabilities of the unions.

In this way, postwar economic growth both required industrial peace and, at the same time, promised to generate the material basis for sustaining it by raising workers' standard of living. Moreover, the new economic doctrines of Keynesianism taught that such a burst of new consumption by working families would itself contribute to the process of economic expansion. This wealth in turn made it possible for government to legitimate the new order (based on corporate expansion and international Cold War military policy) by greatly expanding the "social wage": that amalgam of benefits, worker protections, and legal rights that acts to generally increase the social security of the working class.

Achieving labor peace through sharing a greater part of the benefits of economic growth was a new strategy for employers, and one that they only grudgingly accepted. The history of American class relations, between the end of the Civil War and the end of World War II, is filled with confrontation in the workplace between organized labor unions and associations, and increasingly defensive managers who at times resorted to the active police power of local — and even, on occasion, the federal — government to quell labor unrest. It is also a history of labor participation in grass-roots politics, both within the Democratic party and to some extent in third party movements. This direct political activity produced a number of explicitly pro-labor and socialist electoral victories in state and local jurisdictions across the country.

Out of these local electoral victories and influence over national party platforms came a series of public programs to underwrite the social security of workers, whether or not they belonged to unions. The objective was to reduce workers' absolute, immediate dependence on their employers. Nearly all of the legislation that makes up the social wage (widely referred to in this country as the "social safety net") was first written and implemented at the state and municipal level, especially in the populist Midwest and in patrician-paternalistic Massachusetts, and only subsequently rationalized by the national government under Presidents Wilson and Franklin Roosevelt.

For example, the first workmen's compensation law to pay workers for job-related injuries and disability was passed in 1909 in the state of Montana. The principle of unemployment insurance was pioneered in Massachusetts in 1916, although the first bill to actually pass a state legislature was not drafted until the early 1930s in Wisconsin, and a national program was not instituted until 1935 as a provision of the Social Security Act. The first state welfare boards preceded both workmen's compensation and unemployment insurance. Massachusetts appointed the first state board to oversee local relief charities in 1853, but it was not until 1917 that a modern department of public welfare was created in the state of Illinois — followed by Massachusetts in 1919. By 1926 five states had aid programs for widowed mothers and another six had general programs of support for mothers with children, nine years before the federal government created a national minimum in what later became the program of Aid to Families with Dependent Children (AFDC).

In the 1930s a prairie fire of social legislation spread throughout the nation. The utter desperation of the Great Depression, combined with continued labor victories in the workplace and the election booth, instilled not altogether unrealistic fears of an imminent popular uprising in the United States. Within this climate, the national government produced a wave of national laws designed to legitimate, but also to circumscribe, union activity. The Norris-LaGuardia Act of 1932 put a stop to the use of court-ordered injunctions forbidding workers to strike or picket. The Wagner Act of 1935 — often called "Labor's Magna Carta" — created the National Labor Relations Board and gave workers in the private sector the right to organize unions and to collectively bargain with management over wages and work rules. To protect this right, the act prohibited companies from committing a variety of "unfair labor practices," including the blacklisting of prospective employees who were union members or organizers. Finally the Fair Labor Standards Act of 1938 abolished child labor, established the first minimum wages, and institutionalized the eight-hour day.

Under the umbrella of these hard-won legal provisions, labor union activity in the United States blossomed. The movement was bolstered by the tight labor markets created by World War II and by the national priority assigned to the defense industries to push out military production with practically no regard to cost. So greatly was organized labor's power reinforced by these market conditions that by 1946 it could stage strikes over postwar wage and fringe-benefit demands that involved one out of every ten American workers. These actions took place in all parts of the country, in a wide variety of industries, and were often of long duration. The United Automobile Workers struck GM for 113 days. For a major employer like General Electric, the 1946 national strike by the United Electrical Workers was the largest and longest that corporation had ever faced.

An extreme reaction by business was inevitable. The Cold War with the Soviet Union had begun, and fears of Russian expansion abroad and subversion at home were easily fanned under the pretense of fighting communism. The militant wings of the largest industrial unions were purged, under the pressure of a nationwide anticommunist movement whose most visible spokespersons were Senator Joseph McCarthy and then Congressman Richard Nixon. Beginning in the key defense plants, strikes were soon broken throughout the country. Loyalty oaths were introduced to screen out supposed radicals. In short, management was willing to share the proceeds from economic growth to some extent, but it was absolutely unwilling to concede any control over the process of production to what it viewed as "radical elements."

In this context, the almost continuous attempt since 1937 by the National Association of Manufacturers and the Chamber of Commerce to amend the Wagner Act was finally successful. In 1947, over President Truman's veto, Congress compromised the Wagner Act's guarantee of the right to organize, to strike, and to secure a union shop by passing the Taft-Hartley Act. Section 8(b) established a number of unfair labor practices for which *unions* could be held legally accountable, including sympathy strikes and "secondary boycotts." Section 301 made labor contracts legally enforceable, which gave employers the opportunity to sue any union that called a strike in violation of a no-strike clause in the labor-management agreement.

Most important of all, section 14(b) of the new law allowed individual states to override federal statutes and to enact so-called "right-to-work" laws, which outlawed compulsory union membership whether or not a majority of the workers in a unit voted for it. In the years to come, section 14(b) would seriously set back union organizing in the South (whose congressional delegation had worked the hardest for it) and would lead to the decertification of many unions that had previously won representation elections. By making dues-paying voluntary, 14(b) undermined the financial strength of the unions. By 1980 twenty states had passed these "right-to-work" laws . . . The right-to-work states are overwhelmingly concentrated in the South Atlantic, the East South Central, the West South Central, and the Mountain regions.

These political and ideological initiatives by business helped to weaken labor's resistance to *all* forms of postwar corporate reorganization. They made it easier for management to change work rules in the older factories of the Frostbelt and to promote rationalization plans that closed down older productive capacity in order to free corporate resources for southern and global expansion. With labor's leadership internally divided, an overriding Cold War climate, and media campaigns describing the new multinational corporations as the world's greatest "engine of progress," the trade union movement lost a good deal of its momentum. As Solomon Barkin wrote about this period:

The pressures of intensified competition and rising unemployment are limiting union power, and public disapproval of strikes is making trade unions more amenable to the conciliatory process provided by public intervention, thereby diminishing their own bargaining leverage.

Legislators and judiciary have become increasingly responsive to pressures from business interest desirous of undermining union power and its internal strength. They have yielded to demands for laws and interpretations that restrain trade unions. The pendulum has already swung so far as to halt the growth of the labor movement and actually constrict it.

Indeed, after 1954 the proportion of workers belonging to unions began to fall in every region of the country, from an average of 35 percent in that year to only about 24 percent in 1978.

With the difficulties of organizing new workers, particularly in the South, the labor movement shifted its emphasis to improving the wages and working conditions of its existing membership. This was a much easier task to accomplish, especially in those industries such as automobiles, steel, aerospace, and rubber that were benefiting from the postwar economic expansion. From capital's point of view, this was an attractive development. Thus, between *organized* labor and big business, a "new social contract" began to emerge, admittedly with a good deal of strife.

When the United States emerged victorious from the war, with a much greater degree of economic concentration than had been the case prior to the Great Depression, the large corporations were in a position to offer a new type of deal to the unions. *If* the unions would enforce labor discipline, supply labor stability, accept longer contracts, purge the radicals, set up grievance procedures which removed the handling of grievances from the rank and file as much as possible, stay within the two-party system, leave price and other social decisions alone, etc., *then* the employers would recognize the unions, provide dues check-off, increase wages [in some unionized industries] substantially, not resist too strenuously certain types of legislation favorable to labor, grant seniority rights, etc.

What the corporations won with this cease-fire was the avoidance of unacceptable levels of economic disruption at home during a period when American capital had an unprecedented opportunity to expand abroad.

Jack Metzgar calls the result — an amalgam of tacit understandings and formal rules embodied both in the Wagner and Taft-Hartley acts and in various court rulings — the system of "negotiated class struggle." What the corporations were really offering to labor was sustained economic growth and, with it, the promise of both steadily rising real wages and an increase in the social autonomy of the working class.

The freedom to live in its own way within a steadily expanding range of choices was the principal benefit for the working class of the social contract between capital and labor. It seemed a small price to pay for these increases in social autonomy to allow "the company" to make the larger decisions. . . . Whether and where a company does business, the overall direction of an industry and the conditions of the economy are some of those larger decisions. In particular, "shutdowns and cutbacks are not negotiated. They are announced." . . .

Running away from unions was one way for capital to escape the fetter on profit making which the postwar social contract had become, in the context of the heightened global competition and economic crisis of the 1970s. Another response was to fight the unions head-on over wages, work rules, and — with the help of the corporate consultants — the right of a union to represent any particular company's workers at all.

But precisely because so few American workers *belong* to unions, these managerial responses to the crisis were not sufficient to make really significant, long-term dents in labor costs. For that to happen, workers would have to have been made so insecure and desperate for work that they would be forced to become more "flexible," that is, more willing to accept management's new terms with respect to wages, working conditions, and discipline as industry underwent the process of restructuring technologies, plant locations, and job tasks. The only way for capital to achieve this degree of flexibility — that is, to produce the necessary amount of insecurity — was to attack the social wage itself. This is the historical context within which to understand the significance of that extraordinary 1974 *Business Week* editorial . . . , calling for the dismantling of the standard of living to which American workers had become accustomed.

The assault on the social wage began at the state and local level, giving rise to what *Business Week*'s editors have called "the second war between the states." In choosing where to locate their new plants, or where to move existing operations if the present site is somehow undesirable, managers often talk about the local "business climate." What do they mean?

Sometimes, this fuzzy but much used term is nothing more than a euphemism for the presence or absence of unions, or of a local tradition of labor militancy. But corporate managers are usually thinking about more than just unions when this mystifying but nevertheless ubiquitous concern for a "good business climate" is expressed in local newspapers, on television, or in hearings before legislative committees. They are referring to the extent to which the policies of state and local government promote or retard capital's ability to locate where they prefer, especially with consideration of local taxes; to produce as they wish (irrespective of any external costs that production might impose on the area, such as environmental pollution, or on their workers, as with on-the-job health and safety hazards); and to maintain control over the labor process on the shop (or office) floor.

It appears that companies also have in mind the whole panoply of government policies that provide social insurance, welfare and food stamps, and minimum wages. These shelters from the insecurity that comes with being totally dependent on the demands of capital represent the spoils of past political victories by workers and their unions. The social wage is costly to business, and increasingly they want out. *That* is what the corporate demand for a good business climate is mainly about.

In the United States, from the years immediately following World War II, the shifting of capital from the inner cities to the suburbs and the rural peripheries of the country, and from the North to the South and West has been accompanied by often surprisingly up-front demands by corporate managers — or by their advocates in the many private and public local economic development agencies across the country — for a good business climate as a condition for moving in, or staying put. Elected state and local government officials have at best felt helpless before these demands. But it is probably also fair to say that these officials have tended to see state and local tax breaks and other "incentives" to business as plausible development policies — "if we lower their costs of doing business, why *wouldn't* companies invest here?"

Whatever the rationale, the result has been a proliferation of tax breaks and other business subsidies, together with the weakening of pro-labor, pro-consumer regulations on industry. In a veritable orgy of "incentive" granting, state and local governments have been falling over each other to outcompete or, with the ubiquitous availability of such incentives, to just stay on a par with their rival jurisdictions.

In one recent study by the Conference of State Manufacturers' Associations, the "goodness" of a state's "business climate" was defined in terms of low taxes, low union membership, low workmen's compensation insurance rates, low unemployment benefits per worker, low energy costs, and few days lost because of work stoppages — in that order. Mississippi ranked first in the nation on almost every criterion. Texas, which also placed high on the list, has no corporate or individual income tax, no payroll tax, property taxes below the national average, and the lowest unemployment insurance tax rates in the country. In such a climate, it is not at all remarkable for large companies such as J. P. Stevens to demand — and get — what amounts to a perpetual tax holiday (along with lax enforcement of brown-lung regulations) from the typically rural southern jurisdictions in which it has built its textile mills, while over the years gradually shutting down its operations in the North.

Bold demands by private corporations on state governments are of course hardly confined to the Sunbelt. From the earliest days of the *Pax Americana*, companies have been threatening to leave if the local social wage were not relaxed. . . .

The interstate competition in concessions to business has been the subject of a good deal of recent research. But what seems to have been overlooked is that, so intense has the rivalry been, and so successful the corporate blackmailing, by the mid-1970s the interstate differential on business taxes had all but disappeared!

. . . By 1975 the actual differences between the Frostbelt and Sunbelt states amounted to no more than a single percentage point. For instance, corporate income taxes plus property taxes on business added up to about 1.98 percent of total business sales in depressed Rhode Island. In booming Texas, the rate was 1.31 percent — hardly a large enough difference to coax a firm to pack up its capital and set off for the Southwest. Even so-called Taxachusetts imposed a tax burden on its business community that in 1975 (before the advent of more "pro-business" gubernatorial administrations) was no more than 1.7 percentage points higher than in South

Carolina, a state that has traditionally attracted Yankee capital by its claims of, among other things, pro-business-structured taxation.

Despite all the newsprint about Taxachusetts, local business taxes are *not* the chief targets of groups like the Chamber of Commerce and the National Association of Manufacturers. Rather, the regulations that industry complains about most loudly and most often are those that intervene in the workplace relationship between labor and management — laws having to do with minimum wages, affirmative action, and health and safety — and state laws that provide for some form of income maintenance: unemployment insurance and food stamps for those who usually work, and welfare for those who often do not.

In this respect, the northern industrial states that first pioneered in the development of social benefits for workers and their families are the ones that have come most under attack as being "anti-business." The legacy of those past struggles in state politics is reflected in the current interstate differentials in benefits and coverage. Unlike taxes, *these* differentials are quite large. This is particularly true of the welfare programs: Unemployment Insurance (UI), Aid to Families with Dependent Children (AFDC), and General Assistance (GA). The second war between the states is becoming mainly a struggle between those who would preserve these benefits and those who wish to roll back the social wage at the state and local level.

The actual beneficiaries of these programs have much to lose if the more generous states retreat to the standards set in the more miserly, usually southern jurisdictions. For instance, in 1979 the maximum benefit available to unemployed workers in Massachusetts was more than twice the level of that prevailing in Georgia and Alabama. The maximum tax on employers was as much as 50 percent higher in some Frostbelt states, due to a combination of stronger pro-labor support in northern legislatures, and to generally higher unemployment rates there.

Similarly, benefits under AFDC and GA vary enormously across the country, with the highest amounts of cash assistance in states such as Connecticut, Michigan, and California and the lowest in the South. By June 1979, as a direct consequence of each state being allowed to set its own AFDC benefit levels, the range in monthly payments in the continental United States extended from New York at $362.93 to Mississippi with a meager $79.87 per family. Within GA, a wholly state-financed welfare program, the benefits in some states were as much as *twelve times* greater than in others.

To repair these disparities, the South might be thought to be most interested in federal welfare reform. In fact just the opposite is true. The congressional representatives from the southern states have traditionally been the most vocal opponents of any type of expanded welfare program. This is true despite the fact that reform would mean even larger federal subsidies to the lowest benefit states and would hold these states "harmless" — that is, require them to spend no more state funds than at present.

The reason for southern opposition goes to the very heart of the social-wage issue. While low-wage states do not wish to raise taxes and therefore signal a worsening business climate, their legislators are even more concerned about the possibility of providing grants so large that they might *compete* with the minimum-wage levels in their local labor markets, now being trumpeted as an inducement to employers. They fear that the supply of low-wage labor will be reduced by higher welfare benefits, and so they vote to keep welfare families at below-subsistence levels.

What southern mayors and governors are trying to preserve, many northern elected officials are currently trying desperately to re-create. And the struggle goes far beyond welfare payments. Because capital is mobile and communities are not, the pressure is building in every part of the country for a general reduction in the social wage — and with it, the standard of living of *all* working people.

Along with, and perhaps even to some extent growing out of, the fractional, unplanned, often chaotic war between state and local governments to attract industry (or to hold on to what they already have), a *national* conflict has reemerged between the leadership of American industry and working people as a whole — between *capital* and *community* on a grand scale. A concerted attack on the rights, privileges, and standards of living of the general public is under way. In a nutshell, capital has unilaterally ended even lip service to the great postwar social contract.

The election of Ronald Reagan to the presidency in 1980 is in this respect a major watershed in modern American history. For his administration is profoundly committed to "disciplining" labor by fundamentally undermining the social wage. While it is no doubt true that the tax, expenditure, and (de-)regulatory programs of the government are also greatly redistributing income in favor of the rich, the impact of these policies on corporate production and profitability over the long run is of far greater historical importance.

Take the tax program. The massive supply-side tax breaks for individuals are supposed to promote new savings that can be ploughed by institutions into new capital investment, while lower tax rates on businesses are expected to stimulate investment directly. We think this is unlikely to occur (and in any case, there is in fact no shortage of savings . . .). But whatever the expectations about the stimulative effect of the program, there can be no doubt about its drastic impact on the capacity of the government to continue to finance the social wage.

In August 1981, the Treasury Department officially estimated that the cumulative revenue loss by 1986 resulting from these, and a few smaller, business tax breaks would be about $144 billion. State governments also stand to lose massive tax revenues as an indirect result of the federal policy. It has been estimated that, if the state governments do not rewrite their own tax laws to disassociate them from the new federal law, they stand to lose as much as $27.5 billion in tax receipts over the next six years, with an estimated annual tax loss of over $10 billion by 1986. This will cut further into the already rapidly shrinking state collection of business revenue resulting from the war between the states over industrial location and retention.

In the area of deregulation, the policies that the conservatives are pursuing are supposed to unfetter "free enterprise" for a new wave of capital accumulation.

But it is hard to see how — in the context of a slack economy within a global recession — the specific policies being followed will not actually exacerbate the problems treated . . . [here]. For example, consider an amendment to the Clean Air Act called the Steel Industry Compliance Extension Act of 1981. It permits the steel companies to defer compliance with the laws limiting air pollution for three years, provided they use the savings to "invest in modernization." Unfortunately, nothing in the act requires them to modernize their *steel*-making facilities. And by not so stipulating, the act implicitly promotes continued diversification away from steel. . . .

TOWARD A NEW DEMOCRATIC SOCIALISTIC REINDUSTRIALIZATION

We have tried to outline a set of basic principles or guidelines for thinking about a program of democratic socialist reindustrialization. Its key elements are: an alternative set of planning objectives to the narrow pursuit of private profit; recognition of the need for particular strategies to deal with the development or restructuring of sunrise industries, sunset industries, public goods, and corporate bail-outs; a new, more democratic, participatory approach to the management of productive enterprise; and a belief in the principle that any private industry seeking assistance from the public must stand ready to negotiate a *quid pro quo* that would lead to sharing the benefits, along with the costs, from the revitalization of a company. In the context of a renewed commitment to using national policy to enhance the social and personal security of working people and their families, through a strengthening of the social wage and its extension into the realm of public regulation of capital mobility, such a program offers some chance for the re-creation of the conditions for productive economic growth on terms consistent with the needs and aspirations of the great majority of ordinary people.

CHAPTER 3

HOW DO WE SOLVE THE PROBLEM OF TOXIC WASTES?

A Monsanto advertisement claims that, "Without chemicals, life itself would be impossible!" Each day we act as if Monsanto was right. We use chemicals to control pests, plants, plaque, and pain. Household products include such odor- and dirt-eaters as Ajax, Clorox, Glass-Plus, and Lemon Pledge. In the bathroom, Dow Chemical brings us such products as "Bathroom Cleaner With Scrubbing Bubbles." This chemical miracle kills odor-causing germs, staph, and fungus while being "scrub-brush tough on dirt." Yet it is gentle as a bubble on these surfaces! Bathroom cleansers typically contain dimethylbenyl ammonium chlorides and dimethyl ethylbenzyl ammonium chlorides suspended in water, propelled by hydrocarbons, and scented by perfumes.

The Chemical Age is only forty years old. It is the product of the Second World War, when we first discovered the wonders of synthetic compounds for a better life. Since 1945 we have produced billions of tons of plastics, enamels, ceramics, rubber, benzenes, insecticides, and synthetic fibers.

The seamy side of life with chemicals is that we have produced billions of tons of chemical sludge. Toxins threaten our groundwater, air, soil, and food supply. On beaches south of Boston one can see evidence of raw sewage sludge pumped into the ocean by the cities of Boston and Quincy. Thousands of used tampon dispensers wash up during high tide. Environmental problems are not just eyesores. Epidemiologists have been studying the actors and crew of the movie *The Conqueror*, which was shot in the mid-1950s near Yucca Flat, Nevada, just 137 miles from the site of eleven open-air nuclear explosions. John Wayne (who starred as Genghis Khan) and ninety other members of the cast and crew have contracted cancer. John Wayne and forty-five others have already died from it.[1]

Environmental hazards first became a public issue in the early 1970s. The Earth Day teach-ins on college campuses in 1970 called attention to environmental nightmares such as air pollution, water pollution, destruction of the food cycles, and eco-disasters. For many of today's college students, Love Canal was their first chemical nightmare. Love Canal was the product of a callous disregard for the environment and blind stupidity by Hooker Chemical Company. Over a twenty-year period, Hooker dumped tons of toxic ooze into the ground as if the water supply were a giant toilet basin. The silent but deadly sludge did not disappear. When Hooker abandoned its waste site, a developer converted the area into building lots. Hundreds of young couples in their prime childbearing years built their first homes in the vicinity of the toxic dump. Over a period of years, the chemicals leeched into the groundwater supply, seeped into basements, and backed up into a creek. The silent killer sludge percolated up into homes and onto playgrounds. Hundreds of men, women, and children suffered from the destruction of their respiratory, reproductive, and immune systems. Pregnant women drank water laced with toxins. Children played daily on a playground that exposed them directly to known carcinogens. The residents had no warning of the chemical time bomb in their neighborhood. By the time the sludge reached the schoolyard, the homes, and the creek, hundreds of residents had suffered long-term exposure to known toxins. It was too late for the women who miscarried at a rate ten times the national average. It was too late for the children who were born with an alarmingly high rate of birth defects.

The toxic incident at Love Canal is symbolic of a much larger set of social issues. The Environmental Protection Agency estimates that there are 17,000 toxic dump sites and 181,000 pits, ponds, and lagoons in the United States.[2] Toxic waste sites such as Love Canal, Woburn, Massachusetts, and Chester, Pennsylvania, are not the only problem caused by synthetic chemicals. In recent years, toxic incidents have occurred in not only the disposal of toxic wastes but also in their manufacture, treatment, storage, and workplace use.

Of the more than 50,000 chemicals on the market today, 70 percent are classified as potentially dangerous to human health by the Environmental Protection Agency.[3] Preliminary evidence indicates that as many as 20 million jobs involve exposure to toxic substances that pose reproductive hazards.[4] Many of the workplace chemicals include teratogens, which damage the fetus *in vitro*. Some chemicals pose multiple threats. The most insidious reproductive injury is a mutation. Defined simply, a mutation involves a permanent change in the genetic structure of cells. Mutagenic effects can be expected across several generations for an indeterminate period of time. The children of workers exposed to mutagens and their children's children run a known risk of having such anomalies as three rows of teeth, no limbs, or abnormalities of the renal system. These unknown and unknowable distortions of genetic structure can be expected in future generations long after the workplace has been cleaned up.

Unfortunately, millions of workers continue to be exposed to agents known to cause fetal abnormalities. These industrial agents include lead, benzene, solvents, and anesthetic gases. Worse still, the chemical industry admits that the toxicity of 80 percent of industrial compounds is unknown.[5] Yet there is no industrial policy protecting fertile men and women and the offspring of these workers. There is no systematic effort even to catalogue all of the health and reproductive effects of these compounds. Millions of men and women work under conditions that may kill them and damage future generations.

It is not surprising that each party affected by environmental issues tends to define not only the solution but the problem itself in different ways. The conservative and radical articles that follow are best understood against the project of liberalism. Liberals see the law as a neutral mechanism that can resolve all disputes. Through legislative reform and through creative new doctrines of common law, liberals believe we can protect both the health of the environment and of the economy. The corporate world is skeptical, doubting whether this can be done. For the conservative, government regulation constitutes the environment problem: "Get OSHA and the other agencies off my back and out of my pocket!" The radical believes that liberal reforms, however worthwhile, never can solve the problem. In the drive for profits, the environment will be exploited just like the workers. The radical hope is a long-term movement to empower people to deal directly with environmental and work issues.

ENVIRONMENTAL CONTROL THROUGH LAW: LIBERALISM

Senator Paul Tsongas writes that the "potential return to unfettered private enterprise is unacceptable. How many Love Canals are enough?" The solution to environmental problems according to liberalism is to stiffen legal sanctions against hazardous material. Tsongas proposes a three-fold program: (1) licensed hazardous waste disposal; (2) stiff sanctions against the illegal dumping of hazardous waste; and (3) new laws regulating the accidental release of hazardous material.[6]

Liberals believe that the environment can be saved by the legislature and the judiciary. These are the two institutions responsible for public policy. Legislators are made aware of environmental problems through the lobbying efforts of consumer groups, unions, and other interests. Legislators draft bills as a response to the political winds. Policies, to be enacted, must have widespread political legitimacy. Environmental legislation such as the Toxic Substances Act, the Clean Air Act, and the Clean Water Act was the product of years of work by environmental lobbyists, scholars, and informed citizens. Legislators turned ideas from this social movement into bills.

The judiciary is by far the most important of the two institutions in the handling of toxic incidents. Most environmental conflicts are litigated in the course under the tort system of compensation. Liberals believe that litigation between the corporations and citizens under the tort system of compensations helps to fine-tune the common law. Under civil law, a tort is defined as a private wrong for which a court will award damages. The legal liability is triggered when a person or corporation violates a legal duty, and that violation results in damages or injury. For instance, if the Coca-Cola Bottling Company distributes a bottle with a decomposed mouse inside it, the company must take out their checkbook and pay the consumer for any physical or psychic injuries caused by drinking the contents of the tainted beverage. From the perspective of liberal legality, a manufacturer owes a duty to consumers to make their products carefully. If a company falls short of that duty, they are liable for any injuries. Ford Motor was liable for money damages to the passengers who were "torched" as a result of the company's misdesign of the Pinto's gas tank. Kerr-McGee was equally responsible for damages to Karen Silkwood, carelessly exposing her to deadly plutonium, a highly volatile carcinogen. Under the liberal legality framework, every tort, be it intentional as in assault, or the result of negligence, involves some violation of a legal duty. The theory is that social problems caused by carelessness can be solved when individual litigants make their way to the court. Under the tort system, it is deemed just that a commercial enterprise making profit should bear the cost of any unreasonable risk which it creates.

According to liberal practice, the best deterrent to corporate misfeasance is the threat of costly law suits. A corporation will make their products carefully if they are responsible for undoing harm with money damages. Law suits are seen as the best incentive for safety.

In short, liberals believe that the values and interests of the corporations, the governments, and the victims of toxic waste can be mediated through the courts and through new legislation. The corporation or individual who violates the rights of others is punished through costly tort suits. D. J. Manning sums up the liberal legal rights theory in this way:

It is the belief that the liberty and welfare of the individual and the justice and security of society depend upon their being clearly defined and enforced legal relationships between all of its members. No man may rightly be considered outside or above the law.[7]

CONSERVATIVE VIEW OF TOXIC TORTS

In the conservative article, "The Hazards of Helping Toxic Waste Victims," Jeremy Main asserts that new government regulations in favor of the victims of toxic wastes threaten the long-term competitiveness of American industry. Main's argument reflects the conservative concern with the accumulation process. Conservatives believe that the courts have gone too far in their protection of the worker and consumer at the expense of long-term profit. They believe that government intervention has created the threat of increased legal liability by making it easier for injured workers and consumers to plead and prove their case.

For the conservative, liberal legislation such as the Environmental Protection Act and the Toxic Substances Acts are licenses to harass business. They have a similar view of liberal judges who expand corporations' tort liability with a doctrine like strict liability, which does not require a plaintiff to present proof of a corporation's negligence. The conservative believes that it is the government intervention that is the major environmental problem. They see poisonous industrial wastes, carcinogenic chemicals, and dirty air as something to be put up with as an inevitable by-product of a healthy economy. Government regulation by the legislature and judiciary is a parasite that threatens to destroy industry.[8]

RADICAL VIEW: WHAT CAPITALISM CREATES IT WILL NOT CURE

In the article "Toxic Times and Class Politics," radical Ken Geiser links today's life-threatening chemicals to the capitalist mode of production. He argues that the liberal legislation of the 1970s have only encourages industrial enterprises to dump their waste products illegally. Geiser believes that legislation cannot possibly control the problem of toxic wastes because it does not deal with the initial production of wastes.

Legislation only creates pressures on corporations to break the law and dump their wastes by night.

Geiser sees local struggles over toxic chemicals and a wide grass-roots social movement in opposition to the production process as the solution. He is encouraged by the mass movement that has risen against toxic wastes and is hopeful that this activism will extend to other struggles such as control of the workplace.

To radicals, the issue at stake in the environmental issue is the very nature of capitalism. Behind the issue of toxic wastes loom larger questions — such as the social risks of unfettered industrialization. Radicals are unwilling to let common law judges or government officials from OSHA and the EPA deal with the environmental problem. Radicals believe that public policies adopted by the legislature and courts communicate the underlying values of the interests of the producers of the millions of metric tons of waste; those who own the means of production will inevitably define what the law is and how it is to be interpreted. To radicals, the only hope is mass movements in opposition to industry and the state.

References

1. Michael Blomen's account of the cancer rates of the cast and crew of *The Conqueror* appeared in his feature article "The Biggest Bombs in Movie History," *Boston Globe*, March 25, 1984, Section B, p. 6.
2. Lois Marie Gibbs, "Do You Jog Beside a Freeway? Staying Healthy in a Toxic World," *Ms.*, May 1984, p. 166.
3. The data cited on workplace hazards appeared originally in Judith Perrolle and Michael Rustad's "Industry Response to Reproductive Hazards," a presentation to the American Sociology Association, San Antonio, Texas, August 1984.
4. Ibid.
5. Ibid.
6. Paul Tsongas, *The Road From Here: Liberalism and Realities in the 1980s* (New York: Random House, 1982), p. 256.
7. D. J. Manning, *Liberalism* (New York: St. Martin's Press, 1976), p. 14.
8. George Gilder, *Wealth and Poverty* (New York: Basic Books, 1981), pp. 283–84.

7. THE HAZARDS OF HELPING TOXIC WASTE VICTIMS

Jeremy Main

Congress is on the way to enacting a law that answers some large emerging questions about what our society owes people who may have been injured by hazardous chemicals. Among the questions: Under what circumstances can they collect from a company that manufactured or dumped the wastes? What if several companies are involved and it is unclear which wastes caused the cancer, or birth defects, or other medical tragedies? What if there is doubt that these misfortunes are even related to the toxic wastes? What if there is little or no doubt about this but the company was breaking no laws when it acted, years ago, or had no reason to believe that its actions might turn out, years later, to be harmful to innocent bystanders? Is our society prepared to tell these bystanders that nobody can be held liable for their misfortunes — that life in an industrial society carries with it some inescapable risks?

The toxic waste compensation bills now making their way through Congress attempt, in various ways, to make it easier for those who have been injured to seek damages. However, the bills would have some other major effects. The consequences could include yet another costly federal benefit, complete with the bureaucracy needed to administer it. The bills would create basic and sweeping changes in our concepts of evidence and liability. And they represent a threat to the competitiveness if not the solvency of many corporations.

The potential cost of compensating victims of toxic wastes can be seen in the special case of asbestos. Asbestos workers have brought thousands of suits against their employers of decades ago. These suits involve occupational rather than hazardous waste claims and in other ways are quite different from the problems that Congress is considering. But in terms of costs and numbers, the portents are clear.

Asbestos manufacturers have already spent $1 billion on claims, and at that only about 4000 out of the 25,000 claims filed have been closed. Hundreds of new suits are filed every month. Dr. William J. Nicholson of the Mount Sinai School of Medicine in New York City believes that 165,000 people will die from past exposure to asbestos between now and the end of the century. Manville Corporation and two other companies among the 300-plus defendants have sought protection from the blizzard of claims under Chapter 11 of the bankruptcy law. Several manufacturers are suing their insurers over disputes about their coverage.

The toxic waste claims typically concern companies in the chemical and oil industries, some of which are beginning to find themselves in the same fix as the asbestos companies. The cases are piling up. One big case involves Agent Orange: after trying to get disability benefits from the Veterans Administration and being rebuffed, Vietnam veterans have now turned on the manufacturers and sought payment for the illnesses allegedly brought upon them and their children by the defoliant. A class action by 17,000 veterans against five chemical companies is expected to come to trial in federal district court on New York's Long Island next year. Another center of toxic waste litigation is the area around the notorious Love Canal dump in Niagara Falls, New York, where past and present residents have filed over 1400 individual suits, for a total of at least $1 billion against Occidental Petroleum, which inherited the problem when it acquired Hooker Chemical, and other defendants. In idyllic Silicon Valley, 270 residents are suing Fairchild Camera & Instrument Corporation for leaking a solvent that they say got into their water supply and caused miscarriages and heart defects among their children. In Fort Edward, New York, thirty-five residents are suing General Electric for over $100 million, claiming that the company allowed a solvent call TCE to get into their drinking water. These cases are likely only a beginning.

Hardly anyone is happy with the way the cases are handled. The plaintiffs find it hard to win in a legal system designed to deal with the obvious damage caused by something like a bullet or a car, but not with the hidden processes of chemistry. Developing the scientific evidence to back the plaintiffs' claim is extremely expensive and usually inconclusive, particularly when current illnesses may have been caused by exposure decades ago. The defending companies are unhappy because they often face incalculable penalties for damage in connection with actions they may have taken years ago that were then legal and not known to be harmful.

These dissatisfactions have created an irresistible political pressure to do something, and quickly. Congress has before it a score of bills, some designed to help the victims of hazardous waste in general, others targeted on such specific problems as Agent Orange. Recognizing what it belatedly sees as one of the most sensitive issues of the 1980s, the Administration set up a Cabinet-level work group three months ago to pull together the fragments of policy developed by various federal agencies — and to figure out how to hold down the government's liabilities. California, Minnesota, New Jersey, and Washington have enacted compensation laws, and other states have them in the works.

The evidence thus far suggests that politicians are going to find it hard to vote against compensating victims. It also suggests that politicians will have difficulty making some critical distinctions. When should victims be compensated? Certainly not, we would all agree, when they fall victim to risks that are a normal part of living. By driving cars, smoking cigarettes, and drinking alcohol, most Americans tacitly accepts some risks (far greater than those posed by toxic chemicals) in return for certain pleasures and conveniences. Presumably the public will accept some heightened level of general exposure to toxic risks in return for the benefits of the chemicals that produce them. On the other hand, we could presumably agree that the victims should be able to collect when an illness is demonstrably related to a company's negligent handling of dangerous chemicals.

But between these two clear-cut scenarios is a huge gray area in which there is quite a lot to argue about. The legislators and lawyers writing the new laws seem inclined to push the definition of compensable damage to a point at which it pretty much fills up the gray area.

In doing so, they seem to be operating on the unproved assumption that toxic wastes have claimed some enormous number of victims. But it is clear that some who believe themselves victims are wildly wrong. Consider, for example, the phantom toxic leak that afflicted Memphis in the late 1970s. There were all the usual details — reports of unexplained diseases, picketing, emotional meetings, even a congressional hearing. The only thing lacking was a dump or other source of poisonous chemicals. It was never found and a study by the federal Centers for Disease Control determined eventually that there was no unusual incidence of illness. Since it deals with the unknown and the mysterious, chemical terror spreads fast — and the press does its part to pass on each unexamined piece of evidence.

How many have been affected is unclear. The effects of some poisonous substances, such as dioxin and PCBs, seem to have been exaggerated. On the other hand, still unrecognized dangers might lurk. The reality lies somewhere between the claim of Senator Robert T. Stafford, the Vermont Republican who has offered one of the compensation bills, that there are "millions upon millions" of potential victims and the Chemical Manufacturers Association's soothing words that there is no "evidence of a significant health problem from hazardous wastes."

Science and medicine are far from knowing how to link toxic waste and disease. In the case of asbestos the connection is clear — the plaintiffs were heavily exposed to asbestos, mostly as construction and shipyard workers, and asbestos is the only cause of asbestosis and a fatal cancer of the lung lining called mesothelioma. If the workers are suffering from either disease, there's very little doubt how they got it.

But most cases hold no such clear connection. The chronic effects of many chemicals are still being studied. The effects vary with dosage, length of exposure, the individual, and even the combined effects of several chemicals. Often the dosage was low, making the link harder to establish. When a longtime three-pack-a-day smoker gets lung cancer, it seems reasonable to link it to smoking. But what if a three-cigarette-a-day smoker gets lung cancer? Were the cigarettes the cause, or did they combine with other factors, or did they have nothing to do with the cancer? Medicine just doesn't know. Most exposures to toxic chemicals are at the three-cigarette rather than three-pack level.

The case of Agent Orange shows how difficult it is to know or prove what happened. This chemical, used as a defoliant in Vietnam, contained traces of dioxin, which is highly toxic. It causes cancer and other chronic diseases in animals, but so far as humans are concerned, an acute skin disease called chloracne is the only illness that all the experts acknowledge to be caused by dioxin. Many Vietnam veterans claim that their cancers, liver ailments, nervous disorders, deformed children, and other woes were caused by Agent Orange. They may be right, but the proof is not yet there. In fact, it is not even clear that they suffer from these afflictions more than other Americans.

The limited studies conducted by the government so far tend to support its contention that Agent Orange is not responsible. The Air Force announced in July part of the results of a study of 1269 airmen who were massively exposed to Agent Orange when they handled it during the war. The rate and causes of death among these veterans are normal. Results of the more important part of the study, dealing with illnesses rather than death, will be announced this fall. The government is planning to spend $140 million on Agent Orange research, half of it on a massive study by the Centers for Disease Control, which had no trouble getting the Office of Management and Budget [OMB] to approve the full amount of its request. But the study won't be completed until 1987 and even then may not contain the kind of clear answers lawyers need in court. Many of the veterans' ailments are vague — things like fatigue, headaches, and loss of memory, which could have many causes.

Whatever the study may show, by the time it is out, Congress and the courts will long since have acted. Science can be patient, but the victims and the politicians clearly won't wait. When a lame-duck session of Congress hurried through the Superfund law in 1980 to provide for the cleanup of hazardous dumps, a section providing for compensation to victims was dropped at the last minute. The final act provided, however, for a study of victims' compensation. The twelve lawyers appointed to the so-called 301(e) study group — named after the section of the Superfund act that created it — finished their work last year and issued a two-volume report. In rough outline, all the bills before Congress are similar to this report.

The report recommends a two-tier system for helping victims. To get the bulk of claims cleaned up efficiently without swamping the courts, it suggests a federal Tier I to cover medical costs and lost income, but not pain and suffering through a non-fault administrative system similar to workers' compensation. If plaintiffs wanted to make claims for pain and suffering, they would have to go through the full legal process in state court under Tier II; however, the rules would be altered to strengthen the plaintiffs' side.

A major unanswered question about the Tier I federal fund is how it would be financed. Should the present $1.6 billion Superfund simply be expanded without changing the way it collects money? That would impose the whole burden of the system on a few companies, since 88 percent of the Superfund's money comes from oil and chemical companies, which pay on the basis of the feedstocks they use. And even these contributions to the fund do not exhaust the companies' liability for cleanups — a fact dramatically evidenced by the U.S. Army's recent $1.8 billion claim against Shell Oil Company. (The claim was related to the costs of cleaning up some leased Army property on which Shell had been manufacturing pesticides.)

Simply expanding the present Superfund tax base would surely be unfair. Just five companies, Arco, Dow, Exxon, Shell, and Union Carbide, contribute more than half the total. One way or another, the oil and chemical industries will almost inevitably pay for most of the fund. Still, the burden could be spread more fairly than it would be under an expanded Superfund.

The amounts a victim could recover from the Tier I fund would generally be limited to medical expenses and two-thirds of lost income, up to $2000 a month. However, in a presentation made to President Reagan and his Cabinet council in May and then leaked to the press, OMB cited as a warning the case of black-lung compensation, established in 1970 to help coal miners. It was at first billed as a limited plan that might cost $20 million to $40 million a year. But over the years, miners and their dependents came to be treated more and more liberally; today the program costs $2 billion a year.

Not only might the Tier I fund swell into a monster, but the victims receiving payments from it might also be free to pursue unlimited compensation in the courts under Tier II. The OMB paper said these recommendations add up to "the worst of both worlds; an administrative compensation system with liberal evidentiary standards and generous benefits, as well as continued availability of traditional tort law."

The liberalized court standards being proposed are at least as significant as the potential costs. Since the states have a hodge-podge of common law, mostly making it difficult for victims to claim recompense, all the major bills before Congress would create a "federal cause of action." In other words, plaintiffs could sue under federal, not state, law. And under the federal law the rules of the game would be made easier for the plaintiffs.

To pursue a toxic case in state courts is difficult under present rules. "Proof of the causal connection between exposure and injury is an almost overwhelming barrier to recovery," said the 301 report. Negligence is hard to document if a spill took place twenty years ago and witnesses have died and documents been discarded.

Getting proof is expensive. Anthony Z. Roisman, a Washington attorney who has fought many environmental battles, says it costs $100,000 to $200,000 just to gather the necessary scientific and medical evidence. Expert witnesses may charge $1000 or more a day for their testimony. Most plaintiffs and lawyers just can't spend that kind of money in advance. Roisman gets foundation support for his work, and so he is able to carry the expense of developing cases, but most lawyers can't. In a major toxic case that he is handling in Woburn, Massachusetts, Roisman has been able to make use of some extensive research collected by the Environmental Protection Agency, which is studying pollution in the local area.

Another difficulty about proving causal connection is that it may not exist. Science often can't give clear answers. Consider Woburn, where eight families have each had a case of leukemia in the last decade. The families are suing two companies: W. R. Grace, which has operated a small manufacturing plant producing food-wrapping equipment in Woburn since 1960, and Beatrice Foods, which at one time owned John J. Riley, a local tannery. The suit says, for example, that the solvent TCE was dumped by Grace in its backyard, found its way into the water supply, and contributed to causing the leukemia. Anne Anderson, whose son Jimmy died of leukemia in 1981 after a long illness, is convinced she knows what killed her son. "I've always had a feeling it was the water," she says. "We were told it was okay, but it was always very, very bad." Grace admits to having used small amounts of TCE and to burying several drums of unidentified waste in its backyard, 2500 feet from the contaminated wells. Their contents are being examined now. But the whole area is a mess of pollution and has been since the nineteenth century. Woburn used to call itself the tannery capital of the world. The wells lie near the Aberjona River, which drains a whole industrial area. An industrial sewer that has overflowed at times runs nearby. Many other plants are in the area, as well as cemeteries of old cars and for discarded drums and tanks. Woburn offers "an incredibly complex scientific case," according to a EPA official on the scene. To win his case, Roisman will have to prove that TCE got into the wells, that TCE contributes to causing leukemia (not an accepted scientific fact), and that there was enough TCE to do the damage.

The proposals before Congress would make this kind of case easier to prove. Since scientists are never likely to agree that TCE caused the leukemia, the supporters of victims' compensation are pushing for a form of evidence known as "rebuttable presumptions." These have been used in the black-lung law. For instance, if a man had worked in the mines for ten years and later died of a respiratory disease, he was presumed without any need for further proof to have died of black-lung disease, and it was up to the mining company to prove that he died of something else. Congress eliminated this particular presumption in 1981, but other presumptions remain.

If presumptions are included in the toxic victims legislation, the lawyers plan to develop statistical evidence. For example, if a given city normally had 100 deaths a year from liver cancer and that rate went up to 110 some time after dioxin was dumped locally, lawyers could try to use the increase to create a presumption of liability. But this approach would raise a lot of intriguing questions. Would the dioxin be blamed for all 110 cases, or only 10 cases, and if so, which 10? Leslie Cheek III, a vice president of the Crum & Forster Insurance Companies, said in testimony before a congressional committee that any such use of presumptions "would so weaken the evidentiary and burden-of-proof requirements of the common law as to cast upon defendants and their insurers the impossible tasks of identifying which of the millions of Americans with long-latency diseases and other health problems did *not* contract them through exposure to hazardous substances."

Along with easier rules of evidence, the lawyers and legislators are pushing for tougher and broader rules of liability. Normally a plaintiff has to prove negligence to collect damages. But common law has applied "strict" liability — that is, liability without regard to negligence — to extremely hazardous activities such as blasting. In the 1970s the courts began to apply strict liability to suits over defective products. If strict liability were now extended to toxic wastes, then it would do a company no good to plead that it had obeyed the laws and followed approved procedures when it disposed of its wastes. It would still be liable, even if the hazards are seen only in retrospect.

On top of strict liability, the new legislation might create what is known in legal language as "joint and several responsibility." It means that a single defendant can be made to pay all the damages even in situations where many defendants may be guilty. Like strict liability, joint and several responsibility opens up some fearsome risks to business. Will the company that contributed 10 percent or 20 percent of the waste in a dump be held responsible for all damage caused by its toxic releases?

Lawyers can be expected to refine these statutory changes by looking for ways of creating new common law to reinforce their cases. For example, in the Woburn case, Roisman plans to ask for damages not just for those afflicted, but for the other family members, too, the argument being that drinking the polluted water has made them more susceptible to disease in the future.

Clearly these proposed changes add up to a huge potential burden on society. "The plain goal of these proposals is to provide *all* hazardous-substance victims with the best of both nonfault and fault-based remedies: eased evidentiary burdens coupled with generous awards," says Crum & Forster's Cheek. "As laudable as this objective may be in theory, it cannot realistically be achieved if the system's costs are to be controllable, predictable, and, ultimately, insurable." Joint and several responsibility could double or triple insurance rates; it might even create risks that insurance companies would refuse to cover. Says Michael J. Horowitz, general counsel of the OMB and co-chairman of the Cabinet work group: "I know of no greater fiscal threat for the nineties than the whole question of toxic torts and victims' compensation."

Furthermore, the reforms might discourage what should be their ultimate objective: motivating companies to undertake a real cleanup so that there wouldn't be any victims. Fear of a hefty judgment might make a company take better care of its wastes, but if strict liability removes the need to prove negligence, then the negligent company will suffer no more in court than the company that did its best to clean up. With joint and several responsibility, plaintiffs will tend to go after the company that has the deepest pockets, rather than the dirtiest company.

Taken together, the proposals suggest the possibility of one company being held retroactively responsible for an offense committed by another company at a time when the offense was neither illegal nor known to be harmful. George C. Freeman, Jr., a Virginia lawyer who served on the 301 study group, believes that a new law including joint and several responsibility and strict liability, might conflict with constitutional due process requirements, especially if applied retroactively.

The choice facing Congress is between an existing system that satisfies no one and a set of proposals that could prove enormously costly. Of course, doing nothing could also be costly. The present system for compensating victims is appallingly inefficient and wasteful. A recent Rand Corporation study showed that of the

$1 billion spent on asbestos cases by the end of 1982, only $236 million had reached the hands of the plaintiffs. The rest was absorbed by legal fees and costs. In economists' terms, the "transaction costs" paid by society were steep.

All four of the major bills before Congress follow the basic two-tier formulation of the 301 commission report, but differ substantially in detail. They have been proposed by Senator Stafford, Representative John J. LaFalce (whose district includes Love Canal), Senator George J. Mitchell of Maine, and jointly by Representatives Edward J. Markey (who represents Woburn) and James J. Florio of New Jersey. All four would create strict liability, and three would establish joint and several responsibility. The LaFalce bill provides for a modified form of joint and several reponsibility. The Mitchell and Stafford bills would pay for victims' compensation simply by extending the Superfund, with its present tax system; however, the Markey-Florio bill would spread the burden a little more fairly. It would add a tax of 79 cents a barrel to domestic and imported oil, paid by the refiner or importer, and another tax of $2.13 per dry-weight ton of hazardous waste received at the dump, this tax to be paid by the dump operator. None of these bills is likely to come to the floor before next year; although this fall Markey may try to get part of what he wants for the plaintiffs by tacking onto another bill an amendment creating the federal cause of action.

Whatever legislation is finally adopted, the outcome will inevitably be uncomfortable. However, the cost could be contained by a number of limitations, which some of the bills already have. Perhaps the most important is in the Markey-Florio bill, which, surprisingly, would prevent the plaintiffs among Markey's own constituents now in state court in Woburn from collecting damages in federal court: it does not allow retroactive claims. The bill specifies that to be actionable in federal court: the exposure to a chemical must take place after the date of enactment. The Stafford and Mitchell bills would allow the use of rebuttable presumptions in Tier I and Tier II cases, while the other bills would limit their use to Tier I cases. The Markey-Florio bill would soften joint and several responsibility by making generators and transporters to toxic waste responsible for the waste only during the period when it is in their hands. Other limitations of liability desired by industry include a requirement that plaintiffs choose between Tier I and Tier II, and not pursue both types of actions, and the use of Social Security, workers' compensation, and health insurance payments as an offset to awards.

Congressman Thomas A. Daschle, a South Dakota Democrat, has some other approaches that would contain costs related to Agent Orange. His bill, the most likely to succeed among a dozen that have been offered to help Vietnam veterans, would pay compensation for only three ailments: a rare type of cancer, a rare liver disease, and chloracne. Together, they make up less than 1 percent of the claims based on the use of Agent Orange, but they are the diseases most closely connected to dioxin. The Daschle bill would expire automatically when the Centers for Disease Control finish a major study of the effects of Agent Orange. The idea is that when we know more, we can take a fresh look at what we are doing. These are only some of the means of containing the costs and the claims and at the same time helping people with the most serious problems.

Given the large lingering uncertainties about the damage done by toxic chemicals in the past, Congress shouldn't rush to comprehensive legislation. A minimal and temporary no-fault compensation system seems reasonable, however, provided that the standards for accepting claims are fairly tough and the compensation covers only medical costs, lost pay, and property damage. People who feel entitled to collect more should be free to take their chances in court, but it would be a mistake for Congress to fundamentally transform U.S. tort law in an effort to make things easier for plaintiffs and tougher for defendants in toxic waste cases.

Congress is talking about holding business to a stricter standard of responsibility, but the bills now in the pipeline seem unfair in critical respects. Some might even be unconstitutional. They will almost certainly represent bad news for the oil and chemical industries. And in some form or other, at least one of these bills will almost certainly pass within the next year or so.

RADICAL: ORGANIZE

8. TOXIC TIMES AND CLASS POLITICS

Ken Geiser

In the fall of 1982, the North Carolina national guard arrested over 350 protesters, including a number of national civil rights leaders, in a quiet Warren County farm community named Afton. The arrests made front-page headlines all around the country. The form was pure direct action protest similar to the massive civil rights demonstrations of two decades earlier. But the content was different, for the Warren County protest was an incident in a growing national movement against toxic and hazardous chemical contamination.

The specific issue in Warren County was its selection by state officials as the disposal site for 32,000 cubic yards of toxic soil laden with polychlorinated biphenols, or PCBs, one of the most poisonous chemicals ever produced. PBC-contaminated oil had been illegally dumped from moving tank trucks the year before. Faced with the question of where to get rid of it, state authorities had chosen Warren County, whose per capita income is the lowest in the state and 60 percent of whose citizens are black. Organizing a protest group — the Warren County Citizens Concerned about PCBs — the local residents began a letter-writing and media campaign aimed at forcing the governor to reconsider. The governor did back down briefly but alternative sites were deemed unacceptable or even more politically objectionable. Lawsuits also failed. With approval from the federal Environmental Protection Agency (EPA) and $2.5 million in federal "Superfund" money, the state went ahead with the dumping. The road blockade was the last desperate effort of the Afton citizens to prevent the disposal of such a toxic chemical in their community.

While the Warren County protest failed to stop the dumping it did symbolize the character of a reborn environmental movement focused on toxic and hazardous chemical contamination. From the farmlands of Kansas to suburban Denver and inner-city Baltimore, groups of community citizens have come together in neighborhood organizations to protest the neglect and irresponsibility of local industries and the inadequacy of government authorities. Throughout the country local neighborhood people who have only read about Love Canal are finding their own lives and health jeopardized by similar conditions in their own communities.

A broad review of all the various stories suggests that something more is afoot here than simultaneous accidents. Poor handling, use, and discharge of toxic and hazardous materials turn out to be much more ubiquitous than initially expected. Throughout the country there is a growing sensitivity to toxic chemical threats, and community people are spontaneously reacting by organizing themselves wherever such threats occur. Not only is this response national, it is persistent. Once formed, these small neighborhood organizations are continuing and maturing. There are now national conferences, national newsletters, and a growing number of training institutes and resource libraries for supporting these local efforts. What there is here is more than a collection of events: it is an emerging movement — a nationwide anti-toxic-chemical movement.

This emerging new environmental movement is critical of both government and industry. It arises at a time when the traditional "mainstream" environmentalists are engaged in defensive maneuvers with an openly hostile national administration. And the new movement's class base is strikingly different. The people who make up these local protest organizations, not only in Warren County but elsewhere as well, are drawn mostly from the ranks of poor farmers and lower-income urban residents. And there is more here than simple demographics. This new movement is bringing forth an environmental consciousness among people who were unlikely to think of themselves as "environmentalists." Because the movement is so tightly rooted in the immediate experience of people's community and family life, it has an urgency and a concreteness that is incredibly compelling. For these new "environmentalists" environment is not an abstract concept polluted and decreasing in beauty or scientific value. For many it is something which has already exposed them to hazards which are debilitating them and hastening their deaths.

THE NATURE OF THE THREAT

The exposure of working people to health-threatening chemicals is new only in regard to the character of the risks. Much earlier, the rise of industrialization during the mid-nineteenth century had brought a high level of risk from toxic chemicals.

The early tanning industries, foundries, textile mills, and printing industries employed large quantities of acids, oils, and heavy metal compounds. Workers died of lead and arsenic poisoning and were burned and maimed by acid baths. Public health reports as early as the 1860s documented and complained of industrial chemicals polluting rivers and water supplies. But chemical hazards became qualitatively more serious with the advent of the petrochemical industries and the development of synthetic, organic chemicals following World War II. Not occurring in nature, the complex new hydrocarbon chains have proved slow to assimilate or decompose in the natural environment or living organisms. But their versatility, ease of production, and low cost led them to be increasingly substituted for more traditional inorganic chemicals. The total production of synthetic chemicals by U.S. firms increased from about a billion pounds in 1940 to 30 billion in 1950 and 300 billion in 1976. The variety and complexity of these chemicals also increased at an astounding rate during these years. Today it is estimated that there are nearly a quarter of a million chemicals in circulation, of which some fifty thousand are recognized by the federal government as toxic. Increasingly evidence has associated human exposure to these chemicals with birth defects, reproductive complications, respiratory problems, organ damage, and cancer.

The use of synthetic chemicals in American industry has been made possible by an enormous, though implicit, subsidy from the society as a whole. Not only has the cost of industrial disease been shifted from the companies to individual workers, but the companies have been able to evade almost entirely the costs of disposing of chemical wastes. In both cases, the externalization of costs has reduced the relative price of chemicals and thereby set an artificially low price on chemical products. Low prices and a seemingly endless variety of new chemical products were the side of the coin that capitalism liked to expose. But the coin has two sides, and the other side has become increasingly clear.

At the end of World War II, U.S. corporations produced perhaps a billion pounds of hazardous wastes per year. The figure has grown apace, to the point where the federal Environmental Protection Agency now estimates it at about 80 billion pounds a year. Of this amount, 90 percent is estimated to be disposed of improperly. Ironically, steps taken to control the problem in the 1970s had the effect of shifting it and in some ways exacerbating it. The federal Clean Air and Water Pollution acts, along with corresponding state laws, sought to reduce the dispersal of chemicals in the air and water. But because these laws did not challenge the actual generation of toxic wastes by industry, they encouraged the accumulation of large volumes of solid and liquid hazardous wastes. Much of this waste, often in highly concentrated form, was either dumped into on-site pits and lagoons or transported to off-site land disposal dumps. The federal Resource Recovery and Conservation Act was passed in 1976 to confront the problems caused by this patchwork and highly unsafe system of waste disposal. It sought to provide comprehensive "cradle to grave" regulation of toxic and hazardous wastes, but again without dealing with the initial production of the wastes in the manufacturing process. Because this new act raised the costs of managing and disposing of hazardous wastes, it created simultaneously a large new market for private waste disposal facilities and an illegal market for so-called midnight dumpers.

The unforeseen consequence of these various laws and regulations was to concentrate toxic chemical disposal in the ground. Ground disposal appeared at first to be the most benign technique but, insidiously, it provided one of the most direct channels to human exposure. In the ground, toxic chemicals were slowly leached into groundwater, the source of most of the nation's drinking water. By the end of the decade chemical contamination suddenly emerged across the country as the primary threat to private and public water supplies. A combination of well-intended laws and a highly integrated ecological web brought millions of Americans into direct exposure with toxic chemicals in their homes.

LOVE CANAL AND THE EMERGENCE OF A MOVEMENT

Despite the scope of the problem, hazardous waste was hardly heard of outside of environmental circles prior to the incident at Love Canal, which broke into national headlines in 1978. The struggle at Love Canal pitted a handful of committed neighbors against a sophisticated chemical corporation, intransigent city officials, and less than cooperative state government. The issues involved children's health, birth defects, miscarriages, and a multitude of adult diseases. The consequences involved the buyout and evacuation of a whole neighborhood. The national media brought reports of Love Canal into every corner of the country. The plight and struggle of Lois Gibbs and her neighbors became a national drama. Love Canal became synonymous with toxic chemicals. In the aftermath of the evacuation of residents near the Hooker Chemical site, media throughout the country turned to the disovery of hazardous waste dump sites in local communities. With media attention came a heightened sensitivity as neighborhood residents who had once ignored old dump sites began to speculate about the connection between physical ailments and foul-smelling sites or foul-tasting drinking water.

Passage of the ''Superfund'' bill of 1980, rushed through Congress in the months before Ronald Reagan took office, helped to spread the example of Love Canal. The idea of the Superfund was to tax the chemical industry in order to provide federal aid in cleaning up toxic dump sites. The amount of funding finally arrived at was a totally inadequate $1.6 billion, but the law had unintended consequences. Among the compromises worked out to achieve its passage was a provision that Superfund money would be targeted toward at least some dump sites in every state. This simple political agreement meant that the problem of hazardous wastes was immediately recognized and legitimized in every part of the nation. Passage of the law meant that the issues raised at Love Canal had become fully national in scope. Moreover, if there was ever any thought that passage of the bill would calm the political waters and forestall the emergence of militant community protests like the one at Love Canal, that possibility was smothered by the delays and sweetheart deals that characterized the Reagan administration's handling of the Superfund. The scandals which resulted in the EPA firings and resignations in 1983 revealed to community people throughout the country how little they could trust their government. With or without the Superfund, they would have to continue their protests and struggle if their lives were ever to be free of exposure to toxic chemicals.

In fact, Love Canal has been more or less the model for the anti-toxics movement that has arisen in the early 1980s. While targets and tactics have varied quite a bit from one area to another, the consistent theme has been local organizing around local threats. National environmental organizations have been much less important in the struggle than have ad hoc organizations of people concerned about their own communities. The new movement is emerging out of the activism of hundreds of community organizations and thousands of community leaders. Although statewide and even national coalitions are starting to be developed, it is at the local level that the movement's wellspring of anger and commitment is more obvious.

THE GRASS-ROOTS POLITICS OF THE MOVEMENT

The Matagorda County Citizens for Environmental Protection is a protest group formed in May of 1982 in Bay City, Texas. Bay City is a predominantly working-class city of some 11,000 inhabitants located along Texas's Colorado River. Local residents work either in local petrochemical companies or in fishing grounds off the Gulf Coast. The protest grew out of the concerns of neighbors near a site designated by Waste Management, Inc. for a hazardous waste landfill. Convinced that the site was ecologically unsound for maintaining a landfill and that landfills were simply too dangerous a solution to toxic chemical treatment, the citizens protested their concerns to state and local officials. Through petitions and telegram campaigns the group brought its concerns to the governor.

Some members of the group developed rather special skills at organizing graphic demonstrations at the site and at local government offices. These included the construction of a special float in last summer's local Rice Festival parade featuring men in gas masks picnicking alongside a smoking 55-gallon drum.

As the Matagorda Citizens group developed their research skills they also expanded their range of concerns. Research into Waste Management, Inc. soon revealed that other of the company's facilities had been cited for mishandling of wastes and that there were several suits pending against the firm. So incensed were members of the group over the company's unwillingness to communicate effectively that the group raised funds to fly one member to Alabama to testify against Waste Management's plans to construct a waste treatment center there. Most recently the group has developed alliances with other local community groups who are concerned about the practices of the quasi-governmental Gulf Coast Waste Disposal Authority, which operates in the Houston-Galveston area. These groups are now pushing a tightly drawn bill that would ban new hazardous waste projects within 100 miles of the Gulf of Mexico. As for Bay City, the most recent word is that Waste Management is reconsidering its option on the controversial site due to a reassessment of the potential market.

This Texas episode is illustrative of the nationwide anti-toxics movement in several respects. First, the use of a wide range of tactics was typical of efforts elsewhere. Just as residents of Warren County, North Carolina, used letter-writing campaigns and lawsuits along with illegal sit-ins, the Matagorda County Citizens group used tactics that ranged from lobbying with the governor to demonstrations and a parade float. Another feature of the protest was that, while it started in response to a seemingly local problem, the protesters soon found a need to reach out to neighboring (and even out-of-state) communities in order to find allies and multiply their strength. Finally, the degree of support that the group obtained was striking, and is paralleled in countless other cases around the country.

The fight to clean up a hazardous waste treatment facility in Lowell, Massachusetts, presents a similar case. Lowell is the historical archetype of a working-class community, with a history of textile mills dating back a century and a half. The Ayer City neighborhood lies on the outskirts of town along the Merrimack River. It was here that the Silresim Chemical Corporation operated a hazardous waste treatment facility from 1971 until 1977, when it filed for bankruptcy. The state was left with responsibility for 21,000 rusting drums of hazardous waste on the site. While the state worked to clear the site, local neighbors learned that toxic chemicals had also leaked into the soil and water table. Through the local chapter of Massachusetts Fair Share, a statewide citizen action organization, the Ayer City community began to press for cleanup of the ground as well.

Fair Share staff members helped the residents to organize a neighborhood health survey, which revealed a surprising 50 percent miscarriage rate. Local officials were generally uncooperative and the state moved relatively slowly to address the underground contaminants. Seeing this, the citizens began to demand not only cleanup but a comprehensive health survey and a temporary evacuation while ground cleanup operations were conducted. Having identified a local bank as potentially culpable in the worst dumping, the citizens picketed the bank president's house and demanded cleanup compensation. Seizing on the governor's election campaign the residents organized a major neighborhood meeting with the governor where toxic chemical protest groups from around the state united in presenting their demands.

State officials responded to this pressure by contracting for a full health survey of the neighborhood and applying to the federal government for Superfund designation of the Silresim site. The Superfund designation only shifted the focus of the Ayer City residents, and in February the group staged a surprise sit-in at the regional Environmental Protection Agency office. The issue remains stalled at the moment until the results of the health survey are released and a decision is made on the evacuation.

The protest at Lowell employed direct confrontation and civil disobedience tactics. The role of Massachusetts Fair Share was significant not only in providing technical assistance and organizer support, but also in linking the Ayer City neighbors to residents of other communities where toxic chemicals were a health hazard. The unity of groups proved a much more effective political force than possible with a single organization.

The fight in Lowell over the Silresim dumpsite involved an issue similar to the one at Love Canal: leakage from an abandoned disposal site. Perhaps this is the kind of circumstance that is most often associated with the anti-toxics movement. It might be easy to conclude that the problem is simply a lag in disposal techniques: that the sites causing the problems are the ones that were built before companies had enough knowledge of how to handle toxic wastes. But this conclusion would be very misleading. The Matagordo County, Texas, struggle described above is an example of people having to organize to defend themselves against a poorly conceived *new* dump site. There have been many such struggles around the country. And a great many other protest movements have arisen against facilities that are currently in operation. Neighborhood concern arises when poor construction or poor management allows leaks, discharges, or even fires and explosions. Perhaps the most spectacular was a night-long conflagration at an Elizabeth, New Jersey, chemical waste facility that sent thousands of gallons of toxic chemicals into the air breathed by residents of nearby neighborhoods. Thus, it needs to be emphasized that the anti-toxics movement is not directed simply at the residues of improper dumping practices that are now behind us. The problems are ongoing, and they are continuing to generate new local insurgencies.

The pattern of these local protest movements is different from what can be called "mainstream" environmentalism, defined by the large national organizations. Even as the movement had mushroomed in the late 1960s and early 1970s, its predominantly middle-class composition had remained apparent. Small attention was paid to the specific environmental issue of inner-city neighborhoods ("urban problems") or workplaces ("labor problems"). These issues were given nothing more than lip service, and usually not even that. Even in relation to the maintenance of outdoor recreational resources, there was often an element of implicit class conflict. Working-class interest in the outdoors was seen by many upper-middle-class environmentalists as consisting of trailer caravans, dirt bikes, speedboats, and wildlife hunting, and considered an embarrassment. Even as environmental issues were highly popular among all classes of society, there were real obstacles to cross-class participation in environmentalism as an organized movement.

At the same time, the legislative victories won by environmentalism, as they became embodied in well-funded federal and state bureaucracies, carried with them the danger of a diminution in popular participation. By the middle of the 1970s many thousands of public officials, many of them drawn from the ranks of environmentalist groups, were employed in researching and regulating environmental problems. Almost inevitably there was a cooling down in the rhetoric and militancy of environmental advocacy, a tendency for environmentalism to be seen as a technical problem that could be solved with the right adjustment of competing interests.

In contrast, the new anti-toxics movement has grown up very largely among "outsiders" in society: working-class and other lower-income people who would feel out of place at a meeting of a typical chapter of, say, the Audubon Society or the Sierra Club. And the new movement has had an urgency and immediacy that has little patience for the slow workings of governmental bureaucracies. Casting environmental issues in terms of personal health has proved to be a powerful stimulus to social action, especially when the health hazards are identifiable and close at hand.

WORKPLACE AND COMMUNITY

In urban areas, community-based protests have often been a surrogate for struggles at the workplace. That is, the hazards that are opposed are sometimes a threat first and foremost to the workers at the plant which is producing the toxics in the first place. Yet it is in the community that the struggle has taken place. It is important to understand why this is so, and to see the significance of city- and statewide "right to know" laws in that context.

The most obvious reason for the community focus is that workers in a plant are inhibited from speaking out against working conditions. It is not just a matter of individuals being subject to company harassment, but there is the constant threat that if the company is forced to make costly repairs it will "have to" close the plant. This form of corporate blackmail has often proved effective, not only against union demands but against environmental regulations as well.

Added to the threat of job loss, lack of political resources makes it hard to organize around health and safety protections in the context of a single plant. The help that should be readily available from the federal government, in the form of tough national standards that were supposed to be established and enforced by the Labor Department under the Occupational Safety and Health Act of 1970, has rarely been available. It is also hard for most unions to give help in this area. Not only are major unions on the defensive right now, but there is often a built-in cynicism among workers as to how much unions can really change the conditions of work. The feeling often is that the workplace cannot really be changed — that the only recourse is to struggle for higher wages as a compensation for accepting hazards.

In contrast, when a hazard is found to be threatening a neighborhood or town, a different dynamic is set in motion. Concerns about family health and the health of future babies come immediately to the forefront. The leadership of women, often difficult in workplace situations, is a natural occurrence in a neighborhood setting. Women are often the first to take action around suspicions of health risks, and the least ready to accept the assurances of company or governmental officials that everything is under control.

A final weakness in workplace-based organizing around hazards is that, especially among male workers, there is a tendency to deny the risks. In part it is fatalism in the face of economic dependency, in part it is sometimes a kind of machismo that is totally inappropriate when applied to the kind of dangers posed by microscopic chemical particles.

Lois Gibbs's special role as the most visible activist in the Love Canal neighborhood (and her more recent emergence as a national figure in supporting local grass-roots organizing) reveals a common pattern. Many women, like Ms. Gibbs, have had little political experience before they suddenly find themselves involved in organizing their neighborhood around highly emotional issues. Their concern about their family's health is typically the primary motivator, but it soon develops to anger and outrage as they find how little effectiveness they have in gaining quick and serious government response to their concerns. Freedom from the threat of job loss permits community residents to more quickly identify corporate culpability and more directly demand remediation and compensation. This freedom plus the predominance of women often leads corporate managers and government officials to view these new environmentalists as irrational and hysterical. Instead, the protest leaders tend to be quite hardheaded, highly focused, and persistent. The strength of their demands lies in the immediateness with which they feel that their lives are jeopardized by distant corporate managers who are more interested in profits than public health.

Thus, a community focus has often made possible a much stronger response to chemical hazards than would be possible in a strictly workplace setting. Some of the most farsighted leaders of the new movement, however, recognize the need to try to bring community and workplace together. In this regard, the push for "right to know" laws, requiring companies to disclose the toxic chemicals they are using both to their own workers and to community groups, is an important development. Not only do such laws hold the potential for workers and local residents to strengthen protections against chemical hazards, but the type of coalition that is developed in campaigning for the laws may strengthen the working-class composition of the anti-toxics movement.

The Delaware Valley Toxics Coalition was formed in 1979 in Philadelphia to coordinate neighborhood, health, environmental, and labor groups in advocating a worker and community right-to-know ordinance. That ordinance, which passed the city council in 1981 as the first in the nation, provided both community residents and workers with access to information about the toxic chemicals they are exposed to. Prior to 1981 such right-to-know campaigns had been labor-advocated and limited to providing workers alone with such information. Following the Philadelphia victory, efforts to achieve right-to-know legislation in other cities and states have followed the more comprehensive conception and involved broad-based community and labor alliance. In some cases, firefighters have played a key role, exploiting both the prestige attached to their jobs and their ties to local labor federations. In California, for example, unionized firefighters have been instrumental in the efforts of the newly formed Silicon Valley Toxics Coalition to have a model right-to-know ordinance passed by local governments in the San Jose area.

The fight for a statewide right-to-know law in Massachusetts, whose outcome is not yet clear, illustrates the interplay between workplace and community that is often involved. The campaign has been sponsored by the Massachusetts AFL-CIO, but from the start it has been shaped and supported by a coalition in which community-based groups have had a strong input. Some thirty organizations are in the coalition altogether. The bill was drafted carefully so that both union representatives and other qualified people designated by workers in a plant must be given access to company records having to do with the use of toxic chemicals. Community residents can get this same access by examining records sent by companies to local government offices.

The Massachusetts bill, despite overwhelming approval in the state senate, has been attacked fiercely by business groups, who have made it their number one political priority in state politics at the time being. Recognizing that a bill is likely to be passed in some form, they have tried to split the bill's supporters. But the coalition has stood firm in defending all provisions of the bill. Both union leaders and others in the coalition recognize the unique power of a coalition, and they are not about to give that power up. Regardless of the final fate of the Massachusetts bill, the support it has gathered shows the way in which workplace and community rights can be joined together.

FUTURE OF THE MOVEMENT

The consequences of hazardous and toxic chemical use and misuse will not be easily or quickly resolved. The proliferation of local community groups and the development of coalitions adds up to an emerging movement precisely because there will be no speedy or simple solutions. The conditions for the emergence of a movement are already set. Yet the effectiveness of such a movement remains questionable. There are formidable tasks ahead and some serious debates on programs and strategy.

Conceivably, the movement could be bought off by massive infusions of federal revenue for dumpsite cleanup and the development of safe treatment facilities. This is unlikely. The cleanup of these sites is both technologically difficult and highly costly. Estimates range from several million to hundreds of millions of dollars per site.

The movement could also be diverted by the attempts of governmental agencies to tie up the toxics issue in long bureaucratic processes and professional debates. There is a danger that the fervor of local organizing can be dissipated by an elaborate structure of "proper channels." To some extent, there is a possibility that the involvement of mainstream environmental groups can add to the problem, since they are often at home with scientific studies and with governmental labyrinths. Still, in a number of cases, the militancy and unorthodox tactics of local anti-toxics groups have forced governmental officials to cut through the red tape. Lawsuits and lobbying have been used as part of a range of tactics, and the immediacy of the movement has been preserved rather than lost.

A third danger is that the movement could succumb to excessive localism. "Put it anywhere but not in my backyard" could be a natural implicit theme of local protests. It is not inconceivable that an anti-toxic group in one town could support a state's effort to force an unwanted dumpsite onto another community in another corner of the state. To some extent, this danger has been counteracted in practice by the regional coalitions that have sprung up in the anti-toxics movement. More basically, however, there needs to be an expansion of current efforts to reduce the *production* of toxics in the first place. "Source reduction" is not new or untried: a few companies like the 3M Corporation have even used it systematically and found that it saves them money. But it has to be imposed on all firms by tough regulations, preferably at the national level. Estimates of the potential effects of source reduction range as high as an 80 percent alleviation of the flow of toxic wastes.

The central task in advancing the movement, however, must be broadening its base and strengthening its linkages with other parallel movements, in particular labor and public health. The opportunity to effectively link community, health, and workplace organizing around environmental issues must not be underestimated. It is not often that community and workplace issues are so obviously linked. Occupational health and safety, cancer and a multitude of environmentally dependent diseases are easily recognized by outraged community groups as similar issues. Where many of the local community organizations are from working-class neighborhoods, the ties to workplace and labor groups are sources of support and resources. The occupational health sections within the labor movement and the various COSH (Coalition for Occupational Safety and Health) groups are important allies. But the linkages must be broadened to the labor movement as a whole. Building unity between labor and community around environment and health issues serves to propel both movements. The power of the labor movement legitimizes and grounds community health issues, and community health struggles broaden the focus of labor advocacy toward addressing the full quality of life of working people. Issues of occupational disease and job development or reproductive hazards at work and family well-being at home can be raised as singular concerns. Such labor and community unity can link employment rights with civic rights and open opportunities for advancing democracy in both workplaces and neighborhoods.

Working together around the right to know, tightened toxic regulations, reducing toxins at the workplace, or liability issues permits community and worker organizations to build long-term campaigns. Well, they should. The toxic chemical problem will not be easily or readily resolved. Major changes are required in how industry produces products. The goal of these changes must be to fully wean industry of its reliance on chemicals that risk the health and lives of workers and community residents. Those changes will require a toughened struggle, for at the very heart of the changes are questions about who makes decisions about what products are produced and how. The rights of management, the rights of working people, and the rights of community residents must be reexamined, in a way that goes to the very core of our economic system.

CHAPTER 4

SHOULD THE DEATH PENALTY BE USED?

After a defendant has been processed through the court system, if convicted of a crime, she or he passes into the domain of our penal system. Traditionally these two systems have been distinct, and the personnel of each has jealously guarded their own prerogatives and their right to ignore the problems of the other domain. Courts have had a "hands-off" doctrine toward internal prison matters, and wardens and guards have been happy with this arrangement.[1] Two factors substantially reduced system segregation. In the first place, recidivism is a major problem for all of society. Statistics show that many convicted offenders are not deterred from further criminal acts by a served prison sentence. Conservatives argue that ex-convicts fall back into crime because they are criminals at heart and are incorrigible. Liberals believe that institutionalization contributes to the likelihood of future criminal acts, not only because it fosters dependency and infantilism, but also because it so stigmatizes an individual that reintegration into society is extremely difficult. Whatever the causes of recidivism, its existence is a testimony to the intimate relationship between the court and penal systems. Judges cannot expect to eliminate their problems or those of society by giving out sentences or indeed by not meting out sentences.

AN OVERVIEW OF CRIME AND PUNISHMENT

The criminal side of the law is concerned with the adjudication of those accused of violating specific criminal statutes. Crimes are offenses against the public interest, in contrast to civil law, which has to do with the private rights and duties of individuals. The American justice system separates the arrest, trial, and postconviction stages of criminal procedure. In general, the police and magistrates are solely responsible for the arrest stage, which includes the defendant's right to remain silent (under the Fifth Amendment) and the right to be free from unreasonable searches and seizures (under the Fourth Amendment). Similarly, during the trial stage the judge decides matters such as whether evidence is admissible against a defendant or whether an expert witness should be heard. Every criminal defendant has a trial by jury (under the Sixth Amendment). In practice, few defendants trigger this right because of plea bargaining. The accused will often plead guilty to a lesser included charge rather than face a long sentence for the greater charge. It is the role of the judge to accept or reject plea bargains. Judges have great discretion in deciding how to punish. Statutory guidelines allow judges to consider employment history, family ties, social status, the use of weapons, prior convictions, and other mitigating circumstances. Many judges have never even visited the correctional institutions to which they sentence prisoners. Generally, judges are extremely reluctant to supervise prison matters of any kind because they lack both the judicial resources and expertise to carry out the job. Judge Frank Johnson of the federal bench in Alabama is one of the few judges to place a prison under judicial administration. The vast majority of judges relegate prison administration to guards and wardens. Practically, there is little reform initiated by prison administrators, who often favor things as they are in order to safeguard their own prerogatives.

Few are satisfied with the American penal system. The simplest indicator of the failure of the prison system is the rate of recidivism. Recidivism is simply defined as the percentage of prisoners who continue with a life of crime after they have been convicted and punished for an earlier crime. Statistics place the recidivism rate as well over 60 percent in most jurisdictions. Whatever the cause of the high rate of recidivism, it is testimony to the utter failure of the criminal justice system. Conservatives, liberals, and radicals all agree that the American way of punishment is a disaster. As with all other social problems discussed in this book, ideology determines how crime and the penal system are viewed. Conservatives see criminals as the problem, not the criminal justice system. Conservatives argue that exconvicts are criminals at heart and will inevitably seek crime as a career. Punishment should therefore be swift, severe, and certain. Conservatives blame judges for paying too much attention to the Constitutional rights of criminals and not enough attention to the rights of victims. Liberals are concerned with issues of crime control, but are equally concerned with the Constitutional protection of the accused. Liberal lawyers and judges supported the expansion of criminal procedures promulgated by the Warren Court in the 1960s. Liberals are also likely to favor prison reform. Many liberals favor the decriminalization of victimless crimes, such as the possession of small quantities of recreational drugs. For other crimes, liberals favor measures short of prison, such as restitution and treatment, because they believe long sentences foster dependency and infantilism. Worse yet, prison is like a postgraduate school of crime. Young offenders can learn new skills such as safe-cracking and loan-sharking from experienced teachers with virtually unlimited time. Even if a prisoner has a desire to reform, a prison record "stigmatizes" an individual. The "excon" label may foreclose many employment opportunities. Radical criminologists agree with many liberal reforms but feel that they do not go far enough. Radicals see crime as inevitable. As computers and high technology displace production workers, the number of permanently unemployed increase. In the early 1980s minority youth unemployment ranged from 40 to 60 percent. Radicals argue that economic dislocation leads to criminal careers as young people perceive that they have no stake in the system. Radicals see Constitutional guarantees such as the Eighth Amendment ban on cruel and unusual punishment as precious little protection. Constitutional protections do little to create jobs, education, and legitimate avenues to success. To the radical, individual rights to a fair trial mystify the extent to which crime is a product of capitalism.

The death penalty controversy is an emblem of the role ideology plays in the formation of public policy. Before introducing the competing perspectives, it is useful to introduce some background on the purpose of punishment.

LeMar T. Empey suggests in *Alternatives to Incarceration* that theory of punishment has gone through three stages in this country: revenge, restraint, and rehabilitation; a fourth, reintegration, began in the 1960s. In the very early history of the United States, the state used corporal and capital punishment principally to avenge the victim of a crime. The concept of restraint came about when Dr. Benjamin Rush, a Pennsylvania Quaker, and his followers advocated imprisonment of offenders as a reform from corporal and capital punishment. The word *penitentiary* comes from the Quaker notion that a criminal could best be punished in an isolated cell where he or she could experience penitence. The "Auburn system" was devised in 1823 and included the confinement of prisoners in tiny individual cells at night and their congregate employment in fields, shops, or quarries during the day. Penal institutions as we know them today are modeled on the Auburn system because it was viewed as a relatively cheap form of restraint. Products made by prisoners and sold to the public provided revenue for the institutions.

With the advent of social science disciplines and Freudian psychology during the late 1800s, theory of punishment moved away from a purely custodial stance and embraced the idea that if inmates could be made more aware of themselves and the social milieu from which they came, they could be rehabilitated while in prison and return to society as law-abiding citizens. Educational and psychiatric facilities became available in some prisons. In recent years, with growing awareness of the recidivism problem, proponents of reform in punishment have advocated all-out efforts to reintegrate the ex-convict into society before release from prison. The most basic problem in any penal system is to rehabilitate prisoners while maintaining adequate security for wardens, guards, and citizens.

Today public attitudes toward punishment reflect all four theories (revenge, restraint, rehabilitation, and reintegration), and certainly ideology affects a person's position. Although people know that thousands of offenses are never prosecuted and that thousands of offenders are at large in society, people most fear those offenders who have been convicted of a crime. Harry Barnes and N. K. Teeters in *New Horizons in Criminology*, refer to this phenomenon as the *convict bogey*. People tend to be extremely anxious about convicts (as opposed to criminals in general) and are hesitant to endorse programs of rehabilitation and reintegration if they believe their security will be jeopardized.

This disparity between rehabilitation of the offender and protection of society is most visible in the current distinction between prison reform and correctional reform, which erupted in the 1970s. According to John D. Boone, a former commissioner of corrections in Massachusetts, *prison reform* means maintaining tolerable health and living conditions in prison. *Correctional reform*, on the other hand, involves less reliance on penal institutions per se and integration of the criminal within the community as much as possible. Widespread use of probation, parole, work-release, community-based education and training programs, and furloughs are correctional reform measures.

Many conservatives and liberals alike believe that the personnel of penal institutions must discriminate between dangerous and nondangerous criminals for purposes of rehabilitation. Although both conservatives and liberals differ on the particular mix of revenge, restraint, rehabilitation, and reintegration they prefer in punishment, most conservatives favor rehabilitation programs within prisons (prison reform); but liberals have traditionally argued that rehabilitation and institutionalization are mutually exclusive concepts and that efforts must be made from arrest through parole to keep as many offenders as possible in contact with their communities. Some radicals believe, for example, that criminal behavior is a symptom of economic inequality over which offenders have no control. Other radicals say that not only are criminals in many ways victims of society, but any contact with corrections personnel and other convicted offenders increases the likelihood that the offender will return to crime. In other words, the corrections system must divert the *maximum* number of persons away from incarceration altogether and into community-based treatment programs that can operate in lieu of penitentiaries.

During the 1970s, the strategy of reintegration of convicted persons into society, either by putting them on probation rather than incarcerating them or by allowing some contact with the community during imprisonment, encountered serious criticism. The issue was not whether the goal of treatment through various psychiatric and rehabilitative programs was worthwhile, but whether it had any effect. For better or worse, statistics that most concern Americans revolve around incidence of crime and the recidivism rate. Public concern over the rising crime rate had reached such proportions that some states were challenging the Supreme Court ruling that declared capital punishment unconstitutional because of the inconsistent way in which it was applied. Some states have circumvented this criticism by having a mandatory death sentence ascribed to particular statutes, but it is still possible for persons originally charged with the same crime to be convicted under different laws; thus the death penalty can be applied to some persons who engaged in a certain activity and not to others. In any event the tough line that the death sentence obviously represents has spread to other areas of the criminal justice system as well.

In theory punishment of offenders involves three social objectives: (1) protection of the community through isolation of the offender; (2) deterrence — (a) to deter the offender by making him or her aware that repetition of this action would be neither profitable nor comfortable and (b) to deter others who might be similarly inclined by showing that their payoff would be a negative one; (3) establishing usefulness and responsibility within the offender through remedial programs.[2] During the past two or three decades the notion of deterrence fell into considerable disrepute, and treatment of the offender through psychotherapy, widespread probation, educational and vocational training, transforming the offender's milieu into a supportive rather than a punitive one, and manipulation of sentences dominated the penal scene. Numerous studies have been done of the effectiveness of these various strategies, and when their ambivalent and somewhat negative findings have been viewed within the context of escalating crime rates, some criminologists have recently changed the focus from rehabilitation back to deterrence. There are a few criminologists who have literally reversed their positions over the past few years, and many former liberals have gotten on the bandwagon of backlash.

An overview of these studies indicates that no matter what the quality of the inmates in a prison or the rehabilitative programs offered in it, the rate of recidivism — rearrest and conviction — remains at about 50 percent. One of the most extensive studies was done by Lipton, Martinson, and Wilks, who concluded that some treatment programs are working to some extent, but these instances are isolated and lead to no clear pattern that might indicate the efficacy of any particular method of treatment.[3] No one knows exactly why the recidivism rate appears to be basically unaffected by a variety of rehabilitative approaches. Some people argue that these findings reflect a need for a more full-blown commitment to treatment as a strategy. Others who have chosen to view them as a sign of failure and misguided priorities suggest that the deterrent goal of punishment must be revitalized and reinforced with mandatory and lengthy sentences for an assortment of crimes.

What is at issue here is a conflict between the punitive and the treatment approach to corrections. The custodial staffs at prisons usually define their work as containing prisoners and protecting society. Underpinning these rationales is the unspoken mandate from society to assure a revengeful component as well. Americans may not speak in terms of an eye for an eye, but talk of compensating victims has frequently implied this motif. Prison staff members who are involved in treatment programs for inmates often see their roles in terms of promoting convicts' rehabilitation and may charge the custodial staffs with interfering with their work. Given the divergent goals and appropriate settings for carrying out the goals of each, this tense undercurrent may be inevitable. Today criticisms of penal policies touch on the question of whether or not treatment and punishment motifs are either compatible or humane.

Interestingly, conservative, liberal, and radical critics are arguing in some cases that the treatment or medical model of corrections is inhumane. The conservative position charges that a predetermined punishment for a certain offense, be it imprisonment for x number of years or even death, is a more rational and humane response to criminal behavior than the discretionary and indefinite implementation of rehabilitation programs. At least the offender knows what he or she is up against and why. When sentencing and/or parole decisions depend upon psychiatric reports and conformity to somewhat arbitrary and unspecified expectations among mental health personnel, an offender's fate remains a series of unknowns. According to this reasoning, neither society nor the offender gets a clear sense of vindication through a known price paid. And presumably if specific punishments are stated in advance, the rational citizen will weigh the pleasure of committing the offense against the pain of punishment and be deterred.[4] Whether or not a relationship exists between punishment certainty or severity and deterrence remains a contested issue.

Prior to 1950 few scientific studies were done to try to assess the deterrent effect of punishment. More recently both economists and sociologists have conducted studies. Although findings vary a good deal, even when factors known to affect the incidence of crime, such as a population's age distribution and levels of unemployment have been taken into consideration, there are some indications that punishment does deter crime. Studies have also been done to try to determine whether the severity of a sentence or the likelihood of its being imposed is more significant in deterring crime. More often than not researchers have found that the frequency with which a punishment is administered is of greater importance that its severity.[5] People who are advocating mandatory sentences are obviously incorporating the frequency component, and depending upon the length of the mandatory sentence, they may also be trying to control the severity factor as well.

The radical critique of a treatment approach to corrections extends to an assault on the decarceration trend more generally. Since individuals are often kept out of institutions or released early on the recommendation of "helping" personnel — social workers, psychiatrists, and psychologists — the treatment or medical model of deviance is implicated in the criticism of decarceration. According to Andrew Scull, as society's deviants (nonproductive members) went from being defined as *evil* to *sick*, medical and social caretakers played a major role in this redefinition so as to carve out a legitimized professional niche for themselves in tending to society's *sick* deviants — be they criminals, the mentally ill, the aged, or the poor. The latent function of the institutionalizing of deviants which occurred in the 1800s was the removal of nonproductive workers from the community as a severe example so that others would be deterred from avoiding work. Factory owners were thus major beneficiaries of institutionalization of deviants.[6]

Scull goes on to argue that the decarceration efforts launched in the 1960s were not so much motivated by humane concerns about institutionalization per se as by fiscal pressures on governments. And since these same governments had earlier subsidized the costs of capitalist production through social insurance programs (e.g., social security, workers' compensation, unemployment insurance), they (1) were in poor financial shape by the mid-sixties but (2) could use the existence of these programs to rationalize the dumping of deviants back into the community. Presumably former inmates would be assured a minimal income, no matter how ill equipped for survival on the outside they might be. And if some promised to be too threatening within their inner-city deviant ghettos, they could be managed with tranquilizers — a medical tool that revolutionized society's control apparatus.

Although Scull's analysis involves the decarceration of all state-financed inmate populations, it clearly raises questions about motives for wanting decarceration among convicted offenders in particular. Deinstitutionalization of prison inmates worries many citizens who fear victimization, and the process may represent no prize for offenders who have serious violent tendencies or personality disorders.

Liberals' response to criticisms of decarceration strategies, whether they come from radicals or conservatives, is to try and sort out the assets of custodial and treatment goals. Thus they may agree that treatment programs can be punitive rather than rehabilitative, but then ask why known violent offenders cannot be assigned to high-security prisons with little pretense of trying to reform them under such oppressive conditions. And why not develop well-funded rehabilitative programs for the vast majority of inmates, who are nonviolent and who are competent to handle flexibility within their environments — if they *choose* to participate? Liberals make a major distinction between using rehabilitative programs as a mandated and coercive "correctional" measure that is doomed to failure and providing vocational and psychotherapy programs only to those inmates who actively seek them.[7]

For those who see punishment as the goal of corrections and who propose greater protection of society through stiffer sentences, capital punishment has become a symbolic and real cause. The death penalty has been used by some states within the past few years after a long hiatus, and it remains a controversial legal and moral issue. No doubt the debate was intensified when convicted murderer Gary Gilmore requested that his execution be carried out, albeit possibly to suggest the seriousness of having the penalty available in the first place. Many issues surround the controversy — not least of which is the purpose of punishment in America today. Do we in fact want revenge in taking a life for a life? Is our purpose to assure that the condemned person never perpetrates the crimes again? Although we are a secular society, can we address the subject of capital punishment without reference to moral beliefs?

Ernest van den Haag presents some of the classic arguments in favor of capital punishment in "The Death Penalty: Arguments For." He is a highly respected spokesperson for the conservative perspective on many social issues. Note that he draws upon both consensus and labeling theories to some degree in suggesting that the death penalty is a forceful weapon because it symbolizes total expulsion from the community. From a consensus viewpoint, society is bound together by shared norms (including laws), and van den Haag's assumption that potential/convicted offenders are influenced by threat of expulsion implies a reliance upon community for meanings even among deviants. And to the extent that labeled deviants can follow a career path that leads to greater and greater isolation from the dominant society, the labeling of someone as a *condemned killer* leads to social isolation par excellence — death.

David Hoekema addresses some of the arguments made by van den Haag in "Capital Punishment: The Question of Justification," but he essentially disagrees on several points. This article reflects the liberal's concern with unequal application of the law and argues that the death penalty is too serious a weapon to have available for human error and prejudices. The author also raises moral questions about the taking of one life permitting the taking of another.

Notice how the treatment versus punishment debate that has arisen among conservatives, liberals, and radicals — though with different emphases — over the past few years informs both these selections on the death penalty. An issue that liberals and radicals wanted to believe was off the political agenda — the feasibility of employing capital punishment — has been reintroduced as a necessary subject for debate.

References

1. David J. Rothman, "You Can't Reform the Bastille, *The Nation*, March 19, 1973, p. 365.
2. Walter Evans and Frank S. Gilbert, Jr. "The Sentencing Process: Better Methods Are Available," *Federal Probation*, December 1975, p. 30.

3. Robert Martinson, "What Works? — Questions and Answers About Prison Reform," *The Public Interest*, no. 35 (Spring 1974), p. 49.

4. This kind of reasoning reflects a legalistic or classical perspective on crime causation and is most often associated with Cesar Beccaria's *On Crimes and Punishments*, published in 1764.

5. Gordon Tulluck, "Does Punishment Deter Crime?" *The Public Interest*, no. 36 (Summer 1974), pp. 107–8.

6. For the complete development of the thesis presented here, see Andrew T. Scull, *Decarceration: Community Treatment and the Deviant — a Radical View* (Englewood Cliffs, N.J.: Prentice-Hall, 1977).

7. Norval Morris, *The Future of Imprisonment* (Chicago: University of Chicago Press, 1974).

9. THE DEATH PENALTY: ARGUMENTS FOR

Ernest van den Haag

THE PROBLEM

Rehabilitation, concerned with the convicts's conduct after his release, is irrelevant to the death penalty since the convict is not released. And although helpful, death ordinarily is not indispensable for incapacitation. That leaves but one moral and one utilitarian justification for the death penalty. Moral: death may be required, or at least permitted, by considerations of justice; utilitarian: capital punishment may be a more effective deterrent than the alternatives.

TOO SEVERE?

Most people believe that death is a more severe punishment than the usual alternative, life imprisonment. A minority, including Prof. Jacques Barzun (and, therefore, a weighty minority), do not share that belief; some claim that they would rather die than live in prison. However, those actually confronted with the choice have usually preferred life in prison — unwisely, perhaps, but it is hard to argue with them. Fortunately, the question need not be answered. One may advocate death because it is kinder than life in prison, or because it is not. One may also oppose it for either reason. (Prof. Barzun advocates it because he regards death as more humane than prison.)

Most abolitionists regard the death penalty as too severe, and I shall focus on their arguments. Humanitarians object on grounds of justice, or "humanity": to put a man to death deliberately is sometimes unjust but always morally wrong and "inhumane," they feel. Utilitarians (who may be humanitarians as well) claim that imprisonment, lifelong if necessary, would be at least as effective a deterrent as death, which, since it is not required for any useful purpose, is cruel.

THE ONLY THREAT AVAILABLE

It is always difficult is know how many crimes are not committed because of a threat. But it can be shown logically that the death penalty is the only threat that could (could, not necessarily will) deter members of three groups.

1. Convicts already serving a life term are incapacitated insofar as the world beyond prison walls is concerned, but are left quite capable of committing

crimes within. Such crimes are frequent. Without the death penalty, these conflicts are immune to threats of further punishment. It seems unwise to grant convicted criminals this heady immunity not available to non-convicts, who are less dangerous. The federal prison system currently has custody of an offender who, since being confined for murder, has committed three additional murders on three separate occasions while in prison. The following item appeared in *Newsweek*. . . :

Two hard-case inmates apparently wangled their way into the warden's offices and stabbed the warden and his deputy to death with sharpened mess-hall knives.

. . . investigators said that the death mission had been specifically ordered the night before at a meeting of Muslim inmates because Fromhold had resisted their demands "once too often." Fromhold was stabbed thirteen times in the back and chest; Warden Patrick Curran, 47, who dashed into his deputy's first-floor office, was stabbed three times in the back.

Neither inmate had much to lose. Burton was doing life in the cold-blooded execution of a Philadelphia police sergeant, and Bowen was awaiting trial in another cop-killing and the shooting of an elderly couple.

Ways could be found to deprive these inmates of nearly all capacity to harm each other, or the prison personnel. But to achieve this, prisons would have to become truly inhumane. Convicts would have to be permanently chained or isolated. If rehabilitation, or merely decent treatment, is to be attempted, if prisons are to do anything other than to incapacitate inmates totally, the threats of the law are needed to control those who still might commit crimes, including murder. The death penalty is the only threat that could restrain those already serving life terms from further homicides.

2. Without the death penalty, those already threatened with a life term for kidnapping, skyjacking, or murder, but not yet apprehended, have no reason to refrain from additional crimes. They may murder third persons or the kidnap victim. Above all, they will be able to kill the arresting officer with impunity. This won't make the policeman's job easier. The effective impunity granted for additional crimes to suspects already threatened with a life term invites them to murder the officers trying to apprehend them.

   Logically, as long as there are fewer degrees of punishment than of crime, even the threat of the death penalty would not have a restraining effect on *all* further crimes. Once the first kidnap victim had been killed, murdering the second could bring no additional penalty — one can die but once. But, because of the threat of execution, the first victim might never be killed. And if there is some discretion in sentencing, criminals threatened by the death penalty may feel that further murders worsen their situation and that the killing of police officers ensures their own death.

3. Prospective spies in wartime, or violent revolutionaries in acute situations when there is a present danger of the government being overthrown, can be restrained, if at all, only by the death penalty. They believe that they will be released from prison when their side wins. They may even expect a reward. In an acute situation only the threat of an irrevocable penalty could effectively deter them.

Unlike imprisonment, death cannot be revoked; it may cause the expected victory to come too late.

THE DETERRENT EFFECT OF IRREVOCABILITY

Turn now from logic to emotion, to the expectations people are likely to have. Irrevocability probably makes the death penalty more deterrent than life imprisonment. For, however unfounded or irrational, the hope of revocation inheres in all revocable penalties because the possibility does. Even if revocation is *de jure* excluded and the chance remote, a revocable penalty is always less deterrent than an irrevocable one because of the *de facto* "animal faith" that leaves us only with death: "where there is life there is hope." Anyone, if at all deterrable, is more deterred by the threat of death than by the threat of life imprisonment, which can be revoked and usually is. Only death is irrevocable.

ADDITIONAL SOURCES OF FEAR

Unlike prison, death is not known: we have reports on dying but not on being dead. Most people are unable to imagine their own end and fear it more than anything. The intensive fear of the death penalty — suggested *inter alia* by the agitation for abolishing it — in part is fear of the unknown. It also springs from confusion: death is attributed to the penalty as though it caused an otherwise avoidable event. Yet, unlike a prison sentence, the death penalty does not take from us what we otherwise would keep: people not legally deprived of freedom are free, but people not legally deprived of life still die. A death sentence but hastens and sets a date certain for what must happen to all of us. Yet the fear that has death as its original object is displaced to become fear of the penalty that quickens it, as though certain death itself could have been eluded had there been no death sentence.

Since we often hurry death, or risk doing so, by hazardous actions — or by ordinary habits such as smoking — the fear of the death penalty strictly speaking cannot be fear that death will come sooner. That fear does not restrain people from smoking. Nor can the fear be produced by expectations of pain: execution is no more painful than natural death and in most cases probably less so; at least the pain does not last as long as natural pain often does. Much of the fear of the death penalty and of its deterrent effect probably spring[s] from heightened awareness, from the confrontation with an implacable certainty.

Another source of fear may be more important. To be put to death because one's fellow humans find one unworthy to live is a very different thing from reaching the end of one's journey naturally, as all men must. To be condemned, expelled from life by one's fellows, makes death not a natural event or a misfortune but a stigma of final rejection. The knowledge that one has been found too odious to live is bound to produce immense anxiety. Threatened by disease or danger, we usually feel that death is in an indecent hurry to overtake us. We appeal to friends and physicians to save us, to help delay it, and we expect a comforting response. Death is the common enemy, and it calls forth human solidarity. Not for the condemned man. He is pushed across by the rest of us. To die by the inscrutable decree of higher powers — somehow necessary and, perhaps, benevolent, but at any rate addressed to all of us — is one thing. To be singled out as too loathsome, as unfit to live, by the solemn judgment of one's fellow men is the most desolating of rejections.

THE SYMBOLIC MEANING OF ABOLITION

The degree to which penalties stigmatize crime and criminals as hateful depends not only on the social climate in which punishment takes place but also on the penalties themselves: as these become milder, crimes appear less odious and criminals are less ostracized. Traditionally, death has been the expected penalty for murder. The *lex talionis* has psychological plausibility: we expect outraged nature to strike back, to be done to us as we have done to others. That expectation — and its deterrent effect — ultimately ceases when it is no longer met. Social traditions, beliefs, customs, expectations, and fears may linger on long after the circumstances that gave rise to them have changed, long after they are rationally justified. But not forever.

No matter what can be said for abolition of the death penalty, it will be perceived symbolically as a loss of nerve: social authority no longer is willing to pass an irrevocable judgment on anyone. Murder is no longer thought grave enough to take the murderer's life, no longer horrendous enough to deserve so fearfully irrevocable a punishment. When murder no longer forfeits the murderer's life (though it will interfere with his freedom), respect for life itself is diminished, as the price for taking it is. Life becomes cheaper as we become kinder to those who wantonly take it. The responsibility we avoid is indeed hard to bear. Can we sit in judgment and find that anyone is so irredeemably wicked that he does not deserve to live? Many of us no longer believe in evil, only in error or accident. How can one execute a murderer if one believes that he became one only by error or accident and is not to blame? Yet if life is to be valued and secured, it must be known that anyone who takes the life of another forfeits his own.

THE BURDEN OF PROOF

Does the death penalty actually deter more persons, or deter them more effectively, than other punishments? If so, does the added deterrence warrant the added severity?

The general idea of the penal system is that, all other things being equal, the more severe the penalties the more deterrent they are. Higher penalties for drunken driving, rape, or theft deter more than lower ones. This much is borne out by everyday experience and by statistical demonstrations. Death is perceived as the most severe penalty. The claim that it does not add to deterrence runs counter, then, to the known general relationship between severity and deterrence. This does not disprove the claim; the death penalty could be an exception. But those who feel that it is must bear the burden of proof by showing that diminishing returns (of deterrence) set in as severity is added and that marginal returns are reduced to zero as the death penalty is reached.

So far we do not know if and where diminishing returns set in and reach zero as severity is added. No way has been found as yet to determine the exact amount of the marginal (added) deterrence produced for each crime by a specific amount of added severity. The elasticity of the supply of crime — its response to different negative prices (cost) — may vary; each crime may have a specific elasticity of supply. The response of prospective drug addicts to an increase of the average penalty may differ from that of prospective burglars to the same increase. The supply of some kinds of murder, such as murder by professionals and murder in the course of robberies, may be highly elastic; such murders may be much more deterred by the death penalty (by a very high cost) than murder in the course of intrafamilial disputes. (There are good grounds for suggesting as much but little evidence to prove or disprove it.)

Our ignorance of elasticities and of the points where diminishing or zero returns set in extends to all penalties. There is no evidence to show that ten years of prison deter 100 percent more people, or deter them 100 percent more effectively, than five years. Possibly, if we prolong the penalty to fifteen years, the last five years add zero deterrence. Possibly not. No study has established the degree of marginal deterrence by comparing states that impose five years with states that impose ten years of prison for the same crime, or states before and after abolition of the ten-year penalty, or states before and after reinstatement. Proof of added deterrence is not demanded for any other penalty. It is deemed necessary for the death penalty, and the (alleged) lack of proof of marginal deterrence is the most common argument for abolition. . . .

FACTORS THAT INFLUENCE THE CAPITAL CRIMES RATE

It would be a mistake to relate the frequency of marriages exclusively to legal costs and economic benefits. So with crimes. There are historical, moral, psychological, and cultural variables that affect marriage and crime, and they cannot be reduced to costs and benefits. Crime rates, therefore, can change independently of changes in penalties: the threat of legal punishment is only one current in a stream of motivations and nonpenal factors such as opportunities, customs, or stimuli, which contribute to crime rates, as they do, *mutatis mutandis*, to other social actions. The rates at which fiction, sociology textbooks, vitamin C, or pantyhose are produced all depend not only on cost-benefit ratios but also on motivation, opportunity, fashion, etc. There is no doubt, however, that higher costs, e.g., via taxation, do reduce the rate at which anything is produced. The degree of reduction depends on the elasticity of the supply. Changes in costs (penalties) are as likely to influence the supply of crime—including murder—as they are to influence the supply of anything else.

10. CAPITAL PUNISHMENT: THE QUESTION OF JUSTIFICATION

David Hoekema

In 1810 a bill introduced in the British Parliament sought to abolish capital punishment for the offense of stealing five shillings or more from a shop. Judges and
magistrates unanimously opposed the measure. In the House of Lords, the chief
justice of the King's Bench, Lord Ellenborough, predicted that the next step would
be abolition of the death penalty for stealing five shillings from a house; thereafter
no one could "trust himself for an hour without the most alarming apprehension
that, on his return, every vestige of his property [would] be swept away by the
hardened robber." . . .

During the same year Parliament abolished the death penalty for picking pockets,
but more than 200 crimes remained punishable by death. Each year in Great Britain
more than 2000 persons were being sentenced to die though only a small number
of these sentences were actually carried out.

In this regard as in many others, the laws of the English colonies in North America
were much less harsh than those of the mother country. At the time of the Revolution,
statutes in most of the colonies prescribed hanging for about a dozen offenses —
among them murder, treason, piracy, arson, rape, robbery, burglary, sodomy and
(in some cases) counterfeiting, horse theft, and slave rebellion. But by the early
nineteenth century a movement to abolish the death penalty was gaining strength.

The idea was hardly new: czarist Russia had eliminated the death penalty on
religious grounds in the eleventh century. In the United States the movement had
been launched by Benjamin Rush in the eighteenth century, with the support of
such older distinguished citizens of Philadelphia as Benjamin Franklin and Attorney
General William Bradford. By the 1830s, bills calling for abolition of capital
punishment were being regularly introduced, and defeated, in several state legislatures. In 1846 Michigan voted effectively to abolish the death penalty — the first
English-speaking jurisdiction in the world to do so.

In the years since, twelve states have abolished capital punishment entirely.
Although statutes still in effect in some states permit the death penalty to be imposed
for a variety of offenses — ranging from statutory rape to desecration of a grave
to causing death in a duel — murder is virtually the only crime for which it has
been recently employed. There are about 400 persons in U.S. prisons under sentence
of death, but only [two executions have] been carried out in this country in the last
eleven years.

However, the issue of whether capital punishment is justifiable is by no means settled. Since the Supreme Court, in the case of *Furman* v. *Georgia* in 1972, invalidated most existing laws permitting capital punishment, several states have enacted new legislation designed to meet the Court's objections to the Georgia law. And recent public-opinion surveys indicate that a large number, possibly a majority, of Americans favor imposing the death penalty for some crimes. But let us ask the ethical question: Ought governments put to death persons convicted of certain crimes?

First, let us look at grounds on which capital punishment is defended. Most prominent is the argument from *deterrence*. Capital punishment, it is asserted, is necessary to deter potential criminals. Murderers must be executed so that the lives of potential murder victims may be spared.

Two assertions are closely linked here. First, it is said that convicted murderers must be put to death in order to protect the rest of us against those individuals who might kill others if they were at large. This argument, based not strictly on deterrence but on incapacitation of known offenders, is inconclusive, since there are other effective means of protecting the innocent against convicted murders — for example, imprisonment of murderers for life in high-security institutions.

Second, it is said that the example of capital punishment is needed to deter those who would otherwise commit murder. Knowledge that a crime is punishable by death will give the potential criminal pause. This second argument rests on the assumption that capital punishment does in fact reduce the incidence of capital crimes — a presupposition that must be tested against the evidence. Surprisingly, none of the available empirical data shows any significant correlation between the existence or use of the death penalty and the incidence of capital crimes.

When studies have compared the homicide rates for the past fifty years in states that employ the death penalty and in adjoining states that have abolished it, the numbers have in every case been quite similar; the death penalty has had no discernible effect on homicide rates. Further, the shorter-term effects of capital punishment have been studied by examining the daily number of homicides reported in California over a ten-year period to ascertain whether the execution of convicts reduce the number. Fewer homicides were reported on days immediately following an execution, but this reduction was matched by an increase in the number of homicides on the day of execution and the preceding day. Executions had no discernible effect on the weekly total of homicides. . . .

The available evidence, then, fails to support the claim that capital punishment deters capital crime. For this reason, I think, we may set aside the deterrence argument. But there is a stronger reason for rejecting the argument — one that has to do with the way in which supporters of that argument would have us treat persons.

Those who defend capital punishment on grounds of deterrence would have us take the lives of some — persons convicted of certain crimes — because doing so will discourage crime and thus protect others. But it is a grave moral wrong to treat one person in a way justified solely by the needs of others. To inflict harm on one person in order to serve the purposes of others is to use that person in an immoral and inhumane way, treating him or her not as a person with rights and responsibilities but as a means to other ends. The most serious flaw in the deterrence argument, therefore, is that it is the wrong *kind* of argument. The execution of criminals cannot be justified by the good which their deaths may do the rest of us.

A second argument of the death penalty maintains that some crimes, chief among them murder, *morally require* the punishment of death. In particular, Christians frequently support capital punishment by appeal to the Mosaic code, which required the death penalty for murder. "The law of capital punishment," one writer has concluded after reviewing relevant biblical passages, "must stand as a silent but powerful witness to the sacredness of God-given life." . . .

In the Mosaic code, it should be pointed out, there were many capital crimes besides murder. In the book of Deuteronomy, death is prescribed as the penalty for false prophecy, worship of foreign gods, kidnapping, adultery, deception by a bride concerning her virginity, and disobedience to parents. To this list the laws of the book of Exodus add witchcraft, sodomy, and striking or cursing a parent.

I doubt that there is much sentiment in favor of restoring the death penalty in the United States for such offenses. But if the laws of Old Testament Israel ought not to govern our treatment of, say, adultery, why should they govern the penalty for murder? To support capital punishment by an appeal to Old Testament law is to overlook the fact that the ancient theocratic state of Israel was in nearly every respect profoundly different from any modern secular state. For this reason, we cannot simply regard the Mosaic code as normative for the United States today.

But leaving aside reference to Mosaic law, let me state more strongly the argument we are examining. The death penalty, it may be urged, is the only just penalty for a crime such as murder; it is the only fair *retribution*. Stated thus, the argument at hand seems to be the right *kind* of argument for capital punishment. If capital punishment can be justified at all, it must be on the basis of the *seriousness of the offense* for which it is imposed. Retributive considerations *should* govern the punishment of individuals who violate the law, and chief among these considerations are the principle of proportionality between punishment and offense and the requirement that persons be punished only for acts for which they are truly responsible. I am not persuaded that retributive considerations are sufficient to set a particular penalty for a given offense, but I believe they do require that in comparative terms we visit more serious offenses with more severe punishment.

Therefore, the retributive argument seems the strongest one in support of capital punishment. We ought to deal with convicted offenders not as we want to, but as they deserve. And I am not certain that it is wrong to argue that a person who has deliberately killed another person deserves to die.

But even if this principle is valid, should the judicial branch of our governments be empowered to determine whether individuals deserve to die? Are our procedures for making laws and for determining guilt sufficiently reliable that we may entrust our lives to them? I shall return to this important question presently. But consider the following fact: During the years from 1930 to 1962, 466 persons were put to death for the crime of rape. Of these 399 were black. Can it seriously be maintained that our courts are administering the death penalty to all those and only those who deserve to die?

Two other arguments deserve brief mention. It has been argued that, even if the penalty of life imprisonment were acceptable on other grounds, our society could not reasonably be asked to pay the cost of maintaining convicted murderers in prisons for the remainder of their natural lives.

This argument overlooks the considerable costs of retaining the death penalty. Jury selection, conduct of the trial, and the appeals process become extremely time-consuming and elaborate when death is a possible penalty. On the other hand, prisons should not be as expensive as they are. At present those prisoners who work at all are working for absurdly low wages, frequently at menial and degrading tasks. Prisons should be reorganized to provide meaningful work for all able inmates; workers should be paid fair wages for their work and charged for their room and board. Such measures would sharply reduce the cost of prisons and make them more humane.

But these considerations — important as they are — have little relevance to the justification of capital punishment. We should not decide to kill convicted criminals only because it costs so much to keep them alive. The cost to society of imprisonment, large or small, cannot justify capital punishment.

Finally, defenders of capital punishment sometimes support their case by citing those convicted offenders — for example, Gary Gilmore — who have asked to be executed rather than be imprisoned. But this argument, too, is of little relevance. If some prisoners would prefer to die rather than be imprisoned, perhaps we should oblige them by permitting them to take their own lives. But this consideration has nothing to do with the question of whether we ought to impose the punishment of death on certain offenders, most of whom would prefer to live.

Let us turn now to the case *against* the death penalty. It is sometimes argued that capital punishment is unjustified because those guilty of crimes cannot help acting as they do: the environment, possibly interacting with inherited characteristics, causes some people to commit crimes. It is not moral culpability or choice that divides law-abiding citizens from criminals — so Clarence Darrow argued eloquently — but the accident of birth or social circumstances.

If determinism of this sort were valid, not only the death penalty but all forms of punishment would be unjustified. No one who is compelled by circumstances to act deserves to be punished. But there is little reason to adopt this bleak view of human action. Occasionally coercive threats compel a person to violate the law; and in such cases the individual is rightly excused from legal guilt. Circumstances of deprivation, hardship, and lack of education — unfortunately much more widely prevalent — break down the barriers, both moral and material, which deter many of us from breaking the law. They are grounds for exercising extreme caution and for showing mercy in the application of the law, but they are not the sole causes of crimes: they diminish but do not destroy the responsibility of the individual. The great majority of those who break the law do so deliberately, by choice and not as a result of causes beyond their control.

Second, the case against the death penalty is sometimes based on the view that the justification of punishment lies in the reform which it effects. Those who break the law, it is said, are ill, suffering either from psychological malfunction or from maladjustment to society. Our responsibility is to treat them, to cure them of their illness, so that they become able to function in socially acceptable ways. Death, obviously, cannot reform anyone.

Like the deterrence argument for capital punishment, this seems to be the wrong *kind* of argument. Punishment is punishment and treatment is treatment, and one must not be substituted for the other. Some persons who violate the law are, without doubt, mentally ill. It is unreasonable and inhumane to punish them for acts which they may not have realized they were doing; to put such a person to death would be an even more grievous wrong. In such cases treatment is called for.

But most persons who break the law are not mentally ill and do know what they are doing. We may not force them to undergo treatment in place of the legal penalty for their offenses. To confine them to mental institutions until those put in authority over them judge that they are cured of their criminal tendencies is far more cruel than to sentence them to a term of imprisonment. Voluntary programs of education or vocational training, which help prepare prisoners for noncriminal careers on release, should be made more widely available. But compulsory treatment for all offenders violates their integrity as persons; we need only look to the Soviet Union to see the abuses to which such a practice is liable.

Let us examine a third and stronger argument, a straightforward moral assertion: the state ought not to take life unnecessarily. For many reasons — among them the example which capital punishment sets, its effect on those who must carry out death sentences and, above all, its violation of a basic moral principle — the state ought not to kill people.

The counterclaim made by defenders of capital punishment is that in certain circumstances killing people is permissible and even required, and that capital punishment is one of those cases. If a terrorist is about to throw a bomb into a crowded theater, and a police officer is certain that there is no way to stop him except to kill him, the officer should of course kill the terrorist. In some cases of grave and immediate danger, let us grant, killing is justified.

But execution bears little resemblance to such cases. It involves the planned, deliberate killing of someone in custody who is not a present threat to human life or safety. Execution is not necessary to save the lives of future victims, since there are other means to secure that end.

Is there some vitally important purpose of the state or some fundamental right of persons which cannot be secured without executing convicts? I do not believe there is. And in the absence of any such compelling reason, the moral principle that it is wrong to kill people constitutes a powerful argument against capital punishment.

Of the arguments I have mentioned in favor of the death penalty, only one has considerable weight. That is the retributive argument that murder, as an extremely serious offense, requires a comparably severe punishment. Of the arguments so far examined against capital punishment, only one, the moral claim that killing is wrong, is, in my view, acceptable.

There is, however, another argument against the death penalty which I find compelling — that based on the imperfection of judicial procedure. In the case of *Furman* v. *Georgia*, the Supreme Court struck down existing legislation because of the arbitrariness with which some convicted offenders were executed and others spared. Laws enacted subsequently in several states have attempted to meet the Court's objection, either by making death mandatory for certain offenses or by drawing up standards which the trial jury must follow in deciding, after guilt has been established, whether the death penalty will be imposed in a particular case. But these revisions of the law diminish only slightly the discretion of the jury. When death is made the mandatory sentence for first-degree murder, the question of death or imprisonment becomes the question of whether to find the accused guilty as charged or guilty of a lesser offense, such a second-degree murder.

When standards are spelled out, the impression of greater precision is often only superficial. A recent Texas statute, for example, instructs the jury to impose a sentence of death only if it is established "beyond a reasonable doubt" that "there is a probability that the defendant would commit criminal acts of violence that would constitute a continuing threat to society." . . . Such a law does not remove discretion but only adds confusion.

At many other points in the judicial process, discretion rules, and arbitrary or incorrect decisions are possible. The prosecutor must decide whether to charge the accused with a capital crime, and whether to accept a plea of guilty to a lesser charge. (In most states it is impossible to plead guilty to a charge carrying a mandatory death sentence). The jury must determine whether the facts of the case as established by testimony in court fit the legal definition of the offense with which the defendant is charged — a definition likely to be complicated at best, incomprehensible at worst. From a mass of confusing and possibly conflicting testimony the jury must choose the most reliable. But evident liability can be deceptive: persons have been wrongly convicted of murder on the positive identification of eyewitnesses.

Jurors must also determine whether at the time of the crime the accused satisfied the legal definition of insanity. The most widely used definition — the McNaghten Rules formulated by the judges of the House of Lords in 1843 — states that a person is excused from criminal responsibility if at the time of his act he suffered from a defect of reason which arose from a disease of the mind and as a result of which he did not "know the nature and quality of his act," or "if he did know it . . . he did not know he was doing what was wrong." . . . Every word of this formula has been subject to legal controversy in interpretation, and it is unreasonable to expect that juries untrained in law will be able to apply it consistently and fairly. Even after sentencing, some offenders escape the death penalty as a result of appeals, other technical legal challenges, or executive clemency.

Because of all these opportunities for arbitrary decision, only a small number of those convicted of capital crimes are actually executed. It is hardly surprising that their selection has little to do with the character of their crimes but a great deal to do with the skill of their legal counsel. And the latter depends in large measure on how much money is available for the defense. Inevitably, the death penalty has been imposed most frequently on the poor, and in this country it has been imposed in disproportionate numbers on blacks.

To cite two examples in this regard: All those executed in Delaware between 1902 and the (temporary) abolition of the state's death penalty in 1958 were unskilled workers with limited education. Of 3860 persons executed in the United States between 1930 and the present, 2066, or 54 percent, were black. Although for a variety of reasons the per capita rate of conviction for most types of crime has been higher among the poor and the black, that alone cannot explain why a tenth of the population should account for more than half of those executed. Doubtless prejudice played a part. But no amount of goodwill and fair-mindedness can compensate for the disadvantage to those who cannot afford the highly skilled legal counsel needed to discern every loophole in the judicial process.

Even more worrisome than the discriminatory application of the death penalty is the possibility of mistaken conviction and its ghastly consequences. In a sense, any punishment wrongfully imposed is irrevocable, but none is so irrevocable as death. Although we cannot give back to a person mistakenly imprisoned the time spent or the self-respect lost, we can release and compensate him or her. But we cannot do anything for a person wrongfully executed. While we ought to minimize the opportunities for capricious or mistaken judgments throughout the legal system, we cannot hope for perfect success. There is no reason why our mistakes must be fatal.

Numerous cases of erroneous convictions in capital cases have been documented; several of those convicted were put to death before the error was discovered. However small their number, it is too large. So long as the death penalty exists, there are certain to be others, for every judicial procedure — however meticulous, however compassed about with safeguards — must be carried out by fallible human beings.

One erroneous execution is too many, because even lawful executions of the indisputably guilty serve no purpose. They are not justified by the need to protect the rest of us, since there are other means of restraining persons dangerous to society, and there is no evidence that executions deter the commission of crime. A wrongful execution is a grievous injustice that cannot be remedied after the fact. Even a legal and proper execution is a needless taking of human life. Even if one is sympathetic — as I am — to the claim that a murderer deserves to die, there are compelling reasons not to entrust the power to decide who shall die to the persons and procedures that constitute our judicial system.

CHAPTER 5

DO WE NEED A NEW MILITARY BUILDUP?

There is little doubt that relations have worsened between the United States and the Soviet Union in the 1980s. The 1980 Olympics in Moscow were boycotted by the United States to protest the Soviet invasion of Afghanistan. In September 1983, a Korean airliner was shot down over the Soviet Union; in October the United States invaded Grenada; and in November the United States placed Cruise and Pershing missiles in Europe. The Soviets boycotted the 1984 Olympics in Los Angeles. It is clear that there has been a continued deterioration of disarmament talks between the major powers throughout the mid-1980s. All these events derive much of their political significance from the Reagan administration's overall military strategic framework.

B. Bruce-Briggs's essay "A Catechism of Strategic Defense" answers dozens of questions on defense policy from a conservative's perspective. Conservatives on defense generally favor the Reagan administration's policies, such as new missile-defense systems based in the United States and new strategic nuclear weapons in Europe. They accept the feasibility of tactical nuclear war and believe that we can survive a first-strike offensive with the proper defense. Most conservatives would agree with Bruce-Briggs that we had better start adopting a new strategic outlook if we are to defend our homeland from a military attack. Bruce-Briggs contends that the Soviet threat of attack is growing and the need for an "active" defense is becoming urgent. He believes that we need a ballistic-missile defense (BMD) to protect us from Soviet missiles.

Andrew Winnick's article "Rapid Deployment and Nuclear War: Reagan's New Military Strategies" is a radical's guide to the strategic rationale that underlies the current administration's emphasis on the Soviet threat and the expansion of American military capacities. Winnick identifies three components in this military buildup. One component is an expanded and more effective means of intervening in Third World countries and blocking liberation movements or leftist governments. According to Winnick, events in Zimbabwe, Nicaragua, and Iran have each contributed to a sense of American military weakness. The Rapid Deployment Force is a military planner's solution to setbacks from progressive and nationalist forces in the Third World. The second strategic component of the current military buildup calls for creating a capacity to wage local wars using "tactical" nuclear weapons that can be fired by field artillery or aircraft. The third element involves expanding the United States' capacity to wage a "limited" nuclear war. The deployment of the Cruise and Pershing missiles is intended to contribute an ability to wage such a nuclear war. They are designed to enable the United States to have a "first-strike capacity" against the Soviet Union.

Winnick evaluates the impact of these developments on the American economy and concludes that we are weakened by Reagan's new military buildup.

Winnick argues that each new strategic component takes us closer to nuclear annihilation. Winnick states that we must resist a new military buildup because it is dangerously wrong and threatens our survival.

11. A CATECHISM OF STRATEGIC DEFENSE

B. Bruce-Briggs

What is strategic defense and why is it important?

Strategic defense is the defense of the homeland from military attack. The definition establishes its importance.

Why has the United States been paying such scant attention to strategic defense?

Fortunately, the United States historically has been able to downplay strategic defense. In the nineteenth century our major military investment was in coastal defense — forts at the entrances to every vital harbor. At the turn of the century, the United States became flush enough to afford a deep-water navy that could engage a potential attacker far out to sea, thus obviating the need for direct defense of the homeland. In the twentieth century, the United States adopted a strategy of resisting constructive enemies in Eurasia — Imperial Germany, Nazi Germany, the Soviet Union — before they could consolidate sufficient power to strike at America.

The forward-defense strategy will be required for the foreseeable future, so long as Soviet expansion in Eurasia menaces; it is against that threat that the great bulk of U.S. forces are deployed and a considerable alliance system has been erected.

Nonetheless, the threat of attack upon the homeland exists, and is rising, and therefore the need for strategic defense is growing.

What is the strategic threat to the American homeland?

Toward the middle of this century, extraordinarily deadly weapons were invented, together with the means to deliver them at the intercontinental ranges by vehicles that traverse the atmosphere. Lodgments on Eurasia, command of the seas, and coastal fortifications are worthless against attack by this weaponry.

Today the Soviet Union and the United States both have the means effectively to destroy any country in the world, including each other, in a few hours. The United Kingdom and France could do grave damage to any country. The People's Republic of China has that capability vis-à-vis its neighbors and soon it will have worldwide reach. Other countries will join the devastation club in the early twenty-first century. The prospect is bleak.

What has the United States been doing to counter this strategic threat?

Since 1950, the U.S. Government has spent roughly $200 billion (in 1984 dollars) on strategic defense — both active and passive defense.

What do active defense and passive defense mean?

These terms are current strategic jargon: Active defense blocks an attack before it hits its target; passive defense reduces the damage caused by an attack without harming the attacker.

What constitutes passive defense and how has the United States been using it?
Passive defense can be classified under these heads:

Augmentation — Add to the number of targets so that even a successful attack will destroy a smaller proportion of them. The United States did this until the mid-Sixties, by adding bombers and missiles, and then stopped. Recently there has been a return to augmentation by adding intermediate-range and cruise missiles.

Dispersion — Spread out potential targets so that fewer are damaged by individual enemy attacks. U.S. bomber and missile forces are thus dispersed, and there are certainly plans for wider dispersion in crisis and in war. Similarly, at least on paper, plans exist to disperse the civil population in crisis and in war by evacuation from the vicinity of prime targets.

Mobility — Move targets so that they cannot be as easily hit. This is standard practice for our bombers and sea-launched missiles.

Concealment — Hide targets so that the other side cannot easily find them. A good part of the U.S. strategic offensive force is hidden underwater on submarines.

Fortification — Place land-based missiles and certain communications links in heavily fortified bunkers ("hardened silos") to defend them against attack. The headquarters of the North American strategic defense command is buried deep under a Wyoming mountain. Bombers and communication equipment are "hardened" against radiation and other environmental effects of nuclear attack. Furthermore, the government has identified millions of places suitable as bunkers — "fallout shelters" — to protect civilians from most radiation effects of nuclear weapons.

Damage Control — Reduce secondary effects of attack — for example, by providing the treatment of wounds and the control of fires.

How does passive defense relate to civil defense?
Civil defense is the passive defense of the civil population, of industry, of the cities, of everything in the nation except military targets.

Note that most American passive defenses have been of the strategic offensive forces (SOF), to maintain what strategic jargon terms "credible second-strike capability"; that is, to convince a potential attacker that, whatever he does, some of our strategic forces will survive to strike back. It is generally held that this posture is desirable, so investments in the passive defense of strategic forces are as uncontroversial as any of these matters can be.

Purposive passive defense of nonstrategic military forces and of the civil population, economy, and society has been trivial. A modest program was started by President Truman; an attempt at serious expansion under President Kennedy came a cropper. Since that time civil defense has straggled along underfunded, undermanned, and with low morale.

Would passive defense save the nation from attack?
Passive defense of the strategic offensive forces may have already saved the nation by dissuading attack, but we cannot know without access to Soviet decision-making. We may doubt that the civil-defense effort has had any influence on Soviet policy.

Could passive defense save the nation if we were attacked?

That would depend upon the plan of the attack and other factors only roughly calculable. The earlier statement holds: Despite all efforts short of physically redesigning the nation to meet an attack — of fortifying the entire country by building deep blast shelters for people and industry — America could be effectively destroyed in a few hours if the Soviet leaders decided to do so. The effects on that enduring condition on national morale are beginning to sink in.

What kinds of defense are there?

Active defense is the destruction or deflection of incoming weapons. In strategic jargon, there is "point defense" of a single spot on the map, and "area defense" of many points at once. Area defense of cities is called "population defense." Defensive systems are also labeled "thick" and "thin." And active defense is classified according to what is being defended against — "air defense" against vehicles that fly in the air (bombers and guided/cruise missiles) and "ballistic-missile defense" (BMD) against weapons that fall from space.

What has the United States done about active defense?

An enormous amount. When the Soviet Union acquired atomic bombs and began to build a bomber fleet in the 1950s, the United States (together with Canada) constructed perhaps the most elaborate defensive system since the Great Wall of China. Three lines of radar were thrown across North America up to the Arctic Circle and out to sea on ships and offshore towers. Thousands of fighter interceptors, armed with nuclear missiles, were deployed. U.S. cities were ringed by anti-aircraft nuclear missiles at Nike sites. This system was linked together by an intricate communications net directed from the North American Air Defense (NORAD) headquarters under Cheyenne Mountain, Wyoming.

What happened to the air-defense system?

It was outrun by technology. The Soviets cut back their bomber commitment in favor of intercontinental ballistic missiles (ICBMs). Most of NORAD was shut down, because it seemed wasteful to spend so much money defending against bombers when missiles would arrive hours earlier to take out the radars and blind the system. A small air-defense apparatus survives, mostly Canadian and Air National Guard fighters, which is now being bolstered somewhat in anticipation of Soviet deployment of cruise missiles.

Does not the debacle of air defense demonstrate that a defense will be beaten by offensive improvements?

No. Soviet ICBMs were not a reaction to air defense, because they were under development before NORAD. Continental air defense may well have achieved all its objectives, because the best defense is the one that is not attacked.

What about ballistic-missile defense?'

An ICBM is shot up into space by a rocket and falls to earth in the ballistic trajectory described in freshman physics. Hardly were ballistic missiles invented when people tried to think of ways to counter them (one of the last jobs of the Rosenberg spy ring was to deliver early U.S. BMD research to the USSR). The problem has been characterized as that of "hitting a bullet with a bullet."

A BMD system has four related tasks: acquisition, or detecting the incoming missile; discrimination, or determining if the incoming object is a missile or decoy deployed to outfox you; interception, or getting something up to meet the missile; and destruction, or killing, deflecting, or disarming it.

How does BMD work?

The original U.S. BMD research followed the design of air defense. Ground-based radars would pick up the incoming object; ground-based computers would analyze its movement to calculate whether it acted like a real missile or like a decoy; the computers would tell the ground-based interceptor missile when to fire and in what direction, and would continue to give the interceptor orders by radio to put it on a collision course with the incoming missile. When the interceptor was as near to the target as possible, it would explode a nuclear weapon and hope to kill its prey.

Two systems were conceived: The first, an "exoatmospheric," or outside the atmosphere, system, had the advantages of an early intercept and of being able to kill by special nuclear munitions that could project radiation in space to burn the incoming missile at a considerable distance. Because they reach very high altitudes, exoatmospheric weapons can intercept many possible missile trajectories and are considered to be area-defense systems.

The "endoatmospheric," or inside the atmosphere, option had a late kill and required more accuracy, but discrimination was easier because decoys would mostly have been burned away by the atmosphere, or, if they were not, gravity and air resistance would make them fall in a path different from a real missile's. Because of the late kill closer to ground level, endoatmospheric intercepts are associated with point defense.

In the 1960s, BMD research had progressed to the point where deployment was under consideration. The system selected had both an exoatmospheric area-defense weapon and an endoatmospheric point-defense weapon. This produced what is called "layered defense," which takes advantage of the principle of multiple processing — if each layer kills 90 percent, then the first gets 90 percent, the second gets 90 percent of the remaining 10 percent, or 9 percent, and so forth.

Why not just deploy a single system that is 100 percent effective?

That would be a perfect defense, and perfection is an attribute of the Almighty, blasphemous to ascribe to mere man-made systems. It is startling that both advocates and opponents of strategic defense are ignorant (or pretend to be) of such an obvious article of doctrine. A perfect defense is impossible. What is possible and desirable is an effective defense.

What is an effective defense?

An effective defense makes attack more difficult, more costly, and more time-consuming, and therefore makes the defender safer by dissuading the enemy from attacking, reducing damage, and providing time to hit back at the enemy's strike forces. For example, any bank vault can be cracked with enough resources and time; bank vaults are built to dissuade safecrackers, not to defend deposits perfectly.

A defense must also be "cost-effective," in the sense of being a good investment of military dollars compared with other ways to spend money. Defensive costs should also have a favorable relationship to what it would cost the other side to overcome the defense; this is called the "cost-exchange ratio" in strategic jargon. A million-dollar defense that costs a billion dollars to penetrate is a good investment; the converse is not.

What does an effective defense achieve?

Not in any order of importance, an effective BMD can do the following:

1. Either a thick or a thin system can provide a highly credible area defense against small attacks
   (a) by lesser nuclear powers (e.g., China now, and possibly lots more in the twenty-first century).
   (b) launched accidentally (highly unlikely because of elaborate precautions, but not entirely impossible).
   (c) for purposes of demonstration or retaliation by a major power in crisis or war (these are much more likely than major attacks).
   (d) by errant ICBMs aimed at military targets that might stray toward the wrong target.
2. An area or a series of point defenses might slow down an attack on strategic offensive forces, thereby reducing the attacker's confidence in a quick victory and also permitting controlled use of nuclear weapons in prolonged nuclear war. Both of these, of course, dissuade conflict. Because our SOFs are his prime targets, here is where we surely must concentrate our defense.
3. A very thick defense might prevent national destruction from a mass genocidal attack. (Fortunately, this sort of attack is of no military value and commends itself only to the paranoid fantasies of idle housewives, professors, and clergy.)
4. Even poor BMD can prompt an adversary to maintain his offensive capability by spending money that he would otherwise use for other weapons. If our cost-exchange ratio is favorable, we are better off.

Achievement of any of these bolsters national security, and any effective BMD system will provide protection from more than one threat.

Can BMD eliminate fear of nuclear attack?

As a nation, we should fear national destruction by enemy attack, or by occupying forces after capitulation from fear of enemy attack, or after destruction of our strategic offensive forces. But as individuals, we most fear the destruction of ourselves, our family and friends, and our local environment. Because no defense is perfect, we cannot be sure that our home city will be successfully defended. It must be assumed that at least one missile in a serious attack will get through.

And ballistic-missile defense will not deal with other means of delivering nuclear weapons, poisons, and deadly bacteria — by aircraft (although BMD systems have anti-aircraft capability), by ship, or by mail (you can send a small nuclear explosive by parcel post).

What is the relationship between active and passive defense?

They are mutually substitutable and supplementary. An active defense that intercepts half the incoming missiles is equivalent to a passive defense that saves half the targets; within a fixed budget, the system chosen would depend on cost-effectiveness. But passive defense can also supplement active defense by providing another layer of defense.

BMD interacts nicely with civil defense. Thinning out the attack can reduce the civil-defense problem to "manageable" horrors.

What are the arguments against strategic defense?

The theoretical arguments against strategic defense were nicely summarized by the late strategist Herman Kahn, roughly like this:

1. It won't work, and will waste a lot of money.
2. It will work too well, driving the world into an arms race and encouraging aggressive behavior by national commanders.
3. Both

What are the objections to the objections to strategic defense?

The objectors concentrate their fire on the straw man of a perfect defense. As for the rest, the effectiveness can only be judged under attack, and the prime purpose of a defensive system is to dissuade attack. The costs can range from trivial to impossible.

That strategic defense would make the United States more belligerent is refuted by our lassitude today despite our wonderful defense against all nations that lack nuclear weapons. (The best defense remains the unarmament of others.) Further, the United States had such a defense against Soviet strategic attack in the early 1950s, and the United States was at that time markedly more anti-Communist and bellicose than today, yet was not aggressive against the USSR. (However, effective strategic defense might make the Soviets more aggressive.)

Moreover, the argument that strategic defense won't work nicely counters the argument that it will work too well. As pointed out by President Kennedy's BMD research boss, Charles M. Herzfeld, the other side will be dissuaded from attack because the defense might work, and we will be dissuaded from aggressiveness because the defense might not work. BMD opens up a window of uncertainty.

The claim that any defense can be overcome disregards the purposes of strategic defense listed above. The objection is founded upon an obsolete image of nuclear war as the smashing of cities. The only reason that cities were targeted earlier in the nuclear age is that the weaponry was clumsy and inaccurate. (The Nagasaki raid missed by five miles.) Modern weapons can be carefully controlled and directed against military targets, with priority given to strategic offensive forces — in the jargon, this constitutes "counterforce." Whatever uncertainties there are in BMD, no serious person doubts that the SOF can be defended long enough to launch in retaliation.

What is the relationship between strategic defense and deterrence?

"Deterrence" is the influencing of the behavior of others by threat of reprisal. "Defense" includes an ability to protect ourselves from his counteractions before, during, and after the execution of our threat. Obviously, our defense makes our threat more credible, and therefore reinforces deterrence.

(Considerable confusion has been engendered by the false identification of "deterrence" with mass attacks on Soviet cities. Actually, the ability to blow away Soviet cities is no deterrent to the harassment of U.S. diplomats, while our ability to harass their diplomats is a deterrent. The term should only be used in a context of what action is being deterred, and by whom.)

What about the arms-race implications of strategic defense?

"Arms race" is an unfortunate metaphor circulated by ignorant or cynical folk working to block improvements in weaponry, even those that improve security. Apart from the cost, a defensive arms race would be desirable. A race of offense against defense might or might not be desirable, depending on the particular circumstances, not simplistic metaphors.

Can defense eliminate the need for an offense?

Just as a safecracker could penetrate a bank vault with a hand drill if he had enough time, any defense eventually can be broken by a determined offense, so an offensive capability must be maintained to give the defense credibility.

Can we substitute assured defense for assured destruction?

Neither defense nor destruction can be assured, except by divinely perfect military systems. In particular, the inability to assuredly defend cities requires at least a reserve force to threaten reprisal in kind. Effective defenses greatly reduce the need to rely upon threats of reprisal for security, but do not eliminate them altogether.

With so many advantages, why has the United States no active BMD now?

That requires a quick history of ABM.

But first, what is the difference between ABM and BMD?

BMD is the generic term for all types of ballistic-missile defense. ABM was the particular anti-ballistic-missile system developed in the 1960s, officially christened "Sentinel" and "Safeguard," and the term is sometimes used for the contemporary Soviet system. Otherwise, BMD is preferred usage.

What happened to ABM?

In 1967 President Johnson and Defense Secretary McNamara ordered deployment of a thin ABM system. But when Mr. Nixon came to power, most of the Democrats turned against the ABM, and it was strangled in the domestic political wars between Tet and Watergate. Opponents used all the anti-strategic-defense arguments above, but what was certainly central was partisanship and anti-militarism festering from the frustration of the Indochina war. Support for ABM was weak for several reasons: The armed forces wanted the resources for other purposes; the Administration was desperate to cut spending in order to fight inflation; and even BMD advocates were less than enthusiastic about its capabilities — the radars were vulnerable to attack, the ground-to-interceptor communications were subject to confusion under conditions of nuclear combat, and the computers were clumsy and perhaps too slow. Some BMD supporters favored it merely to get a camel's nose in the tent; others opposed it because it would eat up money that could be better used for superior systems.

In the end, Messrs. Nixon and Kissinger bargained away ABM in the Strategic

Arms Limitation Treaty (SALT) of 1972. SALT I restricted the ABM deployments of both sides to two sites of one hundred launchers each. In 1974, this was cut back to one base each, and in 1976 the United States unilaterally shut down its last ABM base. But the radars remain and so do the missiles.

Why the revival of interest in active defense recently?

Political — There has been a great national reawakening of concern about defense in general, effectively exploited by the most vigorous elements of the Republican Party.

Factional — The defeat of ABM left an implacable hardcore BMD underground — in the weapons labs (Livermore, Los Alamos, Oak Ridge), in "think-tanks" (Stanford Research Institute, Institute for Defense Analyses, Hudson Institute), and among Young Turk congressional staff advisors to conservative Republicans and the shrinking band of liberal Democratic hawks — which proselytized tirelessly.

Technological — This is the most important reason. In the twentieth century, technology drives strategy. During the 1970s the Soviet Union greatly improved the accuracy of its ICBM force, increasingly threatening our land-based ICBMs, and passive defenses looked less adequate. The futile search for a plausible basing scheme (i.e., passive defense) for the MX missile led necessarily to reconsideration of active defense.

Meanwhile, technology has swept on. Four developments completely changed the ballistic-missile-defense equation:

1. The capacity, speed, and compactness of today's computers make the 1960s equipment look antediluvian. Now the computers can be put on the missiles, which can thus find their way to the targets without relying upon interruptable radio links.

2. We have better sensors today than in the Sixties. Radars can now look over the horizon. And the last generation has seen the evolution of infra-red sensors that can detect and report the heat of a rocket engine or other trail of heat caused by the friction of a missile hurtling through the atmosphere. Infra-red sensors are much less easily jammed or fooled than radar.

   Together, the computers and sensors vastly improve the chances of endoatmospheric intercepts, and the upgraded accuracy and reliability make a non-nuclear kill by high explosives or even direct impact ("kinetic") a practical possibility. (Not that anyone minds using nukes to kill nukes, but having lots of bombs bursting complicates the defense.) However, infra-red is blocked by clouds, so the sensors must be in the stratosphere, or higher.

3. While ABM was being developed, the world was astounded when the USSR put a grapefruit-sized object in orbit. Now tons easily go into space, and the cost is rapidly dropping. We already have orbiting ICBM launch detection, which spots the plume of the rocket coming up, and we can anticipate space-based BMD that can kill missiles during their slow, visible, and vulnerable boost phase.

4. The last generation as also experienced the swift development of directed-energy technology. Instead of using energy to propel a missile at another

missile, we can now think of directing the energy itself — at the speed of light — to burn or mangle the missile with lasers, particle beams, or even the focusing of radiation from nuclear reactions.

These last two lead to the concept of space-based anti-missile battle stations — the well-publicized "star wars."

Wouldn't that lead the arms race into space?

The German V-2 ballistic missile led the arms race into space in 1944. Can't think of a better place for the arms race than space, and can't imagine a better nuclear war than one where no one gets hurt.

Could not an enemy attack these space systems?

Probably, but they can also probably be defended, and if they cannot, think of them as a screen that gives warning of the attack, forces the enemy to waste weapons breaking the screen, and triggers the counterattack. A good offense will still be a good defense, and the enemy's weapons can also be hit before the boost phase, while they are still on the ground — counterforce.

But will this new technology work?

Some of it already works. The rest shows great promise. The only sure way to find out is to prove it by enemy attack. We would rather not surely know if it will work. Only skilled technicians with access to classified information are qualified to estimate performance, and the most knowledgeable are the most enthusiastic.

But will the cost be prohibitive?

The costs are conjectural at this time. The ground-based BMD systems seem to be within the same range as major weapons systems — in the tens of billions. The space-based systems are up in the air. And the costs cannot be entirely laid on BMD because the same technologies have other uses. Laser research, for example, has wide military and civil applications.

But is not BMD a violation of the SALT treaty?

Depends. The SALT treaty is more porous than the thinnest BMD system. We may now deploy one hundred interceptors in South Dakota. We may do any amount of research and development, testing, and stockpiling. Because SALT only restricts strategic defense, we can develop and deploy tactical defense of ships and overseas bases, and such anti-tactical-missile (ATM) systems could be redeployed to North America in a crisis. We can also build anti-aircraft systems capable of dealing with hyperspeed, high-altitude targets — such as the U.S. Patriot system. SALT limits ABM radars, but says nothing about infra-red sensors; it limits interceptors, but is silent about directed-energy weapons. SALT is already obsolete.

Anyway, international treaties are obeyed insofar as each of the signatories considers it to be in its interests.

What are the arms-control implications of strategic defense?

The objectives of arms control were laid out by a team of Harvard and MIT professors a generation ago:

1. To reduce the risk of war.
2. To reduce the damage of war.
3. To save money.

BMD reduces the risk of war by dissuading attack by an aggressive power. Obviously BMD reduces the damage of war. BMD will almost certainly not save money.

Also, strategic defense eases offensive-arms negotiations because the defense is a safety net against cheating, so negotiators need not be as tough-minded about verification.

What are the Soviets doing in strategic defense?

The Soviets are doing what the Americans are doing, only more so. Like us, they have concentrated on conventional weaponry for Eurasia and on strategic offense. But they have taken strategic defense more seriously than we have: Their air-defense apparatus is very large; their civil-defense program is considerably more ambitious than ours; they seem to match us in passive defense of land-based strategic forces (however, their strategic submarines are not as good). They have kept and upgraded the ''Galosh'' ABM complex around Moscow, and official intelligence leaks suggest that they are pressing the SALT treaty to its limits, if not slightly beyond. There is a suspicious radar net, and they are working on ATM.

The Soviets seem to be behind us in computers and in infra-red technology, about the same in lasers, almost certainly ahead in particle beams, and stronger but less sophisticated in space.

Some people claim to fear a Soviet ''breakout'' — the unmasking of an effective BMD system in time of crisis. Another way to interpret the intelligence reports is that the Soviets are being commendably sensible.

What about the effects of strategic defense on our allies?

A possible retreat into a Fortress America posture does worry them. And they have understandably been averse to being a battlefield, nuclear or conventional, so they have been loath to face up to any type of war short of a total and improbable superpower exchange. But they are already beginning to realize that a more secure America would be a more reliable support.

What about the American public?

Public-opinion polls reveal that a majority of the American people believe that the United States already has a ballistic-missile defense. (One hopes that this is the same majority that does not vote.) We would have a system already deployed except for the agitation by a small but vocal and highly placed anti-defense lobby that has succeeded in making fashionable the pernicious doctrine that international security is promoted by common vulnerability, which assumes that all powers could endure such a permanent threat without breaking under the strain or breaking out to useful superiority.

What about the morality of strategic defense?

One would think that no policy could be more moral than defenses that hurt no one and might save hundreds of millions of lives.

12. RAPID DEPLOYMENT AND NUCLEAR WAR: REAGAN'S NEW MILITARY STRATEGIES

Andrew Winnick

THE MILITARY BUILDUP

A military buildup is now under way that is the largest undertaken by any country in the history of the world with the exception of those of the United States and Germany around the beginning of World War II. For example, the American navy is planned to increase from about 400 ships to more than 700, and an increase is planned in the current American nuclear arsenal from about 25,000 warheads to a new total of more than 42,000, a 70 percent jump. The development of a new 100,000-man Rapid Deployment Force is under way, partly from reorganized units and partly from units to be newly created. A new system of arms depots is planned, to stockpile large amounts of American military equipment: tanks, helicopters, armored personnel carriers, artillery, ammunition, and spare parts. These will be installed at military bases that are now being newly constructed or are planned at various sites around the world. Also planned is the deployment of two whole new generations of bombers (the B-1 and the Stealth), a new generation of tanks (the MX-1) and of armored personnel carriers, and a new generation of nuclear-powered submarines armed with intercontinental missiles (the Trident). Then, of course, there are the new missile systems — the Cruise, Pershing II, and MX. And on top of all this, there are decisions to renew the research and deployment of new chemical weapons (though as of this writing there are some signs that the Congress may block this plan) and to deploy the neutron bomb which destroys people but not property. What we are seeing is the complete re-equipping of the largest military force the world has ever known.

What is happening is not simply a result of Reagan's policies, though he has greatly accelerated the timetable. Except for certain specific weapon-systems decisions, such as the previously cancelled B-1 bomber and neutron bomb, most of these expansion plans were begun within the Carter administration. The development of the Trident submarine, the Rapid Deployment Force, the establishment of military depots such as at Diego Garcia island in the Indian Ocean, and the Pershing and Cruise missile systems were all begun under Carter. The general thrust for this buildup comes from important elements in both the Democratic and Republican parties as well as the corporate structure of the United States. The buildup is six times bigger than that pursued to fight the war in Vietnam. It is a virtual doubling of annual American military expenditures from the already expanded levels pursued in the last years of the Carter administration.

Despite this history, it is necessary to comprehend the extent of the Reagan administration's commitment to this military buildup and to understand that it is being sought in the face of the almost unanimous opposition of leading economists in the United States. From the far left to the far right economists and business leaders have been arguing that the economic consequences of the rapid expansion of military expenditures may be catastrophic for the American economy, by causing unprecedentedly large inflation. Yet Reagan has not been deterred. Why? What pressures move him ahead with his plans? What kind of thinking lies behind such a sense of desperation and a willingness to risk dire economic consequences for the United States?

The key questions then are: just why is this vast expansion of the American military occurring, and why is it occurring now and in the particular form we are seeing? Does this all simply result from a mania for building up the military? Is it due simply to economic pressure to provide money and profits to the war industry, despite the consequences to the rest of the economy? Is this simply the result of a few individual leaders pursuing their own mad dreams? The answer to all of these questions, and ones of this nature, is no! We are not dealing with fools and we are not dealing with people without a strategic vision. There is a very clear conception within the upper levels of the American power structure as to what they are doing and why they are doing it. There is a very clear conception of the underlying strategies that dictate, in most cases, what weapons systems they are choosing to develop.

Three strategic visions are being pursued simultaneously. And the United States is trying to pursue all three at the same time, which is one crucial reason why the cost is so high. While these three strategies are not unrelated, to a striking extent they each have a distinct focus. Therefore, each one, initially, will be looked at separately.

CONTAINMENT AND INTERVENTION IN THE THIRD WORLD

The first strategic conception is that the United States needs to prepare itself militarily to respond in new ways to liberation struggles and other events in the Third World. There is the conviction that, despite the United States' previous military capacity and efforts, the attempts to militarily block Third World liberation struggles have largely failed and the United States has not felt able to intervene in other situations where it might have wanted to choose that option, Libya being an often-mentioned example.

Obviously, the Vietnam experience was a major element in communicating that perception of impotence — the United States had suffered its first major military defeat. But Vietnam has been viewed by America's leaders as part of a larger pattern. American military leaders began to recognize that once a significant guerrilla liberation movement had developed both a strong military presence and a popular base, it could be blocked, if at all, only by such a large-scale deployment of military resources that any such deployment was economically, and even militarily, untenable.

Thus Kissinger's and the Pentagon's desire in 1975 to intervene militarily (not simply via military aid and covert operations) in Angola was blocked by establishment political forces in the United States, who, while they did not want to see the liberation movement there succeed, were unwilling, in the aftermath of Vietnam, to face the political, economic, and military risks involved in direct armed intervention.

Thereafter, the United States pursued an alternative strategy. This conceded that the United States might not have the political or military capacity to stop a given national liberation movement, but that it might still be able to deflect it into an acceptable direction. This alternative strategy underwent three major tests: in Zimbabwe (Rhodesia), Nicaragua, and Iran. But in each of these cases the strategy failed. This alternative policy recognized that it could not forever hang on to pro-American repressive military dictatorships or white, minority governments. The alternative strategy also recognized that the popular movements of democracy and national liberation had become virtually unstoppable, and that these movements had developed in large part as a response to the practices of repressive governments. Nevertheless, the United States hoped that it could channel the popular movements into political and economic arrangements that would be in tune with American interests. This was to be done by identifying middle-class, business-oriented, "pragmatic" sectors of the society and trying to help them into power, withdrawing support from the dictatorial or white minority regime (of Rhodesia or Somoza or the Shah) at a crucial moment (often much to the chagrin of certain elements within the American establishment that were particularly close to that particular regime). The hope was to establish some sort of pro-business, pro-capitalist, pro-Western element within that society in power, in lieu of having a more populist or socialist government. But the strategy did not work in any of the places it was tried.

In Nicaragua the government that came to power, though pluralistic, has not been as pro-business, as pro-capitalist, or as pro-American as originally anticipated; instead it has become more left and more populist than the United States finds acceptable. The strategy did not work in Zimbabwe, where the United States was forced to accept an election outcome that resulted in a government that was much more antagonistic to American positions than had been expected. And clearly it did not work in Iran, where instead of being able to establish and solidify the pro-business, pro-Western Bakhtiar government, a strongly anti-American Khomeini came to power.

In all these cases, the United States found that its middle-of-the-road, "third force" policy did not work. The lesson of Vietnam was reinforced by the more recent experience in El Salvador, where propping up an unpopular, military regime with American money, arms, and military advisers is having little success against an armed liberation movement with a substantial mass base, liberated zones from which to operate, and military sophistication. Similarly, the experience in Nicaragua was proving very frustrating. Efforts at economic and political destabilization and ostensibly covert efforts to apply military pressure (by supporting the Contras) had little likelihood of doing more than containing the actions of the government in Nicaragua. Indeed, they were heightening the risk of a large-scale, regional war.

Even the outgoing chairman of the U.S. Joint Chiefs of Staff publicly admitted that such a war would be a disaster without political support in the United States for what would, of necessity, be a long war. (Support of "friendly" guerrilla movements in Angola and Afghanistan, as well as in Nicaragua, indicates that this may be another new tactic being tested.)

Beginning in the late 1970s, under Carter, and then accelerating in the Reagan years a new strategy is emerging. The decision was made during the Carter administration that the only successful way to block "leftist" liberation movements from coming into power is to intervene massively, quickly, and at an early stage. In this new strategy it is necessary to intervene before the national liberation movement is militarily very strong, before it has developed a large, sophisticated guerrilla movement, and before it has secured significant liberated zones from which it can operate. But the necessity to intervene very quickly and suddenly was dictated by political as well as military considerations. The United States stands virtually alone in the world in being willing to risk such military intervention. There is almost no support in Western Europe for this sort of policy. Hence, if such intervention were to take a significant period of time — by which is meant months, not years — there would almost certainly be a mobilization of worldwide opinion in the United Nations and even among the European allies, so that sustained intervention would become less viable politically. There is also real fear of a new American antiwar movement again rising, and doing so very much quicker than happened in the 1960s. (The success of American progressive elements in quickly mobilizing around the issues of El Salvador and Nicaragua played a major role in deepening this fear.)

Thus the key elements in this new strategy are that the United States must be willing and militarily able to intervene massively and it must be able to do so virtually instantly. To that end it was decided to develop the Rapid Deployment Force (RDF). The RDF is designed to place 20,000 combat troops on the ground anywhere in the world within twenty-four hours, with as many as another 100,000 within a week to ten days. That is the RDF's purpose — massive, instant military intervention.

In the late 1970s the United States did not have the capacity to execute this strategy. It did not have the capacity to get the planned combat troops in place, let alone the needed heavy equipment (tanks, armored personnel carriers, artillery, helicopters) and ammunition required. But now the 101st and 82nd airborne divisions have been reorganized and C-5A aircraft are becoming available to enable the first 20,000 troops to be dispatched. Furthermore, the Army is being reorganized to make available another 100,000 men. In addition to other special units such as the Navy's Seal (a commando unit), the Army's Ranger and Green Beret units are being retrained, re-equipped, and expanded. But that is only the beginning. One can move the first 20,000 troops and their small arms and ammunition, and perhaps even some heavy equipment if the number of C-5A and other transport planes is expanded, as is now happening. But airlifting from the United States the large amounts of heavy equipment that these airborne and similar (e.g., Ranger) units need even for a short operation is simply not yet possible. Sea transport from the

United States is also not a viable means unless the targets are in our "own back-yards"; ships are simply too slow. They take weeks (as the British found out in the Falkland Islands) to go even partly round the world. Therefore, this strategy requires vast stockpiles of heavy equipment, ammunition, and fuel at American military bases around the world. Development of one such depot, for example, has already begun at Diego Garcia island in the Indian Ocean, not far from the Persian Gulf. And efforts are under way to secure or expand bases in East Africa, the eastern Mediterranean, Latin America, the Pacific Far East, and elsewhere.

This is a strategy that requires enormous redundancy in supply efforts. The United States will need to build thousands of tanks and other forms of equipment only to store them. That is very expensive. But all of this is only a part of what is required, and not necessarily even the most expensive part. Successful intervention by the RDF can only be achieved if close support, air and artillery, can be provided from the moment the first troops are landed. The only possible way of providing such support is via the navy.

Naval support takes many forms. First, aircraft carriers must be in position to provide floating tactical air bases for close air support to the ground troops. Second, ships must be immediately available to ferry materials from the supply depots and to act as close-in resupply bases. Third, ships must be available in position with their rockets and large guns to provide support and protection to the resupply efforts, and if possible, directly to the combat troops. Without such naval forces being immediately available as an integral part of a Rapid Deployment Force, this strategy cannot be implemented. But since ships take a very long time to get anywhere, one must have navies close enough to wherever one might want to use them.

To this end, the United States is planning to almost double the size of its navy, from about 400 to more than 700 ships. The Indian Ocean is to have a permanent American fleet for the first time in history. The Pacific, South Atlantic, and Mediterranean fleets are to be expanded. One part of achieving this naval expansion is to build two new aircraft carriers and their accompanying fleet of ships.

The first elements of the RDF have already been deployed in a particularly disturbing way. The United States, together with seven other countries, is participating in the United Nations Peacekeeping Force in the Sinai Desert which has interposed itself between the Egyptians and the Israelis. The United States' initial contribution to that Peacekeeping Force was the 3rd Battalion of the 82nd Airborne Division, a part of the RDF. The general in charge has specified that he will be rotating other battalions of the 82nd division through that position for training, and he has conceded that one of the reasons these particular units are being employed is so that they can act as the lead element for the RDF anywhere in the Middle East.

Other indications of this emerging new strategy are the upsurge in military maneuvers in Egypt and East Africa, and, of course, in Honduras, and the sending of naval forces, complete with aircraft carriers and even the recently refitted battleship *New Jersey*, to both the Caribbean and Pacific waters bordering Central America. (The *New Jersey* has recently been rotated from Nicaragua's coast to

Lebanon.) In both El Salvador and Nicaragua it is already far too late to try the new RDF strategy. However, in both Honduras and Guatemala, should a guerrilla movement emerge with any potential to pose a threat to the current pro-American governments, the new strategy would certainly be used.

The only way that the United States' military power can have any effective *political* impact in the Third World is if likely use of that military force is truly believed in. Kissinger and others in both the Carter and Reagan administrations have long argued that given the Vietnam Syndrome (i.e., the fear of intervening militarily and getting bogged down, which kept us out of Angola), the only way our threat to use force will again become believable is if we use it again, somewhere, and do so soon. For that reason, Honduras and Guatemala, and also Libya and the Middle East are particularly vulnerable to being used as ''an example'' in the near future.

This new strategy for containing and defeating Third World liberation struggles and for dealing with other problems in the Third World by employing a Rapid Deployment Force is the first of the new triad of United States military strategies for which America is re-arming.

As this article was about to go to the printer the United States invasion of Grenada occurred. It sadly, but all too accurately, reflects the validity of the analysis just presented and reveals two additional elements that were overlooked.

The invasion of Grenada employed Airborne, Ranger, Seal, and Marine units backed up by naval artillery and air support, in a massive, surprise invasion right out of the RDF planning book. The fact that Grenada is so close to the United States allowed the use of home bases as staging areas rather than the not-yet-ready far-flung network of new depots. The negative reaction of the European allies and of the Organization of American States was as expected, but also, as expected, offered no barrier to the invasion so long as the military planners felt that it could be executed and completed quickly.

The withdrawal of most, but by no means at all, of the American troops had the desired result of quickly quieting the political outcry in Europe and Latin America and at home. But how long those last American units remain and what the nature of their role is as an occupying force raise issues that are yet to be resolved.

The Grenada invasion also brought to light two other elements of the RDF strategy. First, the virtually complete news blackout. As a device to limit the political outcry that might, as in Vietnam, follow the viewing of American military force in action in a Third World nation, control of the news media was almost complete. The efforts of Johnson and Nixon to manipulate the media during the war in Vietnam pale in comparison to the censorship employed by Reagan. This censorship and the manipulation of the news media is a facet of the RDF strategy that one should expect to see again.

Second, we also wanted the device of using military units from nearby nations to blunt the visibility of the United States' responsibility. This is, of course, a very old tactic, often used by the major powers. It is one we should expect to see used when the RDF is employed in the future, as surely and sadly it will be.

THE CAPACITY FOR TACTICAL NUCLEAR WAR

The second new element in U.S. military strategy requiring a vast expansion in expenditures is the decision to develop a capacity to wage tactical nuclear war anywhere in the world, but especially anywhere near the borders of the USSR and China, and to be able to do so within the context of an "integrated" battlefield — i.e., one in which conventional, nuclear, and chemical weapons are employed. It is necessary to distinguish between tactical and limited nuclear war, for these are two different things. This may seem like an absurd distinction (which is some ways it is), but unfortunately it is an important one in understanding emerging U.S. military strategies.

The tactical use of nuclear weapons refers to using "small" bombs in "theater operations"; that is, weapons that can be used on the battlefield to stop the advance of an attacking army or to destroy it in its staging and supply areas. These weapons should be distinguished from larger weapons that can be used against military, industrial, and population centers deep behind an opposing army and in its homeland. Tactical nuclear weapons, as they now exist and are envisioned, are fired by artillery pieces, carried in small missiles, or delivered by tactical aircraft within a range of from five to two hundred miles. On the other hand, "limited nuclear war" envisions using large-scale weapons directly against selected targets or areas; e.g., attacking only military, not industrial or population, centers, avoiding a full world war.

The tactical nuclear weapons have been the strategic choice in the "European theater" since the mid-1950s. The United States, together with its NATO allies, decided that rather than matching the buildup in Soviet and Warsaw Pact conventional forces, especially of armored and armored infantry divisions (tanks, motorized artillery, and armored personnel carriers of infantry) the West instead would deploy short-range, low-yield nuclear weapons. These weapons are targeted on West Germany itself, in the theory that to stop an army invading from the east one must shoot in front of it and at its leading units. Needless to say, many residents of West Germany have, for some twenty-five years now, not been thrilled at the prospect of being attacked by NATO-launched nuclear weapons in order to save them from an attack by Warsaw Pact conventional forces.

Under Carter, and now Reagan, this tactical nuclear option, so long employed in Europe, is part of a new strategy of containment. It is at the heart of the so-called Carter Doctrine to maintain Western control of the Persian Gulf's oil riches by military force. If the USSR chose to intervene militarily in the Persian Gulf, it could take the oilfields there as "easily" and "quickly" as the United States could take those of Mexico. There would be nothing the United States could do, militarily, to stop it; there is no possibility that the United States could place enough troops or equipment on the ground to stop such a Soviet takeover of the Middle Eastern oilfields. Even the deploying of a conventionally armed RDF would be ineffective. American military officials have conceded that the RDF, if deployed in those circumstances, would be overrun and destroyed within twenty-four to forty-eight hours.

What then was Carter talking about when he stated that the United States was committed to intervening militarily in order to prevent a takeover of any Middle Eastern oilfields? He was talking about one strategy, and one strategy only — tactical nuclear warfare. That is the only way the United States could block, militarily, such a Soviet move. If any Soviet troops were to cross the border, let us say, between the Soviet Union and Iran, the United States would *immediately* employ nuclear weapons. Timing is the crucial part of this concept — it only works if it is the first, initial, and immediate response. Once Soviet troops have crossed the border passes, once they are in Iran, they could reach the Persian Gulf and take control of the oilfields within at most thirty-six to forty-eight hours, just as the United States could do in Mexico. If one waits a day or two, one is left with the option of blowing up the oilfields one is trying to save. One achieves nothing if one waits even a day. This means that the Carter Doctrine indicates American willingness to make a nuclear wasteland along that border through which nobody could move.

These tactical weapons would be delivered by carrier-based aircraft or launched by naval artillery or short-range, ship-based missiles. In the Reagan program, the United States would make these weapons immediately available to the expanded naval and Rapid Deployment Forces throughout the world. This would result in a mammoth expansion of the United States' tactical nuclear arsenal. Virtually every major combat ship in a vastly expanded navy, and many land- and aircraft-carrier-based planes, as well as the RDF, would be provided with a full array of tactical nuclear weapons. This accounts for a large proportion of the planned increase of 70 percent in the number of American nuclear weapons, from about 25,000 to more than 42,000, and for the planned development of whole new generations of tactical nuclear weapons.

The other component of this strategy is the concept of the "integrated battlefield," one on which are employed not only conventional and nuclear weapons, but also chemical ones. To this end, Reagan has ordered a new research and development effort aimed at deploying a new generation of chemical weapons. Moreover, once such battlefield conditions are envisioned, all tanks, trucks, and personnel must be re-equipped with protective devices adequate to allow them to function in a chemical environment, whether produced by one's own weapon or the enemy's. This effort accounts for yet another component of the vastly expanded American military expenditures. Whether political opposition in Congress will be successful in blocking this element in Reagan's military planning remains to be seen.

THE PURSUIT OF LIMITED NUCLEAR WAR: DEPLOYMENT OF THE CRUISE AND PERSHING II MISSILE SYSTEMS

Since the early 1960s, the fundamental strategy of the United States with regard to the USSR has been one labeled, appropriately, MAD — mutually assured destruction; from all indications, this strategy has been, reciprocally, that of the USSR as well. Each country maintains intercontinental ballistic missiles, bombers, and missile-armed submarines (the so-called triad of strategic weapons) in sufficient number and with sufficient security that enough would survive a first strike to make it credible to the other that, if either side attacks first, the other would retain the ability to totally destroy the first side's country.

However, neither side is confident of its ability to absorb a first strike and still be able to respond "adequately." Moreover, neither side has any interest in absorbing such a first strike voluntarily, allowing a significant portion of its military capacity to be destroyed "unused" — to say nothing of the millions of civilian deaths and the inevitable economic and political consequences. The real deterrent power each has is predicated on the presumption that either side can get its counterattack launched before the other's attack lands. The satellite observation systems and other monitoring systems are designed to give either the Soviet Union or the United States instant notice of the launching of the other's missiles the moment they leave the ground or break the surface of the sea. The current decision-making structure upon which the mutually assured destruction strategy is based requires either side having forty-five minutes to an hour warning of an attack. That is, because of the necessary scale of a first strike, there would be about a forty-five-minute to one-hour notice that the other side has begun the attack. That provides about forty minutes to confirm that, in fact, an attack is on its way before "having to" launch the counterattack.

It is frightening to discover that on a number of occasions U.S. military forces moved more than twenty to twenty-five minutes through the countdown to launching American missiles because of various communication failures, confusing satellite information, human error, or computer failures. Presumably the same thing has occurred in the Soviet Union. The world has been that close to Armageddon.

The new limited nuclear war strategy that underlies the United States' desire to place a new generation of missiles, the Pershing II and Cruise systems, in Western Europe radically alters the set of assumptions upon which the existing strategy of MAD is based. These new missiles, the deployment of which is now begun, change the whole time-frame for decision-making and the entire strategic understanding that underlie MAD. These missiles have the following characteristics:

First, from the time the Pershing IIs are launched to the time they would land on Soviet and Eastern European territory is under fifteen minutes; in fact, some estimates are as low as six to ten minutes from launch to impact. This reduces the response-decision-making time available to the USSR from forty minutes or more to less than ten minutes. Second, these missile systems are incredibly accurate — if the projections are correct, they can be placed within 100 feet of the intended target instead of a current accuracy usually estimated at no better than 1500 yards. Third, the Cruise missiles are designed to fly very low, going up and down over the countryside, staying within 50 to 150 feet above ground obstacles, making their detection by currently deployed ground-based radar almost impossible.

Characteristics of these new missiles significantly change the balance of power between the United States and the USSR. Once these missiles were in place, the USSR would find (1) that its greatly reduced response time to decide whether to launch a counterattack meant a greatly increased danger of launching in error, and (2) that due to the greater accuracy of the new missiles they had a lower probability of their own missiles surviving a first strike, hence "necessitating" an immediate response to a *suspected* American attack. That is, the combined effort of short response time and high accuracy leaves the USSR little choice but to adopt a dangerous new strategy — "launch upon warning" — in place of the current policy of launching upon "confirmed attack." In fact, Andropov himself has recently made this point. The world would thereby be brought much closer to possible disaster.

These new European-based American missiles also make possible a new limited nuclear war strategy — one that allows the launching, or the threat of launching, a first strike against the USSR designed so that "only" Western Europe, and not the United States itself, is the site of a nuclear war. Thus, eleven former NATO generals and admirals, including Bastian and Vollmer of Germany, Sanguinetti of France, Pasti of Italy, Harbottle of England, and von Meyenfeldt of the Netherlands, took the unprecedented step of signing a public statement which reads:

American first-strike weapons on the doorstep of the Soviet Union are the most appropriate fuse for touching off a nuclear war. Americans, we beseech you: Do not deploy Pershing II and Cruise missiles in Europe! For the sake of humankind — Don't do it!

A first strike would be aimed "only" at Soviet and Warsaw Pact military installations — i.e., at major troop staging areas, military bases, missile sites, and naval bases. The attack would be designed to destroy the Soviet Union's military capacity. At the same time, according to this scenario, the United States would announce to the Soviet Union that it has two choices: (1) It may absorb this attack, thereby giving up its status as a world power militarily, but not suffer any direct attacks on major industrial or population centers. (Of course, the radioactive fallout from the attack on the military targets would inevitably endanger most of the peoples of Eastern Europe and the USSR.) Or (2) it could choose to respond by launching a counterattack against the United States itself, in which case the United States would then launch all of its United States–based missiles, nuclear-submarine-based missiles, and strategic bombers, none of which would have been employed to that point, directly at the population and industrial centers of the USSR. Even under option 1 the USSR might try to stop the initial incoming missiles, which would mean "accepting" Soviet missiles exploding over Western Europe. West Germany in particular would be devastated even under the first option as a "necessary" sacrifice to this limited nuclear war strategy. So the Soviet Union would be given the choice either to give up its military, but save (as best it could) its population and industrial capacity and continue to exist as a nation; or to cease to exist, as both sides destroyed each other.

This then is the third part of the United States' new military strategy for which the Cruise and Pershing II missiles are being deployed in Europe. They are designed to enable the United States to have a newly conceived first-strike capacity against the USSR so that only Western Europe, and not the United States, would be endangered, and which would in any event drastically alter the strategic balance of power.

THE MYTH OF DEFENSIVE PURPOSES

It is essential to understand that these missiles are fundamentally offensive, not defensive, in character. They are designed to allow the United States to begin a nuclear war with the Soviet Union which the United States thinks it can "win." If the concern is with the possibility of a Soviet invasion of Western Europe, NATO already has the ground-based tactical nuclear weapons needed to adequately respond to that. And these can be strengthened without deploying Pershing II or Cruise missiles. In fact, in recent months, U.S. Army General Bernard Rogers, commander-in-chief of NATO (backed up by a chorus of "experts" and journalists including Michael Howard of the International Institute of Strategic Studies and Flora Lewis of the *New York Times*) has publicly stated that *if* the NATO allies agree to increase their conventional arms spending by a full 4 percent above the rate of inflation (which means a nominal increase of 10 to 15 percent) every year for the next six to eight years, NATO would be sufficiently strong to deter the USSR and its Warsaw Pact allies without the use of *any* nuclear weapons, that is, without either the introduction of the Pershing II and Cruise missiles, or even the use of smaller tactical nuclear weapons. Rogers and the others envision a greatly expanded deployment of new high-tech "smart" weapons that are accurate and hard to detect, and which could be used against both the lead forces and the second-echelon forces of the Warsaw Pact. These could be deployed in large numbers.

Although the NATO allies had previously agreed to a target of 3 percent (above inflation) growth in military spending per year, not even the new conservative government of Kohl in West Germany plans more than a 1 percent increase. Hence the new proposal may be a fall-back position designed to be used as much with our own NATO allies as with the USSR. For underlying the statements by Rogers and others, there seem to be four related goals, aside from the obvious military one:

1. To shift a major portion of the cost of "defending" Western Europe onto the allies there. The United States would avoid the cost of further developing and deploying the Pershing II and greatly reduce the number of Cruise missiles (which unlike the Pershing, have planned uses outside of Europe) that have to be produced.
2. To force European allied governments to take funds from budgets already strained by the need to maintain social programs in the face of the severe worldwide recession, thus reducing the "drift toward socialism" in these countries. Rogers, in referring to costs of this new strategy, which has been code-named "Airland Battle 2000," conceded that it would require "sacrifices in social benefits."

3. To (a) strengthen the United States' economy by expanding the export of American-produced conventional weapons which are essential to the profits of many American corporations; and/or (b) weaken the competitive position of European, especially West German, civilian industry by forcing a significant shift of those countries' research, engineering, and industrial resources to the expansion of their armaments industry.
4. To isolate and embarrass the European peace movement by, in essence, declaring to it:

If you are sincerely against nuclear weapons, but want a strong Western Europe that can maintain the military balance necessary to secure peace, then prove it and support the (4 percent) buildup in conventional arms in lieu of the deployment of the Pershing II and Cruise missiles. (General Rogers has even been quoted in the *International Herald Tribune* as saying that "the anti-nuclear groups want the same things as I do."

But, if you fail to support this alternative, you make it clear that (a) you really have no desire for a strong and peaceful Europe, and (b) you are, in fact, either dupes of, or agents for, the USSR in its efforts to first neutralize, then dominate Western Europe.

Moreover, the claim that the Pershing II and Cruise systems are a necessary defensive response to the USSR's deployment of its SS-20s, as undesirable as that deployment may be, is absurd. The United States and NATO already have large numbers of nuclear weapons in submarines in the Mediterranean and Baltic seas, attack bombers throughout Western Europe, and intercontinental ballistic missiles based in the United States, all of which pose a strategic threat to the USSR. In addition, England and France have, between them, 162 nuclear missiles, all capable of reaching the USSR, which they maintain outside the NATO command structure. The United States refuses to include any of these strategic systems when evaluating the balance of power in Europe and the ostensible threat of the SS-20s. There can be little doubt that a new offensive capacity is being envisioned. It is this that has brought new life to the European peace movement, which includes, for the first time, major military figures.

THE GENEVA DISARMAMENT TALKS

Even from its inception, the planned introduction of the new strategic nuclear weapons into Europe has elicited cautious reactions from most Europeans, even among the more conservative leadership. It was Europeans who insisted on the "two-track" plan — to begin preparations for the deployment, but at the same time to pursue disarmament talks in Geneva and use the threat of deployment to win more concessions from the USSR, with the hope of never having to actually deploy the new missiles. But while most Europeans anticipated a mutual reduction in arms, the United States pursued a policy that offered to forgo the deployment of these new weapons only in exchange for massive, unilateral arms reductions by the USSR. It is hard to believe that anyone in the U.S. government seriously thought the USSR would accept this position. Hence, one must conclude that the United States was very committed to actually implementing this third element of its new military strategy, while the Europeans, even ranking military officers such as those cited above, were very afraid of this happening.

But during the summer of 1983, the United States had begun to adopt a somewhat more flexible tone in Geneva. There were three main reasons for this: First, the USSR had made it clear that it considered the deployment of the new missiles to amount to a major provocation. (One might compare it to a role-reversal of the Soviet attempt to put missiles in Cuba in the early 1960s.) Second, the European and American peace movements has succeeded in putting a good deal of pressure on the United States and NATO governments. Third, and most important, the Soviet Union, via various public statements, had made it clear that the principal strategic purpose for which these missiles are designed would not succeed. They announced that in the event even one of these missiles was launched against them, they would immediately launch everything they have directly at the United States. The USSR had thus made it clear that it will not, under any circumstances, absorb a so-called "limited" first strike.

There is some reason to think that this statement has been heard and believed in Washington, making the deployment of these missiles largely useless, except as a propaganda and face-saving gesture for Reagan and for some of the conservative leadership in Europe which had already gone out on a political limb in favor of deployment. This changed situation may also have accounted for the new alternatives proposed by General Rogers, and for the recent opposition to deployment being voiced by such establishment figures as Robert McNamara, who now argues against the limited nuclear war strategy, stating that "nuclear weapons serve no military purpose whatsoever. They are totally useless except only to deter one's opponent from using them." On the other hand, the shooting down of the Korean airliner by Soviet forces has engendered a new anti-Soviet mood which the Reagan administration has clearly seen as enabling it to again adopt a more hardline position in Geneva and on the subject of deployment.

RECENT CONGRESSIONAL BUDGET CUTS

Under pressures brought on by the unprecedented budget deficits being run up by Reagan (three times higher than any in history), with their attendant effects on interest rates, our balance of payments, and the overall health of the economy, and with the worldwide pressure from a growing peace movement, Congress has reduced the rate of increase in the military budget from that originally requested by Reagan. But, unfortunately, little that is positive has been gained. For what Reagan has been forced to give up has been a substantial portion of the planned increases in military salaries, some retirement benefits, plans to improve military housing and other service facilities, and some of the additional personnel he had wanted. But not a single major weapon system has been permanently blocked. And, especially, the so-called off-budget authorizations (as compared to the on-budget allocations) are about on his original schedule, except for the items noted above.

There are signs of serious grumblings among military personnel who are suffering from the cutbacks that have occurred, and this will affect re-enlistment, especially among the more highly trained maintenance personnel for whom some jobs exist in the private economy. But given the continuing high unemployment rate, there is little danger of the military not getting its authorized personnel. As for the RDF, the training of the 100,000 back-up troops will be slowed a bit and some more of them will have to come from reassignments rather than new personnel, but overall, it, too, is on schedule.

The key point is that unless and until the peace movement and the Congress address the budget cuts to the particular elements highlighted in this article, little will be accomplished in thwarting the development of these new strategies.

CONCLUSION

The vast expansion in American military expenditures and military capacity now under way must be understood within the context of long-term decisions by both the Carter and Reagan administrations to implement the three new strategic military designs outlined above, rather than being viewed as a more or less irrational desire on the part of one man, Reagan, simply to strengthen and expand the American military. But once this in done, progressive people who do not wish to see such an expansion in military power and who do not wish to see the American people saddled with the enormous economic burden of such an expansion, must come to grips with the strategic issues and consequences. Otherwise, we run the risk of being dismissed as "mere moralists," as "naïve, though well meaning," or as "unconscious dupes of the USSR."

We must be able and willing to confront these new military strategies directly, explicitly stating that:

1. We understand the purpose of, and therefore do not want, the United States to develop a Rapid Deployment Force.
2. We are unwilling to accept the use of tactical nuclear war as a strategy, whether in Europe, the Persian Gulf, or elsewhere.
3. We do not want the United States to gain a first-strike capacity *of any sort* against the Soviet Union.
4. We consider the idea that either a limited or tactical nuclear war could be contained within any reasonably acceptable level of destruction to be dangerously wrong.

Only if the peace movement is willing in this way to demonstrate that we understand and are willing to confront the full range of military strategies underlying the American arms buildup now under way should we expect to be taken seriously. Moreover, we have an obligation to educate people honestly as to what is going on and *why it is happening* so that they can decide for themselves the course they wish their governments to take.

PART II

SOCIAL
CONTROL
VERSUS
PRIVATE
CHOICE

CHAPTER 6

SHOULD FAMILY LIFE BE A PRIVATE AFFAIR?

Neoconservative sociologists Brigitte and Peter Berger view the contemporary war over the family as a battle between the "New Class" and everyone else that is "fed up with the pretensions and power aspirations" of said class. Private matters, like the family, are problematized as public issues by this new "knowledge class," which includes "the vast educational system, the therapeutic-'helping' complex, sizable portions of government bureaucracy, the media and publishing industries, and others." The state cannot be indifferent to the family, they claim, but public policy should only focus on children.[1]

W. Norton Grubb and Marvin Lazerson, on the other hand, feel that children are not well served by being the focus of public policy with regard to the family. The government intervenes on behalf of children only when there is evidence of family failure. Yet the "private family" is a false image in today's world. Resolving the problems of child care and child welfare necessitates that attention be paid to and collective action be directed at broad social and economic issues previously beyond the scope of child advocates.[2] The emphasis Grubb and Lazerson place on structure, class, and gender equality makes their position neoliberal or progressive.

Commentators in the 1980s from every ideological position see the American family as an institution in crisis. Public debate often centers on individual social problems blamed on the family: illiteracy, teenage pregnancy, sexual immorality, inadequate child care, and high divorce rates. Few critics of the family agree on the cause of today's crisis in the family.

Conservatives see the death of the traditional family as a product of too much meddling by the state. For example, they see legislation such as Title VII of the 1964 Civil Rights Act as a cause of family instability. Title VII prohibits employment policies with the intent or purpose to discriminate against women because of their sex. Title VII and other sex discrimination laws are accused of being a prime cause of women withdrawing from their traditional feminine roles. For conservatives, the state has no business intruding on sex roles or other family affairs. The conservative argument is to get the government off the backs of families. Every government program has only made things worse for the family.

To liberals, government inaction is the cause of today's crisis in family policy. Liberals believe that social services programs can save the family. Modern liberals believe that it is government's role to solve social problems, such as day care, work — family interference, and family violence. Whereas conservatives view the family as a private affair, liberals emphasize public policies, such as income support programs and social supports. The liberal hope is that the state can develop policies that not only shore up the family but also help individuals achieve equal opportunity in a class society.

Radicals see the emphasis on the family as a source of social problems as misplaced. Radical feminists challenge the traditional family as a source of oppression. Marxists link social problems of the family to the political economy. Economic inequality is blamed for the poverty of many children, inadequate child care, and illiteracy. Radicals believe that state programs can never solve the problems besetting children and family that keep reemerging from economic inequality.

W. Norton Grubb and Marvin Lazerson call for a liberal transformation of family policy in their section "Broken Promises." As a response to conservatism, the authors argue for a government that attempts to improve children's lives. Their argument is that children have not been well served by public policy because the government has not gone far enough. The government now enters the family's intimate environment only when something is terribly aberrant. For example, the state intervenes with support services when a child is sexually abused. The government intervenes on behalf of children only when there are definite legal grounds of family failure. A social worker interviews parents at the point that shattered bones appear on x rays. By the time the state interferes it is often too late to salvage children's lives. Yet the "private family" as defined by the American state is distorted. If the government is to solve such problems as child care and welfare, it must direct "collective attention at issues previously thought to be beyond the scope of child advocates."[2] Grubb and Lazerson do not place much emphasis on issues of structure, class, and gender inequality, which are the concerns of Marxists and radical feminists. In contrast to radicals, nonliberals such as Grubb and Lazerson believe that family goals can be achieved within the framework of capitalism. A coherent family policy would modify the abuses of capitalism and lead to greater equality.

Neoconservative sociologists Brigitte Berger and Peter Berger completely disagree with liberals who blame the family for social problems in the 1980s. They argue that many problems supposedly created by the family are inventions of the new knowledge class. Private matters, like the family, are viewed as public problems by this new knowledge class, which includes "the vast educational system, the therapeutic helping complex, sizable portions of government bureaucracy, the media and publishing industries, and others." The Bergers argue that the state cannot be "indifferent" to the family, they claim, but public policy should focus only on children.[2] Conservatives are alarmed at any interferences by the government in family affairs. They believe that no national family policy can ever replace the affection and autonomy of the traditional family. The government should stay in Washington, where it belongs.

The articles in this section are diametrically opposed in nearly every assumption about family life. The issues reflect real fears, angers, and aspirations found in public debate about the government's role in the intimate environment of the family.

References

1. W. Norton Grubb and Marvin Lazerson, *Broken Promises* (New York: Basic Books, 1982) p. 269f.
2. Brigitte Berger and Peter L. Berger, *The War over the Family,* (Garden City, N.Y.: Anchor Press, Doubleday, 1983). Note that the Bergers evidently hold a liberal position on abortion. They consider it "absurd" to conflate abortion with family policy. Separation of the two issues is not standard procedure on the right. Cf. Kristin Luker, *Abortion and the Politics of Motherhood* (Berkeley: University of California Press 1984), and Linda Gordon and Allen Hunter, "Sex, Family, and the New Right," *Radical America,* Nov. 1977–Feb. 1978 issue.

13. BROKEN PROMISES: HOW AMERICANS FAIL THEIR CHILDREN

W. Norton Grubb and Marvin Lazerson

Public discussions of childrearing problems have inevitably turned to public resolutions because individual approaches to complex issues like poverty and social cohesion are patently inadequate. In every period of "family crisis," concern for children has led to an expansion of public responsibilities. The nineteenth-century movements establishing public schools to socialize children appropriately, the early twentieth-century efforts at "child saving" through child labor legislation and rudimentary welfare programs, the social programs of the New Deal and Johnson's War on Poverty have institutionalized a set of public obligations to children: to spare innocent children the ravages of poverty, to provide for those children whose parents are unable or unwilling to nurture them, to provide every child a decent opportunity for adult success. In these efforts we have provided public support for children where we are unwilling to reform conditions for adults, and children's institutions have been made responsible for creating a just and equitable society from one riddled with inequities. Yet our implicit promises to children have been only partially fulfilled. Childhood poverty remains first on the list of family problems, and equality of opportunity remains as distant now as it did in the mid-nineteenth century. The same problems besetting children and families keep re-emerging because the reforms to treat them have always been contradictory and incomplete. The recurring cycles of crisis and reform are evidence of our broken promises.

Our task is to analyze the possibilities and limits of public responsibility for children and families, to understand the relationship between the American state and children. That relationship has been paradoxical. On one hand, the boundaries between the private and the public — between the private family and the public world of government and the economy — have shifted constantly, especially with the expansion of the state, so that the distinction between the public and private has become blurred. Yet our rhetoric and public policies continue to refer to the family as a private and personal sphere insulated from the world outside, even as the state's activities have become more elaborate. Ideologically, the family remains the "basic unit of society," even though our economic and social policies make clear that the family is not the primary unit of production nor even the only institution socializing children. In part, we continue to insist on the family's privacy because we have nothing to replace it as a refuge of affection and intimacy. But this insistence has generated the central dilemma: if the state must assume some responsibilities for children, how can it discharge those responsibilities when childrearing is still considered a private responsibility? The dominant solution ever since the early nineteenth century has been to allow the state to intervene into childrearing only when families are considered to have failed. This constraint — the doctrine of *parens patriae* — has itself limited and distorted public programs for children. . . .

The ugliest blotch on the myth of American affluence has been the persistence of poverty. In urban slums, in Appalachian hollows, on Indian reservations, in the backwaters of the South, poverty has been a constant reminder that the American form of capitalism, powerful though it may be, has left many people out. More than 11 percent of all individuals and almost 16 percent of children were "officially" in poverty in 1978, and racial differences make the official figures still more grim: 27 percent of Hispanic children and 41 percent of black children were poor. Despite extensive efforts in every period of social reform to reduce childhood poverty — most recently in Lyndon Johnson's War on Poverty — children continue to be the most impoverished group in the population, and the prospects for improvement are disheartening.

Poverty has been a continuing thorn for Americans brought up on the expectation that hard work and a munificent environment would bring individual and social wealth. These optimistic expectations have been challenged ever since the progressive era, as Americans began to acknowledge that poverty could be caused by economic and social institutions rather than individual failure. Yet that acknowledgment has been slow and grudging. Americans still prefer to ignore poverty or to embrace the ethic of private responsibility that blames individuals and families for their own poverty. Unequal earnings continue to be seen as a legitimate reflection of unequal skills and effort, despite the poverty they imply. This has been the dark side of the American dream: while individualism and hard work could lead to success, individuals could also fail. In either case, the process has been considered both "private" and individual. Only during the most severe periods of social instability — the 1890s, the Great Depression of the 1930s, the 1960s — has the assumption that opportunity is individually determined been widely opposed by one that attributes poverty to structural conditions beyond individual control: discrimination, unequal access to education and to job opportunities, and an economic system that fails to provide enough jobs for those seeking them.

The issue of responsibility for poverty has generated the major conflicts in social welfare policy and has divided conservatives who stress the individual and private roots of poverty from liberals who assert its social and public causes. Still, from every ideological perspective, childhood poverty has always been treated as a special horror. Americans have been outraged by reports of children abused by poverty, even when they are indifferent to the plight of poor adults. As John Spargo, a progressive era reformer, wrote in *The Bitter Cry of the Children* (1906):

Poverty, the poverty of civilized man, which is everywhere coexistent with unbounded wealth and luxury, is always ugly, repellent and terrible either to see or to experience: but when it assails the cradle, it assumes its most hideous form.

Childhood poverty has been especially hideous from an instrumental perspective: liberals and conservatives alike have complained that poverty entails a waste of human resources, stunting the development of little children and generating social burdens rather than productive citizens. Poverty among children is also special because individual failure as the cause of poverty cannot be extended to the young. Instead, children, the innocent and blameless, are the victims of other people and other institutions — their parents and economic conditions, and more recently, "government bureaucrats" and "do-gooders."

Despite a consensus that childhood poverty is economically inefficient, as well as immoral and cruel, efforts to eliminate it have invariably been incomplete. The hostility to "other people's children" and instrumental rationales for public spending on children have limited and distorted public efforts to reduce poverty. The assumption that poor parents have failed their children as a precondition for public support — *parens patriae,* once again — means that poor parents are invariably condemned as immoral, and their children are made to suffer the consequences of reduced support. Indeed, that is a fundamental characteristic of the American approach to poverty: the young are punished for what are considered the transgressions of their parents and the failures of private responsibility. Because it is difficult for Americans to view children distinct from their parents and almost impossible to develop public policies that would do so, public policies are caught in the dilemma that supporting poor children requires assisting their parents as well, contrary to the political demands that public aid should not undermine labor markets, the work ethic, and the prevailing conception of family income as "private." In practice, the short-run needs of the labor market have usually prevailed over longer-run interests in preventing the "stunted development" of future workers. When the welfare of children conflicts with economic constraints, children lose.

As a result, childhood poverty remains higher than for any other group. In 1978, 17.2 percent of children under five and 15.5 percent of children between five and seventeen were below the official poverty thresholds, compared to 8.7 percent of those eighteen to sixty-four and 13.9 percent of those over sixty-five. Children therefore constitute a large fraction of the poor: 40.5 percent of those defined as officially poor in 1978 were under eighteen. Moreover, those figures conceal as much as they reveal. The official poverty line, intended to reflect a level of income necessary for survival, is based on the Economy Food Plan (now the Thrifty Food Plan) of the Department of Agriculture, designed for "temporary or emergency use when funds are low"; the department estimates that only 10 percent of the people using the plan can manage to eat an adequate diet. The official poverty standards are thus too low for continued survival. A more realistic alternative is to use half the median income as the poverty standard, since interview data indicate that many people consider this to be a better conception of poverty. By this measure, 19.7 percent of individuals and 24.5 percent of children were poor in 1974, compared to official figures of 11.2 percent and 15.1 percent. With more acceptable definitions of poverty, then, one-quarter of all America's children are poor. The special plight of minority children is even more obvious: perhaps 40 percent of black children are poor.

There has been some decrease in the incidence of poverty in the past two decades, partly as a result of the economic boom during the 1960s and partly because welfare programs were expanded. But the progress of children in moving out of poverty lags behind that of other population groups. Between 1966 and 1970 the incidence of official poverty for the elderly dropped from 28.5 percent to 24.6 percent, while for children it fell at a somewhat lower rate from 17.4 percent to 14.9 percent. Between 1970 and 1978, while official poverty among children was increasing to 15.7 percent, the incidence for adults aged eighteen to sixty-four decreased slightly from 9.6 percent to 8.7 percent, and the incidence for the elderly dropped dramatically, from 24.6 percent to 13.9 percent. The social welfare programs of federal, state, and local governments have thus been much less effective in moving children out of poverty, compared to most other population groups. The programs that transfer funds to the poor vary considerably in their generosity, and children are most affected by the least generous program, Aid to Families with Dependent Children (AFDC). Furthermore, because of limited state coverage and various restrictions, the AFDC-U program for two-parent families with unemployed fathers reaches very few children, and so the 42 percent of officially poor children in two-parent families have been helped very little by welfare programs. As a consequence, in 1972 only 23 percent of poor families with children were made ''nonpoor'' by government programs, compared to 68 percent of families with an aged head. Clearly the power of transfer programs to reduce poverty among children has been weak.

Here, then, is one way of viewing the welfare ''mess'': generations of reformers have addressed the ''hideous form'' of childhood poverty, but public programs have made little difference. The tremendous expansion in welfare programs during the 1960s was limited in moving children out of poverty, and even the small progress in alleviating childhood poverty was reversed in the 1970s. The weakness of the economy during the 1970s and the growth of single-parent families have increased the number of children who need public aid even to survive, yet resistance to providing the benefits necessary for decent living standards has intensified. In a period of fiscal retrenchment and taxpayer revolts, public opinion polls suggest that welfare programs are the most favored areas for cuts in government spending, and conservatives have singled out welfare programs and social services to the poor as the most flagrant of all government ''give-aways,'' supposedly responsible for federal deficits, inflation, declining productivity, and a host of other evils. The contrast between these conservative reactions and the rhetoric that has historically condemned childhood poverty is enormous and testifies to the difficulty of principled politics on behalf of other people's children.

The welfare system illustrates, better than any other children's institution, a central limitation of *parens patriae*. Although public institutions promise to provide for children when their parents cannot, it proves impossible (except in extreme conditions) to separate children from their parents, either physically or conceptually. Providing for poor children therefore means providing for their parents at the same time. But we are unwilling to support poor adults, who despite all evidence to the contrary remain suspected of sloth, dissolute living, and the destruction of American values. Rather than support their parents we choose to minimize our responsibilities to poor children. The result is the steady abandonment of poor children, despite the abundance that surrounds them. As one welfare rights organizer and welfare recipient declared:

When I see money being wasted — sending men to the moon to play golf, dumping nerve gas in the ocean, burning potatoes, killing off hogs, mutilating them, just getting rid of them — and then I see hungry and raggedy children running around, this is the kind of country we live in, and this is what just burns me up. I feel the only way changes will be made, especially in the welfare system, is through poor people, welfare people organizing and raising a lot of hell . . . which is all we can do.

Welfare at the onset of the 1930s was a ramshackle affair. In the mothers' pensions begun in the progressive era and in the private charity based on nineteenth-century principles of "scientific philanthropy," welfare efforts were designed to support the "deserving" poor, especially widows and children who found themselves poor through no fault of their own. The greatest fear of philanthropists, public officials, and charity workers, was that the dole would "pauperize" recipients, causing them to abandon efforts to work themselves out of poverty. To guard against this possibility and reinforce work norms, the "undeserving" poor and the "employables" received no support. Even those judged "deserving" received meager support, accompanied by invasions of privacy, curtailment of rights, and moral exhortations. The degradation of welfare recipients guaranteed that there would be no incentive even for "unemployables" to go on welfare.

Neither these assumptions nor the methods of providing welfare were able to cope with depression levels of unemployment and poverty, a fact as apparent in the 1890s as in the 1930s. But in the Great Depression, individualistic conceptions that blamed poverty on the poor were considerably less tenable. As the unemployed became increasingly strident in their demands and as civil disorders increased, the Roosevelt administration moved to establish a federal relief program for "all needy unemployed persons and/or their dependents" through the Federal Emergency Relief Act (FERA). Federal aid defused civil disorders, but the source of FERA's effectiveness was also its most vulnerable point. Extending aid to all who needed it was unacceptable to a wide range of people who wanted to tie relief to work. The most immediate efforts to transform public assistance into work programs, making aid contingent on job participation, were the Public Works Administration, the Civil Works Administration, and the Social Security Act of 1935, which resurrected the division between employables and unemployables. For employables — or, more accurately, those who had been employed — a system of social insurance was instituted, including unemployment insurance and an old age security system conditioned on prior wages. For unemployables — principally the aged poor, the blind, and children — the legislation established federal grants to support state and local efforts rather than the comprehensive plan that had been the basis of FERA. For children, benefits were restricted to those deprived of economic support "by reason of the death, continued absence from the home, or physical and/or mental incapacity of a parent" (usually meaning a father).

The structure of federal grants allowed the states to reproduce the old systems of mothers' pensions, with all the inequities and inadequacies of those programs:

states were allowed to set levels of support which were often pitifully low and which varied drastically around the country; the moral judgments used in distinguishing the "deserving" from the "undeserving" poor persisted; and dependent children who were poor despite the presence of their fathers were not helped. A variety of techniques developed during the 1940s and 1950s to discipline the welfare population and to insure that public assistance would not undermine local labor markets. Aid levels were invariably set below the minimum wages available in local areas. State and local administration allowed support levels and eligibility standards to vary among states and within states. The low-wage agricultural labor markets of the South were accompanied by the lowest levels of public assistance in the country, and in seasonal labor markets (as in agricultural areas), welfare recipients found themselves cut off the rolls when seasonal work began.

Closely allied to concerns that local labor markets not be undermined were the "employable mother" and "unsuitable home" provisions. "Employable mother" rules required that mothers receiving AFDC grants go to work when "suitable" employment was found and when provision for day care existed. "Unsuitable home" restrictions drew upon nineteenth-century assumptions that charity should not support those homes in which the mother was so dissolute, immoral, or otherwise incompetent that the home was "unsuitable" for children. Both restrictions were used against black mothers more than white mothers, and in the South more than in the North. Both shifted decisions about whether a mother should work and about how best to care for her children to caseworkers and welfare administrators. The unsuitable home restriction provided a rationale for examining the sexual conduct of AFDC mothers and allowed moral judgments by caseworkers to have serious material consequences; although formally terminated in the late 1950s, it continued to influence local practices through the 1960s. Other restrictions, especially the "substitute father" and "man in the house" regulations, were similarly used to eliminate from the rolls those families that had an able-bodied man, and served as the excuse for unannounced visits and infamous "midnight raids" to see if there were any men in the house.

The 1940s and 1950s were thus a period of extreme local discretion coupled with repressive practices to keep families off the AFDC rolls and prevent children from receiving aid. Despite some demographic changes that should have expanded the rolls — increases in the number of small children and female-headed families, and migration from low-eligibility southern states to the urban North — the growth in the number of families on welfare was a modest 17 percent between 1950 and 1960. While it is difficult to determine causality, the various discretionary methods combined with continuing popular views about the kind of people who "go on welfare" undoubtedly had a sizable impact, both by discouraging potential welfare recipients from applying and by providing the grounds for denying eligibility to those who otherwise qualified.

The turmoil of the 1960s — the militancy of the poor, the frantic efforts to reform AFDC, and above all a huge expansion in the AFDC rolls and levels of support — replaced the stable conditions of the 1950s. At least part of the growth in AFDC families was demographic; an increase in female-headed families of 30 percent between 1960 and 1970 meant that the population most eligible for AFDC expanded relative to the population as a whole. But this growth was small compared to the increases in the AFDC rolls and overall spending levels, which are comprehensible only as a response to increased militancy during the decade. Once again, as they had in the 1930s, the poor found themselves with political clout. The civil rights movement, the threat of social disorder created in the ghetto riots, legal advocacy by poverty lawyers, and organizations like the National Welfare Rights Organization institutionalized and legitimized the struggle for expanded welfare benefits and made poor people aware of those benefits. Some of the worst administrative abusers were curbed, including some of the discretionary power of caseworkers. Legal strategies during the 1960s slowly established welfare as a right with certain legal and procedural safeguards. As a result, participation rates jumped during the late 1960s from around three-fifths of those eligible in 1967, indicating a large pool of families either unaware of welfare, unwilling to apply, or wrongly denied benefits, to almost 100 percent in 1971. Simultaneously, another result of the militancy of the 1960s was the enactment of new programs to distribute specific goods to the poor — principally food stamps and Medicaid. By 1975, when total AFDC payments were $9.2 billion, subsidies under the food stamp program equaled $4.4 billion and Medicaid subsidies were $12.3 billion. Some of the subsidies went to those ineligible for AFDC payments, but the additional resources available to the poor from in-kind programs were substantial.

These developments did not go uncontested, as efforts to limit the expansion of welfare costs by reducing welfare rolls emerged. . . .

In the cycles affecting welfare over the past fifty years, we can see the two different forces of the liberal democratic state operating simultaneously. On the one hand, democratic pressures and the threat to social stability from those unable to earn a subsistence wage, during the Great Depression and the 1960s, forced the expansion of public assistance. Once these threats subsided, assistance programs suffered periods of retrenchment and greater restrictiveness, as they did during the 1950s and again in the 1970s and 1980s. The cycles themselves suggest that, given the inability of the poor to develop a permanent and powerful interest group, the power to threaten social peace — "raising a lot of hell" — has been considerably more potent than moral arguments on their behalf. The cycles also reveal the second force acting on the state — the continuing influence of nineteenth-century liberalism, which views economic conditions as the product of private decisions and individual initiative. In this view, any gain that is not achieved through individual initiative in the private market is wasteful and unproductive. When public assistance is necessary, it must always be less than can be gained in the labor market. This argument, rooted in the tenet of nineteenth-century liberalism that required that the state not undermine private labor markets and that market incentives remain intact, has been more consistently argued, and argued from a wider range of ideological viewpoints, than the impulse simply to reduce welfare spending. It continues to be a prime concern among modern liberals as well as conservatives in the desire to reduce the work disincentives implicit in the welfare system.

These two sets of forces are necessarily antithetical. If the poor gain high welfare benefits, the costs of welfare and its potential for undermining labor markets increase. Conversely, mechanisms to reduce welfare costs and to force welfare recipients into labor markets with few job opportunities reduce support for the poor. This antithesis has been recognized in conservative and liberal discussions as the "great trade-off" among grant levels, costs, and work disincentives, and in neo-Marxist analyses as a contradiction between the state's role in supporting capitalist institutions (like labor markets) and its role in legitimizing the social system by limiting poverty. No matter what the vocabulary, the contradictory pressures on welfare policy — the need to provide a decent subsistence for the poor versus the need to limit support so that a pool of inexpensive labor is available and labor market incentives are maintained — are deeply rooted in the social and economic system. Gains in public assistance have therefore been open to reversal, are always politically controversial, and have been achieved not through moral arguments or within the context of traditional interest group politics, but through various forms of protest.

Children are affected by the contradictory forces within the welfare system as a whole, since the benefits available to them have gone up and down with its restrictiveness or expansiveness. But another set of tensions affects children and helps explain why children are so shabbily treated. A basic assumption of most public assistance programs that benefit children is that *children* should be supported, not poor individuals or poor families. The AFDC system, the earned income tax credit for the working poor, and some proposed revisions like Nixon's Family Assistance Plan have been aimed at families with children and have by design left out childless households. Yet the government's inability to separate children from their parents and the public unwillingness to support certain kinds of parents have led to practices that remove innocent children from the rolls — the "unsuitable homes" and "man in the house" regulations, and more recently, the Child Support Enforcement Program, which in part refuses support to children whose mothers are considered "immoral." Such practices ignore the possibility that these children might be precisely those most in need of assistance, and they deny that the "immorality" of the mother ought not affect the welfare of the blameless child. In effect, poor children are not considered innocent: the state requires them to bear some of the burdens of their mothers' presumed sins.

The state's attitude toward fathers has been no better. One goal of welfare systems, from mothers' pensions to the present, has been to preserve the family, generating the concern that welfare programs not include incentives for the father to leave. Yet in practice the imperative has been stronger not to support able-bodied fathers, who are presumed to have no legitimate reason (as mothers might) for staying out of the labor force. Until 1962 AFDC extended aid only to families with the father absent. Even now the AFDC-U system, which extends aid to families with an unemployed father, has been adopted in only twenty-three states and the District of Columbia, and because of serious restrictions accounts for only 3.7 percent of families and 5.1 percent of all welfare recipients. The "man in the house" and "substitute parent" regulations and the Child Support Enforcement Program are other devices to insure that able-bodied men are not inadvertently supported. As a consequence, children with both a mother and a father fare the worst under present programs; they are only half as likely to be moved out of poverty, compared to children with an absent father. Every reform proposal has mimicked the current welfare system by maintaining differentials between families with an able-bodied man and female-headed families, providing incentives to form female-headed families. The incentives for splitting up families are not accidental, however, but reflect the constraint that public assistance not undercut labor markets by supporting able-bodied men. Children are again penalized for the "sins" of their parents, in this case the "sin" of remaining together.

The inability to break the link between parents and children and the strong tie between income support and employment are clearest in the treatment of different kinds of poor children. Children whose parents have insufficient independent income are supported at very different levels under social insurance programs — primarily Old Age, Survivors, Disability, and Health Insurance (OASDHI or Social Security) and unemployment insurance — and under public assistance programs (primarily AFDC, with a few children supported by Supplemental Security Income). In theory, social insurance programs are distinguished by their connection to employment: wage earners and employers contribute part of earnings, and benefits are presumed to represent previous earnings. In practice these programs are a mixture of insurance and assistance: benefits are not precisely tied to past earnings, and there is some redistribution from high earners to low earners in insurance as well as assistance programs. Despite the fact that the difference between social insurance and welfare programs is imprecise, it remains strong enough in the public consciousness so that social insurance benefits are considered to be "earned rights"; the stigma attached to welfare dependency is relatively absent from Social Insurance programs, and many citizens opposed to welfare spending support Social Security and unemployment insurance. As a result, the payment per child in 1979 under Social Security was $205 per month for the child of a deceased worker, $120 for the child of a retired worker, and $95 for the child of a disabled worker; the average family under unemployment insurance received $336 per month; while the average family on AFDC received $271 per month and the average recipient received $93. This differential treatment reflects a class bias: unemployment insurance and Social Security benefits go to families that have had a regular connection to employment and are therefore part of the working class. AFDC benefits, with lower support levels, go to a marginal class with a much less regular connection to production. Children are again differentially treated according to characteristics of their parents, in this case their class status.

A further ambivalence embedded within the AFDC program concerns the mother-child relationship. In the mothers' pension movement and in the Social Security Act of 1935, the purpose of providing aid was to enable the mother to devote full time to the care of her children. Yet a contrary view of the mother's role has always been present as well: that she ought to get to work as quickly as possible, to become self-sufficient rather than dependent on government benefits. This view has gained prominence as the "employable mother" rules in AFDC have been institutionalized in the WIN program and in the expanded category of "employables." Now only mothers with children under six are clearly thought to be necessary in the home, and mothers with school-age children are generally considered "employable"; and Reagan has proposed that mothers with children over three be eligible for "workfare." Of course, attitudes toward maternal employment have changed drastically since 1909. But rather than expanding the options available to poor women, these changing attitudes have been used against them, restricting their decisions by forcing them into the labor market. In contrast to the nonwelfare population, the decision to work or not has been taken out of the hands of welfare mothers and has been made by welfare regulations and caseworkers. The "workfare" impulse and the imperative to get mothers back to work thus undercuts the original purpose of AFDC: to provide resources so that children can have the benefit of their mother's presence.

The ambivalence toward maternal employment and the reluctance to support able-bodied but underemployed fathers provide two examples of how the welfare system, originally intending to "support the family" by providing basic resources, in fact undermines families by taking decision-making power away from parents and by providing requirements and incentives contrary to family ideals. Other examples exist, like the Child Support Enforcement Program, which theoretically "supports" family units by insuring that fathers will not abandon their families, but in practice may disrupt extended kin networks and may expose the mother to violent retaliation. In these destructive practices and in the failure of welfare programs to reduce poverty substantially, one fundamental issue dwarfs all others: the treatment of poor children is dictated by considerations unrelated to their welfare. Instead, the interest of taxpayers in reducing welfare costs, a punitive attitude toward unemployed fathers (and, increasingly, unemployed mothers), and moralistic attitudes toward welfare mothers have dominated. In the process, the imperative that public welfare protect those children most in need of the state's assistance has been destroyed. . . .

A . . . proposal for restructuring welfare emerged during the 1970s . . . : a "three-track" system that recognized that the poor do not constitute a homogeneous group and included three programs directed at different groups. President Carter's Program for Better Jobs and Income, presented in 1977, is an example of a three-track system. "Unemployables" — the aged, disabled, and single parents with children six and under — would have a relatively high guarantee level (approximately 65 percent of the poverty line) with benefits reduced by fifty cents for each additional dollar of earnings. "Employables" would have a much lower guarantee of less than half the poverty line, and would therefore have to work to earn an adequate income; however, for those unable to find jobs in the private sector (including "regular" government jobs), the program would have provided one public job per family at the minimum wage. Finally, for the working poor — those who have regular employment at low wages — an expansion of the existing earned income tax credit would have supplemented their earnings. Like other three-track proposals, the Program for Better Jobs and Income was designed to preserve income differentials between those who work and those who do not. Like its antecedents, it maintained the integrity of the private labor market by ensuring that public service employment went only to those unable to find a job in the private labor market, by making the income associated with public employment lower than that in private employment, and by aiding the working poor through an earnings subsidy rather than through cash grants requiring no employment. But unlike other proposed reforms, the three-track approach deals forthrightly with the inadequacies of the private labor market, it faces squarely the fact that many jobs available do not pay enough to prevent families from slipping into poverty and the fact that there is not enough employment for all those in the labor force.

Yet as progressive as the three-track plans are, they do not overcome basic structural problems. Children would be affected by the imperatives of the labor market in the continued ambiguity over whether mothers should work or not and in the differential treatment of those who do not work. Children six and under are more likely to be in families of "unemployables," as long as mothers with young children are considered "unemployables." Although the basic benefit levels for them would be higher than for children of "employables," the support levels proposed by Carter were still grotesquely inadequate — 65 percent of the official poverty standard, a standard that has itself been designed to cover only short-term emergencies. Thus, as is currently true, "unemployables" would be forced to work or to pool incomes in kin networks in order to survive. In the resources available to them and in the strain on their mothers, these children — the youngest and most vulnerable children — would still suffer relative to the children of "employables." As always, the welfare of children remains subordinate to the goal of maintaining the status of employment.

A second potential problem involved what is in many ways the most progressive aspect of the three-track proposals, the program of public service employment. With such a program, welfare would begin to transcend its role as a mechanism for merely redistributing income and would begin to provide a clear alternative to labor markets as a way of generating goods and distributing income. But a strong caveat is necessary: public employment is subject to the same constraints as all other public programs, and in a welfare context it could easily be transformed into work relief rather than being a mechanism of economic independence. Since the jobs created under such a program would be neither in the private sector nor in the conventional public sector, they would be considered the least valuable. Employers and labor unions would press to eliminate from public employment any work that could be contracted to private employers, such as public works. Wages for those participating would be politically determined rather than determined by market forces, generating intense political battles. (For example, the AFL-CIO opposed Carter's Program for Better Jobs and Income on the grounds that the public service wage — set at the minimum wage — was lower than the prevailing wage in local labor markets and would thus undermine wages.) With the wage rate set lower than that available in the private labor market, but higher than what nonworkers get in direct grants, public service employment would appear like work done to qualify for a grant rather than work performed because of its value in a market sense. These conditions constitute a set of incentives to create "make-work" programs rather than programs where output and jobs are inherently valued. Finally, work requirements in the context of welfare programs have been associated with some of the worst treatment of welfare recipients, and therefore public service employment is too closely connected to past "workfare" efforts to be supported by recipients themselves. Even three-track proposals, then, were unable to escape the dilemmas inherent in the welfare system, despite their complexity and their efforts to address the different sources of poverty and the inadequacies of the private labor market.

Despite the pressure for reform, none of the proposals advanced during the 1970s proved politically acceptable. Nixon's Family Assistance Plan failed because of inadequate benefit levels; Carter's Better Jobs and Incomes plan was politically dead almost as soon as its details had been unveiled, unacceptable to too many interest groups despite being the result of the most thorough study of reform alternatives ever made. There is no greater testimony to the difficulty of reforming welfare than the inadequacy and political unacceptability of every major approach to reform considered during the 1970s; there is no better evidence of the inability of our political system to act on its deepest convictions.

In retrospect, the reform impetus of the 1970s failed to consider the rising tide of anger at welfare programs. That rage reflected racial hostility toward blacks and Hispanics, but it also reflected the deterioration of economic conditions and the frustration of many Americans with a government unable to resolve its problems. The failure of costly welfare programs to reduce poverty substantially generated hostility toward the whole enterprise and allowed Americans to see in the welfare system everything wrong with public programs: excessive government intervention into private life, outrageous expenditures on people who did not work, public support for "immoral" and "deviant" ways of life. With the election of Ronald Reagan, the ever-present hostility toward the poor has become permissible, even fashionable. The "solution" has been not to propose any real reforms but to reduce transfer payments and social programs, to abandon the effort at federal policy making in favor of state discretion, and to act as if poverty is both trivial and unworthy of public attention. In the retreat to defining childhood poverty as the responsibility of parents, the Reagan proposals create the conditions for more misery, the progressive alienation of the poor, another round of urban riots and another stage in the repeating cycles of crisis and reform.

No one can be complacent about the welfare system. Welfare reform has been on the national agenda almost constantly for two decades, and serious efforts to alleviate poverty through government programs stretch back to the progressive era. The same debates over levels of support and over fears of fraud and "pauperization" have been constantly recapitulated. The same kinds of practices keep reemerging, including distinctions between the "deserving" and the "undeserving" poor and between "unemployables" and "employables." The hope that the welfare population will "wither away," particularly with the initiation of work programs, constantly reappears. Yet the structure of American capitalism guarantees a relatively large welfare class; the causes include the persistence of business cycles and periodic high levels of unemployment, an upward trend in the unemployment rate and high levels of underemployment, and increased number of female-headed families unable to support themselves because of discrimination. Given these conditions, the central preoccupations that keep recurring — to minimize the welfare rolls and to maintain work incentives — ignore the causes of poverty and guarantee the inadequacy of welfare programs.

Redistributive programs — programs like AFDC that redistribute income from the majority of taxpayers to a vulnerable minority — cannot eliminate poverty under any conception of poverty. Under conditions in which the state can alleviate poverty only by taxing away the "private" earnings of individuals and corporations, providing for the poor will always generate resistance. At best, the poor can make limited advances during some periods, especially when they exercise the threat of social disruption; in other periods, redistributive programs are cut back. In a society where incomes are considered private and where other people's children are viewed with such hostility and distrust, redistributive systems lurch back and forth between levels of insufficiency and levels of disaster, fundamentally inadequate to the tasks of eliminating poverty.

For real reform, it will be necessary to move beyond merely redistributive mechanisms of income support. To alleviate the poverty of female-headed families, which constitute such a large proportion of poverty, policies should deal directly with the sexual and racial discrimination and unequal skill levels that cause women to have insufficient earning power. Those concerned about the proliferation of unstable, low-skilled jobs have advocated programs to stimulate the transformation of such jobs into more stable, skilled positions, a policy that would reduce the group moving in and out of poverty. Programs to deal honestly with insufficient employment — for example, public employment without the compromises and constraints that now tend to turn such employment into short-term, unskilled work of marginal value, and public employment that provides the basis for regional development and economic growth — ought to be part of any system of income supports. But these alternatives would interfere with "private" labor markets as they currently operate, and none of them have been taken seriously as welfare reforms. Real solutions — ones aimed at the roots of poverty — must await the relaxation of constraints on the state in a capitalist economy.

In the meantime, the early promise of the welfare system — to support those children, themselves blameless, who are impoverished and unlikely to develop "to the full limit of their potential" — remains empty. Even the instrumental argument that the present costs of providing for poor children will yield future returns has failed to have much weight. In practice, the welfare of poor children is determined by more immediate calculations: children are denied aid if adequate support might threaten the integrity of labor markets, the solvency of the public treasury, or the moral standards of the community. In the process, the promise of *parens patriae* — that the state will provide for children whose parents cannot provide — is effectively vitiated. Instead, we so desperately distrust and dislike lower-class adults that we are willing to let their children suffer as well.

CONSERVATIVE: YES

14. THE FAMILY AND DEMOCRACY

Brigitte Berger and Peter L. Berger

As the twentieth century draws to its close, the overriding question is likely to be the capacity of Western-style democracy to survive; for some, especially among intellectuals, it is whether this type of society is even worthy of survival. Put differently, people are asking more frequently just what it is that our kind of society stands for. Clearly, it cannot be our task here to present a comprehensive philosophical defense of Western society in general and of its political heritage in particular. Also, we are, of course, well aware of the fact that there are sharp differences of viewpoint on this matter within Western society (not to speak of its critics elsewhere). All the same, it seems to us that there is a wide consensus, spanning various ideological divides, on the following propositions:

Western society stands for the value of the individual, regardless of race, social background, or physical endowment. Closely related to this is the belief that every individual has the right to freedom from constraints to which he has not assented, and this right includes freedom of beliefs and ways of life. Implied in this, logically, there is an acceptance of a pluralism of beliefs and ways of life, since free individuals will make various choices. Also implied in this is the democratic assumption that freedom is the right of *every* individual — that is, freedom is not the prerogative of an elite but of the common people as well. These notions of individual rights must be institutionalized; democracy, as it has developed in Western society, is precisely the political system in which this body of convictions has been institutionalized. Democracy, then, rests on a number of basic assumptions about human nature; these assumptions are both cognitive (in terms of what human beings *are*) and normative (in terms of the moral demands human beings are entitled to make).

Political philosophers have put these and similar propositions much more elegantly than we have; the present statement will do for our purposes. But we must now point to an important aspect of this matter: While democracy is clearly based on a set of normative beliefs, it is *also* based on the cognitive assumption that these norms are capable of empirical realization. Thus one may say philosophically that human beings are entitled to freedom; saying this, however, one assumes that there are concrete human beings capable of taking advantage of this entitlement. For democracy to exist, there must be self-reliant and independent-minded individuals capable of making use of the institutional provisions for freedom and capable of resisting the manifold social pressures toward conformity. It follows that a vital question for democracy is that of the psychological and social conditions under which such individuals are likely to emerge. Shortly after the demise of the Franco regime, when the democratic forces of Spain were faced with the problem of how to deal politically with the authoritarian parties of both the right and the left, one liberal politician remarked: "If you want to build a democracy, you must do it with democrats." This sentence can serve a wider purpose: Democracy will be a meaningless abstraction (and probably a short-lived one at that) unless there are living human beings who require it, demand it, and have the ability to make use of its institutional arrangements for their own aspirations toward freedom. *Where are such people to be found?*

Ever since de Tocqueville, if not earlier, there have been passionate debates over the question whether democracy, despite the value of the individual that it has always espoused, may not in fact tend to operate against individual autonomy, pushing people toward conformity and herdlike existence. Aristocrats, of course, have always believed this, and in this they are in curious agreement with critics of "bourgeois democracy" on the left. In recent years this old debate has taken new forms. There has been much concern over the alleged decline of public virtue (certainly a presupposition of democracy), with a tendency of large numbers of people to withdraw from political involvement into private, hedonistic, and even narcissistic concerns. Thus David Riesman saw this shift in the passage from the "inner-directed" to the "other-directed" character type — the former self-reliant and autonomous, the latter pliant and conformist to the changing circumstances of the social milieu. Erich Fromm, more on the left than Riesman, perceived a similar shift as being due to modern capitalism, with individuals acquiring an overall "marketing orientation" and finally perceiving their own personality as a marketable commodity, with the result that they become alienated from themselves as well as from others. In recent American sociology (much of it left of center at least in tendency), C. Wright Mills initiated a whole school of interpretation whereby contemporary "mass society" is understood as the very antithesis of the "public" on which democracy was originally based. A large number of other authors could be cited, all deploring in various ways the decline of the public and with it the impending demise of democracy. Those who view the situation in this way (ranging ideologically from the democratic right to democratic socialists), whatever else may divide them, agree that the danger to democracy is a negative development not only politically but in terms of deeply held human values.

. . . The family (at least in its "bourgeois" form) has been widely accused of being a prime cause of this decline — promoting selfishness and privatism and thus standing in opposition to the common good and the civic virtues. In this perspective, true democracy would have to be anti-familistic. The family constitutes the last and most harmful barrier between the individual and society. . . . There has recently been some important change in this perspective on the family. While there continues to be the notion that the public has been in decline, the family now tends to be seen as a *victim*, rather than a *cause*, of this process. Thus, for instance, Richard Sennett sees the family as but another victim of what he calls "the fall of public man," a paradoxical development characterized on the one hand by an escape into the private sphere and, on the other hand, by a fusion between public and private that is detrimental to both. Even more sharply, Christopher Lasch has bestowed victim status on the family in his description of the alleged devastations of private life by modern capitalism. And of course, on the right there are many people deploring the assaults on the family by an imperialistic welfare state and its professional allies.

We completely disagree with those who would blame the family — and especially the bourgeois family — for the social problems of our time. Compared to this anti-familism, we may further say, the recent emphasis on the family as victim is preferable. But this later view also falls far short of what we would consider an adequate view of the situation: It is not so much a matter of seeing the victimization of the family (though such victimization there has certainly been); it is much more important to see that *the family, and specifically the bourgeois family, is the necessary social context for the emergence of the autonomous individuals who are the empirical foundation of political democracy.* This has been so historically. There is every reason to think that it continues to be so today.

It has frequently been pointed out that the treatment of the family in moral philosophy and political theory is a good indicator of the vision of society being propagated. This has always been so, at least in Western thought. There is one tradition, reaching from Plato through Rousseau to Marx, in which the family is viewed as a barrier to the achievement of virtue, justice, and equality in society. There is another tradition, going back to Aristotle and continued by Locke, Hegel, and de Tocqueville, which declares the family to be the cornerstone of social order. Present-day attacks on the bourgeois family have been most influenced by Marx and by the later developments of Marxist theory. Marx and Engels insisted that "civil society" of the bourgeois type and the bourgeois family developed conjointly. Both social formations are organized around private property, and they continue to reinforce each other, forming a breeding ground for the alleged ills of capitalist society. Marx and Engels were sympathetic to some of the ideals of the early bourgeois family — such as mutual love, equality, and shared work — but they maintained that these ideals were necessarily debased under capitalism. These notions were elaborated by Engels in his seminal work on the origins of the family. . . . An important linkage between Marxism and contemporary feminism is to be found in the writings of the so-called Frankfurt School, especially in the works of Max Horkheimer, Theodor Adorno, and Herbert Marcuse.

Special mention should be made here of Adorno's influential work *The Authoritarian Personality,* published in 1950. The argument here is that (right-wing) authoritarianism has its roots in the type of family produced by bourgeois-capitalist society. This type of family is supposedly characterized by lack of affection and the demand for strict conformity to conventional modes of conduct. Individuals raised in this way are supposed to feel fundamentally weak and insecure and are therefore supposed to admire power and toughness, to despise weak out-groups, and to be prone to succumb to strong leaders. It follows that, as long as the bourgeois family lasts, authoritarianism will remain a constant danger. Conversely, real democracy will be frustrated by the authoritarian patterns reproduced by the family. The connection between bourgeois family patterns and authoritarianism (equated here with fascism) is made even more strongly in the works of Wilhelm Reich, another neo-Marxist German writer who came into his own, somewhat belatedly, in the late 1960s in America. It is but one small step from there to the kind of analyses advanced by R. D. Laing, David Cooper, and other recent radical theorists, who look upon the bourgeois family as the major obstacle to healthy and non-repressed individuals, who alone can be the harbingers of a just social order.

This type of thinking has been very influential in the past two decades in the commune movement in America and Western Europe. The commune is to produce a new kind of human being, freed from the egoism deemed to be intrinsic to the bourgeois way of life and ready to live in collective structures of mutual affection and shared responsibility. This movement has been strongly anti-individualistic and (logically enough) has blamed modern individualism on the bourgeois family. Living communally, within a sharing economy, commune members seek to achieve a collective consciousness radically different from that of the old, individualistic values created by the bourgeois family. The anti-democratic propensities of these groups should not surprise us. Indeed, far from creating the non-authoritarian personalities dreamed of by their original proponents, the communes of recent decades have been the context of some of the most rigidly authoritarian and destructive movements of our time. If any phenomenon can, then the communes constitute the most telling empirical falsification of the theory that the destruction of the bourgeois family is the precondition of freedom. The depressing record of the commune movement may also have contributed to the greater readiness today to reconsider the much-maligned bourgeois family and even to ask anew whether this institution may not be a necessary prerequisite for a democratic society.

We have already made it amply clear that our own position is diametrically opposed to the position of those who see the family and freedom as antithetical phenomena. Nor is our position dependent on the sorry record of recent experiments in anti-bourgeois life-styles. We have tried to show how the bourgeois family developed historically in close correlation with the forces that created modern democracy, and we believe that this historical linkage continues to be of great importance. This belief, however, must be spelled out further.

Aristotle's famous view that if children did not love their parents and family members, they would love no one but themselves, is one of the most important statements ever made about the relation between family and society. The family permits an individual to develop love and security — and most important, the capacity to trust others. Such trust is the prerequisite for any larger social bonds. Only in the family are the individual's social tendencies aroused and developed and with these the capacity to take on responsibility for others. A person who has developed no family bonds will have a very hard time developing any larger loyalties in later life. The normal process of such a development begins in the family and then "moves out" to larger social groupings. In the words of the German ethologist Eibl-Eibesfeldt, "The human community is based on love and trust: and both are evolved through the family."

This, of course, has always been true. That is, these are not aspects of human life that are limited to the modern era or to the specific family type developed by the bourgeoisie. Aristotle has *all* social orders in mind. But a society that puts a premium on individual responsibility, as any democracy must, will have to be particularly mindful of the institutions that nurture this personal trait. As we have tried to show, the bourgeois family, more than any other, at least in modern times, provides this nurture. That is why the attack on the bourgeois family *in the name of democratic values* is peculiarly perverse. So is the attack on the basis of the alleged possessiveness of bourgeois family life — the possessiveness which, ever since Marx, has been ascribed to capitalist notions of private property. Bourgeois education does not emphasize possessiveness but, rather, sharing with others — as any visit to an American playground or nursery school will show. Yet, paradoxically, Marx *was* right in a way: Only if the child has a sense of what is properly his can he share that property with others; in the absence of private property of any sort, there can be no deliberate acts of sharing; the child, in other words, has nothing that he *could* share. By the same token, private property is the precondition of *any* notions of a "private" realm — and finally, of a "private" self, which can in principle be free of others. This has obvious implications, concerning the relation of private property and democracy, that we cannot pursue here. But we do want to point once again to the evidence that children who are deprived of all possessions become severely frustrated and, in consequence, resentful of others. Human culture includes the love of things, of objects. There is no culture in which individuals do not have some things that they can call their own and for which they have "private" responsibility. Possessing things is a prerequisite for the development of individuality and of social development. *This* does not pertain to the bourgeois family as such; what *does* pertain is the value of sharing one's possessions with others and being responsible for their productive use. In Puritan terms, the value of "stewardship" loses plausibility as religious conviction wanes, which once again brings out the importance of religion for the moral base of modern society.

In any event, quite apart from the issue of private property, the bourgeois family has been the single most important context for the value of individual responsibility. No substitute has emerged. We would argue that, because of this, this type of family is essential for the survival of a democratic polity.

More generally, there is the question of the moral foundation of any human society, and especially of a democratic polity. Emile Durkheim was one classical social theorist who has argued that, at its core, every human society is a moral community; conversely, he tried to show how, in the absence of shared moral values, a society must begin to disintegrate. This general sociological truth about society is doubly valid when a society organizes itself politically as a democracy. The reason for this is simple: In the absence of moral consensus, coercion remains the only instrument for the maintenance of even minimal social integration. Such coercion, however, cannot coexist with democracy. Where, then, are the institutions that instill basic moral values in individuals? Durkheim (in this respect, very much in the tradition of the Enlightenment) thought that education might perform this function; John Dewey, coming from a very different intellectual tradition, represented an American version of the same faith. We would argue that the experiences of this century give little support to this notion. This is not to denigrate the values of education. But the school as an institution appears to be quite ineffective in instilling basic moral values — *unless* it serves to reinforce values already instilled in the individual by his homelife. Very much the same is true of the churches. The law, which in America has arrogated to itself (or, more likely, been saddled with by others) the role of moral source or guide, is also singularly unsuited for this function; it is far too abstract, far too remote from the concrete social contexts in which individuals find meaning and identity. The family, today as always, remains the institution in which at any rate the very great majority of individuals learn whatever they will ever learn about morality. It is very unlikely that this will change. Once again, this means that the family has a political function of the greatest importance, especially in a democracy.

No amount of legislation and court decisions can produce in the individual such basic moral ideas as the inviolability of human rights, the willing assent to legal norms, or the notion that contractual agreements must be respected. What legislatures and courts can do, of course, is to reinforce such moral values and to impose sanctions on the minority that offends against them. But neither the state nor the judiciary can be moral authorities in and of themselves. When they try to do this, they either are ineffective (the usual case in democracies) or they start out on a path at the end of which lies totalitarianism, in which the political order tries to absorb into itself all values and all institutions in the society (in which case democracy must come to an end). We would further argue that the primacy of the family as the empirical fountainhead of morality is endangered by the decline of religion, but this point cannot be pursued here.

It is a truism to say (but thereby no less true) that modern society has had serious problems articulating the moral foundation on which it rests. Secularization and pluralism have greatly contributed to this moral crisis. Today, in Western countries, there appears to be a particular crisis of legitimacy for the political order. Why should one obey the law? Is the political order nothing but a collection of practical arrangements, a compromise between competing vested interests? What are the foundations of patriotism — or, even more basically, for *any* sentiments of collective loyalty? Why should one make sacrifices for society? These questions are very difficult to answer in the absence of religious beliefs in the ultimate accountability of human actions. Yet there must be plausible answers if society is not to degenerate either into tyranny or into a sort of public convenience (in the full pejorative sense of the phrase). The family alone, in the absence of a religious world view giving ultimate legitimacy to moral actions, cannot reestablish the civil virtues presupposed by a democratic polity. The family, however, remains the indispensable mediator of these virtues wherever they still exist. This is why the protest of many parents, in various countries, against the moral arrogations of the state and especially of the state-supported school system is an important political event. This is not to endorse any particular protest. And, to be sure, there are protests grounded in bigotry or other reprehensible sentiments. On balance, though, it is the state, rather than parents, which has been responsible for the worst moral perversions of our era; conversely, the resistance against the moral imperialism of state and school, on balance, has been a force conducive to democracy and to the moral order on which it must rest.

Closely related to the issue of moral order is the issue of stability. Social order is impossible unless the conduct of individuals is predictable. In human beings, predictability of conduct depends on the development of a stable character and of reliable habits. Everything we know about social psychology indicates that both have their origins in family life. And as we tried to show earlier, the bourgeois family has been particularly effective in providing a haven of stability in a rapidly changing society. The tensions of modernization, even under relatively benign circumstances, are trying for the individual; the family is the most important institution in which the child is prepared to withstand these tensions and in which, later on, the adult is given the emotional support to continue withstanding them. While providing this stability, the bourgeois family at the same time cultivates individual independence and initiative — again, personality traits that are particularly important under conditions of rapid social change.

The bourgeois ethos arose historically in opposition to "mere tradition," challenging the latter's authority in the name of reason and of individual freedom. This challenge, as the bourgeoisie won its battles against the old order, was itself institutionalized in structures that were both durable and flexible—among these structures notably those of the democratic polity, itself a curious blend of tradition and innovation, of the authority of law and of the autonomous rights of individuals. Such political and legal institutions, however well designed, derive their stability from the personal traits of the many individuals who live under them. The "balancing act" of democracy, therefore, is a faithful reproduction of the "balancing act" of the bourgeois family. Historically, the bourgeois family preceded what we now know as democracy. We would also maintain that the bourgeois family, in its essential features, can survive under nondemocratic or even totalitarian polities; indeed, the evidence from the Communist world indicates how the family becomes extremely important for the individual who wishes to retain any sense of personal autonomy or worth in the face of the all-embracing state. But we doubt very much that the reverse is true; that is, we doubt whether democracy could survive the bourgeois family.

We are, of course, well aware of ideas of freedom that are antagonistic to the bourgeois tradition, notably those related to one or another version of the socialist vision. While we can appreciate the humane ideals of this anti-bourgeois tradition, we are highly skeptical of its possibilities for empirical realization. The term "bourgeois democracy" is a favorite term of opprobrium to many in the socialist tradition. The plain fact is that no other democracy exists, except in the imagination, and at least one reason for this (not the only one, we think) is that the downgrading of the bourgeois family is almost certain to lead to consequences that are incompatible with democracy — or, for that matter, with the freedom of the individual.

In recent decades there has been the cultivation in some social milieus of an extreme individualism, consciously posited in opposition to the bourgeois ethos.

There have been a plethora of "liberationist" gospels. Seen in our historical perspective, this has been an ideal of freedom *without* the bourgeois "balancing act." We are not surprised, therefore, that this type of "liberation" has proved itself to be transitory at best, often an illusion from the beginning, frequently a prelude to an abject surrender of individual autonomy to this or that collective authoritarianism. Individual freedom pushed to an extreme inevitably changes its initial quality. It becomes self-absorption once it is separated from the moral principles that initially both inspired and restrained it. It brings with it a sense of disorientation and loneliness. The individual in this condition comes to turn against the very ideal of freedom that first motivated him. Freedom itself becomes an oppression. In Erich Fromm's apt phrase, the individual now seeks an "escape from freedom" and in consequence becomes ready for any authority that promises him a feeling of belonging and stability. In other words, the individual becomes ready for totalitarian movements or ideologies, which "repress" him far more effectively and comprehensively than any of the authorities he first experienced as oppressive. This is the basic social-psychological dynamics of the revolt against the bourgeois ethos. It is distressing to see it work itself out in the lives of individuals. It is also distressing politically, if one has a stake in the survival of democracy in the modern world.

Thus the bourgeois family and its distinctive ethos have a political significance far beyond the level of individual biography. To be sure, an intact democratic society can survive any number of individuals or subcultures of an anti-bourgeois character; indeed, such tolerance of deviance and nonconformity has been the pride of democracy. However, when such anti-bourgeois values and life-styles become widespread, and when they gain the status of respectability in elite milieus of the society, the matter ceases to be innocuous. A society can absorb only a certain amount of dissolution of its moral substance; a democratic society, paradoxically perhaps, is even more vulnerable than a nondemocratic one to such moral erosion.

Democracy is, by its very nature, a highly precarious human artifact. It cannot survive too much coercion. It must always seek consensus, balancing conflicts and compromises. It must therefore be composed and ongoingly reconstructed by at least a majority of individuals with the personality traits making such a feat possible. Very probably, such individuals must be particularly strongly represented in its elites. How can a society produce individuals who are capable of this sort of balance — who can successfully resist the only seemingly opposite temptations of extreme individualism and a total surrender of individual autonomy to an authoritarian collectivity? This question is the basic sociopsychological issue for any democracy. The bourgeois family is one centrally important institution that has, for several centuries now, provided an *empirical* answer to the question; that is, it has answered the question not just in theory but in its social reality.

. . . We are fully aware of the deep-rooted structural forces of advanced industrial societies and their effects on the family. Thus, of course, we are not advocating that the bourgeois family today should be what it was in an earlier period (even if, as is obviously not the case, it were capable of being this). There has been mounting uncertainty as to the proper purposes of the various roles in the family and in the biographical stages of the individual; this uncertainty is not just a matter of intellectual confusion, but derives directly from the structural changes in society. The contemporary youth culture can be viewed initially as a spontaneous creation of individuals having to cope with uncertainty at a crucial stage of biography. This would not have occurred (for better or for worse) if the family had not lost much of its authority with regard to children and teenagers. Young individuals came to be deprived of the protection traditionally provided them by the family and thus became an "open" category, in the sense that new definitions of what it means to be young could be made. "Youth," in other words, could be radically redefined.

The fate of the youth culture since its virtually Messianic advent in the 1960s provides a very clear illustration of the cycle of "liberation" and disappointment that appears to be endemic to the rebellions against the bourgeois ethos. The earlier sense of mission of the "youth revolution" was well caught in Bob Dylan's song "The Times They Are A-Changin'.". . .

Yet the problems involved in the creation of new institutions were little understood (as, of course, is usually the case with "revolutionary" movements). Despite the heady sense of mission, the real alternatives were limited. It did not suffice to be anti-institutional, as many of the experiments discovered. Above all, it was not understood that institutions are culturally produced forms that must give coherence and continuity, and the enthusiastic people embarked on most of these experiments had little coherence and little capacity to create enduring structures. In consequence, the "new road" was a disappointment to very many of those who set out on it. In some cases, it turned out to be not so new at all, a temporary way station for individuals headed for conventional careers, not too different from earlier versions of "sowing wild oats" before settling down to the "serious" obligations of life. In other cases, the "new road" led to segregated subcultures, many of them cultic or half-crazed. In the worst cases, it was a road to political or religious fanaticism. Large-scale social change in the direction of countercultural ideals of communalism, socialism, or mysticism did not occur, either by radical political transformation of society or by the expansion of new, psychedelic life-styles. It became clear that there are limits to change in the "iron cage" of industrialized/bureaucratized modern society.

But one important change did take place, at least in elite milieus of the society: a far-reaching delegitimation of bourgeois culture, and with this a stripping away of moral authority from various social institutions — not just the family and marriage, but also government, law, business, and organized religion. As one astute observer put it: "The conflict between utilitarian culture and counterculture in the 1960's left *both* sides of the battlefield strewn with expired dreams and ideological wreckage. It resulted in the disillusioned withdrawal of the young and old, hip and straight alike, away from active concern with public institutions and back into the refuge of private life." This could not be a simple "return to normalcy." Delegitimation had gone too far, in both the private and the public spheres. The family did not reassert its moral authority. Education could not fill the gap, but could only serve as a credentialing machine, without the capacity to provide moral guidance. Young people — disillusioned both in their private lives and by the public institutions in the political and economic sector primarily — appear more at bay than ever before in the history of modern Western societies. The extreme cases of this (of which Jonestown has become a terrible symbol) are only the salient angle of the phenomenon. The great majority of young people do not belong to extremist cults, but the disorientation and malaise that provides recruits for these cults are very widespread indeed.

It may well be that Western society no longer has the vitality and the cultural resources to regain its moral self-assurance and its sense of political purpose. But if such a revitalization is possible at all, it will have to be accompanied by a reconstruction of the institutional context in which self-reliant and responsible individuals can develop. This context will have to be very similar to that of the bourgeois family. Paraphrasing Bakunin's reflection upon Voltaire, one might say that if it did not exist, the bourgeois family would have to be invented. It is fortunate that such reinvention is not necessary. As we have seen, the demise of the bourgeois family was proclaimed prematurely. It is still here, despite all the uncertainties about it, and provides a solid foundation for any enterprise of moral reconstruction.

As Max Weber understood very well, modern society is characterized by a "polytheism" of values. To cope successfully with the modern world requires both an honest recognition of this fact and a degree of assurance about one's own value; that is, it requires a delicate balance of tolerance and moral certainty. This is a requirement both for individual sanity and for the survival of a democratic polity. Very clearly, public institutions, including the state, cannot generate these qualities by themselves. As Daniel Patrick Moynihan put it: "In particular, Government cannot cope with the crisis in values that is sweeping the Western world. It cannot respond to the fact that so many of our young people do not believe what those before them believed, do not accept the authority of institutions and customs, whose authority has heretofore been accepted, do not embrace or even very much like the culture that they inherited."

But the isolated individual cannot cope with this crisis either. Human beings are social by their very nature, and the individual bereft of reliable social ties cannot acquire moral assurance in childhood and will have great difficulty in retaining it as an adult. What is essential, then, to a modern society, and especially to a democracy, is the existence of what have been called *mediating structures* — that is, institutions that stand between and meaningfully link the isolated individual and the mega-institutions of modernity. The family is not the only such institution. In Western societies one may add the church, the neighborhood, the voluntary association, and the institutional formations of racial or ethnic subcultures. In non-Western societies there are yet others: clan, village, tribe, and caste. Some of these mediating structures are old, premodern institutions that acquire new functions under modern conditions; others are new creations of the recent period. This is not the place to go into the details of this. Yet one thing is very clear: The family is the most important of these institutions, everywhere in the world — in Emile Durkheim's phrase, ''the key link of the social chain of being.'' In a democratic society, though, this must be a certain type of family, as we have described it — to wit, the bourgeois family, or such a reasonable facsimile of it as will retain its essential features.

There is one further point that must be taken up here: the place of the bourgeois family in a *pluralistic* society. Democracy in general, and American democracy in particular, is committed to the coexistence of a plurality of world views and values. How, then, can our insistence on one particular family type and its particular ethos be reconciled with our allegiance to democracy? As we have pointed out earlier, the argument can be made (and has been made) that it is inaccurate to speak of ''the family'' today and that even the ''bourgeois family'' rarely exists in its ideal form. Empirically, this is correct. There have always been considerable differences in families in terms of class, ethnicity, and race. More recently, attention has focused on single-parent and second-marriage families. While one may point out that very frequently ''non-bourgeois'' families are a matter of necessity, rather than choice, it still remains true that there are significant differences, both in values and in actual practice.

American society in particular has always been highly heterogeneous, and it has become more so in recent history. It can be argued that while class cleavages — certainly in life-styles — have become less pronounced, racial and ethnic subcultures have become more so. What is more, the old ''pockets'' of homogeneity, as in small towns and rural areas, have become ''invaded'' by the national pluralism, with new values and life-styles being accepted, however grudgingly. The coexistence of these very different groups has naturally created tensions and even strife. Yet there is one remarkable fact in all of this: Americans have been ready to accept differences *as long as,* and *only* as long as, the different groups could plausibly be perceived as sharing some common values of the society. In that case, ordinary and initially prejudiced Americans are quite ready to conclude that these different people are ''really okay.'' What are these common values? Mostly, they pertain to interpersonal relations in the private sphere: reliability, honesty, industriousness, respect and concern for others, willingness to take on responsibility. As long as these values are shared by otherwise different groups, there can be a sense of community despite the many differences — in the best sense of *E pluribus unum.* The copious evidence on how Americans overcome racial, ethnic, or religious prejudice bears out this point. Needless to say, this does not deny the ugly history of prejudice in America — with racism its ugliest aspect — but, despite the imprecations of various social critics, it is remarkable how tolerant Americans can be even in the face of drastically different newcomers in their midst. One may contrast this with the sharp resistance to newcomers who do *not* exhibit this allegiance to shared values — as has happened in communities where various countercultural or cultic groups have recently tried to establish themselves.

We would contend that these shared values, making possible a sense of community across the pluralistic spectrum of differences, are in fact the basic values of the bourgeois ethos, and in particular of the bourgeois family. This is not only a matter of outsiders' observations. Rather, people living in situations of intergroup contact and tension perceive things in this way: *They* are really okay: They, too, care for the education of their children; they respect property; they work hard; they try to be helpful to others in the neighborhood. In other words, "they," too, whatever their origins and their continuing differences, can participate in the civil ethos that has been the creation of the bourgeoisie. In this connection it is noteworthy that overcoming prejudices is very often accomplished *via children,* as concerned parents get together on problems that cut across all their differences. This has even happened in situations of acute racial conflict; in such situations, if there is one line that has a chance of carrying the day, it is the proposition "Let's think of the kids first." Now, let it be stipulated that these are values that are not solely exhibited by the bourgeois family. But, in American society, it has been the bourgeois family that has represented them most clearly in the lives of individuals. The bourgeois family, with its values, continues to be the single most important institution capable of bridging differences between groups and subcultures, and thus of providing a plausible basis for democratic pluralism.

Finally, despite the empirical differences between the many forms of family arrangements in contemporary society, it is important to stress that the *ideals* of family life have changed much less than the practice of it. As we have tried to show, it is only a minority, and a highly class-specific one at that, which has directly challenged the ideals. Most people, even if constrained by necessity to live under other-than-ideal circumstances, regret this fact and continue to uphold the old ideal of parents living together and sharing responsibility for their children and for each other — the old ideal, in short, of the bourgeois family. Even many of those who started out rebelling against the bourgeois family find, after they have children, that they "reinvent" arrangements that are remarkably similar to the family type they originally repudiated. This is very important sociologically. A society must be perceived as much in terms of its ideals as of its actual practice. On this level of ideals, the bourgeois family continues to occupy a very prominent place indeed. This, too, is a political as well as a private matter, for it points to one central value set that permits the maintenance of a democratic consensus.

CHAPTER 7

ABORTION RIGHTS: WHERE DO WE GO FROM *ROE* V. *WADE*?

It has been more than a decade since the United States Supreme Court legalized abortion in the case of *Roe* v. *Wade* (1973).[1] The hysteria over abortion continues to brew as one of this country's most unsettling social issues. In the post-*Wade* period there has been an average of more than one million legal abortions per year. Social movements have sprung up to reverse *Roe* v. *Wade*. The National Right to Life Committee (NALRC) involves millions of involved citizens dedicated to stopping abortion at any cost. In contrast, the pro-choice movement has faced off against the right-to-lifers to preserve women's access to abortion. Feminists see the issue somewhat differently. While favoring the right of personal autonomy described in *Roe* v. *Wade,* they see the issue as deflecting attention away from broader issues of women's equality.

Each of the political perspectives presented in this chapter has *Roe* v. *Wade* as its starting point. Therefore it is helpful to examine the reasoning and holding of Justice Harry Blackmun's majority opinion. First, the case came to the Court as a constitutional challenge to a Texas abortion statute holding that procurement of an abortion was a crime — punishable with a two-to-five-year prison sentence — unless it was obtained on "medical advice for the purpose of saving the life of the mother."[2] At the time of the decision, there were great disparities in state abortion laws. In the 1960s, a social movement emerged that defined illness and death from illegal abortions as the social problem and proposed the liberalization of abortion laws. States such as Hawaii, California, New York, and Washington passed laws allowing therapeutic abortions. By the time *Roe* v. *Wade* was decided, seventeen states had passed laws that were more permissive.[3] Yet there were countervailing movements as well. In New York, the permissive abortion law passed by the state legislators was repealed. In Michigan and North Dakota permissive abortion laws were defeated by popular vote.

At the time of the abortion decision, the country was bitterly divided. But worse was the unfairness in the application of state laws. If a woman had the misfortune of desiring an abortion in a conservative state such as Texas, she risked both the penalties of the criminal law and illness and death at the hands of a back-alley abortionist. On the other hand, legalized abortion was available to a woman with means in states with more liberal abortion statutes.

Justice Blackmun opened his opinion of the Court with a frank acknowledgment of the hysteria over abortion. The vigorous opposing views were divided along lines of religion, philosophy, and one's very attitude toward life itself. In addition, Justice

Blackmun observed that the abortion issue was muddied by attitudes toward population control, pollution, poverty, and race.[4]

The task of the Court in such controversies as abortion is to interpret some clause of the Constitution to resolve a dispute with finality. In judicial decision making, past cases or precedents are used to support constitutional interpretation. In *Roe* v. *Wade,* Justice Blackmun acknowledged that there was no explicit mention of a person's right of personal autonomy in the Constitution. (Of course, there was no explicit reference to a woman's right to abortion.) Justice Blackmun relied on right-to-privacy cases such as *Griswold* v. *Connecticut* (1965) to support the Court's decision. In *Griswold,* the Court struck down a state statute banning contraceptive sales to all purposes. The appellant in that case was a licensed physician who provided contraceptive information, instruction, and medical advice to married persons. The Court ruled that a state could not "search the sacred precincts of marital bedrooms for telltale signs of the use of contraceptives. The very idea is repulsive to the notions of privacy surrounding the marriage relationship."[5]

Justice Blackmun relied on the precedent of *Griswold* and other cases bearing on the privacy right to hold that the right of personal privacy protects the abortion decision. The Court held that a women's decision to terminate her pregnancy in the first trimester was absolutely protected by her right of privacy. However, the court did not hold that a woman had an absolute right to abortion regardless of stage of pregnancy. Instead, the Court held that at some point the state's interest in the fetus outweighs a woman's privacy interest. For the stage after the first trimester, the Court allows the state to regulate the abortion procedure. For example, it is not a violation of the privacy right to require abortions to be performed in hospitals rather than in doctors' offices. For the stage after viability, the state may regulate and proscribe abortions. After a fetus reaches viability — the point at which a fetus has the potential to live outside the mother's womb with artifical aid — a state is free to deny any abortion and impose criminal sanctions to protect what the Court called "the potentiality of life." Under modern medical technology, viability is usually placed at about twenty-eight weeks.

To summarize and repeat, *Wade* holds that in the earliest stage of pregnancy, a woman's privacy interest in securing abortion outweighs a state interest in fetal life. As the fetus develops to the last trimester, the privacy interest gives way to the state's interest in the fetus.

THE ABORTION CONTROVERSY IN THE POST-*WADE* PERIOD

Roe v. *Wade* nullified all state criminal abortion statutes that allowed abortion only as a lifesaving procedure on behalf of the mother. After *Wade,* abortion statutes had to be tailored to the stage of pregnancy or be struck down as violative of the privacy interest protected by the Due Process Clause. But unlike other divisive areas such as obscenity, desegregation, and voter rights, the opponents of *Roe* v. *Wade* have not settled into complacency. The opponents of the abortion decision have stiffened. Pro-choice advocates have been unable to extend abortion funding to poor people as a new entitlement. Opposition to abortion has become entangled with the politics of the Equal Rights Amendment.[6] One study described post-*Wade* abortion politics as engendering "a high degree of emotionalism, widespread involvement by the mass citizenry, and persistence over time."[7] This chapter presents three views on the abortion issue, which fall roughly under conservative, liberal, and feminist categories.

Peter Steinfels argues in "The Search for an Alternative" that it is consistent and even desirable for Roman Catholics liberal on such issues as labor and the nuclear freeze to have a conservative view on abortion. The traditional conservative view on abortion is that conception is the point at which nonhuman genetic material becomes human. Once the humanity of the fetus is recognized, abortion is morally reprehensible.[8] Legal protection of the fetus, therefore, must begin at conception.

Right-to-life activists of all religions are popularly depicted as reactionaries by the media and by many social commentators. One journalist described right-to-lifers as "implacable," "nasty," "full of rationalizations," and "inflicting the sting of fetal politics."[9] Yet, the abortion struggle does not always involve such simplistic divisions between the right and the left of center. Peter Steinfels's view represents a moderate conservative position. His position is that the pro-life and the pro-choice views represent extreme political stances difficult to justify. Steinfels argues that liberal Roman Catholics should continue to oppose *Roe* v. *Wade,* but they should do so with a new strategy. Rather than defend life from conception, conservatives (on abortion) should consider supporting abortion up until the first eight weeks of fetal development. It is at eight weeks when the fetus has an unborn human identity, according to Steinfels. This argument addresses the typical liberal justifications for abortion. For instance, such early abortions would allow for freedom of choice when the mother's health was endangered. It would also allow abortion in the early weeks of a pregnancy that was the result of incest, rape, or youthful indiscretion. In short, the revised conservatism proposed by Steinfels short-circuits the most compelling arguments of the pro-choice position. He believes that a more pragmatic opposition to abortion will help move us a decisive step back from *Roe* v. *Wade.*

Charles Hartshorne supports the liberal position in "Concerning Abortion: An Attempt at a Rational View." He argues for the preservation of *Roe* v. *Wade* because it makes pregnancy a matter of human decision. He contends that if we step back from *Roe* v. *Wade,* the coercive arm of the state will be dictating what should be a matter of individual choice, the right to decide whether a fetus should be carried to term. Hartshorne disagrees with Steinfels on the significance of differences between a two- and three-month fetus. To Hartshorne, a two-month fetus is little more than a cell colony a long way from recognizable human feelings. A three-month fetus is not much more. He argues that a fetus cannot speak. A fetus cannot reason or judge between right and wrong. He argues that these are the very qualities which separate humans from higher-order primates such as chimpanzees and orangutans. Traditional conservatives on abortion, such as William Buckley, argue that if a fetus is not fully human, then neither is an infant. An infant, like a fetus, cannot speak, reason, or judge between right and wrong. Hartshorne answers this argument that an infant is not fully human but much closer to that stage than a three-month fetus. He believes that a diminution in abortion rights is a step toward tyranny by our legal system. Although abortion is an unpleasant moral choice, coercion by the state in such matters is unjustifiable.

Catharine MacKinnon in "The Male Ideology of Privacy: A Feminist Perspective on Abortion" supports the result of *Roe* v. *Wade.* The abortion choice should be available. However, she sees the debate between the conservatives and liberals about whether the fetus is human or not as irrelevant. The abortion choice should be available not because the fetus is not human, but because there is no reason why women should not make life and death decisions. MacKinnon approves of the result in *Roe* v. *Wade* but attacks the reasoning of the Court. Recall that Justice Blackmun found a rationale for the abortion decision in the privacy doctrine. Privacy, in the Court's view, was implicit in the concept of ordered liberty. MacKinnon castigates the privacy doctrine formulated by the Court in *Wade* and applied to the subsequent abortion funding case of *Harris* v. *McRae* in 1980.[10] She sees the privacy doctrine as a tool of legal ideology that masks the fact that men dominate women in the private sphere. The private sphere is the whole complex of the intimate environment. It includes the sphere of sex/marriage/childbearing/child-rearing. The Court separates the private sphere from the public sphere. The public sphere includes the courts, the law, and the institutions of the state. MacKinnon views the extraordinary protection of individual rights in the private sphere as two-edged. On the one hand, women should have the right to be free from the unequal effects of sexuality: pregnancy. On the other hand, the liberal right of privacy is an excuse for the state to do nothing about the inequality which occurs behind closed doors in the intimate environment.

The five-to-four decision in *Harris* v. *McRae* highlights MacKinnon's concern about the privacy doctrine. *McRae* came to the Court as a challenge by poor women to the Hyde Amendment, which drastically limited public funding for abortion. In rejecting the women's challenge to the ban on abortion funding, the Court reasoned that it had no obligation to equalize access to abortions. Justice Stewart explained: "Although government may not place obstacles in the path of a women's exercise of her freedom of choice, it need not remove those not of its own creation."[11]

As MacKinnon observes, the state has made "a very short step from that which the government has a duty *not* to intervene in, as in *Roe* [v. *Wade*], and that which it has *no* duty to intervene in, as in [*Harris* v.] *McRae.*" By saying that sexuality, marriage, and the family is not the concern of the state, men will continue to dominate women and our society will be a long way from sexual equality. On its face, the privacy doctrine appears to favor feminist concerns. But what does privacy mean when women do not enter the sexual relationship on the same terms as men? Women are the victims of social problems such as pornography, wife-battering, and the lack of financial access to abortion. The abortion decisions have the hidden effect of supporting sexual inequality. MacKinnon contends that true sexual equality requires state intervention to change the existing distribution of power and resources between the sexes. The legal right to privacy from intervention is a step backward from broader feminist concerns.

References

1. The text of the case can be found in volume 410 of the *U.S. Reports* beginning at page 113. Any law school library would have the full opinion. The proper cite is, *Roe* v. *Wade,* 410 U.S. 113 (1973). Any student of the abortion controversy should begin with the primary decision rather than relying on commentary.
2. *Roe* v. *Wade,* 410 U.S. 113 (1973).
3. *See* Raymond Tatalovich and Bryon W. Daynes. "The Trauma of Abortion Politics," *Commonweal,* November 1981, pp. 644–45.
4. *Roe,* 410 U.S. at 113.
5. *Griswold* v. *Connecticut,* 318 U.S. 479, 485 (1965).
6. Rhonda Copes, "Abortion Rights: Where Do We Go From Here? *Ms.,* October 1983, p. 146.
7. Tatalovich and Daynes, "The Trauma of Abortion Politics," p. 647.
8. Thomas A. Mappes and Jane S. Zembatty, Introduction to Chapter Nine, "Abortion and Fetal Research" in *Biomedical Ethics* (New York: McGraw-Hill, 1981), pp. 400–01.
9. Roger M. Williams, *Saturday Review,* June 9, 1979 quoted by James R. Kelly, "Beyond the Stereotypes: Interviews with Right-to-Life Pioneers," *Commonweal,* November 20, 1981, pp. 654–55.
10. *Harris* v. *McRae,* 448 U.S. 297 (1980).
11. *Harris,* 448 U.S. at 316.

15. THE SEARCH FOR AN ALTERNATIVE

Peter Steinfels

It is hard to tell whether the present impasse over abortion will be lasting. At the moment both sides are in disarray. The pro-choice lobby has suffered a series of legislative and judicial setbacks, culminating in the election of a theoretically anti-abortion administration. The right-to-life movement, prematurely jubilant over the chances that a human life statute could use Congress's fact-finding power to do an end run around *Roe* v. *Wade,* has watched in dismay as (1) some of its stalwarts developed constitutional scruples and deserted the field; (2) the president appointed an ambiguously pro-choice, certainly not anti-abortion, justice to the Supreme Court; (3) the administration made clear that implementing Milton Friedman's notion of "freedom to choose" had priority over combating Planned Parenthood's. Right-to-life groups remain effectively organized to exercise political muscle. But they are not winning the battle of public opinion; indeed, as more women undergo abortions, or know those who have done so, the difficulties of arguing for a total ban will mount. Thus any victory the anti-abortionists win may be almost as "elitist" and at least as subject to public resistance and reversal as the 1973 pro-choice victory in the Supreme Court.

One would think that liberal Catholics might have a distinctive contribution to make in this painful and apparently irresolvable conflict. By "liberal Catholics" I do not simply mean Catholics who are left of center politically, although the greater portion of them are. Liberal Catholicism emerged from the realization that the old alliance of throne and altar corrupted religion and politics alike. But liberal Catholicism did not limit itself to church-state questions. It entailed a general appreciation, both in society and the church, of dissent, dialogue, and diversity; and — a recognition that many Catholic "absolutes" have been historically conditioned and often served institutional power rather than the Gospel.

There are at least two reasons why such an outlook could play a pivotal role in the abortion debate. First, from long immersion in church-state questions, liberal Catholicism forged a relatively sophisticated theory of law and morality, one that neither divorced nor equated the two. Second, while liberal Catholics refuse to treat traditional moral positions as beyond reexamination, they remain rooted in a philosophical tradition that rejects relativism and moral individualism. Morality is neither a matter of social conditioning, nor of arbitrary "personal" opinion, nor of majority vote. Liberal Catholics cannot, like the Supreme Court or the pro-choice movement, slough off the issue of the moral status of fetal life as just too complicated to be considered.

In fact, liberal Catholicism has remained on the margin of the abortion controversy. Part of the explanation is historical. When the abortion issue surfaced in

American politics, liberal Catholics were not only preoccupied with the war in Vietnam but also absorbed in the aftermath of the Vatican Council. Though the reaction in these circles to the repeal of abortion statutes and then to *Roe* v. *Wade* was negative, the reaction to the bishops' plans for a right-to-life campaign was even more negative. People who were disappointed in the church's implementation of conciliar reforms, and for whom the credibility of church leadership had already been sorely tested by *Humanae vitae,* now saw the bishops embark on a course that promised to repeat many of the errors of the past. The fact that prominent segments of the nascent anti-abortion forces exhibited all the characteristics of past crusades against birth control, dirty books, and the Reds didn't help. Liberal Catholics said and wrote some extremely intelligent things about the abortion question in those early years, but already a pattern of detachment, if not embarrassment, had been established.

The fear that the right-to-life movement would harden resistance to reform and renewal in the church has been succeeded by the fear that the right-to-life movement is reinforcing political and social forces that liberal Catholics see as anti-life. The wariness remains. And yet I believe it is being counterbalanced by the increasing impatience many liberal Catholics feel at the tactics and rhetoric of the pro-choice representatives. It is disturbing when a grass-roots anti-abortionist denounces Bella Abzug not only for being pro-choice but for being "anti-family." It is equally, or even more, disturbing when a sophisticated newspaper like the *New York Times* publishes its umpteenth abortion editorial avoiding any discussion of the value of fetal life and thereby delivering its Olympian advice while begging the question at issue. Or when an article on right-to-lifers in *Mother Jones* resurrects the hoariest of nineteenth-century anti-Catholic canards, that Catholics don't really have to practice the morality they preach because they can always wipe their consciences clean in the confessional. Or when NOW and other pro-choice groups raise the alarm that the anti-abortionists are out to ban birth control. One could go on. Despite recent improvement, the national media have treated the pro-life position and the pro-life movement with obvious condescension and bias.

It would be too much to say that liberal Catholics have been moved *en masse* to root for the right-to-lifers, but at least a good number of them have had their sense of fair play and their natural identification when the underdog aroused by shoddy pro-choice maneuvers.

In the end, however, the character of both the right-to-life and pro-choice movements is a peripheral matter. The central issue remains the meaning of unborn human life. Can its destruction be justified? Who should decide, the individual mother or the society? As the increasing resort to abortion — one and a half million a year — mocks all the hopes that this would be an exceptional last resort, limited to tragic dilemmas, liberal Catholics have had to put aside their dissatisfaction with the contending armies and return to the basic questions.

What they find, upon returning, is not reassuring. Abortion is surely becoming an alternative or "fall-back" form of birth control, with the statistics showing a sharp increase in repeat abortions. Rather than being isolated culturally as a "special case," abortion is now mentioned neutrally in everything from Sylvia Porter's *New Money Book for the 80's* ("How to Shop for — and Reduce the Costs of — an Abortion") to health and sex primers for teenagers. It is just another "option."

Will the logic of abortion, as anti-abortionists have always warned, further undermine what respect and protection we currently afford other human lives when, like the fetus, they are vulnerable, unproductive, and threatening to our psychic or material resources? It is hard to tell how slippery the slope is in America. Both practically and psychologically, abortion *has* opened the way to *in vitro* fertilization and sex selection, both on a small scale. It has become the conventional wisdom that a Down's Syndrome child should not be brought into the world, and cases appear to be multiplying where such children are not medically sustained *after* being brought into the world. Here the logic of abortion is indeed powerful: why hesitate to do to a newborn what one is willing to do to a well-developed fetus a few months earlier? (We can, of course, substitute the medical term "neonate" to reduce distracting emotions about this matter.)

But quite apart from worries about where the logic of abortion may lead, which depends on innumerable sociological factors, the logic itself does not withstand scrutiny. Not at least to those who morally reject infanticide. I do not introduce infanticide as a fright word. It is just that in their emphasis either on the woman's right to choose or on social, interpersonal, relational criteria for "humanness," pro-choice arguments almost always deny the fetus any moral standing in such a way that, except for sheer arbitrariness (and instinctive decency, one might add), moral status should also be denied the newborn. Those familiar with philosophical literature know that, logic being logic, defenses of infanticide are no longer uncommon. (Commenting on two of the more notorious such philosophical articles, published in *Philosophy and Public Affairs,* a scholarly journal with impeccable liberal credentials, Roger Wertheimer wondered why their work seemed unlikely "to create anything comparable to the public outrage generated by the now infamous work of Jensen and Hernstein" on race, class, and IQ. "Why not," he asks, "for their assault on the conscience and intellect of civilized people is surely no less brutal and blundering?" His answer: social scientists are taken seriously; philosophers — for good reason, he thinks — are not.)

Last January, the *Christian Century* published an article that aptly illustrates why liberal Catholics may be moving away from peripheral worries to the central issue. It was not by some hawkish population controller but by the distinguished philosopher Charles Hartshorne. Hartshorne set out to refute the "fanatics against abortion" with the familiar argument that a fetus is not an "actual person" because it lacks "the quality that we have in mind when we proclaim our superior worth to the chimpanzees or dolphins. It cannot speak, reason, or judge between right and wrong. It cannot have personal relations, without which a person is not functionally a person at all." Hartshorne is too conscientious to ignore the objection that an infant does not possess these capacities either. His answer is blunt: "Of course, an infant is not fully human. . . . I have little sympathy with the idea that infanticide is just another form of murder." There may be good social or symbolic reasons for not killing infants but since the infant cannot claim equal rights with "already functioning persons," such killing is not "fully comparable to the killing of persons in the full sense." Hartshorne extends the same distinction to the killing of "a hopelessly senile person."

One can even grant this argument some plausibility. We do not think as badly of primitive societies that practice infanticide as we do of those that practice human sacrifice. We do not think as badly of societies that put their burdensome old folks on ice floes as we do of those that regularly slaughter adults in warfare. But that does not mean we want to slide merrily back to that state of things. People who are angered by glib talk of the "truly needy" cannot rest easy with the recent discovery of the distinction between the human and the "truly human."

In the light of pro-choice rhetoric and pro-choice principles, for many liberal Catholics the oversimplifications and insensitivities of the right-to-life movement no longer loom as large as they once did. But liberal Catholics still remain betwixt and between. On the one hand, they are "personally" opposed to almost all abortion and further reject the idea that abortion-on-demand be accepted as the social norm. On the other hand, they are unhappy with the right-to-life alternative, a constitutional amendment declaring all unborn life inviolable from conception.

If liberal Catholics are going to make a difference in the struggle over abortion, there are two steps they must take. Each involves a break with one or the other side, at least as the dispute is now constituted.

The first step is to give up the idea that this issue can be resolved without legislative restriction on abortion. I have in mind various "compromise" positions that some liberal Catholics have found attractive. In one version, for instance, abortion is to be condemned by the churches (but not too harshly) and deplored by the culture. In a second version, extensive social efforts to assure job opportunities and provide child care are added to cultural disapprobation in order to encourage the pregnant woman to carry her child. In no case is abortion finally disallowed for any woman who seeks it, nor funding for abortion denied any woman who needs it.

The psychological assumption behind these schemes is that women naturally find abortion so painful and morally ambiguous that a religious or cultural reminder — or the provision of real support for childbearing and child-rearing — will suffice to dissuade from abortion almost all but the genuinely tragic cases. This psychological assumption, I suspect, may be a projection of the moral and generative sensitivities of those who make the argument. What they assume is quite likely true of most women; what they are unwilling to face is the strong evidence that millions of women simply do not feel this way. Instinctive rejection of abortion does not prevent them from returning, perhaps with regret, though often, too, with a good deal of self-righteousness, for one, two, three abortions. And while equal life opportunities for women — and vastly strengthened social supports for child-raising — are a crying need quite apart from the abortion question, it is hard to imagine any such system that could move either the trivially motivated woman or the seriously burdened and tested one to prefer lifelong responsibilities to a clinic visit and a ten-minute procedure.

What merit there is in these schemes rests on the hope that psychological or social incentives can allow cultural disapprobation of abortion to coexist with a completely noncoercive legal treatment of it. Whether other societies have been capable of maintaining a strong disapproval of some practice without in any way institutionalizing that disapproval in law or social sanctions, I don't know. This society certainly is not. These days our pluralism itself, combined with the pressures of a homogenized national culture, results in the boundaries of morality being largely marked out by the boundaries of the law. To believe that this society can effectively insist on the value of fetal life while refusing to restrict legislatively any assault that a woman may choose on that value, is to indulge in sociological fantasy. Preachment will gradually fall in line with practice.

"Would you then use the law to *force* a woman to carry through a pregnancy to term?" That is the challenge liberal Catholics must be willing to face if they are to make any difference at all in the moral controversy. Their answer will have to be "Yes." Not for every pregnancy (we'll get to that), but for many pregnancies, yes.

Giving that answer will not be easy, especially for Catholic feminists, both male and female. They are justifiably alert to see in any legal coercion of women not the restraints that all members of a reasonable society must submit to, but an extension of the special fetters and disabilities that have historically been inflicted on women. All the more so since pregnancy is not a condition that affects men except indirectly. And sharing a struggle on so many other fronts, Catholic feminists will be loath to break with allies on this point. Nonetheless that is exactly what they will have to do if their often stated opposition to abortion-on-demand is not to equal a mere verbal protestation.

If the first step requires liberal Catholics to disagree frankly with the pro-choice forces, the second step requires them to do the same with the pro-life movement. Anti-abortionists may be divided on what exceptions to tolerate in a ban on abortion, but they are virtually united on insisting that conception is the decisive moment which should trigger the law's protective shield. Thus the two alternatives: *Roe v. Wade* or a constitutional amendment prohibiting abortion at every stage.

The prudential argument against such an amendment has been made — that it so far departs from public opinion as to risk non-enforcement, bringing the law into disrepute while putting abortion itself into a shadow area where grave abuses are likely to occur. The historical test case is Prohibition.

This prudential argument is impressive. There is little doubt that the same citizenry which has resisted *Roe v. Wade* is even more opposed to banning abortion from conception. Americans, Catholics included, overwhelmingly support abortion when the mother's health (not specifically *life*) is endangered; and, again Catholics included, they support abortion in the first trimester. It is unlikely that a human life amendment would pass; if it somehow passed, it would create martyrs who would find ready public sympathy. The end result would be the certain identification of the pro-life impulse with heartless coercion.

Blocking the search for another solution, however, has been the anti-abortion movement's insistence that there can be no compromise on a matter of human life. The fact that only a minority of their fellow citizens share the pro-life position in its entirety is no more relevant than that a minority of Germans opposed Hitler or that a minority of pre–Civil War Americans followed the Abolitionists. To accept anything but a nearly total ban on abortion would be to surrender the very principle of human life at stake and to become complicit with an evil program of extermination. It would be like going halfway with Hitler — a Semi-Final Solution, the right-to-lifers might say bitterly.

It is at this point, I believe, that liberal Catholics must intervene. They must say quite frankly that *the moral status of the fetus in its early development is a genuinely difficult problem*. It is so *of its nature,* as a unique and boundary-line situation, and not because of the blindness or self-interest of those examining the problem.

It should be understood exactly what kind of a challenge this is, and is not, to the dominant position of the right-to-life movement. Just as the pro-choice movement seems utterly oblivious to biology in discussing (when it does) the issue of "humanhood," the right-to-life movement is naively overconfident in its belief that the existence of a unique "genetic package" from conception onwards settles the abortion issue. Yes, it does prove that what is involved is a human individual and not "part of the mother's body." It does not prove that, say, a twenty-eight-day-old embryo, approximately the size of this parentheses (—), is *then and there* a creature with the same claims to preservation and protection as a newborn or an adult.

I am *not* saying that the anti-abortion argument, with its appeal to potentiality, is untrue. In many respects, I find it persuasive. But it is much less persuasive than most anti-abortionists themselves believe. The theologians and philosophers among them have always recognized these difficulties — and fall back on taking the "safer" course in case of uncertainty.

Argument in this area always proceeds by analogy. We analogize from the end of life to the beginning of it. We analogize from the potentiality of an infant or a sleeping person or someone in a reversible coma to the potentiality of the unborn. We analogize from the physical structure and organic integrity of an adult to that of an embryo or fetus. We analogize from the uncertainty of a hunter who doesn't know whether that moving creature in the bushes is a child or a dangerous animal to the uncertainty we face contemplating the unborn life. Philosophers defending abortion have resorted to the most fantastic analogies yet — "thought experiments" involving Martians, violin players mysteriously hooked without permission to someone's circulatory system, or kittens injected with a chemical so that they develop human brains.

All of these analogies are meant to bring what is obscure and unique into the realm of the visible and more familiar (although one doubts that the last category accomplishes this). But all fall short in this effort, some much farther than others. We are left with a large area where we feel our way, relying on imagination, intuition, and a sense of appropriateness as much as on logic. Although it is not *logically* impossible, for example, to consider the great number of fertilized eggs that fail to implant themselves in the uterus as lost "human beings," a great many people find this idea totally incredible. Similarly, very early miscarriage does not usually trigger the sense of loss and grief that later miscarriage does. Can we take these instinctive responses as morally helpful?

The debate about fetal life always reminds me — I swear — of a Dr. Seuss story called *Horton Hears a Who*. The protective elephant, Horton, rescues a civilization of tiny creatures (the "Who") in a series of wild stanzas each ending with the refrain, "A person's a person no matter how small!" But the endangered creatures Horton saves are, of course, exact but miniscule versions of people — at least grown Dr. Seuss people. I have the impression that the clarity of the anti-abortionists' position rests on an image like that — a homunculus, or at least a microscopic baby, inhabiting not the head of the sperm as in medieval lore but the changing shape of the embryo and fetus. It is such an image that provides the emotional force for analogies to Herod's massacre of the innocents or Hitler's extermination of the Jews.

Such an analogy as the latter — whatever else may be said about its uses and abuses — springs from a neglect of biology as great as that of pro-choice advocates who claim the fetus is "part of the mother." It is simply *not* the case that a refusal to recognize Albert Einstein and Anne Frank as human beings deserving of full legal rights is equivalent to a refusal to see the same status in a disc the size of a period or an embryo one-sixth of an inch long and with barely rudimentary features. The old theories of delayed animation and "formed" and "unformed" fetuses may have been based on bad biology. But it seems to me they were also based on a powerful intuition: that what a thing really is corresponds somehow to an overall physical configuration. Thus Dr. Maurice Mahoney of Yale's medical school, who is surely aware of the "genetic package" argument, testifies, "For me, humanness requires that some process of development has taken place which gives the embryo a human form, so that it has a nervous system, a heart and circulatory apparatus, and indications of human shape."

As a Catholic confronting this question, I am not, to be sure, an isolated moral ponderer. Popes, episcopal conferences (Belgium, Italy, Switzerland, Scandinavia, Germany, Quebec, the United States, France), and theologians have reached a remarkable consensus on the obligation to protect human life from its earliest stages. I am impressed not only with the multiple sources of this agreement but with the general moral sensitivity to related social questions that marks many of these statements. I cannot, however, expect my fellow citizens to appreciate the weight of this testimony as I might. Perhaps someday a combination of philosophical argument, moral credibility gained on other issues, and behavior that proclaims the sanctity of human life at every stage could persuade the majority of Americans to accept the current anti-abortion position. At the present time, I believe the force of differing moral intuitions should be recognized. Liberal Catholics who oppose abortion-on-demand should strive for the protection of unborn life not from conception but from that point when not one but a whole series of arguments and indicators have converged to support the ''humanness'' of the unborn.

The goal, in sum, should be the prohibition of abortion after eight weeks of development. At this point, when the embryo is now termed a fetus, all organs are present that will later be developed fully, the heart has been pumping for a month; the unborn individual has a distinctly human appearance, responds to stimulation of its nose or mouth, and is over an inch in size. Electrical activity in its brain is now discernible. As Jerome Lejeune noted before a Senate hearing, at this point ''with a good magnifier the fingerprints could be detected. Every document is available for a national identify card.''

The argument is not that this is the ''magic moment'' when ''human life begins.'' The argument is rather that this is one moment when an accumulation of evidence should compel a majority, even in a pluralist society and despite whatever obscurities about early life continue to be debated, to agree that the unborn individual now deserves legal protection. After this point, abortion could be permitted only for the most serious reasons: endangerment of the mother's life or risk of her incapacitation. ''Mental'' illness (likelihood of suicide or institutionalization) should not be disallowed as though it were not ''real,'' but the decision-making mechanism has to be one of assured integrity because such indications are undeniably more subjective.

Such should be the minimum national policy, established if necessary by constitutional amendment. States should have the freedom to enact stricter restrictions if they chose. Thus the debate about life from conception would not be foreclosed.

What, in practice, would such a prohibition accomplish? On the face of it, it would prevent fewer than half the current abortions. The 1977 figures showed 50 percent of abortions taking place before the end of the eighth week. Another 25 percent or so take place in the next two weeks — and the pressure of a legal time limit would probably mean many of these would be obtained earlier. Still, to those who believe, as I do, that later abortion is a greater evil and a much greater challenge to our standards of protection for human life, such a measure would make a great difference.

Such a measure would also *lead*, not follow, public opinion. It would be a decisive step back from *Roe* v. *Wade,* and it would put the lie to the notion that widespread abortion is an inevitable part of modern ''progress.'' By declaring the legal inviolability of the greater part of fetal life, and by leaving open to states the possibility of defending the rest, such a prohibition would be a statement about the seriousness and moral precariousness of abortion at any stage.

No one knows whether a ban like this could be successfully legislated, but the chances are certainly far higher than for the current right-to-life proposals. Its advocates would not be burdened with charges about the IUD or rape. It would be utterly clear that they were not insisting that any church's moral code be fully translated into law. They would represent reasonable compromise; the defenders of abortion-on-demand, the extreme.

Furthermore, such a proposal could be enforced without self-destructing. Those claiming to be conscientious in seeking abortion can be presumed to have made use of the leeway it allows. In any case, the emphasis of enforcement can be much more easily, as well as justly, placed on the tangible reality of the heart-beating, brain-active, human-featured fetus rather than on the subjective issue of the mother's motivation, whether it be serious or trivial or anywhere in between.

Although the notion of a ban on abortion after eight weeks will be rejected and even derided by many anti-abortionists, it is not to convert them that I advance the proposal. Despite their recent gains, it is still the regime of *Roe v. Wade* that we live under. Public opinion and elite opinion-makers are still massively opposed to outlawing abortion from conception — and so fall into line, for want of a rational alternative, behind abortion-on-demand. It is to this audience that the possibility of an alternative must be presented. For liberal Catholics, that means:

- They should take every opportunity to voice, without hesitation or embarrassment, their disagreement with *Roe v. Wade* in liberal milieus, and insist on the need for an alternative that is not so blatantly neglectful of the reality of fetal life. They should protest the distortions of the abortion issue and of anti-abortion concerns now being strenuously propagated by Planned Parenthood, the American Civil Liberties Union, the National Organization of Women, the Protestant and Jewish bodies gathered in the Religious Coalition for Abortion Rights.
- If Democrats, they should lobby for the repeal of that party's platform support for abortion and its funding. At the same time, they should make it clear that they utterly reject the belief of some centrist and conservative Democrats, that the party should draw back on a host of other welfare-and-human-services commitments.
- Finally, they should find a way to articulate the kind of prohibition suggested here in legal form and have it entered into the lists in Congress. If the "federalist" amendment supported by Senator Hatch should succeed, then an eight-week prohibition should be a proposal backed in many states.

We cannot rest with the two alternatives of *Roe v. Wade* or a ban on all abortion from the time of conception; the former is morally intolerable; the latter, politically and socially impossible. Liberal Catholics cannot let the present dominance of those alternatives be an excuse for abdication.

> ## 16. CONCERNING ABORTION: AN ATTEMPT AT A RATIONAL VIEW
>
> Charles Hartshorne

My onetime colleague T. V. Smith once wrote a book called *Beyond Conscience,* in which he waxed eloquent in showing "the harm that good men do." To live according to one's conscience may be a fine thing, but what if A's conscience leads A to try to compel B and C to live, not according to B's or C's conscience, but according to A's? That is what many opponents of abortion are trying to do. To propose a constitutional amendment to this effect is one of the most outrageous attempts to tyrannize over others that I can recall in my long lifetime as an American citizen. Proponents of the anti-abortion amendment make their case, if possible, even worse when they defend themselves with the contention "It isn't my conscience only — it is a commandment of religion." For now one particular form of religion (certainly not the only form) is being used in an attempt to tyrannize over other forms of religious or philosophical belief. The separation of church and state evidently means little to such people.

IN WHAT SENSE "HUMAN"?

Ours is a country that has many diverse religious groups, and many people who cannot find truth in any organized religious body. It is a country that has great difficulty in effectively opposing forms of killing that *everyone* admits to be wrong. Those who would saddle the legal system with matters about which consciences sincerely and strongly differ show a disregard of the country's primary needs. (The same is to be said about crusades to make things difficult for homosexuals.) There can be little freedom if we lose sight of the vital distinction between moral questions and legal ones. The law compels and coerces, with the implicit threat of violence: morals seek to persuade. It is a poor society that forgets this difference.

What is the *moral* question regarding abortion? We are told that the fetus is alive and that therefore killing it is wrong. Since mosquitoes, bacteria, apes, and whales are also alive, the argument is less than clear. Even plants are alive. I am not impressed by the rebuttal "But plants, mosquitoes, bacteria and whales are not human, and the fetus is." For the issue now becomes, *In what sense* is the fetus human? No one denies that its origin is human, as is its *possible* destiny. But the same is true of every unfertilized egg in the body of a nun. Is it wrong that some such eggs are not made or allowed to become human individuals?

Granted that a fetus is human in origin and possible destiny, in what further sense is it human? The entire problem lies here. If there are pro-life activists who have thrown much light on this question, I do not know their names.

One theologian who writes on the subject — Paul Ramsey — thinks that a human egg cell becomes a human individual with a moral claim to survive if it has been fertilized. Yet this egg cell has none of the qualities that we have in mind when we proclaim our superior worth to the chimpanzees or dolphins. It cannot speak, reason, or judge between right and wrong. It cannot have personal relations, without which a person is not functionally a person at all, until months — and not, except minimally, until years — have passed. And even then, it will not be a person in the normal sense unless some who are already fully persons have taken pains to help it become a human being in the full value sense, functioning as such. The anti-abortionist is commanding some person or persons to undertake this effort. For without it, the fetus will *never* be human in the relevant sense. It will be human only in origin, but otherwise a subhuman animal.

The fertilized egg is an individual egg, but not an individual human being. For such a being is, in its body, a multicellular organism, a *metazoan* — to use the scientific Greek — and the egg is a single cell. The first thing the egg cell does is to begin dividing into many cells. For some weeks the fetus is not a single individual at all, but a colony of cells. During its first weeks there seems to be no ground regarding the fetus as comparable to an individual animal. Only in possible or probable destiny is it an individual. Otherwise it is an organized society of single-celled individuals.

A possible individual person is one thing; an actual person is another. If this difference is not important, what is? There is in the long run no room in the solar system, or even in the known universe, for all human eggs — even all fertilized eggs, as things now stand — to become human persons. Indeed, it is mathematically demonstrable that the present rate of population growth must be lowered somehow. It is not a moral imperative that all possibilities of human persons become actual persons.

Of course, some may say that the fertilized egg already has a human soul, but on what evidence? The evidence of soul in the relevant sense is the capacity to reason, judge right and wrong, and the like.

GENETIC AND OTHER INFLUENCES

One may also say that since the fertilized egg has a combination of genes (the units of physical inheritance) from both parents, in this sense it is already a human individual. There are two objections, either one in my opinion conclusive but only one of which is taken into account by Ramsey. The one he does mention is that identical twins have the same gene combination. The theologian does not see this as decisive, but I do.

The other objection is that it amounts to a very crude form of materialism to identify individuality with the gene combination. Genes are the chemical bearers of inherited traits. This chemical basis of inheritance presumably influences every-thing about the development of the individual — *influences,* but does not fully determine. To say that the entire life of the person is determined by heredity is a theory of unfreedom that my religious conviction can only regard as monstrous. And there are biophysicists and neurophysiologists who agree with me.

From the gene-determined chemistry to a human person is a long, long step. As soon as the nervous system forming in the embryo begins to function as a whole — and not before — the cell colony begins to turn into a genuinely individual animal. One may reasonably suppose that this change is accompanied by some extremely primitive individual animal feelings. They cannot be recognizably human feelings, much less human thoughts, and cannot compare with the feelings of a porpoise or chimpanzee in level of consciousness. That much seems as certain as anything about the fetus except its origin and possible destiny. The nervous system of a very premature baby has been compared by an expert to that of a pig. And we know, if we know anything about this matter, that it is the nervous system that counts where individuality is concerned.

Identical twins are different individuals, each unique in consciousness. Though having the same genetic makeup, they will have been differently situated in the womb and hence will have received different stimuli. For that reason, if for no other, they will have developed differently, especially in their brains and nervous systems.

But there are additional reasons for the difference in development. One is the role of chance, which takes many forms. We are passing through a great cultural change in which the idea, long dominant in science, that chance is "only a word for our ignorance of causes" is being replaced by the view that the real laws of nature are probabilistic and allow for aspects of genuine chance.

Another reason is that it is reasonable to admit a reverse influence of the developing life of feelings in the fetus on the nervous system, as well as of the system upon the feelings. And since I, along with some famous philosophers and scientists, believe in freedom (not solely of mature human beings but — in some slight degree — of all individuals in nature, down to the atoms and farther), I hold that even in the fetus the incipient individual is unconsciously making what on higher levels we call "decisions." These decisions influence the developing nervous system. Thus to a certain extent we *make our own bodies* by our feelings and thoughts. An English poet with Platonic ideas expressed this concept as follows:

> The body from the soul its form doth take,
> For soul is form and doth the body make.

The word soul is, for me, incidental. The point is that feelings, thoughts, experiences react on the body and partly mold its development.

THE RIGHTS OF PERSONS

Paul Ramsey argues (as does William Buckley in a letter to me) that if a fetus is not fully human, then neither is an infant. Of course, an infant is not fully human. No one thinks it can, while an infant, be taught to speak, reason, or judge right and wrong. But it is much closer to that stage than is a three-month fetus. It is beginning to have primitive social relations not open to a fetus; and since there is no sharp line anywhere between an infant and a child able to speak a few words, or between the latter and a child able to speak very many words, we have to regard the infant as significantly different from a three-month or four-month fetus. Nevertheless, I have little sympathy with the idea that infanticide is just another form of murder. Persons who are already functionally persons in the full sense have more important rights even than infants. Infanticide can be wrong without being fully comparable to the killing of persons in the full sense.

Does this distinction apply to the killing of a hopelessly senile person (or one in a permanent coma)? For me it does. I hope that no one will think that if, God forbid, I ever reach that stage, it must be for my sake that I should be treated with the respect due to normal human beings. Rather, it is for the sake of others that such respect may be imperative. Symbolically, one who has been a person may have to be treated as a person. There are difficulties and hazards in not so treating such individuals.

Religious people (I would so describe myself) may argue that once a fetus starts to develop, it is for God, not human beings, to decide whether the fetus survives and how long it lives. This argument assumes, against all evidence, that human life spans are independent of human decisions. Our medical hygiene has radically altered the original "balance of nature." Hence the population explosion. Our technology makes pregnancy more and more a matter of human decision; more and more our choices are influencing the weal and woe of the animals on this earth. It is an awesome responsibility, but one that we cannot avoid. And, after all, the book of Genesis essentially predicted our dominion over terrestrial life. In addition, no one is proposing to make abortion compulsory for those morally opposed to it. I add that everyone who smokes is taking a hand in deciding how long he or she will live. Also everyone who, by failing to exercise reasonably, allows his or her heart to lose its vigor. Our destinies are not simply "acts of God."

I may be told that if I value my life I must be glad that I was not aborted in the fetus stage. Yes, I am glad, but this expression does not constitute a claim to having already had a "right," against which no other right could prevail, to the life I have enjoyed. I feel no indignation or horror at contemplating the idea that the world might have had to do without me. The world could have managed, and as for what I would have missed, there would have been no such "I" to miss it.

POTENTIAL, NOT ACTUAL

With almost everything they say, the fanatics against abortion show that they will not, or cannot, face the known facts of this matter. The inability of a fetus to say "I" is not merely a lack of skill; there is nothing there to which the pronoun could properly refer. A fetus is not a person but a *potential* person. The "life" to which "pro-life" refers is nonpersonal, by any criterion that makes sense to some of us. It is subpersonal animal life only. The mother, however, *is* a person.

I resent strongly the way many males tend to dictate to females their behavior, even though many females encourage them in this. Of course, the male parent of a fetus also has certain rights, but it remains true that the female parent is the one most directly and vitally concerned.

I shall not forget talking about this whole matter to a wonderful woman, the widow of a philosopher known for his idealism. She was doing social work with young women and had come to the conclusion that abortion is, in some cases, the lesser evil. She told me that her late husband had said, when she broached the subject to him, "But you can't do that." "My darling," she replied, "we *are* doing it." I see no reason to rate the consciences of the pro-lifers higher than this woman's conscience. She knew what the problem was for certain mothers. In a society that flaunts sex (its pleasures more than its serious hazards, problems and spiritual values) in all the media, makes it difficult for the young to avoid unwanted pregnancy, and does little to help them with the most difficult of all problems of self-discipline, we tell young persons that they are murderers if they resort to abortion. And so we should not be surprised that Margaret Mead, that clear-sighted observer of our society (and of other societies), should say, "Abortion is a nasty thing, but our society deserves it." Alas, it is too true.

I share something of the disgust of hardcore opponents of abortion that contraceptives, combined with the availability of abortion, may deprive sexual intercourse of spiritual meaning. For me the sacramental view of marriage has always had appeal, and my life has been lived accordingly. Abortion is indeed a nasty thing, but unfortunately there are in our society many even nastier things, like the fact that some children are growing up unwanted. This for my conscience is a great deal nastier, and truly horrible. An overcrowded world is also nasty, and could in a few decades become truly catastrophic.

The argument against abortion (used, I am sorry to say, by Pearl Buck) that the fetus may be a potential genius has to be balanced against the much more probable chance of its being a mediocrity, or a destructive enemy of society. Every egg cell is a possible genius and also a possible monster in human form. Where do we stop in calculating such possibilities?

If some who object to abortion work to diminish the number of unwanted, inappropriate pregnancies, or to make bearing a child for adoption by persons able to be its loving foster parents more attractive than it now is, and do this with a minimum of coercion, all honor to them. In view of the population problem, the first of these remedies should have high priority.

Above all, the coercive power of our legal system, already stretched thin, must be used with caution and chiefly against evils about which there is something like universal consensus. That persons have rights is a universal belief in our society, but that a fetus is already an actual person — about that there is and there can be no consensus. Coercion in such matters is tyranny. Alas for our dangerously fragmented and alienated society if we persist in such tyranny.

17. THE MALE IDEOLOGY OF PRIVACY: A FEMINIST PERSPECTIVE ON THE RIGHT TO ABORTION

Catharine MacKinnon

> In a society where women entered sexual intercourse willingly, where adequate contraception was a genuine social priority, there would be no "abortion issue." . . . Abortion is violence. . . . It is the offspring, and will continue to be the accuser of a more pervasive and prevalent violence, the violence of rapism.
>
> Adrienne Rich
> *Of Woman Born: Motherhood as Experience and Institution*

In 1973, Roe against Wade held that a statute that made criminal all abortions except to save the mother's life violated the constitutional right to privacy.[1] In 1980, Harris against McRae decided that this privacy right did not require public funding of medically necessary abortions for women who could not afford them.[2] Here I argue that the public/private line drawn in *McRae* sustains and reveals the meaning of privacy recognized in *Roe*.

First, the experience of abortion, and the terms of the struggle for the abortion right, is situated in a context of a feminist comprehension of gender inequality, to which a critique of sexuality is central.[3] Next, the legal concept of privacy is examined in the abortion context. I argue that privacy doctrine affirms what feminism rejects: the public/private split. Once the ideological meaning of the law of privacy is connected with a feminist critique of the public/private division, the *Roe* approach looks consistent with *McRae*'s confinement of its reach. To guarantee abortions as an aspect of the private, rather than of the public, sector is to guarantee women a right to abortion subject to women's ability to provide it for ourselves. This is to guarantee access to abortion only to some women on the basis of class, not to women *as women*, and therefore, under conditions of sex inequality, to guarantee it to *all* women only on male terms. The rest of this is an attempt to unpack what I mean by that.

I will neglect two important explorations, which I bracket now. The first is: what are babies to men? Sometimes men respond to women's right to abort as if confronting the possibility of their own potential nonexistence — at *women's* hands, no less. Men's issues of potency, of continuity as a compensation for mortality, of the thrust to embody themselves or the image of themselves in the world, seem to underlie their relation to babies, as well as to most everything else. The idea that women can undo what men have done to them on this level seems to provoke insecurity sometimes bordering on hysteria. To overlook these meanings of abortion to men as men is to overlook political and strategic as well as deep theoretical issues, is to misassess where much of the opposition to abortion is coming from, and to make a lot of mistakes. The second question I bracket is one that, unlike the first, has been discussed extensively in the abortion debate: the moral rightness of abortion itself. My view, which the rest of what I say on abortion reflects, is that the abortion choice should be available and must be *women's*, but not because the fetus is not a form of life. The more usual approach tends to make whether women should make the abortion decision somehow contingent on whether the fetus is a form of life. Why shouldn't women make life or death decisions? Which returns us to the first bracketed issue.

The issues I will discuss have largely not been discussed in the terms I will use. What has happened instead, I think, is that women's embattled need to survive in a system that is hostile to our survival, the desperation of our need to negotiate with whatever means that same system will respond to, has precluded our exploration of these issues in the way that I am about to explore them. That is, the terms on which we have addressed the issue of abortion have been shaped and constrained by the very situation that the abortion issue has put us in a position to need to address. We have not been able to risk thinking about these issues on our own terms because the terms have not been ours — either in sex, in social life in general, or in court. The attempt to grasp women's situation on our own terms, from our own point of view, defines the feminist impulse. If doing that is risky, our situation as women also makes it risky not to.

So, first feminism, then law.

Most women who seek abortions became pregnant while having sexual intercourse with men. Most did not mean or wish to conceive. In contrast to this fact of women's experience, the abortion debate has centered on the separation of control over sexuality from control over reproduction, and both from gender. Liberals have supported the availability of the abortion choice as if the woman just happened on the fetus.[4] The right recalls that intercourse precedes conception, only to urge abstinence, as if sex were up to women, while at the same time defending male authority, specifically including a wife's duty to submit to sex. Continuing this logic, many opponents of state funding of abortions, such as supporters of the Hyde Amendment, would permit funding of abortions when the pregnancy results from rape or incest.[5] These are exceptions for special occasions on which they presume women did not control sex. What I'm getting at is this convergence: many of abortion's proponents, who want to free women from reproduction in order to have sex, seem to share with abortion's opponents, who want to stick us with the consequences, the tacit assumption that women significantly *do* control sex.

Feminist investigations suggest otherwise. Sexual intercourse, the most common cause of pregnancy, cannot simply be presumed co-equally determined. Feminists have found that women feel compelled to preserve the appearance, which acted upon becomes the reality, of male direction of sexual expression, as if it is male initiative itself that we want, that turns us on. Men enforce this. It is much of what men want in a woman. It is what pornography eroticizes and prostitutes provide. Rape, by contrast, is intercourse with force that is recognized as force. The implicit standard against which rape is adjudicated, though, is not, I think, the power or even primarily the degree of force that the man wields or uses, but the degree of perceived intimacy between the parties. The more intimately acquainted you are with your accused rapist, the less likely a court is to find that what you think was rape is rape. Often indices of such intimacy include intercourse itself. If no can be taken as yes, depending on measures of familiarity rather than mutuality of desire, how free can yes be?

Under these conditions, women often do not use birth control because of its social meaning, a social meaning we did not make. Using contraception means acknowledging and planning and taking direction of intercourse, accepting one's sexual availability and appearing nonspontaneous. It means appearing available to male incursions. A good user of contraception is a bad girl. She can be presumed sexually available, among other consequences; she can be raped with relative impunity. (If you think this isn't true, you should consider those rape cases in which the fact that a woman had a diaphragm in is taken as an indication that what happened to her was intercourse, not rape. Why did you have your diaphragm in?) Studies of abortion clinics have looked into circumstances surrounding abortions, including those of women who repeatedly seek abortions — the repeat offenders, high on the list of the right's villains, their best case for opposing abortion as female sexual irresponsibility. Ask such women why they are repeatedly pregnant, they say something like, the sex just happened. Like every night for over a year.[6] I wonder if a woman can be presumed to control access to her sexuality who feels unable to interrupt intercourse to insert a diaphragm; or worse, *cannot even want to,* aware that she risks a pregnancy she knows she doesn't want. Do you think she would stop the man for any other reason, such as, for instance — the real taboo — lack of desire? If not, how is sex, hence its consequences, meaningfully voluntary for women? Norms of sexual rhythm and romance that are felt interrupted by women's needs are constructed against women's interests. When it appears normatively less costly for women to risk an undesired, often painful, traumatic, dangerous, sometimes illegal, and potentially life-threatening procedure than it is to protect oneself in advance, sex doesn't look a whole lot like freedom. Yet the policy debate in the last twenty years has not explicitly approached abortion in the context of how women get pregnant, that is, as a consequence of sexual intercourse under conditions of gender inequality, that is, as an issue of forced sex.

Now, law. In 1973, Roe against Wade found the right to privacy "broad enough to encompass a woman's decision whether or not to terminate her pregnancy."[7] Privacy had previously been recognized as a constitutional principle in a case that decriminalized the prescription and use of contraceptives.[8] Note that courts implicitly connect contraception with abortion under the privacy rubric in a way that parallels the way I just did explicitly under the feminist rubric. In 1977, three justices observed, "In the abortion context, we have held that the right to privacy shields the woman from undue state intrusion in and external scrutiny of her very personal choice."[9] In 1980, the Supreme Court in Harris against McRae decided that this did not mean that federal Medicaid programs had to cover medically necessary abortions for poor women.[10] According to the Court, the privacy of the woman's choice was not unconstitutionally burdened by the government financing her decision to continue, but not her decision to end a conception. The Supreme Court reasoned that "although the government may not place obstacles in the path of a woman's exercise of her freedom of choice, it may not remove those not of its own creation."[11] Aside from holding the state exempt in any issue of the distribution of wealth, which is dubious, it was apparently a very short step from that which the government had a duty *not* to intervene in, as in *Roe,* and that which it has *no* duty to intervene in, as in *McRae.* That this distinction has consistent parallels in other areas of jurisprudence and social policy — such as in the distinction between negative and positive freedom[12] and in the state action requirement[13] — does not mean that the public/private line that forms their common dimension is not, there as well as here, the gender line. The result of government's stance is also the same throughout: an area of social life is cordoned off from the reach of explicitly recognized public authority. This does not mean, as they think, that government stays out really. Rather, this leaves the balance of forces where they are socially, so that government's patterns of intervention mirror and magnify, thus authorize, the existing social divisions of power.

The law of privacy, explicitly a public law *against* public intervention, is one such doctrine. Conceived as the outer edge of limited government, it embodies a tension between precluding public exposure or governmental intrusion on the one hand, and autonomy in the sense of protecting personal self-action on the other. This is a tension, not just two facets of one whole right. This tension is resolved from the liberal state's point of view — I am now moving into a critique of liberalism — by delineating the threshold of the state as its permissible extent of penetration (a term I use advisedly) into a domain that is considered free by definition: the private sphere. By this move the state secures what has been termed "an inviolable personality" by insuring what is called "autonomy or control over the intimacies of personal identity."[14] The state does this by centering its self-restraint on body and home, especially bedroom. By staying out of marriage and the family, prominently meaning sexuality, that is to say, heterosexuality, from contraception through pornography to the abortion decision, the law of privacy proposes to guarantee individual bodily integrity, personal exercise of moral intelligence, and freedom of intimacy.[15] What it actually does is translate traditional social values into the rhetoric of individual rights as a means of subordinating those rights to social imperatives.[16] In feminist terms, applied to abortion law, the logic of *Roe* consummated in *Harris* translates the ideology of the private sphere into individual women's collective needs to the imperatives of male supremacy.

This is my ten-year retrospective on Roe against Wade. Reproduction is sexual, men control sexuality, and the state supports the interest of men as a group. If *Roe* is part of this, why was abortion legalized? Why were women even imagined to have such a right as privacy? It is not an accusation of bad faith to answer that the interests of men as a social group converge here with the definition of justice embodied in law. The male point of view unites them. Taking this approach, one sees that the way the male point of view constructs a social event or legal notion is the way that event or notion is framed by state policy. For example, to the extent possession is the point of sex, illegal rape will be sex with a woman who is not yours unless the act makes her yours. If part of the kick of pornography involves eroticizing the putatively prohibited, illegal pornography — obscenity — will be prohibited enough to keep pornography desirable without ever making it truly illegitimate or unavailable. If, from the male standpoint, male is the implicit definition of human, maleness will be the implicit standard by which sex equality is measured in discrimination law. In parallel terms, the availability of abortion frames, and is framed by, the extent to which men, worked out among themselves, find it convenient to allow abortion — a reproductive consequence of intercourse — to occur. Abortion will then, to that extent, be available.

The abortion policy debate has construed the issues rather differently. The social problem posed by sexuality since Freud[17] has been seen as the problem of the repression of the innate desire for sexual pleasure by the constraints of civilization. Gender inequality arises as an issue in the Freudian context in women's repressive socialization to passivity and coolness (so-called frigidity), in women's so-called desexualization, and in the disparate consequences of biology, that is, pregnancy. Who defines what is seen as sexual, what sexuality therefore is, to whom what stimuli are erotic and why, and who defines the conditions under which sexuality is expressed — these issues are not available to be considered. "Civilization's" answer to these questions, in the Freudian context, instead fuses women's reproductivity with our attributed sexuality in its definition of what a woman is. We are, from a feminist standpoint, thus defined as women, as feminine, by the uses to which men want to put us. Seen this way, it becomes clear why the struggle for reproductive freedom, since Freud, has not included a woman's right to refuse sex. In the post-Freudian era, the notion of sexual liberation frames the sexual equality issue as a struggle for women to have sex with men on the same terms as men: "without consequences."

The abortion right, to the extent it has been admitted to have anything to do with sex, has been sought as freedom from the unequal reproductive consequences of sexual expression, with sexuality defined as centered on heterosexual genital intercourse. It has been as if it is biological organisms, rather than social relations, that have sex and reproduce the species, and sex itself is "really" a gender-neutral, hence sex-equal, activity. But if you see both sexuality and reproduction, hence gender, as socially situated, and your issue is less how more people can get more sex as it is than who, socially, defines what sexuality — hence pleasure and violation — is, the abortion right becomes situated within a very different problematic: the social and political problematic of the inequality of the sexes. As Susan Sontag said, "Sex itself is not liberating for women. Neither is more sex. . . . The question is, what sexuality shall women be liberated to enjoy?"[18] To address this for purposes of abortion policy, from a feminist perspective, requires reconceiving the problem of sexuality from the repression of drives by civilization to the oppression of women by men.

Most arguments for abortion under the rubric of feminism have rested upon the right to control one's own body, gender-neutral. I think that argument has been appealing for the same reasons it is inadequate. Women's bodies have not socially been ours; we have not controlled their meanings and destinies. So feminists have needed to assert that control while feeling unable to risk pursuing the sense that something more than our bodies singular, something closer to a net of relations, relations in which we are (so far unescapedly) gendered, might be at stake.[19] Some feminists have noticed that our "right to decide" has become merged with an overwhelmingly male professional's right not to have his professional judgment second-guessed by the government.[20] But most abortion advocates have argued in rigidly and rigorously gender-neutral terms.

Consider, for instance, Judith Jarvis Thomson's celebrated hypothetical case justifying abortion, in which a gender-neutral abducted "you" has no obligation to be a life support system for the famous violinist ("he") one is forcibly connected to. On this basis, "one" is argued to have no obligation to support a fetus.[21] Never mind that no *woman* who needs an abortion, no woman period, is valued, no potential an actual woman's life might hold would be cherished, comparable to a male famous violinist's unencumbered possibilities. In the crunch, few women look like unborn Beethovens, even to sex-blind liberals. Not to mention that the under-lying parallel to rape in the hypothetical — the origin in force, in abduction, that gives it weight while confining its application to instances in which force is recognized as force — is seldom interrogated in the abortion context for its applicability to the normal case. And abortion policy has to be made for the normal case. While the hypothetical makes women's rights depend by analogy on what is not considered the normal case, Thomson finds distinguishing rape from intercourse has "a rather unpleasant sound" principally because *fetal* rights should not depend on the conditions of conception. My point is that in order to apply even something like Thomson's parallel to the usual case of need for an abortion requires establishing some relation between intercourse and rape — sexuality — and conception. This issue has been avoided in the abortion context by acting as if *assuming* women are persons sexually will make us persons reproductively, as if treating women in gender-neutral terms analytically will remove the social reality of gender from the situation. By this sentimentality, liberal feminism obscures the unequal gender basis on which it attempts to construct women's equal personhood.

Abortion without a sexual critique of gender inequality, I have said, promises women sex with men on the same terms as men. Under conditions under which women do not control access to our sexuality, this facilitates women's heterosexual availability. It promises *men* women on male terms. I mean, under conditions of gender inequality, sexual liberation in this sense does not free women, it frees male sexual aggression. Available abortion on this basis removes one substantial legitimized reason that women have had, since Freud, for refusing sex besides the headache. Analyzing the perceptions upon which initial male support for abortion was based, Andrea Dworkin says: "Getting laid was at stake."[22] The Playboy Foundation has supported abortion rights from day one; it continues to, even with shrinking disposable funds, on a level of priority comparable to its opposition to censorship. There is also evidence that men eroticize abortion itself.[23]

Privacy doctrine is an ideal legal vehicle for the process of sexual politics I have described. The democratic liberal ideal of the private holds that, so long as the public does not interfere, autonomous individuals interact freely and equally. Conceptually, this private is hermetic. It means that which is inaccessible to, unaccountable to, unconstructed by anything beyond itself. By definition, it is not part of or conditioned by anything systematic or outside itself. It is personal, intimate, autonomous, particular, individual, the original source and final outpost of the self, gender-neutral. Privacy is, in short, defined by everything that feminism reveals women have never been allowed to be or to have, as well as by everything that women have been equated with and defined in terms of *men's* ability to have. The liberal definition of the private does not envisage public complaint of social inequality within it. In the liberal view, no act of the state contributes to, hence properly should participate in, shaping its internal alignments or distributing its internal forces, including inequalities among parties in private. Its inviolability by the state, framed as an individual right, presupposes that it is not already an arm of the state. It is not even a social sphere, exactly. Intimacy is implicitly thought to guarantee symmetry of power. Injuries arise in violating the private sphere, not within and by and because of it.

In private, consent tends to be presumed. It is true that a showing of coercion voids this presumption. But the problem is getting anything private perceived as coercive. Why one would allow force in private — the "why doesn't she leave" question raised to battered women — is a question given its urgency by the social meaning of the private as a sphere of equality and choice. But for women the measure of the intimacy has been the measure of the oppression. This is why feminism has had to explode the private. This is why feminism has seen the personal as the political. In this sense, for women as such there is no private, either normatively or empirically. Feminism confronts the reality that women have no privacy to lose or to guarantee. We have no inviolability. Our sexuality is not only violable, it is, hence we are, seen in and as our violation. To confront the fact that we have no privacy is to confront the intimate degradation of women *as* the public order.

In this light, recognizing abortion under the legal right to privacy is a complicated move. Freedom *from* public intervention coexists uneasily with any right which requires social preconditions to be meaningfully delivered. If inequality, for example, is socially pervasive and enforced, meaningful equality will require intervention, not abdication. But the right to privacy is not thought to require social change to be meaningful. It is not even thought to require any social preconditions, other than nonintervention by the public. The point for the abortion cases is not only that indigency, which was the specific barrier to effective choice in *McRae,* is well within public power to remedy, nor that the state, as I said, is hardly exempt in issues of the distribution of wealth. It is rather that Roe against Wade presumes that governmental nonintervention into the private sphere in itself amounts to, or at the least promotes, woman's freedom of choice. When the alternative is jail, there is much to be said for this argument. But the *McRae* result sustains the meaning of the privacy recognized in *Roe:* women are guaranteed by the public no more than what we can secure for ourselves in private. That is, what we can extract through our intimate associations with men. Women with privileges get rights.

Women got abortion as a private privilege, not as a public right. We got control over reproduction that is controlled by "a man or The Man,"[24] an individual man or (mostly male) doctors or the government. In this sense, abortion was not simply decriminalized, it was legalized; *Roe* set the stage for state regulation of the conditions under which women can have access to this right. Much of the control that women got out of legalization of abortion went directly into the hands of men socially — husbands, doctors, fathers. Much of the rest of it women have had to fight to keep from state attempts, both legislative and administrative, to regulate it out of existence.[25]

It is not inconsistent, in this light, that a woman's decision to abort, framed as a privacy right, would have no claim on public funding and might genuinely not be seen as burdened by that deprivation. Privacy conceived as a right from public intervention and disclosure is the conceptual *opposite* of the relief *McRae* sought for welfare women. State intervention would have provided a choice these women did *not* have in private. The women in *McRae,* poor women and women of color whose sexual refusal has counted for especially little,[26] needed something to make their privacy real. The logic of the court's response to them resembles that by which women are supposed to consent to sex. Preclude the alternatives, then call the sole option remaining "her choice." The point is that the women's alternatives are precluded *prior* to the reach of the chosen remedy, the legal doctrine. They are precluded by conditions of sex, race, and class — the conditions the privacy frame not only assumes, but *works to guarantee.* These women were seen, essentially, as not having lost any privacy by having public funding for abortions withheld, as having no privacy to lose. In the bourgeois sense, in which you can have all the rights you can buy, converging with that dimension of male supremacy that makes the self-disposition money can buy a prerogative of masculinity, this was true. The *McRae* result certainly *made* it true.

The way the law of privacy restricts intrusions into intimacy also bars change in control over that intimacy. The existing distribution of power and resources within the private sphere will be precisely what the law of privacy exists to protect. Just as pornography is legally protected as individual freedom of expression without questioning whose freedom and whose expression and at whose expense, abstract privacy protects abstract autonomy without inquiring into whose freedom of action is being sanctioned, at whose expense. I think it is not coincidence that the very place (the body), the very relations (heterosexual), the very activities (intercourse and reproduction), and the very feelings (intimate) that feminism has found central to the subjection of women, form the core of privacy law's coverage. In this perspective, the legal concept of privacy can and has shielded the place of battery, marital rape, and women's exploited labor, preserved the central institutions whereby women are *deprived* of identity, autonomy, control, and self-definition, and protected the primary activities through which male supremacy is expressed and enforced.

To fail to recognize the meaning of the private in the ideology and reality of women's subordination by seeking protection behind a right *to* that privacy is to cut women off from collective verification and state support in the same act. When women are segregated in private, separated from each other, one at a time, a right *to* that privacy isolates us at once from each other and from public recourse, even as it provides the only form of that recourse made available to us. So defined, the right to privacy has included a right of men "to be let alone"[27] to oppress women one at a time. It embodies and reflects the private sphere's existing definition of womanhood. As an instance of liberalism — applied to women as if we *are* persons, gender-neutral — Roe against Wade reinforces the division between public and private, a division that is not gender-neutral. It is at once an ideological division that lies about women's shared experience and mystifies the unity among the spheres of women's violation, and a very material division that *keeps* the private beyond public redress and depoliticizes women's subjection within it. It keeps some men out of the bedrooms of other men.

There seems to be a social perception that the right has the high moral ground on abortion and the liberals have the high legal ground.[28] I have tried to sketch a feminist ground, a political ground critical of the common ground under the right's morals and liberals' laws.

References

1. *Roe* v. *Wade*, 410 U.S. 113 (1973).
2. *Harris* v. *McRae*, 448 U.S. 297 (1980).
3. I talk about this in "Feminism, Marxism, Method and the State: An Agenda for Theory," *Signs: Journal of Women in Culture and Society* 7, no. 3 (Spring 1982): 515–44.
4. See D. H. Reagan, "Rewriting *Roe* v. *Wade,* " *Michigan Law Review* 77 (August 1979): 1569–1646, in which the Good Samaritan, by analogy, happens upon the fetus.
5. As of 1973, ten states that made abortion a crime had exceptions for rape and incest; at least three had exceptions for rape only. Many of these exceptions were based on Model Penal Code Section 230.3 (Proposed Official Draft 1962), quoted in *Doe* v. *Bolton*, 410 U.S. 179, 205–7, app. B (1973), permitting abortion, *inter alia* in cases of "rape, incest, or other felonious intercourse." References to states with incest and rape exceptions can be found in *Roe* v. *Wade*, 410 U.S. 113, n. 37 (1973). Some versions of the Hyde Amendment, which prohibits use of public money to fund abortions, have contained exceptions for cases of rape or incest. Publ. L. No. 95-205, § 101, 91 stat. 1960 (1972); Pub. L. No. 95-480, § 210, 92 Stat. 1567, 1586 (1978); Pub. L. No. 96-123, 109, 93 Stat. 923, 926 (1979); Pub. L. No. 96-536, § 109, 94 Stat. 3166, 3170 (1980). All require immediate reporting of the incident.
6. Kristin Luker, *Taking Chances: Abortion and the Decision Not to Contracept* (Berkeley: University of California Press, 1975), p. 47.
7. *Roe*, 410 U.S. at 153.
8. *Griswold* v. *Connecticut*, 381 U.S. 479 (1965).
9. *H. L.* v. *Matheson*, 450 U.S. 398, 435 (dissent) (1981); See also *Whalen* v. *Roe*, 429 U.S. 589, 599–600 (1977).
10. *Harris* v. *McRae*, 448 U.S. 297 (1980).

11. *Harris,* 448 U.S. at 316.

12. Isiah Berlin, "Two Concepts of Liberty," in Berlin, *Four Essays on Liberty* (Oxford, 1969).

13. See Paul Brest, "State Action and Liberal Theory: A Casenote on *Flagg Brothers* v. *Brooks,"* 130 U. Pa L. Rev. 1296 (1982).

14. Tom Gerety, "Redefining Privacy," *Harvard Civil Rights — Civil Liberties Law Review* 12, no. 2 (Spring 1977): 236.

15. Thus the law of privacy wavers between protecting the institution of heterosexuality as such and protecting that which heterosexuality is at least theoretically only one instance of, that is, free choice in intimate behavior. For the first proposition, see, e.g., *Griswold* v. *Connecticut,* 381 U.S. 479 (1965) (distribution of contraceptives), *Loving* v. *Virginia,* 388 U.S. 1 (1967) (marriage partners), *Skinner* v. *Oklahoma,* 316 U.S. 535 (1942) (male fertility), as well as *Roe* v. *Wade. Doe* v. *Commonwealth's Attorney,* 403 F. Supp. 1199 (D. Va. 1975) (homosexual conduct not protected, since "no part of marriage, home or family life.") For the second, *New York* v. *Onofre,* 424 N.Y.S. 2d 566 (1980) (invalidating criminal sodomy statute). It is consistent with this analysis that homosexuality, when protected or found officially acceptable, would primarily be in private (i.e., in the closet) and primarily parodying rather than challenging the heterosexual model. Kenneth Karst attempts to include both approaches to privacy in his formation of "intimate association," yet implicitly retains the heterosexual model as central to his definition of the meaning of intimacy. "By 'intimate association' I mean a close and familiar personal relationship with another that is in some significant way comparable to a marriage or family relationships . . . but in principle the idea of intimate association also includes close friendship, with or without any such links." K. L. Karst, "The Freedom of Intimate Association," *Yale Law Journal* 89, no. 4 (March 1980), p. 629. On pornography, see *Stanley* v. *Georgia,* 394 U.S. 557 (1969) and *Lovisi* v. *Slayton,* 539 F.2d 349 (5th Cir. 1976). Taken together, these cases suggest that Mr. Standley's privacy rights encompass looking at pornography regardless of the intrusiveness of its production, while the women depicted in the pornography Mr. Stanley looks at have no privacy rights, if they could not have "reasonably expect[ed]" privacy to attach when they permitted "onlookers" to take sexual pictures. For a discussion of privacy law in the pornography context see Ruth Colker, "Pornography and Privacy: Towards the Development of a Group-Based Theory for Sex-Based Intrusions of Privacy," 1, 2 *Law and Equality: A Journal of Theory and Practice* (forthcoming, 1983).

16. This formulation learned a lot from Tom Grey, "Eros, Civilization and the Burger Court," *Law and Contemporary Problems* 43, no. 3 (Summer 1980): 83–99.

17. Nineteenth-century feminists connected the abortion right with control over access to their sexuality. See Linda Gordon, *Woman's Body, Woman's Right: A Social History of Birth Control in America* [New York: Grossman (Viking), 1976]: esp. 100–115.

18. S. Sontag, "The Third World of Women," *Partisan Review* 40, no. 2 (1973), p. 188.

19. Such a relation has at least two aspects: the women/men relation; and woman/fetus relation. To the latter, see Adrienne Rich on the fetus as "neither as me nor as not-me." *Of Woman Born: Motherhood as Experience and Institution* (New York: W. W. Norton & Co., 1976), p. 64.

20. K. Glen, "Abortion in the Courts: A Lay Woman's Historical Guide to the New Disaster Area," *Feminist Studies* 4 (1978): 1.

21. Judith Jarvis Thomson, "A Defense of Abortion," *Philosophy and Public Affairs* 1, no. 1 (1971): 47–66.

22. A. Dworkin, *Right-Wing Women* (New York: Perigee, 1983). *You must read this book!* The support of men for abortion largely evaporated or became very equivocal when the women's movement produced, instead, women who refused sex with men and left men in droves. The fact that Jane Roe was pregnant from a gang rape, a fact which was not part of the litigation (" 'Jane Roe' Says She'd Fight Abortion Battle Again," *Minneapolis Star & Tribune,* Jan. 22, 1983), is emblematic of the sexual dimension of the issue. As further evidence, see Friedrich Engels arguing that removing private housekeeping into social industry would "remove all the anxiety about 'consequences,' " which today is the most essential social — moral as well as economic — factor that prevents a girl

from giving herself completely to the man she loves.'' *Origin of the Family, Private Property and the State* (New York: International Publishers, 1973, p. 139.

23. Andrea Dworkin's analysis of the Marquis de Sade's statements on abortion reveal that ''Sade extolled the sexual value of murder and he saw abortion as a form of murder . . . abortion was a sexual act, an act of lust.'' *Pornography: Men Possessing Women* (New York: Perigee, 1981), p. 96. One woman complaining of sexual harassment said the codirector of the abortion clinic she worked at had asked to be present during her abortion: ''He said he had a fantasy about having sexual intercourse with a woman on an examining table during an abortion,'' she reported. ''Woman accuses clinic chief of sexual harassment,'' *Minneapolis Star & Tribune,* May 28, 1982. Ponder *Hustler's* cartoon depicting a naked man masturbating enthusiastically reading a book labeled *Fetal Positions* in the corner of an operating room where a woman lies on the operating table, knees agape in stirrups. A male doctor is holding up what he has just delivered with tongs, saying ''Want a piece of ass, Earl? This one's stillborn.'' WAVPM Slide Show. This slide show is described in Teresa Hommel, ''Images of Women in Pornography and Medicine,'' VIII, 2 *NYU Review of Law and Social Change* (1978–79): 207–14.

24. Johnnie Tillmon, ''Welfare is a Women's Issue,'' *Liberation News Service,* February 26, 1972, in *America's Working Women: A Documentary History, 1600 to the Present,* ed. Baxandall, Gordon, and Reverby (New York: Vintage Books, 1976), pp. 357–58.

25. *H. L. v. Matheson,* 450 U.S. 398 (1981) (upholding statute requiring physicians to notify parents of ''dependent, unmarried minor girl'' prior to performing an abortion), *Bellotti v. Baird,* 443 U.S. 672 (1977) (Bellotti II) (holding that parents may not have absolute veto power over their minor daughter's decision), *Doe v. Gerstein,* 517 F.2d 787 (5th Cir, 1975), *aff'd* 417 U.S. 281 (1974) (mandatory written consent requirements of husbands' parents unconstitutional). In *Planned Parenthood of Mo. v. Danforth,* 428 U.S. 52 (1976) the Supreme Court held that a state cannot by statute allow a man to veto a wife's abortion choice in part because the state cannot give a husband rights over the woman's reproductive choice that the state itself does not have. This leads one to wonder where the states got their power to regulate (under some circumstances preclude) abortions in the second and third trimesters, where apparently ''public'' considerations can weigh against the woman's ''private'' choice. Could states, by statutes, allow husbands to veto abortions then? Whether courts can do by injunction what states cannot do by statute is discussed if not resolved in *Hagerstown Reproductive Health Services and Bonny Ann Fritz v. Chris Allen Fritz,* 295 Md. 268, 454 A. 2d 846 (1983). See also, *City of Akron v. Akron Center for Reproductive Health,* 103 S. Ct. 2481 (1983) (invalidating five city ordinances regulating where abortions may be performed (hospitals), who needs written consent by a parent (girls younger than 15), what doctors have to tell women prior to the procedure (e.g., tactile sensitivities of a fetus), when an abortion can be performed (24 hours after consent), and how the ''fetal remains'' must be disposed of.

26. The following statistics were reported in 1970: 79 percent of New York City's abortion deaths occurred among black and Puerto Rican women; the abortion death rate was 4.7 times as high for Puerto Rican women, and 8 times as high for black women as for white women. Lucinda Cisler, ''Unfinished Business: Birth Control and Women's Liberation,'' in *Sisterhood Is Powerful: An Anthology of Writings from the Women's Liberation Movement,* ed. Robin Morgan (New York: Vintage, 1970), p. 291.

27. The classic article formulating privacy as ''the right to be let alone'' is S. D. Warren and L. D. Brandeis, ''The Right to Privacy,'' *Harvard Law Review* 4 (1890), p. 205. But note that *state* constitutional privacy provisions are sometimes interpreted to require funding for abortions. *Committee to Defend Reproductive Rights v. Meyers,* 29 C. 3d 252, 172 Cal. Rptr. 866, 625 P. 2d 779 (1981), *Moe v. Society of Administration and Finance,* 417 N.E. 2d 387 (Mass. 1981).

28. I owe this conception of public debate to Jay Garfield, Hampshire College, Amherst, Massachusetts.

CHAPTER 8

DECRIMINALIZATION: HEALTHY, WEALTHY, AND WISE

Chapter 8 raises the question, Shall we decriminalize drugs? The selections in this chapter lay out some of the debate regarding current attitudes towards specific illegal drugs, discusses some of the controversies in the area, and looks to the future in terms of policy directions.

The conservative selection, "Heroin," is from James Q. Wilson's classic *Thinking About Crime*. Wilson argues that society has the right to protect itself from the crimes commited by heroin users — specifically from theft and its effect on innocent victims and from the sale of heroin. Wilson states that an increase in penalization would possibly deter a novice user and also have an impact on the addict-dealer who, because of severe penalties, might choose not to sell to a potential user.

Wilson also argues that society has a commitment to responsibility and therefore the right to help enhance the well-being of users. He bases this intervention on the assumption that, for a large number of users, heroin is destructive. An element of "compulsion" is Wilson's solution — whether it be probation, prison, or some type of mandatory treatment program. Wilson concludes by adding that some individuals might ultimately choose not to use heroin by the mere fact of its illegality.

Andrew Weil is a counterculture figure who presents a more unorthodox approach to illegal drugs. In his essay "Marijuana Reconsidered," he ignores the issues of decriminalization and illegality, discussing instead the characteristics of good and bad relationships with marijuana. Included in his definition of a good relationship are an understanding of the nature of the drug, getting a positive effect from it, and being able to separate from the drug. Bad relationships ignore the drug aspect of use and may result in negative health consequences such as bronchial irritation.

Weil, who is a medical doctor, also spends time discussing the medicinal properties of the drug. He argues that marijuana may be useful in treating such problems as glaucoma, nausea, and spastic paralysis.

Weil acknowledges that he ignores the issue of illegality. He also ignores policy questions like decriminalization. He argues that bad laws create black markets, prevent good drug relationships, and interfere with scientific research. His final emphasis is on accepting the reality of drug use and teaching the "principles of safe interaction with them."

Bruce MacMurray, Thomas Shapiro, and Maureen Kelleher have the last word on the chapter question regarding decriminalization. In "Decriminalization: The Law, Society, and the User," they discuss decriminalization as a policy option and from a liberal perspective point out advantages and disadvantages by focusing on marijuana- and heroin-related issues.

For example, when discussing law, the authors raise the following issues: drug use as a victimless crime; the often ineffective push for deterrence that ignores the issues of addiction and the appeal of "forbidden fruit"; and the assessment of marijuana decriminalization in eleven states.

The authors also discuss societal impact. In terms of the deviance model, there is no clear evidence that society will view the user in a different way after decriminalization. However, there is a possibility that society will view the business of legal drugs differently. Specifically, social criticisms of pharmaceutical company strategies such as excessive promotion and the encouragement of overprescription of antibiotics and psychoactive drugs may increase.

Finally, the authors argue that in terms of the user, patterns of drug use probably will not change dramatically. However, treatment potential may increase because some of the coercive elements of the treatment option will be modified. The authors conclude that it is impossible to assume that one policy direction will satisfactorily meet all the needs and criticisms of drug users in American society.

18. HEROIN

James Q. Wilson

It has been widely believed that much of the increase in predatory crime is the result of heroin addicts supporting their habits; that heroin use has become a middle-class white as well as lower-class black phenomenon of alarming proportions; and that conventional law-enforcement efforts to reduce heroin use have not only failed but may in fact be contributing to the problem by increasing the cost of the drug for the user, leading thereby to the commission of even more crimes and the corruption of even more police officers. These generally held opinions have led to an intense debate over new policy initiatives to deal with heroin, an argument usually described as one between advocates of a "law-enforcement" policy, which includes shutting off opium supplies . . . and heroin-manufacturing laboratories, . . . arresting more heroin dealers in the United States, and using civil commitment procedures, detoxification centers, and methadone maintenance programs and partisans of a "decriminalization" policy, which includes legalization of the use or possession of heroin, at least for adults, and distribution of heroin to addicts at low costs, or zero costs, through government-controlled clinics.

The intensity of the debate tends to obscure the fact that most of the widely accepted opinions on heroin use are not supported by much evidence; that the very concept of "addict" is ambiguous and somewhat misleading; and that many of the apparently reasonable assumptions about heroin use and crime — such as the assumption that the legalization of heroin would dramatically reduce the rate of predatory crime, or that intensified law enforcement drives the price of heroin up, or that oral methadone is a universal substitute for heroin, or that heroin use spreads because of the activities of "pushers" who can be identified as such — turn out on closer inspection to be unreasonable, unwarranted, or at least open to more than one interpretation.

Most important, the current debate has failed to make explicit, or at least to clarify, the philosophical principles underlying the competing positions. Those positions are sometimes described as the "punitive" versus the "medical" approaches, but these labels are of little help. For one thing, they are far from precise: Putting an addict in jail is certainly "punitive," but putting him in a treatment program, however benevolent its intentions, may be seen by him as no less "punitive." Shifting an addict from heroin to methadone may be "medical" if he makes the choice voluntarily — but is it so if the alternative to methadone maintenance is a criminal conviction for heroin possession? And while maintaining an addict on heroin (as is done in Great Britain and as has been proposed for the United States) is not "punitive" in any legal sense, neither is it therapeutic in any medical sense. Indeed, there seem to be no forms of therapy that will "cure" addicts in any large numbers of their dependence on heroin. Various forms of intensive psychotherapy and group-based "personality restructuring" may be of great value to certain drug users, but by definition they can reach only very small numbers of persons, and perhaps only for limited periods of time.

But the fundamental problem with these and other labels is that they avoid the central question: Does society have only the right to protect itself (or its members) from the harmful acts of heroin users, or does it have in addition the responsibility (and thus the right) to improve the well-being (somehow defined) of heroin users themselves? In one view, the purpose of the law is to insure the maximum amount of liberty for everyone, and an action of one person is properly constrained by society if — and only if — it has harmful consequences for another person. This is the utilitarian conception of the public interest and, when applied to heroin use, it leads such otherwise unlike men as Milton Friedman, Herbert Packer, and Thomas Szasz to oppose the use of criminal sanctions for heroin users. The late Professor Packer, for example, wrote that a desirable aspect of liberalism is that it allows people "to choose their own roads to hell if that is where they want to go."

In another view, however, society has an obligation to enhance the well-being of each of its citizens even with respect to those aspects of their lives that do not directly impinge on other people's lives. In this conception of the public good, all citizens of a society are bound to be affected — indirectly but perhaps profoundly and permanently — if a significant number are permitted to go to hell in their own way. A society is therefore unworthy if it permits, or is indifferent to, any activity that renders its members inhuman or deprives them of their essential (or "natural") capacities to judge, choose, and act. If heroin use is such an activity, then its use should be proscribed. Whether that proscription is enforced by mere punishment or by obligatory therapy is a separate question.

The alternative philosophical principles do not necessarily lead to diametrically opposed policies. A utilitarian might conclude, for example, that heroin use is so destructive of family life that society has an interest in proscribing it (though he is more likely, if experience is any guide, to allow the use of heroin and then deal with its effect on family life by advocating social services to "help problem families"). And a moralist might decide that though heroin should be illegal, any serious effort to enforce that law against users would be so costly in terms of other social values (privacy, freedom, and integrity of officialdom) as not to be worth it, and he thus might allow the level of enforcement to fall to a point just short of that at which the tutelary power of the law would be jeopardized. Still, even if principles do not determine policies uniquely, thinking clearly about the former is essential to making good judgments about the latter. And to think clearly about the former, it is as important to ascertain the effects of heroin on the user as it is to discover the behavior of a user toward society. . . .

The amount of crime committed by addicts is no doubt large, but exactly how large is a matter of conjecture. And most important, the amount of addict crime undertaken solely to support the habit, and thus the amount by which crime would decrease if the price of heroin fell to zero, is unknown. Estimates of the proportion of all property crime committed by addicts range from 25 to 67 percent. Whatever the true fraction, there is no reason to assume that property crimes would decline by that fraction if heroin became free. Some addicts are criminals before they are addicts and would remain criminals if their addiction, like their air and water, cost them virtually nothing. Furthermore, some addicts who steal to support their habit come to regard crime as more profitable than normal employment. They would probably continue to steal to provide themselves with an income even after they no longer needed to use part of that income to buy heroin.

Just as it is wrong to suppose that an unwitting youth has heroin "pushed" on him, so also it is wrong to suppose that these youth only then turn to crime to support their habit. Various studies of known addicts have shown that between half and three-quarters were known to be delinquent before turning to drugs. . . .

Once addicted, however, persons are likely to commit more crimes than they would have had they not become addicted. The common and tragic testimony of street addicts dwells upon their need to find the money with which to support the habit, and this means for many of them "hustling," stealing heroin from other users, dealing in heroin themselves, or simply begging. . . .

The kinds of crimes committed by addicts are fairly well known. Selling heroin is perhaps the most important of these — the Hudson Institute estimated that almost half of the annual heroin consumption in New York is financed by selling heroin and related services (for example, selling or renting the equipment needed for injecting heroin). Of the nondrug crimes, shoplifting, burglary, and prostitution account for the largest proportion of addict income used for drug purchases — perhaps 40 to 50 percent. Though the addict wants money, he will not confine himself to those crimes in which property is taken with no threat to personal safety. Muggings and armed robberies will be committed regularly by some addicts, and occasionally by many; even in a burglary, violence may result if the addict is surprised by the victim while ransacking the latter's home or store.

The amount of property taken by addicts is large, but probably not as large as some of the more popular estimates would have us believe. Max Singer has shown that those who make these estimates — usually running into the billions of dollars per year in New York City alone — fail to reconcile their figures with the total amount of property known or suspected to be stolen. He estimated that no more than $500 million a year is lost to both addicted and nonaddicted burglars, shoplifters, pickpockets, robbers, and assorted thieves in New York. If all of that were taken by addicts (which of course it isn't) and if there were one hundred thousand addicts in the city, then the average addict would be stealing about $5000 worth of goods a year — not a vast sum. Even the more conservative figure of sixty thousand addicts would raise the maximum average theft loss per addict to only $8000.

Despite the fact that many addicts were criminals before addiction and would remain criminals even if they ended their addiction, and despite the fact that the theft losses to addicts are considerably exaggerated, there is little doubt that addiction produces a significant increase in criminality of two kinds — stealing from innocent victims and selling heroin illegally to willing consumers. More accurately, the heroin black market provides incentives for at least two kinds of antisocial acts — theft (with its attendant fear) and spreading the use of heroin further.

Critics of the "punitive" mode of attacking heroin distribution argue that law enforcement has not only failed to protect society against these social costs, it has increased those costs by driving up the price of heroin and thus the amount of criminality necessary to support heroin habits. If by this they mean that law enforcement has "failed" because it has not reduced the heroin traffic to zero — and anything short of this will increase the price of heroin — then of course the statement is true. It would be equally true, and equally misleading, to say that most medical approaches have "failed" because the vast majority of persons who undergo voluntary treatment at Lexington or other hospitals return to heroin use when they are released.

Apart from methadone maintenance, which deserves separate discussion, existing therapeutic methods for treating heroin addiction are extremely expensive and have low success rates. Various investigators have found a relapse rate for addicts discharged from hospitals after having undergone treatment ranging between 90 and 95 percent. . . .

The fact that medical approaches do not "cure" addiction, especially if the addict must volunteer for them, need not trouble the critics of the law-enforcement approach if they believe that only the tangible social cost of addiction (e.g., crime) and not addiction itself is a problem, or if they concede that addiction is a problem but think it wrong for addicts to be compelled to obtain help.

But if law enforcement at present fails to prevent the "external" costs of addiction (i.e., crime), or even increases those costs, this will also remain true under any likely alternative public policy, unless one is willing to support complete legalization of heroin for all who wish it. Yet no advocate of "decriminalizing" heroin with whom I am familiar supports total legalization. Most favor some version of the British system, by which heroin is dispensed at low cost in government-controlled clinics to known addicts in order to maintain them in their habit. Almost no one seems to favor allowing any drugstore to sell, or any doctor to prescribe, heroin to anybody who wants it.

The reason for this reluctance is rarely made explicit. Presumably it is either political expediency (designed to make the British system more palatable to a skeptical American public) or an unspoken moral reservation about the desirability of heroin use per se, apart from its tangible social cost. I suspect that the chief reason is the latter: One's moral sensibilities are indeed shocked by the prospect of young children buying heroin at the drugstore the same way they now buy candy. And if one finds that scene wrong or distasteful, then one should also find the prospect of an adult nonuser having cheap access to heroin wrong or distasteful, unless one is willing to make a radical (and on medical grounds, hard to defend) distinction between what is good for a person under the age of (say) eighteen and what is good for a person over that age.

The total decriminalization of heroin would lead, all evidence suggests, to a sharp increase in its use. . . .

Under any conceivable American variant of the British system . . . a law-enforcement strategy would remain an important component of government policy. Rather than simply rejecting law enforcement as "punitive" (and therefore "medieval," "barbarian," "counterproductive," or whatever), one ought to consider what it might accomplish under various circumstances.

The assumption that law enforcement has no influence on the size of the addict population but does have an effect on the price of heroin (and thus on crime committed to meet that higher price) rests chiefly on the evidence that the majority of known addicts have been arrested at least once; that during his life expectancy, any addict is virtually certain to be arrested; and that, despite this, the addict returns to his habit and to the criminal life needed to sustain it. These facts are essentially correct. The difficulty lies in equating "law enforcement" with "arrest."

Thousands of addicts are arrested every year; a very large proportion are simply returned to the street — by the police, who wish to use them as informants, or by judges who wish to place them on probation or under suspended sentences because they believe (rightly) that a prison term will not cause their cure or rehabilitation. Only a few addicts are singled out for very severe punishment. We do not know for how many addicts arrest is simply a revolving door. In Boston, however, Wheat has done a careful study of the relationship between the level of law enforcement, defined as the "expected costs" of an arrest to the user, and the number of addicts in the city. By "expected costs," Wheat means the probability of being arrested multiplied by the probability of being sentenced to prison and the length of the average prison sentence. Though his numerical estimates are complex and open to criticism, the general relationship between the number of heroin users and the expected "costs" to the addict of law enforcement is quite striking — the "costs" declined sharply between 1961 and 1970, while the estimated number of addicts in Boston increased about tenfold. Furthermore, the largest increases in the number of addicts tended to follow years in which the certainty and severity of law enforcement were the lowest. . . .

If there is a relationship between law enforcement and heroin use, it may result from one or both of two processes. An increase in legal penalties may deter the novice user from further use or it may deter the confirmed addict-dealer (or if he is jailed, prevent him entirely) from selling to a potential user. Lessening the "costs" of the penalty may either embolden the novice users and potential users, or improve their access to a supplier, or both.

There is some clinical evidence that both processes are in fact at work. Robert Schasre's study of forty Mexican-American heroin users who had stopped shooting heroin revealed that over half (twenty-two) did so involuntarily after they had lost their source of supply — their dealer had been arrested or had lost his source, or the user himself had moved to another community where he could find no dealer. Of the remaining eighteen who stopped "voluntarily," most did so in response to some social or institutional pressure; in a third of these cases, that pressure was having been arrested or having a friend who was arrested on a narcotics charge.

Indeed, one could as easily make the argument that law enforcement has not even been tried as the argument that it has been tried and failed. Before making it, please be reassured that such an argument does not bespeak an illusion that prison sentences "cure" addiction nor indicate a desire to "seek vengeance" on the addict. The same argument could be made if one substituted for "sentences to prison," sentences to Synanon, Daytop, methadone maintenance, or expensive psychiatric clinics. The central point is that only a small proportion of heroin addicts will voluntarily seek and remain in any form of treatment, care, or confinement — unless that care involves free dispensation of heroin itself.

One can imagine a variety of law-enforcement strategies that would have a powerful effect on the number of addicts on the street, and thus on the number of street crimes they might commit and other harm they might do to others and themselves. One could arrest every known addict and send him to a "heroin quarantine center" with comfortable accommodations and intensive care programs. Or one could arrest every known addict and send him back onto the street under a "pledge" system requiring him to submit to frequent urine tests which, if omitted or failed, would then lead to confinement in either center or jail.

American society does not do these things for a number of reasons. One is that, despite popular talk, we do not really take the problem that seriously — or at least have not until white middle-class suburbanites began to suffer from a problem only ghetto blacks once endured. Another is that we think that detaining addicts for the mere fact of addiction is violative of their civil rights. (It is an interesting question. We quarantine people with smallpox without thinking that their rights are violated. The similarities as well as the differences are worth some public debate.) Finally, we do not do these things because we labor under the misapprehension that law enforcement should concentrate on the "pushers" and the "big connections" and not on the innocent user.

The last reason may be the weakest of all, even if among tough-sounding politicians it is the most common. In the first place, the "pusher" is largely a myth, or more accurately, he is simply the addict playing one of his roles. And the "big connections" and "top dealers," who indeed exist and who generally are not users, are in many ways the least important part of the heroin market system — because they are the most easily replaced. A new "connection" arises for every one put out of business. The amount of heroin seized by federal agents is only a fraction of what is imported. . . .

[However,] the novice or would-be heroin user is quite vulnerable to changes, even small ones, in the availability of heroin. For one thing, a person who has not yet become a heavy user will not conduct an intensive search for a supply. Some studies have suggested that a "dabbler" may use heroin if it is immediately available, but will not use it if it requires two, three, or four hours of searching. Extending the search time for novices may discourage or reduce the frequency of their use of heroin. In addition, a dealer is reluctant to sell to persons with whom he is not closely acquainted for fear of detection and apprehension by the police. When police surveillance is intensified, the dealer becomes more cautious about those with whom he does business. A casual user or distant acquaintance represents a threat to the dealer when police activity is high; when such activity is low, the casual or new customer is more attractive. Heroin customers can be thought of as a "queue" with the heaviest users at the head of the line and the casual ones at the end; how far down the queue the dealer will do business depends on the perceived level of risk associated with each additional customer, and that in turn depends on how strongly "the heat is on."

The price of heroin to the user will be affected by law enforcement in different ways, depending on the focus of the pressure. No one has the data with which to construct anything but a highly conjectural model of the heroin market; at the same time, there is little reason for asserting that the only effect of law enforcement on the heroin market is to drive up the price of the product. . . .

. . . The long-term effect of law-enforcement pressures on large-scale dealers is probably to force up the price of heroin by either increasing the cash price, decreasing the quality of the produce, or requiring dealers to discriminate among their customers in order to avoid risky sales. But in the short term, anti-dealer law enforcement probably affects access (finding a "connection") more than price.

Suppose that law enforcement were directed at the user and the street-level dealer rather than the top supplier. Taking user-dealers off the streets in large numbers would tend to reduce the demand for, and thus the price of, heroin. Furthermore, with many heavy customers gone, some dealers would have to accept the risks of doing business with novice users who, having smaller habits or no real habits at all, would consume fewer bags per capita and pay lower prices. (Law enforcement aimed merely at known and regular users would not result in the apprehension of many novice users, however, and thus would not take off the streets a large fraction of the sources of heroin "infection.") Suppose, finally, that coupled with law enforcement aimed at known user-dealers there were a selective strategy of identifying and restraining the agents of contagion. This was tried in Chicago on an experimental basis by Hughes and Crawford, with promising though not conclusive results. On spotting a neighborhood epidemic, they intervened by seeking quickly to identify the friends and fellow users of an addict. They found in this case that one addict led them to fourteen other addicts and, most important, to seven persons experimenting with heroin. The doctors were able to involve eleven of the fourteen addicts and five of the seven experimenters in a treatment program; the remainder of the experimenters apparently discontinued heroin use, perhaps because the social structure in which their drug use took place was disrupted.

There is, of course, an alternative way to get many confirmed addicts out of the heroin black market, and that is to offer them heroin legally at nominal prices. A black market would still exist for novice users, unregistered regular users, and registered regular users who wish to supplement their government-supplied maintenance dose with an additional dose that would produce a "high." Furthermore, this black market would be in many ways more attractive to the euphoria-seeking user because, due to competition from government suppliers, prices in it would be lower than the price in the existing market. Under this system, the government-maintained users would remain on the street and some fraction of them would continue to serve as contagion agents, thus causing the size of the addict population to continue to grow. Whether it would grow as fast as it has in the past, no one can say. There is little evidence of any rapid growth in England, but as pointed out above, this may be due to the fact that British addicts are different from American ones and the illegal supply of heroin is much smaller there than it is here. Indeed, any estimate of the future size of the addict population under any set of legal constraints is almost meaningless. We simply do not know how many persons are susceptible to heroin use if exposed to it nor what fraction of the population that is at risk is now using heroin. . . .

If nothing else, this discussion of the complexities of heroin use, marketing, and control should suggest the futility of arguments between the so-called "punitive" and "medical" approaches to addiction, the simplistic nature of unqualified recommendations that we adopt the "British system," and the imprecision of angry disputes between those who wish to "get tough" on "pushers" and those who wish to "decriminalize" heroin.

Beyond that, thinking about heroin requires one first of all to decide how one will handle the underlying philosophical issue — namely, whether the state is ever justified in protecting people from themselves, or whether it can only intervene to protect an innocent party from the actions of someone else. Put another way, the question is whether the state has any responsibility for the quality of human life in those cases where that quality (or lack of it) appears to be the result of freely exercised choice with no external effects on other parties. It is my view that the state does have such responsibilities, though its powers in this regard must be carefully exercised toward only the most important and reasonable goals. Even John Stuart Mill, whose defense of personal liberty is virtually absolute, argued against allowing a man to sell himself into slavery, "for by selling himself as a slave, he abdicates his liberty; he foregoes any future use of it beyond that simple act."

The next question is whether heroin addiction is such a form of "slavery" or is otherwise a state of being which should not be left to free choice. This is a more difficult question to answer in general terms, for somewhat surprisingly, we know rather little about what proportion of all heroin users are seriously incapacitated (or "captured") by it. Obviously, a large number are; but some might remain heavy users and yet hold jobs, lead responsible family lives, and retain other attributes of their humanity. Nobody knows what fraction are in this category, though we do know that the advocates of decriminalization tend to give (with little or no evidence) very generous estimates of it, while proponents of "stamping out" heroin give very small ones. The lives of British addicts have not been carefully studied. But Griffith Edwards of the Addiction Research Institute reports "the impression of many of the clinic doctors" that "the majority of young heroin takers do not settle to a job, or otherwise manage their lives responsibly, do not keep to the prescribed dose, and tend to acquire drugs other than those prescribed." Furthermore, the mortality rate of British addicts, even without the need to steal to support a habit, is twenty-eight times as large as the death rate for the equivalent age group in the British population and twice that of American heroin addicts.

I think it clear that for a sufficiently large number of persons, heroin is so destructive of the human personality that it should not be made generally available. (Defending that view in the context of the current debate is not essential, however, because not even the most zealous advocate of decriminalization supports complete legalization.) I believe this to be the case, though I recognize the rejoinders that can be made. Alcohol, some will say, has consequences for many individuals and for society at least as destructive as those of heroin, yet no one would propose returning to a system of prohibition. Alcohol and heroin are different problems, however, both medically and legally. A far smaller proportion of alcohol users than of heroin users become addicted in any meaningful sense of that term; the risks to the average individual of experimentation are accordingly far less in the former than in the latter case. And of those "addicted" to alcohol, there have been a larger proportion of "cures," although perhaps not as many as one would wish. Finally, alcohol use is so widespread as to be nearly universal, while heroin use remains an exotic habit of relatively few, and thus presents easier problems of control. Perhaps because of this, while no advanced society has been able to eliminate alcohol use, most societies have been able to eliminate, or keep to trifling proportions, heroin use.

If one accepts the view that it is desirable and possible, not only to provide better treatment for present addicts, but to reduce the rate of growth of the addict population, then one must also accept the need for some measure of compulsion; nothing is clearer than the fact that most young addicts enjoying their "run" will not voluntarily choose a life without heroin in preference to a life with it. Such compulsion will be necessary whatever disposition is made of the constrained addict — whether he be put on probation or sent to prison, to a quarantine center, to a methadone program, or to a heroin maintenance program. The compulsion will be necessary to achieve two objectives: to insure that he remains in the appropriate treatment without "cheating" (i.e., simply using the treatment center as a cheap source of drugs to be sold on the street), and to insure that while treated he does not proselytize among nonaddicts and spread the contagion. Furthermore, there is some evidence (inconclusive, to be sure) that the possibility of arrest followed by some penalty deters at least some potential users and makes access to heroin more difficult for others.

Finally, to the extent that people voluntarily elect not to use heroin, the fact of its illegality may contribute to the belief that such use is "wrong," and therefore enhance the probability that a nonuser will remain a nonuser. Or put another way, it is difficult to see how society can assert that heroin use is a grave evil if it also must admit that its use is perfectly legal.

A detailed consideration of the legal policies which might effectively deal with the heroin problem is beyond the scope of this chapter. In general, there are two alternatives — "outpatient" programs (in which the addict is left in the community but under a legally enforced requirement to report periodically for tests and for chemical or other forms of treatment) and "inpatient" programs (in which the addict is separated from the community in detoxification, methadone, or other programs). Each kind of program must deal with both regular addicts and infectious, novice addicts. The legal, medical, and organization issues involved in these alternatives are complex. The important thing, however, is to consider them seriously — which means in turn to stop thinking of "legal" and "medical" approaches as mutually exclusive or separately viable.

Perhaps the most difficult of these issues is to decide what role heroin maintenance itself can play in an overall addict control program. It seems likely that offering low-cost, high-quality heroin is the one positive inducement that will prove attractive to most young addicts still enjoying their "run." Under the British system, the addict who obtains heroin from clinics is under no other obligations; no doctor or government official has the power to compel (and some doctors do not even have the desire to ask) the addict to accept, as a condition of heroin maintenance, any form of therapy, including the gradual substitution of oral methadone for heroin. In the British context, with a tiny addict population composed of persons apparently quite different from the typical American addict, that policy may work well enough, though experience with it is still too short to permit one to be confident of its value.

But whatever the fate of the British experiment, it seems probable that any larger program will involve real risks of sustaining the habits of contagion agents likely to recruit new addicts, and of supplying, through illegal diversions, the existing black market in drugs. With the best will in the world, it is probably impossible to devise a government program run by ordinary mortals that can provide heroin to one or two hundred thousand addicts on an outpatient basis in a way that will avoid subsidizing the growth of the addict pool and supplying debilitating (as opposed to mere maintenance) doses. If that is true, and if our society believes that it has some responsibility for preventing addiction, then a substantial measure of legal compulsion will have to accompany any treatment program, especially one involving heroin maintenance. . . .

UNORTHODOX: UNQUALIFIED YES

19. MARIJUANA RECONSIDERED

Andrew Weil

Marijuana is still the subject of such heated debate that it is hard to get useful answers to simple questions like, "Is it healthy to use marijuana?" or "What are its medicinal properties?" I have studied this controversial plant for a long time and have come to some definite conclusions about it.

Cannabis is one of the oldest known useful plants. It is so closely allied with human beings that we cannot unravel its ancestral history. Truly wild hemp, completely independent of man, is unknown. Cannabis provides us with an edible seed, an edible oil, a fiber, a medicine, and a psychoactive drug. That is a lot for one plant to do, which is why it has always been an important cultivated crop.

In our society, most people who use cannabis smoke it for its psychoactive effect: They use it to get high. I am a great believer in the value of being high. High states of consciousness show us the potentials of our nervous systems. They help us integrate mind and body. They promote health. And they feel good. There are many ways to get high. You can do it through music, dance, athletics, sex, fasting, meditation, drugs, and countless other techniques.

That so many different methods lead to the same experiences suggests that the experiences come from inside us, that they are latent in the human nervous system, waiting to be released. It is important to keep this idea in mind in considering drugs. Drugs do not contain highs; they do not put any experiences into us that are not there already. They simply make us feel physically different for a time, and if we are set to interpret that change in a certain way, we can use it as an opportunity to let ourselves feel high.

Marijuana, by its direct pharmacological actions, causes a number of subtle changes in our mind-body. For example, it increases heart rate, dries up saliva and tears, and alters body perception. These changes are so slight that novice users may not notice them at all. Some people may feel them but not associate them with any interesting changes in consciousness. On the other hand, regular users of marijuana come to associate the changed feeling with a high. That is to say, being high on marijuana is a learned association between an experience that is always on tap within the nervous system and a change in feeling caused by the drug.

Most people who ask questions about marijuana want to know whether it is good or bad. (Usually, they have already decided.) But drugs in themselves are neither good nor bad. They are just drugs, with potentials for both constructive and destructive uses. One reason that research on marijuana is mostly unenlightening is that many researchers set out to prove the goodness or badness of the substance without realizing that they are imposing their own values on it. There has been an enormous amount of research on cannabis in the past ten years. One investigator has commented that we now know more about marijuana than we do about penicillin. Most of this information is irrelevant to our concerns about the drug and gives us little help in deciding what to do with it. A great deal of it is contradictory, reflecting the differing biases of researchers.

Although I feel marijuana is neither good nor bad of itself, I have no hesitation in talking about good or bad uses people make of it. We cannot discuss psychoactive drugs meaningfully apart from people, for everything interesting about the drugs arises from the relationships people form with them.

What are the characteristics of a good relationship with marijuana? A primary aspect of a good relationship with any psychoactive drug is awareness of its nature. When people forget that drugs are drugs, they are on the road to trouble. Look at the extent of serious dependence on coffee in our society. Coffee is a strong psychoactive drug; its direct pharmacological effects are more powerful than those of cannabis. Dependence on it has a marked physiological component. Many coffee-dependent persons suffer withdrawal syndromes each morning: they are uncoordinated, unable to think clearly, and unable to move their bowels until they have their first fix of coffee. Yet most of these people are unaware that they are in a bad relationship with a drug, let alone a strong drug. To them coffee is just a beverage they like to drink.

Another characteristic of a good relationship with a drug is getting a positive and useful effect from it. In the case of marijuana that means getting high when you smoke it. The first thing that goes wrong in relationships with drugs when we use them too frequently is that the experiences we seek in them diminish in intensity. If we keep on using the drugs more and more frequently, the highs will disappear altogether, and we will find ourselves using them just to relieve negative symptoms.

The explanation of this pattern is that highs are not direct effects of drugs but indirect associations between the feelings drugs cause and experiences waiting to be released in our nervous systems. When we use any drug very frequently, the novelty of the feelings it causes wears off. It no longer makes us feel as different as it did initially and so does not serve as well as a trigger for a high. That is why many people report the first highs they ever had from any drug to be the best and why people who are heavily dependent on drugs do not get very intense experiences from them.

Frequency of use is the critical factor. But it is not possible to say what is too frequent use except with reference to a specific individual. For one person, smoking marijuana twice a week may be too much, but for another, smoking four times a day may not be too much. The only criterion is whether the person is able to maintain highs at a given level of use. If you are using marijuana regularly and find that you do not get as high from it as you used to, that is a warning that you are using it too much.

Ironically, many people who begin to lose the high of marijuana as a result of too frequent use try to get it back by smoking more or looking for stronger pot. Of course, those actions simply make the problem worse. Stronger pot may work for a while, but soon you will be in the same predicament as before. The only solution is to abstain from use for a while and then resume at a lower frequency. In general, any psychoactive drug is most effective when used least frequently. Furthermore, people who ignore or misunderstand the significance of highs that diminish with increasing frequency of use will eventually find that they cannot easily stop using the drug.

A third characteristic of a good relationship with a drug like marijuana is ease of separation from it. Can you take it or leave it? Do you always smoke a joint if it is offered to you? How long have you gone without the drug since becoming a user? These are hard questions, especially since we often play games with ourselves about our habits. (Remember Mark Twain's comment about quitting cigarettes: "To cease smoking is the easiest thing I ever did; I ought to know because I've done it a thousand times.") Dependence on marijuana is subtle and not marked by prominent physiological changes like dependence on coffee or alcohol. But heavy marijuana smoking can be a neurotic habit, both unproductive and difficult to break.

As a marijuana user, then, if you remain aware that you are using a drug, if you are able to maintain your highs over time, if you can separate yourself from the use of marijuana easily, and if you do not experience any adverse effects on your health, then you have a good relationship with that substance.

The opposite characteristics mark bad relationships with marijuana. I meet many heavy users who do not consider marijuana a drug. It is just a "smoking herb" to them. Some of these users smoke marijuana day in and day out and do not get as high on it as they did when they first began smoking. They are always on the lookout for stronger forms, such as Thai sticks, potent Hawaiian, or preparations of hash oil. They cannot separate themselves from this habitual use of marijuana and are very good at rationalizing it. ("On, John just came in; let's roll another joint." "We can't eat that ice cream without smoking some Hawaiian." "We've got to get really stoned before we go to the movie.") Some of these people suffer adverse consequences of marijuana on health, although they often deny them.

The final characteristic of a good relationship with any psychoactive drug is that no impairment of health occurs, even over time. The greatest health hazard of marijuana seems to me to be its irritating effect on the respiratory tract. It is unfortunate that smoking has become the universal mode of consuming cannabis in our part of the world. Hemp drugs can be eaten, of course. They are more powerful by mouth, take longer to come on, and produce different effects. It is healthier to eat marijuana than to smoke it, but it is also more trouble to prepare, and a few smokers like to eat it except on occasion.

I meet many marijuana smokers with chronic, dry coughs, typical of bronchial irritation. Many of these people are unaware of their coughing and resentful of having it pointed out to them. One of the silliest scenes of New Age life that I have witnessed again and again is a roomful of people coughing their heads off over some especially harsh preparation of cannabis and pronouncing it "really good stuff."

As we have all read, scientists have attributed a great many horrible medical effects to marijuana, from brain damage to chromosomal damage, but in most cases the research is shoddy, using poor controls and demonstrating mainly the researchers' own prejudices. A few findings are worth mentioning.

Several investigators have reported that marijuana impairs the immune system in human beings by interfering with the activity of certain white blood cells. The workers who first described this effect were rabid antimarijuana crusaders, but some less biased investigators have supported their findings. Other experiments contradict them. Most of the evidence comes from test-tube studies rather than clinical research in real people. Epidemiological studies in populations that use marijuana heavily give us no reason to believe that users are more prone to infections than nonusers. Therefore, the test-tube results, even if confirmed, may have no clinical significance.

Another research finding, much publicized in the past few years, is that marijuana use may decrease blood levels of the male hormone testosterone in men. Again, there are contradictory experiments, and the issue is not settled. Of course, even if marijuana does have this effect, its significance is not clear. High testosterone levels may correlate more with aggressiveness than with sexual adjustment; some men in our society might benefit from a reduction in this hormone.

A more bizarre effect, also well publicized, is that marijuana may stimulate the development of breasts in some men. At first glance, this looks like fantastic antimarijuana propaganda, but, in fact, there are a few documented cases of male users who have developed breasts. This condition, called gynecomastia, is normally quite rare. The active compounds of marijuana have some molecular resemblance to certain female hormones (estrogens). Possibly, some men are born with a bio-chemical idiosysncrasy that causes their bodies to mistake the chemicals in hemp for estrogens. This susceptibility is uncommon, and only a tiny percentage of male users is at risk.

In general, marijuana is a relatively nontoxic drug, especially in comparison with other psychoactive drugs in common use, such as alcohol, tobacco, coffee, and tranquilizers. I repeat that the greatest hazard to health seems to be the irritation from smoking, and individuals are more or less likely to develop respiratory con-ditions as a result of this irritation. If you are prone to chest colds and bronchitis, be careful.

So far I have talked about the use of cannabis as a psychoactive drug. What about its use as a remedy? The plant has long and distinguished history of use in medicine around the world. It was extremely popular in Europe and America in the nineteenth century in the form of a tincture and was used for all sorts of conditions.

The attractiveness of cannabis as a medicine is that it is both powerful and nontoxic. Its ability to make people feel different, especially when they consume it orally, puts it in quite another class from herbs like peppermint and chamomile. Its safety, even in large overdoses, makes it much easier to use than drugs like opium and belladonna.

In nineteenth-century medicine, tincture of cannabis was used mainly as a sedative and antispasmodic. It was dispensed for insomnia, migraine, epilepsy, excitability, childbirth, and menstrual discomfort. Interestingly enough, the medical reports from that time make little or no mention of psychoactive effects. In those days, people's expectations of cannabis were different. Either they did not get high from it because they did not expect to, or if they did, they paid it no attention and did not mention it to their doctors. It is expectation that leads us to associate our inner experiences of highs with the pharmacological effects of drugs.

The drawback of cannabis as a remedy is its extreme unpredictability. Its effects vary greatly from person to person. Doctors like drugs that have constant, repro-ducible effects, and they abandoned cannabis when they found more reliable, though sometimes more toxic, sedatives and antispasmodics.

Once, on reading through a nineteenth-century article on the medicinal properties of Indian hemp, I came across a line that caught my attention: "It is impossible to list the therapeutic indications for cannabis because the drug behaves homeopathically.'' What the writer meant, I think, is that cannabis treats individuals, not conditions. In the homeopathic conception, people get sick in unique ways; there are no ''disease entities'' apart from people. In my experience, this old observation about cannabis is quite true. some people respond favorably to it and can use it to make themselves feel better when they are sick, no matter what they have. Other people do not respond favorably to cannabis and cannot use it at all as a remedy.

I know people who use marijuana successfully to treat headaches, insomnia, stomach, and menstrual cramps, labor pains, and a variety of other minor ills. Some of them smoke it and some of them eat it. In general, they are people who like marijuana but do not use it too often and stay in good relationships with it. Just as marijuana tiggers better highs when it is used less frequently, so also does it work better as a remedy when it is saved for occasions when it is really needed.

How can marijuana work for so many diverse conditions in some people? Such people are probably able to use marijuana as a tool for putting themselves in high states from which they can perceive the physical condition differently and thereby modify it. For example, headaches, like all diseases, are psychosomatic. That is, mind and body are both involved. (*Psychosomatic* just means ''mind-body''; it does not mean ''mind-caused'' or ''not physical.'') The physical discomfort of headache captures the mind's attention, lending more energy to the physical problem in a vicious cycle. Shifting attention to a high, by any method, will break this cycle and permit the physical aspect of the disease to subside. People who respond favorably to marijuana have learned to use it to make this shift in attention.

Aside from these broad effects of marijuana in some people, the plant has certain specific pharmacological properties that may make it useful in the treatment of asthma, glaucoma, nausea, and spastic paralysis.

As a drug for asthma, marijuana has a paradoxical effect when smoked. It relaxes bronchial smooth muscle to permit greater airflow, but the irritation of the smoke may worsen the asthma. Which effect predominates depends on the individual. Some asthmatics report definite relief after smoking a joint, but others say the smoke precipitates fits of coughing. Ingesting the cannabis orally would be one way around this problem. Researchers are also experimenting with aerosol preparations of marijuana compounds that might give the relief without the irritation.

Glaucoma is a disease of the eye due to increased fluid pressure inside the eyeball. It is of unknown cause, and some forms of it lead to severe losses of vision. It is now treated by surgery and by drugs, but the drugs are often not very effective and have significant toxicity. Marijuana lowers intraocular pressure. How it does so is not known. Many glaucoma sufferers have found that their vision improves after smoking pot, and they prefer the side effects of marijuana to those of the conventional medicines. Research is under way to find preparations of cannabis that maximize this effect. At least one patient so far has forced the federal government to supply him with marijuana for his glaucoma.

As an antinausea drug, marijuana seems to have a place in modifying the toxic effects of the very poisonous drugs used in the chemotherapy of cancer. Many of these drugs produce violent nausea and vomiting within minutes of their injection.

Marijuana, taken in advance, counteracts this toxicity, an effect discovered first by teenagers with leukemia who happened to be potheads.

Marijuana may also be effective in the treatment of nausea from other causes, including motion sickness. Officials have not allowed researchers to test marijuana itself as an antinauseant. They have insisted, instead, on the use of chemically pure THC (tetrahydrocannabinol), the so-called active principle of the plant. THC does work when given orally, but as anyone familiar with medicinal plants knows, whole plants are safer and often work better than concentrated chemicals extracted from them. I would like to see more research with marijuana and less with THC. And I am not in favor of the development of analogues of THC with no psychoactivity. With proper expectation, the psychoactivity of marijuana can be a powerful and beneficial psychosomatic influence on illness.

Spastic paralysis (or paralysis with increased muscle tone) results from interruption of central nervous system pathways to muscles. It occurs in birth injuries, multiple sclerosis, stroke, and other conditions, and is an uncomfortable disability. Marijuana, by relaxing muscles, may be a specific treatment.

There are reports on other medicinal properties of cannabis, including antibiotic, antitumor, and antiepileptic effects of some of its derivatives. Other researchers have suggested using it as an appetite stimulant in old people and cancer patients. Here again, individual variability would likely be great and might discourage general use. Appetite stimulation from marijuana seems to be a consequence of expectation rather than a direct pharmacological effect.

If marijuana is to be used medicinally, it should be fresh and of good quality, as with any other medicinal plant. The therapeutic and psychoactive properties are in a resin that is concentrated in the flowering tops. The active compounds in this resin are soluble in oil but extremely insoluble in water. Therefore, infusions or decoctions of marijuana are not effective. Alcoholic tinctures are much more reliable but may not keep well. It is also possible to extract the active constituents in fat, for instance by boiling the plant in a mixture of butter and water, straining the mixture, and chilling it to separate the butter. (Several handbooks of marijuana give instructions for this method.)

Because of the insolubility of cannabis resin in water, it is absorbed unevenly from the gastrointestinal tract. This makes it hard to estimate doses of oral preparations and easy to take an overdose. One reason tincture of cannabis fell into disrepute in this century was the difficulty of establishing a standard dose for the average patient. Overdoses of marijuana are not dangerous, but they can be very uncomfortable. It is much better to err on the side of too little. In the absence of a standardized oral preparation, many users in our part of the world prefer to smoke the plant rather than eat it. Those who wish to use it orally will have to experiment with different forms and doses.

In discussing marijuana I have ignored the obvious fact of its illegality. Although laws on its possession and use are changing slowly, they still have a long way to go. Criminalization of marijuana has created large and unpleasant black markets (high-potency varieties now sell for $2000 a pound and more), promoted bad relationships with the drug, and seriously hampered good scientific research. Marijuana is much less toxic than many legal drugs, but many persons are afraid to use it medicinally because of its illegality and bad reputation. Abuse of marijuana is not uncommon today; to my mind it is a direct result of the approach our society has taken.

Sooner or later we will learn that plants with effects on the body and mind, such as marijuana, are what we make of them. Used intelligently and carefully they can help us. Used irresponsibly they can harm us. The problem is not to try to eradicate the plants (impossible) or stop people from using them (also impossible) but to teach the principles of safe interaction with them. Marijuana is certainly here to stay. I hope our relationships with it will improve.

LIBERAL: QUALIFIED YES

20. DECRIMINALIZATION: THE LAW, SOCIETY, AND THE USER

Bruce K. MacMurray, Thomas M. Shapiro, and Maureen E. Kelleher

Drug policy is one of those areas invested with enormous emotional ferment, but blessed with mixed logic and little social science insight. Present national policy focuses overwhelmingly on a law-enforcement approach aimed at punishing the drug user. Such efforts at legally controlling drug use have been marked by their failure, whether one looks at the dismal national experience involving the prohibition of alcohol (1919–1932) or at the ineffective seventy-year effort to eliminate heroin from the American drug scene.

Policy regarding drugs, whether legal or illegal, is a complex enterprise. Not only must pharmacological effects be addressed (such as increased probabilities of cancers, premature heart diseases, liver or brain damage), but so too should problems associated with the social conditions of use (for example, arrest or fear of arrest, stigmatization and deviance, and drug-related crime to secure illicit drug supplies) (Goode 1984). Particularly important in examining the social use of drugs is the recognition that many of associated problems are the direct or indirect result of drug enforcement policy. Thus, we believe it is time to start considering alternative policies aimed at reorienting national efforts away from criminalization and punishment and toward a concern with users, potential users, and related social problems.

Before changing any policy, however, it is prudent to examine the likely consequences such a change might entail, for drug policy touches on many wide-ranging issues. Among the more important to consider are the following: the legislation of morality and victimless crimes; the deterrence and social control of drug use; the legitimacy of the law and its impact by stigmatizing users; the organization of supplying and distributing legal and illegal drugs; the health of drug users; treatment options; and patterns of subsequent drug use. Discussions of these issues has been organized into three related and overlapping areas — the law, society, and the user.

In evaluating such policy options, we must be clear about our goals and biases. Placing the emphasis on the user and society, this paper suggests the following guidelines. First of all, it should be a fundamental aim of drug policy to minimize social disruption and harm to individuals. As such, policy should not pander to induced paranoia, victim-blaming, social sterotyping, or mere symbolic gestures. Furthermore, policy need not be, nor should it be, monolithic. Rather, it should be flexible and based on the specific drugs and related problems in question. Finally, in examining alternatives, we must remember that by maintaining present policy toward drugs we are also making a conscious choice, one to sustain the status quo.

This article will explore the implications of one alternative proposal — decriminalization. We choose decriminalization for a variety of reasons. First, decriminalization implies a reorientation of drug policy away from punitive law enforcement and toward education, rehabilitation, research, and treatment. Symbolic distinctions, commercial interest, and medical utility presently direct policy, producing a crazy patchwork of laws for different drugs (Kelleher, MacMurray, and Shapiro 1983). Second, decriminalization is worth exploring because it highlights the complexities and shortcomings of drug use and social control, which may have positive effects in sorting out drug policy.

Decriminalization typically involves the removal of a jail sentence for first-time possession of small amounts of a drug. The offense thus becomes a civil, rather than a criminal matter, and the offender pays a fine akin to that for a traffic violation. It should be noted that such a policy does not include a legal, regulated supply of drugs, but merely changes the penalty for personal possession and use.

THE LAW

This section discusses the relation of law and the criminal justice system to the use of illegal drugs. Of particular importance are the issues of: drug use as a victimless crime; the effect of deterrence through drug laws; and the implication of decriminalization policy on the criminal justice system.

Law and the Legislation of Morality

For a sociologist, law in general and criminal law more specifically is the attempt by society to formally lay out norms for the social control of acceptable and unacceptable conduct (Akers and Hawkins 1975). In most areas, there is relative consensus about these social rules for the protection of persons and their property (e.g., murder, assault, robbery and burglary). However, the content of some laws are more controversial. An example of one such area is for laws regarding what sociologists term, "victimless crimes."

Victimless crimes as defined by Schur (1965) involve ". . . the willing exchange, among adults, of strongly demanded but legally prescribed goods or services." Typically included in this category are such offenses as: prostitution, pornography, gambling, and illicit drug use. What distinguishes these crimes from others is that there is no victim harmed by their occurrence, or there is typically no complainant to report the crime and press charges. Following a civil libertarian perspective, some argue the law has no mandate to regulate such private consensual acts of individuals (Morris and Hawkins 1970; Szasz 1972). From this point of view, victimless crimes are prime candidates for potential decriminalization or legalization. Critics, however, maintain that no crimes are truly victimless as the offender and the broader society are both usually harmed by such behavior (Wilson 1975).

Law and Social Control

Laws serve to protect society from wrongdoing on the basis of two related processes: (1) instrumental control, and (2) symbolic features. As Gusfield notes (1963), law operates as an instrument by influencing behavior through enforcement and the arrest, conviction and punishment of law violators. However, just as importantly, the law also functions as a symbol designating and affirming the ideals of society. As such, the law provides a clear sense of what behavior is proper according to the moral norms; expresses the public value of a set of moral beliefs; and enhances the social status of one group, while stigmatizing as deviant those with differing views. In precisely this manner, criminal drug laws provide for both the official prosecution of law violators and also define such behavior as immoral and antisocial.

The symbolic function of law is particularly important, because a society's criminal justice system, no matter how large in number or unlimited in resources, can never depend solely on enforcement to prevent or limit crime. Indeed, in the case of drugs (and other victimless crimes), one might expect particular reliance on the law's symbolic value and informal social control through the process of deterrence.

Deterrence and the Policy of Drug Criminalization

Deterrence is based on the assumption that people typically orient their behavior using rational decision making. For example, if the benefits from a particular drug are seen to outweigh the risks and costs associated with it, an individual should choose to use the drug. Deterrence of drug use, then, involves the process of raising the costs (and/or lowering the benefits) for drugs in order to make them seem less beneficial or desirable, and thus prevent their usage. Perhaps the most straightforward means to accomplish this goal is to pass laws against the use and possession of certain drugs, and vigorously enforce these laws to increase both the risk of apprehension and the punishment costs for such behavior.

Given the emphasis of current U.S. drug policy on deterrence and law enforcement, it seems appropriate to ask how effectively the criminalization of drugs works as a legal and social policy. More precisely, what are this policy's effects on drug use and related social behavior?

Brecher (1972) has noted several problems with the logic of deterrence as applied to drug behavior. First, much drug use is based on addiction. In such cases, usage is neither freely chosen nor based solely on rational criteria, making deterrence extremely difficult. Given this circumstance, laws penalizing addicts may be seen to "blame the victim" (Ryan 1971), rather than to provide treatment or rehabilitation to help ameliorate the problems of drug addiction.

Second, the illegality of drugs such as marijuana and LSD may lead to increased experimentation and recreational use, suggesting a "forbidden fruit" appeal for prospective users (Brecher 1972; Hellman 1975). Similarly, to the extent that criminalization is linked with claims about negative health, psychological, and behavioral effects that conflict with users' own drug experiences, the government, the law, and deterrence may all be seen to lose credibility (Hellman 1975).

Third, as criminalization attempts to deter, but does not and cannot entirely eliminate drug use, this policy leaves a tremendous consumer demand void. And as elementary economics tells us, if there is demand for a product or service, a supply will surely arise to meet it. If not by legitimate means, then through the establishment of a black market economy, as has clearly been the case with illegal drugs.

Drug criminalization also leads to additional problems, specifically in the area of enforcement. Because the use of illicit drugs is victimless, most sales transactions as well as private usage take place unbeknownst to the police. This situation forces law-enforcement agents to use techniques and procedures posing serious threats to the protection of constitutional civil liberties. These threats are particularly likely to occur with respect to surveillance, deception, unlawful or questionable searches and seizures, arrests without probable cause, selective enforcement, and harassment. Additionally, the heavy reliance on informers and undercover work places enforcement officers under extreme pressure and risk regarding perjury, corruption, and criminal involvement (Hellman 1975; Skolnick 1969).

In summary, while making certain drugs illegal serves to indicate society's social disapproval by punishing and stigmatizing users, such a policy does not remove the drugs from society and cannot guarantee the prevention of their use or abuse. Instead, this approach merely moves the drug from licit to illicit, and similarly from aboveground, legitimate use to underground, illegal behavior. And therein lies the problem. For much of what contemporary American society regards as most evil about drugs — drug-related crime, involvement with and financial support of organized crime, overdoses, and drug-poisoning, as well as the escapist "down and out" addict life-style — can all be seen as directly or indirectly linked with the criminalization of drugs.

Decriminalization as a Drug Policy

One proposed alternative to the present law-enforcement approach, though by no means universally endorsed, is decriminalization. This policy has recently been applied to the case of marijuana.

Among those proposing decriminalization for marijuana, probably one of the most influential sources was the National Commission on Marijuana and Drug Abuse. In 1972, this commission concluded that a policy of prohibition and the accompanying intrusion by the law into private behavior by citizens was inappropriate for offenses involving the personal possession of marijuana. In its place, the commission recommended a policy of discouragement based on decriminalization.

Following the release of this report, several states decided to implement a decriminalization policy. Beginning with Oregon in 1972 and ending most recently with Nebraska in 1979, decriminalization regarding possession and use of small quantities of marijuana is now the law (in one form or another) in eleven states.

With the passage of these laws, one can ask what effect decriminalization has had on the criminal justice system's handling of marijuana. Data available from states that have decriminalized suggest conclusions for two areas; law-enforcement costs and demands on criminal justice resources. Discussing the economic impact, Maloff (1981) reports that a California state evaluation found a substantial decrease in total arrests and citations for marijuana as well as little change in trafficking arrests. A significant increase occurred, however, in arrests regarding narcotics and other drug offenses. In Maloof's words, "Summing the total law-enforcement savings, California estimates that costs in the first half of 1976 were $12.6 million less than in a comparable period in 1975" (p. 317), not including increased fees from fines and bail forfeitures totaling $361,000 (a 79 percent increase).

A summary report on decriminalization for Maine noted a similar reduction in police costs, superior court trials, and imprisonment for marijuana possession along with an increase in guilty pleas and income from fines, thus turning a $332,600 government expense into a $16,900 profit for the state. Just as important, the report concludes that the change to decriminization, " . . . substantially improved the quality and uniformity of justice administered to marijuana possession defendants in Maine" (p.318).

This section has sought to indicate how a criminalization approach to drug behavior is designed to operate utilizing law enforcement and deterrence. However, because of difficulties related to the victimless nature of illegal drug use, this prohibitionist approach has been a major failure in its mission. After examining some of the reasons for this result, the policy option of decriminalization is discussed as an alternative.

While such a policy seems quite appealing, however, there are problems and trade-offs with such a proposal. These issues will be discussed in the following sections focusing on decriminalization's likely impact on society and the drug user.

SOCIETY

The preceding section has shown how society can single out and define as illegal certain victimless crimes such as the use of illicit drugs. However, by choosing to legislate such moral norms (Duster 1970) and assign enforcement agents and the criminal justice system to act upon these laws, society almost inevitably creates a subgroup of deviants or criminals at the same time.

Focusing on the decriminalization of drugs and its potential impact on society, two primary themes need to be explored. First, one must examine the issue of deviance and whether decriminalization will alter the effect of this label for drug users. Will decriminalization affect the user subculture? Will the drug seem safer or more alluring? Second, one must address the issue involving the business of drugs, both legal and illegal. Does decriminalization affect the legal side of the drug industry in any meaningful way? Does it alleviate the fear of crime committed to support illegal drug habits?

Deviance and Decriminalization

Deviance is the classic sociological model for analyzing the use of drugs. Merton's (1968) retreatist mode of adaptation to disparity between goals and means provides one explanation for the drug user and his/her life-style. In his analysis, Merton argues that the drug user is a ''double failure'' who has given up the attempt to obtain a piece of the American dream by withdrawing from both legitimate and illegitimate occupational means, retreating instead to escape through drugs. More recently, Goode (1972; 1984) has challenged this position maintaining that the addict life-style is typically characterized by constant and demanding street hustling in order to financially support one's habit.

Labeling theorists, such as Lemert and Becker, have provided a slightly different perspective on deviance. Lemert's (1966) major contribution is his concept of secondary deviance, which involves dramatic changes in one's habits and life-styles in response to negative societal reactions such as arrest or incarceration. For example, Ray's (1961) research on heroin addiction and its related cycles of abstinence and relapse discusses the secondary status characteristics of the addict including the negative self-image as a bum, criminal, or someone who is mentally ill—all of which are highly stigmatizing. If heroin was decriminalized, perhaps the most adverse and damaging aspects of this labeling and resulting self-image could be contained or modified.

One example of recent stigma modification for drug users has occurred in terms of marijuana. In his research on the marijuana subculture of jazz musicians, Becker (1966) argues that the American values of the Protestant ethic and the emphasis on pragmatism and utilitarianism prevented acceptance of marijuana users during the 1950s and early 1960s. However, with the growing use of marijuana by middle-class college students in the 1960s and 1970s, society's view of marijuana has changed: possession penalties have been reduced nationwide; stigma has been tempered and usage more accepted; subcultural aspects have been modified away from a counterculture; and while still subject to arrest, users appear to be better integrated into mainstream society.

Trice and Roman (1970) suggest a different approach to reducing stigma through the process of delabeling. For example, by encouraging strict conformity to internal organization norms and creating a socially acceptable image of the reformed drinker, Alcoholics Anonymous has helped alleviate the stigmatizing negative stereotype of the alcoholic. NORML, an organization calling for the legalization of marijuana, uses another strategy emphasizing relabeling by organizing deviants (i.e., marijuana users) to work for the formal change of societal norms. A final approach involves the process whereby mandated professionals who initially take part in labeling behavior, process this deviance through treatment and create a highly visible de-labeling ceremony pronouncing the user "cured" or rehabilitated.

Business and Drugs

The business of drugs, whether legal or illegal, is a profitable one. On the legal side, the pharmaceutical industry is one of the most profitable in the United States year in and year out (Silverman et al. 1981). However, critics point to problems with how this industry operates, including the amount of promotional money spent to persuade doctors to prescribe one company's drug over another's, or over the option of not prescribing any drugs at all. As a partial consequence of this promotion, Silverman and his coauthors argue, a large proportion of two classes of drugs are prescribed in this country: antibiotics and psychoactive drugs (such as stimulants, tranquilizers, and sedatives).

The overprescription of psychoactive drugs is a high profile controversy. Writers such as Chesler (1972) in her classic discussion of psychiatrists and more recently Hughes and Brewin (1979) both argue that American society in general, and women in particular, are being overly tranquilized through the prescribing practices of physicians. As a means to cope with stress, or simply to help one relax, tranquilizers such as Valium are prescribed to provide instant relief. However, because such legal drugs are habit-forming and physically addictive, overprescription also creates the possibilty for abuse and potential demand for illegally supplied psychoactive drugs. While the medical profession has begun to address some of these problems, users of psychoactive drugs remain the hidden addicts of America, in large part because the drugs involved are legal and because the users do not match the profile of the illegal street addict.

Graham's (1972) research on the scheduling of amphetamines in the federal Comprehensive Drug Abuse Prevention and Control Act of 1970 shows similar evidence that billions of amphetamines are overproduced in this country every year without medical justification. While these drugs are considered useful in treating narcolepsy and hyperkinesis, a more common use is for dietary purposes. Two results of this circumstance are overprescription and diversion of these drugs into illegal distribution channels. Graham notes that Senate and House debates on the 1970 bill focused primarily on the illegal street users or "speed freak" and virtually ignored other categories of abusers, such as housewives, students, businessmen, and truck drivers. Coupled with a wide-ranging examination of the entire American drug scene, decriminalization could contribute to a more well-rounded view of overall drug use and abuse in society, which in turn might lead to serious assessment of the impact of production, promotion, prescription, and overall profits of the legal drug business.

The illegal side of the drug business, of course, is also important to examine. As Salerno (1979) argues, the ''American dichotomy'' (p. 167) of guarding the separation of church and state while at the same time maintaining penal statutes for various victimless crimes (e.g., gambling, prostitution, and drug use) serves as a boon to organized crime. Tracing the history of illegal U.S. drugs from the Harrison Act in 1914 to the emergence of cocaine as a profitable drug in the 1970s, Salerno calls law-enforcement attempts a ''convoluted miasma'' (p. 182) involving organizational fragmentation, competition, and gerrymandering among a variety of enforcement agencies.

To improve this situation, Salerno suggests refocusing laws away from attempts to control and penalize the drug user. As a result, enforcement agencies could better target fewer, but more significant, cases against organized crime, and thus positively redirect resources. For users, a public health model similar to the British system might be instituted to maintain poor drug addicts' habits, while ignoring wealthy and other self-supporting users.

This type of public health policy when linked with decriminalization might also help reduce drug-related crime and its impact on society. While experts disagree on precise numbers, heroin addicts are seen as responsible for committing approximately 50 million crimes per year in this country (Ball et al. 1982), many of a serious nature. These crimes are often nonviolent in nature and are typically motivated by the need for income to support one's habit. Nevertheless, such crimes pose direct costs to the society by victimizing nonusers, and more indirectly through the public fear of crime.

This section has examined current drug policy and the alternative of decriminalization in terms of broad societal impacts. Of particular concern have been issues involving the stigmatization of users through criminal drug offenses, and the legal and illegal business of drugs. As has been suggested, present policy poses particular problems and imposes certain social costs which decriminalization might help relieve. In the next section, we turn to the effect of current policy and the option of decriminalization on the drug user.

THE USER

Previous sections have discussed the impact of decriminalization on law and the society. This final section examines how decriminalization might affect the user in the following areas: the general health and well-being of the user; the operation of available treatment facilities; and subsequent patterns of drug use.

Health and Well-Being for the User

One result which decriminalization alone would not produce is the regulation of quality for illicit drugs. For those drugs that become adulterated to increase black market profits, the user would be plagued by essentially the same health risks as under present criminalization policies. Thus, serious medical problems resulting from impurities and fillers in heroin, cocaine, marijuana, and other drugs would not be alleviated.

Decriminalization would also leave intact many societal causes of user health problems. For example, Goode (1972; 1984) points out that roughly one percent of all U.S. heroin addicts die every year as a result of the social conditions for heroin use. These deaths arise from the fact that heroin must be used illegally, not the pharmacological properties of the drug itself. What is typically sold on the streets as heroin can range from only 3–5 percent purity up to 15–20 percent, the bulk consisting of other, unknown substances. Deaths appearing to be from heroin overdose, then, may actually result from the enormous variability in the drug's potency or such impurities, a situation Brecher (1972) calls Syndrome X.

Other problems associated directly with illegality and commonly liked with heroin addicts in the United States include two diseases — hepatitis and tetanus — which are primarily the consequence of sharing unsterilized needles; as under conditions of drug purity and sanitary usage, heroin is relatively nontoxic (Goode 1972). Aside from physical dependence, which sets in motion all sorts of personal, financial and social problems, the use of heroin and other opiates does not cause permanent physiological damage.

One advantage which decriminalization offers for users is a change in psychological climate. For instance, the panic anxiety reaction characteristic of novice marijuana users is partly attributable to fear of being arrested and subsequent disclosure of such activity to parents, educators, other authorities, and peers (Becker 1967). In general, a drug user in a supportive and informed environment is likely to have a safer and more enjoyable experience than an uneasy novice in a hostile societal environment.

Evidence to support this claim can be found in several areas. For example, Becker (1967) describes the stages by which a drug like marijuana or LSD can become acculturated as individuals accumulate and share experience with new drugs. In this fashion a subcultural consensus develops about such matters as: the drug's subjective effects, the duration of these effects, appropriate dosages, predictable dangers and methods to cope with them, as well as when and where usage of the drug is appropriate.

Additionally, the social organization of drug use through subcultures and individuals' drug experiences can often produce a mode of stable usage. For instance, Jamaica provides stark contrast to the United States in terms of social attitudes toward marijuana use and as a result, the subsequent experience of users is vastly different. Americans smoke marijuana for a variety of reasons: to relax, to enhance an experience, to alter subjective feelings, or simply to entertain themselves. In contrast, in the Jamaican countryside a very large amount of potent marijuana (ganja) is communally shared before engaging in strenuous physical labor. In these two contexts, the purpose, experience and meaning of marijuana are worlds apart (Rubin and Comitas 1976).

Decriminalization and User Patterns

Beyond the physiological and psychological health of drug users, another issue raised by decriminalization is what would happen to drug usage patterns. Decriminalization would lead some to expect a drastic increase in drug use in the absence of deterrence. However, there is evidence to contradict this popular notion.

Most significantly, research from Oregon, California, and Maine provide results on the effects of marijuana decriminalization efforts since the 1970s. Using crude impact measures, similar findings were reported in all three states; consumption patterns for marijuana appear to have changed little or not at all. Thus, although it is premature to reach conclusions about the long-range effects of decriminalization, this policy change has certainly not had alarming consequences in promoting marijuana use in the short run. In sum, removal of the legal deterrence for personal use has not opened the "flood gates" to massive abuse as critics had feared.

Conversely, the 1973 "get tough" drug law in New York State set strict mandatory sentences for various drug offenses. For example, a second conviction for selling heroin meant life in prison. Nevertheless, this law failed to demonstrate any influence on the level of heroin use in the state (Meyers 1980).

Decriminalization and Treatment

A final set of issues centers on how decriminalization would affect drug treatment programs. Research to date shows that the track record for treatment is not strong. In fact, prospects for a successful treatment, one which leads to abstinence from an abused drug, are typically quite low. Consequently, assertions of success must be evaluated very skeptically. For instance, Alcholics Anonymous claims a high success rate, but does not keep records or cite any data to support such claims. When pressed, AA speaks of members who have already been in treatment for one year, excluding all those leaving the program before this time. Similarly, residential treatment communities appear to work for some people, who give sensitive personal witness to how the program has changed their lives. But in fact, the success story touches only a small group of addicts (Retting, Torres, and Garrett 1977).

One explanation for the low prospects of treatment success is that both the reasons why people use drugs, and which kinds of treatment are likely to succeed or fail for which individuals are not fully understood. The resulting variety in available approaches, then, is not so much a testament to pluralism in treatment philosophies as it is a commitment to the search for something that works. In terms of societal resources, treatment, research, and drug education are all a distant second in priority to law enforcement. In fact, since the mid-1970s, treatment facilities for drug users have been increasingly eliminated and existing services dramatically curtailed.

Reorientation of drug policy would allow consideration of alternatives such as the British system of heroin maintenance for addicts. Though the lessons from this program are not all clear-cut or without limitations, Trebach (1982) argues that such a system could be a valuable addition to American treatment approaches. While careful evaluation of the British experience would be necessary first, and modifications incorporating more monitoring or regulation might be required, such an approach should not be automatically ignored.

Ideally decriminalization would also provide a different sort of motivation for the addict seeking treatment. This would only be the case, however, if treatment were given a higher priority in the overall scheme of drug policy. If treatment were viewed as less custodial, then perhaps different treatment strategies could be pursued. Under such circumstances, an addict or drug abuser might no longer be coerced into treatment to avoid prison or to look good before a judge or probation officer. Instead, more positive motivations for treatment might be evident, potentially yielding more successful outcomes.

CONCLUSION

The present discussion has examined U.S. policy toward illicit drugs. In so doing, the primary concern has dealt with two questions: (1) what are the major consequences resulting from the current policy of drug criminalization? (and more specifically, the negative social costs involved); and (2) what changes might be expected with the adoption of a decriminalization approach to drugs?

Current drug policy in this country dates from the prohibitionism of the early 1900s. This policy began with the criminalization of the opiates (and cocaine) in 1914 and later continued with legislation on alcohol (1919) and marijuana (1937). However, this law-enforcement policy has not solved America's drug problems. Indeed, in many ways, this approach has served to aggravate and compound these difficulties.

Beyond simply playing the role of critical "devil's advocate" on drug policy, however, this article has also discussed and examined one of the oft-mentioned alternatives available, decriminalization. As we have sought to indicate, decriminalization is not a panacea. Indeed, the major point of this article is that there probably cannot be any instant, perfect solutions to America's problems with illegal drugs. Decriminalization does, however, provided a focus for rethinking drug policy, its present problems, and the goals it should strive toward.

Using the case of marijuana, where decriminalization has been tried and instituted in a fifth of the states in the United States, we have noted that this policy has not led to the "epidemic" of increased use and new users feared by its opponents. At the same time, considerable savings appear to have occurred for law enforcement regarding marijuana, without any strong evidence that public safety has been increasingly endangered. Presumably some reduction in stigma for marijuana use, and perhaps improved set, setting, and additional subcultural aspects have also taken place.

Marijuana decriminalization, however, has not been an unqualified success. Research in the area has had its share of methodological and statistical problems. In addition, there is some evidence to suggest that decriminalization has led to an increase in driving while under the influence of marijuana (Petersen 1981), and perhaps some increased conflict in police-offender interactions where possession of marijuana is involved.

More importantly for the perspective offered here, decriminalization of marijuana or other drugs does not provide a legitimate supply source, nor does it regulate the quality of the drug purchased. As a result, health problems for the drug user are quite likely to remain after decriminalization. Likewise, users will still be forced to obtain their drugs from illicit suppliers. In this situation, it is doubtful that decriminalization would have much effect on income-generating crimes committed by users to support their drug habits. Thus, to the extent that association with illegal suppliers is seen as socially unacceptable and perhaps risky in terms of exposure to other drugs and criminal activities, shifting to a policy of decriminalization would produce little real change.

For society, decriminalization may help remove some of the stigma associated with illegal drug use. To the degree that this means less formal (i.e., arrest, conviction, punishment, and establishment of a criminal record) and informal (stereotype and prejudiced attitude) negative consequences and fears for otherwise law-abiding citizens, decriminalization may have a quite beneficial impact on society. Indeed, such a policy might lead to specific settings that would make possible enjoyment of the more positive effects of given drugs (analogous to drinking alcohol at the corner bar) while emphasizing norms of moderate use and appropriate conduct when under the influence (Becker 1967; Cavan 1966; MacAndrew and Edgerton 1969; Rubin and Comitas 1976.

For addicts or those individuals interested in quitting or limiting their drug use, decriminalization might invigorate treatment efforts, both through: (1) broader social support and less stigma of drug use and the moral character of drug users, thus placing more emphasis on treatment rather than prison as a potential solution; and (2) the creation of supportive subcultural ties which informally advocate responsible drug use and a reputable life as social citizen, above and beyond one's drug use.

More generally, decriminalization would help get the government out of the business of legislating morality for private, victimless acts, and away from the philosophy of deterrence which has been so unsuccessful in this area.

As Petersen (1981) has noted, society needs to develop more rational approaches to drug policy. However, we should not and probably cannot be entirely consistent and uniform. For some drug issues and problems, decriminalization may be both useful and successful, as seems to be the case for marijuana from the information available so far. For other problems, however, such an approach may be quite unsound and inadequate. For example, in a case such as PCP ("angel dust") it would probably be unwise to decriminalize and lift any sanctions, indeed perhaps even stiffer penalties are warranted given this drug's negative effects (Graevan et al. 1981). In a similar fashion, the imposition of penalties for tobacco might be urged based on this substance's negative health effects and addictive properties. Alternatively, for heroin, decriminalization may be a step in the right direction, but simply not go far enough.

Decriminalization of small amounts of heroin for personal use would probably do little to affect the life-style of the user, usage of the drug, or the link to organized crime. Decriminalizing heroin will not reduce the costs of the drug to the addict, nor guarantee the purity of the drug, nor provide the money to obtain it. In this sense, we would expect decriminalization to dismally fail at reducing: (1) heroin-related crime, (2) the problems of the user's life-style and addiction, (3) the black market and strength of organized crime, and (4) health problems related to heroin use. Thus, heroin decriminalization would provide a negligible improvement over our current approach. In this case, a more radical approach toward controlled regulation and legalization (similar to the British approach) might be more adequate at producing changes and reducing heroin problems for this society.

Finally, decriminalization is only one option among a host of alternatives to present drug prohibition. Other available approaches might involve: over-the-counter regulation, drug maintenance and long-term treatment, a public health model, or a pure food and drug model. This article has focused on decriminalization as a vehicle for beginning to rethink current drug policy in America. As has been suggested, decriminalization has the potential to positively change some problems with drug use, but will undoubtedly also create new ones and fail to do anything about others. Decriminalization offers a relatively imperfect policy and not a magical solution. In order to formulate an improved policy toward drugs much more discussion, experimentation, and research is necessary. Thus, we must move beyond the recognition that present policy is a dismal failure and move to the consideration, critical evaluation and eventual implementation of other options. What this discussion has emphasized is that the user and society, directly and indirectly, bear the brunt of present policy failures. Decriminalization would be a large step toward recognizing and addressing this situation. We cannot and must not simply accept the status quo.

References

Akers, Ronald L., and Richard Hawkins. 1975. *Law and Control in Society*. Englewood Cliffs, N.J.: Prentice-Hall.

Ball, John C., Lawrence Rosen, John A. Flueck, and David N. Nurco. 1982. "Lifetime Criminality of Heroin Addicts in the United States." *Journal of Drug Issues*, Summer 1982: 225–38.

Becker, Howard S. 1966. *Outsiders: Studies in the Sociology of Deviance*. New York: The Free Press.

———. 1967. "History, Culture and Subjective Experience." *Journal of Health and Social Behavior* 8: 163–76.

Brecher, Edward M., and the Editors of Consumer Reports. 1972. *Licit and Illicit Drugs*. Boston: Little, Brown and Co.

Bonnie, Richard J., and Charles H. Whitebread II. 1974. *The Marihuana Conviction: A History of Prohibition of Marihuana in the United States*. Charlottesville, VA: University of Virginia Press.

Cavan, Sherri. 1966. *Liquor License: An Ethnography of Bar Behavior*. Chicago: Aldine Publishing Co.

Chesler, Phyllis. 1972. *Women in Madness*. New York: Avon Books.

Duster, Troy. 1970. *The Legislation of Morality: Law, Drugs and Moral Judgment*. New York: The Free Press.

Goode, Erich. 1972. *The Drug Phenomenon: Social Aspects of Drug Taking*. New York: Newsday, Inc.

————. 1984. *Drugs in American Society* (2nd edition). New York: Alfred A. Knopf.

Graeven, David B., Jeffrey G. Sharp, and Stephen Glatt. 1981. "Acute Effects of Phencyclidine (PCP) on Chronic and Recreational Users." *Journal of Drug and Alcohol Abuse* 8: 39–50.

Graham, James. 1972. "Amphetamine Politics on Capitol Hill." *Transaction* 9: 14–22, 53.

Gusfield, Joseph R. 1963. *Symbolic Crusade: Status Politics and the American Temperance Movement*. Champaign, Ill: University of Illinois Press.

Hellman, A. D. 1975. *Laws Against Marijuana*. Champaign, Ill.: University of Illinois Press.

Heimer, John. 1975. *Drugs and Minority Oppression*. New York: Seabury Press.

Hughes, Richard, and Robert Brewin. 1979. *The Tranquilizing of America: Pill Popping and the American Way of Life*. New York: Warner Books.

Kelleher, Maureen E., Bruce K. MacMurray, and Thomas M. Shapiro. 1983. *Drugs and Society: A Critical Reader*. Dubuque, Iowa: Kendall-Hunt Publishing.

Lemert, Edwin. 1966. *Social Pathology: A Systematic Approach to the Theory of Sociopathic Behavior*. New York: McGraw-Hill Book Co.

Maloff, Deborah. 1981. "A Review of the Effects of the Decriminalization of Marijuana." *Contemporary Drug Problems* 10: 307–22.

MacAndrew, Craig, and Robert B. Edgerton. 1969. *Drunken Comportment: A Social Explanation*. Hawthorne, N.Y.: Aldine Publishing Co.

Merton, Robert. 1968. *Social Theory and Social Structure*. New York: Macmillan Publishing Co.

Meyers, Eric. 1980. "American Heroin Policy: Some Alternatives." In *The Facts About Drug Abuse* (by The Drug Abuse Council). New York: The Free Press.

Morris, Norvil, and Gordon Hawkins. 1969. *The Honest Politician's Guide to Crime Control*. Chicago: University of Chicago Press.

Musto, David F. 1973. *The American Disease*. New Haven, Yale University Press.

Petersen, Robert C. 1981. "Decriminalization of Marijuana: A Brief Overview of Research-Relevant Policy Issues." *Contemporary Drug Problems* 10: 265–76.

Ray, Marsh. 1961. "Abstinence Cycles and Heroin Addicts." *Social Problems* 9: 132–40.

Retting, Richard, Manual J. Torres, and Gerald R. Garrett. 1977. *Manny: A Criminal-Addict's Story*. Boston: Houghton-Mifflin Co.

Rubin, Vera, and Lambros Comitas. 1976. *Ganja in Jamaica: The Effects of Marijuana Use*. Garden City, N.Y.: Anchor Press/Doubleday.

Ryan, William. 1971. *Blaming the Victim*. New York: Vintage Books.

Salerno, Ralph. 1979. "Organized Crime and Justice, Beyond 1984." In *Crime and Justice in America: Critical Issues for the Future*, edited by John T. O'Brien and Marvin Marcus. New York: Pergamon Press.

Schur, Edwin M. 1965. *Crimes Without Victims: Deviant Behavior and Public Policy*. Englewood Cliffs, N.J.: Prentice-Hall.

Silverman, Milton, Philip R. Lee, and Mia Lydecker. 1981. *Pills and the Public Purse*. Berkeley, CA: University of California Press.

Skolnick, Jerome. 1969. *Justice Without Trial*. New York: John Wiley and Sons, Inc.

Szasz, Thomas S. 1972. "The Ethics of Addition." *Harper's Magazine*, April: 74–79.

Trebach, Arnold S. 1982. *The Heroin Solution*. New Haven: Yale University Press.

Trice, Harrison, and Paul Roman. 1970. "Delabeling, Relabeling and Alcoholics Anonymous." *Social Problems* 17: 536–48.

Wilson, James Q. 1975. *Thinking About Crime*. New York: Basic Books.

Zinberg, Norman E., and Wayne M. Harding. 1979. "Control and Intoxicant Use: A Theoretical and Practical Overview." *Journal of Drug Issues,* Spring: 121–43.

CHAPTER 9

SHOULD EUTHANASIA BE LEGALIZED?

In the present debate our goal is to assess the current state of the controversy over the proposed legalization of euthanasia and to explore briefly the relevance of the hospice alternative to euthanasia. The term *euthanasia* is used to refer to the act of painlessly putting to death persons suffering from a terminal disease or disability; such an action is also referred to as *mercy killing.*

The euthanasia issue, sometimes referred to as the *right to die* or *death with dignity* issue, has been receiving increasing attention in recent years. One reason is that significant advances have been made in medical life-support technology. As a result it is now possible to keep some people alive for weeks, months, or even years who would have died if this were twenty-five years ago. For many people these medical breakthroughs have added years of healthy and meaningful life. But for some the added time has been of questionable value. It is one thing to add a few more good years; it is quite another to add several years of very poor health, confinement to bed, or pain related to chronic illness. A case can be made that for some people these technological advances have contributed to a prolongation of dying rather than of life. Those who are "saved" sometimes end up in an irreversible coma, confused and disoriented, or severely paralyzed with wires and tubes coming out of every body orifice. Such evidence has made it clear that breakthroughs in medical technology originally thought to have only humanitarian consequences have a very real potential for dehumanization of those who are dying. These medical advances and their unanticipated negative consequences have given new impetus to euthanasia, an issue that has had its advocates and critics for many years.

By the late nineteenth century it was clear that the administration of heavy doses of narcotics in connection with an effort to control the pain associated with the terminal phases of certain diseases such as cancer tended to hasten the onset of death. Large doses risked death due to respiratory failure. Since the motive for giving the narcotic was to control pain, not to hasten the onset of death, the practice has never been very controversial. Euthanasia advocates argue that this practice is a form of euthanasia; they refer to it as *indirect euthanasia.* Many other observers refuse to agree that this practice is a form of euthanasia.[1]

One of the most important distinctions in debates about the proposed legalization of euthanasia is between active and passive euthanasia. With *active euthanasia* some positive action is taken to end the person's life, for example, the administration of an overdose of a narcotic with the explicit goal of ending the person's life. In the case of *passive euthanasia* death results from the omission of certain procedures that would be necessary to prolong life.[2] An example would be the decision not to begin dialysis treatment for kidney failure in a person with advanced cancer. The patient and physician decide not to start dialysis treatment knowing that the decision will lead to death within a month or so. The distinction between active and passive euthanasia is not always clear. There would be some disagreement with respect to the classification of the act of terminating dialysis treatment knowing that the action would lead to death. Some people would consider this a positive action (active euthanasia) and others would consider it an omission (passive euthanasia).

Some observers argue that *assisted suicide* is a form of euthanasia. Consider the patient with terminal cancer who asks his or her physician how much of what drug could be used to induce a painless death or asks a spouse to obtain a lethal dosage of such a drug to have available "just in case." Those who support euthanasia tend to minimize the distinction between the physician who administers a lethal drug at the patient's request and the physician who provides the patient with the drug to take (or not to take) at the time of his or her choosing.

Most proposals calling for the legalization of euthanasia specify that passive and/or active euthanasia should be made legal under certain conditions.[3] Most would be restricted to situations in which the person to die initiates the request for euthanasia. The term *voluntary euthanasia* is used to distinguish this situation from *nonvoluntary euthanasia,* an act in response to a request from the relatives or caregivers of those who are incapable of making such decisions. Included in the latter category are acts of euthanasia with severely deformed infants, the insane, and those in a state of irreversible coma. When the term euthanasia is used without qualification the reference is typically to *voluntary active euthanasia,* but in the debate over the legalization issue, distinctions between the various subcategories become relevant.

During the past twenty years Americans have become increasingly concerned about quality-of-life issues including ecology and the environment, the various therapies and quasi-religions of the human potential movement (Transcendental Meditation, EST, encounter groups), and the right to die with dignity. The trend is toward greater emphasis on individual responsibility for the quality of life. In the past most people felt that it was up to God to decide what their experience of dying would be like. More recently people tended to feel that this was a matter best left up to their physicians. Today we find an increasing number of people want to have their own say; they want to have some control over the decisions made during the terminal stage of life.

During the past thirty years there has been a liberalization of attitudes toward the legalization of euthanasia. In a 1947 Gallup poll a cross section of Americans were asked, "When a person has a disease that cannot be cured, do you think doctors should be allowed by law to end the patient's life by some painless means if the patient and his family request it?" At that time slightly over one-third indicated approval. The same question was repeated in 1973, and slightly over one-half of those questioned indicated approval.[4]

In Nazi Germany from 1940 to 1945 there was a so-called euthanasia program in which some 275,000 Germans were put to death.[5] It eventually evolved into the genocide program in which millions of Jews, Poles, and Russians were murdered. Although the Nazis used the term euthanasia as a euphemism, the program did not qualify as an example of euthanasia by any widely accepted definition of the term in existence then or today. It was not a program of mercy killing; rather it was one of murder aimed primarily at those in state-run mental institutions, particularly the mentally incompetent, those with severe neurological conditions, and deformed children. No attempt was made to find out whether the individual involved wanted to die. Many if not most would have been able to make the decision, and we can assume they would not have chosen death.

The first proposal calling for the legalization of euthanasia in the United States was introduced into the Ohio state legislature in 1906; it was defeated. No such bill has ever been introduced in the United States Congress or Senate. In fact no nation in the world has a law that legalizes voluntary active euthanasia.

During the late 1960s and the 1970s a number of bills were introduced into various state legislatures; some would have legalized passive euthanasia and a few would have legalized active euthanasia, but the term *euthanasia* was avoided in these bills. Because of the opposition of some groups to anything so labeled, it is politically more acceptable to refer to *natural death, death with dignity,* or the *right to die.* The one bill that did pass was California's so-called Natural Death Act, enacted in 1976.[6] This act legalized what we have described as passive nonvoluntary euthanasia. As a result it is now legal in California (as well as in several other states) to discontinue so-called heroic life-support measures when a person is suffering from an incurable terminal condition and is no longer mentally competent to request that such efforts be discontinued. Persons who have recently signed a specified form and who become mentally incompetent due to irreversible coma or other such condition will be allowed to die as opposed to having their life "artificially prolonged."

In this chapter we deal with two articles that consider the euthanasia issue. The article by O. Ruth Russell summarizes the arguments in support of the decision to legalize the practice of euthanasia under some circumstances. The article by Williamson, Evans, and Munley takes a different position. The various arguments that have been offered in opposition to the legalization of euthanasia are summarized by way of introduction to a discussion of the hospice as a possible alternative to euthanasia. Both articles are written from what would most appropriately be described as a liberal perspective.

In "The Case for the Legalization of Euthanasia." O. Ruth Russell describes the various justification that she feels can be made for euthanasia and its legalization. One argument is compassion: people should not be forced to endure useless suffering and the indignity of a prolonged and humiliating death. Another closely related argument is that the right of an individual to die with dignity should be recognized as a basic human right. It should be one of those unalienable rights along with the right to "life, liberty, and the pursuit of happiness." Russell points out that a number of very well respected theologians and physicians have argued that both active and passive euthanasia are justified under some circumstances. Related to this is her argument that what is morally right should be made legal. In this article she goes on to discuss some of the most obvious situations in which she feels euthanasia is appropriate. She gives emphasis to persons suffering from a painful terminal illness and to severely defective infants.

In what sense are the arguments in this reading consistent with a liberal ideology? The liberal is a strong protector of civil liberties. The right to a death with dignity is not one of the civil liberties mentioned in the Bill of Rights, but it is very consistent, as Russell points out, with the Bill. The liberal is generally viewed as favoring compassion toward vulnerable population subgroups such as the poor, the elderly, orphans, and in this case the dying; Russell offers compassion as one of her arguments for euthanasia as an alternative to useless suffering and the humiliating helplessness of a slow death from a terminal illness. Russell argues that there should not be a conflict between what is merciful and what is legally permissible; this again relates to the liberal commitment to compassion toward vulnerable groups.

There are other liberal arguments for euthanasia that Russell does not explicitly make. The liberal is concerned with protecting the rights of the consumer against the power of those who provide essential services such as health care. In this context euthanasia could be viewed as an alternative to a slow death in a dehumanized institutional environment. The liberal respects choice by democratic decision making. If a majority of the people in the nation favor the legalization of euthanasia, then the liberal would argue that it should be legalized.

The Russell article is very much in the liberal tradition, but it does contain some arguments that are consistent with tenets of conservative ideology. The individualist-conservative places a very high value on individual freedom and autonomy. This would include the freedom to ask for an end to life when the alternative is a slow and painful death. Russell's argument in favor of the right to die with dignity is consistent with conservative ideology in this sense. Russell does not mention any radical arguments for euthanasia, but some do exist. One argument is that opposition today is based more on economic grounds (the physician's fear of legal suit) than on ethical grounds. People are being kept alive to protect the physician's economic interest, which does not always reflect the best interest of the patient. The radical would argue that such behavior is to be expected given the capitalistic organization of our economic system.

In their article "Why the Legalization of Euthanasia Is Feared," Williamson, Evans, and Munley point out that a number of arguments can be made in opposition to the proposal to legalize euthanasia. They begin by briefly defining several different categories of euthanasia including indirect, active, passive, voluntary, and nonvoluntary euthanasia and assisted suicide. Typically the term is used in referring to voluntary active euthanasia, but when we take a close look at the arguments on both sides of the euthanasia debate, it is clear that much attention is given to other forms of euthanasia. The authors argue that the legalization of euthanasia might increase the extent of corruption among physicians. Of particular concern in this context are possible payoffs from relatives with a financial stake in the patient's death. They also point to the heavy financial burden of keeping some of these people alive. It is possible that a double standard would evolve with respect to how great an effort were made to prolong a person's life. For the rich a number of very expensive procedures might be considered, but for the poor, euthanasia might be seen as a more expedient alternative. The so-called euthanasia program in Nazi Germany is a reminder of what can happen when the decision is made to put aside the historical commitment of the medical profession to the struggle against disease and death.

In recent years there have been major advances in organ transplant technology; unfortunately there has also been a chronic shortage of donor organs. The legalization of euthanasia would increase the supply of organs (a positive outcome), but it might also influence the extent of the effort some physicians made to keep certain patients alive, particularly those in an unfavored category of the population such as the poor, the old, and drug addicts (a negative outcome). Today the patient knows the physician is on his or her side, but if the physician were to assume the responsibility for administering lethal doses of drugs, the change might undercut patient confidence and affect the quality of the doctor/patient relationship more generally.

Williamson, Evans, and Munley point to the liberalization in attitudes toward euthanasia that has taken place in recent years; today a majority of the population supports euthanasia under some circumstances. But they also point to the recent evolution of the concept of the hospice and what some refer to as the hospice movement. Euthanasia advocates seek to assist those who would prefer death to futile suffering, whereas hospice advocates point to the alternative of keeping the situation of the dying patient from becoming meaningless, degrading, and filled with unnecessary suffering. The hospice is organized around the goal of making the process of dying as free from physical pain, anxiety, and depression as is possible.[7] It is an effort to humanize the process of dying and avoid many of the negative aspects typically associated with dying in a hospital or nursing home.

The overall thrust of Williamson, Evans, and Munley's article would most appropriately be described as liberal, but many of their arguments are also consistent with a radical perspective. A number of dangers associated with the legalization of euthanasia are mentioned which are due to economic expediency. The authors give relatively little emphasis to the theological arguments one would expect from a more conservative perspective. A theme that runs through much of what they say is that the legalization of euthanasia may result in a decrease rather than an increase in the compassion shown terminal patients. Many of the arguments reflect their concern that the interests of vulnerable patients would be subverted by those around them, reducing rather than increasing the quality of the health care provided. Their fear is that patients would end up being manipulated by greedy relatives and impersonal health care institutions. This line of reasoning is consistent with the liberal's commitment to the protection of vulnerable population subgroups.

The hospice alternative described in this reading is consistent with left-liberal ideology. It calls for a fundamental reorganization of the way in which health care is provided for dying persons, but it does not call for a fundamental reorganization of our capitalist economic system. Implicit is the assumption that substantial improvement is possible within the context of the existing economic structure. But many of the characteristics of nursing homes and hospitals that make them oppressive and dehumanizing can be linked to economic factors such as the need to provide efficient care at a reasonable price. From a radical perspective this concern with cost efficiency is a reflection of the dehumanizing consequences of the priorities of a capitalist economy. The new left radical would point to the bureaucratic nature of hospitals and nursing homes. From this perspective health care in the context of any large bureaucratic institution is likely to be dehumanizing.

A case can be made that the hospice alternative to euthanasia represents a radical break with liberalism. The hospice advocate is critical of the dehumanizing potential of modern life-support technology and the bureaucratic structure of large health care facilities. In this respect the advocate of the hospice alternative adopts much of Marcuse's new left ideology. A central component of hospice philosophy is the importance of providing care in the context of an institution that provides a strong sense of community for patients and staff. This emphasis on the importance of creating a sense of community is another component of radical ideology. To this extent, it can be argued that the case against euthanasia and in favor of the hospice alternative is consistent with a radical perspective. The hospice concept does not call for some minor changes in the existing health care system. Rather it calls into question some of the basic assumptions being made, and it calls for a very fundamental reorganization of the context in which health care is provided.

References

1. John B. Williamson, Linda Evans, and Anne Munley, *Aging and Society* (New York: Holt, Rinehart and Winston, 1980), p. 412.
2. Elizabeth S. Johnson and John B. Williamson, *Growing Old: The Social Problems of Aging* (New York: Holt, Rinehart and Winston, 1980), p. 160.
3. For a description of all the euthanasia bills up through the mid-1970s, see the appendix in O. Ruth Russell, *Freedom to Die*, rev. ed. (New York: Human Sciences, 1977).
4. Williamson, Evans, and Munley, *Aging and Society*, p. 421.
5. Leo Alexander, "Medical Science Under Dictatorship," *New England Journal of Medicine*, vol. 241 (1949), pp. 39–47. Also see Alexander Mitscherlich and Fred Mielke, *Doctors of Infamy: The Story of Nazi Medical Crimes*, translated by Heinz Norden (New York: Schuman, 1949).
6. For the content of California's Natural Death Act, see Sandra Galdieri Wilcox and Marilyn Sutton, *Understanding Death and Dying* (Port Washington, N.Y.: Alfred, 1977), pp. 451–53.
7. See Sandol Stoddard, *The Hospice Movement: A Better Way of Caring for the Dying* (New York: Vintage, 1978). Also see Cicely M. Saunders, *Care of the Dying*, 2nd edition (London: Macmillan Journals, 1976) and Anne Munley, *The Hospice Alternative: A New Context for Death and Dying* (New York: Basic Books, 1983).

21. THE CASE FOR
THE LEGALIZATION OF EUTHANASIA

O. Ruth Russell

GROUNDS FOR JUSTIFYING EUTHANASIA AND ITS LEGALIZATION

1. *Compassion and plain common sense for today's world must be the basis of any consideration of euthanasia.* A person should not be required to endure useless suffering or the indignity of prolonged and humiliating helplessness and deterioration of mind or body or both, when there is no reasonable possibility of meaningful recovery. If euthanasia were legally permissible, the fear many people now have of prolonged dying and dependency would be greatly reduced. It is only logical that society allow useless suffering to be ended.

2. *The right to die with dignity should be recognized as a basic human right.* Just as the right to live is a fundamental human right, to be protected from all incursions, so the right to die should also be recognized and protected.

The Declaration of Independence states that "life, liberty and the pursuit of happiness" are unalienable rights. It does not, however, state that there is any compulsion to live when the pursuit of happiness is impossible because of irremediable incapacitation of body or mind. Nor does any other legal document state that the right to live implies compulsion to live.

The preamble to the U.N. Declaration of Human Rights declares that we aspire to "A world in which human beings shall enjoy . . . freedom from fear," but today fear of prolonged suffering, helplessness and dependency are being recognized, more and more, as the greatest fear of the elderly and others. The preamble states also, "The recognition of the inherent dignity . . . of all members of the human family is the foundation of freedom." Article 5 of the Declaration states, "No one shall be subjected to torture," but countless incapacitated, aged, and dying persons have to endure torture today while waiting for death, even though, of course, no intent to torture is involved.

As long ago as 1891, the U.S. Supreme Court stated, "No right is held more sacred, or is more carefully guarded, by the common law, then the right of every individual to the possession and control of his own person, free from all restraint or interference of others, unless by clear and unquestionable authority of law" (*Union Pacific* v. *Botsford*).

Cardozo in the 1914 *Schloendorff* case held, "Every human being of adult years and sound mind has a right to determine what shall be done with his own body." Brandeis spoke of the *Olmstead* case in 1928 of "the right to be left alone," and a Kansas court in the 1960 *Nathanson* case held, "Each man is considered to be master of his own body and he may, if he be of sound mind, expressly prohibit the performance of life-saving surgery, or other medical treatment.'' . . .

Thus it would seem that the right of a person to choose permanent relief from suffering or a meaningless existence is a basic right; also it would seem that parents or other guardians should not only have the right but be encouraged to accept the responsibility of requesting that persons entrusted to their care be spared useless suffering or a tragic existence.

Those who oppose euthanasia on moral or religious grounds have, of course, the right to do so. But they should not be permitted to block legislation that would permit others with different beliefs to exercise their right to choose death for themselves or for persons for whom they are legally responsible. The epithets of murderer or executioner, often hurled freely by opponents of euthanasia, are patently inapplicable to the act of mercifully ending a painful and meaningless life.

It should be noted, however, that ''the right to die with dignity'' can be interpreted in various ways. To some it means only the right to be left alone to die without unnatural prolongation of life by modern techniques and skills. To others it means the right to choose an end to life and to have the services of a qualified doctor in bringing it about painlessly. There can be little doubt that as long as we permit the former of these interpretations, while forbidding the latter, we will find ourselves faced with increasingly inconsistent and hypocritical moral situations.

3. *Numerous highly regarded theologians, ethicists, physicians and others have expressed the conviction that euthanasia, both active and passive, is morally justified in certain circumstances.* Although this is not in itself justification for administering euthanasia, it is impressive and significant that so many responsible people now believe that it is morally indefensible to deny release from hopeless suffering or the indignity of helplessness. Indeed, they believe that society is not justified in denying release from hopeless suffering or indignity. Though some persons still believe in the redemptive value of suffering and condemn euthanasia for anyone, there is now widespread agreement that the relief of useless, hopeless suffering is morally justified and that at least passive euthanasia should be permitted in certain circumstances. And . . . numerous religious leaders have indicated that it is their view that active euthanasia is also permissible in many cases, and that to deny it is morally indefensible.

While the Catholic Church and many fundamentalist and other conservative groups strongly condemn any intentional hastening of death, and such action is still a criminal act according to current law, Pope Pius XII stated that it is morally right to take action to alleviate pain and suffering even if by so doing it would hasten the death of the dying patient; few would disagree with this view, though opinions still differ regarding the ethics of intentionally ending a life. But it is evident that there is a rapidly growing number of persons of all religious faiths who approve of the right to positive as well as negative euthanasia in certain circumstances and believe that the freedom to choose death should not be denied to irremediably ill persons.

4. *What is morally right should be made legally permissible.* The Judeo-Christian

ethic demands of man that he act mercifully. Yet mercy and legality — as it now stands—can pull a man in two opposite directions at once. Some kindly physicians obey the injunction, "Do unto others as you would that they should do unto you," and without legal authority prescribe or administer a lethal drug or take other action that has the effect of ending the life of a dying or hopelessly incapacitated patient. Surely it should not be necessary for a doctor to have to choose between such merciful action and violation of the law. Society has the duty to make legally permissible action that is merciful and widely recognized as morally right. It is a dangerous course to encourage secret action in violation of the law.

A sound euthanasia law would be permissive — not mandatory — and no doctor, nurse, or other person would be required to take any action contrary to his wishes, judgment, conscience, or religious principles and no patient would ever be required to submit to either positive or negative euthanasia against his will.

WHO SHOULD BE ELIGIBLE FOR EUTHANASIA? AND WHO SHOULD DECIDE?

To answer these questions it might be helpful to consider the following:

If it were legally permissible for a physician to follow the course requested, which course do you think you would want for your self if suffering from a condition from which there was no reasonable hope of meaningful recovery, remission, or happiness? Would you request (a) that the physician use every possible means to prolong your life as long as possible regardless of uncontrollable suffering, economic consequences, and grief or hardship for your family, (b) that treatment be terminated and suffering be kept to the minimum until "natural" death occurs, even if that would result in increased distress or being drugged into unconsciousness, or (c) that death be induced painlessly in accordance with your wishes and legal safeguards?

And if you were in an irreversible state of unconsciousness, senility, or otherwise not testamentary capacity, which of the above courses do you think should be followed, provided your next of kin or legal guardian requested it?

Also, if you for any reason you think you would never ask for euthanasia — either passive or active — for yourself or for anyone for whom you might be legally responsible, do you think you are justified in opposing laws that would make it permissible for others?

A Special Plea on Behalf of Severely Defective Infants

. . . In ancient times and in many cultures, seriously defective children were not allowed to live, and until recently, a high proportion of these infants died soon after birth. But the successes of modern medicine now provide defective infants with a greatly increased life span, thus adding to the extent of the problem for the children themselves, their parents, and society. And as long as society and parents adhere to the teaching that life must be prolonged as long as possible, the problem is bound to continue to grow. . . .

I myself became convinced that it was cruel to keep severely defective infants alive as the result of experiences in state hospitals for the mentally defective. As a college professor I arranged annually for senior students in abnormal psychology to visit the state hospital. The sight of one little boy in particular made a lasting impression that can never be erased. On our first visit the boy, a hydrocephalic, was about four years old. He was lying on his back in his crib with his monstrous head on the pillow, and his eyes, like those of a trapped animal, peered out from their sunken sockets. His tiny arms thrashed about wildly, hitting his huge head, which was badly bruised from such beating. The next year we visited him he had been provided with padded gloves to ease the blows he kept giving his head, but his head, nevertheless, had many sores both from the knocks he had given it and from the sheer weight of its rubbing on the pillow. The following year that pathetic little boy was still there. This time his arms were tied to the sides of the crib so he could no longer beat his head.

Many of the students and their teachers came away convinced that our society has a strange concept of what is right or Christian when we permit such cruelty to an innocent little child. Who can justify it? Though the fluid was drained off occasionally to reduce the inner pressure on the child's head, there was absolutely no possibility of his ever being anything but a helpless, hopeless bed patient. Is it not perfectly clear that such a defective child should be painlessly put out of his misery either at birth, or as soon thereafter as diagnosis makes it possible for physicians to predict with reasonable certainty that life can be nothing but tragic? Can anyone honestly argue that it is more moral or humane to have such a severely deformed and mentally defective child institutionalized for the rest of his life, or cared for at home at the risk of the health and happiness of his family, rather than have his life ended?

Although the various euthanasia societies have not included such cases in their bills — these have applied only to those capable of requesting euthanasia for themselves — it is significant that many of the doctors who have been the pioneers of the movement to legalize euthanasia have made a special plea on behalf of defective infants. One critic of any euthanasia. Yale Kamisar, has chided the euthanasia societies for excluding tragically defective infants from their proposed bills. He said that if compassion is the chief justification for euthanasia, surely these helpless infants should be in the forefront of consideration. . . .

WHAT WOULD YOUR CHOICE BE?

It would be helpful if every adult would ask himself or herself which he things he or she would choose — if circumstances arose when there was no reasonable chance of a remission or recovery, as was the case in each of the following instances:

An eighty-five-year-old patient described by Dr. Walter Sackett in testimony before the 1971 White House Conference on Aging who had a terminal blood condition received three blood transfusions daily, to a total of sixty-five, and the emergency resuscitation team was called six times before the man was allowed to die.

An eighty-nine-year-old woman whose physician described her as "a poor old soul who is totally deaf, totally blind, cannot speak and is totally paralyzed." She was being kept alive by intravenous feeding which the physician told the hospital superintendent she would like to order stopped. Permission was refused.

A veteran of World War II with no sight or hearing, no arms or legs, just a torso lying helplessly on a bed.

Many readers will doubtless recall some friend or member of their family who had a long period of senseless suffering before death finally came. Cases range from profoundly defective infants to chronic senility or helplessness and dependency at the other end of life. Prognosis may be certain and death near, or there may be some slight possibility of a temporary remission, and death still some distance away. What cannot be called into question is the extent of human suffering in all these cases.

Undoubtedly if a good euthanasia law were enacted, many difficult decisions would have to be made. Such difficult decisions are far preferable, however to the moral side-stepping of current law. Each individual case would be decided upon only after adequate consideration of all factors, and the concurrence of at least two physicians would be required to ensure well-reasoned and humane action.

LIBERAL: PRO-HOSPICE ALTERNATIVE

22. WHY THE LEGALIZATION OF EUTHANASIA IS FEARED

John B. Williamson, Linda Evans, and Anne Munley

Before turning to a consideration of why the legalization of euthanasia is feared, it is relevant to consider what is typically included in such legislative proposals.[1] There is no serious support for the legalization of all forms of euthanasia. What is being proposed is the legalization of certain very specific categories of euthanasia. Most of the proposed bills would make it legal to grant the request for an end to life made by the patient suffering from the painful terminal phase of a disease such as cancer. This request would be granted only after a number of preconditions designed to safeguard the patient had been met. One is that the patient be examined and a prognosis made by at least two physicians, one of whom is selected in such a way as to assure no financial interest in the patient's estate. Another is that the request for euthanasia originate with the patient. Application would be made to and approved by a court of law. In some bills a representative of the court would interview the patient and close relatives, but not all bills have such a provision.

Many categories of persons who might want euthanasia or who might be considered for euthanasia by others would be excluded from coverage. Most bills would exclude those in no imminent danger of death even if they are suffering from a painful chronic condition. They would not cover severely deformed infants whom physicians or parents might want to put to death or let die. They would not include any who were mentally incompetent, such as persons in an irreversible state of coma, the insane, and the severely retarded. This would be true even if these individuals were suffering considerable pain due to a condition such as terminal cancer. These bills would not legalize any form of involuntary euthanasia, that is, putting to death those who do not want to die.

It is also of interest to note that some forms of euthanasia are legal under present laws. What some refer to as indirect euthanasia is not illegal; a physician can prescribe a strong dosage of narcotics to a patient if it is necessary to control pain, even though it is known that this dose is likely to hasten death. It is legal because the motive is the reduction of pain, not putting the patient to death. Some forms of passive euthanasia are legal. For example, a patient can refuse an operation which is necessary to prolong life, and parents can sometimes refuse permission for the corrective surgery which would be necessary if a deformed newborn is to survive. In addition suicide is legal in every state, and assisted suicide is legal in thirty-two states.

The American Medical Association and other organizations speaking on behalf of the medical profession have consistently opposed legislation to legalize euthanasia. One of their fears is that it would lead to the corruption of some physicians; for example, there might be payoffs from relatives with a financial interest in the patient's death.

Such a law might contribute to the growth and diffusion of norms condoning less effort to keep alive terminal patients who are placing heavy financial burdens on their families. With mounting pressure to hold down hospital costs, it is possible that a set of norms would evolve supporting a double standard with respect to when euthanasia is considered appropriate, one for those who can afford long-term hospitalization (the rich) and another for those who cannot (the poor). More generally, such legislation could lead to a subtle shift in norms and values among physicians in the direction of less commitment to the struggle against disease and death, and less commitment to the value of human life. Such a shift in attitude among physicians in Nazi Germany is a stark reminder of what can happen when these commitments are undermined. Thousands of Germans were killed in connection with a so-called "euthanasia" program in which many German physicians actively participated.

In recent years advances have been made in the technology of organ transplants. One consequence of these advances has been an increase in the demand for donor organs. Some physicians fear that the demand for donor organs could begin to influence the effort that goes into keeping a patient alive, particularly if that patient is a derelict, very old, severely retarded, or a member of some other unfavored category of the population. The more recent euthanasia proposals include safeguards designed to assure that at least one of the doctors approving the euthanasia request has no interest in the patient's organs for transplant purposes. However, such safeguards do not protect against a general shift in attitude among physicians with respect to when a patient's condition is sufficiently hopeless to justify euthanasia followed by organ transplant.

Another potential danger is that seriously ill patients will come to fear their doctors. Traditionally the patient has viewed the physician as being dedicated to the struggle against disease and death. But if [physicians] become involved in putting the incurably ill to death or in making the judgment that the time has come to give up the struggle to prolong life, patients' confidence and trust in their physicians could be undermined. Most euthanasia proposals would require that the request for euthanasia originate with the patient, and this should serve to offset any fear that such a fate will be imposed by a physician against the patient's will.

But even if the request for euthanasia must be initiated by the patient, this does not assure that all of those who make such requests really do prefer the alternative of death. At least some will be responding to subtle or not so subtle pressures from relatives and those who are taking care of them. The physician might not explicitly say that the time has come to request euthanasia, but if this is how he or she feels, some patients will be able to pick it up. As the practice of euthanasia become common, norms might evolve which lead those who are responsible for taking care of the dying to expect that at a certain point the patient will request euthanasia. Some patients would become aware of these expectations and request euthanasia out of a feeling of obligation rather than from a genuine desire for release.[2] Others would resist any pressure to request euthanasia, but would come to feel guilty at not meeting expectations of those who are caring for them and at being a burden on their families.

Many who intend to commit suicide and request a lethal dose of a drug that will do the job, find they cannot bring themselves to actually take it. There are a variety of possible interpretations of this phenomenon. One is that when all things are considered, this person is not yet ready to die. The pain may be great, but the fear of the unknown or the will to live is even greater. Consistent with this interpretation one can argue that this reluctance to act points to the importance of making the patient take the final step as opposed to having it carried out by the physician; it becomes an argument for assisted suicide in those situations for which some would consider active euthanasia appropriate.

Many physicians have had patients who pleaded to be released from life, a request which went unheeded. In some instances the physician was able to bring about substantial improvement in the patient's condition and in a few, a complete cure. Often these patients have ended up thanking the physician for not granting their requests. A similar argument can be made with respect to those who have a disabling injury. At first some feel they would rather be dead than live the life of an invalid which lies before them. But many are able to make the adjustment and to derive a great deal of satisfaction from life.

There is always a chance that a breakthrough will be made during the coming weeks or months that could make possible a substantial improvement in the patient's condition, if not a complete cure. An example that is often mentioned when making this argument is the discovery of penicillin.[3] The advance could come in the form of a new drug which proves effective against a form of cancer previously considered incurable. It could come in other ways too, such as the invention of a new life-support machine such as the pacemaker.

Most euthanasia proposals would restrict mercy killing to those situations in which the patient is known to be dying. This assumes that it is possible to accurately determine whether or not the patient's condition is fatal. But this is sometimes difficult to do. Patients often live weeks, months, or even years longer than their physicians had anticipated; and a few recover entirely from a condition which had been considered fatal. The physician is often faced with making a probabilistic prognosis on the basis of previous experience with patients showing similar symptoms. In view of the probabilistic nature of this judgment, it is appropriate to ask at what point the probability of recovery is sufficiently remote to justify euthanasia.[4] Should it be restricted to those with one chance in 1000 of recovery? How about one chance in 100 or five chances in 100? Where do we draw the line? Wherever the line is drawn, it is going to be arbitrary and subject to criticism.

If euthanasia were legalized, there might be an increase in euthanasia with deformed babies. As a result some who otherwise might have had near normal lives [would] never have the opportunity. While infant euthanasia would not be legalized by any bills proposed to date, it is possible that the legalization of some aspects of euthanasia would give other forms of euthanasia a respectability which they do not today enjoy. The result might be an increase in the proportion of physicians who were willing to carry out euthanasia on deformed infants.

While euthanasia is practiced today in spite of being illegal, it tends to be restricted to extreme situations in which the case for euthanasia is quite compelling. As long as the practice remains illegal, physicians will be forced to be very cautious. When conservative criteria are used in deciding whether or not to grant a patient's request for euthanasia, it is rare that the physician is indicted for the action, and all but unheard of to be found guilty. But if euthanasia were legalized, it is quite possible that the practice would spread to a number of much more controversial situations. In at least some of them it would turn out to be wrong decision. While the present system which keeps euthanasia illegal calls for a certain amount of duplicity on the part of the physicians who practice it, the system does have what many would consider a positive function, encouraging conservative criteria as to when the practice is appropriate.

It is possible that some physicians would attempt to short-circuit a number of the safeguard procedures when sure that a patient falls into the category of persons for whom euthanasia is legal. To avoid all the paperwork, some might decide to resort to euthanasia without going through the elaborate application procedure called for in the law. While this would undoubtedly save the physician a great deal of time and might well save the patient the patient much suffering, it would also undercut the safeguards which have been built into the legislation.

Euthanasia legislation would establish a potentially dangerous precedent, the legalization of killing. While only the least controversial situations would be covered in the bills presently being considered, once the precedent was established there would be nothing to prevent additional legislation at some future point from expanding the range of situations covered. As Leo Alexander points out, it is a short step from the position that there are some lives that are not worth living to the position that we should get rid of all "useless eaters."[5] The Nazi "euthanasia" program is often used to illustrate this argument. While some patients might well benefit from the proposed legislation, against the potential gain we must weigh the risk inherent in establishing the precedent of legal killing.

Despite the evidence of public opinion polls showing a trend toward greater support for the legalization of euthanasia, it is quite possible that no such legislation will be enacted in the foreseeable future.[6] One of the developments which could undercut the euthanasia movement is the hospice movement. Euthanasia advocates seek to assist those who would prefer death to futile suffering. By contrast, the objective of the hospice movement is to take whatever steps are necessary to keep the situation of the dying patient from becoming meaningless, degrading, and filled with unneccessary suffering.

THE HOSPICE ALTERNATIVE

In the late 1960s a new kind of medical institution opened in London: it was St. Christopher's Hospice. Hospitals are organized around the goals of curing illness and prolonging life. In contrast, the hospice is organized around the goal of making the process of dying as free from physical pain, anxiety, and depression as is possible.[7] Consistent with this difference in objectives, there is very little in the way of modern life-support technology at St. Christopher's — there is no heart-lung machine, no intensive care unit, and no resuscitation equipment. If a patient develops pneumonia, as is not uncommon for those with terminal cancer, it would typically go untreated even though failure to treat this condition with antibiotics is likely to hasten the patient's death.

In the discussion that follows we focus on St. Christopher's because it is the most well known of the modern hospices, and it serves as the primary model for most others. However, it should be recognized that hospice principles are already in operation in the United States, most often in special units for the dying within general hospitals such as St. Luke's Hospital in New York City or in hospitals for the terminally ill.[8] The hospice movement in this country is expanding rapidly. By 1978 there were a dozen hospice groups in full operation and 170 hospice groups in various stage of development in thirty-nine states.[9] Before long hospice care will be available throughout the country. In some areas inpatient care will be available in special units within general hospitals or in independent hospice facilities. In other areas hospice groups will operate home-care programs without inpatient facilities in an effort to maintain patients at home as long as possible.

It is part of the hospice philosophy to make relatively little effort to prolong the life of the terminally ill, but a great deal of effort is made to deal with pain and depression. A majority of those admitted to St. Christopher's complain of severe pain, but hospice caregivers are successful in bringing this pain under control for just about all of their patients and in at least reducing it for most of the others.[10] While medication is not generally directed at the cure of the illness, a variety of drugs are used to deal with the patient's pain as well as anxiety and depression. The objective is to achieve these goals without ending up with patients so sedated that any possibility of communicating with loved ones is precluded. Through expert use of drugs, hospice physicians are usually able to keep the patient alert and active until death is quite imminent. They make extensive use of morphine and diamorphine, painkillers which are also very effective in dealing with depression and anxiety. In most patients hospice pain medication creates a sense of well-being without the side effect of lethargy. By making medication available on a regular basis, physicians are able to anticipate and control the patient's pain. This fosters the development of more positive self-images among patients by minimizing their feelings of dependency on the drugs and those who supply them.

A prime goal for the hospice staff is to bring pain and other symptoms accompanying lingering terminal illness under control. After that has been done, caregivers turn to other tasks such as providing patients with psychological, social, and spiritual support. It is part of the hospice philosophy that communication can be very therapeutic. If the patient wants to talk about fears of dying, reconciliation with God, friends, or family members, the well-being of a spouse who will be left, or other such issues, there are always people available to listen and offer support. At St. Christopher's the nursing staff is assisted by a number of volunteer workers, some of whom are relatives of former patients. The objective is to provide a supportive environment and the assurance that there are people who care and who will offer support to the end. No effort is made to deny the reality of impending death; it is an issue to be faced and discussed openly when a patient wants and needs to do so. After this issue has been addressed, it is possible to deal with a variety of other matters which are also sources of concern to patients and their families, such as the economic adjustments the surviving spouse will have to make after the death of the patient.

Another of the major objectives at St. Christopher's is to bring the family together. Often the prolonged illness which preceded hospice admission has adversely affected the quality of interaction between the patient and his or her family. To part on unpleasant terms can be extremely stressful both to patients and their families. It can contribute to feelings of guilt among those who survive and to a sense of abandonment for the person who is dying. One aspect of the effort at St. Christopher's to reunify the family is the provision of counseling for family members. This counseling and support continues to be available after the patient has died. An effort is made to make the family feel welcome and at ease while visiting the hospice. They can come whenever they want and stay as long as they want; they can also take responsibility for feeding, washing, and in other ways caring for the patient. This participation in the care for a dying relative or spouse is not without its therapeutic value. Those who participate tend to suffer less from feelings of guilt after the death of a family member.

Like many other hospice advocates, Cicely Saunders, the founder of St. Christopher's, has been an outspoken critic of proposals to legalize active euthanasia. Undoubtedly one reason for this opposition is that legalization of active euthanasia would reduce the pressure for such reforms as the introduction of hospices.

One of the arguments for euthanasia is that if offers a merciful alternative to slow, painful death in a dehumanizing environment. But hospice advocates are quick to point out that it is possible to control terminal pain for almost everyone and it is possible to create an environment for the patient far superior to that found in most hospitals. To legalize euthanasia is a cop-out. It is viewed as a cheap, expedient solution to the problem at the expense of the patient's best welfare. In a hospice it would be possible for many who might otherwise prefer the alternative of death to enjoy their last days or weeks. Often this time can be spent in such worthwhile activities as coming to terms with one's impending death, assisting one's spouse in preparing for the adjustments that will be necessary, and in bringing together family members who have grown distant due to the strains of the illness.

If it turns out to be possible to duplicate the success of St. Christopher's on a large scale in the United States, the hospice movement will quite likely undercut the perceived need and public support for the legalization of euthanasia. But it is too soon to judge the ability of the hospice to meet the needs of many different kinds of people facing chronic illness and death. In particular, it may prove difficult to replicate the spectacular success of St. Christopher's.[11] The rapid expansion of the hospice movement in the United States in recent years might lead one to conclude that it is indeed possible to repeat St. Christopher's success here. However, this same rapid expansion may prove to be problematic. Some authorities are concerned that rapid expansion may lead to exploitation and scandal similar to that which occurred with the explosive growth of the nursing home industry during the late 1960s and early 1970s. Robert Butler is quoted in *Newsweek* (May 1, 1978) as saying, "We don't want to go overboard and create death houses."

While the growth of the hospice alternative may represent a defeat for the euthanasia movement in one sense, it represents a victory in another. A case can be made that the kind of death made possible by the hospice is a form of euthanasia. The reference here is to the original meaning of the term. For more than two hundred years (1646 to 1869) *euthanasia* referred to an easy but painless death and efforts to assure that death would be as free of pain as possible. There was no reference to hastening the onset of death. It would seem that the modern hospice is very much what the euthanasia advocates of the seventeenth, eighteenth, and early nineteenth century had in mind. If euthanasia in this sense of a "good death" is possible, then arguments for euthanasia in the sense of the intentional putting to death of persons suffering from a painful and incurable condition lose their power.

Contemporary hospices are a promising social solution for resolving the euthanasia debate. This humanitarian model of terminal care does not "put people out of their misery," the goal of euthanasia proponents. Rather, hospices provide warm, supportive environments where people benefiting from expert methods of symptom and pain control are able to spend the final period of their lives in meaningful living instead of despondent dying.

References

1. For a brief description of the various euthanasia bills up through the mid-1970s, see O. Ruth Russell, *Freedom to Die*, revised edition (New York: Human Sciences, 1977).
2. Ibid.
3. Sissela Bok, ''Euthanasia and the Care of the Dying,'' in John A. Behnke and Sissela Bok, eds., *The Dilemmas of Euthanasia* (New York: Doubleday, 1975).
4. Ibid.
5. Leo Alexander, ''Medical Science Under Dictatorship,'' *New England Journal of Medicine*, vol. 241 (1949), pp. 39–47.
6. Elizabeth S. Johnson and John B. Williamson, *Growing Old: The Social Problems of Aging* (New York: Holt, Rinehart and Winston, 1980), p. 161.
7. See Cicely M. Sanders, *Care of the Dying*, 2nd edition (London: Macmillan Journals, 1976); see also Cicely M. Sanders, ed., *The Management of Terminal Disease* (London: Edward Arnold, 1978).
8. Joan Craven and Florence S. Wald, ''Hospice Care for Dying Patients,'' *American Journal of Nursing*, vol. 75 (1975), pp. 1816–22.
9. Sylvia Lack and Robert W. Buckingham, III, *First American Hospice: Three Years of Home Care* (New Haven: Hospice, Inc., 1978).
10. Sandol Stoddard, *The Hospice Movement: A Better Way of Caring for the Dying* (New York: Vintage, 1978).
11. Robert J. Kastenbaum, *Death, Society, and Human Experience* (St. Louis: C. V. Mosby, 1977).

PART III

SCIENCE,
TECHNOLOGY AND
WORK

CHAPTER 10

COMPUTERS: WHAT IS THEIR SOCIAL IMPACT?

In evaluations of the social impact of technology, conservatives, liberals, and radicals often disagree among themselves as well as with one another. Conservative positions on the computer range from neo-Luddite arguments that we should not use them at all to arguments that they should be employed extensively for such purposes as criminal surveillance or checking welfare payments in order to maintain our existing social and political arrangements. Noted computer scientist Joseph Weizenbaum, for example, takes a very negative view of the computer's effects upon our traditional human values.

Liberals tend to view computers as mixed blessings, emphasizing their positive contributions in such areas as medicine, libraries, and education, but worrying about such issues as personal privacy, unemployment, and computerized warfare. Most of the contemporary debates surrounding computers in our society involve differences of opinion among liberals as to the relative social costs and benefits of various computer applications. "Pro-computer" liberals are those who feel that the use of computers will result in more and better jobs and improvements in social equity. "Anti-computer" liberals are concerned that computers may cause massive unemployment and increase racial and gender inequities in society. Where the liberals agree is in their belief that social control over computer technology should be and can be exerted by society through its democratic political process.

At one extreme of the radical positions are those who believe that computer technology is bringing us into a new information age in which everyone will be free for creative activity. Popular writers like Alvin Toffler tend to dismiss the political and social concerns of both conservatives and liberals as belonging to a "dying" culture. Sometimes, like Fritjof Capra, they express an almost mystical faith in a new age. Marxist radicals, on the other hand, focus on the economic impact of computers. Analysts such as Mike Cooley and Harley Shaiken argue that computers are being used by companies to control workers, lower wages, and eliminate labor unions.

Both of the articles selected for this chapter consider the possibility that the widespread use of computers in our society will cause problems for the democratic process. In looking at the computer, both authors combine a technical with a social science perspective. Herbert A. Simon was a pioneer in the field of artificial intelligence and received the Nobel Prize in economics for his contribution to the study of decision making. Judith A. Perrolle, an M.I.T. graduate and former computer professional, is a sociologist specializing in the social impact of technology. She was also a political activist who participated in one of the earliest attempts to organize a computer programmers' labor union.

Simon takes a liberal view of the social impact of the computer on the centralization of power, pointing out the technology's positive contributions to decision making, yet identifying a possibly negative tendency toward centralization. He argues from a pluralist perspective that computers will not be used to centralize political power, because we will be able to make decisions that prevent such an outcome. He thinks that computers will greatly enhance our ability to make informed decisions and that power will remain decentralized as a result of our political choices.

Perrolle, arguing from a radical perspective, claims that the major impact of the computer will be to centralize economic power (and thus political power) by creating a new division of labor that will eliminate a large part of the middle class. She believes that we will not be able to halt this trend with our present political system because the decisions that produce it are being made in the workplace and are defined as economic rather than political choices.

In evaluating these two articles, consider the following differences in their arguments:

1. Will information as a commodity become cheaper and more widely available, as Simon claims, or will "ownership" of information become more centralized and will it tend to be produced under "factory" conditions, as Perrolle argues?
2. Will expert systems facilitate decision making, as Simon argues, or will they replace human expertise in the workplace, as Perrolle maintains?
3. Do computer users retain their autonomy, as Simon suggests, or do they become alienated from their "mental labor," as in Perrolle's analysis?
4. Do we have the political power to control the use of computer technology or are the crucial decisions being made economically and outside of our political process?

References

Capra, Fritjof. 1982. *The Turning Point*. New York: Bantam.

Cooley, Mike. 1980. *Architect or Bee?* Boston: South End Press.

Shaiken, Harley. 1984. *Work Transformed: Automation and Labor in the Computer Age*. New York: Holt, Rinehart and Winston.

Toffler, Alvin. 1980. *The Third Wave*. New York: Bantam.

Weizenbaum, Joseph. 1976. *Computer Power and Human Reason*. San Francisco: W. H. Freeman.

23. THE CONSEQUENCES OF COMPUTERS FOR CENTRALIZATION AND DECENTRALIZATION

Herbert A. Simon

Today, the terms *centralization* and *decentralization* are heavily laden with value. In general, decentralization is the good thing and centralization the bad thing. Decentralization is commonly equated with autonomy, self-determination, or even self-actualization. Centralization is equated with bureaucracy (in the pejorative sense of that term) or with authoritarianism and is often named as a prime force in the dehumanization of organizations and the alienation of their members. If the reader shares these common attitudes toward centralization and decentralization, I shall ask him to hold them in suspension until I have inquired more closely into their meanings.

THE NATURE OF CENTRALIZATION AND DECENTRALIZATION

Picture a typical organization in hierarchical form with various decision-making functions being carried out at the nodes. Centralization is any transfer of such functions from a lower node to a higher one, decentralization any transfer from a higher node to a lower one. Centralization is always a relative matter, for decision making is never fully concentrated at the very top or at the very bottom of an organization. When we ask what effect computers will have on the centralization and decentralization of the institutions and organizations of our society, we are asking in what direction they will move the balance. It is perfectly possible, of course, for both movements to go on concurrently in an organization, some functions being passed upward at the same time that others are passed downward. Thus, in the 1950s, many production and marketing decisions in large American corporations were being decentralized to product divisions at the same time that labor relations decisions were being centralized.

Functions of Centralization

There are three main motives for centralizing decision functions: to gain economies of scale, to coordinate interdependent activities, and to control lower-level activities in the interest of higher-level goals.

1. In decision making, economy of scale means mainly creating central units for handling certain classes of decisions expertly, where it would be too costly to distribute experts more widely through the organization — a classic application of Adam Smith's principle of the division of labor, although in this case the labor is mental, not physical.

2. The interdependencies that make coordination desirable are those that the economist calls *externalities*; that is, actions whose consequences fall on a part of the organization other than the one making the decision. These external consequences may be undervalued or ignored if decisions are not centralized. It may be possible, however, so to design the reward system that a decentralized decision-making unit will be charged fully with the indirect consequences of its actions, in which case interdependence ceases to be a reason for centralization. Pricing mechanisms provide an important means for reconciling decentralization with interdependence whenever appropriate prices can be assigned to all of the relevant consequences of an action. On the other hand, prices that do not reflect important externalities can be a cause for divergence between decentralized decisions and higher-level goals, and hence a motive for centralization.

3. Even without interdependencies among units, some measures of centralization may be thought necessary in order to guarantee that the actions of individual organization units will reflect the goals of the whole organization. Successful decentralization assumes that lower-level administrators can be motivated to make their decisions in terms of higher-level goals.

Decision Premises

Making a decision involves weaving together many diverse premises — goal premises, constraints, side conditions, and factual assumptions based on data and theory — and deriving from them the choice of a course of action. Centralization need not involve transporting the whole decision process from one node in an organization to a higher one but may consist in establishing and communicating from the higher node one or more decision premises, with the injunction that they be employed in making the decision. One organization unit may provide another with objectives, with rules and constraints, or with facts. A single decision, then, may be manufactured out of a diversity of component materials that were themselves fabricated elsewhere in the organization.

It is important to view decision making as more than just the final signing on the dotted line. The decision-making process in an organization encompasses (1) determining what items will be on the agenda and receive attention; (2) inventing and designing alternative plans of action; (3) evaluating alternatives and making the choice; and (4) postauditing decisions and their consequences. If we take a longer view, we also have to include in the decision process all the varieties of investigation and research that build the organization's understanding of its environment and of the laws by which it operates. It is from this understanding that the invention of plans of action proceeds, as well as the estimation of decision consequences.

Decision making begins, then, with activities directed toward understanding the environment, proceeds through attending to selected aspects of the environment and the problems it presents, to devising courses of action, choosing among them, and reevaluating them by hindsight. For example, the energy shortage and rising energy prices may cause a company management to attend to the reliability of its energy supply and the efficiency of its use of energy. Means may be sought, discovered, and adopted for insulating buildings, reducing the energy requirements of manufacturing processes, or remodeling power plants to enable them to use alternative fuels. This whole stream of activities constitutes the decision-making process.

Decision premises do not only flow downward through the organization's channels of formal authority; they also flow upward and sideward. If the higher organizational levels provide authoritative instruction and information for decision making at the lower levels, the lower levels also provide much of the information that goes into higher-level decisions. In the unhappy history of the Vietnam War, no small part was played by the "body counts" and other local assessments of the battle situation that flowed upward to the top command in Saigon and thence to Washington. Whether this information was believed, or only partly believed, it provided a substantial part of the "facts" on which the decisions of war or peace were based. The information received by the top organizational levels is not always as bad, fortunately, as it was in this instance. In any event, it is typical of organizations that a large proportion of the facts for decision making at all levels originate either near the bottom or in specialized units outside the chain of command that perform one or another kind of expert or intelligence function (e.g., economic forecasters, market analysts, research and development departments).

Where decisions involve resource allocation, as they commonly do, much of the needed information can be encapsulated in the form of prices of inputs and outputs to each particular organization unit. Clearly the dissemination of this kind of information is not limited to any particular communication channels. Hence, where prices can be used to represent interactions, the decision-making process can be carried out in close proximity to the points where the decisions will be executed. Whether an increased communication flow to a decision center means more or less centralization of decision making depends, therefore, on whether the flow is from a lower level in order to inform decisions at a higher level, from a higher level to control decisions at a lower level, or from some expert source to a collateral point of decision making. Reduced autonomy for a high-level decision maker may imply a greater degree of decentralization (i.e., increased reliance on decentralized information sources) rather than centralization.

Perception of Autonomy

The premises of any particular decision may have their origins far back in time and may be stored in a variety of repositories — human memories, organization records, or books — before they are brought to bear on that decision. How centralized or decentralized we regard the decision as being will depend on whether we trace back these premises or consider only where they were stored at the time the decision was made. Herbert Kaufman, in his classic work *The Forest Ranger*, describes a highly decentralized decision-making system in which the district ranger in the

Forest Service exhibits great autonomy within his district. But Kaufman also shows how the forest ranger's training and indoctrination have instilled in his memory the decision premises — both goals and techniques — that give the organization confidence that he will work toward its objectives and will do so expertly and predictably. Thus, in this case and many others, autonomy in decision making goes hand in hand with the internalization of goals and the knowledge that make decentralization safe from the viewpoint of the higher levels of the organization.

From the standpoint of the autonomous decision maker's attitudes and motivation, it makes a great difference whether the premises on which he is acting have been received in the form of directives from other parts of the organization or whether they have come from his own memory, where they have long resided and become part of himself. But suppose one of his decisional premises comes neither from a directive nor from his memory, but from a reference book? Does he then view himself as acting autonomously, or under direction? Suppose it resides in a computer memory that he interrogates from a terminal? Is he acting autonomously, or is he being controlled by the computer?

His perception of his autonomy in these circumstances may depend on what motivated him to consult the book or computer memory in the first place. Was he instructed to do so by an organizational directive? Did his professional training teach him to turn to this source? What confidence does he have in the validity of the information? Clearly, autonomy resides in the mind of the decider and in his identification or nonidentification with the various parts of his informational environment. Any conclusions we draw about the implications of computers for centralization, and particularly its psychological consequences, must be carefully weighed in terms of the decision maker's attitudes toward the sources of information on which he draws and the extent to which he has internalized his recourse to those sources.

Feasibility of Centralization

Finally, the degree to which decisions are centralized or decentralized in an organization depends not only on the desirability of one or the other mode of operation but also on its feasibility. Any change in technology that makes it cheaper and easier either to centralize or to decentralize decisions will tip the balance in that direction.

COMPUTERS AND COMMUNICATION

An analysis of the consequences of computers for centralization and decentralization must take account of the electronic communications systems in which computers are embedded. It may even be that the communications systems, with or without computers, are of more import than the computers themselves.

Effects of Modern Communications Technology

Modern communications technology was introduced long before the computer. First the telegraph and cable, then the wireless, and then the telephone revolutionized communication at long distance. Already in the nineteenth century, the autonomy of ambassadors was greatly curtailed by the possibility of communicating almost instantaneously with the foreign ministry in the home capital. The same is true of overseas executives of corporations. On the other hand — and there almost always is another hand — the speeding up and cheapening of international communication and transportation greatly increased the volume of international transactions.

As a consequence of these countervailing trends, it is not obvious that the foreign representative of a governmental or business organization perceives himself as having less decision-making responsibility than his ancestors had. On the one hand, it is easier to instruct him. On the other hand, there is much more to instruct him about. Moreover, these communication links are two-way links; they enable the foreign representative to inform and advise the home office as readily as they enable the home office to inform and instruct him. As the costs of long-distance communication go down and the volume of information that can be transmitted increases, the opportunities for low-level inputs to high-level decisions are greatly enhanced. As I have already shown, this is a force toward greater decentralization.

These comments apply, of course, not only to international communications but also to communications within a single country, a single city, or even a single office building. Large volumes of information can flow electronically between any two points in an organization where it pays to install a broadband communication link, and the cost of such a link decreases each year.

The fact that information can be transmitted to a decision point does not mean that it can and will be used there. The world of modern communications is an information-rich world, in which the problem of absorbing information is generally perceived as more acute than the problem of generating or transmitting it. A decade ago, the U.S. State Department ''modernized'' its communications system by installing fast line printers to handle the traffic of messages from foreign embassies. Nothing was said about how the department staff would deal with the inundation of messages. Today, improvements in the efficiency of such a system would certainly encompass information filtering and information compression, as well as transmission.

Characteristics of the Computer

What can be done faster and better with a computer than without it? A computer can analyze the behavior of systems with many interacting variables — systems much too large to analyze without its help. It can store sizable bodies of information, indexed so as to meet a great variety of information needs. It can copy, input, and output information with great speed. And it can do all of these things not only with numerical data but with information in various forms, including natural-language texts and other nonnumerical information. Moreover, next year its descendants will be able to handle more information faster and cheaper than it can.

Modeling and Analyzing Interdependent Systems

The ability of the computer to model systems with many interdependent variables was exploited in one of its early management applications: making ordering, inventory, production, and shipping decisions for large, geographically dispersed manufacturing operations. These were decisions that had previously been made by factory and warehouse inventory managers and schedulers; hence the introduction of the computer has brought about a substantial centralization of these activities in many companies, where it has produced large reductions in average inventory holdings. It is undoubtedly the most striking example of computer-produced centralization, but it is perhaps not typical of the ways in which computers have been used.

A different use of computers to analyze complex systems of interdependent variables are the models of energy systems or combined energy and environmental systems that have been constructed in the past several years to help guide the formation of public policy. Here is another case where the power of the computer is needed to assemble a previously fragmented structure of numerous interacting mechanisms. But in instances like this it would be misleading to say that the computer brings about centralization. It would be more accurate to say that it allows a systematic, analytic approach to problems that previously were addressed in an unsystematic, almost chaotic way. It is not that energy policy was previously arrived at in a decentralized way; it is that there was no energy policy. The cause of centralization, if there has been any, is not the computer but the need to address the whole problem rather than isolated fragments of it. The computer enhances our ability to do this; it does not create the necessity for it.

Similarly, building a model of the economic and market environment of a corporation does not centralize management decision making so much as it allows top management to adopt an orderly, analytic approach to decisions it had already been making — but by seat-of-the-pants methods. Taking account of relevant variables that had previously been ignored is not to be confused with centralizing the locus of the decision process.

Two related fields of research, operations research and artificial intelligence, have built tools to enlarge the capabilities of computers for modeling complex systems and have devised more and more powerful analytic techniques for this purpose during the past thirty years. Of course these tools are applicable to a particular set of phenomena only to the extent that the phenomena themselves are understood. But the combination of research on systems analysis techniques with basic scientific research is permitting us each year to approach complex decision problems in business organizations and in the public domain with greater sophistication.

Information Storage and Retrieval

One form of centralization, although not necessarily of decision making, is the gathering of large bodies of information into central computer memories as the basis for information retrieval systems of one kind or another. An airlines reservations system is an interesting application of this sort, particularly because it involves remote access to the central memory over long distances. It can be seen that in this instance hardware centralization does not bring about any centralization of decision making. On the contrary, it allows each of the decentralized decision points to take actions independently, confident that automatic updating by the central memory will take care of all interactions among decisions.

An example of a different sort is the computerized systems for medical diagnosis that are just on the verge of moving from research and development into practical application. Let us suppose that a perfected version of such a system existed in some central location where it could be accessed from remote terminals. By an interactive procedure, information about the patient would be entered, say, from the local hospital. The system could request additional information or ask that additional tests be performed on the patient before arriving at a diagnosis. By any reasonable definition, such a system would represent a centralization of the decision-making process, even if its diagnoses were only advisory. But the important question is the psychological one: would the physician perceive the system as replacing him in his diagnostic function, or would he perceive it as a tool — like penicillin or an X-ray machine — to help him carry out his task? The answer to this question probably depends on the way the system is introduced and the institutional framework within which it is used. Physicians, after all, do not usually regard reference books as threatening automation of their functions, however good the answers or advice they may obtain by consulting them. The automated diagnostic system can simply be regarded as a more powerful and more easily consulted reference book — or it can be regarded as a "robot doctor." What it "really" is lies mainly in the mind of the physician.

TRENDS IN COMPUTER TECHNOLOGY

During the first twenty or so years that computers were on the scene, they had two characteristics that suggested their widespread use would inevitably move decision making toward centralization. The first was that the efficiency of computers increased rapidly with their size: a single large computer was substantially cheaper (perhaps by a factor of three) than ten small computers of the same aggregate computing power. The economies of scale seemed to argue for one or a few centrally located computers rather than many computers distributed through an organization. The second characteristic of early computer systems was that they could only by used by someone in physical proximity to them. Therefore, if the computers were geographically centralized, so would be their use.

In the past decade advances in technology have made drastic changes in these two characteristics, and the shift is still continuing. Minicomputers have been developed that for many purposes compete very well in efficiency with the largest computers. Economies of scale no longer provide a conclusive argument for centralization. Second, and perhaps even more important, with time sharing and remote access, many users in different locations can share the same central computer. (As the examples of the plane reservation system and the medical diagnosis system show, not only can processing capacity be shared, but also access to a memory bank.)

With the new and emerging computer technology of minicomputers, time sharing, and remote access, the decisions about where to locate components of the decision-making process can be pretty completely detached from decisions about the hardware configuration. Of course, long-line access to computers is not without cost, but the costs are relatively low today and still dropping, so that it is not at all unreasonable to look toward the development of nationwide networks. In fact, several experimental networks of this kind (in addition to special-purpose networks like the reservations systems) already exist.

THE IMPACT OF COMPUTERS ON ORGANIZATIONS

Although the computer revolution is far from having run its course, it has been under way for thirty years, and by now we have accumulated a considerable body of experience that should help us predict its direction. Its most visible consequence to date has been the automation of many clerical information-processing functions in accounting departments, insurance companies, and banks. This development, however important it may be from other standpoints, has no particular implications for centralization or decentralization.

Operations Research

Another consequence of the computer revolution is the centralization of middle-management decisions relating to inventory, production scheduling, and the like. At the same time, there has been a great expansion in the use of formal operations research models for making many kinds of middle-management decisions. At the outset, the introduction of such models probably caused some centralization of decision making in special operations research departments, but this was a transitory phase of a kind that often occurs when a new technology requiring specialized knowledge is introduced into an organization. As soon as knowledge of operations research techniques was diffused widely enough to become a part of the standard equipment of industrial engineers and other managers at middle levels, the decision-making responsibilities tended to return to their previous locations in the factory and departmental organizations. Middle managers now make some different kinds of decisions than they did traditionally, and use management-science tools in making many of them, but the management-science tools have become *their* tools and are not generally viewed as removing them from the decision process.

Strategic Planning

The spread in the use of complex models as an aid to decision making has not been limited to middle-management decisions. I have already mentioned the governmental use of models to aid in making decisions about energy and environmental policy. Increasingly, corporate planning at top management levels is being informed and assisted by a variety of computerized analytic techniques (systems analysis), including modeling of the firm itself and its economic environment.

The growing use of modeling as a component of strategy formulation and strategic planning has led to some expansion of corporate planning staffs and their counterparts in government agencies to carry out this function, producing new flows of information and advice from these staffs to top management. Again, it is difficult to interpret this development as an increase in centralization. What it principally means is that a considerable amount of managerial and technical effort all up and down the line, which previously was devoted to day-to-day decision making, is now devoted to the design of the decision process itself and to developing and maintaining the basic models and data bases required for strategic analysis. The change in managerial role is analogous to the change in supervisory role with the introduction of automated control into processing plants, where the main task of foremen and supervisors shifts from making operating decisions to maintaining and monitoring the performance of the automated decision system.

I should insert parenthetically, because there has been some confusion on this point, that the development of strategic planning systems and techniques has had relatively little to do with the development of so-called ''management information systems'' (MIS). Most of the MIS work has been aimed at computerizing existing internal accounting and production records systems and incorporating in them procedures (usually elaborate) for producing reports addressed to management at various levels. Experience with management information systems has generally been disappointing, mainly because insufficient thought was given to the nature of the management decisions they were to inform and because it was not realized that the important function of computers in organizations is not to multiply information but to analyze it so that it can be filtered, compressed, and diffused selectively. The systems that have been designed under the strategic planning label are generally more relevant for these purposes than are typical MIS systems.

The Qualitative Change in Decision Making

In summary, the very large impact that computers are having on business and governmental organizations cannot be described in terms of centralization and decentralization. What is occurring is a profound qualitative change in the decision-making process, which is being formalized, made explicit, and subjected to deliberate planning.

As decision processes become more explicit, and as their components are more and more embedded in computer programs, decisions and their underlying analyses become more and more transportable. If the method of analysis is explicit and the informational and other premises that enter into it can be specified, then it does not matter very much at what organizational locations the analysis is carried out. As a matter of fact, it becomes increasingly feasible to carry out alternative analyses, using different assumptions and even different decision frameworks and analytic techniques, and employ them all as inputs to the final decision process. With all sorts of organizational and extraorganizational sources providing inputs, the locus of decision making becomes even more diffuse than it has been in the past. The organizational hierarchy remains as a critical mechanism for monitoring the process, but an increasing part of the flow of decisional premises overlaps the boundaries of the formal hierarchy.

IMPLICATIONS FOR THE POLITICAL SYSTEM

Decentralization has entered the political rhetoric of our time in the discussion of two related questions about the organization of our governmental system. The first of these is the question of the relations among the different levels of government: national, state, and local. The second is the question of the participation of citizens in the governmental process. Although often discussed together, these really are separate issues which should be looked at individually.

Federal, State, and Local Relations

There is a long-standing myth abroad in America that local government is "closer to the grass roots" than state government and state government closer than the federal government. In the purely numerical sense that each person represents a larger fraction of the electorate of his city than of his state, and of his state than of the nation, the claim is undeniably true. But it does not follow from this arithmetic that each person has a greater influence on local decisions than on state decisions, or on state decisions than on national ones. It could be argued, in fact, that because it is easier to focus public attention on major national issues than on state or local ones, there is greater popular influence on national decisions than on the others — the Vietnam War and the impeachment of Nixon being cases in point. The principal mass media in this country, and particularly TV and the news magazines, attend largely to national affairs, attracting public attention to them — to the relative neglect of what is going on at the state and local levels. While political participation is highly selective at all levels of government, it is probably most selective at the state and local levels.

As a matter of fact, the transfer of power from national to local government, a policy that has had wide popularity during the past few years and especially during the Nixon administration, is not motivated primarily by the desire for greater public participation in government decisions. Part of the support for the movement does come from advocates of participatory democracy, but a much larger part has had two other motives: (1) equalization of the disparate financial capacities of the states and cities to provide governmental services; and (2) the desire of a conservative administration faced by a liberal Congress to put power back in the hands of state and local governments believed to be more congenial than Congress to the administration's point of view.

That government in the United States has tended to become more centralized over the years cannot be doubted. It has become more centralized as activities throughout the nation, and particularly economic activities, have become more interdependent. A highly integrated economy with a highly mobile population cannot behave as though it were fifty independent states or three thousand independent counties. Any important trend toward decentralized decision making is unlikely to occur unless technical means can be found to deal with the real interdependencies that exist.

All of this is preliminary to putting two questions about computer technology: (1) Has the computer contributed, or is it contributing, to the movement toward centralization in American government? (2) Does the computer provide means for checking or reversing that movement? From what has just been said, it is reasonably clear that the answer to the first question must be no. The trend toward centralization long predated the computer, and is adequately explained by other causes. Nothing I have said about computer technology suggests a positive answer to the second question, either. However, there have been some claims, and even some experiments to verify them, alleging that the computer could become an important means for enabling citizens to participate more fully in public decisions. I should like to examine those claims next.

Participatory Democracy

A few years ago, a well-known physicist proposed putting a simple electronic voting device in all homes, so that a referendum could be held almost instantaneously on any issue. The same suggestion has been made by others, and an experiment along these lines appears to be under way at the present time in a West Coast community. Such a device would certainly go a long way toward solving one problem — that of ascertaining the state of opinion of any citizen on any issue at any time. (I hope provision would be made for a "no opinion" response!) The question is whether this is the problem that needs to be solved in order to enhance anything that could justifiably be called citizen participation.

The genius of democratic government is not arithmetic; it is informed consensus. Most questions of public policy do not begin life as dichotomies that can be decided by yes or no. Yet courses of action must be framed and decisions about them reached. Democratic institutions define a process for getting issues on the agenda, generating proposed courses of action, and modifying and amending those proposals until some measure achieves enough support to be enacted, but only in the most specious sense can we say that the chosen course represents the will of the majority. There is almost never a single action that is preferred by a majority over all alternative actions. There may, of course, be a majority preference for that action among all politically feasible actions — where "politically feasible" is defined by the decision process itself.

Different democratic systems define differently the processes for forming majorities.In many European democracies, the legislative body consists of members of numerous political parties, each having a more or less definable ideology and none commanding a majority. In such systems, the formation of coalitions among parties, a process in which each of them relinquishes some of its ideological purity, plays a central role in the formation of majorities. In the American system, with two amorphous political parties with almost unidentifiable ideologies, one of which is usually able to form a legislative majority, the formation of majorities is accomplished primarily through the process that creates and maintains the parties themselves.

This is not the place to enter into a lengthy discourse on political institutions, beyond demonstrating that they are not merely or mostly mechanisms for counting noses. To be sure, elections play a major role in our system and referenda a significant role in some states. But the question to be asked about elections and referenda is not whether the alternative finally chosen obtained a majority or plurality vote, but whether the process by which the decision was reached commanded consensus, whether the decision bore some reasonable relation to informed preferences, and whether — a point I wish to elaborate — the process was spacious enough to accommodate fact and reason along with all the other factors that enter into the formation of public opinion.

The political process, then, is not simply a mechanism for recording a majority of opinions already formed. It is a process for reaching decisions, often about complex matters of policy, in the light not only of already existing goals but also of the probable consequences of alternative courses of action. When we have legislative and public debate about measures to be taken to protect the environment, it is not that there are some people who are "for" the environment and others who are "against" it. There are deep disagreements, some about values, but most about the magnitude and seriousness of the consequences that would follow protection or failure to protect. Is the benefit to public health that will be gained by reducing the nitrogen oxide emission standard for automobiles to 0.4 grams per mile substantial enough to justify the expenditure of several billions of dollars to achieve it? On many, if not most, questions of this kind, disagreement stems much less from conflicts of interest than from uncertainties about outcomes. Even where both are involved, we probably would regard it as an improvement in the democratic process if its participants could make more accurate estimates of where their interests lay.

Informing Public Opinion

If the computer has any implications for the effectiveness of democratic institutions, it has to do with the processes for forming and informing opinion rather than the processes for recording it. The computer enters as a tool that permits policy alternatives to be examined with a sophistication and explicitness that would otherwise be impossible.

Already one can begin to point to examples where the computer, used in conjunction with the tools of systems analysis, is beginning to play such a role. The debate on federal financing for the SST is one such example, the debate on the antiballistic missile is another. In both these cases, intelligent public debate was facilitated by analyses, some of them aided by computer, of what might result from choosing one alternative over another. With such analyses available, their assumptions explicit and open to examination and question, a layman could acquire not merely an opinion on the policy issue but an informed opinion.

Over the next decade, I think it is predictable that the computer is going to play an even more important role in helping us to understand the choices with which we are faced in matters relating to energy and the environment. The complexities here are an order of magnitude greater than in the SST or ABM decisions, and there is probably greater consensus about the values to be served by the decisions. But the computer is simply a tool in the process that enables us to calculate interactions better than we could without it. It will help us only to the extent that we have valid scientific theories of the systems whose behavior we are trying to model and predict. (It will help us too, of course, in developing and testing those theories.)

The effectiveness of democratic institutions, as well as people's confidence in them, depends in part on the soundness of the decision-making processes they use. Democracy does not require a town meeting in which every member of the public can participate directly in every decision. But it is enhanced by an open and explicit decision process that enables members of the public to judge on what premises the decisions rest and whether the decisions are informed by the best available facts and theories. In fact, such a decision process is a precondition to intelligent public participation of any kind. To the extent that computers can contribute to its growth, they can strengthen democratic institutions and help combat public feelings of helplessness and alienation.

CONCLUSION

I began by arguing that there are three main motives for centralizing the decision-making process: to gain economies of scale (expertness), to coordinate interdependent activities, and to control lower-level activities in the interest of higher-level goals. I went on to examine the implications of computer technology for centralization and decentralization in both management decision making and the formation of public policy. What remains is to show how the introduction of the computer affects the motives favoring centralization, hence tipping the balance in one direction or another.

The computer is making major contributions to raising the level of expertness in decision making on complex matters. It is doing this, however, not by concentrating the decision process at higher levels of management but by either (1) facilitating the construction and use of systems models that can incorporate expert knowledge about system structure and system behavior or (2) permitting the assembly of expert knowledge in large data banks that can be consulted readily from any organizational location provided with a terminal. It is a psychological question whether these sophisticated aids to decision making will be perceived as reducing the autonomy of executives or as enlarging and extending their capabilities. If care is taken with the ways in which computerized decision aids are introduced into organizations and employed in them, there is no reason why they should either be or appear to be centralizing mechanisms.

There probably exists a continuing long-term trend toward the centralization of decision making in both business and government as the matters about which decisions have to be made become more and more interdependent. It has perhaps been slowed but certainly not halted by the use of price and market mechanisms to reconcile interdependence with decentralization. It does not appear that computers have contributed to this trend. What they have contributed, through the modeling capabilities already mentioned, are powerful new means for decision makers to deal with problems involving large numbers of interacting variables. Decisions will not be more centralized as a result of the introduction of computers, but centralized decisions will be made in a far more sophisticated way, taking a fuller account of the real-world complications of the situation, than was possible before.

The use of computers in decision making has important implications for control over the goals to which administrative action and policy are directed, but these implications can as easily support broader as narrower participation in goal setting. What computers do in this respect is mainly to open the decision process to inspection. They objectify the process and make fully explicit the premises of fact and value that enter into it. As a result, the use of the computer will facilitate top management's control over decisions made elsewhere in the organization — in this way reconciling the notion of central control over goals with the notion of decentralization of the actual decision process.

More generally, the use of computers will permit multiple inputs into the decision process from a variety of sources, along with mutually independent alternate analyses of problems. In this way, computers will facilitate — and already have facilitated — a more extensive participation of both experts and laymen in debates on public policy, not by providing means for expressing uninformed opinions but in enabling opinions to be better informed.

Modern communications and computers have moved us from a world in which information was a scarce, valuable commodity to be cherished and preserved, to a world so full of information that what is scarce is the capacity to attend to it. The computer has often been used incorrectly, as in many MIS systems, as a producer of information. Increasingly,we are learning to use it as a compactor of information, reducing the amount of data that managers and policymakers must absorb and shouldering an important part of the burden of analysis that transforms a multitude of premises and predicted consequences into a decision to embark on a course of action.

Whether we employ computers to centralize decision making or to decentralize it is not determined by any inherent characteristics of the new technology. It is a choice for us to make whenever we design or modify our organizations. The technology does offer us a wide range of alternatives for fitting our decision-making systems to our requirements, whatever they may be.

References

Kaufman, Herbert. 1960. *The Forest Ranger: A Study in Administrative Behavior.* Baltimore: Johns Hopkins Press.

Sackman, Harold, ed. 1972. *Computers and the Problems of Society.* Montvale, N.J.: AFIPS Press.

Sackman, Harold, and Barry W. Boehm, eds. 1972. *Planning Community Information Utilities.* Montvale, N.J.: AFIPS Press.

Simon, Herbert A. 1977. *The New Science of Management Decision.* 3d edition. Englewood Cliffs, N.J.: Prentice-Hall.

———. *Administrative Behavior.* 1976. 3d edition. New York: Free Press. Chapters 13 and 14.

Whisler, Thomas L. 1970. *The Impact of Computers on Organizations.* New York: Praeger.

RADICAL

24. COMPUTERS AND CAPITALISM

Judith A. Perrolle

This article argues that the spread of computer technology is part of a transformation of the capitalist mode of production in the world's political and economic system (Perrolle 1983b). As Karl Marx argued in *The Poverty of Philosophy* (1973:110–26), the introduction of new machinery into the process of production requires a particular division of labor. The division of labor has consequences for the division of society into social classes, which in turn has political consequences. Although Marx is often quoted as saying that the hand mill produced feudal society and the steam mill produced modern capitalist governments, his theory was not one of simple technological determinism. Before new machinery can be introduced into the workplace, work must be reorganized to accommodate the equipment by those who have the power to redefine tasks and products. It is from this reorganization of work in the new information age that the social and political consequences of computer technology will emerge. The "electronic mill" will give us a worldwide society dominated by transnational corporations, not because such political and economic arrangements are inherent in computers, but because those who have the power to decide how computers will be used are reorganizing the division of labor in society in their own interests.

THE ELECTRONIC MILL

Computer technology has been, from its beginning, a tool for rationalizing capitalist industrial production. Charles Babbage, whose 1833 design for the "analytic engine" was the prototype of the modern computer, owned factories organized around the principle that:

Human labor is similar to capital, raw materials, etc. It is therefore subject, or ought to be subject, to similar input/output analyses, measurement, standards and controls (Babbage 1982).

The techniques which led to the eventual development of robots and other automated industrial processes appeared first on factory assembly lines with manual workers serving as semiautomatic components. In fact, the word "computer" was first used to describe the jobs of women who performed calculations and wired hardware for the pioneering ENIAC. Norbert Weiner, whose mathematical theory of information became the foundation for all later work on industrial control systems, called his theory "cybernetics, or control and communication in the animal and the machine" (1948). Weiner's theories provided industrial management with the techniques for realizing Babbage's labor principle and allowed designers to create automatic equipment to replace human labor altogether in many industrial applications.

Yet, if computers in capitalist industry were limited to the assembly line, they could hardly be considered anything more than a continuation of the mode of production laid down in English factories during the Industrial Revolution. The substitution of machinery for labor was an early part of the production process; Marx agreed with Babbage's definition of a machine as a division of labor in which a single engine links particular operations performed by a single instrument (1973:120–21). On the assembly line the electronic mill is simply an extension of the steam mill. However, computer technology does make possible a transformation of the capitalist mode of production through what Norbert Weiner called a "second industrial revolution" in which "the sporadic design of individual automatic mechanisms" is replaced by "communication between machine and machine" (1967:208). This integrated technology involves a new division of labor in which skilled mental work can be treated as a factor of production and a widespread geographical division of centrally managed labor is possible.

Information as a Commodity

In the century that elapsed between Marx's analysis of capitalism and Weiner's analysis of information, theorists working in the Marxist tradition have tended to treat clerical, technical, and managerial workers quite distinctly from workers engaged in the production of *commodities* — items made by wage laborers in order to be sold at a profit. For example, according to Harry Braverman's work on labor and monopoly capitalism, "commercial and financial labor add nothing to the value of the commodities represented by the figures or papers which they handle" (1974:414).

Yet the industrial proletariat was considered a class by Marx not because it produced material objects, but because it was organized in a mode of production that systematically exploited the value of the labor of workers and added value to what the workers produced. By considering certain types of information as commodities, many of the theoretical insights of Marx's analysis of class can be more directly applied to the rapidly expanding proportion of the capitalist labor force who are in "computerized" jobs.

Certainly all information is not property, nor do all information workers produce commodities. Most forms of information are still *means* — of control over workers and political processes or of maintaining ideology and cultural hegemony of the dominant classes. Yet the objective economic situations of some information workers are beginning to resemble those of factory workers as they perform routine tasks that contribute to the construction of marketable software and data. In this production process, information is not a means for workers but a raw material to be fashioned according to the requirements of their job into a new information product.

Information becomes a commodity when it is "made" by wage laborers and sold at a profit, and when the social and legal institutions of nations accord such products the status of corporate property. Weiner's mathematical quantification of information made the first step in "the establishment of socially recognized standards of measure" that Marx (1967:199) identified as an important characteristic of commodities. The current legal trends in the advanced industrial countries toward the treatment of information as property are apparent in recent tax cases and in laws designed to protect corporate data bases from theft (Perrolle 1983a:33–36). Knowledge as private property based upon personal work is being replaced by information as private property based on wage labor (Marx 1979:336; 1967:Chapter 30).

The ownership of the means of information production is heavily concentrated in a single country — the United States — and in the hands of a few multinational corporations which monopolize microelectronic technology (NACLA 1982:25; Saunders et al. 1983:63–67). The United States controls "60–70 percent of the market for exporting information by computer and has a near monopoly of scientific-technological information" (Mattelart 1982). Information products in the form of news and mass media broadcasts so predominantly reflect the culture and interests of the dominant powers that they can best be described as a form of "electronic colonialism" (McPhail 1981). Throughout the world those who control the means of producing information products are also able to determine the social organization of the "mental labor" which produces them.

The Alienation of Mental Labor

The history of capitalism has been a history of the reduction of thoughtful labor to routine, automatic processes. The skill and decision making of craftsmen was transformed in the factory to simple manual tasks. These in turn were gradually mechanized. Intellectual, or "white-collar," work was subjected to increasing bureaucratic organization, although it generally escaped automation. While the use of computers in management and the professions is being widely heralded as a technology for enhancing human skills, in reality it is a technology for the further routinization and in some cases actual automation of intellectual work.

As professional, managerial, and technical work becomes more organized and subject to the analysis needed to divide it into less skilled operations as part of production organized around computer-based information and control systems, an alienation process occurs. First, the technology physically removes the worker from the object of the work, as more and more labor is done on abstract information about the world rather than on material objects in the world. Second, the technology reduces the scope of a worker's activity to a small portion of a much larger product. In structured programming, for example, each programmer works on a small portion of a larger program according to specifications so rigid that in some cases computer programs are used to edit the work and remove any nonstandard lines of code. Third, the machinery often paces the worker. While this trend is much clearer for routine clerical and sales workers whose keystrokes per minute or items sold per hour can become part of their efficiency reports, it is also part of the design of such technologies as management information systems, intended to routinize higher-level white-collar work. The effect of machine pacing is to subject information workers to the same sort of labor discipline as was imposed upon assembly line workers in industrial production. Even in socialist societies, cybernetics is being used as a tool for rationalizing intellectual labor (Mulej 1980:213).

Workers subjected to such conditions are "deskilled" (Cooley 1980) in the sense that their labor requires less thought than before and gives them fewer decisions to make. If mental labor is increasingly organized for commodity production and if educational and intellectual institutions increasingly reflect capitalism's "need" for such deskilling, then even "creative" work may become a set of learned reflexes suitable for a machine environment. Work as a source of human satisfactions and social relationships will be further degraded, and education is likely to be redesigned in ways that blunt the intellectual and critical faculties of all but the elite.

The Distribution of Labor

The computer technology that maintains centralized control over workers who are physically distanced from their work and from one another facilitates a new international division of labor. Multinational corporations are increasingly able to integrate unskilled labor in the peripheral less-developed countries and deskilled labor in the core industrial countries into a geographically dispersed mode of production. This mode of production can be distinguished from earlier forms of international capitalist production by its centralized coordination of the scattered units. Labor is widely distributed while production remains centralized. This has the effects of intensifying Third World underdevelopment (Frobel et al. 1980) and "peripheralizing" labor at the core (Sassen-Koob 1982).

Both the "reindustrialization" policies of core countries like the United States

(Dixon et al. 1982) and the "New International Economic Order" investment policies of Third World nations (McMichael 1982) tend to produce a deskilled, low-wage, international working class which is politically fragmented but becoming economically integrated by the new form of capitalist production. In the periphery, new industrial locations take advantage of cheap unskilled labor in the militarily repressive states; in the core, runaway shops apply downward pressure to wages while the new "high tech" industries produce few "high tech" jobs and many low-paid, unskilled ones. Computer technology also supplies the automated equipment to dislocate the unionized and highly skilled industrial workers of the core and can create a return to nonunion piecework in "electronic cottage" arrangements. Already some clerical work is being distributed to part-time home workers in the United States. As telecommunications infrastructure improves, this sort of work can be done in almost any region which has been opened to electronic capital penetration.

Although proponents of telecommunications development stress the economic advantages that accrue to Third World nations through better communications facilities, the New World Information and Communication Order program proposed by UNESCO seems to some a "technological Trojan Horse" through which the transnational corporations that monopolize communications technology can extend their control over the Third World (NACLA 1982:25–26). If telecommunications is viewed as part of the computer technology base for a new mode of capitalist production, its consequences are clear. As the late Stephen Hymer observed: "To maintain the separation between work and control, capital has erected elaborate corporate superstructures to unite labor in production, but divide it in power" (1977:102–3). Computer technology provides the means for a global separation of work and control.

The Machine as Manager

Computer technology provides some capacity to relocate control over complex production processes from human decision makers to the machine itself. The field of "artificial intelligence" involves the design and production of computer systems and automated equipment with a limited capacity to behave in ways that at least resemble human thought processes. Although artificial intelligence is a new field and has so far shown very meager results, robots, expert systems, and the proposed new military "supercomputers" are being designed to replace the knowledge and judgment of human professionals with machinery. Although they have only just begun to appear as part of the capitalist mode of production, they represent a trend with enormous consequences for the social relations of production.

The main consequence of machine-embodied knowledge is a devaluation of the knowledge of human experts, especially at the lower technical and managerial levels (Perrolle 1984). With the spread of artificial intelligence, we may expect a marked stratification between a small technocratic elite whose expertise is in the development of such systems and a massively deskilled middle class whose "professions" are increasingly subject to automation and computerized controls. Because the computer's intelligence is limited by the narrow range of instrumental logic with which it has been endowed, decision making by computer will accelerate the dehumanizing effects already visible in bureaucratic organizations. In their military applications, decision-making machines increase the possiblity of an accidental triggering of nuclear war. This is partially because the enormously complex technology is prone to failure. But it is also because the electronic reaction speeds of computer-controlled weapons greatly reduces the amount of time available to humans to plan, debate, and negotiate military situations.

The machine as manager permits a complex economic integration of manual and mental labor on a global scale and provides the technology for supervising and disciplining it. This "electronic mill," owned and controlled by multinational corporations and the military-industrial complexes of the core nations, represents a new force of capitalist production. Although now fettered by national economic and military interests, the electronic mill is hastening the "international decentralization and social diversification of material production and reproduction" (Frobel 1982:512) and transforming the world from a "set of nations" to a "network of transnational powers" (Dixon et al. 1983:190). It seems likely that the electronic mill will give us a world-society dominated by transnational enterprise.

CLASS FORMATION

While the spread of computer technology is creating common working conditions for large numbers of individuals in the world-system, the conditions of computerized work do not facilitate the formation of class consciousness in the same way that the early industrial revolution situation of groups of workers in factories did. By allowing workers to be physically separate from their work and from one another (even across international boundaries at great distances), computer technology interferes with the linkages Marx observed between capitalist organization of industrial production and workers' political responses. If workers in the new international division of labor are to become organized into the sort of revolutionary class predicted by Marx, alternative means of creating common culture, easy communications among class members, and political organizations dedicated to economic transformation must develop. Computer technology provides some means by which this may occur, though it also provides means by which efforts to organize international workers can be severely inhibited by the dominant class.

The Information Society Elite

In his analysis of information and telecommunications in "post-industrial" society, Daniel Bell argues that a new "knowledge elite" is forming, consisting of individuals with expertise in the new information technologies. Because he believes that knowledge is the private property of educated individuals and that power is the not-necessarily-related social status based on control over others, Bell does not believe that the information society ''knowledge elite'' will become a ''power elite'' (1980:204). In other words, Bell does not see an individual's relationship to computer technology as a possible basis for his or her economic class position, nor does he see the control over information production as a source of political power. Instead, Bell envisions a society in which the majority of educated people will find interesting and well-paid work with the new technologies. However, the long-range consequences of the commodification of knowledge and the consolidation of information production will be that Bell's information-society elite will be much smaller and more powerful than he imagines. And many of those he assumes will become part of the elite will instead become members of the information-society working class.

The artificial intelligence expert Herbert Simon is more realistic about the effects of computer technology on the relationship between knowledge and power. He sees the technology creating no ''long-term trend towards the centralization of decision making in both business and government'' (1981:226–27). Simon believes that the centralist tendency lies not in the technology, but in our choices of organization structures. Like others who have pointed to computer technology's potential for supporting decentralized networks for pluralist decision making, Simon is optimistic about the prospects for democratic controls over computer technology. Unfortunately, the fundamental changes being introduced by computers are occurring within the workplace, and are considered economic rather than political decisions. The impact of computers on centralized decision making will not occur as a direct use of computer systems in the political process but will occur through a restructuring of social classes.

Terence Hopkins (1977:71), Philip McMichael (1982:143–43), and others have argued that a world capitalist class is consolidating across national boundaries and incorporating the elites of the Third World. Computer technology's contribution to this process is to improve production efficiency by consolidating production control into the hands of fewer but more expert managers, to eliminate large segments of the middle class, and to provide new forms of ideology and labor discipline. The information-society elite will contain a relatively small remnant of the managerial, technical, and professional occupations possessing both decision-making power and knowledge of computer technology.

Although at present there is a division of labor between technical expertise and positions of management, the mixing of ''knowledge-based'' and ''position-based'' power has been advocated by U.S. corporate leaders as being in the interests of production efficiency (Grove 1983). One of the problems of capitalist enterprise has been what Randall Collins calls a consciousness of formalism ''directed away from the material realities of work experience and into the purely relative values of cultural currency'' (1979:72). That this is a problem for capital has been evident in the shift in business management interests from the actual production in factories (Haavind 1983:2) and on farms (Rubin 1983:96) to symbols of power and status. Since in corporate culture the appearances of status and the ability to manipulate information and subordinates yield better returns to managers than actual involvement in production, a consolidation of expertise and status could improve productivity. As computer systems become more "user-friendly," managers will be able to directly manage production processes from their terminals. This will also eliminate the need for many lower layers of managers.

The same computerized integration of production is occurring in socialist societies. Although the Soviet scientist S. A. Heinman believes that "the scientific and technical revolution may provide the basis for a radical solution of socal problems and elimination of social distinctions between men" (1981:51), he also sees that its "potentialities are also connected with the economic integration of the socialist-community countries, which provides extensive potentialities for improving the specialization and cooperation of production" (1981:47). Insofar as there exists a "new class" in the socialist countries, that class seems likely to become stronger and more international as computer technology is applied to international socialist economic integration. If, as Nyiri argues, the world-system incorporates both a capitalist world-economy and a socialist world-economy which are becoming more interdependent, then there may be for the socialist elite some "blurring" (which Nyiri sees as impossible) of "the social differences between the two systems into some third form" (1982:21).

The spread of a world "corporate culture" of rather uniform patterns of electronically based production and ways of conducting international business may produce a worldwide information-society elite dedicated to the overthrow of nationalist political interference with their global accumulation process, to the incorporation of Third World and "socialist" ruling classes, and to the consolidation of social status and political power into their expert hands.

The Information Society Working Class

One of the most visible signs of the progress of the second industrial revolution has been the automation of highly skilled jobs of the "labor aristocracy." These workers, largely through strong unions, had escaped many of the consequences of the proletarianization process of the first Industrial Revolution. Now that computerized industrial robots have been designed with enough "intelligence" to perform skilled manual operations on the assembly line, the unionized blue-collar worker's highly paid position in industrial society is seriously threatened. The significant feature of the robotics phenomenon is the use of expensive machines to replace expensive labor. Robots pay for themselves within five years; more important, they do not join unions. Within a generation they will have broken the power of the industrial unions and restricted membership in the middle class by eliminating the high-wage blue-collar segment.

As the application of computer technology to traditional assembly lines reduces industrial wages, its application to office work is raising productivity and rationalizing working conditions. The new automated offices are information factories; clerical and data-processing workers are the new information assembly line workers. Although in the beginning, the office automation phenomenon expands opportunities in what have been traditionally women's jobs, eventually much of this work will be automated to the point where jobs can be eliminated. Already bank tellers and supermarket clerks are being replaced by machines; other office work can be similarly computerized. Advertisements promise that word processors will free secretaries from drudgery; studies of VDT screen use report serious eye and back problems, to say nothing of boredom. By 1985, 85 percent of the major U.S. corporations are expected to have begun office automation ("The Office Automation Challenge" 1984). As each pink-collar worker is more heavily capitalized, it becomes increasingly important to management to optimize the use of the equipment, not the comfort of the workers. Downward pressure on pink-collar wages is provided by the trends towards "electronic cottage" piecework (Mattera 1983) and "electronic runaway shops" ("9 to 5 in Barbados" 1984). Already a fifth of the U.S. labor force works part-time, and the majority of the part-time workers are women (Serrin 1983).

Optimistic analysts of the computer revolution tend to dismiss the devaluation of blue- and pink-collar wages as a transitional phenomenon. They focus their attention on the promise of expanded opportunities for creative, highly paid jobs in the professions as a solution to computer-generated unemployment and worsening working conditions. However, a relatively little known branch of computer science is threatening to make possible the automation of skilled mental work as well as the more routine forms of information handling. Expert systems, a type of "artificial intelligence" computer program, are bringing automation to the professions (Drake and Perrolle 1984). Such programs can ask for needed information, can interpret information in terms of "best guesses" based upon their problem-solving experience, can draw inferences from data, and can modify their own behavior as a result of the outcome of their previous actions. The practical success of expert systems that play chess, infer chemical structures from molecular data, and diagnose illnesses indicate quite clearly that artificial intelligence is being put to work at industrial and professional tasks, despite theoretical objections (Dreyfus 1972; Weizenbaum 1976) that what they do isn't really the same as human thought. The applications in which they are used are those in which the knowledge of human experts is characterized by great rationality; claims that they will eventually be able to perform in all areas of human expertise are essentially claims that all human knowledge can be made rational and automatable.

The computer software industry is often pointed to as a prime example of the new opportunities for creative work in high tech industry. Based on its rapid expansion in recent decades and its relative openness to women, software production was widely believed to be a positive example of the new employment pattern. Unfortunately, a recent major study of the software industry (Kraft 1984) finds that there are virtually no black programmers; that women reach career dead ends early, are paid less than men in all positions beyond the entry level, and are concentrated in documentation and customer support (the high tech version of "women's work"); and that there are unemployed programmers. The U.S. pattern of employment discrimination by race and gender persists in the information age. Indeed, given our cultural beliefs about women's and minorities' lower capacities for mathematical and analytic thinking, we may find worsening job discrimination. Finally, a technological development called "structured programming" is being used to break large computer programming tasks into small interchangeable parts. Even as software production is thus being rationalized, expert systems are being designed to automate the programming itself.

In engineering and production control new "embedded systems" are being designed to make production processes fully integrated and automated, from purchasing decisions through process design, production optimization, pricing, and marketing. These developments will soon begin to cut into the bottom ranks of industrial and business management. As can be seen from the recent recession's effects on managers (Main 1984), the computerization of information and decision making eliminates managerial as well as technical functions.

As highly paid blue-collar workers lose their jobs, information workers are organized into production work, and even skilled white-collar workers find themselves downwardly mobile, the new information age working class is being formed. As competition for jobs requiring little skill becomes more intense, those already in the working class will suffer the brunt of the unemployment and declining benefits. The explanations and justifications for the decline of the middle class at the expense of the lower class will be terms of international competition, individual lack of "computer literacy," and the inevitability of progress. It is with great reluctance that the middle class population will identify itself by its new economic status; already an ideology is emerging to explain the new information society in ways which avoid any consideration of the basic economic transformation which is under way.

References

Babbage, Charles. 1982. Cited in Philip Kraft, Butler-Cox Foundation Lecture, Davos, Switzerland.

Bell, Daniel. 1981. "The Social Framework of the Information Society." In Michael L. Dertouzos and Joel Moses, eds., *The Computer Age: A Twenty-Year View*. Cambridge, Mass.: MIT Press.

Braverman, Harry. 1974. *Labor and Monopoly Capital: The Degradation of Work in the Twentieth Century*. New York: Monthly Review Press.

Collins, Randall. 1979. *The Credential Society*. New York: Academic Press.

Cooley, Mike. 1980. *Architect or Bee? The Human/Technology Relationship*. Boston: South End Press.

Dixon, Marlene, Susanne Jones, and Ed McCaughan. 1983. "Reindustrialization and the Transnational Labor Force in the United States Today." *Contemporary Marxism* 5:101–15.

———. 1982. "Changes in the International Division of Labor and Low-Wage Labor in the United States." In Albert Bergsen, ed., *Crises in the World-System*. Beverly Hills, Calif.: Sage:173–92.

Drake, Elisabeth M. and Judith A. Perrolle. "Computer-Aided Creativity." American Institute of Chemical Engineers, Winter National Meeting, Atlanta.

Dreyfus, Herbert. 1972. *What Computers Can't Do*. New York: Harper and Row.

Frobel, Folker. 1982. "The Current Developments of the World-Economy." In Edward Friedman, ed., *Ascent and Decline in the World System.* Beverly Hills, Calif.: Sage:115–46.

———, J. Heinrichs, and O. Kreye. 1980. *The New International Division of Labor.* Cambridge: Cambridge University Press.

Grove, Andrew S. 1983. "Breaking the Chains of Command." *Newsweek* (October 3):23.

Haavind, Robert. 1983. "Fast Action Needed in Upgrading Factories." *High Technology* (July):2.

Heinman, S. A. 1981. *Scientific and Technical Revolution.* Moscow: Progress Publishers.

Hopkins, Terence. 1977. "Notes on Class Analysis and World-System." *Review* I, 1:67–72.

Hymer, Stephen. 1972. "The Internationalization of Capital." *Journal of Economic Issues* 6, 1:91–123.

Kraft, Philip. 1984. Preliminary findings presented at Eastern Sociological Society Meetings, Boston (March).

Main, Jeremy. 1984. "The Recovery Skips Middle Managers." *Fortune* (February 6):112–20.

Mattera, Philip. 1983. "Home Computer Sweatshops." *The Nation* (April 2):390–92.

Mattelart, Armand. 1978. "The Crises and Modes of Communication." *LARU Studies* (Toronto) II, 3 (June):38.

Marx, Karl. 1979. Letter to Vera Ivanovana Zassulich, in Saul K. Padover, ed., *The Letters of Karl Marx.* Englewood Cliffs, N.J.: Prentice-Hall.

———. 1973. *The Poverty of Philosophy.* Moscow: Progress Publishers.

———. 1967. *Capital* vol. 1. New York: International Publishers.

McMichael, Philip. 1982. "Social Structure of the New International Division of Labor." In Edward Friedman, ed., *Ascent and Decline in the World System.* Beverly Hills, Calif.: Sage: 115–146.

McPhail, Thomas L. 1981. *Electronic Colonialism.* Beverly Hills, CA: Sage.

Mulej, Matjaz. 1982. "Some Practical Results of the Application of the Dialectic Systems Theory in Business." In *Progress in Cybernetics and Systems Research* vol. X, New York: Hemisphere Publishing Company.

NACLA. 1982. "Toward a New Information Order." Special issue of *NACLA Report on the Americas* XVI, 4 (July–August).

"9 to 5 in Barbados." *In These Times* (April 4–10, 1984):24.

Nyiri, Karoly. 1982. "Towards an Integrated International Division of Labor: The Place of the World Socialist Economy." *Review* VI, 1 (Summer):15–23.

"The Office Automation Challenge: American Business Responds." *The Omni Group*, 1984.

Perrolle, Judith A. 1984. "Expert Systems, Structured Programming, and the Devaluation of Mental Labor." Eastern Sociological Society Annual Meetings, Boston (March).

———. 1983a. "Computer-Generated Social Problems." Society for the Study of Social Problems Annual Meetings, Detroit (August).

———. 1983b. "Computer Technology and Class Formation in the World-System." *Proceedings of the 1983 Conference on Communications, Mass Media, and Development,* Chicago (October).

Rubin, Charles, with Dick Landis. 1983. ''Farming Smarter with a Computer.'' *Personal Computing* (June):96–101.

Sassen-Koob, Saskia. 1982. ''Recomposition and Peripheralization at the Core.'' *Contemporary Marxism* 5:88–100.

Saunders, Robert J., Jeremy J. Warford, and Bjorn Wellenius. 1983. *Telecommunications and Economic Development.* Baltimore: Johns Hopkins Press (for the World Bank).

Serrin, William. 1983. ''Up to a Fifth of U.S. Workers Now Rely on Part-time Jobs.'' *The New York Times* (August 14):1.

Simon, Herbert. 1981. ''The Consequences of Computers for Centralization and Decentralization.'' In Michael Dertouzos and Joel Moses, eds., *The Computer Age: A Twenty-Year View.* Cambridge, Mass.: MIT Press.

Weiner, Norbert. 1967. *The Human Use of Human Beings.* New York: Avon Books.

———. 1948. *Cybernetics, or Control and Communication in the Animal and Machine.* New York: The Technology Press and John Wiley and Sons.

Weizenbaum, Joseph. 1976. *Computer Power and Human Reason: From Judgment to Calculation.* San Francisco: W. H. Freeman.

CHAPTER 11

THE POLITICS OF COMMUNICATION: WHAT ARE THE DANGERS OF NEW MEDIA TECHNOLOGIES?

Communication is an essential activity in any society, but its effect on freedom and the exercise of power depends greatly on the character of the media by which people communicate. In a small, predominantly oral culture, the ability to communicate is open, on a roughly equal basis, to all who are able to speak and to understand the language. With the invention of writing, of printing, and ultimately of complex electronic modes of information dissemination, the act of communication becomes at once more powerful and more restrictive: more powerful because a single message can now reach a much larger audience, more restrictive because the skills and physical resources required to transmit the message become increasingly subject to the monopoly control of a small elite.

The revolutionary changes that are transforming our communications environment in the late twentieth century promise to have profound and far-reaching consequences for the way we work, the way we play, the way we learn, and (perhaps most important of all) the way we practice politics. Some of these consequences were explored in the previous set of readings. In this chapter, two media analysts consider the impact of electronic communications technologies on the future of democracy. A. P. Simonds is the founding director of the Program in Marxist Studies and Associate Professor of Political Science at the University of Massachusetts/Boston. The late Ithiel de Sola Pool was the Ruth and Arthur Sloan Professor of Political Science at the Massachusetts Institute of Technology, and the director of its Research Program on Communications Policy. In spite of their contrasting political views, the two articles have much in common. Both emphasize the importance of changes in media technology for the political process, especially the shift from a print-centered culture to the new dominance of electronic communications media. Both are concerned about the threat to freedom posed by these new technologies. Neither, on the other hand, sees these trends as uniformly negative; both express the hope that by increasing our awareness of the dangers posed by the new communications technologies, the future of democratic government might still be strengthened rather than eroded.

The difference between the radical and conservative perspectives becomes apparent, however, in their contrasting appraisal of the nature of the threat which the emerging electronic media pose to democracy. For Simonds, the most pressing danger comes from the effect of highly concentrated and therefore immensely powerful but privately owned and controlled media upon the ability of citizens to secure access to information, to participate in public debate, and consequently to develop the political competence necessary to exercise real and effective control over their government. Pool worries, on the other hand, that the traditional identification of First Amendment protections with the printed word may lead to an erosion of that freedom as the print media are increasingly displaced by electronic forms of communication subject to governmental regulations that disregard the protection of free speech. In short, Simonds is chiefly worried that the electronic media may undermine the right of citizens to control their government; Pool is chiefly worried that the government may undermine the right of the owners of electronic media to exercise their constitutionally protected freedom of speech.

Simond's argument grows from a premise and a paradox. The premise is that genuinely democratic government is not possible without well-informed citizens. The paradox is that in spite of a highly successful, multimillion dollar "news" industry, survey data consistently show that the public is extremely ill informed. Simonds claims that this is at least in part a result of the logic of information technology in a commodity-producing society. Historically, he claims, the development of a print-based culture was favorable to the growth of liberal democracy. Conversely, the increasing dominance of electronic, nonprint modes of information dissemination threatens to reverse this trend and to make democracy, even in its incomplete liberal form, increasingly shallow, vacuous, and illusory.

Pool's discussion carries the history of media technology forward to the present frontiers of cable, computers, videodisks, and satellites. He shows how closely the constitutional tradition protecting free speech and a free press has been connected to the printed word, and he worries that the kinds of government regulation that have evolved for other sorts of communication ("carriers" such as mail, telegraph, telephone, and "broadcast" media such as radio and television) may come to undermine the First Amendment as the traditional functions of print media are increasingly performed electronically. When the daily newspaper is delivered to a videotex terminal in the home via telephone cable, for example, will the government's role be defined by the principles of a free press (as the newspaper industry is now protected from any prior restraint), by the example of government regulation of monopoly carriers (as the telephone company is now subject to rate and other restrictions), or by the model of public regulation of the airwaves (as television broadcasters are now subject to licensing requirements, rules of "fairness," etc.)?

As you reflect on the political significance of communications media, ask yourself the following questions:

1. To the extent that effective and credible communication requires the use of facilities and equipment costing hundreds of thousands of dollars, is freedom of speech adequately protected by ensuring that the government will not interfere in any way with what the owners of that equipment choose to do with it?

2. What are the advantages and disadvantages of the printed text as a medium for conducting public debate? Compare the specific comments of Simonds and Pool on this point.

3. Is the future of democratic freedom endangered more by the concentration of communications power in the hands of a small elite (as Simonds thinks) or by the prospect of governmental regulation of private media (as Pool believes)?

References

Compaine, Benjamin M., ed. 1982. *Who Owns the Media? Concentration of Ownership in the Mass Communications Industry* (2nd edition). White Plains, N.Y.: Knowledge Industry Publications.

Czitrom, Daniel J. 1982. *Media and the American Mind: From Morse to McLuhan.* Chapel Hill: University of North Carolina Press.

Eisenstein, Elizabeth L. 1979. *The Printing Press as an Agent of Change.* Cambridge: Cambridge University Press.

Smith, Anthony. 1980. *Goodbye Gutenberg: The Newspaper Revolution of the 1980s.* Oxford: Oxford University Press.

Wicklein, John. 1981. *Electronic Nightmare: The Home Communications Set and Your Freedom.* New York: Viking.

RADICAL:ACCESS, PARTICIPATION, AND CITIZEN COMPETENCE

25. ON BEING INFORMED

A. P. Simonds

To read the newspaper is the modern man's morning-prayer.

— Hegel

WHO SHALL BE "MASTERS OF THE SITUATION"?

Although the principles of democracy have commanded near universal assent, at least since World War II, its modern history is still brief, fragmented, and inconclusive. Unfortunately, the familiarity of the first point has often served to distract attention from the importance of the second. That "we are all democrats today" may say something about our good intentions, or about our conceptual confusion, or about our hypocrisy, but it says very little about the future prospects either of the ideal or of efforts to realize it. Certainly we have too much evidence of the fragility of the democratic impulse to continue to hold any Whiggish confidence in its promise as our appointed destiny. The problems of realizing democratic rule are put into useful perspective by recalling some of the arguments that were employed, not so very long ago, when we were *not* all democrats. One of the most influential of the arguments brought against suffrage expansion in the nineteenth century amounted essentially to a rather simple claim: the elimination of political privilege threatened, indeed it promised, the elimination of socioeconomic privilege as well. An equal distribution of the right to vote would lead directly and rapidly to a redistribution of property from the wealthy few to the impecunious many. Here, for example, is the warning issued by Robert Lowe to the House of Commons (and to the entire propertied elite of Britain) in 1866 on the consequences to be expected from extending the franchise to working men:

The first stage, I have no doubt, will be an increase of corruption, intimidation, and disorder, of all the evils that happen usually in elections. But what will be the second? The second will be that the working men of England, finding themselves in a full majority of the whole constituency, will awake to a full sense of their power. They will say, "We can do better for ourselves. We have objects to serve as well as our neighbours, and let us unite to carry those objects. We have machinery; we have our trades unions; we have our leaders all ready. We have the power of combination, as we have shown over and over again; and when we have a prize to fight for we will bring it to bear with tenfold more force than ever before."

Well, when that is the case — when you have a Parliament appointed, as it will be, by such constituencies so deteriorated — with a pressure of that kind brought to bear, what is it you expect Parliament to stop at? Where is the line that can be drawn?...for my part I think Parliamentary life would not be worth preserving on those terms. Look at the position Parliament will occupy. As long as we have not passed this Bill we are masters of the situation. Let us pass the Bill, and in what position are we? That of the Gibeonites — hewers of wood and drawers of water, rescued for a moment from the slaughter that fell on the other Canaanites in order that we may prepare the Bill for redistribution.[1]

This was surely a compelling argument. Give to the humble the power, by virtue of their number, to control the state and why should they not be expected to use it to advance their material interests at the expense of those more privileged but less numerous? Certainly such an assumption was widely shared. It underlay the advocacy of radical democrats in the tradition of Paine as much as the opposition of men such as Lowe. It was largely accepted by the liberal reformers as well, who hastened, on this account, to emphasize the *modesty* of the extension proposed — one that would still leave working men in the minority.[2] It was an assumption, moreover, that would seem far more consistent with common sense than Tory confidence in the perpetual effectiveness of ''natural'' authority, tradition, and habits of deference. And yet the subsequent history of liberal democracy has demonstrated the Lowe's argument, however compelling, was almost entirely false.

More prescient, it turns out, was the observation of the Member for Westminster, Mr. John Stuart Mill: ''They may be able to decide whether a Tory or a Whig shall be elected; they may be masters of so small a situation as that.''[3] This comment was based on the restricted franchise envisioned by the 1866 Bill, but its spirit seems to have applied to the results of universal suffrage as well. Certainly the effects expected by Lowe have not materialized. As one recent summary of the relevant research puts it: ''It is difficult to measure the impact of democratization on redistribution, but the best available evidence suggests that the impact is by no means large and certainly not uniform.[4] Although redistributive policies have been adopted, their overall impact on socioeconomic hierarchy has been limited. Close to a century after substantial manhood suffrage was won in Britain, 20 to 25 percent of all personal wealth is still owned by 1 percent of the population; taxes reduce the income share of the richest tenth from 26.6 percent to 23.2 percent and raise that of the poorest tenth from 2.8 percent to 3.1 percent.[5] This does not look like democracy as it was understood by Mr. Lowe.[6] Nor have the redistributive effects of political equality been significantly different elsewhere. In all the industrial liberal democracies, the Gibeonites of property are still suffered their existence, but instead of hewing wood or drawing water, they rule. . . .

One hundred years ago, the debate over democracy was much exercised by the problem of ''the informed citizen.'' Today this would seem to have become a matter of little theoretical interest, even if it still provides the occasion for a certain amount of public hand wringing. (J. Roland Pennock's recent massive study of democratic theory includes perhaps half a dozen sentences, scattered across more than 500 pages, which can be said to address the problem.[7] The explanation for this is probably fairly simple.Nineteenth-century concern was closely connected to nineteenth-century fears about the threat of political equality to socioeconomic hierarchy, or at least to "sound" government and "prudent" public policy. Twentieth-century indifference reflects the realization that there was nothing to fear — not because the quality of public information is high (most evidence indicates, rather strikingly, the opposite) but because it does not seem to make much difference. Indeed, to the extent that the "ill-informed citizen" has been credited with an impact on the practice of democracy, this has more often been judged benign than malignant, a conclusion that has of course been explained and justified by the "empirical" theory of democracy.[8] But the contrast is less significant than it may first appear. The Victorians' concern was not so much with the conditions requisite to being politically informed as with the problem (as J. S. Mill put it) of "general ignorance and incapacity, or, to speak more moderately, insufficient mental qualifications, in the controlling body."[9] And while modern political science has been little concerned with ideals of civic virtue and public competence, it has devoted enormous resources over the last twenty-five years to clarifying our picture of actual non-elite political behavior. Now even though both of these concerns have implications for the one I want to explore, neither of them can be identified with it. It might be helpful to make these differences explicit.

The problem debated by Mill and the Victorians concerned the validity of the democratic norm itself. For what was at stake in the argument over "mental qualifications" was the fundamental democratic assumption that the ordinary person is, on the whole, a more competent judge of his or her political interests than any other person is.[10] This assumption is not at issue in this paper; my concern with the problem of "being informed" presupposes that the democratic norm is justified. (This does not, of course, mean that it is self-evident; only that I do not intend to make the argument for democracy here!) What I want to consider is not the legitimacy of such judgments but the resources for making them: are the latter adequately developed and equitably distributed? This distinction is an important one, for too often discussion of the health of the polity proceeds on the assumption that critical appraisal of the political competence of citizens is automatically an antidemocratic argument; an implicitly elitist claim to "know the people's interests better than they do" and hence to make their political decisions for them. But this does not follow. One can consistently and reasonably hold that citizen Smith is a more competent judge of his own political interest than any other person, including citizen Brown, and yet also hold that the distribution of resources requisite to effective judgment makes it likely that citizen Brown is a more competent judge of Brown's interest than Smith is of Smith's. Insofar as differences of this kind exist, realization of democratic norms is obstructed. Criticism of such differences and of the conditions that reproduce them consequently serves the opposite purpose from the antidemocratic claim that people are "unfit to rule." It is not such criticism, but the neglect of it, that undermines commitment to democracy.

Can empirical research on political opinion and behavior shed light on the state of development and distribution of the resources for political judgment? The answer is surely yes, but it is a very modest and largely negative sort of back-lighting that is provided. The main conclusion to emerge from the extensive survey research that has been conducted since World War II is that the democratic citizenry is, indeed, ill-informed politically. True, these indications are not uniform: there is some evidence of improvement in the United States during the sixties, though perhaps also some evidence of deterioration in the seventies.[11] But setting aside the fact that even the most positive interpretations of the data make the expectations of traditional proponents of democratic rule look (to use one of the favorite adjectives of the revisionists) "naive," it remains doubtful that such evidence can shed much positive light on the conditions requisite to "being informed." Certainly measures of citizen "information" in the narrow sense of awareness of certain important facts about politics (such as "what party controls the Senate?") can establish only negative results,[12] for the ability to make effective political judgments is only weakly related to the ability to perform successfully in a current-events quiz. More promising, perhaps, are the efforts deriving from the pioneering work of the Michigan group to infer political competence from the extent to which a person's views on one issue are consistent with those on another, and from the extent to which the judgments expressed demonstrate the capacity to employ comprehensive, abstract conceptual tools.[13] But even if the measurement of attitude consistency and level of conceptualization is reliable, the "consistency" and "conceptualization" to which they refer can only be judged as primitive: e.g., that a person inclined to a "liberal" view on one of five major issues areas will also choose the "liberal" answer to questions about the other four; that a person will, in answering certain open-ended questions about candidates and parties, use "ideological" terms (such as *liberal* or *conservative*) or make implicit reference to such terms.[14] But neither identifies in more than the vaguest way the qualities that are required to "be informed" in any significant or substantial sense: the capacity to grasp, interpret, appraise, and draw appropriate inferences from factual information, the ability to follow and evaluate an argument, the ability to comprehend and imply abstract concepts (as opposed simply to using, perhaps blindly, an abstract term), the ability to make connections between events, or ideas, or attitudes — the ability, in short, to "make sense" of the political world. Consequently, such data can provide us with but scant clues respecting the *conditions* favorable to the development of political sophistication. It is such an object that guides my interests in the matter of the "informed citizen." I do not doubt that the extraordinary body of evidence assembled by decades of voting behavior research is instructive with respect to other questions, and I can appreciate the powerful obstacles to using such methods to secure answer to mine; nonetheless I think one must conclude that this kind of data can tell us very little (except, in some cases, negatively) about the development and distribution of resources for political judgment.

Let me endeavor to describe the nature of those resources more precisely. Political competence entails three different sorts of judgment, and thus three different dimensions of "being informed": judgments about what *is*, judgments about what is *good or desirable*, and judgments about what is *possible*.[15] In the first of these, we establish the basic inventory of materials with which and on which political activity must work. This "material" world comprises physical facts, of course — natural resources, populations, stocks of produced wealth, and the geographical distribution of all of these. But it also and more importantly comprises the institutions and practices by which human activities are organized: family, state, market, custom, ritual, and law. Political action of any kind presupposes familiarity with such phenomena, with their material characteristics, and with the rules and shared meanings that define them. What distinguishes political judgments from the majority of everyday social judgments is their greater scope and comprehensiveness. Politics concerns the *public* realm; it involves decisions about conditions that transcend the boundaries of private experience. The steady expansion of global interdependence over the past centuries has broadened this realm; it has meant that what we can know at first hand, from direct experience, accounts for a smaller and smaller part of the knowledge of "what is" that is required in making political judgments. The consequences of this situation are fairly straightforward: (1) the phenomena about which we must know to make sound political judgments are overwhelmingly and increasingly matters that we do not observe or experience directly (say, the passing of a tax bill in the Senate, the harvesting of lettuce in California, the setting of the price of oil at an OPEC meeting); (2) the vast number of such phenomena and the complexity of the interconnections among them means that we can derive political judgments from such knowledge only by means of extremely abstract, synthetic, conceptually complex ideas (such as representative democracy, the labor contract and labor organization, inflation). Even those activities of which we have first-hand experience (such as voting in an election, boycotting a supermarket, or switching to gas heat) can be considered expressions of political will only insofar as they are comprehensible to us in terms of information resources of the sort implied by (1) and (2).

The second sort of judgment, concerning what is *good or desirable*, is what makes politics as a steering activity possible. To be a political agent and not merely a repository of knowledge about the world, one must be informed by normative standards that permit the *evaluation* of "what is." Such norms do not come as standard genetic equipment; they must be acquired by a process that includes becoming informed about one's own interests and those of others, about the conventions and expectations that govern social life generally, and about the principles that underlie and justify (or fail to justify) such conventions.[16] This process is essentially dialogic: it requires the capacity to hear and respond to the initiatives of others, to participate in the kind of discursive interaction that permits generation of shared norms on a basis of moral autonomy and mutual respect. Being informed, in this sense, might be expressed as the capacity to identify the General Will.

But identifying the General Will is not equivalent to realizing it. For steering to be effective, it must be informed about what is *possible*. Political will can be rendered impotent by errors of judgment on this matter in either of two directions: by an overestimation of the limits established by "what is" (nothing is possible), or by an underestimation of them (anything is).[17] But where can we turn to inform ourselves about what is possible? The answer, in some ways paradoxically, seems to be: to the past. It is historical awareness, the capacity to follow a process across time, to identify tendencies (including, but certainly not confined to, the consequences of causal connections) that permits judgments about potential, about limits, and about opportunity.[18] Such judgments, of course, preclude truth claims (for reasons definitively set forth by Karl Popper years ago[19]) but that does not make them irrelevant or indeed unessential to effective political activity. The possibility of historical freedom, of being able to "shape our destiny," depends on our capacity to make informed judgments in this sense.

Each of these dimensions of "being informed" requires at least minimal competence with respect to the preceding levels; that is, moral competence presupposes at least some empirical competence, whereas historical/practical competence presupposes that one is reasonably well informed with respect to both of the other dimensions. By the same token, ideological domination (which has the effect of obstructing or constraining the acquisition of information at any of these levels) is sequential in its effects: a person kept in ignorance and isolation from the rest of the world is unable to participate in the discourse that establishes standards; a person whose norms are undeveloped, unreflectively affirmed, or entirely dependent on the directives of some external authority suffers on that account a diminished measure of historical freedom. The history of ideological forms of domination seem to follow such a sequence. In precapitalist societies, the most powerful ideological obstacle to political competence on the part of the rural producer at the bottom of the system of domination was ignorance: a conception of the world that was narrowly confined within the immediate, the local, and the concrete, coupled with hazy and largely false conceptions of the "good king" somewhere over the horizon.[20] But this condition was altered by the requirements of early capitalist production; labor mobility, the concentration and complex coordination necessary for the production process, and urban life in general all meant that resources for being informed, in the first sense, expanded. The main focus of ideological constraint shifted to the second sense: the inhibition of the development of moral autonomy and the capacity for independent, self-reflective valuative judgments. Enormous emphasis came to be placed on respect for rules of behavior and deportment, deference to the authority from whom these rules issued — scientific, religious, managerial, patriarchal — and willingness to pursue "self-improvement" by the standards thus handed down. In late capitalism, which depends on an increasingly large number of persons whose work — technical, intellectual, professional — requires a highly developed sense of self-direction and independent responsibility, it may be that still another shift is occurring: that the politically most significant constraints on communication are now the ones impeding the acquisition of a historical sense, a sense of political efficacy, and consequently produces an erosion of optimism of the public will. The predictable consequence of such blockages is not ignorance or moral subordination but cynicism, resignation, political withdrawal, and the eclipse of civic virtue. (As forms of domination shift to higher levels, incidentally, there is no reason to suppose they will not continue to function, to some extent at least, at the lower levels as well.)[21]

Now the kinds of resources that make it possible to become informed and thus politically competent vary considerably, as do the techniques for restricting access to such resources and hence for diminishing the political competence of those who are so excluded. A satisfactory account of ideological forms of domination thus depends on a careful and historically nuanced account of the use of both tools of access such as literacy, physical mobility, information decoding and processing skills, "free" time, opportunities to assemble and converse, physical means of transmission — pen and paper, mail service, phone, radio, computer hookup, or whatever — and also of tools of exclusion such as secrecy, censorship, myth, propaganda, intimidation, as well as *any* deprivation, especially selective deprivation, of tools of access. In relation to the history of popular government and democracy, one resource, the printed text, has played a particularly critical role and therefore merits special attention.

POLITICS AND PRINT

The beginnings of the formation of national states in Europe coincided with the explosive proliferation of books, pamphlets, and broadsides that followed the invention of movable type in the middle of the fifteenth century. There is more than chronological coincidence to suggest that the two processes had something to do with one another. Within twenty-five years of Gutenberg's achievement, "printers were set to work turning out synodal constitutions, papal bulls, legal titles, imperial acts and especially diplomatic documents"; in Paris, "the office of royal printer was created as early as 1488." Popular literature, often single sheets, flooded Europe with "news" of matters great and small: invasions, discoveries, battles, natural disasters, ceremonious occasions, and a wide assortment of horrors that ranged from Turks to anabaptists.[22] Over the sixteenth century, the emerging systems of state absolutism made increasingly extensive and adept use of this new resource: to transmit directives, to standardize and therefore integrate administration, to mobilize support and subvert opposition — a practice that quickly secularized the original meaning of *propaganda fidei*.

In France, the regency of Louis XIII saw the last meeting of the Estates General before 1789; it also saw the founding of the first royally sponsored newspaper in Europe. The replacement of the volatile assembly by the controlled weekly *Gazette* is a concurrence symptomatic of the importance Cardinal Richelieu attached to print in his state-building objectives.[23]

But important as such use of the printed word was, and neglected as it has generally been in accounts of European political development, it is in this perspective little different from a wide variety of other facilitating technological innovations that, even if they were not always such sharp and dramatic breakthroughs, may have been equally important as resources for the new state-making processes: e.g., gunpowder, ocean navigation, double-entry bookkeeping, and the mechanical clock.

What was special about the resource of printing was the extraordinary nature of its consequences not just for those who used it but for those on whom it was used. The persons addressed by the medium of the printed text in the sixteenth century were, in an important sense, constituted as a public; they were transformed, in a way that is fascinatingly confused by the etymology of the word, from political *subjects* (in the sense of "a person under the domination of a lord or sovereign" or even "matter worked on") into political *subjects* (in the sense of "the active mind or the thinking agent").[24] For when matters of belief, of conscience, and of expectation that were formerly private matters become public, when they are "published," then they organize social behavior in a different way; when structures of domination come to depend not on personal obligations (of fealty, of deference, of honor) but on public ones (to the law, to the state, to the terms of a contract), the seeds of democracy have been planted.[25] The reason for this seems to be twofold. First, the individual addressed by a printed text is required to be responsive in a peculiarly *active* way; he or she must be able and willing to employ complex skills to read the message, and the more developed these skills the more difficult it is to keep them from running of their own momentum beyond simply receiving the message to analyzing it, evaluating it, and criticizing it. Employed in a system of domination, the printed text threatens to turn its victim from passive object to active and *re*active subject. Second, the printed text proved to be a medium of communication that was at once very powerful and very hard to monopolize or control. In the earliest period, journeymen printers carried their equipment and their knowledge across the entire continent; permanent printing shops were established in more than 200 municipalities by 1500.[26] Alarmed by the incendiary threat of such proliferation, Francis I of France went so far as to forbid, in 1535, the printing of *any* book on penalty of hanging — an order revoked a few weeks later to allow the appointment of just twelve printers who were to be allowed to publish only "those books which are necessary and approved for the public good."[27]

This order, like others with similar intent, was never enforced; indeed, it was largely unenforceable. But publicity and the fear of publicity are a prominent part of all subsequent struggles over social domination and it is therefore not surprising that the modern history of printed texts has been so closely intertwined with that of insurrection, sedition, riots, challenges to authority, movements of reform, and revolution.[28] The contribution of the print medium to the constituting of a politically active public is a topic richly deserving of careful investigation by the student of ideology; it has, to my knowledge at least, been almost entirely neglected. Elizabeth L. Eisenstein's fascinating recent survey is devoted chiefly to the impact of print on Renaissance culture, the Reformation, and the rise of modern science, but her many suggestive marginal comments on politics and her broad inventory of characteristic features and consequences of print communications make it possible to sketch a rudimentary picture of what may be involved.[29] Let me comment briefly on some implications of each of the six features she attributes to the advent of print technology.

1. *Wide Dissemination.*   The power of the press to put a copy of the same text into a very large number of widely dispersed hands at the same time is probably its most obvious advantage, and the implications of this capacity for facilitating the operation of the enormous and complex machinery of modern politics almost equally so. But what may be even more important, as Eisenstein points out, are the implications of this from the side of the reader; that is, the multiplicative powers of the press means not only that one text can have many readers, but also that *one reader can have many texts.* Previously scattered and hence isolated texts can now be brought together — within the reach, perhaps even within the personal library, of a single reader. As a result, scholarship takes on a quite different character: from the activity of authenticating and glossing a single, venerated, and sacrosanct text to that of comparing, cross-referencing, combining, and selecting among many different texts (an activity that also establishes the need to determine what shall count as appropriate "evidence" when the texts disagree). The second activity requires very different habits of mind from the first, for the reader assumes the active role of a textual resource rather than the relatively passive one of recipient and guardian of a textual "Authority." Criticism and reconstruction are built into the new activity just as they are excluded or at least discouraged in the old. The result of this shift for European scholarship was extraordinary: a vast expansion in the breadth of knowledge that a single individual could acquire, a burst of creativity as old but previously isolated ideas could now be brought into contact with one another within the same mind, a general broadening of cross-cultural contact and intellectual interaction, and an increasing independence of disciples (who could now inform themselves "on their own") from masters. It is unlikely that the habits of mind thus engendered were without political consequences as well. Indeed, the expanding practical use of printed texts seems to have favored basic shifts in attitude toward authority that went well beyond the bounds of the scholar's study: "In general," writes Donald R. Kelley, "it was in the context of particular crises that authority was subjected to questioning, and never so massively and so publicly as in the sixteenth century."[30]

2. *Standardization.*   However numerous and widely dispersed they may be, the readers of a printed text share an identical object: a common message.[31] Eisenstein calls attention to some of the many implications of this state of affairs: the broadening of opportunity for collaborative work, the fixing of conventions of style and "image," and the formation of a trans-local sense of common identity. And one of the consequences of establishing "standards," she points out, is that new opportunities are opened for the awareness and assertion of individuality. "Sixteenth-century publications not only spread identical fashions but also encouraged the collection of diverse ones....In this regard one might consider the emergence of a new sense of individualism as a by-product of the new forms of standardization. The more standardized the type, indeed, the more compelling the sense of an idiosyncratic personal self."[32]

3. *Reorganization.* The physical layout of the printed book occasioned a new concern for problems of organizing information: ordering, indexing, cataloging, codifying, systematizing, and rationalizing. The application of such principles and attendant skills to public life had far-reaching effects: rationalization of the legal system, administrative reorganization, and new methods of controlling, supplying, and deploying vast standing armies. But they were also significant in their effects on the information processing skills and attitudes of individual readers: "Increasing familiarity with regularly numbered pages, punctuation marks, section breaks, running heads, indices, and so forth, helped to reorder the thought of *all* readers, whatever their profession or craft. Hence countless activities were subjected to a new 'esprit de système.' "[33]

4. *Data Collection.* Closely related was the effect on attitudes toward data. The printing press seems to have spurred a rapid and expansive accumulation of data, especially in the process of enlarging, refining, and emending works of reference. Of course much of the material collected in, for example, early encyclopedias and atlases served only to disseminate misinformation more widely. Yet because the process was visible and public (unlike the more irregular and hence camouflaged error of scribal texts), it pointed to the methods of revision, criticism, and feedback by which data resources could be strengthened. The very notion of such works of reference would seem to rest on an essentially democratic assumption: viz, that information about the nature of the world is, in principle, publicly accessible — not something that is only revealed by hermetic processes and exclusively to privileged initiates.

5. *Preservation.* By "fixing" the past (against the losses to drifting texts and vanishing manuscripts characteristic of scribal culture), the printing press extended communication across time, as well as across space and social position. It thus expanded the possibilities for cumulative, i.e., self-correcting and self-directing, knowledge. Eisenstein suggests that the use of this resource contributed to the growth of nationalistic sentiment and to the process of dynastic consolidation.[34] But it also encouraged the habit of contesting the authority claimed on behalf of tradition, as rival groups (aristocracy and monarch, yeomen and noblemen, rural cottagers and commercial landholders) learned to scour the historical record for precedents that would ground their interests in "right."

6. *Amplification and Reinforcement.* Repetition reinforces and amplifies any message; the pattern generated by selective repetition — conventions, stereotypes, habits of perception and expression, fads and fashions — all become more complex and potentially more powerful as the theater of discourse shifts from the parochial stage of interpersonal oral or written communication to the public and far more expansive stage of print. The history of print culture shows that such change leads to two very different results: the reinforcement and intensification of hostility,

prejudice, and group rivalry; and the crossing of such divisions to establish a stronger sense of shared humanity.

Paradoxically enough, the same presses which fanned the flames of religious controversy also created a new vested interest in ecumenical concord and toleration; the same wholesale industry which fixed religious, dynastic, and linguistic frontiers more permanently also operated most profitably by tapping cosmopolitan markets.[35]

But if there is a paradox here, it is a comprehensible one; when the communicative conventions that tie human beings to one another are established in print rather than in spoken or written discourse, the circle of identification expands — from family, village, or workshop to nation, the faithful, race, or class.[36] Insofar as such a circle is strengthened, short of the "circle of humanity," conflicts are also intensified. The consequences of print culture seem to have included both the sharper drawing of lines and a continuous pressure to break them, a state of affairs that has colored the whole of modern politics.

The overall implication of these features of printed communication is favorable to democratizing trends: the printed text is egalitarian in the double sense that it is the same for one and all and, even more important, it implies agency, the development and exercise of competence, on the part of *both* sender and recipient of its message. But only a most vulgar technological determinism could reason: if printing press, then democracy (and the historical evidence would immediately disconfirm such an inference). Print culture is a *resource*; even if its structural characteristics ultimately have emancipatory implications, it can be employed very effectively in the service of domination as long as other conditions are maintained — such as restricting access, regulating content, and obstructing or distorting transmission. Although such controls have been exercised in all sorts of ways ranging from the crude (such as the burning of books or even of booksellers) to the ingenious (such as licensing acts, stamp taxes, copyright privileges, or less formal devices for intimidating or discrediting a source), the most effective device has been the simple expedient of excluding people from print culture altogether, or at least of severely restricting their capacity to participate in it. The political significance of literacy has long been appreciated: during the English Civil War the Leveller Richard Overton included in his list of grievances the demand that "Free-Schooles" be "founded, erected, and indowed at the publique charges" throughout England and Wales so "that few or none of the free men of England may for the future be ignorant of reading or writing."[37] At about the same time, the royalist James Howell complained that "people of all sorts though never so mean and mechanical" still pursued literacy, and he opined: "It were to be wished that there reigned not among the people of this land such a general itching after book learning."[38]

Although the history of literacy is shrouded in the mists of very weak and conjectural evidence, at least before the middle of the seventeenth century, certain basic facts stand out clearly. First, the process of general acquisition of the skills of reading and writing begins essentially with the advent of printing (at which time fewer than one person in ten is literate) and extends at least to the nineteenth century (when, in economically advanced areas, the proportion seems to have been reversed).[39] Second, at almost any point between these periods (i.e., between universal illiteracy and universal literacy), the ability to read and write is distributed, with the exception of certain groups for whom it is an occupationally required skill such as members of the clergy, lawyers, or schoolmasters, in almost perfect accordance with social power: gentlemen are more literate than commoners, tradesmen more literate than laborers, men more literate than women, town dwellers more literate than country people.[40] A third point, that — although in some measure already suggested by the first two — is often neglected by those who credit the level of literacy to "natural" differences of cognitive ability and motivation, is that the acquisition of this resource is both a consequence and a cause of the effective exercise of political power. Ruling elites were not always literate. "All learned men are paupers," rants an English gentleman to Cardinal Wolsey's secretary Richard Pace at the beginning of the sixteenth century:

"By God's body, I would rather have my son hanged than he should be studious. Gentlemen's sons should be able to sound the hunting horn, hunt cunningly, neatly train, and use a hawk. The study of literature should be left to the sons of peasants." Pace is provoked into a sharp reply: "when the King needs someone to reply to a foreign ambassador, he will turn not to the horn-blowing gentleman but to the educated rustic."[41]

The gradual reduction of illiteracy over the succeeding century (illustrated in Figure 1) reflects in part the persuasiveness of Pace's argument. Literary skills were an essential part of the political arsenal by which the progressive nobility of England thwarted the absolutizing ambitions of the crown; the English gentry was overwhelmingly literate, with the partial exception of residents of the northeast, by the end of Elizabeth's reign.[42] Illiteracy falls even more sharply in the century following the Civil War, levels off slightly during the industrial revolution, then drops again sharply toward zero after the middle of the nineteenth century. Although it would

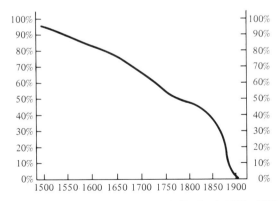

Figure 1. Estimated adult illiteracy in England, 1500–1900.

be a mistake to read too much into these slopes, they are at least consistent with what we might expect if the growth of literary competence were connected to the development of popular government and the successive political assertions of nobility against crown, commercial interests against more traditionist sectors of the aristocracy, and finally labor against owners of capital.

The final point is an important qualification of the preceding one. The historians' discussion of the expansion of literacy might suggest there is an identifiable threshold of competence after which one has "acquired" literacy in much the same sense that one might acquire resources such as property or weapons. This is, of course, not the case and it is a circumstance that, beyond any difficulties of lack of evidence, bedevils the efforts of researchers to construct graphs of the sort offered here. The most recent contribution to this discussion, from which I have drawn my figures, "regards the signatures and marks that men and women made on various documents as the best evidence of literate skills."[43] But it is far from clear that the ability to write one's name can be taken as a reliable indicator of the ability to read or to write more than that name. Moreover, what we mean by "ability to read" is itself open-ended: the sort of competence we have been discussing, capable of informing effective political action, involves considerably more than the capacity to decode a simple and direct printed message. Hence, even much more precise measures than historians usually have at their disposal (e.g., literacy tests) might fail to indicate either the extent to which text-handling skills had been developed or the extent to which they were actually used on a regular basis — two things that, for obvious reasons, tend to go together. We should expect, therefore, that the effective distribution of resources for political competence, insofar as these involve the capacity to use the printed word effectively, will tend to lag behind the chronology indicated by a graph such as this.

"KEEP THE NEWS STRAIGHT, SHORT, UNDERSTANDABLE"

Has the era of "print culture" come to an end? Certainly the shift to a "post-literate" electronic culture has been proclaimed frequently over the last two decades. But in relation to the questions that have concerned us here, this is probably a misleading claim. If the idea of a "print culture" requires that such texts play a central role for the population as a whole and that the capacity for competent and effective use of them is universally distributed, then it cannot be defunct for it has never existed. This is not to deny that significant changes are taking place. The cause for concern, however, is not that the television screen has made the printed text obsolescent but that new modes of information dissemination may have slowed, ended, or even reversed the process of gradual expansion and development of text-using skills — a process that, I have been arguing, had fundamentally democratic implications. The most important medium for the acquisition of political information by a large majority of the public defines its objectives as being (in words attributed to John Chancellor in an advertisement for NBC Nightly News) to "keep the news straight, short, understandable."[44] We must consider whether such an objective has significant ideological implications.

It is instructive, I think, to consider some of the general features of messages that are conveyed by means of different channels of communication. The most important resources for political information can be arranged across a spectrum that has television (the electronic medium par excellence) at one end, books and periodicals at the other. In between we can place a variety of other important resources that exhibit qualities partially reflective of both. Radio is, like television, an electronic medium but it gives far greater salience to the (spoken rather than written) text; newspapers are fully a print medium, but the information services they provide are chiefly competitive with (and to some extent imitative of) television and radio; news weeklies such as *Time* and *Newsweek* are closer in function and structure to newspapers than to resources (which I am here denoting as "periodicals" — e.g., *The New Yorker, Harper's*) that, while addressing public affairs, are not concerned with the comprehensive presentation of fresh facts.[45] An arrangement of this kind is rather impressionistic and certainly imprecise, but it allows one to frame some general hypotheses about the significance of shifts in the predominant forms of information dissemination. The nature of such shifts can be clarified by considering some contrasting attributes of messages at the two ends of the spectrum, summarized in Figure 2.

The first point of contrast concerns the extent to which the material means required to transmit messages are located in a few large or in many smaller enterprises. Obviously the days of the itinerant printer are long past, and those of the traditional independent publishing house seem to be fading rapidly today.[46] But as we move leftward across the spectrum we find that the obstacles to dispersion tend to become more severe and the likelihood of oligopolistic concentration correspondingly greater (although radio is probably out of place on this criterion).[47] The second group of four contrasts concerns what might be called the "temporal form" of the message. First, there is a difference in its permanence. The book is relatively durable; it invites repeated consultation and reconsideration. (It has been remarked that, with

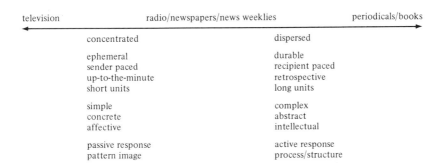

Figure 2. Information resources.

respect to books, the verb "to read" has no past tense.) The television message, in contrast, exists only in the moment: it is sent, it is received, it is finished. It would be a mistake to suppose that the proliferation of videotape recorders will alter this situation — first, because it is unlikely that any but communications scholars and network executives would have any interest in taping news programs, and second, because a collection of taped messages, even if they are available, cannot usefully be consulted or even scanned without an intervening printed transcript. The second temporal contrast is partially connected to this. The electronic media (television and radio) deliver a message within a time structure that is, of necessity, controlled by its sender. One cannot, on receiving a telecast or broadcast, exercise any control over this space: one cannot slow it down, or stop it to think it over, or skim forward, or check back to compare it to what was said a few moments ago. For the same reason, cross-message comparison is made very difficult. Even with a newspaper, it is unlikely that one will be able to juxtapose today's message with that of last week, or last year, in the way that a bookshelf tends to facilitate. If we do not notice this or find it troublesome, it is largely because (to move to the third temporal contrast) our interest, especially on the left side of the spectrum, is focused on the present, on *now*. This has always, of course, been the chief appeal of the "news." But to the extent that "being informed" is increasingly identified with knowing "news," and to the extent furthermore that the technology of transmission reduces the range of *new* from years to months, to days, to seconds, there is a danger of severely impoverishing the concept of information itself. Media toward the right of the spectrum, because they cannot compete on the grounds of currency,[48] are oriented to a different kind of message: one that is retrospective and therefore more inclined to be reflective, interpretive, comparative, evaluative, and analytic. A final temporal contrast concerns the duration or length of the message itself. For reasons that ultimately help to explain television's effectiveness in capturing and holding attention, its demands on a viewer's *span* of attention are typically very low; no message lasts very long. The visual part of the message typically consists of a series of images, each of which lasts but a few seconds — the constant movement and jump-cutting of most advertisements illustrates this technique at its most frenetic. The elements that make up a typical news story are very short: rarely is there more than a "quoted" sentence from the subject of the story; often there is only a fragment of a sentence.[49] The story itself is delivered in a temporal space of some ninety seconds, on the average. A newspaper story is usually longer, but it is presented in the classic top-heavy format designed to allow the reader to break off at any spot without losing the point or missing the most "important" content. Only in the relatively expansive forms at the right of the spectrum is it usually possible to present a message that can incorporate internal qualification and development or offer elaborate supporting evidence, and therefore it tends to be only in such media that *argument*, in the full sense of the word, can be presented.

These features of temporal form entail a number of consequences for characteristics of *content* typical of each medium. There is, first of all, a tendency for the internal structure of the message to become more simplified as we move from books to television.[50] Although there are a number of reasons for this, it suffices to point to the obviously constricting effects of brevity for the development of a complex or nuanced position. There is, second, a tendency to become increasingly concrete and specific. This is particularly the case with television, and follows directly from the need to tie a message to an image: crime becomes a mugger being led away by the police, presidential power becomes Ronald Reagan speaking to a group of congressional leaders, inflation becomes the complaints of shoppers "interviewed" at the supermarket. There is, third, a tendency (again deriving from the greater sensuous immediacy and specificity of such images) for the message to appeal to affect more than to intellect: we feel afraid of the mugger, charmed by the President, annoyed at the plight of shoppers who are, after all, "just like us." Now it is important to emphasize there is nothing inherently wrong with being simple, concrete, or affective; indeed, resources that are devoid of such qualities (a certain sort of social science could serve as an example) must also be judged defective as a means of comprehending the world — of being informed. The danger is that, as we move toward the left of the spectrum, we lose the special capacity of the printed word to handle complex ideas, as well as simple and direct ones, abstract thought, as well as vivid examples, intellectual processing of information, as well as emotional response to it.

The final two points of contrast refer to the *effects* of communication, and in major part are simply derivative from those already mentioned. First, the person addressed by a message that is short, simple, sensuously immediate, isolated, and predominantly emotional may not be stupefied, but he or she is certainly rendered relatively passive. Little or no effort is required to receive the message, few skills are developed in the course of receiving it, no opportunity is provided nor incentive given to work actively on it — to interpret, to compare, to generalize, and to criticize. Second, the conception of the world that is fostered by such messages tends to take what might be called a "pattern image" form: the citizen is offered, each day, a series of discrete images — juxtaposed, but not really connected to one another (as in the layout of a newspaper front page). The sum of those images is a picture of the world: "that's the way it is today." But this picture dissolves, to be replaced tomorrow with another pattern. The connection between today's picture and yesterday's is very difficult to draw, for yesterday's picture is already hard to recall. And so we move forward in time, always gazing at the patchwork of "the world tonight" in the increasingly forlorn hope that it will fall into place and make sense. A marvelous passage from Susan Sontag's *On Photography* is pertinent also to television, and indeed to the tendencies exhibited generally by the information resources toward the left of my spectrum.

A new sense of the notion of information has been constructed around the photographic image. . . . Photography reinforces a nominalist view of social reality as consisting of small units of an apparently infinite number — as the number of photographs that could be taken of anything is unlimited. Through photographs, the world becomes a series of unrelated, freestanding particles; and history, past and present, a set of anecdotes and *faits divers*. The camera makes reality atomic, manageable, and opaque. It is a view of the world which denies interconnectedness, continuity, but which confers on each moment the character of a mystery. . . .

Photography implies that we know about the world if we accept it as the camera records it. But this is the opposite of understanding, which starts from *not* accepting the world as it looks. All possibility of understanding is rooted in the ability to say no.[51]

To the extent that we are informed in such a way as impedes the ability to say no (indeed, to say much of anything) and occludes comprehension of either historical continuity or structural interconnectedness, our political competence is enfeebled and democracy is undermined. If the picture I have sketched has any validity, the possible ideological significance of changing technologies of information dissemination is considerable. Insofar as trends are apparent, they certainly seem to favor an effect of this kind. Media popularity corresponds fairly closely to the order of my spectrum. Most surveys indicate that television passed newspapers as the most popular source of information about the world and also as the most *trusted* source of such information sometime in the early sixties, and has remained decisively on top ever since.[52] Newspapers generally follow in appeal, although an event such as the Washington Post–Pulitzer Prize scandal of 1981 can displace them in public esteem, at least momentarily.[53] Periodicals and books are not, of course, often thought of as sources of ''news'' but we can infer their lesser popularity as sources of information of *any* kind from data about circulation and book-reading habits.[54] Perhaps even more significant than evidence of comparative popularity is the nature of shifts in the character of the print medium itself. Over the last twenty years, to put it simply, books have come to look more and more like television. The volumes that account for the vast majority of sales are precisely the ones whose subject matter, style, format, layout, and intended use correspond *the least* to those qualities I have associated with the printed text as an information resource.

If the above sketch is plausible, it explains the possibility of a society that invests enormous amounts of time and money in ''being informed,'' in which the production and marketing of ''news'' is a vast and extremely profitable enterprise, in which today's newspaper is still ''the modern man's morning-prayer,'' while the nightly television news has become his evening prayer, but in which popular political competence and the general quality of public political understanding still seem to be extraordinarily low. It helps to make more intelligible certain increasingly salient features of the polity — the extraordinary volatility of public opinion, its frequent incoherence, the pervasiveness of expressions of cynicism and impotence among members of the electorate. But can we consider a condition that seems to engender general political debilitation to be a form of ideological domination? Who, in such a situation, can be said to be dominating whom? How, if at all, do class interests come into this picture? Why should we suppose that *democracy* is in any way impaired?

It is probably true that the effect of changes in the technology of information dissemination have been socially pervasive, obstructing the development of political competence on the part of elites, as well as subordinate members of the hierarchy.

(Comparing the transcript of a nineteenth-century legislative debate with contemporary versions of the same thing certainly strengthens such a suspicion.) Nor is it clear or even likely that the common person is, on the average, any less politically competent or well informed than his or her nineteenth-century forebears. In this sense, the capacity to make intelligent political judgments may well be more equitably distributed today than it was in the predemocratic polity, in the sense that the *gap* between the information competence of elites and non-elites may have narrowed. This does not mean, however, that the gap has disappeared or even become small. The resources of political communication, most particularly the capacity to handle texts effectively, continue to be distributed in a fashion that greatly favors persons of property and privilege. Familiarity with, regular use of, and competence with respect to the media at the right side of my spectrum tends to rise in direct proportion to socioeconomic status, and the reasons for this (schooling, stimulus and motivation, leisure time) are not far to seek. To the extent that such maldistribution persists, in particular, insofar as substantial portions of the population are effectively excluded from the use of information resources essential to effective political thinking and action, ideological forms of class domination can be said to exist.

But even if such resources, or such incompetence, were distributed with perfect equality across all socioeconomic classes, a general shift of the sort we have been discussing (i.e., in the direction of diminished political competence) would be favorable to class rule. This is because insofar as constraints on information have a competence-reducing effect on everyone, they tend to make the political realm as such ineffective. But this cannot be counted a neutral result in relation to class interest. For it implies that the exercise of social power, the determination of social decisions, will take place not in the political sphere at all but outside of it in what Marx, following Hegel and the eighteenth-century Scottish moral philosophers, called the sphere of *civil society*. As the democratic state comes into increasing disrepute, effective power moves to "private" institutions that make no pretense of deference to democratic principles: to corporate firms, financial directorates, the commands of the marketplace. Because ruling principles in this sphere correspond not to "one person, one vote" but to "one share, one vote," the effect of such a shift is to assure that property owners such as the heirs of Robert Lowe will indeed continue to be "masters of the situation."

Such considerations pose fundamental questions about the future of liberal democratic institutions. Widely dispersed political competence seems to be a necessary condition for popular rule; on this point, classical democratic ideas exhibit greater realism and empirical acumen than do the assumptions of their pluralist critics. In the absence of the information resources and communicative competence requisite to its exercise, rule of the *demos* is drained of any substance. From the sixteenth to the twentieth century, developing means of information dissemination seem to have favored the expansion of political participation; as the twentieth century closes, however, there is reason to fear that they may serve increasingly to impede or to discourage such participation. Should such a trend prevail, it would threaten the legitimacy not merely of the liberal state, but of the political sphere as such. (It is essential that the democratic left not lose sight of this possibility. The "legitimacy crisis" of the liberal state does not necessarily lead us to socialism; it is just as likely, perhaps more likely, to lead to new forms of state repression or to devolve into nondemocratic forms of power outside of the state altogether.) To the extent that the loss of political competence makes the liberal state increasingly unresponsive, unwieldy, or "out of control" from the perspective of popular interests, the opportunities for nondemocratic solutions to issues of public power are enlarged. In his Inaugural Address, President Reagan remarked that "government is not the solution to our problem; government is the problem." But coming from one who professes the belief that the government in question is a democracy, this statement can be translated into another that would be a more forthright expression of the interests of a property-owning ruling class: "Democracy is not the solution to our problem; democracy is the problem." Perhaps, after all, the debate between Lowe and Mill is still not settled.

References

1. *Hansard's Parliamentary Debates*, 3rd series, 182 (1866), pp. 149–50.
2. The Russell-Gladstone Bill of 1866 would have enfranchised only about 400,000 men, roughly half of them working class; voting roles in England and Wales would have risen from 20 percent to 25 percent of all adult males.
3. *Hansard's*, 3rd series, 182 (1866), pp. 1256–57. With respect to *universal* suffrage, Mill was of course equally worried about rule on behalf of the class interests of manual laborers: see *Considerations on Representative Government* (Bobbs-Merrill, 1958), pp. 92–101.
4. Sidney Verba, Norman H. Nie, and Jae-on Kim, *Participation and Political Equality: A Seven-Nation Comparison* (Cambridge University Press, 1978), p. 3.
5. Figures are for 1974/75; see A. H. Halsey, *Change in British Society* (Oxford University Press, 1978), pp. 30, 33.
6. "Whatever we learnt at Oxford, we learnt that democracy was a form of Government in which the poor, being many, governed the whole country, including the rich, who were few, and for the benefit of the poor," Lowe remarked during the 1866 debate; *Hansard's*, 3rd series, 182 (1866), p. 2095.
7. *Democratic Political Theory* (Princeton University Press, 1979), pp. 155, 227, 243–44, 439. I have probably missed some others, but certainly the problem of being informed must be counted one of the book's lesser concerns.
8. The argument initiated by Schumpeter and Berelson has been on the defensive for some time now. But those who have endeavored to revivify a more activist conception of democracy have thus far not shown much more than marginal interest in the problem of securing the conditions for political competence; it is, for example, of little relevance to the small-unit, shared-interest situations explored by Jane J. Mansbridge, *Beyond Adversary Democracy* (Basic Books, 1980). The problem of information dissemination is given prominence by Michael Margolis, *Viable Democracy* (Penguin Books, 1979), pp. 158–70, but in a fashion concerned almost exclusively with questions of technological hardware.
9. Mill, *Representative Government*, p. 86.
10. This fundamental democratic claim must be taken to include the possibility of deciding that one's interest is best served by deferring to the expertise of others; see Robert A. Dahl's formulation in *After the Revolution?* (Yale University Press, 1970), p. 35.

11. See the very elegant overview of Philip E. Converse, "Public Opinion and Voting Behavior," in Fred I. Greenstein and Nelson W. Polsby, eds., *Handbook of Political Science,* vol. 4: *Nongovernmental Politics* (Addison-Wesley, 1975), pp. 75–169; also Norman H. Nie, Sidney Verba, and John R. Petrocik, *The Changing American Voter,* enl. ed. (Harvard University Press, 1979), esp. ch. 20. (On the latter, see the important corrections included in the "Communication" cited below, n. 14.)

12. Certain kinds of extraordinary misunderstanding can be taken as convincing evidence that the resources for judgment are absent: for example (we all have a favorite example), I was told, while canvassing door-to-door in the early sixties, that American boys were being attacked by red gorillas in Asia — an impression that, one can safely assume, precluded effective judgment about U.S. foreign policy at the time. On the other hand, the *absence* of such misunderstanding cannot establish that the resources for effective political judgment are *present*.

13. See especially Philip E. Converse, "The Nature of Belief Systems in Mass Publics," in David Apter, ed., *Ideology and Discontent* (Free Press, 1964), pp. 206–61, and Angus Campbell, Philip E. Converse, Warren E. Miller, and Donald E. Stokes, *The American Voter* (John Wiley, 1960).

14. On these measures, see the critical observations of Robert E. Lane, "Patterns of Political Beliefs," in Jeanne N. Knutson, ed., *Handbook of Political Psychology* (Jossey-Bass, 1973), esp. pp. 98–105, and Eric R. A. N. Smith, "The Levels of Conceptualization: False Measure of Ideological Sophistication," *American Political Science Review* 74 (1980), pp. 685–96; see also the "Communication" in the same journal, 75 (1981), pp. 146–54.

15. These dimensions are not, of course, independent of one another, but they do involve different sorts of information problems and hence different opportunities for ideological distortion. Cf. Therborn, pp. 18–20, 93–100 for a different use of a somewhat similar schema.

16. Lawrence Kohlberg's account of the stages of moral development sheds light on the nature of this process: see *The Philosophy of Moral Development: Moral Stages and the Idea of Justice* (Harper & Row, 1981); the stages are summarized on pp. 409–12.

17. We scarcely need to be reminded of errors of judgment in the latter direction, for utopian fantasy has been the ruin of any number of prominent political projects; it is important, however, not to ignore the opposite sort of error, of which the following passage from Joseph de Maistre's 1796 *Considerations on France* provides an instructive and amusing example: "The particular institutions of English America inspire no confidence in me. For example, the towns, inspired by a rather unworthy jealousy, were not able to agree on a place where the Congress should sit; none of them was willing to surrender this honor to another. Consequently, it has been decided to build a new town as the seat of government. The site was chosen on the banks of a great river; it was decided that the town should be called *Washington*; the situation of all the public buildings was marked out; the work has been set in hand and the plan of the capital city is already circulating throughout Europe. In essentials, there is nothing in this beyond human powers; a town can very easily be built; nevertheless, there is too much deliberation, too much of mankind in all this, and it is a thousand to one that the town will not be built, or that it will not be called *Washington*, or that Congress will not sit there." *The Works of Joseph de Maistre* (Macmillan, 1965), pp. 84–85.

18. The notion of tendency is central, of course, to the Marxian emancipatory project; for an exemplary discussion of what this does and does not entail, see Alan Wood, *Karl Marx* (Routledge & Kegan Paul, 1981), esp. pp. 104–8.

19. *The Poverty of Historicism* (Routledge & Kegan Paul, 1961).

20. This has nothing to do with cognitive incapacity or with nonsense about "the idiocy of rural life." Cf. E. P. Thompson's wise observation: "It may perhaps be argued that experience is a very low level of mentation indeed: that it can produce no more than the grossest 'common sense.' . . . I don't think that this is so; on the contrary, I consider that the supposition that this is so is a very characteristic delusion of intellectuals, who suppose that ordinary mortals are stupid. In my own view, the truth is more nuanced: experience is valid and effective but within determined limits: the farmer 'knows' his seasons, the sailor 'knows' his seas, but both may remain mystified about kingship and cosmology." *The Poverty of Theory and Other Essays* (Monthly Review Press, 1979), p. 7.

21. The historical sketch in this paragraph is obviously speculative in the extreme; it is intended mainly to be suggestive of the sort of processes that a theory of ideological domination must investigate.

22. Donald R. Kelley, *The Beginning of Ideology: Consciousness and Society in the French Reformation* (Cambridge University Press, 1981), pp. 224–26.

23. Joseph Klaits, cited in Elizabeth L. Eisenstein, *The Printing Press as an Agent of Change: Communications and Cultural Transformations in Early-Modern Europe*, one vol. ed. (Cambridge University Press, 1980), p. 135.

24. Cf. Raymond Williams, *Keywords: A Vocabulary of Culture and Society* (Fontana, 1976), pp. 260–61.

25. Neither the public nor democracy were created by print culture, of course, but their incarnation in the context of oral-script culture was confined to a relatively intimate context: the classical city-state. If oral-script culture suffices to enable direct democracy, print culture would seem to be requisite to representative democracy.

26. See the map in Lucien Febvre and Henri-Jean Martin, *The Coming of the Book: The Impact of Printing 1450–1800* (NLB, 1976), pp. 184–85.

27. Ibid., p. 310. Cf. Kelley, *Beginning of Ideology*, pp. 18, 238.

28. "In 1789, did not the fall of the Bastille signify something of particular importance to men of letters in comparison with all other social groups? Over eight hundred authors, printers, booksellers, and print dealers had been incarcerated there between 1600 and 1756. Its image as a dreadful symbol of royal tyranny had been built up by publicists who had been 'embastillé' " Eisenstein, *Printing Press*, p. 147.

29. In her Preface, Eisenstein promises a further volume on problems pertaining to political movements.

30. Kelley, *Beginning of Ideology*, p. 326.

31. Of course compositor's error and worn or damaged type, both of which were very extensive in early printed works, make the word "identical" an idealization; nonetheless, as Eisenstein points out (pp. 80–81, 108–9), it is an idealization brought significantly closer to realization once printed texts replaced hand-copied manuscripts because errors could now be located and emended on a systematic rather than an ad hoc basis.

32. Ibid., p. 84, cf. p. 132.

33. Ibid., pp. 105–6.

34. Ibid., pp. 117–18.

35. Ibid., p. 139; cf. pp. 445–47.

36. For a discussion of the ethical implications of this process, see Peter Singer, *The Expanding Circle: Ethics and Sociobiology* (Farrar, Straus & Giroux, 1981), esp. pp. 111–24.

37. "Certaine Articles for the good of the Common wealth, presented to the consideration of his Excellencie, Sir *Thomas Fairfax*, and to the Officers and Souldiers under his Command," in Don M. Wolfe, ed., *Leveller Manifestoes of the Puritan Revolution* (Thomas Nelson, 1944), p. 194.

38. Quoted in David Cressy, *Literacy and the Social Order: Reading and Writing in Tudor and Stuart England* (Cambridge University Press, 1980), p. 45.

39. There are, of course, anomalous cases. In relatively undeveloped Sweden, literacy was close to 100 percent in the middle of the eighteenth century. *Ibid.*, p. 178.

40. For England, see *ibid.*, pp. 118–41.

41. Quoted in Eisenstein, p. 396. Such attitudes were even more widespread among the French nobility, whose "boorishness was notorious, giving rise to the frequent charge that they had disqualified themselves [from royal appointment of public office] by illiteracy, backwardness, and general incompetence." Davis Bitton, *The French Nobility in Crisis, 1560–1640* (Stanford University Press, 1969), p. 47.

42. Cressy, *Literacy and Social Order*, pp. 123, 142–45.

43. Ibid., p. 42.

44. It appeared in *The New York Times*, 12 May 1981.

45. There are, of course, many other means by which we become informed about the world but they are marginal in relative importance or are largely derivative from the resources mentioned (e.g., personal conversations), or else they predominantly serve different interests in information; thus,

in addition to an interest in *political competence*, we might identify interests in *entertainment* (for which it would be necessary to extend the spectrum to the left and include resources such as human interest and consumer magazines, theatrical film, popular music) and also *scholarly/commercial* interests (for which we might extend the spectrum to the right to include technical monographs, documents, data sources, computer hookups). There is, of course, considerable overlap among these "interests in information" and some media, for instance *The New York Times*, clearly endeavor to serve all three.

46. See Thomas Whiteside, *The Blockbuster Complex: Conglomerates, Show Business, and Book Publishing* (Wesleyan University Press, 1981). Most of this very interesting survey of recent trends appeared in *The New Yorker* (29 September, 6 October, 13 October, 1980).

47. A very convenient compilation of data on this subject is Benjamin M. Compaine, ed., *Who Owns the Media? Concentration of Ownership in the Mass Communications Industry* (Harmony Books, 1979).

48. Even this is decreasingly true. I recall a memorial biography of John Lennon appearing in bookstores within days of his death.

49. The implications of this point are particularly well developed by William Gibson, "Network News: Elements of a Theory," *Social Text* 3 (Fall 1980), pp. 88–111.

50. This claim will be disputed by those who think that I improperly reduce "complexity" to "verbal complexity" and who are impressed with the capacity of television to develop complex visual and visual-aural structures of meaning. Clearly this is not the place to pursue such an argument (I think, in any case, that it is far less persuasive applied to television than to theatrical film). But my position, in any case, is concerned solely with complexity of *thought*, and to the extent that television is not implicitly tied to a text, I would argue that it is equally liable to Mary McCarthy's claim about film, viz., that it "cannot be an idea-spreader; its images are too enigmatic." *Ideas and the Novel* (Harcourt Brace Jovanovich, 1980), p. 63.

51. (Farrar, Straus & Giroux, 1977), pp. 22–23.

52. See the results of surveys by the Roper Organization for the Television Information Office, 1959–1978, presented in *Public Opinion* (August/September 1979), pp. 30–31.

53. See, for instance, the results of the poll reported in *Newsweek* (4 May 1981), p. 51, in which the news weeklies place second.

54. A "periodical" such as *Harper's* has one tenth the readership of *Time* or *Newsweek*; cf. Table 8.1 in Compaine, *Who Owns the Media?*, p. 324, which indicates that consumer spending on newspapers, magazines, and sheet music in 1976 was more than twice that spent on books and maps, while both combined amounted to only 57 percent of what was spent on audiovisual media.

CONSERVATIVE: FIRST AMENDMENT FREEDOMS

26. TECHNOLOGIES OF FREEDOM

Ithiel de Sola Pool

Once upon a time companies that published newspapers, magazines, and books did very little else; their involvement with other media was slight. They reviewed plays and movies, they utilized telephones and telegraphs, they reported on the electrical industry, but before about 1920 they had limited business ties with any of those industries. This situation is changing, and with implications adverse to freedom.

A process called the "convergence of modes" is blurring the lines between media, even between point-to-point communications such as the post, telephone, and telegraph, and mass communications such as the press, radio, and television. A single physical means — be it wires, cables or airwaves — may carry services that in the past were provided in separate ways. Conversely, a service that was provided in the past by any one medium — be it broadcasting, the press, or telephony–can now be provided in several different physical ways. So the one-to-one relationship that used to exist between a medium and its use is eroding. That is what is meant by the convergence of modes.

The telephone network, which was once used almost entirely for person-to-person conversation, now transmits data among computers, distributes printed matter via facsimile machines, and carries sports and weather bulletins on recorded messages. A news story that used to be distributed through newsprint and in no other way nowadays may also be broadcast on television or radio, put out on a telecommunication line for printing by a teletype or for display on the screen on a cathode ray tube (CRT), and placed in an electronic morgue for later retrieval.

Technology-driven convergence of modes is reinforced by the economic process of cross-ownership. The growth of conglomerates, which participate in many businesses at once, means that newspapers, magazine publishers, and book publishers increasingly own or are owned by companies that also operate in other fields. Both convergence and cross-ownership blur the boundaries which once existed between companies publishing in the print domain that is protected by the First Amendment and companies involved in businesses that are regulated by government. Today, the same company may find itself operating in both fields. The dikes that in the past held government back from exerting control on the print media are thus broken down.

The force behind the convergence of modes is an electronic revolution as profound as that of printing. For untold millennia humans, unlike any other animal, could talk. Then for four thousand years or so their uniqueness was not only that they could move air to express themselves to those immediately around them but also that they could embody speech in writing, to be preserved over time and transported over space. With Gutenberg a third era began, in which written texts could be disseminated in multiple copies. In the last stage of that era phonographs and photographs made it possible to circulate sound and pictures, as well as text, in multiple copies. Now a fourth era has been ushered in by an innovation of at least as much historical significance as the mass production of print and other media. Pulses of electromagnetic energy embody and convey messages that up to now have been sent by sound, pictures, and text. All media are becoming electronic.

The word "electronic" implies more than electrical. The dictionary tells us that electronics is the science of the behavior of electrons in gases, vacuums, and semiconductors. Long before the vacuum tube was invented, telegraph and telephone messages flowed over electrical wires, but the flow was not subject to much control. Except for noise and attenuation, the current that went in was the current that came out. From Lee de Forest's vacuum tube of 1906, through computers, to today's computers on a chip, progress in electronics has allowed manipulations such as storing, amplifying, and transforming electrical signals. In today's electronic communication, the electrical pulses are stored in computer memories as arrays of on-off switches, which are usually represented in verbal explanations as zeros or ones and called bits. Transmission from sender to receiver also flows in such digital codes. To say that all media are becoming electronic does not deny that paper and ink or film may also continue to be used and may even be sometimes physically carried. What it does mean is that in every medium — be it electrical, like the telephone and broadcasting, or historically nonelectrical, like printing — both the manipulation of symbols in computers and the transmission of those symbols electrically are being used at crucial stages in the process of production and distribution. . . .

If computers become the printing presses of the twenty-first century, will judges and legislators recognize them for what they are? At issue is the future of publishing. The law till now may have infringed the First Amendment for newer media, but for the printed word, freedom from licensing, from prior restraint, from taxation, and from regulation has remained sacrosanct. When written texts are published electronically, that may not remain true. The law on the use of print, the mails, telecommunications, and broadcasting is by now cast in a mold of precedents that is sometimes libertarian, sometimes less so. But for still newer technologies where the law is in gestation, precedents are in the process of being set, often in ways to cause alarm. Practices are now being canonized in regard to cable television, computer networks, and satellites which may someday turn out to be directly relevant to publishing. People then may ask in puzzlement where protections of the free press have gone.

Calamity is not foreordained. The trends in freedom have not been one-way. The technological trends are favorable, though the political response to them has been less so. Eternal vigilance there has not been; more often what has prevailed is unawareness that actions taken had First Amendment implications. Regulations are set for technical reasons or for the protection of established interests, and only in retrospect are they seen to impair free speech. Then in a burst of occasional vigilance a court may blow the whistle. Having previously sanctioned a path that led to abuse, judges then find a line of reasoning to distinguish the case at hand from those that led up to it. This has been the pattern so far. There is reason for concern about where it will leave freedom as the publishing of books, pamphlets, magazines, and newspapers becomes electronic.

Publishing is becoming electronic for reasons of both convenience and cost. Large, complicated arrays of bits of information can, using computer logic, be edited, stored, transmitted, and searched with a flexibility that is impossible for ink records on paper. Millions of words can be scanned in seconds and transmitted across the world in minutes. Up to now, however, this convenience was bought at a price. Electronic text handling was powerful but expensive; paper records were cheaper. That situation is reversing. It is becoming cheaper to handle words electronically than to handle them physically, to the point where the physical mode is becoming too expensive for ordinary use.

People are not going to stop reading from and writing on paper, or carrying pieces of paper in their pockets and purses. Nothing on the horizon is yet the full functional equivalent of this most useful technology. People did not stop talking when they learned to write, and they did not abandon pens when typewriters were invented. Use of paper is likewise not likely to be given up for any alternative that can be anticipated today. Cathode ray tubes (CRTs), television screens, or microfiche readers are often less comfortable to handle than printed sheets. Yet increasingly the most economical way of moving, storing, and displaying words is electronically. The use of paper is becoming a luxury.

Of four distinguishable functions in the processing of words — input, storage, output, and delivery — storage is already cheaper in computers than in filing cabinets. At the moment, the most promising storage technology is that of videodisks. An optical digital six-disk pack is anticipated to appear shortly with a total capacity of a trillion bits or over a hundred thousand books. At an estimated cost of $51,000 for this device, a book as a stored object — not including its editoral, composition, or distribution costs — would cost 40 cents. One hundred such videodisk packs, or the equivalent of the Library of Congress, would cost $5 million and fit in a medium-sized room. Other longer-term projections for different videodisk approaches arrive at cost estimates of a cent to a nickel per book. Clearly the significant costs will not be those of storing the data.

To transmit material electronically is also far cheaper than to print it and carry it by plane or truck. Compare the Hewlett-Packard Company's interplant electronic message system's cost of about a penny per hundred-word average message for domestic transmission with the cost of a first class stamp. For storage and delivery the choice is clear: computer memories and networks far outdistance paper as the most economical medium. The balance between paper and computer is less one-sided for input and output. Higher than the cost of electronic storage and transmission is the cost of getting a microscopic record that is on tape, disk, film, or bubble memory back out again to someone who wants it in a form in which it can be read, and still higher is the cost of input.

In costs for retrieval, electronic means are gaining the advantage. The cost of labor for finding one sheet of paper in a file containing millions of sheets is rising, while the cost of computing hardware is falling by a factor of about 40 percent a year. There is little doubt that searching for a record in computer memory and displaying it on a screen, or even printing it out again on a sheet of paper that can be thrown away because the permanent record is still in the computer, will become, even if it has not yet become, cheaper than getting it out manually.

The main continuing use of paper in a mature electronic communication system is likely to be as a medium for active handling and short-run retention, and this use may grow enormously. The probable style of such usage is illustrated by a Xerox laser printer, which is both a copier and a computer on a network. To retrieve a manuscript from a file in the memory of any other computer on the network, someone calls the document up, specifies the format, type fonts, and other visual details, and the laser printer instantly runs off one copy or as many as are immediately needed. The important difference from a 1970s photocopy machine is that no paper original has to exist to be copied.

The paperless office or paperless society is probably a fantasy. Though for both storage and transmission, paper is likely to become a rarity because of its cost, the use of paper for display, reading, and current work may grow, partly in fact because it will not be economical to retain the paper copies. The paper industry has cause for optimism. Experience shows that when word processors are introduced into offices, paper consumption increases, since with a word processor it is easier, when minor corrections are made, to run a whole new version of a document rather than tediously to correct the old copies. So too, when no paper files are kept because bulk storage of them is too expensive, a new paper copy may be derived from the bulk electronic files every time an item needs to be seen, and then that copy can be thrown away.

These points apply not only to office records and memos but equally to books, articles, and reference materials. There is no reason to stockpile printed paper when a laser printer can produce a paper copy whenever a customer wants one. Even in the 1960s far-sighted library planners looked forward to the day when people would never take out the library's unique copy of a work but would instead get their own instantly printed copy.

This may seem wasteful of both forests and money. It is, and paper will be used only because it is the most convenient if rarely the cheapest way to display text. A screen display, if acceptable, is generally less costly. Just how much cheaper is a question that will vary with time, depending on electronic and paper technology, both of which are changing. Recycled paper, erasable ink, synthetic paper, and cultivated cellulose instead of trees could all affect the calculations. But nothing on the horizon suggests that physical storage and transmission, or even retrieval, will be able to compete with the electronic alternatives.

The balance of costs between paper and computer is least one-sided with regard to input. Off in the dreamland of inventors is an optical character reader (OCR) that can look at any font of type or any handwriting and turn it correctly into digital representation, but such a reader does not yet exist. Success has been achieved cheaply and reliably only with well-defined fonts. Without such a device, the entry of text into electronic form requires the manual operation of retyping, and this is horrendously expensive. Without an optical reader or its equivalent, the Library of Congress will never be put into computer memory. No one will pay the cost of typing it all.

In short, to put records into computer-readable form is rarely economically justified if the purpose for doing it is solely to file them. However, if for other reasons the records need to be put into computer-readable form, then it becomes more economical to file and retrieve them that way than to print them out and preserve them in hard-copy form. Since more and more of everything that gets written does at some time appear in computer representation, its further handling in electronic form is dictated by economics. In the near future, virtually everything published in print will surely be typeset by computer. So too with the coming of word processors, whatever is done by the present 4.8 million stenographers, typists, and secretaries in America will exist in electronic form and be accessible for computer storage, transmission, formatting, and editing. Thus economics dictates the fact that most text handling will become electronic.

The very definition of ''publishing'' is changed by convergence between books, journals, and newspapers, which deliver information in multiple copies, and information services, office automation, and electronic mail, which deliver information in editions of one. A distinction between publishing and the provision of individual information was a product of Gutenberg's mass media revolution, when for the first time in history written texts could be mass produced cheaply. With contemporary communications technologies, singly produced copies are no longer much more expensive than mass-produced ones.

The Xerox copier was a major breakthrough in reducing the economic advantage of mass printing. For people who do not put a high price on their own time and are insensitive to the law, making a copy of a printed publication today is highly competitive with buying one in a store, which has to bear the costs of inventory and distribution. Computer processing of text is pushing the process further. Data communications, a point-to-point medium, is falling . . . toward cost levels like those of print mass media and is rising correspondingly in volume of use. In electronic publishing it is not necessarily economical to preprint multiple copies and physically store and distribute them. It can be cheaper for the source text to exist in some microdigital form, to be published later in units of one on reader demand.

Such on-demand publishing is increasingly used for technical literature. It is estimated that of the 2.5 billion copies of journal articles published each year in America, 250 million, or only one in ten, are ever read. Providing each reader with selected sets of articles reflecting an individual profile of the reader's interests rather than sending entire, uniform journals has clear advantages. Services of this sort are growing.

Electronic publishing and office information processing are both being revolutionized by the same technologies, so they tend to converge, even though a difference in purpose remains. Publishing remains a business devoted to organizing texts and information and offering this material widely, either in the marketplace or for free. Whether a publisher preprints and warehouses multiple copies or prints on demand is a matter of market strategy, not of cultural substance. Publishing's strategies may change, while it retains in an electronic era as vital a function as ever. It remains the vascular system of science, democracy, and culture. The cause for fear is that when its technology looks like that of an office, the law may see it as commerce, not publishing, and thus subject to regulation like any business. . . .

The electronic information marketplace of the future will thus be a complex, changing arena of monopolistic competition among many players — probably more than in print publishing today — where narrow natural software monopolies are reinforced by copyright. Such pluralism is at least possible if public policy does not prevent it. Technology will provide a variety of delivery vehicles and forms of information display. The content that publishers will offer over these vehicles will be in voice and video, in addition to text. The messages delivered can at some cost be multimedia spectaculars, but even at low cost they can mix audio and visuals with text. Today one can buy a book or magazine, perhaps beefed up with pictures, and one can buy a cassette or disk of a movie, perhaps clarified with captions; but electronic technology will create options for mixes not yet dreamed of. Entrants into electronic publishing may therefore come from many directions — not only from book, magazine, and newspaper publishing, but also from cablecasting, television, Hollywood, the computer industry, and the telecommunications industry. As long as all these vigorous competitors can obtain access to the major carriers, monopoly among electronic publishers will not arise easily.

Although paper will not vanish, electronic publishing may in the long run evolve to something radically different from what we know today. Though pluralistic, competitive, and economical, like print, it may differ markedly in content from what is now found in magazines, newspapers, and books. Automobiles looked like horseless carriages at the start but not forever; it may be the same with electronic publishing.

One change that computers seem likely to cause is a decline of canonical texts produced in uniform copies. In some ways this change will signal a return in print to the style of the manuscript, or even to the ways of oral conversation. Since Gutenberg, books, articles, manuals, and laws have been available in diverse locations in identical form. From this availability followed footnoting. When the work and the edition are named, anyone anywhere can locate an identical version. From this also followed cataloguing and the compiling of bibliographies. The identification of a printed publication by an entry in a catalogue or bibliography is unambiguous. One can even say with some precision whether a bibliography in a particular field is fairly complete or not.

Contrast this situation to the world of manuscripts where every copy was unique, with its own variations. Variations engendered a central problem in scholarship; careers were devoted to inferring the original version. Scribal rituals focused largely on preventing deviation, and in some traditions, error in transcribing a sacred manuscript was a sin.

The contrast is even greater between the modern canonical book and the world of oral dialogue. Neither in Plato's Academy nor in a modern seminar does scholarly procedure allow for cataloguing or footnoting of the ideas expressed. There is no fixed unit in which ideas occur. Their flow is amorphous.

Electronic publishing returns to these traditions. A small subculture of computer scientists who write and edit on data networks like the Arpanet foreshadow what is to come. One person types out comments at a terminal and gives colleagues on the network access to the comments. As each person copies, modifies, edits, and expands the text, it changes from day to day. With each change, the text is stored somewhere in a different version.

Computer-based textbooks may exist in as many variants as there are teachers. All teachers on occasion desire to correct or modify the textbooks they use; if texts are in a computer, they can and will do that. Each teacher will create a preferred version, which will be changed repeatedly over the years. Or in a literature or drama course one exercise might be to take a text and try to improve it. Reading thus becomes active and interactive. Penciled scribbles in the margin become part of the text and perhaps even part of a growing dialogue as others agree or disagree.

There are problems with this kind of fluid dialogue. Scientists, who were among the earliest users of computer information networks, are of two minds about the possible displacement of refereed journals by the more informal flow in computer-linked interest groups. In many endeavors in law and humanities as well, one needs to identify the original or official version. Conventions will certainly develop for constraining and labeling variant versions, but they cannot stop proliferation. Before a person can read a text on a computer terminal, the text must somehow be stored in the computer's memory. Once there, it can be copied, modified, and retransmitted at will.

The implications for scholarship are mind boggling. Blue sky writings on the wonders of the computer age often describe how scholars will be able to call up instantly at their terminal any book or article from the world's literature. Wrong! The proliferation of texts in multiple forms, with no clear line between early drafts and final printed versions, will overwhelm any identification of what is "the world's literature."

For copyright, the implications are fundamental. Established notions about copyright become obsolete, rooted as they are in the technology of print. The recognition of a copyright and the practice of paying royalties emerged with the printing press. With the arrival of electronic reproduction, these practices become unworkable. Electronic publishing is analogous not so much to the print shop of the eighteenth century as to word-of-mouth communication, to which copyright was never applied.

Consider the crucial distinction in copyright law between reading and writing. To read a copyright text is no violation, only to copy it in writing. The technological basis for this distinction is reversed with a computer text. To read a text stored in electronic memory, one displays it on the screen; one writes it to read it. To transmit it to others, however, one does not write it, one only gives others a password to one's own computer memory. One must write to read, but not to write.

Or consider the case of computer-authored texts. A computer program may operate on raw numerical data and from that data generate a readable report on trends, averages, and correlations. Another program may operate on articles and, without human intervention, generate abstracts of them. Certainly the computer program that does this is itself a text and is copyrightable under present law. But what of the text that the program generates? Who is the author of the computer-written report or abstract? The computer? The idea that a machine is capable of intellectual labor is beyond the scope of the copyright statues. Can a computer infringe copyright?

In short, the process of computer communication produces multitudinous versions of texts, which are partly authored by people and partly automatic. The receivers may be individuals, or they may be other machines that never print the words in visible form but use the information to produce something else again. So some of the text that is used exists electronically but is never apparent; some is flashed briefly on a screen; and some is printed out in hard copy. What starts out as one text varies and changes by degrees to a new one. Totally new concepts will have to be invented to compensate creative work in this environment. The print-based notion of copyright simply will not work. . . .

Electronics is changing publishing only gradually. A reporter today writes a story on a word processor, whereby editing and page makeup are computer aided; but what comes out at the end is a newspaper looking just the same as it always did. Eventually electronic publishing may become more like an electronic game, permeated by lights and sound along with words. The players will initiate, and the machine answer back, in an interactive conversational process. It may be for fun, for management of daily life, or for work. Whatever it is, it will probably in the end resemble present-day publishing no more than does the business or product of today's Time-Life conglomerate resemble that of the scriptorium of a monastery.

If such drastic changes occur in the publishing industry, great changes could occur in First Amendment practices, too. The industry is a complex structure imposed on a flow that starts in institutions of culture and science where knowledge and art are produced, and goes through institutions where editing and packaging take place, to printing plants and then distributors. In the print tradition of the First Amendment the entire flow has been free of government controls. In various cases about academic freedom and reporters' rights, the search for knowledge has been recognized by the courts to be part of speech. So too has the integrity of records and files. The courts protect the acts of speaking, parading, picketing, distributing handbills, and selling publications. They also protect the physical plant which is used; printing presses are beyond the reach of government licensing. For print communication the one element of the flow that was a monopoly was the post office, whose authority the courts have curtailed so as to protect the freedom of the users.

Among print publishers the structure of the flow ranges all the way from almost complete vertical integration to almost complete disintegration. Newspapers are typically at the integrated extreme. Stories are researched and written by their own hired staff, they have their own printing plants, and they often bypass the postal monopoly, delivering papers through their own trucks and newsboys. At the other end are publishers who have only an office and no plant at all. They contract with authors, printers, binders, and distributors, and themselves perform just an organizing function.

Electronic publishing has to carry out all the same functions and may do so in an equal variety of ways. In electronic publishing, as in print publishing, only one — and the same one — of these various linked functions is generally monopolized, the physical transmission. Electronic publishers depend on access to the basic carrier just as print publishers depend on access to the postal system.

Whether that monopoly element will be more important or less in the electronic system that it is in the print system is likely to vary with time. Postal delivery was more important for newspapers in the early years of the country that it is today. The telephone and telegraph monopolies were much stronger before there were alternative technologies for transmission, such as microwaves, satellites, and cable. Monopoly seems likely to be even further eroded in the future.

Despite these technical forces in favor of competition and the FCC's recent policy favoring competition even in physical carriage, the degree of monopoly is likely to remain significant in transmission plants. There will continue to be only one microwave link on many routes and almost everywhere only one cable television trunk and one set of telephone wires. Common carrier principles, including compulsory nondiscriminatory access, will continue to be appropriate to these parts of the transmission plant, but by analogy with print publishing, it seems plausible to expect that all the other elements of electronic publishing will, by constitutional requirement, be fully unregulated. Just as with print, electronic publishers might set themselves up at will with various patterns of vertical integration. Some electronic publishing organizations would, like newspapers, carry on most activities in-house. Other publishers would, on the analogy of book publishing, be vertically disintegrated. The British Prestel videotex system is more like the former; the United States electronic information market is more like the latter, with data base preparation, archiving, computer networking, and physical transmission all now usually done by different companies. It might be assumed that, except where there are elements of monopoly, the government would have no say about how electronic publishing is organized and done; that would be left, under the First Amendment, to be determined by the free marketplace of ideas. But this is certainly not the case today. . . .

As computers become the printing presses of the twenty-first century, ink marks on paper will continue to be read, and broadcasts to be watched, but other new major media will evolve from what are now but the toys of computer hackers. Videodisks, integrated memories, and data bases will serve functions that books and libraries now serve, while information retrieval systems will serve for what magazines and newspapers do now. Networks of satellites, optical fibers, and radio waves will serve the functions of the present-day postal system. Speech will not be free if these are not also free.

The danger is not of an electronic nightmare, but of human error. It is not computers but policy that threatens freedom. The censorship that followed the printing press was not entailed in Gutenberg's process; it was a reaction to it. The regulation of electronic communication is likewise not entailed in its technology but is a reaction to it. Computers, telephones, radio, and satellites are technologies of freedom, as much as was the printing press. . . .

In most countries the constitution sets the framework for communications policy. America's basic communications policies are found in three clauses. Article 1, Section 8, gives Congress the power to establish post offices and post roads. The next clause gives Congress the power "To promote the Progress of Science and useful Arts, by securing for limited Times to Authors and Inventors the exclusive Right to their respective Writings and Discoveries." And the very first amendment prohibits Congress from passing any law abridging freedom of speech or of the press. This package of provisions provided publishers with the support they needed but barred the government from interfering with their free expression.

In the comparatively simple American society of the eighteenth century, when the media depended largely on the slowly changing technology of the printing press and when government consisted of the relatively spare mechanisms of the courts, Congress, and a tiny executive branch, communications policy issues were few. They arose most often from the ability of the government to use its fiscal powers both for and against the press. The American people did not oppose the government's use of its fiscal powers to support the press. The authorities did so through the postal system, official advertising, and sinecure appointments. The idea that government should stand at arm's length from the press developed later; the earliest federal policy was to foster the media. The other possibility, that government might employ its coercive powers against the press, was prohibited by the First Amendment.

As Congress, the executive branch, and the courts dealt with innovations in communications technologies and, during the two centuries following adoption of the First Amendment, sought to formulate polices appropriate to them, the Amendment's original principles were severely compromised. The three main decades of such change occurred at intervals a half-century apart. In the 1870s Congress and the courts extensively restructured postal policies, imposing censorious restrictions. Also in that decade, and shortly before it, the system of common carrier regulation of telegraphy evolved. Fifty years later, in the 1920s, radio broadcasting began. For that medium Congress required that broadcasters be chosen and licensed by the state. Then half a century later, in the 1970s, computer networks, satellites, and cable systems came into extensive use. Some of the regulatory responses to them seem quite unconstitutional.

Both the 1870s and the 1920s were decades of ambivalence about civil liberties. In the 1870s a rising reform movement about both morals and economics challenged the prevailing philosophy of laissez faire. Movements for temperance, prudery, voter registration, and labor protection clashed with ideas of minimal governance. Reformers pressed for acceptance of the regulation of mail as an instrument of censorship. The 1920s saw the Palmer raids on the one hand, and the Brandeis-Holmes dissents and decisions on the other. The sensitivity of the Supreme Court to the First Amendment, starting in the 1920s and particularly after World War II, led it to blow the whistle and stem the trend toward postal censorship.

It was in the 1920s, however, that communications policy in the United States most seriously lost its way. Without adequate thought, a structure was introduced for radio which had neither the libertarian features of the common carrier system nor those of the free market. The assumption of the new system was that spectrum was extremely limited and had to be allotted to chosen users. In Europe the chosen user was generally the government itself; in America it was private licensees. Since only a few would be privileged to broadcast, government felt it must influence the character of what they broadcast. The broadcasting organizations, unlike common carriers, selected and produced programs, but unlike print publishers, who also select what appears, there was no free entry for challengers. So government stepped in to regulate the radio forum and shape the broadcasters' choices.

By this process of evolution there came to be three main communications structures in the United States: the print model, free of regulation in general; the common carrier model, with government assuring nondiscriminatory access for all; and the broadcast model, with government-licensed private owners as the publishers. The choice between them is likely to be a key policy issue in the coming decades. A convergence of modes is upsetting what was for a while a neatly trifurcated system. Each of the three models was used in its particular industries and for different types of communications. As long as this was the case, the practices in some industries might be less true to the First Amendment than the practices in others, but it did not much affect those media that remained in the domain of the First Amendment. What happened in one industry did not matter greatly for what happened in another.

If this situation were a stable one, there would not be much cause for worry, for if the nation retained a free printed press through which all viewpoints could be expressed, it would not lose its freedom even if broadcasting were totally government controlled. Having print as an island of freedom might be assurance enough against total conformity to authority. But the situation is not stable.

Very rapidly all the media are becoming electronic. Previously the print media were affected, but not themselves transformed, by the electronic media. The electronic media grew and enlarged their field of action but left the older media fundamentally what they had been before. This is no longer the case. With electronic publishing, the practices of the electronic media become practices of the print media too. No longer can one view electronic communications as a circumscribed special case whose monopolistic and regulated elements do not matter very much, because the larger realm of freedom of expression still encompasses all of print. Telecommunications policy is becoming communications policy as all communications come to use electronic forms of transmission.

Soon the courts will have to decide, for vast areas that have so far been quite free of regulation, which of the three traditions of communications practice they will apply. The facts that will face the courts will be a universally interconnected electronic communication system based on a variety of linkable electronic carriers, using radio, cable, microwave, optical fiber, and satellites, and delivering to every home and office a vast variety of different kinds of mail, print, sound, and video, through an electronic network of networks. The question is whether the system will be governed as are the regulated electronic media now, or whether there is some way of retaining the free press tradition of the First Amendment in that brave new world.

Historically, some media operate by different rules under the First Amendment from those applied to publications in print because of the existence of scarcities in the resources used in producing them. Abundance and scarcity of resources are the two ends of a continuum. At one end, communication is entirely unconstrained by resources; in the middle are situations in which there is constraint, but everyone can nonetheless have some ration of the means to communicate; and at the other end the constraints are such that only a privileged few can own those means.

Conversation illustrates the optimal situation in which communication is totally without resource constraints; the only limit is one's desire. There is also sidewalk enough in most places that anyone can picket a building without excluding others from passing by, though not when hundreds want to picket in the same place at once. In practice there is no resource bar to forming a congregation to worship together, as witnessed by storefront churches and congregations that meet in members' homes. Similarly anyone can send a petition or write a letter or protest. The property required to carry out these acts is trivial.

Even in such domains, where normally anyone can communicate at will without noticeably reducing the opportunities for others, there are exceptional situations in which one person's wants do constrain others. Conversation may be abundant, but conversation with a particular partner is an imposition on that person. Assemblage as a congregation can be almost costless if in a member's home, but building a large church on a desirable lot is not. In each of these situations the cliché formula is that people have the right to do as they wish, so long as they do not interfere with the rights of others. But communication in such situations involves so few resource constraints that no special institutions are set up to deal with them.

The situation is more complex when the resources for communication, while not unlimited, are available enough that by reasonable sacrifice and effort a person can get hold of some. In this situation allocation by the institutions of property and the market becomes a useful norm. An example is the printed magazine. Even the poor, by scrimping and cooperating, can produce periodicals, and some of them do. There are church bulletins for modest congregations, labor and protest papers, adolescent club and school papers. There are thousands of little magazines with stories and poems by unknown amateurs. To convert a publication into a success requires talent, capital, and energy; if the talent and energy are there, the capital may even be borrowed.

In such situations of moderate scarcity, however, not all people can have whatever means of communication they want. The means are rationed. The system of rationing may or may not be equitable or just. There are an infinity of ways to partition a scarce resource. The method may be strictly egalitarian, as that which requires all legal candidates to be offered the same amount of air time under the same terms during an election campaign. The method may be meritocratic, as that which gives free education to those who score high in exams. The method may recognize privilege, as that which allows a descendant to inherit a communications medium or a seat in the House of Lords. The method may recognize cultural values, as that which occurs when a foundation makes grants to museums or symphonies. The method may reward skill and motivation, as that which allows communications institutions to earn profits that depend on their efficiency.

Each of these criteria for allocation has its value, and actual public policy represents different mixes of them. Equality may have both rhetorical appeal and a great deal of merit. Yet few people would opt for totally equal access to scarce means of communication, quite independent of considerations of talent, motivation, or social value in their use.

Property rights in the means of communication are a major method of allocation, but different property schemes produce different allocations. In some property schemes, if people who have radio frequencies do not use them, their right lapses and the frequencies revert to the allocating agency. This is like the small print which reads, "This ticket is nontransferable." In a market scheme, however, the owners may, within the limits of the law, pass on their resource to someone else as a gift or as part of a deal. A market scheme is predicated on a lack of faith in administered wisdom; it treats whatever allocations exist as a starting point only. It assumes that the distributed wisdom among the property holders is greater than that of a central planner.

The law creating a market defines the mix of deals that may be made and specifies some as illegal. A person moving may sell a house, but perhaps under zoning laws it may not be turned into a tavern. A shipowner with a radio license may sell a ship, including the radio facilities, but may not turn the ship's frequency to broadcasting. A cablecaster may sell a system to someone else but, under American rules, may not sell it to the owner of a television station in the same town.

Property is, in summary, simply a recognized partition of a resource that is somewhat scarce. A market is a device for distributing the use of that property. It measures the value people attach to different uses; it allows for shifts in the uses; and it depoliticizes decisions by decentralizing them. But a market is not a single device; it is a class of devices, and public policy defines the market structure.

Where some resource is either very scarce or not easily divisible, ordinary markets function badly. Spectrum, given the way it is now administered, is scarce enough that every small group cannot have its own television station. A telephone system is indivisible in that what is needed is a universal system. In such cases of monopoly or partial monopoly of the means of communication there are problems for free societies. It was for such situations that the common carrier approach was developed in the nineteenth and early twentieth centuries. Common carriers are obligated to offer their resources to all of the public equally. In the American constitutional system this is an exceptional fallback solution. The basic American tradition of the

First Amendment is either the free-for-all or free speech or the competitive market of the early press.

Since scarcity and indivisibility of resources compel a departure from the print model, it is important to estimate what major scarcities and indivisibilities will appear in the evolving electronic media. Despite the profusion of means of communication that are coming out of the technology of the late twentieth century, a number of truly scarce or indivisible elements will remain in the communications system. Despite the cliché of broadcast regulation that frequencies are exceptionally scarce, spectrum is not one of them. If spectrum were allotted by sale in a market, the prices would not be prohibitive, for there are now numerous alternatives, such as data compression or transmission by coaxial cables or optical fibers, which would become economic in the presence of relatively low costs for air rights. Spectrum is only of medium scarcity.

The orbit for satellites is today what spectrum was in 1927, something that at first glance seems inherently and physically scarce. If the technology of orbit usage remained that of the 1970s, orbital slots in the Western hemisphere would have run out by about the time this book got published, and in many other places shortly thereafter. However, techniques for orbit and spectrum saving are multiplying. The real problem is spectrum, not real estate on the orbit. There is abundant space for the satellites themselves. The difficulty is to find frequencies for communicating to and from the satellites without causing radio interference. Polarization, spot beams, time-division multiplexing, on-board switching, and direct satellite-to-satellite microwave or laser links are among the techniques that help. These require agreement to use technically efficient methods, which may not be the cheapest ones. The orbit problem turns out to be a special case of the familiar spectrum problem. To keep prices down requires agreement on and compliance with efficient standards and protocols. But at a price, as much of the resource as is wanted is likely to be available.

Though neither spectrum nor orbital slots are too scarce to be handled by normal market mechanisms, there are other more severe elements of monopoly in the system. One is the need that basic communications networks be universal in reach. If anyone is to be able to send a message or talk to anyone else, there must be universal connectivity, directory information, agreed standards, and a legal right to interconnect.

Another element of communications systems that makes for central control is the need to traverse or utilize the public's property. The social costs of not granting the right of eminent domain for transmission routes are very high. Also streets have to be dug to lay cables. These requirements affect many people who are not direct participants in the arrangements.

Finally, there are areas of natural monopoly where the larger the firm, the more efficient its operation, so in the end the smaller competitors are driven out of business. This has been the case for American newspapers. They depend heavily on advertising by merchants. Where there is more than paper in a town, merchants find it more efficient to advertise in the larger one, and the smaller ones wilt. The situation was similar when there was more than one phone company in a city; customers joined the larger system because there were more people whom they could then call. Customers would also pick the larger cable system if more than one served a neighborhood. The larger system that shared the fixed plant costs among more subscribers could charge less, and with more revenue it could offer more or better programs.

In communications, economies of scale are found especially in wire or cable transmission plants. The large investment in conduits reaching everywhere dominates the equation. There is no such strong economy of scale either in over-the-air transmission or ordinarily in programming or enhanced services. Where economies of scale and therefore natural monopolies do exist, some form of common carriage access is appropriate. It exists in phone service. Common carriage in some form may well come for cable as well.

Although there are elements of natural monopoly in both newspaper and electronic carrier markets, common carrier procedures have been applied in one and not the other. A newspaper may be the only one in its town, yet still it enjoys all the privileges of the ordinarily competitive printed media. Under the First Amendment, as interpreted in the *Tornillo* case, it cannot be forced to yield access to anyone. The issue of whether, as a monopoly, it should be so compelled is not a trivial one. Barron's argument in *Tornillo* was not dismissable lightly, but the Court did reject it and continued to give newspaper owners full autonomy of editorial decision.

The fact that the newspapers have maintained such freedom from a requirement that normally goes with monopoly distinguishes them from cablecasters, who are ordinarily required by their franchises to provide some access. Historical complexities, not simple logic, account for this paradox. In both cases, but especially for newspapers, the scope of the monopoly is incomplete. At least as important is the fact that newspapers, reared in the tradition of a free press, have behaved so as to discourage the issue from arising. Newspapers, as they moved into the status of monopolies, had the wisdom to defuse hostility by acting in many respects like a common carrier. Aware of their vulnerability, they voluntarily created something of an access system for themselves. Unlike their nineteenth-century ancestors, they see themselves as providing a forum for the whole community. They not only run columnists of opposite tendency and open their local news pages willingly to community groups, but also encourage letters to the editor. Most important of all, they accept advertising for pay from anyone. Only rarely does a newspaper refuse an ad on grounds of disagreement. If newspapers were as opinionated as they used to be in the days when they were competitive, public opinion would have long since acted against their unregulated monopoly.

Furthermore, newspapers are far from having a complete monopoly. Newspaper publishers, like cablecasters, argue that they are not a monopoly in a appropriately defined market. Even if there is only one newspaper in a town, there are many ways in which opinions get distributed in print. A handbill or periodical of opinion competes with a newspaper in the marketplace of ideas. News magazines and suburban papers also compete. . . .

Electronic media, as they are coming to be, are dispersed in use and abundant in supply. They allow for more knowledge, easier access, and freer speech than were ever enjoyed before. They fit the free practices of print. The characteristics of media shape what is done with them, so one might anticipate that these technologies of freedom will overwhelm all attempts to control them. Technology, however, shapes the structure of the battle, but not every outcome. While the printing press was without doubt the foundation of modern democracy, the response to the flood of publishing that it brought forth has been censorship as often as press freedom. In some times and places the even more capacious new media will open wider the floodgates for discourse, but in other times and places, in fear of that flood, attempts will be made to shut the gates.

The easy access, low cost, and distributed intelligence of modern means of communication are a prime reason for hope. The democratic impulse to regulate evils, as Tocqueville warned, is ironically a reason for worry. Lack of technical grasp by policy makers and their propensity to solve problems of conflict, privacy, intellectual property, and monopoly by accustomed bureaucratic routines are the main reasons for concern. But as long as the First Amendment stands, backed by courts which take it seriously, the loss of liberty is not foreordained. The commitment of American culture to pluralism and individual rights is reason for optimism, as is the pliancy and profusion of electronic technology.

CHAPTER 12

WHAT CAN BE DONE ABOUT THE DEGRADATION OF WORK?

Our contemporary understanding of what constitutes the degradation of work owes much to Karl Marx, a nineteenth-century social theorist. His key work, *Capital*, Volume I, was an analysis of the capitalist mode of production, and not a blueprint for a socialist society. Marx believed the essence of human nature to be activity, especially creativity and productivity in work. In working, human beings create their selves. This process is most meaningful and fulfilling when the individual is aware of the total creative process and has or shares control over the product of his or her labor. In modern capitalism, with its mechanized factory setting and system of ownership and labor, this humanizing process of productive labor is shattered. The individual becomes alienated from the product of his or her labor. Because this product is a deep expression of self, one thus becomes alienated from oneself. Labor becomes forced. Work becomes something to finish so that one may relax and be human.[1]

If radicals find work to be a degrading experience under the capitalist division of labor, liberals tend to agree that the benefit of increased productivity outweighs the costs. Yet radicals are not the only ones to identify relationships of domination and subordination in the workplace. Pope John Paul II's recent Encyclical *On Human Work*, portions of which follow, is an elegantly written and important document by a traditional thinker. He finds work degrading when it damages the "dignity" of a person. The rights of workers are secured by "union activity" that aims at the good of social justice.

Peter Rachleff's "Working the Fast Lane" is, obviously, not an abstract treatise but a concrete description of the workplace in the U.S. Postal Service. We might recall that "after a nationwide strike by postal workers in 1970, broken in part by the use of federal troops, the Post Office was made a semi-independent corporation modeled after private industry."[2] The implicit argument of Rachleff's piece is that work will remain alienated practice until a change to a more democratic, participatory economic system is made. Unions sometimes accept the introduction of new technologies that are not conducive to democracy in the workplace.

References

1. See Erich Fromm, *Marx's Concept of Man* (New York: Ungar, 1961); Shlomo Avineri, *The Social and Political Thought of Karl Marx* (Cambridge: Cambridge Univesity Press, 1971); David McLellan, ed., *Karl Marx: Selected Writings*, (Oxford: Oxford University Press, 1977).
2. See the editor's introduction to *Radical America*, vol. 16, Nos. 1&2, 1982: p. 10.

27. ON HUMAN WORK

Pope John Paul II

Through work man must earn his daily bread and contribute to the continual advance of science and technology and, above all, to elevating unceasingly the cultural and moral level of the society within which he lives in community with those who belong to the same family. And work means any activity by man, whether manual or intellectual, whatever its nature or circumstances; it means any human activity that can and must be recognized as work, in the midst of all the many activities of which man is capable and to which he is predisposed by his very nature, by virtue of humanity itself. Man is made to be in the visible universe an image and likeness of God Himself, and he is placed it in order to subdue the earth. From the beginning therefore he is *called to work*. *Work is one of the characteristics that distinguish* man from the rest of creatures, whose activity for sustaining their lives cannot be called work. Only man is capable of work, and only man works, at the same time by work occupying his existence on earth. Thus work bears a particular mark on man and of humanity, the mark of a person operating within a community of persons. And this mark decides its interior characteristics; in a sense it constitutes its very nature.

Since May 15 of the present year was the *ninetieth anniversary* of the publication by the great Pope of the ''social question,'' Leo XIII, of the decisively important encyclical which begins with the words *Rerum novarum*, I wish to devote this document to *human work* and, even more, to *man* in the vast context of the reality of work. As I said in the Encyclical *Redemptor hominis*, published at the beginning of my service in the See of St. Peter in Rome, man ''is the primary and fundamental way for the Church,'' precisely because of the inscrutable mystery of redemption in Christ; and so it is necessary to return constantly to this way to follow it ever anew in the various aspects in which it shows us all the wealth and at the same time all the toil of human existence on earth.

Work is one of these aspects, a perennial and fundamental one, one that is always relevant and constantly demands renewed attention and decisive witness. Because fresh *questions* and *problems* are always arising, there are always fresh hopes, but also fresh fears and threats, connected with this basic dimension of human existence: man's life is built up every day from work, from work it derives its specific dignity, but at the same time work contains the unceasing measure of human toil and suffering, and also of the harm and injustice which penetrate deeply into social life within individual nations and on the international level. While it is true that man eats the bread produced by the work of his hands — and this means not only the daily bready by which his body keeps alive but also the bread of science and progress, civilization and culture – it is also a perennial truth that he eats this bread by *"the sweat of his face,"* that is to say, not only by personal effort and toil but also in the midst of many tensions, conflicts and crisis, which, in relationship with the reality of work disturb the life of individual societies and also of all humanity.

We are celebrating the ninetieth anniversary of the Encyclical *Rerum novarum* on the eve of new developments in technological, economic and political conditions which, according to many experts, will influence the world of work and production no less than the industrial revolution of the last century. There are many factors of a general nature: the widespread introduction of automation into many spheres of production, the increase in the cost of energy and raw materials, the growing realization that the heritage of nature is limited and that it is being intolerably polluted, and the emergence on the political scene of peoples who, after centuries of subjection, are demanding their rightful place among the nations and in international decision making. These new conditions and demands will require a reordering and adjustment of the structures of the modern economy and of the distribution of work. Unfortunately, for millions of skilled workers these changes may perhaps mean unemployment, at least for a time, or the need for retraining. They will very probably involve a reduction or a less rapid increase in material well-being for the more developed countries. But they can also bring relief and hope to the millions who today live in conditions of shameful and unworthy poverty.

It is not for the Church to analyze scientifically the consequences that these changes may have on human society. But the Church considers it her task always to call attention to the dignity and rights of those who work, to condemn situations in which that dignity and those rights are violated, and to help to guide the above-mentioned changes so as to ensure authentic progress by man and society. . . .

The Church is convinced that work is a fundamental dimension of man's existence on earth. She is confirmed in this conviction by considering the whole heritage of the many sciences devoted to man: anthropology, palaeontology, history, sociology, psychology and so on; they all seem to bear witness to this reality in an irrefutable way. But the source of the Church's conviction is above all the revealed word of God, and therefore what is *a conviction of the intellect* is also *a conviction of faith.* The reason is that the Church — and it is worthwhile stating it at this point believes in man: she *thinks of man* and addresses herself to him *not only* in the light of historical experience, not only with the aid of the many methods of scientific knowledge, but in the first place in the light of the revealed word of the living God. Relating herself to man, she seeks to *express* the eternal *designs* and transcendent *destiny* which *the living God*, the Creator and Redeemer, has linked with him.

The Church finds *in the very first pages of the book of Genesis* the source of her conviction that work is a fundamental dimension of human existence on earth. An analysis of these texts makes us aware that they express — sometimes in an archaic way of manifesting thought — the fundamental truths about man, in the context of the mystery of creation itself. These truths are decisive for man from the very beginning, and at the same time they trace out the main lines of his earthly existence, both in the state of original justice and also after the breaking, caused by sin, of the Creator's original covenant with creation in man. When man, who had been created "in the image of God . . . male and female," hears the words: "Be fruitful and *multiply, and fill the earth and subdue it,"* even though these words do not refer directly and explicitly to work, beyond any doubt they indirectly indicate it as an activity for man to carry out in the world. Indeed, they show its very deepest essence. Man is the image of God partly through the mandate received from his Creator to subdue, to dominate, the earth. In carrying out this mandate, man, every human being, reflects the very action of the Creator of the universe.

Work understood as a "transitive" activity, that is to say an activity beginning in the human subject and directed towards an external object, presupposes a specific dominion by man over "the earth," and in its turn it confirms and develops this dominion. It is clear that the term "the earth" of which the biblical text speaks is to be understood in the first place as that fragment of the visible universe that man inhabits. By extension, however, it can be understood as the whole of the visible world insofar as it comes within the range of man's influence and his striving to satisfy his needs. The expression "subdue the earth" has an immense range. It means all the resources that the earth (and indirectly the visible world) contains and which, through the conscious activity of man, can be discovered and used for his ends. And so these words, placed at the beginning of the Bible, *never cease to be relevant.* They embrace equally the past ages of civilization and economy, as also the whole of modern reality and future phases of development, which are perhaps already to some extent beginning to take shape, though for the most part they are still almost unknown to man and hidden from him.

While people sometimes speak of periods of "acceleration" in the economic life and civilization of humanity or of individual nations, linking these periods to the progress of science and technology and especially to discoveries which are decisive for social and economic life, at the same time it can be said that none of these phenomena of "acceleration" exceeds the essential content of what was said in that most ancient of biblical texts. As man, through his work, becomes more and more the master of the earth, and as he confirms his dominion over the visible world, again through his work, he nevertheless remains in every case and at every phase of this process within the Creator's original ordering. And this ordering remains necessarily and indissolubly linked with the fact that man was created, as male and female, "in the image of God." This *process* is, at the same time, *universal;* it embraces all human beings, every generation, every phase of economic and cultural development, and *at the same time* it is a process that takes place *within each human being,* in each conscious human subject. Each and every individual is at the same time embraced by it. Each and every individual, to the proper extent and in an incalculable number of ways, takes part in the giant process whereby man "subdues the earth" through his work.

This universality and, at the same time, this multiplicity of the process of "subduing the earth" throw light upon human work, because man's dominion over the earth is achieved in and by means of work. There thus emerges the meaning of *work in an objective sense*, which finds expression in the various epochs of culture and civilization. Man dominates the earth by the very fact of domesticating animals, rearing them and obtaining from them the food and clothing he needs, and by the fact by being able to extract various natural resources from the earth and the seas. But man "subdues the earth" much more when he begins to cultivate it and then to transform its products, adapting them to his own use. Thus agriculture constitutes through human work a primary field of economic activity and an indispensable factor of production. Industry in its turn will always consist in linking the earth's riches — whether nature's living resources, or the products of agriculture, or the mineral or chemical resources — with man's work, whether physical or intellectual. This is also in a sense true in the sphere of what are called service industries, and also in the sphere of research, pure or applied.

In industry and agriculture man's work has today in many cases ceased to be mainly manual, for the toil of human hands and muscles is aided by *more and more highly perfected machinery*. Not only in industry but also in agriculture we are witnessing the transformations made possible by the gradual development of science and technology. Historically speaking, this, taken as a whole, has caused great changes in civilization, from the beginning of the "industrial era" to the successive phases of development through new technologies, such as the electronics and the microprocessor technology in recent years.

While it may seem that in the industrial process it is the machine that "works" and man merely supervises it, making it function and keeping it going in various ways, it is also true that for this very reason industrial development provides grounds for reproposing in new ways the question of human work. Both the original industrialization that gave rise to what is called the worker question and the subsequent industrial and post-industrial changes show in an eloquent manner that, even in the age of ever more mechanized "work," *the proper subject of work continues to be man*.

The development of industry and of the various sectors connected with it, even the most modern electronics technology, especially in the fields of miniaturization, communications and telecommunications and so forth, shows how vast is the role of technology, that ally of work that human thought has produced, in the interaction between the subject and objects of work (in the widest sense of the word). Understood in this case not as a capacity or aptitude for work, but rather as *a whole set of instruments* which man uses in his work, technology is undoubtedly man's ally. It facilitates his work, perfects, accelerates and augments it. It leads to an increase in the quantity of things produced by work, and in many cases improves their quality. However, it is also a fact that, in some instances, technology can cease to be man's ally and become almost his enemy, as when the mechanization of work "supplants" him, taking away all personal satisfaction and the incentive to creativity and responsibility, when it deprives many workers of their previous employment, or when, through exalting the machine, it reduces man to the status of its slave.

If the biblical words "subdue the earth" addressed to man from the very beginning are understood in the context of the whole modern age, industrial and post-industrial, then they undoubtedly include also *a relationship with technology*, with the world of machinery which is the fruit of the work of the human intellect and a historical confirmation of man's dominion over nature.

The recent stage of human history, especially that of certain societies, brings a correct affirmation of technology as a basic coefficient of economic progress; but, at the same time, this affirmation has been accompanied by and continues to be accompanied by the raising of essential questions concerning human work in relationship to its subject, which is man. These questions are particularly charged with *content and tension of an ethical and social character*. They therefore constitute a continual challenge for institutions of many kinds, for states and governments, for systems and international organizations; they also constitute a challenge for the Church.

In order to continue our analysis of work, an analysis linked with the word of the Bible telling man that he is to subdue the earth, we must concentrate our attention on *work in the subjective sense*, much more than we did on the objective significance, barely touching upon the vast range of problems known intimately and in detail to scholars in various fields and also, according to their specializations, to those who work. If the words of the book of Genesis to which we refer in this analysis of ours speak of work in the objective sense in an indirect way, they also speak only indirectly of the subject of work; but what they say is very eloquent and is full of great significance.

Man has to subdue the earth and dominate it, because as the "image of God" he is a person, that is to say, a subjective being capable of acting in a planned and rational way, capable of deciding about himself, and with a tendency to self-realization. *As a person, man is therefore the subject of work.* As a person he works, he performs various actions belonging to the work process; independently of their objective content, these actions must all serve to realize his humanity, to fulfill the calling to be a person that is his by reason of his very humanity. The principal truths concerning this theme were recently recalled by the Second Vatican Council in the Constitution *Gaudium et spes*, especially in chapter one, which is devoted to man's calling.

And so this "dominion" spoken of in the biblical text being meditated upon here refers not only to the objective dimension of work but at the same time introduces us to an understanding of its subjective dimension. Understood as a process whereby man and the human race subdue the earth, work corresponds to this basic biblical concept only when throughout the process man manifests himself and confirms himself *as the one who "dominates."* This dominion, in a certain sense, refers to the subjective dimension even more than to the objective one: this dimension conditions *the very ethical nature of work*. In fact there is no doubt that human work has an ethical value of its own, which clearly and directly remains linked to the fact that the one who carries it out is a person, a conscious and free subject, that is to say, a subject that decides about himself.

This truth, which in a sense constitutes the fundamental and perennial heart of Christian teaching on human work, has had and continues to have primary significance for the formulation of the important social problems characterizing whole ages.

The ancient world introduced its own typical differentiation of people into classes according to the type of work done. Work which demanded from the worker the exercise of physical strength, the work of muscles and hands, was considered unworthy of free men, and was therefore given to slaves. By broadening certain aspects that already belonged to the Old Testament, Christianity brought about a fundamental change of ideas in this field, taking the whole content of the Gospel message as its point of departure, especially the fact that the one who, while *being God*, became like us in all things, devoted most of the years of His life on earth to *manual work* at the carpenter's bench. This circumstance constitutes in itself the most eloquent "Gospel of work," showing that the basis for determining the value of human work is not primarily the kind of work being done but the fact that the one who is doing it is a person. The sources of the dignity of work are to be sought primarily in the subjective dimension, not in the objective one.

Such a concept practically does away with the very basis of the ancient differentiation of people into classes according to the kind of work done. This does not mean that, from the objective point of view, human work cannot and must not be rated and qualified in any way. It only means that *the primary basis of the value of work is man himself*, who is it subject. This leads immediately to a very important conclusion of an ethical nature: however true it may be that man is destined for work and called to it, in the first place work is "for man" and not man "for work." Through this conclusion one rightly comes to recognize the preeminence of the subjective meaning of work over the objective one. Given this way of understanding things, and presupposing that different sorts of work that people do can have greater or lesser objective value, let us try nevertheless to show that each sort is judged above all by *the measure of the dignity* of the subject of work, that is to say the person, *the individual who carries it out*. On the other hand, independently of the work that every man does, and presupposing that this work constitutes a purpose — at times a very demanding one — of his activity, this purpose does not possess a definitive meaning in itself. In fact, in the final analysis it is always man who is *the purpose of the work*, whatever work it is that is done by man — even if the common scale of values rates it at the merest "service," as the most monotonous, even the most alienating work. . . .

When dealing with human work in the fundamental dimension of its subject, that is to say, the human person doing the work, one must make at least a summary evaluation of developments during the ninety years since *Rerun novarum* in relation to the subjective dimension of work. Although the subject of work is always the same, that is to say man, nevertheless wide-ranging changes take place in the objective aspect. While one can say that, by reason of its subject, *work is one single thing* (one and unrepeatable every time), yet when one takes into consideration its objective directions one is forced to admit that *there exist many works*, many different sorts of work. The development of human civilization brings continual enrichment in this field. But at the same time, one cannot fail to note that in the process of this development not only do new forms of work appear but also others disappear. Even if one accepts that on the whole this is a normal phenomenon, it must still be seen whether certain ethically and socially dangerous irregularities creep in, and to what extent.

It was precisely one such *wide-ranging anomaly* that gave rise in the last century to what has been called "the worker question," sometimes described as "the proletariat question." This question and the problems connected with it gave rise to a just social reaction and caused the impetuous emergence of a great burst of solidarity between workers, first and foremost industrial workers. The call to solidarity and common action addressed to the workers — especially to those engaged in narrowly specialized, monotonous and depersonalized work in industrial plants, when the machine tends to dominate man — was import and eloquent from the point of view of social ethics. It was the reaction *against the degradation of man as the subject of work*, and against the unheard-of accompanying exploitation in the field of wages, working conditions, and social security for the worker. This reaction united the working world in a community marked by great solidarity.

Following the lines laid down by the Encyclical *Rerum novarum* and many later documents of the Church's Magisterium, it must be frankly recognized that the reaction against the system of injustice and harm that cried to heaven for vengeance and that weighed heavily upon workers in that period of rapid industrialization was justified *from the point of view of social morality*. This state of affairs was favored by the liberal sociopolitical system, which, in accordance with its "economistic" premises, strengthened and safeguarded economic initiative by the possessors of capital alone, but did not pay sufficient attention to the rights of the workers, on the grounds that human work is solely an instrument of production, and that capital is the basis, efficient factor, and purpose of production.

From that time, worker solidarity, together with a clearer and more committed realization by others of workers' rights, has in many cases brought about profound changes. Various forms of neo-capitalism or collectivism have developed. Various new systems have been thought out. Workers can often share in running businesses and in controlling their productivity, and in fact do so. Through appropriate associations, they exercise influence over conditions of work and pay, and also over social legislation. But at the same time various ideological or power systems, and new relationships which have arisen at various levels of society, *have allowed flagrant injustices to persist or have created new ones*. On the world level, the development of civilization and of communications has made possible a more complete diagnosis of the living and working conditions of man globally, but it has also revealed other forms of injustice, much more extensive that those which in the last century stimulated unity between workers for particular solidarity in the working world. This is true in countries which have completed a certain process of industrial revolution. It is also true in countries where the main working milieu continues to be *agriculture* or other similar occupations.

Movements of solidarity in the sphere of work — a solidarity that must never mean being closed to dialogue and collaboration with others — can be necessary also with reference to the condition of social groups that were not previously included in such movements but which, in changing social systems and conditions of living, are undergoing *what is in effect "proletarianization"* or which actually already find themselves in a "proletariat" situation, one which, even if not yet given that name, in fact deserves it. This can be true of certain categories or groups of the working "intelligentsia," especially when ever wider access to education and an ever increasing number of people with degrees or diplomas in the fields of their cultural preparation are accompanied by a drop in demand for their labor. This *unemployment of intellectuals* occurs or increases when the education available is not oriented towards the types of employment or service required by the true needs of society, or when there is less demand for work which requires education, at least professional education, than for manual labor, or when it is less well paid. Of course, education in itself is always valuable and an important enrichment of the human person; but in spite of that, "proletarianization" processes remain possible.

For this reason, *there must be continued study of the subject of work* and of the subject's living conditions. In order to achieve social justice in the various parts of the world, in the various countries, and in the relationships between them, there is a need for ever new *movements of solidarity of* the workers and *with* the workers. This solidarity must be present whenever it is called for by the social degrading of the subject of work, by exploitation of the workers, and by the growing areas of poverty and even hunger. The Church is firmly committed to this cause, for she considers it her mission, her service, a proof of her fidelity to Christ, so that she can truly be the "Church of the poor." And the "poor" appear under various forms; they appear in various places and at various times; in many cases they appear as a *result of the violation of the dignity of human work*: either because the opportunities for human work are limited as a result of the scourge of unemployment, or because a low value is put on work and the rights that flow from it, especially the right to a just wage and to the personal security of the worker and his or her family.

Remaining within the context of man as the subject of work, it is now appropriate to touch upon, at least in a summary way, certain problems that *more closely define the dignity of human work*, in that they make it possible to characterize more fully its specific moral value. In doing this we must always keep in mind the biblical calling to "subdue the earth," in which is expressed the will of the Creator that work should enable man to achieve that "dominion" in the visible world that is proper to him.

God's fundamental and original intention with regard to man, whom He created in His image and after His likeness, was not withdrawn or cancelled out even when man, having broken the original covenant with God, heard the words: "In the sweat of your face you shall eat bread." These words refer to *the sometimes heavy toil* that from then onwards has accompanied human work; but they do not alter the fact that work is the means whereby man *achieves that "dominion"* which is proper to him over the visible world, by "subjecting" the earth. Toil is something that is universally known, for it is universally experienced. It is familiar to those doing physical work under sometimes exceptionally laborious conditions. It is familiar not only to agricultural workers, who spend long days working the land, which sometimes "bears thorns and thistles," but also to those who work in mines and quarries, to steelworkers at their blast furnaces, to those who work in builder's yards and in construction work, often in danger of injury or death. It is likewise familiar to those at an intellectual workbench; to scientists; to those who bear the burden of grave responsibility for decisions that will have a vast impact on society. It is familiar to doctors and nurses, who spend days and nights at their patients' besides. It is familiar to women, who, sometimes without proper recognition on the part of society and even of their own families, bear the daily burden and responsibility for their homes and the upbringing of their children. *It is familiar to all workers*, and, since work is a universal calling, it is familiar to everyone.

And yet, in spite of all this toil — perhaps, in a sense, because of it — work is a good thing for man. Even though it bears the mark of a *bonum arduum*, in the terminology of St. Thomas, this does not take away the fact that, as such, it is a good thing for man. It is not only good in the sense that it is useful or something to enjoy; it is also good as being something worthy, that is to say, something that corresponds to man's dignity, that expresses this dignity and increases it. If one wishes to define more clearly the ethical meaning of work, it is this truth that one must particularly keep in mind. Work is a good thing for man — a good thing for his humanity — because through work man *not only transforms nature*, adapting it to his own needs, but he also *achieves fulfillment* as a human being and indeed, in a sense, becomes "more a human being."

Without this consideration it is possible to understand the meaning of the virtue of industriousness, and more particularly it is impossible to understand why industriousness should be a virtue: for virtue, as a moral habit, is something whereby man becomes good as man. This fact in no way alters our justifiable anxiety that in work, whereby *matter* gains in *nobility, man* himself should not experience a *lowering* of his own dignity. Again, it is well known that it is possible to use work in various ways *against man*, that it is possible to punish man with the system of forced labor in concentration camps, that work can be made into a means for oppressing man, and that in various ways it is possible to exploit human labor, that is to say, the worker. All this pleads in favor of the moral obligation to link industriousness as a virtue with *the social order of work*, which will enable man to become, in work, "more a human being" and not be degraded by it, not only because of the wearing out of his physical strength (which, at least up to a certain point, is inevitable), but especially through damage to the dignity and subjectivity that are proper to him. . . .

. . . It is obvious that, when we speak of opposition between labor and capital, we are not dealing only with abstract concepts or "impersonal forces" operating in economic production. Behind both concepts there are people, living, actual people: on the one side are those who do the work without being the owners of the means of production, and on the other side those who act as entrepreneurs and who own means or represent the owners. Thus *the issue of ownership or property* enters from the beginning into the whole of this difficult historical process. The Encyclical *Rerum novarum*, which has the social question as its theme, stresses this issue also, recalling and confirming the Church's teaching on ownership, on the right to private property even when it is a question of the means of production. The Encyclical *Mater et magistra* did the same.

The above principle, as it was then stated and as it is still taught by the Church, *diverges* radically from the program of *collectivism* as proclaimed by Marxism and put into practice in various countries in the decades following the time of Leo XIII's encyclical. At the same time it differs from the program of capitalism practiced by liberalism and by the political systems inspired by it. In the latter case, the difference consists in the way the right to ownership or property is understood. Christian tradition has never upheld this right as absolute and untouchable. On the contrary, it has always understood this right within the broader context of the right common to all to use the goods of the whole of creation: *the right to private property is subordinated to the right to common use*, to the fact that goods are meant for everyone.

Furthermore, in the Church's teaching, ownership has never been understood in a way that could constitute grounds for social conflict in labor. As mentioned above, property is acquired first of all through work in order that it may serve work. This concerns in a special way ownership of the means of production. Isolating these means as a separate property in order to set it up in the form of "capital" in opposition to "labor" — and even to practice exploitation of labor — is contrary to the very nature of these means and their possession. They cannot be *possessed against labor*, they cannot even be *possessed for possession's sake*, because the only legitimate title to their possession — whether in the form of private ownership or in the form of public or collective ownership — is *that they should serve labor*, and thus, by serving labor, they should make possible the achievement of the first principle of this order, namely, the universal destination of goods and the right to common use of them. From this point of view, therefore, in consideration of human labor and of common access to the goods meant for man, one cannot exclude the *socialization*, in suitable conditions, of certain means of production. In the course of the decades since the publication of the Encyclical *Rerum novarum*, the Church's teaching has always recalled all these principles, going back to the arguments formulated in a much older tradition, for example, the well-known arguments of the *Summa Theologiae* of St. Thomas Aquinas.

In the present document, which has human work as its main theme, it is right to confirm all the effort with which the Church's teaching has striven and continues to strive always to ensure the priority of work and, thereby, man's character as a *subject* in social life and, especially, in the dynamic *structure of the whole economic process*. From this point of view the position of "rigid" capitalism continues to remain unacceptable, namely the position that defends the exclusive right to private ownership of the means of production as an untouchable "dogma" of economic life. The principle of respect for work demands that this right should undergo a constructive revision, both in theory and in practice. If it is true that capital, as the whole of the means of production, is at the same time the product of the work of generations, it is equally true that capital is being unceasingly created through the work done with the help of all these means of production, and these means can be seen as a great workbench at which the present generation of workers is working day after day. Obviously we are dealing here with different kinds of work, not only so-called manual labor but also the many forms of intellectual work, including white-collar work and management.

In the light of the above, the many proposals put forward by experts in Catholic social teaching and by the highest Magisterium of the Church take on special significance: *proposals* for *joint ownership of the means of work*, sharing by the workers in the management and/or profits of business, so-called shareholding by labor, etc. Whether these various proposals can or cannot be applied concretely, it is clear that recognition of the proper position of labor and the worker in the production process demands various adaptations in the sphere of the right of ownership of the means of production. This is so not only in view of older situations but also, first and foremost, in view of the whole of the situation and problems in the second half of the present century with regard to the so-called Third World and the various new independent countries that have arisen, especially in Africa but elsewhere as well, in place of the colonial territories of the past.

Therefore, while the position of "rigid" capitalism must undergo continual revision, in order to be reformed from the point of view of human rights, both human rights in the widest sense and those linked with man's work, it must be stated that, from the same point of view, these many deeply desired reforms cannot be achieved by an *a priori elimination of private ownership of the means of production*. For it must be noted that merely taking these means of production (capital) out of the hands of their private owners is not enough to ensure their satisfactory socialization. They cease to be the property of a certain social group, namely the private owners, and become the property of organized society, coming under the administration and direct control of another group of people, namely those who, though not owning them, from the fact of exercising power in society *manage* them on the level of the whole national or the local economy.

This group in authority may carry out its task satisfactorily from the point of view of the priority of labor; but it may also carry it out badly by claiming for itself *a monopoly of the administration and disposal* of the means of production and not refraining even from offending basic human rights. Thus, merely converting the means of production into State property in the collectivist system is by no means equivalent to "socializing" that property. We can speak of socializing only when the subject character of society is ensured, that is to say, when on the basis of his work each person is fully entitled to consider himself a part-owner of the great workbench at which he is working with every one else. A way towards that goal could be found by associating labor with the ownership of capital, as far as possible, and by producing a wide range of intermediate bodies with economic, social, and cultural purposes; they would be bodies enjoying real autonomy with regard to the public powers, pursuing their specific aims in honest collaboration with each other and in subordination to the demands of the common good, and they would be living communities both in form and in substance, in the sense that the members of each body would be looked upon and treated as persons encouraged to take an active part in the life of the body.

Thus, *the principle of the priority of labor* over capital is a postulate of the order of social morality. It has key importance both in the system built on the principle of private ownership of the means of production and also in the system in which private ownership of these means has been limited even in a radical way. Labor is in a sense inseparable from capital; in no way does it accept the antinomy, that is to say, the separation and opposition with regard to the means of production that has weighed upon human life in recent centuries as a result of merely economic premises. When man works, using all the means of production, he also wishes the fruit of this work to be used by himself and others, and he wishes to be able to take part in the very work process as a sharer in responsibility and creativity at the workbench to which he applies himself.

From this spring certain specific rights of workers, corresponding to the obligation of work. They will be discussed later. But here it must be emphasized, in general terms, that the person who works desires *not only* due *remuneration* for his work; he also wishes that, within the production process, provision be made for him to be able to *know* that in his work, even on something that is owned in common, he is working *"for himself."* This awareness is extinguished within him in a system of excessive bureaucratic centralization, which makes the worker feel that he is just a cog in a huge machine moved from above, that he is for more reasons that one a mere production instrument rather than a true subject of work with an initiative of his own. The Church's teaching has always expressed the strong and deep conviction that man's work concerns not only the economy but also, and especially, personal values. The economic system itself and the production process benefit precisely when these personal values are fully respected. In the mind of St. Thomas Aquinas, this is the principal reason in favor of private ownership of the means of production. While we accept that for certain well-founded reasons exceptions can be made to the principle of private ownership — in our own time we even see that the system of "socialized ownership" has been introduced — nevertheless the personalist *argument still holds good* both on the level of principles and *on the practical level*. If it is to be rational and fruitful, any socialization of the means of production must take this argument into consideration. Every effort must be made to ensure that in this kind of system also the human person can preserve his awareness of working "for himself." If this is not done, incalculable damage is inevitably done throughout the economic process, not only economic damage but first and foremost damage to man. . . .

After outlining the important role that concern for providing employment for all workers plays in safeguarding respect for the inalienable rights of man in view of his work, it is worthwhile taking a closer look at these rights, which in the final analysis are formed within the relationship *between worker and direct em-ployer. . . .*

Besides wages, various *social benefits* intended to ensure the life and health of workers and their families play a part here. The expenses involved in health care, especially in the case of accidents at work, demand that medical assistance should be easily available for workers, and that as far as possible it should be cheap or even free of charge. Another sector regarding benefits is the sector associated with the *right to rest.* In the first place this involves a regular weekly rest comprising at least Sunday, and also a longer period of rest, namely the holiday or vacation taken once a year or possibly in several shorter periods during the year. A third sector concerns the right to a pension and to insurance for old age and in case of accidents at work. Within the sphere of these principal rights, there develops a whole system of particular rights which, together with remuneration for work, determine the correct relationship between worker and employer. Among these rights there should never be overlooked the right to a working environment and to manufacturing processes which are not harmful to the workers' physical health or to their moral integrity.

All these rights, together with the need for the workers themselves to secure them, give rise to yet another right: *the right of association*, that is to form asso-ciations for the purpose of defending the vital interests of those employed in the various professions. These associations are called *labor or trade unions.* The vital interests of the workers are to a certain extent common for all of them; at the same time however each type of work, each profession, has its own specific character which should find a particular reflection in these organizations.

In a sense, unions go back to the medieval guilds of artisans, insofar as those organizations brought together people belonging to the same craft and thus *on the basis of their work.* However, unions differ from the guilds on this essential point: the modern unions grew up from the struggle of the workers — workers in general but especially the industrial workers — to protect their *just rights* vis-à-vis the entrepreneurs and the owners of the means of production. Their task is to defend the existential interests of workers in all sectors in which their rights are concerned. The experience history teaches that organizations of this type are an indispensable *element of social life*, especially in modern industrialized societies. Obviously, this does not mean that only industrial workers can set up associations of this type. Representatives of every profession can use them to ensure their own rights. Thus there are unions of agricultural workers and of white-collar workers; there are also employers' associations. All, as has been said above, are further divided into groups or subgroups according to particular professional specializations.

Catholic social teaching does not hold that unions are no more than a reflection of the ''class'' structure of society and that they are a mouthpiece for a class struggle which inevitably governs social life. They are indeed *a mouthpiece for the struggle for social justice*, for the just rights of working people in accordance with their individual professions. However, this struggle should be seen as a normal endeavor ''for'' the just good: in the present case, for the good which corresponds to the needs and merits of working people associated by profession; but it *is not a struggle "against" others*. Even if in controversial questions the struggle takes on a character of opposition towards others, this is because it aims at the good of social justice, not for the sake of "struggle" or in order to eliminate the opponent. It is characteristic of work that it first and foremost unites people. In this consists its social power: the power to build a community. In the final analysis, both those who work and those who manage the means of production or who own them must in some way be united in this community. *In the light of this fundamental structure* of all work — in the light of the fact that, in the final analysis, labor and capital are indispensable components of the process of production in any social system — it is clear that, even if it is because of their work needs that people unite to secure their rights, their union remains a constructive factor of *social order* and *solidarity*, and it is impossible to ignore it.

Just efforts to secure the rights of workers who are united by the same profession should always take into account the limitations imposed by the general economic situation of the country. Union demands cannot be turned into a kind of *group or class "egoism,"* although they can and should also aim at correcting — with a view to the common good of the whole of society — everything defective in the system of ownership of the means of production or in the way these are managed. Social and socioeconomic life is certainly like a system of "connected vessels," and every social activity directed towards safeguarding the rights of particular groups should adapt itself to this system.

In this sense, union activity undoubtedly enters the field of *politics*, understood as *prudent concern for the common good*. However, the role of unions is not to "play politics" in the sense that the expression is commonly understood today. Unions do not have the character of political parties struggling for power; they should not be subjected to the decision of political parties or have too close links with them. In fact, in such a situation they easily lose contact with their specific role, which is to secure the just rights of workers within the framework of the common good of the whole of society; instead they become *an instrument used for other purposes*.

Speaking of the protection of the just rights of workers according to their individual professions, we must of course always keep in mind that which determines the subjective character of work in each profession, but at the same time, indeed before all else, we must keep in mind that which conditions the specific dignity of the subject of the work. The activity of union organizations opens up many possibilities in this respect, including their *efforts to instruct and educate* the workers and to *foster their self-education.* praise is due to the work of the schools, what are known as workers' or people's universities and the training programs and courses which have developed and are still developing this field of activity. It is always to be hoped that, thanks to the work of their unions, workers will not only *have* more, but above all *be* more: in other words, that they will realize their humanity more fully in every respect.

One method used by unions in pursuing the just rights of their members is *the strike* or work stoppage, as a kind of ultimatum to the competent bodies, especially the employers. This method is recognized by Catholic social teaching as legitimate in the proper conditions and within just limits. In this connection workers should be assured the *right to strike*, without being subjected to personal penal sanctions for taking part in a strike. While admitting that it is a legitimate means, we must at the same time emphasize that a strike remains, in a sense, an extreme means. *It must not be abused*; it must not be abused especially for ''political'' purposes. Furthermore it must never be forgotten that, when essential community services are in question, they must in every case be ensured, if necessary by means of appropriate legislation. Abuse of the strike weapon can lead to the paralysis of the whole of socioeconomic life, and this is contrary to the requirements of the common good of society, which also corresponds to the properly understood nature of work itself.

RADICAL: CHANGE THE ECONOMIC SYSTEM

28. WORKING THE FAST LANE: JOBS, TECHNOLOGY AND SCIENTIFIC MANAGEMENT IN THE U.S. POSTAL SERVICE

Peter Rachleff

Scientific management and machine technology have gone hand in hand down the years causing a progressive dehumanization of work, disruptions in the work process, alienation of workers, and, frequently, unemployment. As one author noted years ago, ''unlike generals, who win their wars by recruiting armies, captains of industry win their wars by discharging armies.'' The pattern of mechanization and reorganization found in private industry since the turn of the century has repeated itself in the handling of the nation's mails in the short span of only one decade. The impact on jobs and working conditions has been no less severe. Understanding what has happened would seem a logical first step for postal workers — and the public — in trying to protect jobs and job rights and to maintain the integrity of an essential public service.

THE POSTAL SERVICE BECOMES A BUSINESS

For nearly 200 years the U.S. Post Office Department had functioned as a federal agency and as such had been largely immune from the pressures for higher profits and capital accumulation facing business enterprises. The delivery of the nation's mail relied almost exclusively on manual labor, with management in the hands of political appointees. Congress determined policies governing the Post Office Department, established appropriations for running it, and evaluated its performance. In July 1971, with the passage of the Postal Service Reorganization Act, all of this changed. Once seemingly immune to goals of business and distant from the havoc created by new technology, in the decade of the 1970s the postal service now moved into the economic mainstream.

As the volume of all mail more than doubled between 1940 and 1970, and first-class mail tripled in volume, the postal service compensated by adding to its workforce, becoming the second largest employer in the entire country. Postal facilities became increasingly crowded, with both mail and workers, and the quality both of service and of working conditions went steadily downhill. In 1969 a postal-union official told a House of Representatives committee:

> The average mail handler working in one of these poorly lit, dirty, cluttered, depressing, and inefficient operations, usually bears the brunt of the Post Office's backwardness. He finds himself lugging around an 85- to 100-pound sack that could be transported far more efficiently and easily by machines operated by mail handlers. Many of our major post offices are so inadequate for today's needs that mail handlers and other postal employees are literally falling all over one another trying to get their job done.

In 1970, this deterioration of the postal service came to a head for both management and workers. Drawing strength and confidence from the movement of public-employee unionism in the 1960s, rank-and-file postal workers, from mail handlers to letter carriers, defied their national union leaders and launched a nationwide wildcat strike. For one week, the nation's mail was disrupted as postal workers held firm and, in some cities, threatened to expand their strike to other dissatisfied public employees. Administrators, meanwhile, had become convinced — some before, some during the strike — that full-scale "reorganization," wedded to massive capital improvements, mechanization, and "modernization," was the solution to their problems.

Postal workers were united in their quest for significant wage increases. At the time, their average annual income fell well below the Department of Labor's minimum standards for a family of four. There were even stories of full-time workers receiving public assistance. Postal workers had no intention of going back to work, whatever their union leaders told them, until they got their due. It did not take long for management to make conciliatory noises, as even Wall Street tottered on the brink of shutdown. President Nixon told the public that postal workers had been underpaid for the past twenty-three years. Within the halls of Congress, rumors of substantial wage increases were leaked out. Even then, even after all this talk, it took the deployment of 25,000 federal troops into the New York City postal facilities — the very center of the strike — to finally push postal workers back to the job.

Postal management, for its part, was thinking beyond the immediate termination of the strike to full-scale reorganization. An elaborate plan took shape, whose implementation would change the postal service from top to bottom. Part of this plan was, first, the convincing of union officials that their members' demands for decent wages and working conditions could only be met through reorganization and mechanization, and then, secondly, to use the union leaders to convince their members of the same. Over the 1970s, the first would prove easier to accomplish than the second.

In 1971, a new, semi-independent United States Postal Service was born, with a new, "nonpolitical" management structure and new, corporate goals. The new USPS was given "broad borrowing authority," the right to float bonds to finance capital improvements. "Efficiency," cost cutting, attrition, mechanization, productivity, and "self-sufficiency" became the watchwords of the new management. Here, then, was the ultimate answer to the threat which had been posed in the 1970 national wildcat.

One of the first steps taken by USPS was to seek binding collective bargaining agreements with a limited number of nationwide trade unions, along industrial rather than craft lines. With rapid job transformation and work reorganization in the offing, postal management knew that an industrial-union structure would prove more amenable to the job loss and transfers that would result. The agreements also specifically denied postal workers the right to strike. A highly formalized grievance procedure with arbitration as the final step was negotiated for solving questions that arose under the contracts. Each agreement contained a "management rights" clause patterned after those in private industry. It read, in part:

The Employer shall have the exclusive right, subject to the provisions of this Agreement and consistent with applicable laws and regulations:

A. To direct employees of the Employer in the performance of official duties;

B. To hire, promote, transfer, assign, and retain employees in position within the Postal Service and to suspend, demote, discharge, or take other disciplinary actions against such employees;

C. To maintain the efficiency of the operations entrusted to it;

D. To determine the methods, means, and personnel by which such operations are to be conducted.

In short, the USPS was given a free hand to "reorganize" postal work as it saw fit.

Mechanization was seen as the way to reduce the total labor costs of the USPS, which management feared would outstrip its ability to pay — especially in light of the wage concessions that had been necessary to end the 1970 wildcat. Many hoped that mechanization would eventually bring immunity to the disruption of strikes. Frederick R. Kappel, then chair of the USPS Board of Governors, was asked by a congressional committee in early 1973:

Q: What would we do if we had an occurrence of the strike of a couple of years ago? Do we have any machinery now that would work any better then we had before?

Mr. Kappel responded:

A. No, we do not. I do not know what you could do about it. I think we have some mechanization, but it only feeds into a place where there isn't any, and I think we are still in a very serious condition should a strike occur.

Overall, mechanization was seen as the ultimate strategy for making the new Postal Service economically self-sufficient.

Of course, the introduction of expensive machines could only be economically justified where there was an adequate, and regular, volume of machine-processable mail. Zip codes, originally intended primarily for use by large-volume mailers, were now promoted for adoption by all users of the postal service. Postal management also began a long — and ongoing — campaign for relative uniformity in envelope and postcard dimensions. But, most importantly, their strategy centered on accumulating large volumes of mail at a limited number of locations, volumes large enough to justify the capital investment in new, costly machines. Peter Dorsey, then the regional postmaster for New York and later the USPS's primary strategist in its mechanization campaign, told a congressional committee in 1973: "I suppose the ideal thing would be to have a long conglomeration of equipment hooked up sequentially where you could dump raw mail in one end and have it come out sorted to the carrier at the other end."

The early 1970s saw the piecemeal introduction of such notions, with chaotic and catastrophic results. New machines were installed in antiquated and overcrowded postal facilities in major cities. Moe Biller, then president of the New York Metro local postal workers union, told a congressional committee in 1973:

The mechanization program, which runs into billions, will yet prove the biggest bust of all. You can't quarrel with the idea of mechanization in 1973, just as we're all for motherhood and against sin. Let's look at the New York experience in this regard. The introduction of letter-sorting machines into the general post office, a building built in 1910. That is a crying shame. The noise is unbearable. The machines are not cleaned enough; frequently there are paper lice. . . . The workers on these machines have mostly night work and most of them work weekends even though, initially, management advertised these jobs as mostly weekends off. Management's comment? The people must be where the mail is.

At the same time, during the early seventies, the new postal management also adopted the strategy of reducing total labor costs through attrition, actively encouraging early retirement and even imposing a hiring freeze in 1972. They sought quick results, and they got them: 55,000 postal employees opted for early retirement. In New York for example, total postal personnel fell by 13 percent between 1970 and 1973. Needless to say, such across-the-board reductions failed to mesh with the mechanization program and created even more chaos in the postal service. Letter carriers certainly didn't have their loads lightened. With their ranks reduced, they found their routes lengthened, their traditional work patterns disrupted by such directives as crossing lawns rather than walking on sidewalks, and their actual work observed by timekeepers and monitored by devices in their vehicles. Local union officials across the country reported an increase in heart attacks among letter carriers. Inside postal facilities, the reduced work forces were called upon to put in long overtime hours, actually increasing labor costs of many facilities. New York regional postmaster Peter Dorsey admitted to Congress in 1973: "We may have gone too far, we were hell-bent on saving money as opposed to service." James H. Rademacher, then president of the National Association of Letter Carriers, summed it all up in his testimony before the same committee:

We can state without fear of contradiction by the general public that the level of mail service is at the worst stage in history and the quality of the nation's mail service is the poorest it has ever been.

Indeed, no one contradicted him.

By 1973, the business-oriented management of the new USPS had introduced new machines in existing postal facilities with high mail volumes and had reduced their total work force through an attrition campaign. All observers, inside and outside the postal service, were agreed: the immediate results had been disastrous. The USPS was no closer to "self-sufficiency" than it had been in 1970 at its establishment. The quality of mail service had become a national scandal. And working conditions inside postal facilities had deteriorated even further. Despite the no-strike clause in the contract, management feared another major disruption of the nation's mails upon the contract's expiration in 1973. Apparently, the business-oriented management's new strategies had backfired all around.

In this context, postal management moved to drastically reorganize the postal system, seeking to *create* large accumulations of mail in specific locations. A single, centralized facility would process all the originating mail for a given geographical region. And the entire range of new mail-handling and processing machines would be installed in these new buildings, constructed according to new, "modular" specifications. Similar plans were laid for the construction of twenty-one new bulk-mail facilities, which would transform the handling of parcels and other non-first-class items. Peter Dorsey, now promoted to senior assistant postmaster general for operations despite his problem in New York, reported in 1974:

Inside a Bulk Mail Center or Auxiliary Service Facility we will replace today's manual single sorting operations with high-speed machine processing designed to maintain a continuous flow of mail through the facility. Our aim is to reverse the present 80 percent manual, 20 percent mechanical ration in processing mail. . . .

Put very simply, the basic idea behind the national Bulk Mail Service is to centralize mail processing so that it is more efficient to utilize mechanization.

Thus relocation and mechanization became inseparable strategies as postal management moved to put the service on a more businesslike basis. Without relocation to concentrate the mails, mechanization would not be profitable — and without mechanization, relocation would make no sense at all.

Having reorganized the workplace and the whole mail-handling system, management established standards for the output expected from each type of job within the post office. It also prescribed the most "efficient" methods for performing individual tasks. Now it resorts to discipline or discharge for those who fail to meet the standards or refuse to follow established methods.

In the short span of one decade the U.S. Post Office Department, a federal agency which provided an essential service, was reorganized, and in the process of that reorganization it acquired new goals.

THE POSTAL SERVICE MOVES TO THE SUBURBS

It was part of postal management's overall strategy to locate many of the new facilities for accumulating mail outside of central cities. Publicly, postal officials offered a range of weak excuses for this major decision. Traffic was too congested in central cities, they argued, and it would slow the transportation of mail to and from the new facilities. But it turned out that many of the new locations were on major commuter arteries, and no less prone to traffic tie-up than urban streets. Land was too expensive in the cities, they also argued. But then they went out and paid exorbitant sums for suburban acreage. Of course, under the new United States Postal Service structure, they did not really have to convince anyone of the justice of their argument. What was behind their strategic relocation of major postal facilities?

The center of the 1970 wildcat had been in the major postal facilities in large cities. In Detroit, Pittsburgh, Philadelphia, and New York, some 50 to 75 percent of the workers — and strikers — had been black. Moving to the suburbs was designed to alter the composition of the work forces at the major postal facilities. Forest Park, Illinois, for example, was selected as the site for a new facility to replace the major Chicago center. In the old post office, a majority of the employees were black. In Forest Park, a lengthy commute from South Chicago, there were no black families — not one. It was unlikely that many black postal workers would make the transfer. Similar concerns were voiced in city after city.

The suburban location of the new facilities would alter the composition of the work force in other ways as well. Many workers would choose not to transfer, either seeking jobs elsewhere in the postal system or retiring altogether. Administrators would thus have considerable latitude in hiring new workers or reassigning veteran workers, and, with their strengthened hand, could shape the work force more in accordance with their own preference and needs. An added weapon, of course, was that workers transferring in had to be able to master the operation of new machinery. The location of new facilities at some distance from the currently operating centers therefore gave management a tremendous opportunity to reorganize the work forces inside the centers of the postal system.

But the implications of this relocation extended even further, for it simultaneously undermined two major sources of postal workers' strength. With the reorganization of work and the work force which accompanied relocation, informal work groups which had developed over many years were suddenly torn apart. Men and women who had come to trust and understand each other would never work together again. Moving to a new facility was an individual decision, and many chose not to go. Even accepting reassignment offered little promise of keeping work groups together, for the new machines in the new facilities demanded a reorganization of the work itself. Management in the new, mechanized facilities could thus operate, at least initially, with little concern for the workplace powers developed by experienced work groups.

The impact of relocation was even more wide-ranging. Traditionally, the bars, taverns, and restaurants surrounding a large workplace have served as centers of socializing and discussion by the workers employed there. These establishments, and the neighborhood within which they are located, have been a critical element to whatever strengths their patrons and residents exercised at work. The old, central-city postal facilities were situated within such a framework, one which helped consolidate and extend the postal workers' immediate work-group relationships. But the new facilities were constructed "in the middle of nowhere," surrounded by miles of concrete in every direction.

The new postal facilities were not located in the heart of any neighborhoods, surrounded by various social institutions. Nor have such institutions developed. Most postal workers live too far from the new facilities to be willing to add to their time away from home by hanging around after work. The prospect of an hour's drive in heavy traffic is enough to sour any man or woman on relaxed socializing.

One postal worker gave the following account of a postal relocation in Pennsylvania:

On July 28, 1979, a new General Mail Facility (GMF) was opened in Lancaster, Pennsylvania. The new facility was designed to further consolidate the handling of dispatch mail within a three-county area. It also serves the purpose of breaking community ties around the former facility and changing the relationship between employees.

Before occupation of the GMF facility, mail was collected from the county offices and processed for dispatch in each of the three counties within the Sectional Center. When the GMF became operational, all the collected mail from the three counties — including local mail — began being trucked to Lancaster for processing and dispatch. This means that mail going to a post office five miles down the road may be trucked forty miles to Lancaster and forty miles back to the destination. The reason given for consolidation was to improve efficiency through increased use of mechanization in Lancaster. . . .

The GMF is on the outskirts of town. While the facility is only 2.56 miles from the old building, the setting is totally different. The old building is three blocks from the center of Lancaster. A convenience store and sandwich shops are literally across the street or around the corner. Banks and stores in the downtown area can be walked to during lunch break or after work. Numerous bars and taverns are within walking distance.

In contrast, the GMF is surrounded by acres of grass and farmland. There is no store or sandwich shop within walking distance. Employees are thus subtly encouraged to stay in the building. Except for the administrative offices, there are no windows in the building. The building consists of a one-story 156,000 square foot concrete slab. The warehouse atmosphere is cold and sterile.

Postal management officials have designed these bleak facilities in such a way as to maximize their control over workers. The results are strikingly similar to a prison yard. (Postal workers noted that even the newly remodeled facilities in central cities look very much like fortresses and prisons.)

On the basis of efficiency and financial return on the dollars invested, however, the relocation strategy did not make a particularly good showing. The bulk mail centers soon became the subject of much public criticism. In February 1979 the nationally syndicated columnist Jack Anderson sent one of his staff into a bulk mail center as a postal employee and then published the following impressions, under the headline "BULK MAIL CENTER: AUTOMATED NIGHTMARE":

The bulk main center is a machine-powered world modeled after Charlie Chaplin's movie, *Modern Times*. Automated carts filled with mail run along trolley tracks, heedless of parcels that fall off and people who get in the way. Overhead trays carry mail through the building, tipping their contents into chutes on command from the control room.

Operators in the control room can tell how the mail is moving by watching the flow on video screens. Unfortunately the screens don't show the plight of a worker frantically trying to load a truck as fast as the conveyor belt spews the mail out. It also doesn't show the assemblyline workers who can't keep pace with the relentless machines and can't shut off or slow down the conveyor belt. The parcels often spill off the belt onto the floor, where they remain for days.

Employees at the Washington center have their own wry slogan: "You mail 'em, we maul 'em." It's not the humans who are doing the mauling, though, it's the machines. Like the sack shake-out rig that empties parcels — including those marked "Fragile — Glass" — from mail sacks and lets them fall four feet onto a belt.

Packages that get jammed in the automatic conveyors are ripped apart. Attempts are made to patch them up, but the many Humpty Dumpty irreparables end up in a parcel graveyard — a room designated "loose in the mail" and off-limits to all but a few employees. Our reporter got inside for a look around, and found thousands from books to homemade Christmas presents. There were so many books that they had been arranged by topic on metal shelves. . . .

The billion-dollar bulk mail system was supposed to save the Postal Service $300 million a year. Recent estimates have now reduced the potential savings to $40 million — a return of 4 percent on the money invested.

Nor is there any evidence that the bulk mail system saves time. A package en route from El Paso to Midland, Texas, for example, is sent 1,483 miles out of the way to be processed by a bulk mail center.

WHEN MACHINES REPLACE PEOPLE

Traditionally, mail had been sorted manually by experienced clerks, working in "teams" around a shared table. Each person had to memorize complex sorting "schemes," and all were able to maintain virtually 100-percent accuracy. A great deal of pride and experience went into learning "schemes," and tight-knit informal work groups developed within the post office. All this was wiped out by the introduction of letter-sorting machines (LSMs).

Now clerks sit before keyboards and screens. Letters — already faced, cancelled, and placed in position — appearing on the screen at the rate of one per second. Reading the zip code, the clerk then types the appropriate code on the keyboard. Each clerk sits, fixated before the automatically placed screen, in a separate cubbyhole. Communication with workmates is virtually impossible. The LSMs are very noisy — so noisy that many operators contend they exceed OSHA noise levels. At any rate, the level of noise presents a major obstacle to normal conversation. But that doesn't concern postal management, since normal conversation among LSM operators is prohibited in most facilities.

The new LSMs rely on electronic memory banks, which allow operators to sort mail into an immediate 277 separations, far superior to the 77 which had been standard under the manual-sort system. The new machines reduce the number of sorts necessary overall, and, intermeshed with the accumulation of mail volumes in a limited number of locations, their use made possible a significant reduction in the sorting work force employed in mail processing. The LSM alone, according to postal management, was at least 57 percent more productive than the manual sorting system.

Nowhere in management's productivity claims did it count the human toll. Here is the description offered by one worker, Jack Katzmire:

Although I am no longer an LSM Operator, I spent the better (or worse) part of six years as a "Trained Monkey" so most of my comments will deal with problems in and around the LSM. I started in the Postal Service in 1973, being hired under the LSM Training Program, whereby I had to qualify on the LSM or lose my job. I did qualify, and worked on the LSM for about six years, in which time I went physically and emotionally downhill. . . .

Prior to working on the LSM, I had never needed glasses, but finally got my first pair in 1976 — and should have had them before that. Anyone can look down a row of people sitting on the LSM and see how few *don't* have glasses — the few that don't being relatively new to the LSM, it being only a matter of time until they need their first pair.

I haven't had my ears professionally tested to determine what degree of hearing loss I have actually suffered, but there has been a definite hearing loss — not only have I noticed it myself, but those close to me pointed it out repeatedly.

The main physical problem I experienced, and one of the major factors in my decision to bid off the LSM was my hands. My hands cramped up constantly and gave me an arthritis-like pain the entire time I coded. I got to the point where I coded with only one finger on each hand, as this helped to ease the pain compared to coding normally with all my fingers. I went to our medical unit, but neither the nurse nor the doctor were any help in determining what was causing the problem or what to do to alleviate the problem. . . .

I hated the job and everything about it so much, that I took it out (unwittingly) on those around me. When I finally bid off that dehumanizing LSM, my wife told me how completely different I was and how thankful she was I had gotten off — and then she told me she didn't know how much more she could have taken had I stayed on the machine: only then did I learn how close I had come to ruining my marriage.

I realize that everything affects each individual differently and there are literally thousands of jobs that where some people enjoy them, others would hate and would not be able to handle, but the LSM has to be in a class of its own. Here is a job that I thoroughly enjoyed initially, but later came to hate as it became more and more boring and tedious and dehumanizing as I became used to it and it became "automatic" whereby I became more aware of the "Pavlov Dog" treatment. I worked "outgoing" mail initially, and then moved on to "incoming secondary" mail, each time enjoying the change because it was a bit of a challenge at first, but as I learned it, it became automatic and boredom set in again.

The letter-sorting machine was not introduced alone. Rather it was interfaced with a host of other innovations, which brought mail processing close to a continuous flow operation. Mechanical cullers, face-cancellers, and edgers fed mail into the LSMs. Operators processed letters at the rate of one every second, and trays were automatically swept, the letters bagged for transportation to their post office of destination. The labor needed for first-class mail handling dropped sharply.

Postal management was — and still is — very interested in yet another innovation which which could be interfaced with the LSM, further boosting productivity
and displacing labor. This technological wonder — the optical character reader, or
OCR — has long held a particular fascination for postal management. J. P. Lee,
the San Francisco sectional center manager, pulled no punches when he told a
congressional committee in 1973:

The only piece of machinery that we have no problem with is the OCR. But as long as you
put a human being at one of those LSMs, we do have a problem because it is getting this
human being adjusted to the machinery.

While there are technical problems to be overcome before the OCR can be
introduced on a system-wide basis, when it does come the OCR will eliminate the
LSM operator's job.

This, then, is the modern facility where most first-class mail is processed. Clearly,
it has cost postal workers a great deal. Interestingly, it has not seemed to solve the
USPS's problems. More mail than ever is sent through private carriers. Overnight
delivery remains a pipe dream for most first-class mail. Postal rates have continued
to climb, while the goal of "self-sufficiency" remains as elusive as ever. Missent
mail floats throughout the system. But there is no denying that this reorganization
has strengthened postal management's hand vis-à-vis its employees. In this sense,
and in no other, the reorganization of first-class mail processing can be termed a
"success."

The second main area of postal reorganization and mechanization has been bulk
mail. Changes in this area have proven even more disastrous for postal workers.

In the early 1970s, the new management of the USPS earmarked more than $1
billion for the construction of a complete, integrated, mechanized bulk mail system.
Twenty-one BMCs and eleven auxiliary Service Facilities were to be constructed
by the mid-1970s. Here, as with the relocation of major postal facilities, management's public justification was questionable. The stated goal was to win back the
parcel-post business which had been lost to UPS and other private carriers. However,
a study commissioned by the Postal Service itself in 1973 had concluded that, even
if it worked perfectly, the new bulk-mail system, with its complicated rerouting of
packages over thousands of miles between facilities, would never be competitive
with UPS within a 600-mile range of delivery — precisely the area in which UPS
has captured the largest share of USPS business. Even before the new bulk-mail
system became operational, then, it was clear to postal management that it could
not magically recapture the lost business.

But this did not deter postal management. The new system — with its centralized
control, relocation of centers to suburban areas, recomposition of the work force,
and reorganization of work — remained attractive to them. Despite a series of
construction delays and equipment failure, the new system was put into operation
in the later 1970s. George R. Cavell, the first program director of the Bulk Mail
Processing Department, explained to Congress what was supposed to happen in
each facility:

The equipment in question consists of high-speed sorting machines into which parcels are introduced from a series of automatic induction units. When the machinery is running, unsorted parcels are brought on conveyors to employees who, by operating simple keyboards, feed the zip code of each package into a computer. Once a package has been through this key code operation, it is automatically transferred to one of a number of shallow trays mounted on chair-driven carriages. These trays move by at a rate of 160 per minute, and, following an oval path, carry the packages past a series of slides each of which leads to a different collection point. The computer "remembers" which individual collection point each package is destined for, and as the tray comes up to the particular slide into which its package should be deposited, the computer activates a tripping device that tilts the tray and lets the parcels slide out.

It sounds pretty smooth. But in 1976, Representative Charles Wilson opened his subcommittee's hearings on the Bulk Mail System by calling it, "a dream gone sour, or, more appropriately, a management blunder of the first magnitude, which will cost the American public millions of dollars."

Witnesses told Wilson's subcommittee of packages caught between conveyor rollers, parcels being run over by containers, small parcels being damaged in induction unit slides by heavier parcels, and packages being smashed upon dropping from sack shake-out machines. William Anderson, Deputy Director of the General Government Division of the GAO, which had just released its study of the bulk mail system, testified:

We believe much of the damage is caused by the equipment in the centers. Unlike the other problems the Postal Service may have, the personnel have very little to do with this one. It's just a case of the machinery.

Missent and misdirected parcels remained a much larger percentage of total volume than was expected as well. Instead of the targeted maximum of 5 percent, for example, the Washington, D.C., regional facility was rarely below 10 percent in 1975 and 1976, and occasionally above 20 percent.

The BMCs were also quite unsafe. Accident rates were high from the day the centers opened, and they have remained high to the present day. In 1978, for example, USPS figures ranged between twelve and fourteen injuries per million work hours, triple the nationwide average. The brand new buildings with brand new machinery were proving as unsafe as the old, antiquated facilities which were being closed. GAO investigator William Anderson testified in 1976:

The walkways are really tough to stick to and then these towveyors are moving downward. There are a lot of instances, and I know we had to dodge them all over the place walking through the plant here. The work floor is just so crowded, and these things are coming sporadically and if you don't keep your — if you're not intent all the time on trying to spot a coming towveyor, I can understand how people can be getting hurt.

It is unfortunate indeed that frequently the public placed the responsibility for postal services inefficiencies on the postal employees rather than on poor management and ineffective machinery. Employees who have traditionally prided themselves on both speed and accuracy in handling the nation's mails have thereby been hit hard from both sides. The new technology has eliminated jobs and degraded those that remain. And when the new technology fails, the workers get blamed.

Summoning up the USPS's success in making the mails more efficient, one union leader made the following critique in 1976:

What has $3 billion in plant and mechanization accomplished? The Bulk Mail System cost $1 billion, and high-speed letter-sorting machines and other mechanization cost nearly $2 billion. Let's look at the Postal Service when it was labor intensive. During that time, missent, misdirected and damaged mail amounted historically to about one-half of the 1 percent of the volume during the decade proceeding the Postal Reorganization Act of 1970. Today the Bulk Mail System damage is 1 percent and the missent is approximately 5 percent. This error rate is machine error, not human error. In the letter sorting machine operation the error rate (machine) is 4 percent. . . .

Who now thinks of "self-sufficiency" as a feasible goal for the USPS? Postal rates increase, subsidies increase, and postal service remains a public laughingstock. It is now important to ask ourselves why have these been the results of the new strategies of postal management.

One is tempted to answer the question glibly by dismissing the USPS's condition as merely another typical example of government bureaucracy in action. To be sure, instances of mismanagement, ignorance, stupidity, and perfidy can be cited ad infinitum. But, was there not a method to this madness? Are there not some long-run advantages to management which will outweigh the costs and confusion which we have noted? It seems so.

The one critical, shared feature of the measures taken by the new business-oriented management was that they all attacked postal workers' sources of power. Not only was the work force reduced and the postal unions tightly restricted, but the attack also targeted the informal work groups, the neighborhoods around the postal facilities, and the once-crucial importance of the workers' skill and knowledge to the daily operation of the postal service. Work was simplified, mechanized, routinized, and subjected to the automatic pace of machines and the centralized control of management. Parking lots look like prison yards, surrounded by high gates. Management's concern with gaining control dictated the strategies which have resulted in the continuing deterioration of the quality of postal service, but these same strategies now place management in the driver's seat for determining, without challenge or interruption, the future of the postal service.

IN GENERATIONS TO COME

Mechanized mail processing grew from 25 percent of total volume in 1971 to 70 percent in 1979, while the work force fell through attrition, by 80–90,000. One-time American Postal Workers Union official David Johnson estimated that 250,000 to 300,000 postal workers will be eligible to retire between now and 1985, reflecting the big postwar expansion of postal employment. How many will remain, and what will they do, will largely depend on postal management's implementation of two major technological innovations. How postal workers and their union will cope with these impending innovations will determine the future of their jobs and the future of the postal service.

In retrospect, it certainly seems that postal management blundered into, and through, its reorganization, construction, and mechanization programs of the 1970s. Historically, management's quest for the "rationalization" of production has always generated chaos for its employees, whatever the industry, whatever management's expertise. However, this sort of problem certainly seemed profound in the Postal Service in the 1970s, and the resulting levels of workplace chaos and disorganization were extreme.

On the other hand, had postal management really "had its act together," so to speak, in its reorganization and mechanization programs, the consequences for postal workers might well have been all the more extreme. Tens of thousands of postal workers might have found themselves out of work altogether, at a time of ever-tightening labor markets. Maybe we should be thankful that postal management was so inexperienced and so inept. Had they not been, the present situation might be even worse that it is.

However, there is little solace in such observations, for contemporary postal management is moving towards the implementation of electronic message systems with little of its previous uncertainty and confusion. They have hired experts from NASA and contracted for the services of the nation's most advanced computer and electronic firms. After a decade of stumbling, postal management now knows precisely what it is doing in the area of electronic message systems, and they have carefully worked out plans that would eliminate most postal workers' jobs in the next twenty years.

It is important to take a close look at the two major technological innovations that postal workers can expect to face in the 1980s: (1) widespread use of advanced optical character readers (OCRs) with both "read" and "code" capacities, inter-faced with a battery of multiposition letter-sorting machines, and (2) a full-fledged electronic message system (EMS), which would do away with most mail handling and processing as we know it. If postal workers are to cope with these innovations, it will be necessary to understand them.

Neither of these technological innovations is genuinely new, in the strict sense. Postal management has expressed an interest in their development since the mid-1960s. But only in the last few years has postal management committed itself to developing and using these new technologies. Now, after the spending of millions of dollars on research and pilot projects, full system-wide implementation is around the corner.

In 1977, Roger K. Salaman of the U.S. Department of Commerce told a congressional committee that some 60 percent of the Postal Service's first-class mail consisted of financial transactions which could be completed through the new, privately operated system of "electronic funds transfers." He predicted conservatively that, within the next decade, up to 40 percent of first-class mail might disappear. Congressman Hanley responded to Salaman's testimony: "Because of the development of this technology of electronic transfer of funds, I think it is fair to say that we kiss [this mail] right off, say good bye to [it]."

But other witnesses argued against such a fatalistic concession. They suggested that the USPS develop its own electronic message system with all deliberate speed. Not to do so, warned Dr. Rader of the National Research Council, would mean: "mounting costs, decreasing volumes, and continually rising deficits, a 'no-win' situation leading inevitably to a deterioration of services and a growing dependency on subsidies." In short, then, one of the reasons for management's current interest in computer and electronic innovations is that reorganization and mechanization in the 1970s failed to ensure the continued adequacy of mail volume necessary to justify the mechanization itself.

At the same time, the new centralized control that management gained in the 1970s now gives it much more of a free hand in its latest plans for the introduction of new technology. Postal management now believes it can introduce new technologies, bringing a massive loss of jobs, with little collective opposition from their workforce.

Most postal workers are familiar with optical character readers. They are computer-controlled machines that scan addresses and then route the envelopes to the proper bins of the LSMs with which they are interfaced. Linked to the introduction of nine-digit zip codes, OCRs will sort much of the nation's mail automatically. Prototypes have been developed which are reportedly capable of sorting upwards of 80,000 pieces of mail in an hour. The introduction of OCRs will, quite simply, replace all LSM operators, who read addresses visually and then key in codes. In short, the very occupation will disappear.

The development of the OCR has been plagued with problems, mostly stemming from the machine's inability to "read" all mail. The inability, or unwillingness, of people to address their letters uniformly has created the greatest problems. However, between 70 and 80 percent of first-class mail volume is generated by business, who have already shown a willingness to dovetail their mailing operations with the technological requirements of postal machinery. They are already addressing their envelopes in such a way as to make them "machine-readable."

To date, where OCRs have been introduced, they have been directly interfaced with standard LSMs. In short, they simply replace the LSM operators. A greater challenge lies in the interfacing of OCRs with electronic message equipment, such as facsimile transmission. This is the wave of the future.

Postal management has divided its research into electronic message systems into three stages — the so-called Generation I, Generation II, and Generation III. Let's look at them in turn.

Generation I substitutes electronic transmission of information for a portion of the mail stream. Functionally, this is similar to the World War II "V-mail" service, in which a letter was photographed and reduced to microfilm which was transported to an overseas location for reproduction. Today's technology enables letters or messages to be converted to electronic signals for transmission and reconversion to hard copy.

In Generation II, information enters the mail stream at a postal installation close to the recipient. Prior to the production of a hard copy at this postal installation, the information exists in electronic form, possibly with a concurrent hard copy for local record purposes. All transmission and sorting is electronic. An example of Generation II is Mailgram, developed jointly by Western Union and the USPS. Mailgrams may originate at a terminal (Telex, TRW, or InfoCom), at a computer (direct or via a Western Union office), by a toll telephone call, by acoustically coupled terminals (facsimile, word processor, or teletypewriter), or across-the-counter at a public telegraph office. Once entered into the system, the information is switched and transmitted electronically to a post office near the addressee, and a hard copy is produced. The hard copy is put into an envelope by USPS personnel and dropped into the conventional mail stream for delivery.

The conceptual model of Generation II suggests telecommunication services similar to Mailgram, with electronic inputs entered directly at a postal installation near the originator. It is estimated that 80 percent of all letter mail originated by government and 40 percent originated by business would yield to input in electronic form. As Generation II service grew, addresses would receive an increasing proportion of their mail in the form of messages that have been transmitted electronically and converted to hard copy for delivery.

Looking beyond this, it will become feasible to replace physical delivery with electronic delivery for each individual recipient, depending upon the specific circumstances. Two main elements are required for Generation III to operate widely: The engineering problems here are immense, but USPS management thinks they can be overcome. As early as 1977 William J. Miller, the director of advanced mail systems development, testified before Congress:

Q: How soon do you foresee the opportunity of having what some refer to as "the black box" in the home, an inexpensive means by which every individual household could receive its message?
A: Miller said: '1990.'

To be sure, much controversy has followed these plans. Private firms have challenged the USPS's expansion into this area, especially its quest for a legally sanctioned monopoly. The FCC and Congress, traditionally responsive to business demands, have failed to grant the USPS the free hand it has sought. Other critics have expressed concerns about the potential violation of privacy such systems could occasion. In Generations I and II, what will happen to the originating copies of letters? Will they be returned to the sender? destroyed? or stored? Who might gain access to them? Our knowledge of the traditional cooperation between USPS management and the FBI and other agents of domestic surveillance gives us little confidence in glib assertions that electronic mail poses no threat to individual privacy. Similarly, though, our knowledge of the government's's growing disregard of individual civil liberties is hardly reassuring. Unless there is a strong outpouring of public sentiment on this issue, the USPS and the government will do as they see fit.

Given what we know about the available technology there is no denying that the future is exceedingly grim for postal workers. Postmaster General Bolger told a congressional subcommittee in 1978 that the adoption of electronic message systems would displace three fourths of the processing work force, without even eliminating the uses of "hard copy" at both ends of the operation. Can we comfortably agree with the GAO's William Anderson's contention that: "Anything that will make the Postal Service less labor intensive has to be to the Nation's good"?

LAST THOUGHTS

The introduction of new technology involves more than a simple quest for improved productivity, or the general "march of progress." The development and introduction of new technologies is governed by social decisions. Those in power have always sought out and promoted precisely those technological innovations which will increase their control over other human beings, be it the consumers of energy or the workers in their plants.

In the workplace, the availability, development, and introduction of new technologies has consistently provided management with a powerful weapon to disrupt workplace organization, reorganize production, routinize work, and increase control over the employees. It was the growing demands and militancy of postal workers in the late 1960s, reflected in their national wildcat in 1970, that pushed postal manageement in the direction of wholesale reorganization. The replacement of human labor by machines and scientific management of the workplace became the order of the day. But this was not all that happened. The new technologies which were introduced broke up work groups and the social networks of support, regimented the work of all postal employees, and centralized management's immediate control within each facility. This strategy, we have seen, was disastrous for both postal workers and postal patrons. The quality of the nation's mail service plummeted. But these technologies had served their purpose for management, for they significantly shifted the balance of power in their direction.

Interestingly, two figures in the rank-and-file militancy of the early 1970s, then presidents of New York City locals of the APWU and the National Association of Letter Carriers, now head their respective unions. Together, they negotiated a post-deadline contract with postal management this past summer. Most impressive was the size of the money package in the contract (at a time of "takeback" bargaining) and the maintenance of the cost-of-living escalator, which Postmaster General Bolger had publicly targeted for extinction. Amidst preparations by both local management and rank-and-file groups for a wildcat strike upon the expiration of the old contract, the new agreement caught everyone by surprise.

Both Moe Biller and Vinnie Sombrotto appear tamed in their new roles. Neither opposes technological change in the post office. Despite their "militant" pasts, they, too, have been part of the consensus that has seen technological development as the answer to the postal service's woes. Perhaps their faith was rewarded by the 1981 settlement, which surely strengthened their hand within their union. Postal management obviously preferred to strengthen the influence of those "responsible" leaders by letting them deliver the goods (in terms of money, anyway) to their members, rather than face more than 600,000 angry workers outside of their union leaders' control. Postal workers themselves had shown a willingness to exchange wage increases for technological development, even in the tumultuous early seventies. And, in 1978, they had agreed to a two-tier system within their union, with lifelong security promised to those hired before 1978, but six years of continuous service required of those hired afterwards in order to be covered (not unlike the now notorious "A" and "B" systems of unionized longshoreworkers).

While there were some postal workers who remained dissatisfied with the contract, they had little hope of galvanizing other union members into a wildcat walkout. Barely a month later, while many postal workers were still pondering how to cast their ballots, President Reagan sent them, and all other unionized workers, a strong message, when he fired the striking air traffic controllers. The new administration chose an inexperienced, small, isolated union, with supposedly well-paid members, to make its point — that public-sector workers could now expect to be punished for striking in the face of no-strike laws, oaths, and clauses.

All this, especially in the shadow of the destruction of Solidarity by the Polish military and Communist Party, underlines the hollow nature of state ownership as a working-class goal. There has to be much more. What this could mean in an agency like the postal service is suggested in an editorial appearing in the newsletter of the Prince Georges County, Maryland, local of the APWU. Written by *Union Dispatch* editor Danny Betman, it says in part:

My very modest proposal is really simple. Get rid of the current make-up of the Postal Service, the PMG, the Board of Governors, the whole mess. In its place, turn over the operation and running of the Postal Service to the only people who know how to run it correctly — the people who do the work day in and day out. This could be done by working through the Union structure. Let the Congress stake us to just three years' Postal Subsidy to cover the period of reorganization, and we would be breaking even at the end of those three years. How would we organize it differently in order to do this? Easy!

The problem with the PO isn't the hopeless situation of trying to provide a cheap, efficient service to the people and it is not with the workers themselves. The real problem is with top management who sit down in L'Enfant Plaza in air-conditioned and carpeted offices and play around with computers, adding machines, pushing a lot of paper and juggling a lot of figures. The problem is that they don't know the first thing of what it is like on the workroom floor, of what it is like actually trying to move the mail. The average worker on the floor knows more about his/her job than any so-called "expert" and there is nothing that cannot be learned by the workers about the rest of the operations.

We would run the PO democratically. The first step would be the elimination of all craft distinctions, and the equalization of salaries for all Postal workers. All supervisory and managerial positions would be filled by democratic vote, all would be subject to recall, and would receive salaries no higher than the rest of the workers. This would insure that only people with an interest in the welfare of the service and of all would want these positions.

Any grievance concerning working conditions, safety, etc. would be heard by a committee of elected co-workers who would solve these problems. All rules and regulations concerning work, salary, etc. would be decided democratically. The workers would elect representatives to make policy for the running of the business. The postal service would remain as the property of the people of the United States, run and operated by the workers as a non-profit service to the public.

The problem with the PO is not the workers. The problem is the system under which the PO is run. Even the politicians who are hell-bent upon destroying the Postal Service say this. Their solution is give it away to business and the public and workers be dammed. We see the same problem but offer a different solution, one that can provide a cheap, reliable service to the public and safeguard our welfare, our safety and our livelihood. So, Mr. PMG, give away the postal service, not to those who only want to use it for their own profit, but to those who are the only ones capable enough and caring enough to do the job.